THE MANUAL OF THE
ARMED CONFLI

THE MANUAL OF THE LAW OF ARMED CONFLICT

UK Ministry of Defence

OXFORD
UNIVERSITY PRESS

OXFORD

UNIVERSITY PRESS

Great Clarendon Street, Oxford OX2 6DP

Oxford University Press is a department of the University of Oxford.
It furthers the University's objective of excellence in research, scholarship,
and education by publishing worldwide in

Oxford New York

Auckland Cape Town Dar es Salaam Hong Kong Karachi
Kuala Lumpur Madrid Melbourne Mexico City Nairobi
New Delhi Shanghai Taipei Toronto

With offices in

Argentina Austria Brazil Chile Czech Republic France Greece
Guatemala Hungary Italy Japan Poland Portugal Singapore
South Korea Switzerland Thailand Turkey Ukraine Vietnam

Oxford is a registered trade mark of Oxford University Press
in the UK and in certain other countries

Published in the United States
by Oxford University Press Inc., New York

British Library Cataloguing in Publication Data

Data available

Library of Congress Cataloguing in Publication Data

Data available

Typeset by Newgen Imaging Systems (P) Ltd., Chennai, India
Printed in Great Britain
on acid-free paper by
Biddles Ltd, King's Lynn

ISBN 0–19–924454–5 (Hbk.)   978–0–19–924454–6 (Hbk.)
ISBN 0–19–928728–7 (Pbk.)   978–0–19–928728–4 (Pbk.)

1 3 5 7 9 10 8 6 4 2

Foreword

By the Chief of the Defence Staff and the Permanent under Secretary, Ministry of Defence

Law, both domestic and international, plays an increasingly important part in Defence activities these days. When undertaking operations, Commanders must take into account a broad and increasingly complex body of operational law. The Law of Armed Conflict is a part of that wider body of applicable law, but it merits a manual in its own right because of its great importance to all those involved in the use of force and in wider military activities.

This is the first major statement of the British approach to the Law of Armed Conflict since 1958. During the intervening years, there have been numerous expressions of the UK's position on aspects of this law, but nothing as comprehensive as this Manual. In this fast moving world, some issues cannot of necessity be stated in absolute terms. What follows is, however, a clear articulation of the UK's approach to the Law of Armed Conflict.

In the same fast moving world, the law itself evolves, and to that end this publication will be subject to periodic revision, the resulting amendments being published as noted in the Preface.

The United Kingdom has long appreciated the practical, policy and legal importance of conducting the full range of its military activities in accordance with applicable legal norms. The publication of this Manual should be seen as another step in stating publicly the UK's interpretation of what the Law of Armed Conflict requires. This Manual will form the basis for training of UK military personnel in this body of law, and will be used widely to inform practical decision making.

CDS PUS

Preface

This Manual is a reference work for members of the United Kingdom's Armed Forces and officials within the Ministry of Defence and other departments of Her Majesty's Government. It is intended to enable all concerned to apply the law of armed conflict when conducting operations and when training or planning for them.

It has distinguished antecedents. Chapter XIV of the *Manual of Military Law*, published by the Army in 1914, was written jointly by Colonel J E Edmonds and Professor Lassa Oppenheim. This was revised in 1936 and was the principal source of guidance throughout the Second World War and Korean War. During the 1950s the law of armed conflict element of the *Manual of Military Law* was completely redrafted to form a volume entitled *The Law of War on Land, being Part III of the Manual of Military Law* (London, HMSO, 1958). This volume was written by Sir Hersch Lauterpacht QC with the assistance of Colonel (later Professor) Gerald Draper OBE and came to be regarded internationally as a classic text on its subject. The current volume owes a great deal to the work carried out by these earlier authors but, clearly, has been influenced a very great deal by changes that have taken place within the law of armed conflict since the 1950s. It is also, significantly, a Joint Service Publication and not merely a manual for use by the Army during land operations. As such, it incorporates the relevant law dealing with both maritime and air operations.

This new Manual is the result of work put in by a great many people over a long period of time, almost 25 years. The need for a new manual became apparent when the 1977 Additional Protocols to the Geneva Conventions of 1949 were adopted and drafting first got underway in 1979. The full list of contributors during the years since then would be too great to reproduce and an attempt to compile it would, in any case, risk offence by leaving out some whose input was significant at the time but whose names are no longer on record. Nevertheless, mention of some key contributors is appropriate. The first General Editor was Colonel (later Major General) Michael Fugard, with the first full version of a draft text completed by 1986 under the general editorship of Colonel (later Major General) David Selwood. At that point publication was delayed to await the United Kingdom's ratification of the Additional Protocols. However, it took a further 12 years for ratification to occur. In the meantime, in the period 1994–97, as ratification became increasingly likely, Colonel Charles Garraway took on the general editorship and carried out a complete revision of the draft to take account of international legal developments, particularly those arising from the Gulf conflict of 1991. At that stage, Professor Christopher Greenwood was enlisted as Academic Consultant, a position he has retained ever since.

Following the ratification of the 1977 Additional Protocols by the United Kingdom on 28 January 1998, the draft has been thoroughly revised once again to prepare it for publication, taking account of more recent developments and conflicts, notably the jurisprudence of the International Criminal Tribunals for the former Yugoslavia and for Rwanda and the adoption of the Rome Statute of the International Criminal Court. Sponsorship of the Manual was assumed by the newly established Joint Doctrine and Concepts Centre (JDCC) in 1999 and a new General Editor, Major General (Retired) Anthony Rogers, was appointed to co-ordinate work to bring the Manual fully up to date. This was achieved under the supervision and active assistance of an Editorial Board convened and chaired by the JDCC. This was composed of representatives of the three Services, the Ministry of Defence and Foreign and Commonwealth Office Legal Advisers, and the Academic Consultant, listed alphabetically as follows:

> Commodore Jeffrey Blackett Royal Navy, Chief Naval Judge Advocate
>
> Group Captain William Boothby, Royal Air Force Legal Services
>
> Colonel Charles Garraway CBE, Army Legal Services
>
> Professor Christopher Greenwood CMG, QC, London School of Economics (Academic Consultant)
>
> Commander Steven Haines Royal Navy, Joint Doctrine and Concepts Centre (MOD Central Staff Sponsor and Chairman, Editorial Board)
>
> John Hudson Esq, Ministry of Defence Legal Advisers
>
> Miss Ruma Mandal, Foreign and Commonwealth Office (FCO) Legal Advisers
>
> Major General (Retired) Anthony Rogers OBE, Fellow of the Lauterpacht Research Centre for International Law, University of Cambridge (General Editor).

The Editorial Board has also received a great deal of assistance since 1999 from a number of people whose contribution deserves acknowledgement: Martin Eaton Esq CMG, FCO Legal Advisers; Professor Vaughan Lowe, Chichele Professor of Public International Law in the University of Oxford (who provided particular advice on Chapter 13 on Maritime Warfare); Professor Sir Adam Roberts KCMG FBA, Fellow of Balliol College, Oxford (who read and commented on a draft of the whole text); Michael Meyer Esq OBE of the British Red Cross Society (who read and commented on 12 draft chapters); and Miss Elizabeth Wilmshurst CMG, who has read and commented on several complete drafts and who has striven hard to improve its quality. Last but not least, the full text was read by Sir Michael Wood KCMG (FCO Legal Adviser) and Martin Hemming Esq CB (MOD Legal Adviser) prior to its formal adoption on 1 July 2004 as the United Kingdom's official manual on the subject.

Although the Manual represents the United Kingdom's interpretation of the law, there were several meetings over the years up to the ratification of the Additional Protocols, with service lawyers from other English-speaking countries, principally Australia, Canada, New Zealand, and the USA. The comparison of drafts and the exchange of ideas generated by these meetings proved invaluable in the development of the Manual.

EDITORIAL NOTES

In the text each legal rule or proposition is set out in a numbered and headed paragraph, followed in sub-paragraphs by any necessary definitions, explanations, or examples. Where a legal rule is based on the terms of a treaty, the treaty text has usually been summarized or paraphrased. Sometimes it is quoted and, if so, it appears in inverted commas. The Manual is intended to be issued along with A Roberts and R Guelff, *Documents on the Laws of War* (3rd edn 2000), which contains the texts of most of the law of armed conflict treaties referred to in the Manual. That does not mean that the treaties or treaty articles set out in that work are necessarily binding on the United Kingdom, nor that the views expressed in that work necessarily reflect those of Her Majesty's Government. The Appendices to the Manual contain additional documents that are not to be found in Roberts and Guelff.

Readers may detect a slightly different style in Chapters 12 (Air Operations), 13 (Maritime Warfare), and 14 (Peace Support Operations) from that of the other chapters. The reason for this is that experts had to be called in to draft those chapters. The Air Operations chapter was based on a draft originally prepared by Group Captain Christopher Eadie. As for the chapter on Maritime Warfare, various drafts were initially prepared by naval lawyers but these were eventually rejected in favour of a new text based substantially on that of the *San Remo Manual on International Law Applicable to Armed Conflicts at Sea*. Nevertheless, it was not possible simply to repeat the San Remo text and Chapter 13 differs from it in a number of respects. This chapter is the combined work of Professor Lowe, Commodore Blackett, Commander Haines, and Miss Wilmshurst. The chapter on Peace Support Operations was drafted by Professor Greenwood.

Although efforts have been made to eliminate duplication, and to limit the Air Operations and Maritime Warfare chapters to matters specific to those types of operations, inevitably there will be some overlaps. Cross-references within the chapters are included to avoid confusion and these invariably point to the place in the Manual where a particular topic is dealt with in greatest detail.

The Manual applies only in international armed conflict except where otherwise specified. The most obvious example of an exception to this is Chapter 15, which is specifically devoted to internal armed conflict.

The Manual is intended as a description of the law as at 1 July 2004. However, it does not commit Her Majesty's Government to any particular interpretation of the law. Every effort has been made to ensure the accuracy of the Manual at this date but it must be read in the light of subsequent developments in the law.

Despite the care that has been taken, errors and omissions may well have occurred and the Editorial Board accepts full responsibility for them. Any comments, particularly about errors and omissions, should be reported to:

Director-General Joint Doctrine and Concepts
Ministry of Defence
Shrivenham
Swindon, Wiltshire, SN6 8RF

Amendments of this Manual will be prepared from time to time and will be published at www.mod.uk.

Contents

Table of Cases

Tables of Legislation

Abbreviations

AA	Army Act
AC	Appeal Cases
AD	Annual Digest
ADIZ	Air Defence Identification Zone
AFA	Air Force Act or Armed Forces Act, depending on the context
All ER	All England Law Reports
AP	Additional Protocol 1977 to the Geneva Conventions 1949
App	appendix
Art	article
BR 11	Book of Reference No 11 (Manual of Naval Law)
BWC	Biological Weapons Convention 1972
BYIL	British Yearbook of International Law
CC	Chicago Convention 1944
CCW	Conventional Weapons Convention 1980
Ch	Chapter
CM(A)A	Courts-Martial (Appeals) Act
Cmnd	Command Paper
CPC	Cultural Property Convention 1954
CWC	Chemical Weapons Convention 1993
ECHR	European Convention on Human Rights
EEZ	Exclusive Economic Zone
ENMOD	Environmental Modification
GC	Geneva Convention
GCA	Geneva Conventions Act
GC(A)A	Geneva Conventions (Amendment) Act
HC	Hague Convention 1907
HMSO	Her Majesty's Stationery Office
HR	Hague Regulations annexed to Hague Convention IV 1907
ICAO	International Civil Aviation Organization
ICC	International Criminal Court
ICCA	International Criminal Court Act
ICC(S)A	International Criminal Court (Scotland) Act
ICJ	International Court of Justice
ICJ Rep	International Court of Justice Reports
ICRC	International Committee of the Red Cross
ICTR	International Criminal Tribunal for Rwanda

ICTY	International Criminal Tribunal for the former Yugoslavia
ID	Identity
IHL	International Humanitarian Law
ILM	International Legal Materials
ILR	International Law Reports
IMT	International Military Tribunal
ITU	International Telecommunications Union
IW	Information Warfare
JAG	Judge Advocate General
JSP	Joint Service Publication
JWP	Joint Warfare Publication
LOAC	Law of Armed Conflict
MAFL	Manual of Air Force Law
MML	Manual of Military Law
MOD	Ministry of Defence
NATO	North Atlantic Treaty Organization
NBC	nuclear, bacteriological, and chemical
NDA	Naval Discipline Act
NOTAM	Notice to Airmen
OSCE	Organisation for Security and Co-operation in Europe
OST	Outer Space Treaty 1967
PSO	Peace Support Operation(s)
PW	Prisoner of War
QR (Army)	Queen's Regulations for the Army 1975
QRRN	Queen's Regulations for the Royal Navy
RAF	Royal Air Force
RN	Royal Navy
ROE	Rule(s) of Engagement
RPV	Remotely Piloted Vehicle
SI	Statutory Instrument
SSR	Secondary Surveillance Radar
STANAG	Standardization Agreement
UK	United Kingdom
UN	United Nations
UNC (or UN Charter)	United Nations Charter 1945
UNCLOS	United Nations Convention on the Law of the Sea 1982
UNESCO	United Nations Educational, Scientific and Cultural Organization
UNGA	United Nations General Assembly

UNGAR	United Nations General Assembly Resolution
UNSC	United Nations Security Council
UNSCR	United Nations Security Council Resolution
US	United States
USA	United States of America
WA	Written Answer
WCR	Law Reports of Trials of War Criminals 1946–49
WWI	First World War
WWII	Second World War
YIHL	Yearbook of International Humanitarian Law
2HP	Second Protocol 1999 to the Cultural Property Convention 1954

1

Historical and General Background

A. INTERNATIONAL LAW

NATURE AND SCOPE OF INTERNATIONAL LAW

Nature of international law

International law principally governs relations between states. It is sometimes **1.1** known as public international law or the law of nations.[1]

Scope of international law

International law governs international relations both in time of peace **1.2** and in time of armed conflict. It covers, for example, the delimitation of international boundaries, international trade, the law of the sea, air and space law, human rights, protection of the environment, and diplomatic relations. It also regulates the circumstances in which states may use armed force (traditionally termed '*jus ad bellum*') and the way in which armed

---

[1] Private international law governs international dealings between individuals.

force is actually used (traditionally termed '*jus in bello*' or 'the law of war'). This manual is concerned with the latter, today more frequently known as 'the law of armed conflict' or 'international humanitarian law applicable in armed conflict' or more simply 'international humanitarian law', or 'IHL' for short.

USE OF FORCE IN INTERNATIONAL RELATIONS

Prohibition on use of force

1.3 States are required to refrain in their international relations from the threat or use of force against the territorial integrity or political independence of any state.[2]

Exceptions to the prohibition on use of force

1.4 First, the *Security Council* of the United Nations (UN) may authorize the use of force if it determines that there is in existence a threat to the peace, breach of the peace, or an act of aggression.[3]

1.5 Secondly, states have the inherent right of individual or collective *self-defence* if an armed attack occurs, until the Security Council has taken measures necessary to maintain international peace and security.[4] They must immediately report the measures taken to the Security Council. Self-defence may include the rescue of nationals where the territorial state is unable or unwilling to do so.

1.5.1 Under Article 5 of the North Atlantic Treaty 1949, states party agree that an armed attack against one or more of them in Europe or North America is to be considered an armed attack against all of them. This is an example of collective self-defence.

1.6 In addition, cases have arisen (as in northern Iraq in 1991 and Kosovo in 1999) when, in the light of all the circumstances, a limited use of force was justifiable in support of purposes laid down by the Security Council but without the Council's express authorization when that was the only means to avert an immediate and overwhelming humanitarian catastrophe. Such cases are in the nature of things exceptional and depend on an objective assessment of the factual circumstances at the time and on the terms of

---

[2] Charter of the United Nations 1945 (UN Charter), Art 2, para 4.
[3] UN Charter, ch VII.   [4] Reaffirmed in UN Charter, Art 51.

relevant decisions of the Security Council bearing on the situation in question.[5]

Requirement to comply with the law of armed conflict

Regardless of the justification for or the legitimacy of any resort to force, **1.7** individual members of the armed forces must act in accordance with the law of armed conflict. If they fail to do so, they will be acting illegally.

B. LAW OF ARMED CONFLICT

(1) INTRODUCTION TO THE LAW OF ARMED CONFLICT

PURPOSE AND SCOPE OF THE LAW OF ARMED CONFLICT

Purpose of the law of armed conflict

The main purpose of the law of armed conflict is to protect combatants and **1.8** non-combatants from unnecessary suffering and to safeguard the fundamental human rights of persons who are not, or are no longer, taking part in the conflict (such as prisoners of war, the wounded, sick, and shipwrecked) and of civilians. At sea, the law also serves to identify and protect ships flying the flag of states not parties to the conflict. By preventing the degeneration of conflicts into brutality and savagery, the law of armed conflict aids the restoration of peace and the resumption of friendly relations between the belligerents.

Components of the law of armed conflict

The law of armed conflict was traditionally divided into two parts, each **1.9** named after the city where much of the law was devised. Hague law was largely concerned with how military operations are conducted; Geneva law was concerned with the protection of the victims of armed conflict. The two bodies of law have now merged. However, there is still a distinction between the law relating to armed conflicts between states, known as international armed conflicts, and armed conflicts within the territory of a state, known as internal (or non-international) armed conflicts. This Manual deals with the law relating to international armed conflict except where otherwise specified, for example Chapter 15 dealing specifically with internal armed conflict.[6]

---

[5] See *Hansard* (House of Lords), 16 November 1998, WA 140, Baroness Symons of Vernham Dean, written answer to Lord Kennet.   [6] See also, eg, paras 3.5 to 3.9 and 16.34.

Binding nature of the law of armed conflict

1.10 The law of armed conflict, being part of international law, is binding on states but it also regulates the conduct of individuals.

1.10.1 A violation of the law of armed conflict by the armed forces of a state involves the international responsibility of that state, which may be liable to pay compensation for the violation.[7] A violation may also involve the prosecution of the individuals concerned for war crimes. Membership of the armed forces thus requires knowledge of the law of armed conflict.

1.10.2 On 30 September 1946, the International Military Tribunal sitting at Nuremberg rejected the assertion that the law of armed conflict only applies to states.[8] The decisions in hundreds of war crimes trials conducted after the Second World War have reinforced the principle of individual criminal responsibility of members of the armed forces or others who violate the law of armed conflict. This principle has been confirmed in the Statutes of the Yugoslavia and Rwanda War Crimes Tribunals and in the Statute of the International Criminal Court.[9]

SOURCES OF THE LAW OF ARMED CONFLICT

1.11 The law of armed conflict is to be found in:

a. customary law—rules developed from the practice of states which are binding on states generally; and

b. treaty law—rules expressly agreed upon by states in international treaties which are only binding on states party to those treaties.[10]

---

[7] Hague Convention IV 1907 Respecting the Laws and Customs of War on Land (Hague Convention IV), Art 3; Geneva Protocol I 1977 Additional to the Geneva Conventions of 12 August 1949 and Relating to the Protection of Victims of International Armed Conflicts (Additional Protocol I or AP I), Art 91.

[8] 'Crimes against international law are committed by men, not by abstract entities, and only by punishing individuals who commit such crimes can the provisions of international law be enforced': Trial of the Major War Criminals before the International Military Tribunal (IMT), vol XXII, 477.

[9] See the Statute of the International Tribunal for the Prosecution of Persons Responsible for Serious Violations of International Humanitarian Law Committed in the Territory of the Former Yugoslavia since 1991 (ICTY Statute), adopted by UN Security Council Resolution (UNSCR) 827(1993), Art 7. The corresponding provision in the Statute for the Tribunal for Rwanda (ICTR Statute), established by UNSCR 955(1994) is Art 6. See also the Rome Statute of the International Criminal Court of 17 July 1998 (Rome Statute 1998), Art 25.

[10] At one time, most treaties included a general participation clause, which stipulated that the treaty did not apply in an armed conflict unless all the belligerents were parties to the treaty. However, modern treaties apply as between states party to a treaty even if a non-party is also involved in the conflict.

Customary law

Customary international law consists of the rules which, as a result of state **1.12** practice over a period of time, have become accepted as legally binding.

A rule of customary law is created by widespread state practice coupled **1.12.1** with what is known as *opinio juris*, namely, a belief on the part of the state concerned that international law obliges it, or gives it a right, to act in a particular way.

The existence of a customary rule is dependent on widespread, but not **1.12.2** necessarily unanimous, state practice. Although much of the law of armed conflict has now been codified in treaties, important aspects of belligerent activity, especially in naval warfare, continue to be regulated by customary law.[11]

Treaty provisions declaratory of customary law

When treaty law provisions are declaratory of customary law, the rules they **1.13** embody are binding on all states even if they are not parties to the treaty concerned. In some cases a treaty as a whole may be viewed as customary law while in other cases only certain of a treaty's provisions may be so viewed.

There have been important judgments and opinions indicating that the **1.13.1** Hague Regulations[12] and Common Article 3 of the Geneva Conventions 1949[13] are accepted as customary law and thus binding on all states.

In the Gulf conflict of 1991, Additional Protocol I was not applicable as Iraq **1.13.2** and several coalition powers, including the United Kingdom, were not parties to it.[14] However, coalition rules of engagement were constructed so as to take into account those provisions of the Protocol that embodied rules of customary law.

---

[11] The Preamble to Hague Convention IV 1907 provided, in a passage known, after its drafter, as the 'Martens Clause' that: 'the high contracting Parties clearly do not intend that unforeseen cases should, in the absence of a written undertaking, be left to the arbitrary judgment of military commanders. Until a more complete code of the laws of war has been issued, the high contracting Parties deem it expedient to declare that, in cases not included in the Regulations adopted by them, the inhabitants and the belligerents remain under the protection and the rule of the principles of the law of nations, as they result from the usages established among civilized peoples, from the laws of humanity, and the dictates of the public conscience'.

[12] IMT, vol XXII, 497. This was endorsed in *Advisory Opinion on the Legality of the Threat or Use of Nuclear Weapons*, International Court of Justice, 1996 ICJ Rep 226, 258, though the court was vague about the extent to which other treaties might be considered to embody customary law.

[13] The International Court of Justice in the *Military and Paramilitary Activities in and against Nicaragua (Nicaragua v United States) Case* (1984) 76 ILR 1, 448, referred to the rules in Common Art 3 as constituting 'a minimum yardstick' in international armed conflicts.

[14] The UK ratified the Protocol on 28 January 1998.

Treaties

1.14 In general, treaties between states in public international law may be compared with contracts between individuals in national law in that they bind only the parties as between themselves and in accordance with their terms. Most treaties on the law of armed conflict do not take effect immediately on signature but require ratification by the state concerned. Provision is usually made for states which were not original signatories to become parties at a later date by accession.

Reservations to treaties

1.15 A reservation is a statement made by a state whereby that state purports to exclude or modify the legal effect of certain provisions of the treaty in their application to that state. A state is only allowed to make a reservation as long as this is not prohibited under the terms of the treaty and the reservation itself is not incompatible with the object and purpose of the treaty.

1.15.1 Reservations should be distinguished from interpretative statements (sometimes known as declarations) as the latter simply set out the state's understanding of the meaning of certain provisions of the treaty.

1.15.2 When considering a state's obligations under a treaty, it is necessary to have regard to any relevant reservations and interpretative statements it has made and, indeed, the reaction of other parties.

1.15.3 As customary international law is always binding on a state, any reservations to a treaty provision codifying a rule of custom will not affect the continued application of the customary rule.

(2) HISTORY OF THE LAW OF ARMED CONFLICT

EARLY HISTORY OF THE LAW OF ARMED CONFLICT

Ancient civilizations

1.16 Evidence of practices intended to alleviate the sufferings of war can be found in the writings of the ancient civilizations of India and Egypt. Agreements on the treatment of prisoners of war existed in Egypt around 1400 BC. The edicts of the Indian Emperor Asoka of about 250 BC were based on principles of humanity. In Europe, the idea of imposing rules on the conduct of warfare seems to have emerged in the Middle Ages as a result of the combined influences of Christianity and chivalry. It is said, however, that the first systematic code of war was that of the Saracens, based on the Koran, and principles of the law of armed conflict presented themselves in many different parts of the world.

England

In England, as early as the reign of Richard II in the fourteenth century, rules **1.17** of conduct in war were issued. By the early fifteenth century, all men-at-arms had to be included in an official muster and subject to a disciplinary code including rules with regard to the taking and distribution of booty. By the seventeenth century, England had a full system of Articles of War[15] regulating the behaviour of the armed forces, forbidding marauding of the countryside, individual acts against the enemy without authorization from a superior, private taking or keeping of booty, or private detention of an enemy prisoner.

Europe

The early writings on the law of nations were primarily concerned with **1.18** describing the law of war, the relations between states during such periods, and the duties of soldiers rather than with the relations that would exist during peacetime. In fact, most of the early classical writings, if not dealing with military matters as such, were given such titles as 'Concerning the Law of War and of Peace'.[16]

Through the eighteenth and into the nineteenth century, scholars were **1.19** writing texts of what they considered to be the rules regulating the conduct of armed conflict.[17] However, these texts were sometimes more indicative of the views of the writer as to what the law should be, even though they purported to be reflective of what states did in fact do, or were considered obliged to do.

MODERN HISTORY OF THE LAW OF ARMED CONFLICT

Lieber Code 1863

The most important early codification of the customs and usages of war **1.20** generally was the Lieber Code issued by President Lincoln to the Union forces in the American Civil War as General Order 100.[18]

---

[15] Laws and Ordinances of Warre 1639.

[16] See Grotius, *De Jure Belli ac Pacis* (1625), often described as the first textbook on international law, although there were earlier works on which, to some extent, he based his text.

[17] For example, E de Vattel, *Le Droit des Gens* (1758).

[18] Instructions for the Government of Armies of the United States in the Field.

Paris Declaration Respecting Maritime Law 1856

1.21 This declaration is of historical importance because it derived from the practical concerns of allies who had fought together during the Crimean War 1853–56 to harmonize their practices with regard to the treatment of enemy vessels and property as distinguished from neutral vessels and property.

Geneva Convention 1864

1.22 In the second half of the nineteenth century, greater emphasis was placed on codifying the law of war in treaty form. In 1864, at the invitation of the Swiss government, a conference, attended by the representatives of 16 states, was held in Geneva to draw up a Convention for the Amelioration of the Condition of the Wounded in Armies in the Field. This launched Geneva law as the body of the law of armed conflict that was concerned with the treatment and protection of persons rendered *hors de combat* (out of action), civilians, and other non-combatants.[19]

St Petersburg Declaration 1868

1.23 An early agreement dealing with the means[20] and methods of warfare was the St Petersburg Declaration 1868. Of great importance are the principles, set out in the Preamble, which are relevant to much of the law of armed conflict:

> That the progress of civilization should have the effect of alleviating as much as possible the calamities of war;
> That the only legitimate object which States should endeavour to accomplish during war is to weaken the military forces of the enemy;
> That for this purpose it is sufficient to disable the greatest possible number of men;
> That this object would be exceeded by the employment of arms which uselessly aggravate the sufferings of disabled men, or render their death inevitable;
> That the employment of such arms would, therefore, be contrary to the laws of humanity.

Brussels Declaration 1874 and Oxford Manual 1880

1.24 The first comprehensive international code of the law of armed conflict was the Brussels Declaration 1874, but this never entered into force. The Institute of International Law prepared a manual on the laws of war on land, known as the Oxford Manual, in 1880 but this had no binding force.

[19] The Geneva Convention was revised in 1906, 1929, and 1949.
[20] For means of warfare, that is weapons, see Ch 6.

Hague Declarations 1899 and Hague Conventions 1907

Both the Brussels Declaration and the Oxford Manual were, however, **1.25**
influential in the negotiations at the 1899 and 1907 peace conferences
that followed at The Hague. The conventions and declarations prepared
at the conferences concerned the conduct of armed conflict and underlie
that body of the law of armed conflict still known as Hague law. Although
these conventions and declarations contained a general participation
clause,[21] many of their provisions were, or have become, declaratory of
customary law.[22]

One declaration of 1899 is still relevant today, Hague Declaration 3, which **1.25.1**
prohibits the use of dum-dum bullets. Another, which would become
relevant to the use of gas during the First World War, was the Hague
Declaration of 1899 concerning asphyxiating gases. This prohibited 'the use
of projectiles the sole object of which is the diffusion of asphyxiating or
deleterious gases'.

The 1907 conference resulted in 13 conventions and one declaration. States **1.25.2**
party to Hague Convention IV 1907 were required to issue instructions to
their land forces in accordance with the regulations, now known as the
Hague Regulations, annexed to the Convention. For the first time, states
were required to pay compensation for violations of the Regulations.

However, the Convention did not provide for the prosecution of indi- **1.25.3**
viduals who violated the Regulations. Trials of these persons were
conducted by national tribunals[23] applying customary international law,[24]
the Hague Regulations,[25] or, in the case of their own personnel, the national
military or criminal code.[26]

---

[21] A clause stating that the treaty would cease to be binding if a state not party to the treaty
became involved in the war, see n 10. [22] See para 1.12.
[23] In the case of the German trials held at Leipzig after the First World War against German
accused, these were in accordance with the Treaty of Versailles 1919, Art 228.
[24] For the German trial of Captain Fryatt in 1916 for attempting to ram a German submarine
when captain of a merchant vessel, see M Lachs, *War Crimes* (1945) 33. See also *The Llandovery
Castle Case* (1920) 2 Annual Digest (AD) 436 (Case No 235), in which the officers of a U-boat
were sentenced by the Leipzig Supreme Court for firing upon and killing contrary to international law survivors of a torpedoed hospital ship carrying a number of Canadian medical
personnel; *The Peleus Trial* (1946) 1 Law Reports of Trials of War Criminals (WCR) 1, another
case of attacking the shipwrecked; and *The Hadamar Trial* (1947) 1 WCR 46, which was concerned with the killing of allied civilian nationals contrary to international law.
[25] See *The Dreierwalde Case* (1947) 1 WCR 81, which was concerned with the killing of
captured RAF personnel contrary to Art 23(c).
[26] For recent examples, see the US trials of personnel accused of crimes against prisoners
of war or enemy civilians during the Korean and Vietnam wars, eg, *US v Keenan* (1954)
14 CMR 742; *US v Calley* (1969/71; 1973) 46 CMR 1131; 48 CMR 19; 1 Mil Law Reporter 2488.

Experience of the First World War

1.26 During the First World War, it became clear that the law of armed conflict was inadequate with regard to the treatment of the wounded and sick and prisoners of war and with regard to the use of gas.

1.26.1 In 1929, two new Geneva Conventions were drafted, the first dealing with the wounded and sick and up-dating the earlier Conventions of 1864 and 1906, and the second dealing with prisoners of war, building on provisions in the Hague Regulations.

1.26.2 Aerial bombardment and its attendant problems have existed as long as man has had the technology to conduct it. The Hague Peace Conference 1899 forbade the dropping of bombs for a period of five years. This was followed by the Hague Regulations 1907.[27] During the First World War, air bombardment from aeroplanes at first consisted of no more than dropping hand-held bombs into enemy lines. Later in the war, bombarding the enemy on his own territory from the air became the strategy of all states capable of undertaking it. The belligerents claimed that they were restricting air bombardment to military objectives. While instructions and intentions on both sides reflected a proper regard for the principles of the law of war, the circumstances and techniques of the time prevented accurate bombing and there were many instances of loss of civilian life and damage to civilian objects disproportionate to the military advantage gained.

1.26.3 An attempt was made in 1923 to arrive at some measure of international agreement with the Draft Hague Rules of Aerial Warfare (Hague Rules 1923).[28] Although these draft rules were never adopted by states, they did to a large extent reflect general principles and customary rules and were treated as an attempt to apply these to air operations. During the period between the World Wars, however, there were several instances of bombardment conducted with little or no regard to the distinction between military targets and civilian objects. However, one leading expert on the law of war wrote in 1933:

> If a military objective is situated in such a densely populated neighbourhood, or if the circumstances of the case are otherwise such that any attack upon it from the air

The Canadian and Belgian cases arising out of UN operations in Somalia in 1993 (*Korad Kalid v Paracommando Soldier, Osman Somow v Paracommando Soldier, R v Boland*, and *R v Seward*) are abstracted in M Sassoli and A A Bouvier, *How Does Law Protect in War?* (1999) 1062–1085.

[27] The only clear rule of air bombardment to be found in the Hague Regulations 1907 (HR) is the prohibition of the bombing of undefended places, HR, Art 25.

[28] For an exposition of the Draft Hague Rules of Aerial Warfare 1923 (Hague Rules 1923), see A Roberts and R Guelff (eds), *Documents on the Laws of War* (3rd edn 2000) (Roberts and Guelff, *Documents*) 139–153.

is likely to involve a disastrous loss of non-combatant life, aircraft are bound to abstain from bombardment.[29]

The law of air warfare is dealt with in Chapter 12.   **1.26.4**

Geneva Gas Protocol

One treaty of the inter-war years that is still significant today is the Geneva   **1.27** Gas Protocol 1925.[30] In practice, having regard to the many reservations, it amounted to a prohibition of the first use of chemical and biological methods of warfare.

The 1899 Declaration had a very limited scope and has been replaced   **1.27.1** by the Geneva Gas Protocol 1925. That Protocol prohibited 'the use in war of asphyxiating, poisonous or other gases, and of all analogous liquids, materials or devices'. It did not, however, prohibit their manufacture or acquisition. Some states, including the United Kingdom,[31] entered reservations on ratification to the effect that the Protocol would cease to be binding if the enemy failed to respect its provisions. For these states, the Protocol amounted to a ban on the first use of chemical weapons. In the years since 1972, some states that earlier made reservations to the Protocol have withdrawn those reservations either partially or completely, principally on account of the prohibition contained in the Biological Weapons Convention or the Chemical Weapons Convention.[32]

In 1970, the United Kingdom stated that CS and other such gases were   **1.27.2** outside the scope of the Protocol. The USA, on ratification of the Protocol in 1975, declared their understanding that it did not apply to riot control agents and chemical herbicides but that, as a matter of policy, the use of riot control agents and chemical herbicides would be restricted.[33] Of course, the Protocol only applies in time of armed conflict so has no bearing, in any event, on the use of CS gas in the course of peacetime riot control.

---

[29] J M Spaight, *Air Power and War Rights* (2nd edn 1933) 210. See also speech by Prime Minister Neville Chamberlain to Parliament on 21 June 1938, *Hansard* (House of Commons Debates) vol 1337, col 937.

[30] Protocol for the Prohibition of the Use in War of Asphyxiating, Poisonous or Other Gases, and of Bacteriological Methods of Warfare 1925 (Geneva Gas Protocol 1925).

[31] The first such reservation was that of France and provided '(1) The said Protocol is only binding on the Government of the French Republic as regards States which have signed or ratified it or which may accede to it. (2) The said Protocol shall *ipso facto* cease to be binding on the Government of the French Republic in regard to any enemy State whose armed forces or whose Allies fail to respect the prohibitions laid down in the Protocol'. Similar statements, or statements to the effect that the Protocol would be applied on the basis of reciprocity, were made by many states.   [32] See Roberts and Guelff, *Documents*, 156.

[33] See Roberts and Guelff, *Documents*, 165–167.

1.27.3 The Geneva Gas Protocol was the principal basis for asserting the illegality of the use of chemical weapons in the Iran–Iraq conflict 1980–88.[34]

Experience of the Second World War

1.28 The Second World War was a watershed for the law of armed conflict. The inadequacies of the existing law were again exposed. This was in part due to the fact that not all the belligerents were parties to the Geneva Conventions 1929. The treatment accorded to prisoners of war often fell well below acceptable international standards.[35] The Hague Regulations were insufficient to guide properly the authorities in control of vast areas of occupied territory and even these rules were frequently ignored and harsh measures were adopted to counter the activities of partisans. The notion of total war, where civilians were heavily involved in war-supporting industries, area bombing methods, siege warfare, long-range rockets, and atomic weapons together led to extremely heavy civilian casualties. Above all, there was an absence of treaty provisions to protect civilians who were subjected to deportation and extermination as part of a concerted policy of genocide.

1.28.1 The Second World War witnessed extensive bombing offensives, which resulted in the destruction of many civilian areas in the United Kingdom, Germany, Poland, Japan, and elsewhere. During this period of conflict there was no written code of law specifically governing air warfare and binding on the belligerents. Air operations, especially when directed against ground targets, were, however, arguably subject to the same general principles of customary international law and certain treaty obligations as bound armed forces on land.[36] Similarly, certain rules of naval warfare, such as those requiring respect for hospital ships, were applicable to air operations against naval targets.

War crimes trials

1.29 As a result of events during the Second World War, International Military Tribunals were established at Nuremberg and Tokyo to try the major war criminals of the Axis powers. These tribunals had the power to deal not only with war crimes but also with crimes against peace and crimes against humanity. The latter were defined, and identified as crimes under international law.[37] Whilst there is considerable overlap between crimes against humanity and war crimes, war crimes (violations of the laws and customs

---

[34] See Roberts and Guelff, *Documents*, 157.

[35] See, eg, *The Nuremberg Judgment* (1947) XXII IMT 451–453.

[36] Although in the Charter of the Nuremberg International Military Tribunal indiscriminate bombardment was made a crime cognizable by the tribunal, the judgment did not contain any definite reference to the subject.   [37] Under Art 6 of their respective charters.

of war) are directly related to a state of armed conflict whereas crimes against humanity (inhumane acts committed against the civilian population in peace or in time of armed conflict) are not necessarily linked to a state of armed conflict.[38] The Nuremberg Tribunal confirmed that the Hague Regulations were recognized by all civilized nations, and were regarded as being declaratory of the laws and customs of war[39] and, as such, applicable to all belligerents whether parties to the Convention to which the Regulations were annexed or not. Although subsequent attempts were made to codify principles established by the Nuremberg Tribunal, such codes did not meet with universal acceptance.[40] However, Article 7 of the ICTY Statute and Article 6 of the ICTR Statute,[41] address the matter of individual criminal responsibility and both embody important Nuremberg principles. This approach has been taken further by the Statute of the International Criminal Court (ICC).[42]

After the Second World War, apart from international military tribunals, **1.29.1** there were many war crimes trials in national courts of various types (both civil and military) in countries occupied by Allied forces. British military tribunals so acted under the authority of the Royal Warrant for the Trial of War Criminals of 14 June 1945.

Geneva Conventions 1949

Geneva law was totally revised in 1949 with four new Conventions dealing **1.30** with the protection of:

a. the wounded and sick (replacing the Conventions of 1864, 1906, and 1929);[43]

b. the wounded, sick, and shipwrecked at sea (replacing Hague Convention X 1907);[44]

c. prisoners of war (replacing the Convention of 1929);[45] and

d. civilians.[46]

---

[38] See *The Barbie Case* (1987) 78 ILR 125, 136; ICTY Statute, Art 5; ICTR Statute, Art 3; Rome Statute, Art 7.   [39] *Nuremberg Judgment* (1947) XXII IMT 467–497 (see n 8).
[40] International Law Commission, Draft Code of Offences Against the Peace and Security of Mankind 1954.   [41] See para 1.36.
[42] See para 1.38.
[43] Geneva Convention I 1949 for the Amelioration of the Condition of the Wounded and Sick in Armed Forces in the Field (Geneva Convention I or GC I).
[44] Geneva Convention II 1949 for the Amelioration of the Condition of Wounded, Sick and Shipwrecked Members of Armed Forces at Sea (Geneva Convention II or GC II).
[45] Geneva Convention III 1949 Relative to the Treatment of Prisoners of War (Geneva Convention III or GC III).
[46] Geneva Convention IV 1949 Relative to the Protection of Civilian Persons in Time of War (Geneva Convention IV or GC IV).

1.30.1 All four Geneva Conventions apply:

a. in any international armed conflict, whether war is declared or not, and even if one of the parties does not recognise the existence of a state of war;[47] or

b. if there is a partial or total occupation of another state's territory, even if the occupation has met with no armed resistance.[48]

1.30.2 Unlike the Hague Conventions 1907, the Geneva Conventions expressly reject the 'general participation clause' approach and apply as between parties even though one of the other belligerents is not a party to the Conventions. In addition, if a state which is not a party to the Conventions abides by their provisions, the belligerents who are parties are also obliged to observe the Conventions in relation to that state.

1.30.3 In practice, the Geneva Conventions are of virtually universal application and are generally considered to embody customary law.

1.30.4 The Geneva Conventions extend to internal armed conflicts a minimum of humanitarian protection,[49] see Chapter 15.

1.30.5 The Conventions also establish for the first time an express obligation on states to bring to justice individuals who commit certain war crimes. States are obliged to bring before their courts persons in their jurisdiction, whatever their nationality, who are alleged to have committed 'grave breaches'[50] of the Conventions, or, if they prefer, hand such persons over for trial by another party to the Conventions which has made out a *prima facie* case against the alleged offender.[51] For the trial of war crimes, see Chapter 16.

Cultural Property Convention 1954

1.31 In response to the destruction and looting of cultural property that had taken place during the Second World War, the Hague Convention for the Protection of Cultural Property in the Event of Armed Conflict (Cultural Property Convention) was concluded in 1954 under the auspices of the United Nations Educational, Scientific and Cultural

---

[47] Whether an international armed conflict exists is a question of fact.

[48] Common Art 2 of all four Geneva Conventions.

[49] Common Art 3 of all four Geneva Conventions.

[50] The definition of grave breaches is in GC I, Art 50; GC II, Art 51; GC III, Art 130; and GC IV, Art 147.

[51] GC I, Art 49; GC II, Art 50; GC III, Art 129; GC IV, Art 146. The United Kingdom (UK) gave effect to the Conventions in UK law by the Geneva Conventions Act 1957. Section 1 of the Act makes the commission of a grave breach by any person, whether in or outside the UK, an offence under UK law, triable by UK courts.

Organization (UNESCO).[52] A Second Protocol to this Convention was adopted in 1999.[53] For details, see paragraph 5.26.

This Convention places an equal obligation on defenders and attackers by requiring states to refrain from uses of cultural property that would expose it to danger in armed conflict and to refrain from acts of hostility against cultural property. **1.31.1**

Cultural property is 'movable or immovable property of great importance to the cultural heritage of every people'.[54] **1.31.2**

Biological Weapons Convention 1972[55]

Biological weapons were finally prohibited under this Convention. See, further, paragraph 6.5. **1.32**

Additional Protocols I and II 1977

A major development in the law of armed conflict was the adoption in 1977 of two Protocols Additional to the Geneva Conventions of 1949.[56] Additional Protocol I deals with international armed conflicts and Additional Protocol II deals with internal armed conflicts. **1.33**

International armed conflicts

Additional Protocol I codifies existing principles of customary law and introduces important new treaty provisions relating to international armed conflicts. It sets out detailed rules on targeting and the means and methods of warfare and expands on the concept of grave breaches. It extends the range of persons entitled to combatant status as well as **1.33.1**

[52] Although the UK is not yet a party to the Convention or either of its Protocols, it is intended to ratify the Convention when implementing legislation has been introduced and passed by Parliament. No timetable has yet been set for this. In the meantime, UK forces, though not strictly bound by the terms of the Convention, should apply the principles it contains. There are also provisions for the protection of cultural property in AP I, which UK forces are required to apply, see para 5.25.

[53] Second Hague Protocol for the Protection of Cultural Property in the Event of Armed Conflict 1999 (Second Hague Protocol).

[54] Hague Convention for the Protection of Cultural Property in the Event of Armed Conflict 1954 (Cultural Property Convention 1954 or CPC), Art 1.

[55] The UN Convention on the Prohibition of Development, Production and Stockpiling of Bacteriological (Biological) and Toxin Weapons and on their Destruction 1972 (Biological Weapons Convention 1972 or BWC).

[56] Additional Protocol I, see n 7; Geneva Protocol II 1977 Additional to the Geneva Conventions of 12 August 1949 and Relating to the Protection of Victims of Non-International Armed Conflicts (Additional Protocol II or AP II). The UK gave effect to these Protocols by the Geneva Conventions (Amendment) Act 1995, which came into force on 28 July 1998.

the rights and guarantees afforded to civilians and medical services. It includes provisions on civil defence, mercenaries, and the protection of the environment. The definition of international armed conflict is itself expanded to include certain conflicts fought by peoples 'in exercise of their right of self-determination'.

Internal armed conflicts

1.33.2 Additional Protocol II develops and supplements the humanitarian protection provided by Common Article 3 of the Geneva Conventions of 1949 in internal armed conflicts.

1.33.3 International law has historically regulated relations between states. A state's internal affairs, including responsibility for the maintenance of law and order and the defence of territorial integrity against domestic insurgents, were largely regarded as the exclusive business of the state concerned. The notion of international law regulating a conflict occurring within a state would generally have been regarded as being at variance with this approach. However, it was possible for insurgents in an internal armed conflict to be recognized as belligerents and for the law of armed conflict to apply.

1.33.4 The internal use of force against criminal and terrorist activity is not regulated by the law of armed conflict unless the activity is of such a nature as to amount to armed conflict. However, human rights law would apply.[57] Sometimes, as a matter of policy, governments and armed forces have applied basic principles drawn from the law of armed conflict, in such matters as the treatment and interrogation of detainees, even in situations in which the law of armed conflict did not formally apply.

1.33.5 Although the Geneva Conventions 1949 dealt primarily with international armed conflict, an attempt was made, in Article 3 common to each Convention, to provide basic rules in internal armed conflicts for the protection of those who take 'no active part in hostilities, including members of the armed forces who have laid down their arms or those placed *hors de combat* by sickness, wounds, detention, or any other cause'. Additional Protocol II builds on that basic framework.

1.33.6 In practice, many armed conflicts have at the same time certain aspects which have the character of an internal armed conflict, while other aspects are clearly international. For example, an internal conflict may become internationalized, with the armed forces of outside states actively involved. Different parts of the law of armed conflict may, therefore, apply

---

[57] AP II, Art 1(2) excludes internal disturbances and tensions such as riots and isolated and sporadic acts of violence, as not being armed conflicts.

to different phases or aspects of the conflict. There is thus a spectrum of violence ranging from internal disturbances through to full international armed conflict with different legal regimes applicable at the various levels of that spectrum. It is often necessary for an impartial organization, such as the International Committee of the Red Cross, to seek agreement between the factions as to the rules to be applied.

Conventional Weapons Convention 1980[58]

The Convention has five Protocols dealing with: **1.34**

a. the prohibition of the use of weapons the primary effect of which is to injure by fragments that cannot be detected by X-rays;

b. the regulation of mines[59], booby-traps and similar devices;[60]

c. the prohibition of the use of air-delivered incendiary weapons against targets in populated areas and the regulation of the use of other incendiary weapons;

d. the prohibition of the use of laser weapons designed to cause permanent blindness; and

e. explosive remnants of war.

These Protocols are dealt with in Chapter 6.   **1.34.1**

Chemical Weapons Convention 1993[61]

This Convention introduces a complete ban on the development, production, **1.35** stockpiling, retention, transfer, or use of chemical weapons, see Chapter 6.

International criminal tribunals

International criminal tribunals were established by the UN Security Council: **1.36**

a. in 1993 to deal with grave breaches, war crimes, genocide, and crimes against humanity committed in the former Yugoslavia since 1991;[62] and

---

[58] UN Convention on Prohibitions or Restrictions on the Use of Certain Conventional Weapons Which May be Deemed to be Excessively Injurious or to Have Indiscriminate Effects 1980 (Conventional Weapons Convention 1980 or CCW).

[59] Anti-personnel mines are prohibited altogether by the Ottawa Convention 1997, see para 1.37.

[60] There are two such Protocols: the original version of 1980 and an amended version of 1996. Some states are parties to the original and some to the amended Protocol. The UK is a party to both Protocols.

[61] Convention on the Prohibition of the Development, Production, Stockpiling and Use of Chemical Weapons and on their Destruction 1993 (Chemical Weapons Convention 1993 or CWC).   [62] UNSCR 827(1993).

b. in 1994 to deal with genocide, crimes against humanity, and violations of Common Article 3 of the Geneva Conventions and of Additional Protocol II committed in Rwanda or by Rwandans in neighbouring states in 1994.[63]

Ottawa Convention 1997[64]

1.37 This Convention prohibits the use, development, production, acquisition, stockpiling, retention, or transfer of anti-personnel mines and requires the destruction of stocks. It does permit the retention of small stocks for training purposes.[65]

International Criminal Court

1.38 On 17 July 1998, another milestone in the development of the law of armed conflict was reached with the Rome Statute of the International Criminal Court. The court has jurisdiction over genocide, crimes against humanity, and war crimes committed after the entry into force of the Statute.[66]

1.38.1 The Statute applies to a wider range of situations than armed conflict because of the extent of the concept of crimes against humanity. The Statute is explained in Chapter 16.[67]

Naval warfare

1.39 This outline of the history and development of the law of armed conflict has concentrated mainly on the law relating to armed conflict on land and in the air. Prize law, as part of international law exclusively applicable in wartime, was well developed by the sixteenth century. The Paris Declaration 1856 was the first multilateral treaty to deal with naval warfare. The Geneva Convention 1864 was adapted for maritime warfare in 1899 and several of the Hague Conventions 1907 deal with naval matters. These subjects are dealt with more fully in Chapter 13.

---

[63] UNSCR 955(1994).

[64] Ottawa Convention on the Prohibition of the Use, Stockpiling, Production and Transfer of Anti-Personnel Mines and on their Destruction 1997.

[65] The Convention was implemented in the UK by the Landmines Act 1998.

[66] The ICC also has jurisdiction over the crime of aggression, but only after a definition and conditions for the exercise of jurisdiction have been agreed to and included in the Statute under the amendment procedure; see Art 5(2) of the Statute.

[67] The International Criminal Court Act 2001 and the International Criminal Court (Scotland) Act 2001 were enacted to enable the UK to ratify the Statute.

United Nations operations

UN peacekeeping operations have consistently been viewed as subject **1.40** to the 'principles and spirit' (later 'principles and rules') of the general international conventions.

In recent years, the increased role of the UN in dealing with both interna- **1.40.1** tional and internal armed conflicts has raised questions about the applica- tion of the law of armed conflict to UN forces or forces operating under a UN mandate. There is no treaty specifically dealing with this matter but the regulations for such forces from the earliest deployments provided that they are to follow the general principles of the law of armed conflict.[68] Members of national contingents in UN operations are, in any event, bound by their own states' adherence to treaties.

UN peace support operations and the rules applying to them are dealt with **1.40.2** in Chapter 14.

United Nations role in relation to the law of armed conflict

The UN Security Council has played an increasingly active role in this **1.41** area. It has passed numerous resolutions calling on states to comply with the law of armed conflict, has initiated inquiries into violations and has estab- lished international tribunals for the trial of war crimes and other offences.

(3) NEUTRALITY

INTRODUCTION

The traditional law of neutrality defines the relationship under inter- **1.42** national law between states engaged in an armed conflict and those that are not participating in that conflict. Traditionally, the law has incorporated the principle of non-participation in armed conflict and also impartiality in certain dealings with the belligerents.

In numerous conflicts, including the two World Wars, some non-belligerent **1.42.1** states departed from a strict interpretation of the impartiality principle in certain respects, whether by taking non-violent discriminatory measures against states seen as having unlawfully resorted to force, or by giving extensive support to one side. Certain terms, such as 'qualified neutrality' and 'non-belligerence' have been used to describe a status which, while departing from certain traditional neutral duties, was still based on avoid- ance of active participation in hostilities.

---

[68] See the Basic Principles in Ch 2.

1.42.2 The development of the prohibition on the use of force, through the Pact of Paris and the UN Charter, has important implications for the traditional law of neutrality. Since the end of the Second World War and the establishment of the United Nations, the traditional law of neutrality has been affected by and, to a large extent, superseded by the UN Charter. First, the conduct of armed conflict is subject to the limitations imposed by the Charter on all use of force. Secondly, UN member states are required to give the UN every assistance in any action it takes, and refrain from giving assistance to any state against which the UN is taking preventive or enforcement action.[69] UN members are further bound to accept and carry out the decisions of the UN Security Council,[70] and join in affording mutual assistance in carrying out the measures decided upon by the Security Council under Chapter VII of the Charter.[71]

1.42.3 A number of treaties concluded since the establishment of the UN implicitly accept that non-participation in hostilities continues to be a valid position, and that it can take different forms: such treaties contain references to 'neutral or non-belligerent powers'[72] and 'neutral and other States not Parties to the conflict'.[73]

BASIC PRINCIPLES

1.43 Certain fundamental principles of neutrality law remain applicable:

    a. Neutral states must refrain from allowing their territory to be used by belligerent states for the purposes of military operations. If a neutral state is unable or unwilling to prevent the use of its territory for the purposes of such military operations, a belligerent state may become entitled to use force in self-defence against enemy forces operating from the territory of that neutral state. Whether or not they are so entitled will depend on the ordinary rules of the *jus ad bellum*.[74]

    b. Given the duties of neutral states, targets in neutral territory cannot be legitimate military objectives and they must not be attacked by belligerent states. Nor may belligerent states conduct military operations in neutral territory (including territorial waters). This prohibition applies also to military operations that infringe the rights of a neutral state in any other of its maritime zones: for example, targeting oil installations or erecting military installations on its continental shelf.[75]

---

[69] UN Charter, Art 2(5).   [70] UN Charter, Art 25.   [71] UN Charter, Art 49.
[72] eg, GC III, Arts 4B(2) and 122.   [73] eg, AP I, Arts 9(2)(a), 19 and 31.
[74] See para 1.2.
[75] The two principles detailed in this paragraph are examples and are not necessarily exhaustive.

2

Basic Principles of the Law of Armed Conflict

INTRODUCTION

At the outset of any consideration of the law of armed conflict, it must **2.1** be emphasized that the right of the parties to the conflict to choose methods or means of warfare is not unlimited.[1] Despite the codification of much customary law into treaty form during the last one hundred years, four fundamental principles still underlie the law of armed conflict. These are military necessity, humanity, distinction, and proportionality. The law of armed conflict is consistent with the economic and efficient use of force. It is intended to minimize the suffering caused by armed conflict rather than impede military efficiency.

MILITARY NECESSITY

Military necessity permits a state engaged in an armed conflict to use only **2.2** that degree and kind of force, not otherwise prohibited by the law of armed conflict, that is required in order to achieve the legitimate purpose of the conflict, namely the complete or partial[2] submission of the enemy at

---

[1] This general principle is firmly rooted in the law of armed conflict, see Hague Regulations 1907 (HR) Art 22, Additional Protocol I 1977 (AP I), Art 35(1). AP I, Art 36 also places an obligation on states party to recognize this principle in the development of new weapons.

[2] The traditional wording omits 'partial'. However, armed conflict can have a limited purpose, as in the termination of the occupation of the Falkland Islands in 1982 or of Kuwait in 1991.

the earliest possible moment with the minimum expenditure of life and resources.

2.2.1 The principle of military necessity contains four basic elements:

    a. the force used can be and is being controlled;

    b. since military necessity permits the use of force only if it is 'not otherwise prohibited by the law of armed conflict', necessity cannot excuse a departure from that law;

    c. the use of force in ways which are not otherwise prohibited is legitimate if it is necessary to achieve, as quickly as possible, the complete or partial submission of the enemy;

    d. conversely, the use of force which is not necessary is unlawful, since it involves wanton killing or destruction.

2.2.2 Military necessity was defined as long ago as 1863 in the Lieber Code as 'those measures which are indispensable for securing the ends of the war, and which are lawful according to the modern law and usages of war'.[3] The principle is encapsulated in the Preamble to the St Petersburg Declaration 1868 that the only legitimate object which states should endeavour to accomplish in war is to weaken the military forces of the enemy and that for this purpose it is sufficient to disable the greatest possible number of men.

2.2.3 The practical application of the principle of military necessity has been described, in the context of belligerent occupation, as follows:

Military necessity permits a belligerent, subject to the laws of war, to apply any amount and kind of force to compel the complete submission of the enemy with the least possible expenditure of time, life and money. In general, it sanctions measures by an occupant necessary to protect the safety of his forces and to facilitate the success of his operation. It permits the destruction of life of armed enemies and other persons whose destruction is incidentally unavoidable by the armed conflicts of the war; it allows the capturing of armed enemies and others of peculiar danger, but it does not permit the killing of innocent inhabitants for purposes of revenge or the satisfaction of a lust to kill. The destruction of property to be lawful must be imperatively demanded by the necessities of war. Destruction as an end in itself is a violation of international law. There must be some reasonable connection between the destruction of property and the overcoming of the enemy forces. It is lawful to destroy railways, lines of communication, or any other property that might be utilized by the enemy. Private homes and churches even may be destroyed if necessary for military operations. It does not admit the wanton devastation of a district or the wilful infliction of suffering upon its inhabitants for the sake of suffering alone.[4]

---

    [3] Lieber Code, Art 14.
    [4] *The Hostages Case (United States v List and others)* (1980) 8 WCR 34.

Military necessity cannot justify departure from the law of armed conflict

It was formerly argued by some that necessity might permit a commander **2.3** to ignore the laws of war when it was essential to do so to avoid defeat, to escape from extreme danger, or for the realization of the purpose of the war.[5] The argument is now obsolete as the modern law of armed conflict takes full account of military necessity.[6] Necessity cannot be used to justify actions prohibited by law. The means to achieve military victory are not unlimited. Armed conflict must be carried on within the limits of international law, including the restraints inherent in the concept of necessity.[7]

Humanity

Humanity forbids the infliction of suffering, injury, or destruction not **2.4** actually necessary for the accomplishment of legitimate military purposes.

The principle of humanity is based on the notion that once a military purpose **2.4.1** has been achieved, the further infliction of suffering is unnecessary. Thus, if an enemy combatant has been put out of action by being wounded or captured, there is no military purpose to be achieved by continuing to attack him. For the same reason, the principle of humanity confirms the basic immunity of civilian populations and civilian objects from attack because civilians and civilian objects make no contribution to military action.

However, civilian immunity does not make unlawful the unavoidable **2.4.2** incidental civilian casualties and damage which may result from legitimate attacks upon military objectives, provided that the incidental casualties and damage are not excessive in relation to the concrete and direct military advantage anticipated. This is the principle of proportionality.[8]

The principle of humanity can be found in the Martens Clause in the **2.4.3** Preamble to Hague Convention IV 1907.[9] It incorporates the earlier rules of

---

[5] These arguments were mainly advanced by German theorists, such as Lueder, between 1871 and 1914, and are summed up in the translated maxim 'The purpose of war overrides its usages'.

[6] There are numerous examples of allowances for military necessity in the Geneva Conventions 1949, the Hague Cultural Property Convention 1954, and AP I, see the list in WA Solf and J Ashley Roach (eds), *Index of International Humanitarian Law* (1987) 152.

[7] See J Cameron (ed), *The Peleus Trial* (1948) where the defendant claimed unsuccessfully that he was under an operational necessity to protect his boat and crew. Similarly, self-preservation or military necessity can never provide an excuse for the murder of prisoners of war. See also para 8.32.   [8] Which is explained in paras 2.6 and 5.33.

[9] '[I]n cases not included in the Regulations . . . the inhabitants and the belligerents remain under the protection and the rule of the principles of the law of nations, as they result from the

chivalry that opposing combatants were entitled to respect and honour. From this flowed the duty to provide humane treatment to the wounded and those who had become prisoners of war.

<h2 style="text-align:center">DISTINCTION</h2>

2.5 Since military operations are to be conducted only against the enemy's armed forces and military objectives, there must be a clear distinction between the armed forces and civilians, or between combatants and non-combatants, and between objects that might legitimately be attacked and those that are protected from attack.

2.5.1 The principle of distinction, sometimes referred to as the principle of discrimination or identification, separates combatants from non-combatants and legitimate military targets from civilian objects. This principle, and its application to warfare, is given expression in Additional Protocol I 1977.[10]

2.5.2 Only combatants[11] are permitted to take a direct part in hostilities.[12] It follows that they may be attacked. Civilians may not take a direct part in hostilities and, for so long as they refrain from doing so, are protected from attack.[13] Taking a direct part in hostilities is more narrowly construed than simply making a contribution to the war effort. Thus working in a munitions factory or otherwise supplying or supporting the war effort does not justify the targeting of civilians so doing. However, munitions factories are legitimate military targets and civilians working there, though not themselves legitimate targets, are at risk if those targets are attacked. Such incidental damage is controlled by the principle of proportionality.[14]

2.5.3 As with personnel, the attacker also has to distinguish between civilian objects and military targets. This obligation is dependent on the quality of the information available to the commander at the time he makes decisions. If he makes reasonable efforts to gather intelligence, reviews the intelligence available to him and concludes in good faith that he is attacking a legitimate military target, he does not automatically violate the principle of distinction if the target turns out to be of a different and civilian nature.

usages established among civilized peoples, from the laws of humanity, and the dictates of the public conscience.' A more recent version of this clause can be found in AP I, Art 1(2) and AP II, Preamble.

[10] AP I, Arts 48 and 49(3). Although the application of AP I to naval warfare is somewhat limited, the principle of discrimination is inherent in customary law.

[11] AP I, Art 43(1), (2).   [12] AP I, Art 43(2).   [13] AP I, Art 51(2), (3).

[14] See paras 2.6 and 5.33.

PROPORTIONALITY

The principle of proportionality requires that the losses resulting from **2.6** a military action should not be excessive in relation to the expected military advantage.

Additional Protocol I is the first treaty to set out the principle of pro- **2.6.1** portionality specifically. Despite its importance, proportionality is not the subject of a separate article but is to be found in two different references. In the first, it features as an example of an attack that is prohibited because it is indiscriminate.[15] In the second, it appears in almost identical language in the article dealing with precautions in attack.[16] That article requires commanders to cancel, suspend, or re-plan attacks if they may be expected to offend the proportionality principle.

The principle of proportionality is a link between the principles of military **2.6.2** necessity and humanity. It is most evident in connection with the reduction of incidental damage caused by military operations.

A munitions factory may be such an important military objective that the **2.6.3** death of civilians working there would not be disproportionate to the military gain achieved by destroying the factory. A more significant factor may be the number of incidental casualties and the amount of property damage caused among civilians living nearby if the factory is in a populated area. The explosion of a munitions factory may cause serious collateral damage but that is a risk of war that would not automatically offend the proportionality rule. In such a case, the likely civilian casualties must be weighed against the military advantages which are expected to result from the attack.

Applying the principle of proportionality

Modern, smart weaponry has increased the options available to the **2.7** military planner. He needs not only to assess what feasible precautions can be taken to minimize incidental loss but also to make a comparison between different methods of conducting operations, so as to be able to choose the least damaging method compatible with military success.

The application of the proportionality principle is not always straight- **2.7.1** forward. Sometimes a method of attack that would minimize the risk to civilians may involve increased risk to the attacking forces. The law is not

---

[15] '[A]n attack which may be expected to cause incidental loss of civilian life, injury to civilians, damage to civilian objects, or a combination thereof, which would be excessive in relation to the concrete and direct military advantage anticipated': AP I, Art 51(5)(b).

[16] AP I, Art 57(2)(a)(iii) and (b).

clear as to the degree of risk that the attacker must accept. The proportionality principle does not itself require the attacker to accept increased risk. Rather, it requires him to refrain from attacks that may be expected to cause excessive collateral damage. It will be a question of fact whether alternative, practically possible methods of attack would reduce the collateral risks. If they would, the attacker may have to accept the increased risk as being the only way of pursuing an attack in a proportionate way.

2.7.2 Even where human shields are being used,[17] the proportionality rule must be considered. However, if the defenders put civilians or civilian objects at risk by placing military objectives in their midst or by placing civilians in or near military objectives, this is a factor to be taken into account in favour of the attackers in considering the legality of attacks on those objectives.

2.7.3 It is reported that, during the Gulf War of 1991, Iraq pursued a deliberate policy of placing military objectives near protected objects, for example, near mosques, medical facilities, and cultural property. Examples included dispersing military helicopters in residential areas, storing military supplies in mosques, schools, and hospitals, including a cache of Silkworm missiles in a school in Kuwait City, placing fighter aircraft near the ancient site of Ur and chemical weapons production equipment in a sugar factory.[18]

Proportionality in the use of force in international relations

2.8 It is also necessary to take account of the legal basis on which force is exercised as this may impose additional constraints on the level of force used. It is generally accepted that the use of force must be proportionate to its overall objective. In this respect, it is important to distinguish between the limitations on the level of force which is required to achieve the overall objective of the armed conflict (for example, national self-defence) and the legal limitations on the level of force required to achieve a particular military objective.

2.8.1 Self-defence may also place limitations upon the choice of targets and weaponry. Even an attack on a legitimate military target may be an unjustifiable escalation of the conflict. Thus a minor frontier incursion by infantry may not be sufficient to justify an artillery barrage against a concentration of units well away from the area of incursion. However, what is proportionate can only be judged in the particular circumstances of the case.

2.8.2 In the Falklands conflict, 1982 and the Gulf conflict, 1991, there were defined and limited goals: to re-take the occupied territories, not to pursue a war of conquest against Argentina or Iraq.

---

[17] Such use is, in any event, unlawful, see AP I, Art 51(7).
[18] US Department of Defense, *Conduct of the Persian Gulf War*, Final Report to Congress (1992) (Department of Defense Report) 613.

3

The Applicability of the Law of Armed Conflict

WHEN THE LAW OF ARMED CONFLICT APPLIES

The law of armed conflict applies in all situations when the armed **3.1**
forces of a state are in conflict with those of another state or are in occupation of territory. The law also applies to hostilities in which some of
those involved are acting under the authority of the United Nations
and in internal armed conflicts. Different rules apply to these different
situations.

The term 'armed conflict', rather than 'war', is preferred today because it **3.1.1**
is wider in scope than the term 'war' which was, and indeed still is, a technical term with certain legal implications. The Geneva Conventions refer
to 'cases of declared war or of any other armed conflict'.

The law of armed conflict was developed in the context of war between **3.1.2**
states. Until comparatively recently, it applied only to conflicts of an international nature and had no application to internal conflicts, such as civil
wars and rebellions. The only exceptions occurred in the case of large-scale
civil wars in which the participants were internationally recognized as having belligerent status and thus regarded by the international community as
engaging in war.[1]

In this chapter the application of the law of armed conflict in the various **3.1.3**
types of conflict is explained.

---

[1] The classic examples are the American Civil War and the Spanish Civil War.

ARMED CONFLICTS BETWEEN STATES

**Application of law of armed conflict not dependent
on declaration of war**

3.2 A formal declaration of war is not required to bring the law of armed
conflict into effect. It applies whenever there is an armed conflict between
states or a belligerent occupation of all or part of the territory of another
state, even if it is not resisted by armed force.

3.2.1 Under Hague Convention III 1907 there was a requirement that hostilities
would commence only after a formal declaration of war or following an
ultimatum containing a conditional declaration of war if certain demands
were not met.[2] Many armed conflicts have commenced without any
declaration, although the victim of attack or its allies have occasionally
responded with a formal declaration. The demise of the declaration of war
has thus obscured the boundary between peace and war and raises doubt
about when the law of armed conflict applies.

3.2.2 Today, states are required to settle their international disputes by peaceful
means. The United Nations Charter requires states 'to refrain in their international relations from the threat or use of force against the territorial
integrity or political independence of any State'.[3] A declaration of war or an
ultimatum could in some circumstances be regarded as evidence that
a state had contravened the provisions of the United Nations Charter.
However, Article 51 of the Charter preserves the right of individual or
collective self-defence.[4]

3.2.3 The modern law applies to any armed conflict between states, whether or
not they are at war in the technical sense and, indeed, even if the state of war
is not recognized by one of them.[5] The law will apply even if none of the

[2] Hague Convention III 1907 (HC III), Art 1 provided that hostilities should not commence
'without previous and explicit warning, in the form either of a declaration of war, giving
reasons, or of an ultimatum with conditional declaration of war'. There was, however,
nothing to impose any period of delay between the issue of notification and the beginning
of hostilities. In 1939, Germany attacked Poland and declared war simultaneously.
[3] Art 2(3), (4).
[4] United Nations (UN) Charter, Art 51. See UN Security Council Resolution (UNSCR)
661(1990) 'affirming the inherent right of collective self-defence, in response to the armed
attack of Iraq against Kuwait'. The UK's actions in recovering the Falkland Islands in 1982
were based throughout on self-defence. This conflict also showed that the right of self-defence
is not placed in abeyance merely because the Security Council has been able to pass a resolution calling for one of the parties to a conflict to withdraw.
[5] Geneva Conventions I–IV (GC I–IV), Common Art 2.

parties recognize the existence of a state of war[6] provided that an armed conflict is in fact in existence. Common Article 2 of the Geneva Conventions also applies the Conventions, and hence Additional Protocol I,[7] to all cases of partial or total occupation of the territory of a party, even if that occupation meets with no armed resistance. Even though some of the older treaties are expressed as applying in the event of 'war',[8] it is now generally accepted that the provisions of these agreements are also applicable to all armed conflicts between states. The term 'war' is thus largely void of current international legal significance except in the case of declared war, where the law of armed conflict would apply even where there is no actual fighting, in the field of neutrality, and in the law of prize in naval warfare. Customary international law is certainly not confined to 'wars' and applies to both international and internal armed conflicts.[9]

Definition of armed conflict

Neither the Geneva Conventions nor Additional Protocol I contain any definition of the expression 'armed conflict' but the following guidance has been given: **3.3**

a. 'any difference arising between States and leading to the intervention of members of the armed forces is an armed conflict';[10]

b. 'an armed conflict exists whenever there is a resort to armed force between States or protracted armed violence between governmental authorities and organised armed groups within a State'.[11]

These definitions do not deal with the threshold for an armed conflict. Whether any particular intervention crosses the threshold so as to become an armed conflict will depend on all the surrounding circumstances.[12] For example, the replacing of border police with soldiers or an accidental border incursion by members of the armed forces would not, in itself, amount to an armed conflict, nor would the accidental bombing of another country. At the other extreme, a full-scale invasion would amount to an armed conflict. **3.3.1**

---

[6] See J Pictet (ed), *Commentary on the Geneva Conventions of 12 August 1949* (1952) (Pictet, *Commentary*), vol I, 29.   [7] Additional Protocol I (AP I), Art 1(3).

[8] eg, HC IV.

[9] The Appeal Chamber of the International Criminal Tribunal for the former Yugoslavia held that customary law also applied to internal armed conflicts in *Prosecutor v Tadić* (1996) 105 International Law Reports (ILR) 419, 425.   [10] Pictet, *Commentary*, vol III, 23.

[11] *Prosecutor v Tadić* (1996) 105 ILR 419, 488.

[12] See also Additional Protocol II (AP II), Art 1(1), (2) dealing with internal conflicts.

ARTICLE 1(4) OF ADDITIONAL PROTOCOL I

3.4 Article 1(4) of Additional Protocol I applies the Protocol, and by extension the 1949 Conventions, to armed conflicts in which 'peoples are fighting against colonial domination and alien occupation and against racist regimes in the exercise of their right of self-determination'.

3.4.1 Conflicts of this nature within the territory of a state had hitherto been regarded as internal. Under the Protocol, such conflicts are treated as if they were international armed conflicts.

3.4.2 Three conditions must be complied with before this provision comes into effect:

a. First, there must be an 'armed conflict'. The threshold of violence required to render the situation an armed conflict is the same as that required for internal armed conflicts, see paragraph 15.3.

b. Secondly, the people concerned must genuinely be 'fighting against colonial domination and alien occupation and against racist regimes in the exercise of their right of self-determination'. It is not sufficient for the authority representing the people simply to claim that this is happening. This condition has to be assessed objectively. A substantial degree of international recognition of the legitimacy of the 'liberation movement' is necessary, as a minimum recognition by the appropriate regional inter-governmental organization.

c. Thirdly, the authority representing the people must undertake to apply Additional Protocol I and the Geneva Conventions. This undertaking is given by means of a unilateral declaration addressed to the Swiss government.[13] The effect of the undertaking is to impose upon both the state and the authority all the rights and obligations created by Additional Protocol I and the Geneva Conventions, so that they become responsible for ensuring the due observance of those rights and obligations.[14] Authorities cannot become parties to the Protocol or the Conventions since this status is reserved for states.

3.4.3 The United Kingdom, on ratification of Protocol I, stated that it would not be bound by an authority's declaration unless the United Kingdom expressly recognized that it was made by a body which was genuinely an authority representing a people engaged in this type of armed conflict.

---

[13] See AP I, Art 96(3). The Swiss Federal Council is the depositary of the Conventions and Protocol, see Art 93.

[14] AP I, Art 96(3). The Swiss government does not list any such declarations. This is partly due to the fact that states most likely to be affected by such conflicts have not become party to AP I. For the position relating to the Palestine Liberation Organization, see A Roberts and R Guelff, *Documents on the Laws of War* (3rd edn 2000) 362.

INTERNAL ARMED CONFLICTS

Applicability of the law of armed conflict to internal armed conflicts

If the situation in a country amounts to an armed conflict, the law of armed **3.5** conflict applies. The body of law that applies is less detailed than that applying to international armed conflicts and its precise content depends on the situation. Customary law applies in any case. If it is an armed conflict between the armed forces of a state and dissident or anti-government armed forces, or it is an armed conflict between factions within a state, Common Article 3 of the Geneva Conventions applies. If, however, the dissident or anti-government armed forces exercise sufficient territorial control as to enable them to carry out sustained and concerted military operations and implement Additional Protocol II, that Protocol applies in addition to Common Article 3.

As has already been stated,[15] the term 'armed conflict' is not defined. **3.5.1** State practice since 1949 indicates that banditry, criminal activity, riots, or sporadic outbreaks of violence and acts of terrorism do not amount to an armed conflict.[16] 'Situations of internal disturbances and tensions, such as riots, isolated and sporadic acts of violence and other acts of a similar nature' do not amount to armed conflict.[17] The law of armed conflict has no application.[18]

Until 1949, armed conflicts which were not of an international character **3.5.2** were regarded as being governed exclusively by the domestic law of the state in which they occurred.

Common Article 3

Common Article 3 of the Geneva Conventions is a mini-convention **3.6** covering all cases of armed conflict *not* of an international character occurring in the territory of one of the parties to the Conventions. It

---

[15] In para 3.3.

[16] Between 1954 and 1956, the French government dealt with the Algerian uprising under domestic law, only formally accepting the additional applicability of Common Article 3 in June 1956. The Nigerian government in the Biafra conflict never openly acknowledged the applicability of the article but, in practice, went further than its terms required, even treating Biafran prisoners as 'prisoners of war'.   [17] AP II, Art 1(2).

[18] International human rights law will apply, for example, the European Convention for the Protection of Human Rights and Fundamental Freedoms 1950 (ECHR), though derogations are permissible from certain provisions of human rights law 'in time of war or other public emergency threatening the life of the nation': ECHR, Art 15(1).

requires each party to the conflict to apply as a minimum certain basic humanitarian provisions during the course of a conflict.[19] These are set out in Chapter 15.

3.6.1 The point at which situations of internal disturbances and tensions develop into an armed conflict is open to interpretation. Although Common Article 3 specifically provides that its application does not affect the legal status of the parties to a conflict, states have often been reluctant to admit to such a development. Traditional factors that might be used to indicate the existence of an armed conflict, such as recognition of a status of insurgency by third parties, or indeed the recognition of belligerent status, have lessened in importance.[20] Pictet, in his *Commentary on the Geneva Conventions*, lists a number of possible criteria but at the same time welcomes the lack of definition. The terms of Common Article 3 are in fact merely 'rules which were already recognized as essential in all civilized countries and embodied in the national legislation of the states in question, long before the convention was signed'.[21] It follows, therefore, that whilst states may not be willing to admit to the application of Common Article 3 as a matter of law, its provisions are frequently applied in fact.

Additional Protocol II

3.7 For Additional Protocol II to apply, there must be an armed conflict of an internal nature between the forces of a state party to the Protocol and dissident armed forces or other organized armed groups under responsible command. The dissident forces are required to have a territorial base and to exercise such control over a part of the state's territory as to enable them to carry out sustained and concerted military operations and to implement the Protocol.[22]

3.7.1 Once it comes into effect, the Protocol applies, without adverse distinction, to all persons affected by the armed conflict and continues to apply both during the conflict, and, for those deprived of their liberty or whose liberty

---

[19] Some of those provisions are similar to those in the Universal Declaration of Human Rights 1948, the International Covenant on Civil and Political Rights 1966, and the ECHR. The International Court of Justice in *Military and Paramilitary Activities in and against Nicaragua (Nicaragua v United States)* (1984) 76 ILR 1, 448, referred to the rules in Common Article 3 as constituting 'a minimum yardstick' in international armed conflicts as well.

[20] A recognition of insurgency was effectively an international recognition of an internal war but left states free to assist the legitimate government. Assistance to the rebels, however, would be an illegal interference in the internal affairs of the state concerned.

[21] See Pictet, *Commentary*, vol III (1960), 35–37.

[22] It is unclear whether the dissident forces must manifest the ability to apply the Protocol by doing so or whether it is sufficient that they have the ability to do so.

has been restricted for reasons relating to such conflict, until the end of that deprivation or restriction of liberty.[23]

Agreements to supplement the law

The parties to an internal armed conflict may agree to apply more than just **3.8** Common Article 3 or Additional Protocol II, perhaps the whole of the law of armed conflict.[24]

Spectrum of conflict

The application of the law of armed conflict to internal hostilities thus **3.9** depends on a number of factors. In the first place, it does not apply at all unless an armed conflict exists. If an armed conflict exists, the provisions of Common Article 3 apply. Should the dissidents achieve a degree of success and exercise the necessary control over a part of the territory, the provisions of Additional Protocol II come into force. Finally, if the conflict is recognized as a conflict falling within Additional Protocol I, Article 1(4), it becomes subject to the Geneva Conventions and Protocol I.

THE BEGINNING AND END OF APPLICATION

Period of application

The law of armed conflict applies from the beginning of an armed conflict **3.10** until the general close of military operations.[25] However, in the case of occupied territories, its application continues until the termination of the occupation, even if military operations, if any, ceased at an earlier date.[26] Additionally, persons in the power of the adversary continue to benefit from the relevant provisions of the Conventions and Protocol until their final release, and repatriation or re-establishment.[27]

---

[23] AP II, Art 2.

[24] GC I–IV, Art 3. A memorandum of understanding was entered into between the various factions in Bosnia-Herzegovina on 1 May 1992 to supplement Common Article 3 by, among other things, dealing with the wounded and sick in accordance with GC I, giving captured combatants the treatment provided for in GC III, and in applying Arts 35–42 and 48–58 of AP I as well as the Mines Protocol of 1980. The text of the memorandum is set out in M Sassoli and A A Bouvier (eds), *How Does Law Protect in War?* (1999) 1112.

[25] This does not necessarily mean on the conclusion of a formal peace treaty. In 1951, the UN Security Council refused to accept Egypt's claim to be exercising belligerent rights in respect of shipping passing through the Suez Canal over two years after the 1949 armistice had put an end to the full-scale hostilities between Israel and Egypt. [26] See para 11.8.

[27] AP I, Art 3.

Denunciation

3.11   Although a party to the Geneva Conventions and Additional Protocol I has the right to denounce those treaties,[28] denunciation does not take effect immediately. For parties not involved in armed conflict, denunciation takes effect one year after the receipt by the depositary of the notification of denunciation. For parties engaged in armed conflict:

a. in the case of the Geneva Conventions, at the time of the notification, or

b. in the case of Additional Protocol I, at the end of that year,

the denunciation does not take effect before the end of the conflict or, if appropriate, occupation and not in any case before operations connected with the final release, repatriation, or re-establishment of protected persons have been terminated. Any denunciation can have no effect on obligations under customary law.

UNIVERSAL APPLICATION OF THE LAW OF ARMED CONFLICT

3.12   One of the most important characteristics of the law of armed conflict is its universal application. It applies with equal force to all parties engaged in an armed conflict, whether or not any party is considered to be 'an aggressor' or 'a victim of aggression'.

3.12.1   Equally, every victim of armed conflict is entitled to the protection afforded by the law. The fact that he is a national, or member of the armed forces, of any particular state or that he has particular religious convictions or political opinions is irrelevant in this context. A party to an armed conflict cannot evade its obligations under international law by purporting to change the status of territory (for example, by annexation) or individuals (for example, by forced changes of nationality).[29] Similarly, members of regular armed forces who are taken prisoner cannot be denied prisoner of war status on the ground that they profess allegiance to a regime that is not recognized by the state which has captured them.[30]

LEGAL STATUS OF PARTIES TO THE CONFLICT

3.13   The application of the law of armed conflict does not affect the legal status of parties to the conflict or the status of any occupied territories.[31] This is

[28]   See GC I, Art 63; GC II, Art 62; GC III, Art 142; GC IV, Art 158; AP I, Art 99.

[29]   GC IV, Art 47.   [30]   GC III, Art 4A(3).

[31]   AP I, Art 4. Previously, such a statement had only been made in relation to non-international armed conflicts (see Common Art 3(4)). However, it was felt necessary to extend this in order to make it unequivocally clear that the sole aim of the Conventions and Protocols

also true in respect of non-international conflicts. Nothing in Additional Protocol II may be 'invoked for the purpose of affecting the sovereignty of a State or the responsibility of the government, by all legitimate means, to maintain or re-establish law and order in the State or to defend the national unity and territorial integrity of the State'.[32]

was humanitarian. See Y Sandoz, C Swinarski, and B Zimmermann (eds), *Commentary on the Additional Protocols of 8 June 1977 to the Geneva Conventions of 12 August 1949* (1987) (*ICRC Commentary*) 72.

[32] AP II, Art 3(1).

4

The Armed Forces of the Belligerents

COMBATANTS AND NON-COMBATANTS

The law of armed conflict protects members of the civilian population by **4.1** making a distinction between combatants, who take part in the fighting, and non-combatants, who do not take part in the fighting and who must be shielded, as far as possible, from its effects. Combatants have the right to attack and to resist the enemy by all the methods not forbidden by the law of armed conflict.[1] Conversely, it is legitimate to attack and resist them by lawful methods, so long as they continue to fight. Once they have become ill or have been injured or captured, and as a result in any such case have stopped fighting, they have a right to humane and honourable treatment as prisoners of war.[2] Their lives must be spared and it is the duty of their captors to protect and maintain them. Non-combatants, by contrast, are not permitted to take a direct part in hostilities and are liable to trial and punishment if they commit, or attempt to commit, hostile acts. So long as they do not take a direct part in hostilities, non-combatants are not legitimate targets of attack.[3]

The distinction between combatants and non-combatants became blurred in **4.1.1** many of the conflicts of the twentieth century but the distinction between these two classes continues to be of the utmost importance. Each class has distinct rights and duties. An individual who belongs to one class is not permitted at the same time to enjoy the privileges of the other class.

---

[1] For these prohibitions, see Ch 5.   [2] See Ch 8.
[3] See Ch 5. There are exceptions, eg see para 4.2.3, and also in the law of war at sea, eg, blockade runners, see Ch 13.

DEFINITION OF COMBATANT

4.2 Members of the armed forces of a party to a conflict (other than medical personnel and chaplains)[4] are combatants and have the right to participate directly in hostilities.[5]

4.2.1 The expression 'combatant' has in the past been used in two senses. Sometimes it has been used to describe any person who actually engages in hostile acts in an armed conflict on behalf of a party to the conflict, whether or not he is permitted to do so. It has also been used to describe only those persons with a right to take a direct part in hostilities. For this reason, it has often been qualified by the use of the adjectives 'lawful' or 'unlawful'. 'Combatant' is now defined, as set out in paragraph 4.2, by Additional Protocol I 1977. For the meaning of 'participating directly in hostilities', see paragraph 5.3.3.

4.2.2 The distinction between combatants and non-combatants is similar, but not identical, to the distinction between the armed forces of a state and the civilian population. Some members of the armed forces of a state (medical personnel and chaplains)[6] are classed as non-combatants and do not have the right to take a direct part in hostilities. Although members of the civilian population are normally forbidden to participate in hostilities, they may do so in the exceptional circumstances of a *levée en masse*,[7] in which case they become combatants.

4.2.3 The expression 'medical personnel' is not confined to doctors and nurses but also embraces a wide range of specialists, technicians, maintenance staff, drivers, cooks, and administrators provided that they are exclusively assigned to the medical staff.[8] Non-combatant members of armed forces who participate directly in hostilities may expect to forfeit that non-combatant status. They also render themselves liable to trial and punishment. Non-combatant members of the armed forces are, however, legally permitted to defend themselves against acts of violence which are directed against them and, for this purpose, the use of firearms may be justified. Medical personnel do not forfeit their protection under Geneva Convention I 1949 by being armed and by using those arms in their own defence or in the defence of the wounded and sick in their charge.[9]

---

[4] Although still combatants as defined by Additional Protocol I (AP I), Art 43(2), members of the armed forces assigned to civil defence duties have protected status akin to that of non-combatants, so long as they do not take a direct part in hostilities, AP I, Art 67(1)(e), see para 5.48.   [5] AP I, Art 43(2).

[6] Members of the armed forces assigned to civil defence duties also have protected status, see para 5.48.   [7] See para 4.8.

[8] AP I, Art 8(c), see para 7.11.

[9] Geneva Convention I (GC I), Art 22. For chaplains, see para 7.30.

THE ARMED FORCES

The armed forces of a party to a conflict are 'all organized armed forces, **4.3**
groups and units which are under a command responsible to that Party
for the conduct of its subordinates, even if that Party is represented by
a government or an authority not recognized by an adverse Party'. Armed
forces are to be 'subject to an internal disciplinary system which, *inter alia*,
shall enforce compliance with the rules of international law applicable in
armed conflict'.[10]

Additional Protocol I supplements the Hague Regulations 1907 and **4.3.1**
Geneva Convention III 1949,[11] which laid down strict criteria for combatant
and prisoner of war status.

An organized guerrilla group or resistance movement that meets the **4.3.2**
requirements of paragraph 4.3 is as much part of the armed forces as
a regular unit.

The requirement that an armed force should be under a command **4.3.3**
responsible to a party to the conflict for the conduct of its subordinates is
satisfied if the commander is regularly or temporarily commissioned as an
officer or is otherwise recognized as a commander by the party concerned.
However, particularly in the case of resistance movements in occupied territory, formal state recognition is not essential and an organization may be
formed spontaneously and appoint its own officers. The essential feature
of the requirement is that the commander should accept responsibility for
the acts of his subordinates and equally his responsibility to, and his duty
of obedience to the orders of, the power or authority upon which he
depends. Partisans or paramilitary forces acting on their own initiative do
not comply with that requirement and so are not members of an armed
force.[12]

To ensure that armed forces comply with the law of armed conflict, they **4.3.4**
must be subject to an effective disciplinary system which enables compliance with the law to be enforced. Any force, group, or unit which in the
course of its operations systematically fails to obey the law runs the risk of
being regarded as not being subject to an effective disciplinary system and
therefore not being a legally recognizable armed force under international
law.[13] The members of such a force would not be entitled to combatant

---

[10] AP I, Art 43(1).   [11] Hague Regulations (HR), Arts 1 and 2; GC III, Art 4.
[12] Furthermore, many would be unlikely to meet the test of organization.
[13] The decision to deny an armed group the status of 'armed force' under international law
is not one for the commander in the field and must be taken at governmental level.

status and would be liable to trial and punishment in the same way as other non-combatants who participate directly in hostilities.

4.3.5 In the United Kingdom, the reserve forces are included in the definition of armed forces and comprise the following:

a. the Royal Fleet Reserve, the Royal Naval Reserve, and the Marine Reserve;

b. the Army Reserve and the Territorial Army;

c. the Royal Air Force Reserve (which includes the Royal Air Force Volunteer Reserve (Training), the Royal Air Force Volunteer Reserve (University Air Squadrons), and the Royal Auxiliary Air Force).

Members of university officer training units (University Royal Naval Units, the Officer Training Corps, and University Air Squadrons) are members of the reserve forces. However, most members are either exempt from call out or have a reduced call out liability. Similarly, officers who are commissioned into the reserve forces solely for the purposes of serving in the Army Cadet Force, the Air Training Corps, or the Combined Cadet Force are members of the armed forces though they too are either exempt from call out or have a reduced liability.

4.3.6 To avoid confusion, the law requires that 'whenever a Party to a conflict incorporates a paramilitary or armed law enforcement agency into its armed forces it shall so notify the other Parties to the conflict'.[14]

4.3.7 Armed forces increasingly rely on the technical and administrative support of civilians. Civilians who are authorized to accompany the armed forces in the field in such capacities remain non-combatants, though entitled to prisoner of war status,[15] so long as they take no direct part in hostilities. They may not be directly attacked. However, they share the dangers of war of the members of the armed forces they support. They should not wear military uniform[16] and must carry a special identity card confirming their status. The law is silent on the question of whether such civilians may be issued with weapons. To ensure retention of non-combatant status, they should be issued with small arms for self-defence purposes only. It should be borne in mind that, if they carry arms, they are likely to be mistaken for combatants. It follows that, so far as possible, such civilians should not be deployed to places where they are liable to come under enemy fire or to be captured.

---

[14] AP I, Art 43(3). The Belgian government, on ratification, declared, in accordance with Art 43, that the *gendarmerie* formed part of their armed forces.   [15] See para 8.3.1.
[16] It may be necessary for them to be issued with NBC suits and other protective items. In that case any military insignia should be removed.

The Duty of Combatants to Distinguish Themselves from the Civilian Population

General rule

'In order to promote the protection of the civilian population from the **4.4** effects of hostilities, combatants are obliged to distinguish themselves from the civilian population while they are engaged in an attack or in a military operation preparatory to an attack.'[17]

The law of armed conflict requires that combatants should be distinguished **4.4.1** from civilians. Failure on the part of combatants to distinguish themselves from civilians can only result in a real risk that civilians will be mistaken for combatants. Whilst that might benefit some irregular fighters, it would gravely add to the dangers of war for civilians. The Hague Regulations and Geneva Convention III require the carrying of arms openly and the wearing of a fixed distinctive sign.[18] However, the negotiators of Additional Protocol I considered that the observance of these strict provisions was impracticable in some circumstances of modern warfare and so laid down the general rule set out in paragraph 4.4 but introduced a special exception, dealt with in paragraph 4.5.

Additional Protocol I does not specify the manner in which combatants **4.4.2** should distinguish themselves. There is no difficulty in the case of regular troops, whose uniform or combat gear provides a sufficient distinction.[19] Irregular forces that do not habitually wear uniform must take some positive steps to identify themselves as being combatants rather than civilians. The open carrying of arms and military equipment and the wearing of some form of uniform or a fixed distinctive sign visible at a distance would clearly suffice.[20] Unlike the old law in the Hague Regulations and Geneva Convention III, however, there is no rigid requirement that an irregular combatant should distinguish himself from the civilian population by

---

[17] AP I, Art 44(3).

[18] HR, Art 1; GC III, Art 4A(2). Four conditions are laid down. These are:

a. being commanded by a person responsible for his subordinates;
b. having a fixed distinctive sign recognizable at a distance;
c. carrying arms openly;
d. conducting their operations in accordance with the laws and customs of war.

These rules would still apply in a conflict against a state not party to AP I.

[19] AP I, Art 44(7).

[20] See, however, the special rule in para 4.5. Guerrilla or partisan forces are often seen, at least before the media, in camouflage pattern fatigues and displaying a special badge or patch. This would be sufficient to constitute uniform or distinction from the civilian population.

wearing a fixed distinctive sign. The criterion is whether members of the adversary forces are able to recognize the person concerned as a combatant, and therefore a legitimate target, rather than a civilian who is protected under international law. The issue is one of fact. It may have to be determined by any tribunal before whom a person accused of violating the rule of distinction is brought.

4.4.3 The general obligation for a combatant to distinguish himself from the civilian population now applies only when the former is engaged in an attack or in a military operation preparatory to an attack.[21] In order that the civilian population should be adequately protected, the expression 'military operation preparatory to an attack' must be given a wide meaning.[22] Members of the armed forces who do not wear uniform, combat gear, or an adequate distinctive sign and whose sole arm is a concealed weapon, or who hide their arms on the approach of the enemy, will be considered to have lost their combatant status.

Exceptional case

4.5 'There are situations in armed conflicts where, owing to the nature of the hostilities, an armed combatant cannot so distinguish himself'. In such situations, a special rule applies and the individual will retain his status as a combatant provided that he 'carries his arms openly: (a) during each military engagement, and (b) during such time as he is visible to the adversary while he is engaged in a military deployment preceding the launching of an attack in which he is to participate'.[23]

In these exceptional situations, there is no obligation for a combatant to distinguish himself from the civilian population at any other time. The combatant is permitted, in effect, to disguise himself as a member of the civilian population and thereby seek to obtain the protection from attack given to the latter, except during the period of the attack and deployment.

4.5.1 Wide application of this special rule would reduce the protection of civilians to vanishing point. Members of the opposing armed forces would come to regard every civilian as likely to be a combatant in disguise and, for their own protection, would see them as proper targets for attack. The special rule is thus limited to those exceptional situations where a combatant is truly *unable* to operate effectively whilst distinguishing himself in accordance with the normal requirements. The United Kingdom, together

---

[21] Even in time of armed conflict, members of the armed forces may be authorized to wear civilian clothes when off duty away from the combat zone.
[22] Such operations would include deployments, as to which, see para 4.5.3.
[23] AP I, Art 44(3).

with other states, made a formal statement on ratifying Additional Protocol I that this exception could only apply in occupied territory or in conflicts to which Additional Protocol I, Article 1(4) apply. Even in those cases, there are many occasions on which combatants can still comply with the general rule of distinction, which remains in force, when the special rule would not apply.

Members of irregular armed forces, whether they comply with the rule of distinction or not, are legitimate objects of attack when taking a direct part in hostilities.   **4.5.2**

Even when the special rule applies, it requires, as a condition of retaining combatant status, that arms be carried openly in two cases. The first is during a military engagement, that is, when the combatant is in contact with the enemy. The second is during such time as he is visible to the adversary while engaged in a military deployment preceding the launching of an attack in which he is to participate. The term 'deployment' includes individual as well as group deployments. On ratifying Additional Protocol I, the United Kingdom, together with other states, made a formal declaration that the expression 'military deployment' means any movement towards a place from which an attack is to be launched. The requirement to carry arms openly during any such movement is limited to such time as the combatant is *visible* to the adversary. In the light of modern technical developments, 'visible' cannot be construed as meaning only 'visible to the naked eye'. A combatant is accordingly required to carry his arms openly if he is visible through binoculars or, during the night, visible by the use of infra-red or image intensification devices. The test is whether the adversary is able, using such devices, to distinguish a civilian from a combatant carrying a weapon. If such distinction can be made, the combatant is 'visible to the adversary'. The wide availability of these devices means that combatants who are seeking to take advantage of the special rule should carry their arms openly well before they are actually in contact with the enemy.   **4.5.3**

Combatants who comply with the requirements set out above will not be regarded as committing perfidious acts,[24] such as the feigning of civilian, non-combatant status.[25]   **4.5.4**

Effect of failure to comply with the rule of distinction

The position of a person who takes a direct part in hostilities while failing to comply with the rule of distinction is as follows. If he falls into the power of   **4.6**

---

[24] AP I, Art 37.   [25] AP I, Art 44(3).

the enemy while engaged in an attack or a military operation preparatory to an attack, and is not at that time complying with the requirements of the general rule (or, where applicable, the special rule set out above), he forfeits his combatant status and may be tried and punished for unlawful participation in hostilities. If he has disguised himself as a civilian, he will also be guilty of perfidy if he kills, injures, or captures an adversary by resort to that disguise.[26] He also forfeits his right to be treated as a prisoner of war unless, in spite of the circumstances, he still falls within one of the categories entitled to prisoners of war status under Geneva Convention III.[27] He must, however, be accorded treatment equivalent to that of a prisoner of war, so that he is entitled, for example, to the protection afforded to prisoners of war at his trial.[28] If he falls into the power of the adversary while he is not engaged in a military engagement or in a military operation preparatory to an attack, he does not forfeit his rights to be a combatant or a prisoner of war by virtue of his past activities,[29] though he remains liable to trial in respect of those activities, if they were unlawful. Any person who has taken part in hostilities but who is not entitled to prisoner of war status, and does not benefit from more favourable treatment as a civilian in the hands of a party to the conflict, is nevertheless entitled to certain basic humanitarian guarantees.[30]

SPECIAL CASES

Special missions and airborne troops

4.7 Members of armed forces on hostile missions behind enemy lines, whether conveyed to enemy or enemy occupied territory by air, land, or water, and also airborne troops whether landed by parachute or aircraft (even if they are operating by highly skilled methods of surprise and combat) retain their combatant status, whether operating alone or in company. As is true for all uniformed forces, they must comply with the law of armed conflict including distinguishing themselves from the civilian population in accordance with the rules set out in paragraphs 4.4 and 4.5. These provisions are equally

---

[26] AP I, Art 37(1)(c).

[27] AP I, Art 44(4) and (6). The categories entitled to prisoner of war (PW) status under GC III are set out in GC III, Art 4. It is highly unlikely that anyone who fails to meet the requirements of AP I, Art 44(3) as set out in para 4.5 will qualify for PW status under GC III, Art 4. Courts in the Commonwealth and the United States have held that a member of a belligerent's regular armed forces who was captured while engaged in an operation in which he was not distinguished from members of the civilian population was not entitled to be treated as a PW. See the decisions of the Judicial Committee of the Privy Council in *Mohammed Ali v Public Prosecutor* [1968] 3 All ER 488 and the Supreme Court of the United States in *United States v Quirin* 317 US 1 (1942).   [28] AP I, Art 44(4).

[29] AP I, Art 44(5).   [30] AP I, Arts 45(3) and 75. See, further, Ch 9 Pt B.

applicable to members of armed forces on sabotage missions. The earlier rules, which equated saboteurs with spies, have been superseded.

Levée en masse

A *levée en masse* occurs where the 'inhabitants of a territory not under **4.8** occupation . . . on the approach of the enemy, spontaneously take up arms to resist the invading troops without having had time to organize themselves'.[31] These inhabitants are treated as combatants provided that they carry arms openly and respect the laws and customs of war. However, it should be stressed that the rules relating to the *levée en masse* apply only to inhabitants of territory not yet occupied who are reacting to the approach of the enemy. The inhabitants of territory already occupied who rise in arms do not enjoy such privileges and are not entitled to be treated as prisoners of war unless they are members of organized resistance or liberation movements.[32]

Spies

'Any member of the armed forces of a Party to the conflict who falls into the **4.9** power of an adverse Party while engaging in espionage shall not have the right to the status of prisoner of war and may be treated as a spy.'[33] Nevertheless, he is to be treated humanely and his trial must respect established judicial safeguards.[34] A spy may not be punished without first having been tried and convicted.

A spy is any person who, acting clandestinely or on false pretences, obtains **4.9.1** or endeavours to obtain information in territory controlled by an adverse party, with the intention of communicating it to the opposing party.[35]

It follows that soldiers on a reconnaissance patrol who are in uniform and **4.9.2** driving in a military vehicle at the time of capture could not have been acting clandestinely.

The obtaining of intelligence about the enemy is an important military **4.9.3** activity. It can be done in many ways, from monitoring signal traffic to reconnaissance by satellites and drones. Sometimes long-range patrols or

---

[31] HR, Art 2; GC III, Art 4A(6); GC I, Art 13(6). This concept arose from the wish of smaller countries at the Hague Conference to retain the ability to defend themselves without the need to maintain conscription or large standing armies.

[32] And complying with AP I, Art 43.   [33] AP I, Art 46(1).

[34] HR, Art 30; AP I, Art 75.

[35] HR, Art 29; see also AP I, Art 46(3). Agents in neutral territory would not fall within these provisions although they may be subject to trial under the domestic law of the state that has captured them (which may be a neutral state).

agents have to deploy behind enemy lines. The Hague Regulations[36] formally sanctioned the employment of measures necessary for the obtaining of intelligence in enemy-held territory. The collection of such information *openly* by combatants wearing uniform is a recognized branch of the art of warfare. The obtaining of such information by *secret* methods is governed by different rules. Thus it is lawful to employ spies and secret agents but the fact that these methods are lawful under international law does not prevent the punishment under domestic or occupation law of individuals who are engaged in procuring intelligence in other than an open manner.

4.9.4 'A member of the armed forces of a Party to the conflict who, on behalf of that Party and in territory controlled by an adverse Party, gathers or attempts to gather information shall not be considered as engaging in espionage if, while so acting, he is in the uniform of his armed forces.'[37] This is because, in wearing uniform, he would not be 'acting clandestinely or on false pretences'. Similarly, a member of an armed force (presumably, in these circumstances, a resistance group) 'who is a resident of territory occupied by an adverse Party and who, on behalf of the Party on which he depends, gathers or attempts to gather information of military value within that territory shall not be considered as engaging in espionage unless he does so through an act of false pretences or deliberately in a clandestine manner'.[38] There is no requirement here that he should be in uniform. Moreover, if captured, he will remain entitled to prisoner of war status unless captured whilst actually engaged in espionage. These provisions do not apply to a member of an armed force who is *not* a resident of the occupied territory though he too does not lose his right to prisoner of war status and may not be treated as a spy 'unless he is captured before he has rejoined the armed force to which he belongs'.[39]

4.9.5 Civilians in occupied territory, even outside the zone of operations, who furnish information to the enemy, fall outside the provisions of Additional Protocol I and will usually be dealt with under the law of the belligerent or occupying power against whom their activities are directed.

4.9.6 In the United Kingdom, espionage is dealt with in the Official Secrets Acts 1911–89.[40] This legislation enables a wide range of establishments, public utility works, and means of communication to be declared to be 'prohibited places'. It is an offence to approach or inspect such places. The legislation

---

[36] HR, Art 24.   [37] AP I, Art 46(2).   [38] AP I, Art 46(3).

[39] AP I, Art 46(4). The phrase 'unless he is captured before he has rejoined the armed force to which he belongs' is intended to apply to both the question of PW status and treatment as a spy, see Y Sandoz, C Swinarski, and B Zimmermann (eds), *Commentary on the Additional Protocols of 8 June 1977 to the Geneva Conventions of 12 August 1949* (1987) (*ICRC Commentary*), paras 1771, 1781, and 1782. HR, Art 31, by inference, supports this interpretation.

[40] See MML, part II, ch 6; MAFL, vol II, part IV; BR 4005, QRRN J7.0003.

also deals with disclosure of information prejudicial to the safety or interests of the state and the protection of various other forms of official information. During large-scale armed conflicts, Parliament may enact special legislation to deal with espionage, such as the Treachery Act 1940, enacted during the Second World War.

Spies are usually tried by civilian courts under the domestic legislation of **4.9.7** the territory in which they are captured.

Mercenaries

Mercenaries are not entitled to combatant status. If captured, they are not **4.10** entitled to prisoner of war status.[41]

A mercenary is[42] any person who: **4.10.1**

a. is specially recruited locally or abroad in order to fight in an armed conflict;

b. does, in fact, take a direct part in the hostilities;

c. is motivated to take part in the hostilities essentially by the desire for private gain and, in fact, is promised, by or on behalf of a party to the conflict, material compensation substantially in excess of that promised or paid to combatants of similar ranks and functions in the armed forces of that party;

d. is neither a national of a party to the conflict nor a resident of territory controlled by a party to the conflict;

e. is not a member of the armed forces of a party to the conflict; and

f. has not been sent by a state which is not a party to the conflict on official duty as a member of its armed forces.[43]

Before 1977, there was no restriction in the law of armed conflict upon the **4.10.2** use of mercenaries in armed conflict and any form of discrimination towards prisoners of war was forbidden.[44] However, Additional Protocol I denies combatant and prisoner of war status to mercenaries.[45]

---

[41] AP I, Art 47(1). This provision does not prevent a party to a conflict extending PW status to mercenaries if it so wishes, see GC III, Art 6.   [42] AP I, Art 47(2).

[43] Gurkhas are not mercenaries because they are part of the British armed forces, are not paid substantially in excess of the pay of other soldiers, and are not recruited especially for one conflict. The same is true of the French Foreign Legion.

[44] See, eg, GC III, Art 16. In relation to specific conflicts in Africa, the UN General Assembly recommended prohibition of the use of such personnel against national liberation movements.

[45] See also the International Convention against the Recruitment, Use, Financing and Training of Mercenaries 1989 (1990 29 ILM 89) which came into force on 20 October 2001. However, the UK is not a party.

4.10.3 The definition of mercenary is very tightly drawn. Any member of the armed forces of a party to the conflict, or any member of the armed forces of any other state, who is sent on official duty as a member of its armed forces, is not a mercenary. For example, military observers or advisers who are members of the armed forces of states other than those engaged in hostilities, are not mercenaries.

4.10.4 When Iraqi armed forces invaded Kuwait in 1990, members of the British armed forces seconded to the Kuwaiti armed forces as the Kuwait Liaison Team were captured by the Iraqis. They were not mercenaries because they were members of the British armed forces. Indeed, they were not prisoners of war because, at that stage, the United Kingdom was not involved in an armed conflict with Iraq. Their status was that of civilian protected persons and they were eventually released.

Child soldiers

4.11 Parties to an armed conflict are required to take all feasible measures to ensure that children who have not attained the age of 15 years do not take a direct part in hostilities. They must refrain from recruiting such children into their armed forces. In recruiting children aged 15 and over but under 18, the oldest are to be recruited first. If captured, under-aged members of the armed forces are entitled to be treated as prisoners of war, but are also entitled to the special protection afforded to children.[46]

---

[46] AP I, Art 77(3). See also para 9.9.1. In 2000, an Optional Protocol, on the involvement of children in armed conflict ((2000) 39 ILM 1285), to the Convention on the Rights of the Child 1989 was adopted. It entered into force on 12 February 2002. It raises to 18 the age at which persons may be permitted to take a direct part in hostilities. On signature of the Protocol, the UK declared as follows: 'The United Kingdom of Great Britain and Northern Ireland will take all feasible measures to ensure that members of its armed forces who have not attained the age of 18 years do not take a direct part in hostilities. The United Kingdom understands that article 1 of the Optional Protocol would not exclude the deployment of members of its armed forces under the age of 18 to take a direct part in hostilities where:

(a) there is a genuine military need to deploy their unit or ship to an area in which hostilities are taking place; and

(b) by reason of the nature and urgency of the situation:
  (i) it is not practicable to withdraw such persons before deployment; or
  (ii) to do so would undermine the operational effectiveness of their ship or unit, and thereby put at risk the successful completion of the military mission and/or the safety of other personnel'.

DETERMINATION OF STATUS

It is not for officers and soldiers to concern themselves with the status of **4.12** captured enemy personnel. In all cases of doubt as to the status of a captured person who has taken, or is believed to have taken, part in hostilities, that person must be treated as a prisoner of war until a properly constituted tribunal[47] has determined his proper status.

---

[47] GC III, Art 5; AP I, Art 45(1); see, further, para 8.21.

5

The Conduct of Hostilities

INTRODUCTION

5.1 This chapter deals with the application of the law of armed conflict to the conduct of hostilities. It explains the application of the basic principles[1] of the law of armed conflict and the detailed rules that reflect those principles. It is based on the fundamental rule[2] that hostilities are only to be conducted between opposing armed forces and against military objectives, the civilian population and civilian objects being spared so far as possible. The chapter is in six parts. The first part deals with the basic rules relating to the conduct of hostilities; the second with the rules that apply as between the opposing armed forces; the third with the additional rules that have to be observed for the protection of the civilian population; the fourth with precautions to be taken in attacks; the fifth with precautions to be taken against the effects of attacks; and the sixth with civil defence. The rules on the use of weapons are to be found in Chapter 6. There are also special rules for the protection of those who do not, or no longer, pose a threat to the armed forces: the wounded, sick, and shipwrecked (Chapter 7), prisoners of war (Chapter 8), and civilians in the hands of a party to the conflict (Chapter 9).

[1] Referred to in Ch 2.   [2] Mentioned in Ch 4.

A. BASIC PRINCIPLES AND RULES

The Law of Armed Conflict and Rules of Engagement Distinguished[3]

The law of armed conflict must not be confused with rules of engagement **5.2** (ROE). The latter are 'directions for operational commands that set out the circumstances and limitations under which armed force may be applied by United Kingdom forces to achieve military objectives for the furtherance of United Kingdom government policy'.[4]

The law of armed conflict derives from, and is a part of, international **5.2.1** law and is, to a large extent, universal and settled in its application. ROE are directives for operational commands and will be subject to constant review, within the constraints of law, according to the political and military assessment of national or multinational interest as it relates to the mission to be accomplished and the circumstances facing the force. ROE reflect not only legal considerations but also a wide range of other concerns, such as the need to avoid destroying certain installations which it is sought to capture intact, to avoid politically damaging criticisms, to harmonize practice among allies, and to prevent so-called 'friendly fire'.

Civilian Immunity

'The civilian population as such, as well as individual civilians, shall not **5.3** be the object of attack.'[5] 'Attacks against the civilian population or civilians by way of reprisals are prohibited.'[6]

Civilians are persons who are not members of the armed forces. In **5.3.1** cases of doubt, persons are considered to be civilians.[7] 'The civilian population comprises all persons who are civilians' and 'the presence within the civilian population of individuals who do not come within the definition of civilians does not deprive the population of its civilian character'.[8]

A civilian is a non-combatant. He is protected from direct attack and is to **5.3.2** be protected against dangers arising from military operations. He has

---

[3] For a more detailed exposition of ROE principles, see JWP 3.00 *Joint Operations* 3-29 to 3-33.

[4] United Kingdom Compendium of National Rules of Engagement (JSP 398).

[5] Additional Protocol I (AP I), Art 51(2).   [6] AP I, Art 51(6). However, see para 16.19.1.

[7] AP I, Art 50(1). See Ch 4 for the composition of the armed forces, in particular, para 4.3. Commanders must do everything feasible to verify that a person to be attacked is not a civilian.

[8] AP I, Art 50(2), (3).

no right to participate directly in hostilities. If he does so he loses his immunity.[9]

5.3.3 Whether civilians are taking a direct part in hostilities is a question of fact. Civilians manning an anti-aircraft gun or engaging in sabotage of military installations are doing so. Civilians working in military vehicle maintenance depots or munitions factories or driving military transport vehicles are not, but they are at risk from attacks on those objectives since military objectives may be attacked whether or not civilians are present.[10]

5.3.4 In the practical application of the principle of civilian immunity and the rule of doubt, (a) commanders and others responsible for planning, deciding upon, or executing attacks necessarily have to reach decisions on the basis of their assessment of the information from all sources which is available to them at the relevant time, (b) it is only in cases of substantial doubt, after this assessment about the status of the individual in question, that the latter should be given the benefit of the doubt and treated as a civilian, and (c) the rule of doubt does not override the commander's duty to protect the safety of troops under his command or to preserve the military situation.[11]

MILITARY OBJECTIVES

5.4 'Attacks shall be limited strictly to military objectives.'[12]

5.4.1 The term 'military objective' includes combatant members of the enemy armed forces and their military weapons, vehicles, equipment, and installations. It may include other objects which have military value such as bridges, communications towers, and electricity and refined oil production facilities.[13] Objects are only military objectives if they come within the following definition:

> those objects which by their nature, location, purpose or use make an effective contribution to military action and whose total or partial destruction, capture or neutralization, in the circumstances ruling at the time, offers a definite military advantage.[14]

---

[9] AP I, Art 51(3).   [10] Subject to the rule of proportionality, see para 5.33.
[11] See the statements made by the UK on ratification of AP I.
[12] AP I, Arts 48 and 52(2). The UK made a statement on ratification that this rule prohibits only attacks against objects that are not military objectives. It does not deal with the question of collateral damage resulting from attacks directed against military objectives. Collateral damage is controlled by the rule on precautions in attack, see para 5.32.
[13] These objects were attacked during the Gulf conflict 1991, see US Department of Defense, *Conduct of the Persian Gulf War*, Final Report to Congress (1992) (Department of Defense Report) 96–99.   [14] AP I, Art 52(2).

In cases of doubt, objects that are normally used[15] for civilian purposes **5.4.2** are to be presumed as not being used for military purposes.[16] Such objects would include churches, dwelling houses, residential flats, commercial offices and factories, shopping precincts and markets, schools, and libraries.

These criteria require commanders and others planning, deciding on, **5.4.3** or launching attacks to exercise their discretion. In doing so they must necessarily reach their decisions on the basis of their assessment of the information from all sources which is available to them at the relevant time.[17]

The definition of military objectives contains various elements that require **5.4.4** explanation:

a. The second part of the definition limits the first. Both parts must apply before an object can be considered a military objective.

b. Attacks on military objectives that cause incidental loss or damage to civilians are not prohibited so long as the proportionality rule is complied with.[18]

c. 'Nature' refers to the type of object, for example, military transports, command and control centres, or communications stations.

d. 'Location' includes areas which are militarily important because they must be captured or denied to the enemy or because the enemy must be made to retreat from them.[19] An area of land can, thus, be a military objective.[20]

---

[15] 'Used' is not the same as 'occupied'. Use could occur, for example, when enemy troops take shelter from direct fire behind a house or school.

[16] AP I, Art 52(3). If, for example, it is suspected that a schoolhouse situated in a commanding tactical position is being used by an adverse party as an observation post and gun emplacement, this suspicion, unsupported by evidence, is not enough to justify an attack on the schoolhouse. Where there is doubt about the status of a target, a pilot may not be able to resolve that doubt by visual observation in order to justify the attack. He is entitled to rely on intelligence relayed to him unless his own observation contradicts that intelligence or raises doubts about its reliability.

[17] The UK declared on ratification of the Protocol that 'military commanders and others responsible for planning, deciding upon, or executing attacks necessarily have to reach decisions on the basis of their assessment of the information from all sources which is reasonably available to them at the relevant time'. For the precautions to be taken in attacks, see para 5.32.   [18] See para 5.33.

[19] See Y Sandoz, C Swinarski, and B Zimmermann (eds), *Commentary on the Additional Protocols of 8 June 1977 to the Geneva Conventions of 12 August 1949* (1987) (*ICRC Commentary*) para 2021.

[20] The UK declared on ratification of the Protocol that 'a specific area of land may be a military objective if, because of its location or other reasons specified in Article 52, its total or partial destruction, capture or neutralisation in the circumstances ruling at the time offers definite military advantage'.

e. 'Purpose' means the future intended use of an object while 'use' means its present function.[21]

f. The words 'nature, location, purpose or use' seem at first sight to allow a wide discretion, but they are subject to the qualifications later in the definition of 'effective contribution to military action' and the offering of 'a definite military advantage'. There does not have to be geographical proximity between 'effective contribution' and 'military advantage'. That means that attacks on military supply dumps in the rear or diversionary attacks, away from the area of actual military operations, can be launched.

g. 'Military action' means military action generally, not a limited or specific military operation.

h. The words 'in the circumstances ruling at the time' are important. If, for example, the enemy moved a divisional headquarters into a disused textile factory, an attack on that headquarters would be permissible (even though the factory might be destroyed in the process) because of the prevailing circumstances. Once the enemy moved their headquarters away, the circumstances would change again and the immunity of the factory would be restored.

i. 'Definite' means a concrete and perceptible military advantage rather than a hypothetical and speculative one.[22]

j. 'Military advantage'. The military advantage anticipated from an attack refers to the advantage anticipated from the attack considered as a whole and not only from isolated or particular parts of the attack.[23] The advantage need not be immediate.

5.4.5 The following is a list of examples of possible military objectives. The mere fact that an object is on the list does not mean that it is necessarily a military objective. It must always be tested against the definition in paragraph 5.4.1, especially the question: 'does it make an effective contribution to military action?' The list is not exhaustive.[24]

a. combatant members of the armed forces and those who take a direct part in hostilities without being members of the armed forces;[25]

---

[21] *ICRC Commentary*, para 2022.

[22] M Bothe, K-J Partsch, and WA Solf, *New Rules for the Victims of Armed Conflicts* (1982) (Bothe, Partsch, and Solf, *New Rules*) 326.   [23] UK statement on ratification of AP I.

[24] It follows that attacks on certain types of objects are prohibited. These include cities, towns, and villages as such; buildings used by civilians and not for military purposes such as dwellings, schools, museums, places of worship, and other buildings without military significance; foodstuffs (not intended solely for members of the armed forces) and food producing areas; and water sources for the civilian population. These matters are dealt with in more detail in Part C of this chapter. Special protection is given to medical facilities, internment and prisoner of war camps, see Chs 7, 8, and 9.   [25] So long as they are not *hors de combat*.

b. military equipment, including vehicles, weapons, munitions, and fuel stocks;

c. military works, including defensive works and fortifications;

d. military depots and establishments, including headquarters and command and control centres, barracks, military airfields, military supply depots, defence ministries, and intelligence establishments;

e. other works producing or developing military supplies and other supplies of military value, including metallurgical, engineering, chemical, oil and power industries, and infrastructure supporting the war effort;

f. areas of land of military significance such as hills, defiles, and bridgeheads;

g. means of transportation used for moving military supplies or other supplies of military value, including railways, ports, airfields, bridges, canals, tunnels, and main roads;

h. communications installations used for military purposes, including broadcasting and television stations, telephone and telegraph stations.

B. CONDUCT OF MILITARY OPERATIONS AGAINST ENEMY ARMED FORCES

QUARTER

'It is prohibited to order that there shall be no survivors, to threaten an **5.5** adversary therewith or to conduct hostilities on this basis.'[26]

SAFEGUARD OF PERSONS *hors de combat*

'A person who is recognized or who, in the circumstances, should be recog- **5.6** nized to be *hors de combat* shall not be made the object of attack.' A person is *hors de combat* if:

a. 'he is in the power of an adverse Party';[27]

b. 'he clearly expresses an intention to surrender'; or

c. 'he has been rendered unconscious or is otherwise incapacitated by wounds or sickness, and therefore is incapable of defending himself';

---

[26] AP I, Art 40. The old rule that quarter could be refused to the garrison of a fortress carried by assault, to the defenders of an unfortified place who did not surrender when artillery was brought against it, or to a weak garrison who obstinately and uselessly persisted in defending a fortified place against overwhelming forces, has long been obsolete.

[27] Any combatant who falls into the power of an adverse party becomes a prisoner of war (PW), AP I, Art 44(1).

'provided that in any of these cases he abstains from any hostile act and does not attempt to escape'.[28]

5.6.1 A combatant is entitled to continue fighting up to the moment of his surrender without losing the benefits of quarter and his rights as a prisoner of war. No vengeance can be taken since that person has simply done his duty up to the moment of his surrender. The mere fact that a soldier is wounded does not necessarily mean that he is incapacitated. There have been many examples of soldiers who continued to fight though wounded. It is only when he surrenders or is rendered incapable of fighting because of his wounds that he becomes *hors de combat*.

OCCUPANTS OF AIRCRAFT AND VEHICLES

5.7 'No person parachuting from an aircraft in distress shall be made the object of attack during his descent. Upon reaching the ground in territory controlled by an adverse Party,[29] a person who has parachuted from an aircraft in distress shall be given an opportunity to surrender before being made the object of attack, unless it is apparent that he is engaging in a hostile act. Airborne troops are not protected by this' rule.[30]

5.7.1 This rule follows from the protection of those *hors de combat*. Members of the civilian population must also respect this rule. If an aircrew member should open fire or try to escape at any time during his descent or upon reaching the ground, he would forfeit his protection. If aircrew try to destroy an aircraft that has been forced down, this would be regarded as a hostile act.[31] Parachuting airborne troops are legitimate targets, even if descending from aircraft in distress, though in those circumstances it may be difficult to distinguish airborne troops from aircrew. When the identity of parachutists is in doubt, they should not be attacked. Once on the ground, airborne troops who are not incapacitated must clearly express an intention to surrender to qualify for protection as being *hors de combat*.

5.7.2 The position of combatants leaving disabled tanks or other military vehicles is not specifically dealt with in Additional Protocol I. The general rule on the protection of those *hors de combat* in paragraph 5.6 applies.

UNUSUAL CONDITIONS OF COMBAT

5.8 'When persons entitled to protection as prisoners of war have fallen into the power of an adverse Party under unusual conditions of combat which

---

[28] AP I, Art 41(1), (2). The detailed treatment of these persons is to be found in Chs 7 and 8.
[29] That is, adverse to the person parachuting.   [30] AP I, Art 42.
[31] *ICRC Commentary*, para 1650.

prevent their evacuation as provided for in Part III, Section I, of the Third Convention, they shall be released and all feasible precautions[32] shall be taken to ensure their safety.'[33]

This rule covers cases such as commando operations or long-range recon- **5.8.1** naissance patrols in enemy-held territory. If enemy combatants are captured by or surrender to the commandos the latter are placed in a dilemma. Because they are operating behind enemy lines, the prisoner of war handling and evacuation[34] chain does not exist and, when encumbered with prisoners of war, commandos may be hampered in carrying out their mission or in withdrawing safely afterwards. The rule prevents the killing of prisoners of war in these circumstances; they must be released. Release need not be immediate. It may take place at a time when it is safe for the capturing troops to do so. The capturing power is normally responsible for the safety of prisoners of war from the moment of capture, but the rule recognizes that in circumstances such as these the capturing troops may be very restricted in the precautionary measures they can take. A lot depends on the circumstances. If the captured personnel are close to troops of their own side, few if any precautions will be necessary. If they are a long distance from friendly forces in hostile conditions, they may have to be provided or left with, if available, rations, map, compass, shelter, and, possibly, information about unexploded ordnance in the area.

PERFIDY

'It is prohibited to kill, injure or capture an adversary by resort to perfidy.'[35] **5.9**

Perfidy is defined as 'acts inviting the confidence of an adversary to lead **5.9.1** him to believe that he is entitled to, or is obliged to accord, protection under the rules of international law applicable in armed conflict, with intent to betray that confidence'.

The following acts are examples of perfidy, if done with intent to betray the **5.9.2** enemy's confidence:

a. the feigning of an intent to negotiate under a flag of truce or of surrender;

b. the feigning of an incapacitation by wounds or sickness;[36]

---

[32] The UK has on ratification placed on record its understanding that 'feasible' means that which is practicable or practically possible, taking into account all circumstances ruling at the time, including humanitarian and military considerations. [33] AP I, Art 41(3).

[34] For the evacuation of PW, see para 8.35.

[35] AP I, Art 37(1). Examples of treachery included calling out 'Do not fire, we are friends' and then firing at enemy troops who had lowered their guard, especially if coupled with the wearing of enemy uniforms or civilian clothing; or shamming disablement or death and then using arms. The rule has no effect on the use of civilian aircraft or vessels to transport military cargo.

[36] The feigning of incapacity with the motive not of attacking the enemy but of surviving to fight another day is permitted.

   c. the feigning of civilian, non-combatant status; and

   d. the feigning of protected status by the use of signs, emblems, or uniforms of the United Nations or of neutral or other states not parties to the conflict.[37]

5.9.3 The reason for the prohibition of perfidy is to prevent the abuse, and the consequent undermining, of the protection afforded by the law of armed conflict.

5.9.4 Persons who kill or wound by resort to perfidy commit war crimes and should be put on trial.[38]

RECOGNIZED EMBLEMS

5.10 It is prohibited[39] to:

   a. 'make improper use of the distinctive emblem of the red cross, red crescent or red lion and sun[40] or of other emblems, signs or signals provided for by the' Geneva Conventions or by Additional Protocol I;[41]

   b. 'misuse deliberately in an armed conflict other internationally recognized protective emblems, signs or signals, including the flag of truce,[42] and the protective emblem of cultural property';[43]

   c. 'make use of the distinctive emblem of the United Nations, except as authorized by that Organization'.

5.10.1 Great care must be used to ensure that rules on the use of protective emblems are scrupulously observed. Thus the red cross flag must not be used to cover vehicles used for the transport of munitions or non-medical stores.[44]

---

[37] AP I, Art 37(1). Under AP I, Art 39(3), this rule is expressed as not affecting the existing generally recognized rules of international law applicable to:

a. espionage, see para 4.9. Under Hague Regulations (HR), Art 31, a spy who succeeds in rejoining his own forces cannot, if subsequently captured, be tried for his earlier spying offences. That means that he could not be punished for wearing enemy uniform while committing those offences;

b. the use of flags in the conduct of armed conflict at sea, see paras 13.81–13.83.

[38] In fact, the perfidious use of recognized emblems may amount to a grave breach, see AP I, Art 85(3)(f).

[39] AP I, Art 38. See also Geneva Convention (GC) I, Art 53 and GC II, Art 44.

[40] The use in battle of the insignia of the red cross for the purpose of deceit has long been regarded as a war crime, see *In re Hagendorf* (1948) 13 WCR 146.

[41] eg, the emblems for civil defence and for the protection of installations containing dangerous forces, see paras 5.45 and 5.30.1 respectively.   [42] See para 10.5.

[43] See para 5.26.6.

[44] Vehicles proceeding to forward positions with food, water, and ammunition must not display the distinctive emblem. They could do so on the return journey if they were exclusively used for carrying the sick and wounded on that journey, see AP I, Art 8(k).

A hospital train must not be used to facilitate the escape of combatants. It is forbidden to fire from a tent, building, or vehicle displaying the red cross emblem.[45] A hospital protected by the red cross emblem must not be used as an observation post, military office, or store. Likewise, the flag of truce must not be used merely to gain time to effect a retreat or bring up reinforcements. Surrender must not be feigned in order to take the enemy at a disadvantage when he advances to secure his prisoners. In fact, there is no obligation on the adverse party to expose itself to accept surrender. The onus is on those displaying the white flag to move forward under its protection.[46]

UNIFORMS

It is prohibited: **5.11**

a. 'to make use in an armed conflict of the flags or military emblems, insignia or uniforms of neutral or other States not Parties to the conflict';

b. 'to make use of the flags or military emblems, insignia or uniforms of adverse Parties while engaging in attacks or in order to shield, favour, protect or impede military operations'.[47]

The prohibition of use of such items of states not party to the conflict is **5.11.1** absolute. The prohibition on the use of such items of enemy uniforms only arises in connection with actual military operations, so there would be no objection to enemy uniforms being worn in rear areas for training purposes or by a prisoner of war to facilitate his escape. Members of commando or long-range reconnaissance forces using enemy uniforms, for example, to move freely in enemy-held territory, would contravene this provision but would not forfeit prisoner of war status. If, owing to a shortage of clothing, it becomes necessary to consider using clothing captured from the enemy, badges and insignia should be removed and items should not be used, in the circumstances set out in sub-paragraph 5.11(b), which are readily identifiable as enemy uniforms.

---

[45] Except in the limited circumstances allowed for self-defence, see GC I, Art 22(1).

[46] See further para 10.4 onwards.

[47] AP I, Art 39. This rule is expressed as not affecting the existing generally recognized rules of international law applicable to:

a. espionage, see para 4.9. Under HR, Art 31, a spy who succeeds in rejoining his own forces cannot, if subsequently captured, be tried for his earlier spying offences. That means that he could not be punished for wearing enemy uniform while committing those offences;

b. the use of flags in the conduct of armed conflict at sea, see paras 13.81–13.83.

The rule, as formulated in AP I, clarifies doubts arising from the *Skorzeny Trial* (1949) 9 WCR 90, in which German soldiers were acquitted who had been captured before battle while wearing American uniforms.

SNIPERS

5.12 The use of snipers in warfare is a long-established practice, not prohibited by the law of armed conflict. The provisions of that law apply equally to snipers. In particular, firing at civilians[48] or persons *hors de combat* is prohibited.

ASSASSINATION

5.13 Whether or not the killing of a selected enemy individual is lawful depends on the circumstances of the case. There is no rule dealing specifically with assassination, but the following rules would be applicable in such a case:

a. attacks may not be directed against civilians, see paragraph 5.3;

b. attacks must be limited to military objectives, including enemy combatants, see paragraph 5.4;

c. only combatants have the right to participate directly in hostilities;[49]

d. enemy combatants may not be killed by resort to perfidy, see paragraph 5.9.

OUTLAWRY

5.14 The proscription or outlawing or the putting of a price on the head of an enemy individual or any offer for an enemy 'dead or alive' is prohibited.[50]

5.14.1 The prohibition extends to offers of rewards for the killing or wounding of all enemies, or of a class of enemy persons, such as officers.[51] On the other hand, offers of rewards for the capture unharmed of enemy personnel generally or of particular enemy personnel would be lawful.

---

[48] During the siege of Sarajevo in the Yugoslav conflict of 1992–95, there were many cases of civilians, including elderly people, women, and children, being killed or injured by sniper bullets. The besieging corps commander, Stanislav Galić, was indicted before the International Criminal Tribunal for the former Yugoslavia (ICTY) in respect of sniper attacks on civilians by troops under his command, Case No IT-98-29-I, 26 March 1999.

[49] AP I, Art 43(2). All members of the armed forces are combatants unless they are medical personnel or chaplains, see further para 4.2. They are also protected if they are permanently assigned to civil defence duties, AP I, Art 67(1). Reprisals against protected persons and their property are now prohibited, see GC IV, Art 33 and AP I, Arts 51(6) and 52(1). Civilians who are responsible for assassination or other outrage against the occupation authorities may be tried and punished by duly constituted courts of the occupation authorities functioning in accordance with the requirements of GC IV (see Arts 5, 66 and 67).

[50] See the *Manual of Military Law Part III* (1958) (MML) para 116.

[51] This is because it would lead to or encourage the denial of quarter, see para 5.5.

INTELLIGENCE GATHERING

Gathering information about the enemy and the enemy state is permissible.[52] **5.15**

Intelligence gathering is essential if commanders are to be able to verify poten- **5.15.1**
tial targets as military objectives and take precautions for the protection of the
civilian population.[53] Information can lawfully be gleaned in many different
ways, for example, by the employment of informers or agents in enemy-held
territory, the use of long-range patrols, the questioning of captured persons,
the examination of captured documents or intercepted messages, or the use of
reconnaissance aircraft and satellites.[54] It is lawful to employ spies; to induce
enemy civilians or soldiers to give information, to desert with or without technical equipment, vehicles, or aircraft,[55] to surrender, rebel, or mutiny; or to
give false information to the enemy. It is lawful to incite enemy subjects to rise
against the government in power.[56] It is, however, a grave breach of Geneva
Convention III to compel a prisoner of war to serve in the forces of the hostile
power.[57] Geneva Convention IV contains a provision[58] prohibiting the occupying power from exercising pressure or engaging in propaganda aimed at
securing voluntary enlistment in the armed forces or auxiliary forces of the
occupying power. Neither prisoners of war nor the inhabitants of occupied
territory may be employed on work of a military nature.[59]

SABOTAGE

Sabotage attacks behind enemy lines are lawful provided they are carried **5.16**
out by combatants who distinguish themselves from the civilian population,[60] they are directed against military objectives,[61] and suitable precautions are taken to minimize the risks to the civilian population.[62]

---

[52] HR, Art 24.   [53] As to which, see para 5.32.

[54] For the status of persons gathering intelligence who are captured and of spies generally,
see para 4.9.

[55] eg, to offer a reward to an enemy pilot to fly a new military fighter aircraft over to your
lines, see L Oppenheim, *International Law* (7th edn by H Lauterpacht 1952) vol II, 426.

[56] In the Second World War (WWII) both sides established regular radio services for spread-
ing war news, among the enemy and neutrals. They also resorted on a large scale to propaganda disseminated from aircraft and from the ground. The draft Hague Air Warfare Rules
1923, Art 21, provided that: 'The use of aircraft for the purpose of disseminating propaganda
shall not be treated as an illegitimate means of warfare. Members of the crews of such aircraft
must not be deprived of their rights as prisoners of war on the charge that they have committed such an act'. Although these rules have never been adopted in treaty form, state practice
has been in line with this provision. During the Gulf conflict 1991 the allies dropped leaflets
over Iraqi troop concentrations offering Iraqi soldiers safe conduct if they surrendered.

[57] GC III, Art 130.   [58] Art 51.   [59] GC III, Art 50; GC IV, Art 51.

[60] See para 4.7.   [61] See para 5.4.   [62] See para 5.32.

Ruses of War

5.17   'Ruses of war are not prohibited. Such ruses are acts which are intended
        to mislead an adversary or to induce him to act recklessly but which
        infringe no rule of international law applicable in armed conflict and
        which are not perfidious because they do not invite the confidence of the
        adversary with respect to protection under the law. The following are ex-
        amples of such ruses: the use of camouflage, decoys, mock operations
        and misinformation.'[63]

5.17.1 Ruses of war are, therefore, measures taken to obtain advantage of the
        enemy by mystifying or misleading him. They are permissible provided
        they are not perfidious and do not violate an agreement. Belligerent forces
        must be constantly on their guard against, and prepared for, legitimate
        ruses, but they should be able to rely on their adversary's observance of
        promises and of the law of armed conflict.[64]

5.17.2 Legitimate ruses include: surprises; ambushes; feigning attacks, retreats,
        or flights; simulating quiet and inactivity; assigning large strong-points to
        a small force; constructing works or bridges which it is not intended to
        use; transmitting bogus signal messages and sending bogus despatches
        and newspapers with a view to their being intercepted by the enemy;
        making use of the enemy's signals, passwords, radio code signs, and
        words of command; conducting a false military exercise on the radio while
        substantial troop movements are taking place on the ground; pretending
        to communicate with troops or reinforcements which do not exist; moving
        landmarks; constructing dummy airfields or aircraft; setting up dummy
        guns or tanks; laying dummy minefields; removing badges from uni-
        forms;[65] issuing to personnel of a single unit uniforms of several units
        so that prisoners and the dead may give the impression of a much
        larger force; giving false ground signals to enable airborne personnel or
        supplies to be dropped in a hostile area, or to induce aircraft to land in a hos-
        tile area; and feint attacks to mislead the enemy as to the point of the main
        attack.[66]

---

    [63] AP I, Art 37(2).

    [64] According to the debate that took place at the Hague Conference, a ruse ceases to be per-
missible if it contravenes any generally accepted rule: *Correspondence respecting the Peace
Conference held at The Hague in 1899* (Cmnd 9534) 146.

    [65] Combatants must still distinguish themselves from civilians, see para 4.4.

    [66] During the Gulf conflict 1991, the allies undertook actions to convince Iraqi military
leaders that the ground campaign to liberate Kuwait would be centred on eastern Kuwait and
would include an amphibious assault, whereas the actual main thrust was considerably
further west, see Department of Defense Report 621.

Difference between perfidy and ruses

It would be perfidious to induce the enemy to lay down their arms and **5.17.3** surrender by falsely declaring that an armistice had been agreed, because that would induce them to believe that they were entitled to protection under the law of armed conflict. It would be lawful to summon an enemy force to surrender on the false ground that it was surrounded, or to threaten bombardment when no guns were actually in place. To demand a cease-fire and then to break it by surprise, or to violate a safe conduct or any other agreement, in order to kill, wound, or capture enemy troops would be perfidious. On the other hand, it has been considered a legitimate ruse to utilize an informal cease-fire for the purpose of collecting wounded and dead (which is sometimes arranged during a battle) to withdraw unseen by the enemy.[67] However, if this were done to surround the enemy with a view to capturing them or to manoeuvre into a better position for attacking them, that would be perfidious.

REPRISALS

Reprisals are acts, that would normally be illegal, taken by a belligerent to **5.18** suppress illegitimate acts of warfare by the adversary and are only permissible in very narrowly defined circumstances.[68] They may not be undertaken by UK armed forces without prior authorization at the highest level of government.[69]

ATTACKING FOOD AND WATER USED BY MEMBERS OF
THE ENEMY ARMED FORCES

Military action may only be taken for the purpose of attacking, destroying, **5.19** removing, or rendering useless 'foodstuffs, agricultural areas for the production of foodstuffs, crops, livestock, drinking water installations and supplies and irrigation works' if they are used by an adverse party:

a. 'as sustenance solely for the members of its armed forces'; or
b. 'if not as sustenance, then in direct support of military action'.

In the latter case, no action may be taken against these objects if it 'may be expected to leave the civilian population with such inadequate food or water as to cause its starvation or force its movement'.[70]

---

[67] MML, para 319.   [68] The subject is dealt with in para 16.16 onwards.
[69] UK statement on ratification of AP I. See paras 16.19.1 and 16.19.2.
[70] AP I, Art 54(3). See also *ICRC Commentary*, para 2112. There are additional rules for the protection of the civilian population from starvation. These are dealt with in para 5.27.

5.19.1 The use of the above objects in direct support of military action might occur, for example, where a corn field or orchard is used as cover by advancing infantry or enemy troops take cover behind a barn containing grain.[71]

C. PROHIBITED METHODS OF WARFARE

DEFINITION OF 'ATTACKS'

5.20 ' "Attacks" means acts of violence against the adversary, whether in offence or in defence.'[72]

5.20.1 Not only are civilians and the civilian population protected from direct attack,[73] but the measures set out in this part of this chapter must also be taken to reduce as much as possible the incidental effects on civilians and civilian property of attacks.

5.20.2 An 'act of violence' involves the use of armed forces including means of warfare (that is, weapons).[74] The definition of attack covers not only attacks in the military sense but also the use of armed force to slow or halt an attack by the enemy and counter-attacks. In those circumstances, the defending military commander is also obliged to take steps for the protection of the civilian population.

5.20.3 The following rules apply to all attacks, even attacks in a party's national territory which is under adverse occupation.[75] They also apply to air attacks or attacks from the sea against targets on land or 'which may affect the civilian population, individual civilians or civilian objects on land'.[76]

5.20.4 The definition of attack is wide enough to cover a whole range of situations from that of a single soldier opening fire with his rifle to a massive artillery bombardment preceding a major offensive. It is necessary to test any military action in its context against each specific rule of protection[77] to ascertain whether it is affected by the rule in question. Some states have made statements of understanding on ratification that obligations in attack only apply to commanders at certain levels.[78] It is, however, difficult to apply a general exception such as that in practice since so much will depend on the circumstances and the information available to a commander.

---

[71] See *ICRC Commentary*, para 2110.   [72] AP I, Art 49(1).   [73] See para 5.3.

[74] 'Act of violence' does not include such things as flooding part of one's national territory to inhibit an invasion. These practices are controlled by AP I, Art 54, see para 5.27.

[75] AP I, Art 49(2).   [76] AP I, Art 49(3).

[77] These rules are dealt with one by one in this part of this chapter.

[78] eg, the Swiss declaration that the provisions of AP I, Art 57(2) (precautions in attack, see para 5.32) only create obligations for commanding officers at battalion or group level.

The commander must be judged in the light of the information available to him.[79]

Some states, including the United Kingdom, made statements on ratification of Additional Protocol I that 'the military advantage anticipated from an attack is intended to refer to the advantage anticipated from the attack considered as a whole and not only from isolated or particular parts of the attack'. The effect of this statement is that when judging the responsibility of a commander at a particular level, one has to look at the part of the attack for which he was responsible in the context of the attack as a whole. **5.20.5**

TERROR ATTACKS

'Acts or threats of violence, the primary purpose of which is to spread terror among the civilian population are prohibited.'[80] **5.21**

This rule reinforces the rule[81] that civilians are not to be made the object of direct attack. It would apply, for instance, to car bombs installed in busy shopping streets, even if no civilians are killed or injured by them, their object being to create panic among the population. Threats of violence would include, for example, threats to annihilate the enemy's civilian population.[82] It does not apply to terror caused as a by-product of attacks on military objectives or as a result of genuine warnings of impending attacks on such objectives.[83] **5.21.1**

CIVILIANS NOT TO BE USED AS SHIELDS

'The presence or movements[84] of the civilian population or individual civilians shall not be used to render certain points or areas immune from military operations,[85] in particular in attempts to shield military objectives from attacks[86] or to shield, favour or impede military operations. **5.22**

---

[79] See, eg, the UK statement of understanding made on ratification of AP I: 'Military commanders and others responsible for planning, deciding upon, or executing attacks necessarily have to reach decisions on the basis of their assessment of the information from all sources which is reasonably available to them at the relevant time'.   [80] AP I, Art 51(2)

[81] Set out in para 5.3.   [82] See *ICRC Commentary*, para 1940.

[83] See Bothe, Partsch, and Solf, *New Rules*, 301.

[84] This relates to cases where the civilian population moves of its own accord, see *ICRC Commentary*, para 1988, as in the case of refugees.

[85] During the Gulf conflict 1991, Iraq placed civilians forcibly deported from Kuwait and prisoners of war in or around military targets as 'human shields', see Department of Defense Report, 608, 619.

[86] According to the Department of Defense Report, 613, during the Gulf conflict 1991 the Iraqi government adopted a deliberate policy of placing military personnel, weapons, and equipment in civilian populated areas or next to mosques, medical facilities, or cultural sites in an effort to protect them from attack. For example, Silkworm surface-to-surface missiles were found in a school in Kuwait City and UN inspectors uncovered chemical bomb production equipment while inspecting a sugar factory in Iraq.

The Parties to the conflict shall not direct the movement of the civilian population or individual civilians in order to attempt to shield military objectives from attacks or to shield military operations.'[87]

5.22.1 Any violation by the enemy of this rule would not relieve an attacker of his responsibility to take precautions to protect the civilians affected,[88] but the enemy's unlawful activity may be taken into account in considering whether the incidental loss or damage was proportionate to the military advantage expected.[89]

INDISCRIMINATE ATTACKS PROHIBITED

5.23   'Indiscriminate attacks are prohibited.'[90]

5.23.1 Indiscriminate attacks are:

  a. 'those which are not directed at a specific military objective';[91]

  b. 'those which employ a method or means of combat which cannot be directed at a specific military objective';[92] or

  c. 'those which employ a method or means of combat the effects of which cannot be limited as required' by Additional Protocol I;[93]

  'and consequently, in each such case, are of a nature[94] to strike military objectives and civilians or civilian objects without distinction'.[95]

5.23.2 The following are examples of indiscriminate attacks:

  a. 'an attack by bombardment by any methods or means[96] which treats as a single military objective a number of clearly separated and distinct military objectives located in a city, town, village or other area containing a similar concentration of civilians or civilian objects'; or

  b. an attack which violates the rule of proportionality.[97]

---

[87] AP I, Art 51(7). For the effect of this provision on siege warfare, see para 5.34.

[88] AP I, Art 51(8).   [89] See para 2.7.2.   [90] AP I, Art 51(4).

[91] This prohibits aimless attacks such as the soldier who fires off an automatic weapon at no particular target.

[92] This prohibits the use against targets in populated areas of inaccurate weapons such as the Scud missiles fired by Iraq during the Gulf conflict 1991 at Israel and Saudi Arabia.

[93] This sub-para covers two situations: where the attacker is unable to control the effects of the attack, such as dangerous forces released by it, or where the incidental effects are too great.

[94] An attack would not be indiscriminate if the result was not intended but was caused by something outside the attacker's control, such as the intervening act of another party. The attacking commander would not be responsible if enemy defences or counter-measures deflected a missile from its target, causing it to hit a civilian object.   [95] AP I, Art 51(4).

[96] This includes aerial bombing as well as bombardment by artillery, rocket, or missile.

[97] AP I, Art 51(5), see para 5.33.

It seems that an attack can be indiscriminate even if no civilians are killed or injured by it, but a grave breach only occurs if the civilian population or civilian objects are knowingly and actually affected.[98] Whether an attack is indiscriminate will depend very much on the facts of each case. If the military objective consists of scattered enemy tank formations in an unpopulated desert, it would be permissible to use weapons having a wider area of effect than would be possible if the target were a single communications site in the middle of a heavily populated area. Military objectives dispersed about populated areas have to be attacked separately. There is nothing to prevent the use of artillery covering fire or the laying of anti-tank mines to deny an area of land to the enemy, but other rules would apply to protect the civilian population.[99] Also indiscriminate is any air bombardment technique or device that lacks the precision to ensure a reasonable probability that the targets under attack will be hit.

5.23.3

IMMUNITY OF CIVILIAN OBJECTS

'Civilian objects shall not be the object of attack or of reprisals.'[100]

5.24

'Civilian objects are all objects which are not military objectives.'[101]

5.24.1

The term 'civilian objects' would normally include cities, towns, and villages as such but not military objectives within those places. It also includes foodstuffs and food producing areas, springs, wells, water works and other water sources, buildings and facilities used by civilians (so long as they do not fall within the definition of military objectives) such as housing estates and houses; apartment blocks and flats; factories and workshops producing goods of no military significance; offices, shops, markets and warehouses; farms and stables; schools, museums, places of worship, and other similar buildings; and means of transport such as civil aircraft, cars, railway trains, trams, and buses. Special protection is also given to hospitals, internment and prisoner of war camps.

5.24.2

In cases of doubt, objects are to be considered as civilian.[102]

5.24.3

The fact that a military objective is located in a populated area means that civilians and civilian objects may legitimately suffer indirectly if those objectives are attacked, subject to the rule of proportionality.[103]

5.24.4

---

[98] AP I, Art 85(3)(b).

[99] Such as the requirement to take precautions in attack, see para 5.32.

[100] AP I, Art 52(1). The UK has reserved the right to take reprisal action against civilian objects in certain circumstances, see para 16.19.1.

[101] AP I, Art 52(1). For the definition of military objectives, see para 5.4.1.

[102] AP I, Art 52(3).   [103] See para 5.33.

PROTECTION OF CULTURAL OBJECTS AND PLACES OF WORSHIP

5.25 It is prohibited:

   a. to commit any acts of hostility directed against the historic monuments, works of art or places of worship which constitute the cultural or spiritual heritage of peoples;

   b. to use such objects in support of the military effort;

   c. to make such objects the object of reprisals.[104]

5.25.1 In general, all civilian objects are protected. However, the protection of cultural property and places of worship is given special emphasis in the law of armed conflict, both in respect of protection from attack and in respect of discouraging their use for military purposes, so that the need to attack such property does not arise.

5.25.2 Because of its wording, the prohibition in paragraph 5.25 only applies to very important cultural property of international stature.[105] It is not clear whether 'works of art' includes scientific collections or libraries,[106] but the prohibition certainly applies to more than just buildings and would cover cultural or archaeological sites. Property loses its protection if it is used for military purposes.[107] The protection is against all acts of hostility, not just 'attacks'. Additional Protocol I does not specify any protective emblem for cultural property.[108] However, making clearly recognized cultural property the object of an attack can amount to a grave breach of the Protocol if the property is subject to special protection,[109] extensive destruction is caused, the property has not been used for military purposes, and it is not in the immediate proximity of a military objective.[110] If a monument or work of art is marked with the protective emblem of the Cultural Property Convention (see paragraph 5.26.6) a commander is put on notice that it may also be protected under Additional Protocol I.

---

[104] AP I, Art 53. The UK has reserved the right to take reprisals against cultural property in certain circumstances, see para 16.19.1.

[105] ie, which constitute the cultural or spiritual heritage of peoples. That means objects of more than just local or national importance.   [106] However, see para 5.26.2.

[107] The UK made the following declaration on ratification of AP I: 'if the objects protected by this Article are unlawfully used for military purposes, they will thereby lose protection from attacks directed against such unlawful military uses'.

[108] For parties to the Hague Convention for the Protection of Cultural Property in the Event of Armed Conflict 1954 (Cultural Property Convention 1954 or CPC) (see para 5.26) the protective emblem of that Convention should be used. AP I does, however, prohibit deliberate misuse in an armed conflict of the cultural property emblem, see AP I, Art 38(1).

[109] See para 5.26.4.   [110] AP I, Arts 53 and 85(4)(d). For grave breaches, see para 16.24.

Protocol I needs to be read in conjunction with the Cultural Property 5.25.3
Convention,[111] even for states not party to the latter, because an attack on cultural property is regarded as an aggravated form of attack on a civilian
object, thus necessitating special care in operational planning. The prohibition in the Protocol of the use of cultural property for military purposes is
important because if it is not so used, there is no need to attack it. Thus a
church tower or mosque minaret should not be used as a military observation post. There may be *rare* cases where it is essential to use cultural property for military purposes, for example, an historic bridge that is the only
available river crossing. These cases only occur where there is no choice possible between the use of cultural property for military purposes and another
feasible method for obtaining a similar military advantage.[112] The main
advantage of having special rules for cultural property is in making attacking commanders more aware of the existence of cultural property, especially
if it is marked or contained in a published list which is available to them.[113]

CULTURAL PROPERTY CONVENTION

A comprehensive convention for the protection of cultural property is the 5.26
Hague Cultural Property Convention. The Convention has not been ratified
by the United Kingdom, so does not apply in detail to UK forces.[114] Many
European NATO states are parties to the Convention and it is important,
therefore, to be aware of its basic principles, which are outlined below. This is
only a brief summary of the most important features of the Convention.

The protection of cultural property under the Convention applies in internal 5.26.1
as well as international armed conflicts and during occupations.[115]

For the purposes of the Convention, cultural property is defined as: 5.26.2

Movable or immovable property of great importance to the cultural heritage of every
people,[116] such as monuments of architecture, art or history, whether religious or
secular; archaeological sites; groups of buildings which, as a whole, are of historical or
artistic interest; works of art; manuscripts, books and other objects of artistic, historical

---

[111] See para 5.26.
[112] Second Hague Protocol for the Protection of Cultural Property in the Event of Armed
Conflict 1999 (Second Hague Protocol or 2HP), Art 6.
[113] The Department of Defense Report, 100, contains information about the steps taken by
the allies to protect cultural property during the Gulf conflict 1991. Lists were drawn up of
historical, archaeological, and religious installations in Iraq and Kuwait that were not to be
targeted. Analysts were also asked to look at a six miles radius around proposed targets for
schools and mosques in that area, which would necessitate special care in planning attacks.
[114] The detailed rules of the Convention do not apply to states not party to it, but the general
principles of immunity of cultural property (see para 5.25) do apply to those states.
[115] CPC, Arts 18 and 19.
[116] This means items of international rather than local importance.

or archaeological interest; as well as scientific collections and important collections of books or archives or of reproductions of the property defined above.[117]

The definition extends to buildings or shelters where cultural property is exhibited or stored and to centres containing a large amount of cultural property.[118]

5.26.3 The *basic protection* is threefold. States must avoid using cultural property for military purposes,[119] must not direct hostilities against it,[120] and must protect it from theft, misappropriation, vandalism, requisitioning, or reprisals.[121] Occupying forces also have a duty to safeguard and preserve cultural property.[122]

5.26.4 There are detailed rules for the *special protection*[123] of refuges for the shelter of cultural property, centres containing monuments,[124] and immovable property of very great importance.[125] This property must be entered in a special international register maintained by UNESCO.[126] The transport of cultural property in certain circumstances[127] is also entitled to special protection.

5.26.5 The Convention has been supplemented by two Protocols of 1954 and 1999. Under the Second Protocol, there are also detailed rules for *enhanced protection* of cultural property if it is 'cultural heritage of the greatest importance for humanity'. This is dependent on the following action by the state party to the Protocol having jurisdiction or control of the property: suitable domestic legislation and a declaration that the property will not be used for military purposes or to shield military sites.[128] A Committee for the Protection of Cultural Property is established to monitor and supervise the implementation of the Protocol and, in particular, to establish and maintain a list of cultural property under enhanced protection.[129] The Protocol establishes a list of offences in relation to cultural property that are to be made criminal offences

---

[117] CPC, Art 1(a).   [118] CPC, Art 1(b), (c).

[119] Cultural property or its surroundings must not be used in such a way as to expose it to destruction or damage in the event of armed conflict.

[120] This protection can only be waived where military necessity imperatively requires under Art 4(2). Bearing in mind that the Convention deals with property of international importance, protection should *not* be waived lightly and the situation only arises where the enemy unlawfully uses such property for military purposes and even then attacks on it may not be necessary, see para 5.26.8.   [121] CPC, Art 4.

[122] CPC, Art 5.

[123] The actual protection is the same as for property under ordinary protection, ie hostilities may not be directed against it and the property and its surroundings must not be used for military purposes. For waiver of protection, see para 5.26.8. During armed conflict, cultural property under special protection must be marked with the distinctive emblem, see para 5.26.6, and will be open to a measure of international control, CPC, Art 10.   [124] CPC, Art 8.

[125] CPC, Art 8.

[126] CPC, Art 8(6). Various refuges have been registered, for example, by Austria, Germany and The Netherlands. The only centre containing monuments so far registered is The Vatican City.

[127] CPC, Arts 12 and 13.   [128] 2HP, Art 10.   [129] 2HP, Arts 24 and 27.

under the domestic law of states party to the Protocol.[130] The Protocol also introduces a stricter definition of military necessity, including incorporating some of the Additional Protocol I provisions on precautions in attack,[131] and strengthens rules in occupied territory.

Property protected under the Convention may be marked with the blue and white shield *distinctive emblem* shown in Appendix F. Cultural property under special protection may, and in time of armed conflict must, be marked with the distinctive emblem in the form of a group of three shields in triangular formation (one shield centred below). **5.26.6**

Practical measures to safeguard cultural property by the authorities of the state where that property is located include the following: to compile and publish lists, to register property under special or enhanced protection, to mark property, to set up emergency measures against fire or structural damage, to draw up plans for the removal of property to refuges or to provide *in situ* protection, to establish refuges, to have a policy of non-defended localities and demilitarized zones, and to designate an authority with responsibility for the protection of cultural property. **5.26.7**

The obligations under the Cultural Property Convention can be waived only: **5.26.8**

a. in the case of property under basic protection, at the level of a battalion or equivalent commander or higher;

b. in the case of property under special protection, at the level of a divisional or equivalent commander or higher;

c. in the case of property under enhanced protection, at the highest operational level of command;

and if, in all these cases, the property has become a military objective, there is no feasible alternative method for dealing with the situation and, unless it is a case of immediate self-defence, a prior warning is given with a reasonable time-limit for compliance.[132]

STARVATION; OBJECTS INDISPENSABLE TO SURVIVAL

'Starvation of civilians as a method of warfare is prohibited.'[133] It is also prohibited 'to attack, destroy, remove or render useless[134] objects indispensable to the survival of the civilian population, such as[135] foodstuffs, agricultural areas for the production of foodstuffs, crops, livestock, drinking water installations and supplies and irrigation works, for the specific purpose of denying them for their sustenance value to the civilian population or to the **5.27**

---

[130] 2HP, Art 15.   [131] 2HP, Art 7. See also para 5.32 onwards.
[132] CPC, Arts 4 and 11; 2HP, Art 13.   [133] AP I, Art 54(1).
[134] These words are wide enough to cover use of chemical agents or defoliants against these objects, see *ICRC Commentary*, para 2101.
[135] Use of the words 'such as' indicates that the list is not exhaustive.

adverse Party, whatever the motive, whether in order to starve out civilians, to cause them to move away, or for any other motive'.[136] Reprisals against these objects are also prohibited.[137]

5.27.1 The rule on starvation does not apply where these objects are for the sole use of members of the enemy armed forces or in direct support of military action.[138] In cases of imperative military necessity, a party to the conflict may depart from the prohibition relating to indispensable objects in order to defend its national territory from invasion, but only in those parts of its territory that are under its control.[139] The exception for the defence of national territory might include, for example, the flooding of low-lying areas to impede invading forces.

5.27.2 The law is not violated if military operations are not intended to cause starvation but have that incidental effect,[140] for example, by cutting off enemy supply routes which are also used for the transportation of food, or if civilians through fear of military operations abandon agricultural land or are not prepared to risk bringing food supplies into areas where fighting is going on. For the duties of the occupying power to ensure the supply of food to the population, see paragraph 11.45. For the special rules relating to sieges, see paragraph 5.34. The rules in this paragraph do not affect the law relating to naval blockade, see paragraph 13.67 onwards.[141] The customary law rule that permitted measures being taken to dry up springs and to divert rivers and aqueducts must now be considered as applying only to water sources used exclusively by military personnel or for military purposes.

PROHIBITION OF ENVIRONMENTAL MANIPULATION

5.28 States party to the Convention on the Prohibition of Military or Any Other Hostile Use of Environmental Modification Techniques 1976[142] undertake:

not to engage in military or any other hostile use of environmental modification techniques having widespread, long-lasting or severe effects[143] as the means of destruction, damage or injury to any other State Party.

---

[136] AP I, Art 54(2).   [137] AP I, Art 54(4).   [138] See para 5.19.

[139] AP I, Art 54(5). This exception does not apply to the forces of an occupying power whose commander would not be permitted when withdrawing to carry out a 'scorched earth' policy of destroying indispensable objects, though he would, of course, be permitted to destroy military objectives such as bridges and lines of communications to slow down the enemy's advance, see *ICRC Commentary*, para 2121.

[140] On ratification of Protocol I, the UK made a statement that the paragraph 'has no application to attacks that are carried out for a specific purpose other than denying sustenance to the civilian population or the adverse party'.   [141] See AP I, Art 49(3).

[142] Popularly known as the ENMOD Convention. The UK ratified the Convention on 16 May 1978.

[143] Art I. The text of the Convention was negotiated by the Conference of the Committee on Disarmament and when submitting the text to the United Nations the committee also sent its

The Convention is concerned with the deliberate manipulation of the 5.28.1
environment for hostile purposes to change 'the dynamics, composition or
structure of the Earth, including its biota, lithosphere, hydrosphere and
atmosphere, or of outer space'.[144] Phenomena that could be caused by environmental techniques include 'earthquakes; tidal waves; an upset in the
ecological balance of a region; changes in weather patterns (clouds, precip-
itation, cyclones of various types, and tornadic storms); changes in climate
patterns; changes in ocean currents; changes in the state of the ozone layer;
and changes in the state of the ionosphere'.[145]

ENVIRONMENTAL PROTECTION

Additional Protocol I contains two articles specifically designed to protect 5.29
the natural environment in armed conflicts. The first is in the section
headed 'methods and means of warfare' and is as follows:

It is prohibited to employ methods or means of warfare which are intended, or
may be expected, to cause widespread, long-term and severe damage to the natural
environment.[146]

The second is in the part dealing with the general protection of the civilian
population against the effects of hostilities and is as follows:

Care shall be taken in warfare to protect the natural environment against widespread, long-term and severe damage. This protection includes a prohibition of the
use of methods or means of warfare which are intended or may be expected to cause
such damage to the natural environment and thereby to prejudice the health or
survival of the population.[147]

'Attacks against the natural environment by way of reprisals are
prohibited.'[148]

Additional Protocol I is concerned with the protection of the environment 5.29.1
from the effects of hostilities. As already mentioned, the Protocol deals with
the subject in two separate articles couched in slightly different terms and

understanding of the meaning of these terms as follows:
a. 'widespread': encompassing an area on the scale of several hundred square kilometres;
b. 'long-lasting': lasting for a period of months, or approximately a season;
c. 'severe': involving serious or significant disruption or harm to human life, natural and
economic resources, or other assets.

However, the committee added that these understandings related exclusively to the
Convention and would not affect the interpretation of similar terms used in other international agreements.

[144] ENMOD Convention, Art II.

[145] This was another understanding by the Conference of the Committee on Disarmament.

[146] AP I, Art 35(3).   [147] AP I, Art 55(1).

[148] AP I, Art 55(2). The UK has reserved the right to take reprisal action in certain circumstances, see para 16.19.1.

in sections of the Protocol dealing with different forms of protection. Article 35 deals with direct protection of the environment whereas Article 55 tends more towards protecting the environment from the incidental effects of warfare, especially if it prejudices the health or survival of the civilian population. The only difference of substance is that while Article 35 relates to all methods of warfare whether on land, sea, or in the air wherever in the world they are utilized,[149] Article 55 only relates to environmental damage on the territory or in the territorial sea of a state party to the conflict.

5.29.2 Additional Protocol I relates to widespread, long-term,[150] and[151] severe damage. The terms are not defined. Those who negotiated the Protocol understood 'long-term' as relating to a period of decades and not the damage on the scale of that suffered in France during the First World War or to battlefield damage incidental to conventional warfare.[152] Unfortunately, there was no such understanding as to the meaning of 'severe' or 'widespread'.[153]

5.29.3 These provisions do not automatically prevent certain types of military objectives such as nuclear submarines or super tankers[154] from being legitimate targets nor do they automatically prevent the use of certain means of warfare such as herbicides or chemical agents.[155] The effects of attacking these targets or using these means must be considered. The rules introduced by Additional Protocol I apply exclusively to conventional weapons. In particular, the rules so introduced do not have any effect on and do not regulate or prohibit the use of nuclear weapons.[156] Although the words 'or may be expected' in the Protocol seem to indicate an objective assessment of the risk, commanders should be judged in the light of the information which is available to them at the relevant time.[157]

---

[149] Even on the high seas.   [150] The ENMOD Convention uses the term 'long-lasting'.

[151] The ENMOD Convention uses 'or' rather than 'and'. The effect is that in the case of the Protocol a breach does not occur unless the environmental damage is widespread, long-term, *and* severe.

[152] The Report of Committee III, *Official Records of the Diplomatic Conference* (1978) vol XV, 269, para 27.

[153] During the Gulf conflict 1991, Iraq opened the valves of a Kuwaiti oil terminal causing massive oil spills into the Gulf and sabotaged and set on fire hundreds of Kuwaiti oil wells causing huge emission of sulphur dioxides, nitrous oxide, and carbon dioxide and the deposit of soot on more than half of Kuwait. Iraq was not a party to AP I. Had the Protocol applied, the widespread and severe tests would probably have been satisfied but arguably not the long-term test.

[154] For attacks which cause the release of flood water or radioactivity, see para 5.30.

[155] As to these, see paras 6.5 and 6.8.

[156] See the UK statement of understanding to this effect made on ratification of AP I. Similar statements were made by other NATO states.

[157] The UK made the following statement of understanding on ratification of AP I: 'Military commanders and others responsible for planning, deciding upon, or executing attacks necessarily have to reach decisions on the basis of their assessment of the information from all sources which is reasonably available to them at the relevant time'.

Other provisions of international law, such as the Antarctic Treaty 1959, or **5.29.4** of the law of armed conflict, for example, the Incendiaries Protocol 1980,[158] also serve to protect the environment.

WORKS AND INSTALLATIONS CONTAINING DANGEROUS FORCES

Dams, dykes, and nuclear electrical generating stations 'shall not be made **5.30** the object of attack, even where these objects are military objectives, if such attack may cause the release of dangerous forces[159] and consequent severe losses among the civilian population'.[160] 'Other military objectives located at or in the vicinity of these works or installations shall not be made the object of attack if such attack may cause the release of dangerous forces from the works or installations and consequent severe[161] losses among the civilian population.'[162]

Although it is not a prerequisite for protection, dams, dykes, and nuclear **5.30.1** electrical generating stations may be marked to facilitate their identification with a special sign consisting of 'three bright orange circles placed on the same axis'.[163] For an illustration, and detailed information about the display, of this emblem, see Appendix E.

Commanders are in any event required to take the usual precautions **5.30.2** in attack.[164] In assessing whether the attack 'may' cause these effects, the principle of proportionality would require a party to refrain from the attack if the risk of releasing dangerous forces is so great as to outweigh the military advantage. Only objectively foreseeable risks need be taken into account. Commanders must make their decisions on the basis of their knowledge of the relevant factors (including humanitarian and military considerations) prevailing at the time. A commander's knowledge will depend on factors such as whether the installation is marked with a protective emblem or is identified in a published list[165] or a list made available by the adversary.

---

[158] See para 6.12.

[159] For example, flood water caused by breaching a dam or radioactivity caused by bombing a nuclear reactor. [160] AP I, Art 56(1).

[161] The word 'severe' is not defined and, according to the *ICRC Commentary*, para 2154, is to be interpreted as a matter of common sense and in good faith on the basis of objective elements such as the proximity of inhabited areas and the lie of the land.

[162] AP I, Art 56(1). In fact, parties to the conflict are under an obligation to 'endeavour to avoid locating military objectives in the vicinity of' dams, dykes, and nuclear electrical generating stations, AP I, Art 56(5). Anti-aircraft weapons installed solely for the defence of dams, dykes, and nuclear electrical generating stations, are not to be regarded as military objectives so long as they are used for defensive purposes. [163] AP I, Art 56(7).

[164] AP I, Art 56(3), see para 5.32.

[165] For example, the German Manual, *Humanitarian Law in Armed Conflicts*, Federal Ministry of Defence (VR113) (1992), contains, at para 470, figures showing nuclear electrical generating stations and important dams in the Federal Republic of Germany.

5.30.3 The United Kingdom, on ratification of Additional Protocol I, declared that:

> The United Kingdom cannot undertake to grant absolute protection to installations which may contribute to the opposing Party's war effort, or to the defenders of such installations, but will take due precautions in military operations at or near the installation . . . in the light of the known facts, including any special markings which the installation may carry,[166] to avoid severe collateral losses among the civilian population; direct attacks on such installations will be launched only on authorisation at a high level of command.[167]

5.30.4 Attacks only become unlawful if they may result in the release of dangerous forces and consequent *severe* losses among the civilian population.[168] It is unlikely that a commander would want to attack a dam as such if his aim was to neutralize the hydroelectric power station served by the dam. The attack would, therefore, be aimed at the power station, precautions being taken to reduce the risk of incidental damage to the dam.

5.30.5 In certain exceptional circumstances the protection afforded to dams, dykes, and nuclear electrical generating stations ceases:[169]

    a. 'for a dam or dyke only if it is used for other than its normal function[170] and in regular, significant and direct support of military operations';

    b. 'for a nuclear electrical generating station only if it provides electric power in regular, significant and direct[171] support of military operations';

---

[166] This is a reference to knowledge on the part of the responsible commander that the installation is, eg, a nuclear power station. Unless the protective emblem is displayed, the commander will need to rely on intelligence reports about the nature of the installation.

[167] Where direct attacks are made, commanders will be under a duty to take precautions to minimize collateral damage. It may be possible to put a nuclear power station out of action without damaging the reactor.

[168] Although AP I speaks of 'attacks which *may* cause the release of dangerous forces', it is inconceivable that an attack would be regarded as unlawful which did not actually have that effect. Launching an attack against works or installations containing dangerous forces in the knowledge that such attack will cause excessive loss of life, injury to civilians, or damage to civilian objects, is a grave breach of AP I, see Art 85(3)(c).   [169] AP I, Art 56(2).

[170] This means for any function other than its primary function of containing water, so that if a road on the top of a dam is regularly used as a military supply route or a dyke is incorporated into military defensive works it would run the risk of losing protection, see *ICRC Commentary*, para 2162. If a dam containing drinking or irrigation water is to be breached, the responsible commander will also have to consider the protection of indispensable objects dealt with in para 5.27.

[171] This exception is unlikely to occur in practice since most electricity supplied by nuclear power stations goes into an integrated grid. The mere fact that the station supplies electricity is not sufficient to remove protection, see *ICRC Commentary*, para 2165.

c. 'for other military objectives located at or in the vicinity of' dams, dykes and nuclear electrical generating stations 'only if they are used in regular, significant and direct support of military operations';[172]

and, in the case of a, b, and c, 'if such attack is the only feasible[173] way to terminate such support'.

In addition to the normal precautions to be taken in attack[174] all practical precautions are to be taken to avoid the release of dangerous forces.[175] Compliance may be achieved by using precision-guided munitions or other precision bombing techniques but this would require considerable technical advice and intelligence about the operation of the works or installations concerned. The unpredictability of the movement of airborne radioactive material means that the air commander ordering an air bombardment of a nuclear electrical generating station must consider the civilian population of a much wider area.   **5.30.6**

To avoid the risks to the civilian population, there is an obligation on the parties to the conflict 'to endeavour to avoid locating any military objectives in the vicinity of the works or installations' containing dangerous forces.[176] They may install weapons such as anti-aircraft or anti-missile missiles solely for the defence of these installations and those weapons are also protected from attack so long as they are not used for offensive purposes.   **5.30.7**

Reprisals may not be taken against dams, dykes, and nuclear electrical generating stations or against military objectives there or in their vicinity.[177]   **5.30.8**

The parties to Additional Protocol I in peacetime, and the parties to the conflict in time of armed conflict, are encouraged to conclude agreements between themselves for the protection of these installations.[178]   **5.30.9**

This gives rise to quite complicated considerations for military commanders. They have to be able to distinguish defensive weapons from other military objectives and they have to be able to distinguish offensive from defensive uses of those weapons. No special protection is afforded to military personnel manning the defensive weaponry. It is unlikely in practice that commanders will need to direct attacks against dams and dykes. As for nuclear electrical generating stations, it may be possible to render them   **5.30.10**

---

[172] Military objectives can take many forms. Tanks and troops concentrations would clearly fall within the exception. A nearby railway line would too if it were regularly used for military purposes.

[173] The UK declared on ratification of the Protocol that 'feasible' meant 'that which is practicable or practically possible, taking into account all circumstances ruling at the time, including humanitarian and military considerations'. It might well be possible to attack a road carried on a dam or a railway passing a nuclear power station at a different point with the same military effect.

[174] See para 5.32.   [175] AP I, Art 56(3).   [176] AP I, Art 56(5).   [177] AP I, Art 56(4).

[178] AP I, Art 56(6).

inoperative without causing the release of radioactive material, for example, by a commando action.

LOCALITIES AND ZONES UNDER SPECIAL PROTECTION

5.31 Certain areas are exempt from attack, bombardment, or from military operations. The details are to be found elsewhere in this Manual, but it is convenient to list them here:

   a. undefended towns,[179] villages, dwellings, or buildings;[180]

   b. hospital zones and localities for the protection of the wounded and sick of the armed forces and medical personnel;[181]

   c. safety zones for wounded and sick civilians, old people, expectant mothers, and mothers of small children;[182]

   d. neutralized zones for protection of the wounded and sick, both combatants and civilians, and also civilians who are taking no part in hostilities;[183]

   e. non-defended localities;[184]

   f. demilitarized zones.[185]

5.31.1 In some recent conflicts, zones using different nomenclature (for example, 'safe area', 'safe haven', 'open relief centre') have been established. These zones differ in important respects from the types provided for in treaties on the law of armed conflict as indicated above. For example, in some cases they have been proclaimed without the full consent of the parties to the conflict, and in some cases too they have not been demilitarized or neutralized. Some zones, as with the so-called 'safe areas' in Bosnia in 1993–95, have been declared by the UN Security Council, in which case the resolution will have set out the terms of the zone and will be binding on the parties to the conflict. Some, as in northern Iraq in 1991, have been set up by outside states, but with subsequent consent from the government of the state concerned. Others, such as the open relief centres in Sri Lanka in the 1990s, were set up by international agencies with some agreement from the belligerents. The question of what measures of force may be necessary to defend UN-established safe areas has proved difficult in practice. Following the fall of the 'safe area' of Srebrenica to Bosnian Serb forces in July 1995 and the killing of large numbers of inhabitants, a UN report urged the need for a clearer commitment to the use of forces in the defence of such areas.[186]

---

[179] Sometimes known as open towns.   [180] HR, Art 25, see para 5.37.
[181] GC I, Art 23, see para 5.41.   [182] GC IV, Art 14, see para 5.41.
[183] GC IV, Art 15, see para 5.40.   [184] AP I, Art 59, see para 5.38.
[185] AP I, Art 60, see para 5.39.
[186] See *Report of the Secretary-General pursuant to General Assembly Resolution 53/35: The Fall of Srebrenica*, UN doc A/54/549, New York, 15 November 1999. This is a detailed account of the establishment, maintenance, and fall of the 'safe area' of Srebrenica, and related events.

D. PRECAUTIONS IN ATTACK

PRECAUTIONS IN ATTACK

'In the conduct of military operations,[187] constant care shall be taken to **5.32** spare the civilian population, civilians and civilian objects.'[188]

With respect to attacks,[189] the following precautions shall be taken:[190]

(1) those who plan or decide upon an attack shall:

   (a) do everything feasible[191] to verify that the objectives to be attacked are neither civilians nor civilian objects and are not subject to special protection[192] but are military objectives[193] . . . and that it is not prohibited . . . to attack them;

   (b) take all feasible[194] precautions in the choice of means and methods of attack with a view to avoiding, and in any event to minimizing, incidental loss of civilian life, injury to civilians and damage to civilian objects;

   (c) refrain from deciding to launch any attack which may be expected to cause incidental loss of civilian life, injury to civilians, damage to civilian objects, or a combination thereof, which would be excessive in relation to the concrete and direct military advantage anticipated [the *rule of proportionality*];[195]

(2) an attack shall be cancelled or suspended if it becomes apparent that the objective is not a military one or is subject to special protection [or the attack violates the rule of proportionality];

(3) effective advance warning shall be given of attacks which may affect the civilian population, unless circumstances do not permit.[196]

Where there is a choice between different military objectives whose attack will yield the same military advantage, the one whose attack is expected to cause the least incidental damage should be chosen.[197]

Interpretation

Additional Protocol I lays down a general obligation on the parties to the **5.32.1** conflict to take care in the conduct of military operations to spare civilians

---

[187] Conduct of military operations has a wider connotation than 'attacks' and would include the movement or deployment of armed forces.   [188] AP I, Art 57(1).

   [189] For the definition of attacks, see para 5.20.   [190] AP I, Art 57(2).

   [191] 'Feasible' means that which is practicable or practically possible, taking into account all circumstances ruling at the time, including humanitarian and military considerations.

   [192] Special protection is a wide concept which would include, for example, any of the objects referred to in Part C of this chapter or medical units or prisoner of war camps. It is not limited to cultural property under special protection.   [193] See para 5.4.

   [194] See n 191.   [195] For further discussion of the rule of proportionality, see para 5.33.

   [196] The Conventional Weapons Convention 1980 makes specific provision for warnings to be given for certain uses of mines, booby-traps and similar devices, see para 6.14.

   [197] AP I, Art 57(3).

and their property and to 'direct their operations only against military objectives'.[198] So the commander will have to bear in mind the effect on the civilian population of what he is planning to do and take steps to reduce that effect as much as possible. In planning or deciding on or carrying out attacks, however, those responsible have more specific duties. These are outlined in the following sub-paragraphs.

Target identification

5.32.2 There is a legal obligation to do everything feasible to verify that the proposed target is not protected from attack[199] and that it is a military objective.[200] The problem of verification is obviously different for the air or artillery commander drawing up target lists from a distance than it is for a tank troop commander who has enemy armoured vehicles in his sights. The former has more time to make up his mind; the latter is more easily able to verify the target. Any commander selecting a target will have to pay regard to some or all of the following factors before he makes up his mind to attack it:

a. whether he can personally verify the target;

b. instructions from higher authority about objects which are not to be targeted;

c. intelligence reports, aerial or satellite reconnaissance pictures, and any other information in his possession about the nature of the proposed target;

d. any rules of engagement imposed by higher authority under which he is required to operate;[201]

e. the risks to his own forces necessitated by target verification.[202]

Target lists

5.32.3 It is important that target lists are constantly reviewed in the light of fresh information and changing circumstances. What was a military objective one day because, for example, of the presence of an enemy headquarters, may not be a military objective the next if that headquarters deploys somewhere else.

Means and methods of attack

5.32.4 There is the obligation to select the means (that is, weapons) or methods of attack (that is, tactics) which will cause the least incidental damage

---

[198] AP I, Arts 48 and 51(1).   [199] See Part C of this chapter.   [200] See para 5.4.

[201] Rules of engagement are not law, but they help commanders and soldiers to operate within the law or any political restraints under which they may be operating.

[202] Traditionally commanders have accepted some risk in identifying targets by using, for example, artillery spotters, forward air controllers, and intelligence gatherers operating in enemy-held territory.

commensurate with military success.[203] A direct fire weapon aimed at the target, such as a rifle or a wire-guided anti-tank missile, is less likely to cause incidental damage than indirect fire weapons such as mortar or artillery rounds unless, of course, they miss the target and hit civilian property instead. Free fall bombs are less likely to hit a narrowly defined target, unless dropped at very low altitude, than laser-guided bombs.[204] Cruise missiles are likely to hit the target selected unless there is a malfunction or the missile is deflected by defensive counter-measures. However, it is important that target intelligence is kept up-to-date because an object that was once a military objective may cease to be one because of a change of circumstances. The same considerations apply to the tactics adopted or the way weapons are used. Automatic fire is by its nature less discriminating than single aimed rounds; automatic fire loosed off in the general direction of the enemy may increase the risks to civilians if there are any in the vicinity. Sometimes, especially during fighting in towns, the tactics employed can make a great difference to the control of incidental damage. Artillery fire can cause a lot of incidental damage without any appreciable military advantage. The same military advantage might be just as well achieved by manoeuvre, outflanking or by-passing the objective, rather than direct assault.

Factors to be considered

In considering the means or methods of attack to be used, a commander **5.32.5** should have regard to the following factors:

a. the importance of the target and the urgency of the situation;

b. intelligence about the proposed target—what it is being, or will be, used for and when;

c. the characteristics of the target itself, for example, whether it houses dangerous forces;[205]

d. what weapons are available, their range, accuracy, and radius of effect;

e. conditions affecting the accuracy of targeting, such as terrain, weather, and time of day;

f. factors affecting incidental loss or damage, such as the proximity of civilians or civilian objects in the vicinity of the target or other protected

---

[203] The Department of Defense Report, 99, states that in the Gulf conflict 1991 coalition targeting policy was to minimize collateral damage and civilian casualties. Using precision weapons, targets such as the Iraqi Intelligence Headquarters in Baghdad, were struck, usually with little or no damage to adjacent buildings.

[204] During the Gulf conflict 1991, accuracy in aerial bombardment was improved by the use of Buccaneer aircraft fitted with lasers to designate targets while Tornado crews released laser-guided bombs. These methods were employed to attack bridges and, later, petroleum storage sites, hardened aircraft shelters, and aircraft operating surfaces, see Despatch by the Joint Commander of Operation Granby, Second Supplement to The London Gazette, 28 June 1991, G42.   [205] eg, a chemical weapons factory.

objects or zones and whether they are inhabited, or the possible release of hazardous substances as a result of the attack;

g. the risks to his own troops of the various options open to him.

Timing

5.32.6 The timing of an attack can be important. If it is known, for example, that a bridge is heavily used by civilians during the day but hardly at all at night, a night-time attack would reduce the risk of civilian casualties.

Cancelling, suspending, or re-planning attacks

5.32.7 There is the duty to cancel or suspend attacks if the incidental damage may be expected to be disproportionate to the military advantage anticipated.[206] This, the rule of proportionality, is discussed in the next paragraph. Instead of cancelling or suspending the attack, it can be re-planned so as to bring it within the proportionality principle. Allied to this duty is the duty, where there is a choice of targets offering the same military advantage, to select the target whose attack will cause the least incidental damage.

Warnings

5.32.8 There is a duty to give advance warning of an attack that 'may' affect the civilian population, unless circumstances do not permit. Obviously, the point does not arise as a matter of law if military operations are being conducted in an area where there is no civilian population or if the attack is not going to affect the civilian population at all.[207] In other cases, the warning must be given in advance and it must be effective. The object of warnings is to enable civilians to take shelter or leave the area and to enable the civil defence authorities to take appropriate measures. To be effective the warning must be in time and sufficiently specific and comprehensible to enable them to do this.[208] Warnings can be given by radio and television broadcasts as well as by dropping or distributing leaflets. They can also be given by word of mouth in the case, for example, of resistance forces operating in territory which is controlled by enemy troops. Warnings are not required if circumstances do not permit. Circumstances would not permit if the situation did not allow time to give warnings, for example, where troops have to

---

[206] It is of interest in this connection that during the Gulf conflict 1991, the British air commander had a power of veto of particular targets. This he used twice when he considered that severe collateral damage could have resulted from a malfunctioning of the weapons system, see House of Commons Defence Committee, 10th Report, *Preliminary Lessons of Operation Granby* (1991) xi.

[207] In practice, however, the question of giving warnings can arise even when there is no civilian population present. In the Gulf conflict 1991, Iraqi soldiers were warned in leaflets that their tanks were liable to be attacked but that if they got well clear they would be safer.

[208] For the special rules relating to warnings about the use of landmines, see para 6.14.

respond to an attack upon them or unexpectedly come across a target, where the element of surprise is crucial to the success of the military operation or where the safety of attacking forces would be compromised. In the latter case it might be possible to give a warning couched in more general[209] terms.

Level of responsibility

The level at which the legal responsibility to take precautions in attack rests **5.32.9** is not specified in Additional Protocol I. Those who plan or decide upon attacks are the planners and commanders and they have a duty to verify targets, take precautions to reduce incidental damage, and refrain from attacks that offend the proportionality principle. Whether a person will have this responsibility will depend on whether he has any discretion in the way the attack is carried out and so the responsibility will range from commanders-in-chief and their planning staff to single soldiers opening fire on their own initiative. Those who do not have this discretion but merely carry out orders for an attack also have a responsibility: to cancel or suspend the attack if it turns out that the object to be attacked is going to be such that the proportionality rule would be breached.[210]

Assessing discharge of responsibility

In considering whether commanders and others responsible for planning, **5.32.10** deciding upon, or executing attacks have fulfilled their responsibilities, it must be borne in mind that they have to make their decisions on the basis of their assessment of the information from all sources which is available to them at the relevant time.[211] This means looking at the situation as it appeared to the individual at the time when he made his decision. The obligation to cancel or suspend attacks only extends to those who have the authority and the practical possibility to do so as laid down in national laws, regulations, or instructions or agreed rules for NATO or other joint operations.[212]

---

[209] A warning was given to the German Commander of Münster, Germany, in 1945 that an intensive bombardment would begin unless he surrendered. Under the new rules of AP I, such a bombardment can only be directed against military objectives, see para 5.4, and precautions to protect civilians and civilian objects have to be taken.

[210] During the Kosovo conflict 1999, a pilot who launched an attack against a radar site noticed that the site was close to a church, so pulled his weapon off the target causing it to explode harmlessly in a wood.

[211] The UK made a statement to this effect on ratification of AP I.

[212] The UK declared on ratification that the obligation only extended 'to those who have the authority and practical possibility to cancel or suspend the attack'. During the Gulf conflict 1991, allied aircrew attacking targets in populated areas were directed not to expend their munitions if they lacked positive identification of their targets. When this occurred, aircrew dropped their bombs on alternative targets or returned to base with their weapons, Department of Defense Report, 612. Similar instructions were given to NATO aircrew in the Kosovo conflict 1999 as stated by Air Commodore David Wilbey, at the NATO press briefing on 1 April 1999.

THE RULE OF PROPORTIONALITY

5.33 An attack is not to be launched, or is to be cancelled, suspended, or replanned, if 'the attack may be expected to cause incidental loss of civilian life, injury to civilians, damage to civilian objects, or a combination thereof, which would be excessive in relation to the concrete and direct military advantage anticipated'.[213]

5.33.1 There are many reasons why the risk of civilian casualties is unavoidable even where civilians do not take part directly or indirectly in hostilities. For example:

a. military objectives may not be sufficiently set apart from centres of civilian population;

b. civilians and civilian objects may be improperly located in proximity to military objectives in an unlawful attempt to shield the latter from attack; or

c. civilians may unavoidably be present within a military objective for purposes not directly associated with hostilities.

5.33.2 The principle of proportionality, dealt with in paragraph 2.6, is intended to minimize such civilian casualties. It is an attempt to balance the often conflicting interests of military necessity on the one hand and humanitarian protection on the other when taking precautions in attack. Although a long-standing principle, it was expressed for the first time as a treaty rule in Additional Protocol I in the terms set out in paragraph 5.33.

5.33.3 'Concrete and direct' means that the advantage to be gained is identifiable and quantifiable and one that flows directly from the attack, not some pious hope that it might improve the military situation in the long term. In this sense it is like the term 'definite' used in the definition of military objects.

5.33.4 In deciding whether an attack would be indiscriminate, regard must also be had to the foreseeable effects of the attack. The characteristics of the target may be a factor here. Thus if, for example, a precision bombing attack of a military fuel storage depot is planned but there is a foreseeable risk of the burning fuel flowing into a civilian residential area and causing injury to the civilian population which would be excessive in relation to the military advantage anticipated, that bombardment would be indiscriminate and unlawful, owing to the excessive collateral damage.

---

[213] AP I, Art 51(5)(b) and Arts 57(2)(a)(iii) and (2)(b).

The military advantage anticipated from the attack refers to the advantage **5.33.5**
anticipated from the attack considered as a whole and not only from
isolated or particular parts of the attack.[214] The point of this is that an
attack may involve a number of co-ordinated actions, some of which
might cause more incidental damage than others. In assessing whether
the proportionality rule has been violated, the effect of the whole attack
must be considered. That does not, however, mean that an entirely gratu-
itous and unnecessary action within the attack as a whole would be
condoned. Generally speaking, when considering the responsibility of a
commander at any level, it is necessary to look at the part of the attack
for which he was responsible in the context of the attack as a whole and in
the light of the circumstances prevailing at the time the decision to attack
was made.

SIEGES AND ENCIRCLED AREAS

The principles of the law of armed conflict, particularly the rules relating to **5.34**
attacks, apply equally to situations of siege or encirclement.

Attacks can be costly in casualties and incidental loss or damage. A more **5.34.1**
effective method may be to encircle enemy forces, cutting them off from
supplies and communications with the outside world and forcing their
surrender. The same is true of besieging a town or stronghold. Siege is a
legitimate method of warfare as long as it is directed against enemy armed
forces.[215] It would be unlawful to besiege an undefended town since it
could be occupied without resistance.

Encirclement poses problems for the attacking commander if there are **5.34.2**
civilians in the encircled area, especially if the encircled area is, or contains,
a town which is inhabited by civilians but is defended by enemy armed
forces. In any bombardment, the normal rules on precautions in attack[216]
apply. So do the rules preventing starvation of the civilian population as a
method of warfare or those protecting supplies indispensable for the survival of the civilian population.[217] There is also an obligation to allow essential relief supplies through to the civilian population.[218] The effect of these

[214] The UK declared on ratification of AP I that 'the military advantage anticipated from an
attack is intended to refer to the advantage anticipated from the attack as a whole and not only
from isolated or particular parts of the attack'.

[215] The older customary law practice that permitted a besieging commander to drive escaping civilians back into the besieged area to increase the pressure on the defending commander
to surrender is now obsolete, see AP I, Arts 51(2), (7) and 54(1). [216] See para 5.32.

[217] See para 5.27. [218] See para 9.12.

provisions may be to prolong the siege and render an attack or bombardment more likely, especially if the attacking commander has to act within a limited period. In those circumstances, consideration may be given to allowing all civilians and the wounded and sick to leave the besieged area.[219] He would then be able to prevent food as well as other supplies from reaching the defending troops and he would be less circumscribed in attacking them.

5.34.3 The military authorities of the besieged area might decide not to agree to the evacuation of civilians[220] or the civilians themselves might decide to stay where they are. In those circumstances, so long as the besieging commander left open his offer to allow civilians and the wounded and sick to leave the besieged area, he would be justified in preventing any supplies from reaching that area.

PILLAGE

5.35 Even if a town or place has been taken by assault, pillage is prohibited.[221]

5.35.1 More or less synonymous with 'plundering', pillage involves the obtaining of property against the owner's will and with the intent of unjustified gain.[222]

5.35.2 Once a defended locality has surrendered, or been captured, only such further damage is permitted as is demanded by the exigencies of war, for example, removal of fortifications, demolition of military structures, destruction of military stores and measures for the defence of the locality. It is not permissible to destroy a public building or private house because it was defended. Looting is prohibited and the rules for the protection of civilians and civilian objects continue to apply.

---

[219] Under GC IV, Art 17, there is an obligation on the parties to a conflict to endeavour 'to conclude local agreements for the removal from besieged or encircled areas of wounded, sick, infirm and aged persons, children and maternity cases, and for the passage of ministers of all religions, medical personnel and medical equipment on their way to such areas'. Personnel of a state not party to the armed conflict who have diplomatic status would, in any event, have the right to leave a besieged area. That would extend to the personnel protected by the UN Convention on the Safety of United Nations and Associated Personnel 1994, see Arts 7(1) and 8 of that Convention. The establishment of evacuation corridors is in accordance with the principles of the law of armed conflict. Such corridors must be as safe as conditions permit and should, preferably, be monitored by an international organisation such as the ICRC or OSCE. For the special provisions on the evacuation of children, see para 9.14.

[220] This might amount to a breach of AP I, Art 51(7) and a war crime under Art 8(2)(b)(xxiii) of the Rome Statute for the International Criminal Court 1998, but see para 5.36.

[221] HR, Art 28; GC IV, Art 33.

[222] R Bernhardt (ed), *Encyclopaedia of Public International Law* (1997) vol 3, 1029–1030.

E. PRECAUTIONS AGAINST THE EFFECTS OF ATTACKS

PRECAUTIONS TO BE TAKEN

Parties to a conflict are required,[223] to the maximum extent feasible,[224] to: **5.36**

a. endeavour to remove[225] the civilian population, individual civilians and civilian objects under their control from the vicinity of military objectives;[226]

b. avoid locating military objectives within or near densely populated areas;

c. take other necessary precautions to protect the civilian population, individual civilians and civilian objects under their control against the dangers resulting from military operations.

Some of these obligations rest primarily on the civilian authorities, though **5.36.1** they may look to the military authorities for assistance, and close co-operation between them is essential. Steps such as planning the location of fixed military installations, civil defence planning, the earmarking of protected control centres, evacuation plans, or the provision of air raid shelters may be taken in peacetime or at an early stage in hostilities. Other measures affecting the civilian population such as the location of mobile military units or the laying of minefields would depend on the tactical situation, and here the responsibility for taking precautions would rest primarily with military commanders. The evacuation of civilians from areas likely to be attacked is advisable when there is immediate danger and where it would be likely to involve less hardship and danger to civilians than leaving them in place.

It is not prohibited to use urban terrain for military purposes, in particular **5.36.2** the location of military headquarters in urban areas, when military necessity so dictates, but the potential danger to the civilian population is an important factor to be considered in making decisions. As for locating military objectives near to works containing dangerous forces, see paragraph 5.30.

---

[223] AP I, Art 58.

[224] 'Feasible' means that which is practicable or practically possible, taking into account all circumstances ruling at the time, including humanitarian and military considerations.

[225] Arrangements must comply with GC IV, Art 49, which protects the inhabitants of occupied territory from unwarranted evacuations and transfers.

[226] For military objectives, see para 5.4.

5.36.3 Consideration should be given to declaring certain areas as undefended or setting up demilitarized or safety zones.

UNDEFENDED LOCALITIES

5.37 'The attack or bombardment, by whatever means, of towns, villages, dwellings, or buildings which are undefended is prohibited.'[227]

5.37.1 The reason for this rule is that there is no military need to attack a place that is not being defended. It can simply be occupied without resistance or bypassed. Enemy armed forces are likely to have withdrawn. Any remaining members of the enemy armed forces in the place can be taken prisoner of war and their weapons and military equipment captured. The concept of an undefended place does not apply to places in rear areas behind enemy lines,[228] only to places that are open to occupation by ground forces.

NON-DEFENDED LOCALITIES

5.38 'It is prohibited for the Parties to the conflict to attack, by any means whatsoever, non-defended localities.'[229]

5.38.1 The term 'non-defended locality' has a special meaning. It is one where all the following conditions are met:[230]

 a. all combatants,[231] as well as mobile weapons and mobile military equipment must have been evacuated;

 b. no hostile use shall be made of fixed military installations or establishments;

 c. no acts of hostility shall be committed by the authorities or by the population; and

 d. no activities in support of military operations shall be undertaken.

5.38.2 This rule is an extension of the rule on undefended localities but depends on more formal arrangements. Where opposing ground forces are in contact, a commander might decide to withdraw from an inhabited area and

---

[227] HR, Art 25.

[228] Places in rear areas are covered by the general rules prohibiting attacks on civilians, civilian objects, and protected areas and installations, prohibiting indiscriminate attacks, requiring attacks to be limited to military objectives, and the rule of proportionality.

[229] AP I, Art 59(1).   [230] AP I, Art 59(2).

[231] That does not include military personnel who are wounded or sick or medical personnel or who are assigned to a civil defence role nor does it include police (including military police, though their use for this purpose is not recommended because it can lead to misunderstanding) retained for the sole purpose of maintaining law and order: AP I, Art 59(3).

allow the enemy to occupy it to avoid bloodshed among the civilian population or to preserve important historical or cultural sites. He can declare the place a non-defended locality.

The declaration of a non-defended locality should define as precisely as **5.38.3** possible the limits of that locality and should be addressed to the adverse party[232] who should acknowledge its receipt and then treat the locality as non-defended unless any of the conditions mentioned above is not fulfilled. In that event, it must inform the party making the declaration.[233] It follows that a non-defended locality can be created without express agreement between the parties. It remains a non-defended locality until the party making the declaration withdraws it. Although no procedure for withdrawal is laid down, it should not take effect until notice of withdrawal had been given to the opposing party.[234]

Even if all the conditions are not met, the parties may agree between them- **5.38.4** selves to treat an area as a non-defended locality.[235] The agreement should be in writing and should specify the exact geographical limits of the locality, the date and time of the entry into force of the agreement and its duration, rules on marking the locality and agreed signs, persons authorized to enter the locality, methods of supervision (if any), whether and under what conditions the locality may be occupied by enemy troops.[236]

If, in any case, an area is to be treated as non-defended, the party controlling **5.38.5** it is responsible for marking it with agreed signs, especially on its perimeter and on highways.[237] Some ingenuity will be required to devise signs visible from aircraft. Distinctive radio or electronic signals may be needed instead.

Even if it loses its non-defended status, the locality will benefit from other **5.38.6** protection available under international law.[238]

DEMILITARIZED ZONES

'It is prohibited for the Parties to the conflict to extend their military **5.39** operations to zones on which they have conferred by agreement the status of demilitarized zone, if such extension[239] is contrary to the terms of this agreement.'[240]

---

[232] By direct contact through a parlementaire or communications system, or through diplomatic channels, the protecting power or an organization such as the UN or ICRC.
[233] AP I, Art 59(4).   [234] See *ICRC Commentary*, para 2268.   [235] AP I, Art 59(5).
[236] *ICRC Commentary*, paras 2287–2297.   [237] AP I, Art 59(6).
[238] AP I, Art 59(7), eg, the rules prohibiting attacks on civilians or civilian objects, attacks on undefended places, or indiscriminate attacks.
[239] ie, the extension of military operations.   [240] AP I, Art 60(1).

5.39.1 To qualify as a demilitarized zone, the following conditions[241] should usually[242] be fulfilled:

    a. 'all combatants,[243] as well as mobile weapons and mobile military equipment, must have been evacuated';

    b. 'no hostile use shall be made of fixed military installations or establishments';

    c. 'no acts of hostility shall be committed by the authorities or by the population'; and

    d. 'any activity linked to the military effort must have ceased'.[244]

5.39.2 Demilitarized zones may only be set up by agreement between the parties to the conflict. Their precise status will depend on the terms of the agreement but, generally speaking, these zones will not be used by any party for the conduct of military operations. Their purpose is to protect the areas themselves, or the people in them, from hostilities or as refuges for the civilian population.[245]

5.39.3 The main differences between demilitarized zones and non-defended localities[246] are that the former depend on agreement between the parties, are not necessarily inhabited places, and are not necessarily in the contact zone and open to occupation, so may be anywhere. Protection of non-defended localities is temporary and ceases when they are occupied by enemy forces; protection of demilitarized zones continues[247] for as long as may be specified in the agreement. Agreements about the creation of demilitarized zones may also be concluded in peacetime.

5.39.4 The agreement for the establishment of a demilitarized zone:

    a. must be express;[248]

    b. may be concluded orally or in writing;[249]

    c. may be made through direct contact with the opposing party or through a Protecting Power or an impartial humanitarian organization;[250]

    d. may consist of 'reciprocal and concordant declarations';

---

[241] Which are similar to those for non-defended localities.

[242] The conditions can be varied by agreement between the parties.

[243] That does not include military personnel who are (a) wounded or sick, (b) medical personnel, or (c) assigned to a civil defence role nor does it include police (including military police, though their use for this purpose is not recommended because it can lead to misunderstandings) retained for the sole purpose of maintaining law and order: AP I, Art 60(4).

[244] AP I, Art 60(3).   [245] See Bothe, Partsch, and Solf, *New Rules*, 387.

[246] See para 5.38.   [247] See Bothe, Partsch, and Solf, *New Rules*, 378.

[248] ie, it must be expressly for the purpose of creating a demilitarized zone. It cannot be implied.   [249] Obviously, a written agreement is to be preferred.

[250] Such as the ICRC.

e. should 'define and describe, as precisely as possible, the limits of the demilitarized zone and, if necessary, lay down the methods of supervision';[251]

f. may specify conditions to be complied with or provide interpretation of terms, for example, on the meaning of 'fixed military installations', 'acts of hostility', 'activity linked to the military effort', or 'purposes related to the conduct of military operations', or specify perimeter signs or specify who may be admitted to the demilitarized zone or as to what is to happen in the event of a breach of any of the conditions or if the fighting draws near to the zone.[252]

The party controlling the demilitarized zone is responsible for marking it **5.39.5** with agreed signs, especially on its perimeter and on highways.[253]

'If the fighting draws near to a demilitarized zone, and if the Parties to the **5.39.6** conflict have so agreed, none of them may use the zone for purposes related to the conduct of military operations or unilaterally revoke its status.'[254]

A material breach by one party of its obligations under sub-paragraphs **5.39.7** 5.39.1 or 5.39.6 will release the other party from its obligations under the agreement but the zone will continue to benefit from any other protection available under international law.[255]

NEUTRALIZED ZONES

Neutralized zones[256] may be established in regions where fighting is **5.40** taking place to shelter the wounded and sick, whether combatants or non-combatants, and civilians[257] from the effects of war.

These civilians may not perform work of a military character while they **5.40.1** reside in the zone. For the purpose of establishing such zones, the written agreement of the parties to the conflict is required. That agreement may be reached either directly or through a neutral state or humanitarian organization. The agreement must define the location and area of the zone, its commencement and duration, and also the arrangements for its administration, food supply, and supervision.[258] A neutralized zone is likely to be

---

[251] AP I, Art 60(2).　　　[252] AP I, Art 60(3), (4), (6).　　　[253] AP I, Art 60(5).

[254] AP I, Art 60(6). The terms of the agreement will be crucial. It might recognize the continuance of demilitarized status even when the area in which it is located falls into enemy hands, or it might, in these circumstances, envisage occupation and loss of demilitarized status.

[255] AP I, Art 60(7), eg, the rules prohibiting attacks on civilians or civilian objects, attacks on undefended places, or indiscriminate attacks.　　　[256] GC IV, Art 15.

[257] For a definition of civilians, see para 5.3.1.

[258] During the Falklands conflict of 1982, a neutralized zone was set up in the centre of Port Stanley, comprising the cathedral and a clearly defined area around it. This was done at the suggestion of the ICRC representative and with the consent of the Argentine and British authorities.

established in an area where the fighting is taking place. It is likely to be a very limited area and its purpose is very limited.

Hospital and Safety Zones

5.41 Hospital and safety zones and localities may be established in peacetime or in time of armed conflict and in occupied territory 'to protect from the effects of war, wounded, sick[259] and aged persons, children under fifteen, expectant mothers and mothers of children under seven'.[260]

5.41.1 After the outbreak of hostilities, the parties to the conflict may conclude agreements on the mutual recognition of these zones. The agreement may be modelled on the draft annexed to Geneva Convention IV.[261] This draft agreement provides for marking of the zones by means of oblique red bands on a white ground, these markings being placed on buildings and the outer precincts of the zone. It is also permissible to mark zones reserved exclusively for the wounded and sick with the distinctive red cross or red crescent emblem. The protecting powers and the ICRC are invited to lend their good offices to facilitate the institution and recognition of these zones. Similar provisions apply to the hospital and safety zones for the wounded and sick of the armed forces.[262]

F. CIVIL DEFENCE

Protection

5.42 Civil defence organizations and their personnel must be respected and protected.[263] They must also be allowed to perform their civil defence tasks except in case of imperative military necessity.[264] This protection extends to civilians responding to calls for assistance from the competent authorities and performing civil defence tasks under their control.[265] Buildings and materiel used for civil defence purposes and shelters provided for the civilian population[266] have the same protection as civilian objects[267]

---

[259] For definition of 'wounded' and 'sick', see AP I, Art 8(a) and see para 7.2.

[260] GC IV, Art 14.   [261] At Annex I. For the text, see Appendix D.

[262] GC I, Art 23.

[263] If civilians or civilian objects, they benefit from the civilian protection afforded to civilians and civilian objects. They also benefit from the special rules on civil defence.

[264] AP I, Art 62(1), ie, they may be prevented from carrying out their tasks if they would impede military operations. According to the ICRC, 'what it amounts to is that such tasks may only be forbidden or curtailed when the authorities are placed before the alternative of either changing major operational plans or doing without civil defence personnel', see *ICRC Commentary*, para 2445. Civil defence personnel should not normally be interned except for imperative security reasons, see *ICRC Commentary*, para 2446.   [265] AP I, Art 62(2).

[266] Not necessarily those provided by civil defence organizations.   [267] See para 5.24.

but, in addition, objects used for civil defence purposes must not be destroyed or diverted from their proper use except by the party to which they belong.[268]

Under Additional Protocol I:[269]　　　　**5.43**

Civil defence is the performance of certain humanitarian tasks[270] that are **5.43.1** 'intended to protect the civilian population against the dangers, and to help it to recover from the immediate effects, of hostilities or disasters[271] and also to provide the conditions necessary for its survival'.

Civil defence tasks are warning; evacuation; management of shelters; man- **5.43.2** agement of blackout measures; rescue; medical services, including first aid, and religious assistance; fire-fighting; detection and marking of danger areas;[272] decontamination and similar protective measures; provision of emergency accommodation and supplies; emergency assistance in the restoration and maintenance of order in distressed areas; emergency repair of indispensable public utilities; emergency disposal of the dead; assistance in the preservation of objects essential for survival; complementary activities necessary to carry out any of these tasks including, but not limited to, planning and organization.[273]

Civil defence organizations are 'those establishments and other units which **5.43.3** are organized or authorized by the competent authorities of a Party to the conflict to perform any [civil defence tasks], and which are assigned and devoted exclusively[274] to such tasks'.[275]

Civil defence personnel are 'those persons assigned by a Party to the conflict **5.43.4** exclusively to the performance of' civil defence tasks 'including personnel

---

[268] AP I, Art 62(3). That party would still be responsible for taking other precautions against the effects of attacks, see para 5.36.　　　　[269] AP I, Art 61.

[270] ie, some or all of those listed under 'civil defence tasks'.

[271] This includes natural disasters, see *ICRC Commentary*, para 2349.

[272] This would not include the detection and marking of minefields for combat purposes, see Bothe, Partsch, and Solf, *New Rules*, 395–396.

[273] AP I, Art 61(a). This is an exhaustive list of civil defence tasks, see *ICRC Commentary*, para 2344.

[274] AP I, Art 61(b). Rather like medical transports, exclusive assignment to civil defence tasks can be of a temporary nature. The fact that the armed forces may derive incidental benefit from civil defence actions does not necessarily deprive those actions of their civil defence character. Bothe, Partsch, and Solf, *New Rules*, 398, give the example of civil defence fire fighters putting out a fire at a military fuel dump to protect the adjacent civilian homes. Not all the bodies providing these services, eg, those providing routine, peacetime medical and burial services, necessarily qualify as civil defence organizations. They must be under the responsibility of the relevant public authorities.　　　　[275] AP I, Art 61(b).

assigned by the competent authority of that Party exclusively to the administration of these organizations'.[276] The definition includes members of the
armed forces and military units permanently assigned and exclusively
devoted to the civil defence tasks. The latter may not take part in hostilities
nor commit acts harmful to the adverse party.[277]

5.43.5 *Civil defence materiel* means 'equipment, supplies and transports[278] used by'
civil defence organizations for the performance of their tasks.

IDENTIFICATION

5.44 The parties to the conflict must endeavour to ensure that their 'civil defence
organizations, their personnel, buildings and materiel' are identifiable and
recognizable 'while they are exclusively devoted to the performance of civil
defence tasks. Shelters provided for the civilian population should be
similarly identifiable.'[279]

5.44.1 It follows that, for example, personnel should not be identifiable as civil
defence personnel when they are not exclusively devoted to civil defence
tasks and that civilians responding to appeals for assistance are not to
be identified as civil defence personnel. Identification can be by means of
the international distinctive sign of civil defence.[280] Civilian[281] civil defence
personnel are required to display this sign and carry a special identity card
in occupied territory and in places where fighting is taking place or likely
to take place.[282] The sign may also be used in peacetime for civil defence
identification purposes, provided the competent national authorities
agree.[283] The sign may be supplemented by agreed distinctive signals.[284]
Medical and religious personnel are also entitled to use the red cross and
red crescent emblems.[285]

DISTINCTIVE SIGN

5.45 'The international distinctive sign of civil defence is an equilateral blue triangle on an orange ground when used for the protection of civil defence organizations, their personnel, buildings and materiel and for civilian shelters.'[286]

---

[276] AP I, Art 61(c).   [277] AP I, Art 67.

[278] AP I, Art 61(d). Transports can be by land, sea, or air: Bothe, Partsch, and Solf, *New
Rules*, 399.   [279] AP I, Art 66(1).

[280] AP I, Art 66(3).

[281] Military personnel assigned to civil defence duties are required to display the sign and
carry the identity card at all times, see para 5.47.   [282] AP I, Art 66(2).

[283] AP I, Art 66(7). In the UK, the competent authority is the Secretary of State, see Geneva
Conventions (Amendment) Act 1995, ss 2, 3.   [284] AP I, Art 66(5).

[285] AP I, Art 66(9).   [286] AP I, Art 66(4). The sign is illustrated at Appendix E.

For detailed rules on the sign and card, see Appendix E. Measures must be   **5.45.1**
taken to supervise the display of the sign and to prevent any misuse.[287]

CESSATION OF PROTECTION

'The protection to which civilian[288] civil defence organizations, their per-   **5.46**
sonnel, buildings, shelters and materiel are entitled shall not cease unless
they commit, or are used to commit, outside their proper tasks, acts harmful to the enemy.[289] Protection may, however, cease only after a warning has
been given setting, whenever appropriate, a reasonable time-limit, and
after such warning has remained unheeded.'[290]

The following are *not* considered to be acts harmful to the enemy:[291]   **5.46.1**

a. that civil defence tasks are carried out under the direction or control of the
    military authorities;

b. that civilian civil defence personnel co-operate with military personnel in the
    performance of civil defence tasks, or that some military personnel are attached
    to civilian civil defence organizations;

c. that the performance of civil defence tasks may incidentally benefit military
    victims, particularly those who are *hors de combat*.[292]

Although there is no requirement for civil defence personnel to be armed,   **5.46.2**
the bearing of light, individual weapons by civil defence personnel for the
purpose of maintaining order or for self-defence is allowed.[293] In areas
where land fighting is taking place, or is likely to take place, the parties to
the conflict are required to limit the weapons to handguns, such as pistols
or revolvers, in order to assist in distinguishing between civil defence

---

[287] In the UK, these measures are contained in the Geneva Conventions (Amendment) Act
1995, ss 2, 3.   [288] ie, not military.

[289] Compare para 7.13.1 on similar language used in connection with medical units.

[290] AP I, Art 65(1). There are circumstances, however, where it might not be feasible to
give advance warning of the cessation of protection when civilian civil defence personnel are
working closely alongside military personnel who are not assigned to civil defence duties,
especially within or near a military objective. In those circumstances, any death or injury to
civilian civil defence personnel would be incidental to the attack on the military objective.
Similarly, this provision does not affect the use of delayed action munitions in attacks on
military objectives.

[291] This list is not exhaustive. Other cases would have to be examined on their merits.

[292] AP I, Art 65(2).

[293] The position is similar to that for medical personnel, see para 7.15. Civil defence personnel
are not combatants and, therefore, may not use their arms in combat or to resist capture. They
may use their arms in self-defence if unlawfully attacked, and that would extend to civilians in
their care who are unlawfully attacked, and, so far as national law permits, against marauders
and criminal groups or individuals, see *ICRC Commentary*, para 2624.

personnel and combatants. However, even if carrying other light, individual weapons,[294] civil defence personnel are to be 'respected and protected as soon as they have been recognized as such'.[295]

5.46.3   'The formation of civilian civil defence organizations along military lines, and compulsory service in them, shall also not deprive them' of protection.[296]

Members of Armed Forces, and Military Units, Assigned to Civil Defence Organizations

5.47   Members of the armed forces, and military units, may be assigned to civil defence organizations to carry out civil defence tasks and, during that assignment, are entitled to the same respect and protection as apply to those organizations. The assignment must be permanent and exclusive and those assigned must not perform any other military duties during the conflict. Assigned military personnel are subject to the same rules on weapons as apply to civilian civil defence personnel. They must not 'participate directly in hostilities'.[297] They, and the assigned military units, must not 'commit, or be used to commit, outside their civil defence tasks, acts harmful to an adverse Party'. Such personnel and units may 'perform their civil defence tasks only within the national territory of their Party'.[298] They must be 'clearly distinguishable from other members of the armed forces by prominently displaying the international distinctive sign of civil defence' and must carry the special identity card for civil defence personnel.[299] Buildings, major items of equipment and transports of military units so assigned must be clearly marked.[300]

5.47.1   Although assigned military personnel carrying out civil defence tasks are immune from attack, they may be captured by the enemy armed forces. In that event, they become prisoners of war. In occupied territory, such prisoners of war may be employed on civil defence tasks as the need arises but only in the interests of the civilian population of that territory. If so, only volunteers may be employed on dangerous tasks.[301]

---

[294] The carrying of heavy weapons would result in the loss of protection.

[295] AP I, Art 65(3).   [296] AP I, Art 65(4).

[297] If they do, they not only lose protection but commit a breach of the law of armed conflict, AP I, Art 67(1), last sentence.

[298] That means that they cannot be lent to the civil defence organization of an ally or to a party to a conflict in which the sending state is not involved or be used in occupied territory, see *ICRC Commentary*, para 2728.

[299] In addition to their combatant identity card which they need for the purposes of PW status, see para 8.19.   [300] AP I, Art 67(3).

[301] AP I, Art 67(2). The occupied territory will normally be the occupied home state of the prisoners of war, where they will have performed their civil defence duties before capture,

The materiel and buildings of assigned military units falling into the hands **5.47.2** of the enemy are subject to the law of armed conflict.[302] They may not be diverted from their civil defence purpose unless they are no longer required for that purpose, or adequate provision for the civil defence of the civilian population has been made, or the diversion is required for reasons of imperative military necessity.[303]

CIVILIAN CIVIL DEFENCE ORGANIZATIONS OF THIRD PARTIES

Neutral states and other states not party to the conflict may make their **5.48** civilian[304] civil defence organizations available to a party to the conflict but only with the consent and under the control of that party who becomes responsible for them.[305] In that event, they are entitled to the same respect and protection as civil defence organizations, personnel, and materiel of a party to a conflict.[306] Notification of such assistance must be given to the adverse party as soon as possible.

Although this assistance is not to be regarded as interference in the **5.48.1** conflict,[307] it must be performed with due regard to the security interests of the parties to the conflict concerned. In appropriate cases, the parties should facilitate the international co-ordination of such civil defence actions and the relevant international organizations are then covered by the civil defence provisions as well.[308]

---

see AP I, Art 67(1)(f). Dangerous tasks in this context would include the detection and marking of danger areas. This must also be read in the light of GC III, Art 52. For prisoner of war status, see para 8.3 onwards, and for prisoner of war employment, see para 8.83 onwards.

[302] This is a reference to the provisions governing the destruction or seizure of enemy property and war booty, see para 11.75 onwards.　　　　　　　[303] AP I, Art 67(4).

[304] ie, not military.　　　　[305] See *ICRC Commentary*, para 2540.

[306] However, a party to the conflict would not be entitled to requisition the civil defence materiel of a third party.　　　　[307] ie, participation in the conflict or a breach of neutrality.

[308] AP I, Art 64. Such an international organization is the International Civil Defence Organization, of which the UK is not a member. An occupying power may not exclude or restrict third party assistance if it cannot adequately perform civil defence tasks from its own resources or from those of the occupied territory, see AP I, Art 64(3).

6

Weapons

A. GENERAL PROVISIONS

GUIDING PRINCIPLE

'It is prohibited to employ weapons, projectiles and material and methods of **6.1**
warfare of a nature to cause superfluous injury or unnecessary suffering.'[1]

Historical background

The use of weapons is as old as war itself. The authors of the Preamble **6.1.1**
to the St Petersburg Declaration 1868 accepted that the use of weapons to

---

[1] Additional Protocol I (AP I), Art 35(2).

disable members of the enemy armed forces, even by killing them, was permissible. But it has also been recognized that the right to choose weapons is not unlimited.[2] Weapons use is restricted by international conventions, protocols and declarations, and by the customary law of armed conflict.[3] Moreover, there are the compelling dictates of humanity, morality, and civilization to be taken into account. The idea of humanity is expressed in the Preamble to the St Petersburg Declaration thus: 'this object would be exceeded by the employment of arms which uselessly aggravate the sufferings of disabled men, or render their death inevitable'. It has been said that 'commanders are quite ready to admit the claims of humanity to the extent of forgoing the use of any engine of war whose military effect is disproportionate to the suffering it entails'.[4] Any weapon that goes beyond what is needed to achieve the military object of disabling the enemy combatant would be difficult to justify on the grounds of military necessity.

6.1.2   While in 1868 warfare may have been waged principally against enemy combatants, things have become more complicated nowadays. Anti-material weapons have been developed that only incidentally have anti-personnel effects. The law does not specify the permissible level of disablement. In contemporary military operations, while the killing of enemy combatants is still contemplated, so is wounding them to put them out of action. This may cause them permanent injury. In either case suffering is implicit. But the law does not define unnecessary suffering, and views can differ markedly. Some are horrified by the prospect of blindness, others by the blast injuries caused by mines, and many regard burn injuries as particularly serious, but it is difficult to compare one type of injury with another and say that it necessarily signifies unnecessary suffering. In considering the control of weapons, therefore, all that can be done, in very general terms, is to try and balance the military utility of weapons with the wounding and incidental effects that they have. Comparisons may be made with the effectiveness and effects of existing weapons that are required for the same purpose.

6.1.3   A projectile designed to incapacitate at 300 metres or more may do more damage at closer ranges. At short range more force may be needed to make sure an enemy combatant is quickly rendered *hors de combat*. Powerful weapons designed to pierce the armour of tanks are likely to cause very serious injury to tank crews. Numerous other factors can

---

[2]   Hague Regulations 1907 (HR), Art 22; AP I, Art 35(1).

[3]   In the absence of any rule of international law dealing expressly with it, the use which may be made of a particular weapon will be governed by the general principles of the law of armed conflict.   [4]   JM Spaight, *War Rights on Land* (1911) 75.

affect wounding, for example, deformation or deflection of a projectile through armour plating, vegetation, body armour, or even atmospheric conditions.

Although use of weapons is an integral feature of armed conflict, there **6.1.4** have been several attempts over the centuries to ban certain weapons or to restrict their use. More recent international treaties on the use of weapons have been formulated in one of two ways. The first approach is an absolute ban on the use of a specific weapon or projectile. This has the advantage of precision, simplifying compliance and verification. On the other hand, the ban may be easily circumvented by equipping forces with another weapon that achieves the same result but is not caught by the precise terms of the prohibition. The second approach takes a more general form by referring to the effects of weapon use. But here there may be room for argument about whether the weapon use has that effect. An example of the first approach is the Hague Declaration 2 Concerning Asphyxiating Gases 1899 in which the parties agreed to abstain from 'the use of projectiles the sole object of which is the diffusion of asphyxiating or deleterious gases'. The use of canisters to release gas carried by the wind in the direction of the enemy lines was not caught by this treaty. An example of the second approach is the prohibition in Article 23(e) of the Hague Regulations of the employment of 'arms, projectiles, or material calculated to cause unnecessary suffering'. Arguments continue to this day about whether certain weapons that have undoubted military utility cause unnecessary suffering.

The current practice is to combine the two approaches by regarding **6.1.5** the 'unnecessary suffering' provision as a guiding principle upon which specific prohibitions or restrictions can be built.

Application of the Guiding Principle

The correct criterion is whether the use of a weapon is of a nature to cause **6.2** injury or suffering greater than that required for its military purpose.

In deciding the legality of use of a specific weapon, therefore, it is necessary **6.2.1** to assess:

a. its effects in battle;
b. the military task it is required to perform; and
c. the proportionality between factors (a) and (b).[5]

---

[5] See M Bothe, K-J Partsch, and WA Solf, *New Rules for Victims of Armed Conflicts* (1982) (Bothe, Partsch, and Solf, *New Rules*) 196.

6.2.2 However, even if the use of a weapon is considered under this test to be generally lawful, its use in certain ways, or in certain circumstances, may still be unlawful.

Weapons and the Environment

6.3 It is prohibited to employ weapons that are intended, or may be expected, to cause widespread, long-term, and severe damage to the natural environment.[6]

Indiscriminate Weapons

6.4 It is prohibited to employ weapons which cannot be directed at a specific military objective or the effects of which cannot be limited as required by Additional Protocol I and consequently are of a nature to strike military objectives and civilians or civilian objects without distinction.[7]

6.4.1 This provision operates as an effective prohibition on the use of weapons that are so inaccurate that they cannot be directed at a military target. The V1 flying bomb used in the Second World War and the Scud rocket used during the Gulf conflict of 1990–91 are examples of weapons likely to be caught by this provision.

B. SPECIFIC WEAPONS

Bacteriological or Biological Weapons

6.5 The development, production, stockpiling, acquisition, retention, and use of bacteriological, biological, and toxin weapons are prohibited.[8]

6.5.1 This does not interfere with the right of states to participate in the exchange of equipment, materials, and scientific and technological information for the use of bacteriological and biological agents and toxins for peaceful purposes such as the prevention of disease.

[6] AP I, Art 35(3). The subject of environmental protection is dealt with in para 5.29.

[7] AP I, Art 51(4). The word 'limited' is a reference, *inter alia*, to the rule of proportionality, see para 5.33.

[8] Geneva Gas Protocol 1925; Convention on the Prohibition of the Development, Production and Stockpiling of Bacteriological (Biological) and Toxin Weapons and on Their Destruction 1972 (Biological Weapons Convention 1972 or BWC). The BWC was ratified by the UK, the USA, and the USSR, as the co-depositaries, on 26 March 1975. The BWC does not explicitly prohibit use, but the states party confirmed at the Fourth Review Conference in 1996 that Art 1 effectively prohibits use. The UK withdrew its reservation concerning biological weapons in 1991. Since entry into force of the Chemical Weapons Convention 1993, the UK has also withdrawn its reservation on retaliatory use of chemical weapons.

The term 'toxin' refers to agents that are chemical poisons of types that can **6.5.2** be produced naturally by biological processes or synthesized artificially. The terms 'bacteriological' and 'biological' are not defined in the relevant treaties.

BAYONETS, SWORDS

Stabbing or cutting weapons such as lances, swords, bayonets, or knives **6.6** are lawful provided they are not of a nature to cause superfluous injury or unnecessary suffering, for example, because they have barbed heads or serrated edges or are spread with substances designed to inflame wounds.

BOOBY-TRAPS

The use of booby-traps is permitted provided certain conditions are **6.7** complied with. First, they must be directed against combatants and may not under any circumstances[9] be directed against civilians. Secondly, indiscriminate use is prohibited. That means that the method used, or the circumstances, must be such that there is a reasonable prospect that only combatants will become victims of the booby-traps and that the risk to civilians does not outweigh the military advantage of laying booby-traps. Care has to be taken to ensure that civilians do not become the unwitting victims of booby-traps. So, thirdly, feasible precautions must be taken to protect civilians from their effects. Feasible precautions are those which 'are practicable or practically possible taking into account all circumstances ruling at the time, including humanitarian and military considerations'.[10] Further prohibitions of, or restriction on the use of, booby-traps are set out in sub-paragraphs 6.7.3. to 6.7.7.

A booby-trap is 'any device or material which is designed, constructed or **6.7.1** adapted to kill or injure, and which functions unexpectedly when a person disturbs or approaches an apparently harmless object or performs an apparently safe act'.[11] For example, in the case of a booby-trapped doorway, opening the door would be an apparently safe act with respect to the door.

A military logistic installation that is being abandoned in a hurry during a **6.7.2** withdrawal could be booby-trapped, but with signs to that effect posted on the perimeter of the installation as a warning to civilians not to enter it.

[9] Not even by way of reprisals, as to which, see para 16.16 onwards.
[10] Amended Protocol II 1996 on Prohibitions or Restrictions on the Use of Mines, Booby-Traps, and Other Devices (Amended Mines Protocol) to the Convention on Prohibitions or Restrictions on the Use of Certain Conventional Weapons Which May be Deemed to be Excessively Injurious or to Have Indiscriminate Effects 1980 (Conventional Weapons Convention 1980 or CCW), Art 3(10).   [11] Amended Mines Protocol, Art 2(4).

Prohibitions and restrictions on use of booby-traps

6.7.3 Where combat between ground forces is neither taking place nor appears imminent, booby-traps may not be used at all in populated areas unless either:

  a. 'they are placed on or in the close vicinity of a military objective';[12] or

  b. 'measures are taken to protect civilians from their effects, for example, the posting of warning [signs, the posting of] sentries, the issue of warnings or the provision of fences'.[13]

6.7.4 'It is prohibited to use booby-traps in the form of apparently harmless portable objects which are specifically designed and constructed to contain explosive material.'[14] This prohibition relates to booby-traps made to look like watches, personnel audio players, cameras and the like. This is to prevent the production of large quantities of dangerous objects that can be scattered around and picked up by civilians, especially children. It does not prohibit, subject to paragraph 6.7.5, the booby-trapping of existing items of that sort.

6.7.5 It is also prohibited in all circumstances to use booby-traps 'attached to or associated with':

  a. 'internationally recognized protective emblems, signs or signals';[15]

  b. 'sick, wounded or dead persons';

  c. 'burial or cremation sites or graves';

  d. 'medical facilities, medical equipment, medical supplies or medical transportation';

  e. 'children's toys or other portable objects or products specially designed for the feeding, health, hygiene, clothing or education of children';

  f. 'food or drink';[16]

  g. 'kitchen utensils or appliances except in military establishments, military locations or military supply depots';

---

[12] For a definition of military objective, see para 5.4. This formulation is less restrictive than in the Mines Protocol 1980 which read: 'they are placed on or in the close vicinity of a military objective belonging to or under the control of an adverse party' (Art 4(2)(a)). It was thought then that in cases in populated areas where booby-traps were under one's own control, it should be mandatory to take measures to protect civilians.

[13] Amended Mines Protocol, Art 7(3)(b). The words in square brackets appeared in the Mines Protocol 1980, Art 4(2)(b) and their omission in the Amended Protocol must be a drafting error.

[14] Amended Mines Protocol, Art 7(2).   [15] Such as the red cross emblem.

[16] At first sight, this seems to imply that the practice of booby-trapping refrigerators containing food will now be unlawful. However, the next sub-paragraph deals specifically with kitchen utensils or appliances, so they must be regarded as a separate category. It follows that the booby-trapping of refrigerators in military installations remains permissible.

h. 'objects clearly of a religious nature';

i. 'historic monuments, works of art or places of worship which constitute the cultural or spiritual heritage of peoples';[17]

j. 'animals or their carcasses'.[18]

It is also prohibited in all circumstances to use any booby-trap which is **6.7.6** designed to cause superfluous injury or unnecessary suffering.[19] Although these would be prohibited under the guiding principle set out at the beginning of this chapter, the drafters of this provision had in mind booby-traps specifically designed to cause a cruel or lingering death, their purpose being to intimidate through terror.

It is further prohibited to use booby-traps which are designed to be deto- **6.7.7** nated by mine detectors.[20]

Recording

Recording the location of booby-traps is required. This not only protects **6.7.8** civilians but also protects one's own or allied troops and also enables booby-traps to be deactivated as soon as they are no longer required.[21]

For details of the making of records, the use of records, the protection of **6.7.9** United Nations forces or missions, and the removal of booby-traps, see the corresponding provisions in respect of landmines in paragraph 6.14.6.

CHEMICAL WEAPONS[22]

Chemical Weapons Convention 1993

Under the Chemical Weapons Convention,[23] states party undertake never **6.8** under any circumstances:[24]

a. 'to develop, produce, otherwise acquire, stockpile or retain chemical weapons, or transfer, directly or indirectly, chemical weapons to anyone';

b. 'to use chemical weapons';

c. 'to engage in any military preparations to use chemical weapons';

---

[17] See paras 5.25 and 5.26.   [18] Amended Mines Protocol, Art 7(1).
[19] Amended Mines Protocol, Art 3(3).   [20] Amended Mines Protocol, Art 3(5).
[21] Amended Mines Protocol, Art 9.
[22] For the prohibition on the use of poison, see para 6.19. Herbicides are dealt with in para 5.29.3.   [23] Which entered into force on 29 April 1997.
[24] Art I(1). The words 'never under any circumstances' would also prohibit use by way of reprisals in response to an earlier unlawful use. Reservations to the articles of the Convention are not permitted: Art XXII.

    d. 'to assist, encourage or induce, in any way, anyone to engage in any activity prohibited to a State Party' under the Convention.

6.8.1 The Convention contains, for the first time, a definition of chemical weapons as follows:[25]

'chemical weapons' means the following, together or separately:

(a) Toxic chemicals[26] and their precursors,[27] except where intended for purposes not prohibited[28] under this Convention, as long as the types and quantities are consistent with such purposes;

(b) Munitions and devices, specifically designed to cause death or other harm through the toxic properties of those toxic chemicals specified in sub-paragraph (a), which would be released as a result of the employment of such munitions and devices;

(c) Any equipment specifically designed for use directly in connection with the employment of munitions and devices specified in sub-paragraph (b).

6.8.2 States party also undertake not to use riot control agents as a method of warfare.[29]

6.8.3 Permitted uses of chemicals include industrial, agricultural, research, medical, pharmaceutical, or other peaceful purposes; purposes directly related to protection against toxic chemicals and chemical weapons; military purposes not connected with the use of chemical weapons and not dependent on the use of the toxic properties of chemicals as a method of warfare; and law enforcement, including domestic riot control purposes.[30]

6.8.4 The Convention also requires states party to destroy existing chemical weapons and chemical weapons production facilities. It establishes an Organization for the Prohibition of Chemical Weapons and contains very detailed provisions, outside the scope of this work, for verification, including

[25] Art II.

[26] Defined as 'any chemical which through its chemical action on life processes can cause death, temporary incapacitation or permanent harm to humans or animals. This includes all such chemicals, regardless of their origin or of their method of production, and regardless of whether they are produced in facilities, in munitions or elsewhere': Art II(2). Some of these are listed for verification purposes in Schedules to the Convention. There is some overlap with the BWC in the area of toxins produced artificially by chemical means and those produced by plant or animal means.

[27] Defined as 'any chemical reactant which takes part at any stage in the production by whatever method of a toxic chemical. This includes any key component of a binary or multi-component chemical system': Art II(3). Precursors identified for the purposes of verification are listed in Schedules to the Convention.

[28] The Convention does not prohibit peaceful use of chemicals, see para 6.8.3.

[29] Art I(5).   [30] Art II(9).

short-notice challenge inspections. In the United Kingdom the responsible authority is the Department of Trade and Industry.[31]

Dum-dum Bullets

It is prohibited to use in international armed conflicts 'bullets which expand or flatten easily in the human body, such as bullets with a hard envelope which does not entirely cover the core or is pierced with incisions'.[32]   **6.9**

This prohibition is aimed at soft-nosed bullets that mushroom on impact or bullets whose casing is designed to fragment on impact causing, in either case, unnecessarily serious injuries.   **6.9.1**

Explosive or Incendiary Bullets

The practice of states indicates that the use of explosive or incendiary bullets[33] designed solely for use against personnel is not permissible under customary law.   **6.10**

The reason for this is because a solid round will achieve the military purpose of disabling the enemy combatant; if a round explodes on impact it would uselessly aggravate the injury. That does not prevent the use of tracer. Nor does it prevent the use of explosive or combined-effects munitions of, for example, 0.5 or 20 mm calibre for defeating materiel targets, even though personnel may be incidentally wounded by them.   **6.10.1**

The parties to the St Petersburg Declaration 1868 undertook 'mutually to renounce, in case of war among themselves, the employment by their military or naval troops of any projectile of a weight below 400 grammes, which is either explosive or charged with fulminating or inflammable substances'. Although it is not clear from the declaration itself whether anti-materiel, as opposed to anti-personnel, uses of explosive or incendiary bullets were also contemplated,[34] it may be inferred from state practice that it was not.   **6.10.2**

---

[31] The Chemical Weapons Act 1996 gives effect to the United Kingdom's obligations under the Convention.

[32] Hague Declaration 3 1899 Concerning Expanding Bullets. Although originally only binding on the parties to the Declaration, it now seems that states regard themselves as prohibited from using dum-dum bullets in international armed conflicts. In the light of this state practice, the Declaration should be regarded as reflecting customary international law and binding on all states and all individual combatants.

[33] Incendiary weapons are considered in para 6.12.

[34] It seems that explosive bullets were introduced in the Russian Army in 1863 for attacking ammunition vehicles but the Russian War Minister considered that they should not be used against troops and wanted states to renounce their use: see A Roberts and R Guelff (eds), *Documents on the Laws of War* (3rd edn 2000) (Roberts and Guelff, *Documents*) 53.

The Hague Rules of Aerial Warfare 1923,[35] provided that 'the use of tracer, incendiary or explosive projectiles by or against aircraft is not prohibited'. During the Second World War such projectiles were used by the air forces of all belligerents[36] and tracer and incendiary ammunition has since been in general use by armed forces. Incendiary weapons are not prohibited by the Conventional Weapons Convention.[37] The 400 gram limit in the St Petersburg Declaration is, in any event, obsolete as states have developed 20 mm and 25 mm combined-effects munitions which weigh less than 400 grams. The use of tracer, or small incendiary or explosive projectiles, must be considered to be lawful if it is directed against inanimate military objectives, including aircraft, or is used for range-finding or target indication. It is also lawful to use tracer mixed with normal ammunition for range-finding or target indication at night against combatant personnel, for snipers to use combined-effects munitions against either materiel or personnel targets, and for aircraft to strafe enemy combatants in the open.

Fragmentation Weapons

6.11 The general rule[38] prohibiting the infliction of unnecessary suffering or superfluous injury does not preclude the use of hand-grenades and other fragmentation weapons.

6.11.1 The general rule must be taken as banning the use of weapons or projectiles that discharge broken glass, nails, and the like.[39]

6.11.2 The use of 'any weapon the primary effect of which is to injure by fragments which in the human body escape detection by X-rays' is prohibited.[40]

Incendiary Weapons

6.12 It is prohibited 'in all circumstances to make any military objective located within a concentration of civilians the object of attack by air-delivered incendiary weapons'.[41] Subject to that, the use of incendiary weapons,

---

[35] Art 18. These rules were never adopted in legally binding form.

[36] See JM Spaight, *Air Power and War Rights* (1947) 214.

[37] Their use is restricted, however, see para 6.12.   [38] AP I, Art 35(2).

[39] L Oppenheim, *International Law* (7th edn by H Lauterpacht 1952) (Oppenheim, *International Law*), vol II, 340.

[40] Protocol I on Non-Detectable Fragments (Non-Detectable Fragments Protocol) to the CCW.

[41] Protocol III on Prohibitions or Restrictions on the Use of Incendiary Weapons (Incendiaries Protocol) to the CCW, Art 2(2). This is the only really new provision in the Incendiaries Protocol. It prohibits the type of attacks on cities that were common during the Second World War. The civilian population, civilians, and civilian objects may not be attacked with any weapons, let alone incendiary weapons. Although reprisal action against the civilian population may be

including incendiary bombs, napalm, and flamethrowers, against military objectives is not prohibited under customary or treaty law.

Although these weapons can cause severe injury to personnel, their use is **6.12.1** lawful provided the military necessity for their use outweighs the injury and suffering which their use may cause.

An incendiary weapon is 'any weapon or munition which is primarily **6.12.2** designed to set fire to objects or to cause burn injury to persons through the action of flame, heat, or a combination thereof, produced by a chemical reaction of a substance delivered on the target'.

Such weapons can take the form of, for example, 'flamethrowers, fougasses, **6.12.3** shells, rockets, grenades, mines, bombs and other containers of incendiary substances'.

The following are not considered incendiary weapons: 'munitions which **6.12.4** may have incidental incendiary effects, such as illuminants, tracers, smoke or signalling systems'; nor do they include 'munitions designed to combine penetration, blast or fragmentation effects with an additional incendiary effect, such as armour-piercing projectiles, fragmentation shells, explosive bombs and similar combined-effects munitions in which the incendiary effect is not specifically designed to cause burn injury to persons, but to be used against military objectives, such as armoured vehicles, aircraft and installations or facilities'.[42]

A 'concentration of civilians' is widely defined to include the inhabited parts **6.12.5** of cities or inhabited towns or villages but also temporary concentrations as in camps or columns of refugees or evacuees, or groups of nomads.[43] An attack on a military objective in a concentration of civilians with incendiary weapons other than air-delivered ones may only take place if the military objective is clearly separated from the concentration and all feasible precautions[44] are taken to limit the incendiary effect to the military objective and to avoiding or minimizing incidental loss, injury, and damage to civilians.[45] Forests and 'other kinds of plant cover' may not be attacked with incendiary weapons unless they are 'used to cover, conceal or camouflage combatants or other military objectives, or are themselves military objectives'.[46]

---

taken in exceptional circumstances (see para 16.16 onwards), Art 2(1) of the Protocol, which prohibits incendiary attacks on the civilian population, civilians, and civilian objects 'in all circumstances', would preclude the use of incendiary weapons for the purpose of reprisals.

[42] Incendiaries Protocol, Art 1(1).   [43] Incendiaries Protocol, Art 1(2).

[44] Feasible precautions are those which are practicable or practically possible taking into account all circumstances ruling at the time, including humanitarian and military considerations: Incendiaries Protocol, Art 1(5).   [45] Incendiaries Protocol, Art 2(3).

[46] Incendiaries Protocol, Art 2(4).

6.12.6 Use of weapons such as napalm and flamethrowers against combatant personnel is not dealt with specifically in the Conventional Weapons Convention or any other treaty. Such uses are governed by the unnecessary suffering principle so that they should not be used directly against personnel but against armoured vehicles, bunkers, and built-up emplacements, even though personnel inside may be burnt. The same applies to white phosphorous, which is designed to set fire to targets such as fuel and ammunition dumps or for use to create smoke, and which should not be used directly against personnel.

LANDMINES

Anti-personnel landmines

6.13 Parties to the Ottawa Convention 1997, including the United Kingdom, accept a prohibition on the possession or use of anti-personnel landmines as well as assistance, encouragement, or inducement to any other person to possess or use these mines.[47] Members of the United Kingdom armed forces will not, however, be guilty of an offence merely by reason of taking part in joint operations with forces of an ally not bound by the Ottawa Convention which deploy landmines.[48]

Anti-vehicle landmines

6.14 The use of anti-vehicle landmines[49] is permitted so long as:

    a. they are not designed to be detonated by mine detectors;[50] and

    b. any anti-handling device is deactivated when the mine deactivates;[51] and

[47] Ottawa Convention on the Prohibition of the Use, Stockpiling, Production and Transfer of Anti-Personnel Mines and on their Destruction 1997 (Ottawa Convention), Art 1. This Convention came into force on 1 March 1999. Anti-personnel mines, which for parties to the Convention are now prohibited, have been used to make the clearance of anti-tank minefields more difficult, to deny areas, airfields, and similar military objectives to enemy infantry, or to protect defensive positions from surprise attack. However, because of the risk of their misuse, it was considered that the humanitarian interest in their prohibition outweighed any military advantage in their use.   [48] Landmines Act 1998, s 5.

[49] Anti-tank mines are used to deny mobility to, slow down, or channel enemy armoured formations giving the defenders time to meet the threat. They may be laid in the ground or may be 'off route' mines where a sensor fires a projectile at the side of any passing tank. Sensors are becoming increasingly sophisticated so that they can detect certain types of tanks and other vehicles by differentiating between track patterns or vibrations. There are detailed legal provisions on transfers of mines, clearance after hostilities, detectability, and deactivation but, since these are primarily aimed at the states party and the manufacturers and procurers of mines, they are not set out in this Manual.

[50] Amended Protocol II on Prohibitions or Restrictions on the Use of Mines, Booby-Traps and Other Devices 1996 (Amended Mines Protocol), Art 3(5).

[51] Amended Mines Protocol, Art 3(6).

c. they are either:

   (1) cleared before the area where they are laid is abandoned, or

   (2) handed over to another state that assumes the responsibilities laid down in this paragraph.[52]

In the case of remotely delivered anti-vehicle mines, they must be self-deactivating and their location must be recorded.[53]

Definitions

The mines referred to in this paragraph are those used on land or laid to **6.14.1** interdict beaches, waterway crossings, and river crossings.[54] This paragraph does not apply to anti-ship mines used at sea or in inland waterways.[55] 'Mine' means 'a munition placed under, on or near the ground or other surface area and designed to be exploded by the presence, proximity or contact of a person or vehicle'. 'Remotely-delivered mine' means a mine 'not directly emplaced but delivered by artillery, missile, rocket, mortar or similar means, or dropped from an aircraft'.[56] Mines laid from a land-based system from less than 500 metres are not considered remotely delivered.[57] Anti-vehicle mines equipped with anti-handling devices are not considered to be anti-personnel mines as a result of being so equipped.[58]

Restrictions on use

The following rules apply to anti-vehicle mines: **6.14.2**

a. they may only be deployed against or to protect military objectives;

b. they may not be directed against civilians, even by way of reprisals;

c. indiscriminate use is prohibited;

d. feasible precautions must be taken to protect civilians from their effects;[59]

e. effective advance warning must be given of any deployment of mines that might affect the civilian population unless circumstances do not permit; and

f. mines must not be of a nature to cause superfluous injury or unnecessary suffering.[60]

---

[52] Amended Mines Protocol, Arts 5 and 10.   [53] Amended Mines Protocol, Art 6.
[54] Amended Mines Protocol, Art 1(1).   [55] See para 13.52 onwards.
[56] Amended Mines Protocol, Art 2(1), (2).
[57] Amended Mines Protocol, Art 2(2). Those delivered by helicopter are remotely delivered; those laid by a vehicle, such as a bar-mine layer or the Ranger system, are not remotely delivered.
[58] Ottawa Convention 1997, Art 2(1).
[59] Feasible precautions are those which are practicable or practically possible taking into account all the circumstances ruling at the time, including humanitarian and military considerations.   [60] Amended Mines Protocol, Art 3.

Civilian protection factors

6.14.3 In considering the protection of the civilian population, regard should be had to the following factors, though these are not exclusive:

a. the short and long-term effect of mines on the local civilian population for the duration of the minefield;

b. possible measures to protect civilians (for example, fencing, signs, warning, and monitoring);

c. the availability and feasibility of using alternatives to mines;

d. the short and long-term military requirements for a minefield.[61]

Self-deactivation

6.14.4 It is prohibited to use remotely delivered anti-vehicle mines 'unless, to the extent feasible, they are equipped with an effective self-destruction or self-neutralization mechanism and have a back-up self-deactivation feature, which is designed so that the mine will no longer function as a mine when the mine no longer serves the military purpose for which it was placed in position'.[62]

Warning symbol

6.14.5 There is an international warning symbol for mined areas.[63]

Recording

6.14.6 The recording of information about minefields, mined areas and mines (as well as booby-traps and other devices) is mandatory[64] and is to be done as follows:[65]

a. Except in the case of remotely-delivered mines, locations are to be 'specified accurately by relation to the coordinates of at least two reference points and the estimated dimensions of the area containing these weapons in relation to those reference points'.

b. 'Maps, diagrams or other records shall be made in such a way as to indicate the location of minefields, mined areas, booby-traps and other devices in relation to reference points, and these records shall also indicate their perimeters and extent'.

c. For the purposes of detection and clearance of mines, booby-traps, and other devices, the records are also to contain 'complete information on the type, number, emplacing method, type of fuse and life time, date and

---

[61] Amended Mines Protocol, Art 3(10).   [62] Amended Mines Protocol, Art 6(3).

[63] Amended Mines Protocol, Technical Annex; Ottawa Convention 1997, Art 5(2). See the illustration in Roberts and Guelff, *Documents*, 732.

[64] Amended Mines Protocol, Art 9(1).

[65] Amended Mines Protocol, Technical Annex, para 1.

time of laying, anti-handling devices (if any) and other relevant information on all these weapons laid. Whenever feasible the minefield record shall show the exact location of every mine, except in row minefields when the row location is sufficient. The precise location and operating mechanism of each booby-trap laid shall be individually recorded'.

d. In the case of remotely-delivered mines, the estimated location and area is to be 'specified by coordinates of reference points (normally corner points) and shall be ascertained and when feasible marked on the ground at the earliest opportunity. The total number and type of mines laid, the date and time of laying and the self-destruction time periods' are also to be recorded.

e. Copies of records are to be 'held at a level of command sufficient to guarantee their safety as far as possible'.[66]

Protection[67]

If requested by the head of a relevant force or mission, and in the case of UN forces or missions so far as they are able, armed forces in conflict are required to protect the following from the effects of mines: **6.14.7**

a. UN peacekeeping forces or missions;

b. any of the following if they have the consent of the state in whose territory they are operating:

    (1) UN missions under Chapter VIII of the UN Charter;

    (2) UN humanitarian and fact-finding missions;

    (3) missions of the International Committee of the Red Cross or national Red Cross or Red Crescent Societies or similar humanitarian missions.

The protection that can be afforded will depend on the circumstances and the tactical situation but commanders will need to consider: **6.14.8**

a. clearance of devices or clearing lanes or routes;

b. giving information to the head of the mission about the location of devices or about safe routes.

Any information provided is to be treated in strict confidence by the recipient and not released outside the force or mission without the express authority of the giver of the information. **6.14.9**

Clearance

The Amended Mines Protocol contains detailed provisions on the clearance of mines and booby-traps after the cessation of active hostilities. Basically **6.14.10**

---

[66] The Technical Annex is set out in full in Appendix F.
[67] Amended Mines Protocol, Art 12.

states are responsible for devices they have emplaced and for the areas under their control. There are provisions for international exchanges of information and co-operation in this respect.[68]

LASER WEAPONS

6.15 'It is prohibited[69] to employ laser weapons specifically designed, as their sole combat function or as one of their combat functions, to cause permanent blindness[70] to unenhanced vision.'[71] These weapons must not be transferred[72] to other states or non-state entities.[73]

6.15.1 Other laser systems may be employed against military objectives, for example, against military optical equipment[74] even though this may cause incidental effects, including blindness, to the users of that equipment.[75]

6.15.2 'In the employment of laser systems, . . . all feasible precautions'[76] must be taken 'to avoid the incidence of permanent blindness to unenhanced vision'.[77]

OTHER DEVICES

6.16 Some of the restrictions that apply to use of mines and booby-traps apply equally to the uses of 'other devices'. These are the restrictions set out in paragraphs 6.7.3 to 6.7.7 and 6.14.2.[78] Recording is also mandatory, as laid down in paragraph 6.14.6.[79]

6.16.1 'Other devices means manually-emplaced munitions and devices including improvised explosive devices designed to kill, injure or damage and which are actuated manually, by remote control or automatically after a lapse of time.'[80]

6.16.2 Although the definition covers a bomb operated by remote control when a patrol or vehicle passes or designed to explode at a pre-set time, the definition

---

[68] Amended Mines Protocol, Arts 3(2), 10, and 11.

[69] Protocol IV on Blinding Laser Weapons (Lasers Protocol) to the CCW.

[70] Permanent blindness means irreversible and uncorrectable loss of vision, which is seriously disabling with no prospect of recovery. Serious disability is equivalent to visual acuity of less than 20/200 Snellen measured by using both eyes. See Lasers Protocol, Art 4.

[71] Unenhanced vision means that of the naked eye or the 'eye with corrective eyesight devices' (Lasers Protocol, Art 1) such as spectacles or contact lenses.

[72] Lasers Protocol, Art 1.   [73] Such as warring factions or rebel movements.

[74] Including binoculars, periscopes, night vision goggles, and the like. Lasers may also be used for range-finding, against sensors and aircraft, and for causing temporary dazzling.

[75] Lasers Protocol, Art 3.

[76] For example, training members of the armed forces in the correct uses of laser systems and other such practical measures.   [77] Lasers Protocol, Art 2.

[78] Amended Mines Protocol, Arts 3, 7.   [79] Amended Mines Protocol, Art 9.

[80] Amended Mines Protocol, Art 2(5).

is not limited to such devices nor is it limited to weapons that kill or injure by explosion.

Nuclear Weapons

There is no specific rule of international law, express or implied, which **6.17** prohibits the use of nuclear weapons. The legality of their use depends upon the application of the general rules of international law, including those regulating the use of force[81] and the conduct of hostilities.[82] Those rules cannot be applied in isolation from any factual context to imply a prohibition of a general nature.[83] Whether the use, or threatened use, of nuclear weapons in a particular case is lawful depends on all the circumstances. Nuclear weapons fall to be dealt with by reference to the same general principles as apply to other weapons. However, the rules introduced by Additional Protocol I 'apply exclusively to conventional weapons without prejudice to any other rules of international law applicable to other types of weapons. In particular, the rules so introduced do not have any effect on and do not regulate or prohibit the use of nuclear weapons'.[84]

The threshold for the legitimate use of nuclear weapons is clearly a high **6.17.1** one.[85] The United Kingdom would only consider using nuclear weapons in self-defence, including the defence of its NATO allies, and even then only in extreme circumstances.

The United Kingdom has given a unilateral assurance that it will not use **6.17.2** nuclear weapons against non-nuclear weapons states parties to the Treaty on the Non-Proliferation of Nuclear Weapons 1968. The assurance does not apply in the case of an invasion or any other attack on the United Kingdom, its Overseas Territories, its armed forces, its allies, or on a state towards which it has a security commitment, carried out by a non-nuclear weapon state in association or alliance with a nuclear weapon state. An assurance

---

[81] See para 1.3 onwards.   [82] See Ch 5.

[83] For example, the argument that attacks with nuclear weapons are necessarily indiscriminate.

[84] Statement made by UK on ratification of AP I to reflect the terms on which the negotiations leading to AP I were entered into. See also the statements relating to nuclear weapons made on ratification of AP I by Belgium, Canada, Germany, Italy, The Netherlands, and Spain and on signature by the USA: Roberts and Guelff, *Documents*, 499–512. France made a similar statement when it acceded to AP I on 11 April 2001.

[85] In its Advisory Opinion of 8 July 1996, (1974) 110 ILR 163, 165–166, the International Court of Justice declared (unanimously) that 'there is in neither customary nor conventional international law any comprehensive and universal prohibition of the threat or use of nuclear weapons as such' but (by a majority) that 'the threat or use of nuclear weapons would generally be contrary to the rules of international law applicable in armed conflict'. The court stated, however, that it could not definitively conclude whether the threat or use of nuclear weapons would be lawful or unlawful in an extreme circumstance of self-defence in which the very survival of the state was at stake.

in virtually identical terms has been given in memoranda signed with Belarus, Kazakhstan, and Ukraine. Further, the United Kingdom has given treaty-based assurances in the same terms to the states in Latin America and the South Pacific which are parties to the treaties establishing nuclear weapons-free zones in those regions.[86] The Antarctic Treaty[87] prohibits any nuclear explosion in Antarctica. There are various other prohibitions, for example on installing or testing nuclear weapons on the seabed[88] and in outer space.[89]

NON-LETHAL WEAPONS

6.18 There is no treaty dealing specifically with non-lethal weapons as such and so the general principles enunciated in paragraphs 6.1 to 6.4 apply. When assessing their legality, each device and its effects would need to be examined to establish whether its use was in accordance with existing international law.

6.18.1 Non-lethal weapons are weapons that are explicitly designed and developed to incapacitate or repel personnel, with a low probability of fatality or permanent injury, or to disable equipment, with minimal undesired damage or impact on the environment.[90]

6.18.2 Devices such as water cannon, plastic bullets, CS gas, stun grenades, electronic jammers, and laser weapons would fall within this category. So would acoustic devices or those causing metal embrittlement or entanglement. CS gas and laser weapons are dealt with in paragraphs 6.8 and 6.15.[91]

6.18.3 Generally speaking, devices that temporarily incapacitate combatants or that have only anti-materiel applications are, from the legal point of view, to be preferred to lethal weapons or those that cause permanent harm to individuals.

---

[86] Once Protocol 1 to the African Nuclear-Weapon-Free-Zone Treaty comes into force, a similar assurance will be in place for states party to that Treaty.

[87] Antarctic Treaty 1959.

[88] Treaty on the Prohibition of the Emplacement of Nuclear Weapons and Other Weapons of Mass Destruction on the Seabed and the Ocean Floor and in the Subsoil Thereof 1971.

[89] Treaty on Principles Governing the Activities of States in the Exploration and Use of Outer Space, including the Moon and Other Celestial Bodies 1967.

[90] Annex to C-M (99) 44 dated 14 September 1999, Final Report of the Non-Lethal Weapons Policy Team (NLWPT), approved by the North Atlantic Council under the silence procedure on 27 September 1999.

[91] Electronic and computer warfare is not considered to be part of non-lethal warfare but is separately addressed as information warfare (IW).

POISON

It is prohibited 'to employ poison or poisoned weapons'.[92]   **6.19**

The prohibition applies to any use of poison, including the poisoning or con-   **6.19.1**
tamination of water supplies. Such poisoning or contamination would not
be made lawful by the posting of a notice informing the enemy of the fact.[93]

Special rules have been developed for certain weapons. For toxic weapons,   **6.19.2**
see paragraph 6.5, for gas and chemical weapons, see paragraph 6.8, and for
nuclear weapons, see paragraph 6.17.

C. LEGAL REVIEW OF NEW WEAPONS

States party to Additional Protocol I are under an obligation 'in the study,   **6.20**
development, acquisition or adoption of a new weapon, means or method
of warfare . . . to determine whether its employment would, in some or all
circumstances, be prohibited by [Additional Protocol I] or by any other rule
of international law'.[94]

This obligation is imposed on all states party, not only those that produce   **6.20.1**
weapons. To this end each state is required to have effective review procedures operating in accordance with the rules of international law but there is
no requirement that the findings from these proceedings should be published. In the UK the weapons review process is conducted by the Ministry
of Defence in a progressive manner as concepts for new means and
methods of warfare are developed and as the conceptual process moves
towards procurement. Qualified legal staff contribute to the weapon development process. The review process takes account not only of the law as it
stands at the time of the review but also attempts to take account of likely
future developments in the law of armed conflict.

D. EXPLOSIVE REMNANTS OF WAR

In order to minimize the risks posed by explosive remnants of war[95] after   **6.21**
armed conflicts have ceased, Protocol V to the Conventional Weapons

---

[92] HR, Art 23(a), re-affirming customary law.
[93] In 1915, Lt Col Franke, commander of German troops in South-West Africa, sought to
justify his poisoning of the drinking water by such a notice, but the practice has been
condemned: see Oppenheim, *International Law*, 340, n 5 and Garner, *International Law and the
World War* (1920), vol 1, para 190.   [94] AP I, Art 36.
[95] Explosive remnants of war for these purposes comprise unexploded ordnance and abandoned explosive ordnance.

Convention places responsibilities on High Contracting Parties to the protocol and on parties to the armed conflict.[96] The effect is that a state or party in control of affected territory is required as soon as feasible after the cessation of active hostilities to mark and clear, remove or destroy explosive remnants of war in that territory.[97] Where the user of ordnance that has become explosive remnants does not control the affected territory, there is a requirement where feasible to provide assistance to facilitate marking, clearance, etc.

6.21.1 The Protocol requires states and parties to a conflict, as far as practicable, to record and retain information about where explosive ordnance has been used or abandoned.[98] Similarly, there are detailed provisions concerning the transmission of that information to the party in control of the affected area. The Protocol also requires states and parties to a conflict to take precautions in territory under their control to protect civilians, civilian objects, humanitarian missions and organizations from the effects of explosive remnants.[99]

6.21.2 Protocol V comprises a legally binding element, which has been summarized above, and a Technical Annex, which contains suggested best practice for achieving some of its objectives. The Technical Annex is voluntary in nature and does not therefore give rise to legal obligations.

---

[96] Protocol V to the CCW was adopted in Nov 2003. It has not yet been ratified by the UK.
[97] Protocol V, Art 3.   [98] Protocol V, Art 4.   [99] Protocol V, Arts 5 and 6.

7

The Wounded, Sick, and Dead and Medical Services

A. THE WOUNDED AND SICK

INTRODUCTION

7.1 It was the plight of the sick and wounded that led to the first Geneva international conference of 1863 and, subsequently, to the Geneva Convention 1864 dealing with the Amelioration of the Condition of the Wounded in Armies in the Field. The law has gradually developed from that point with the major conventions, now Geneva Conventions I and II 1949, the first dealing with the wounded and sick in land warfare and the second with the wounded, sick, and shipwrecked in maritime warfare. The latter only applies to forces at sea and is dealt with in Chapter 13. Once they are put ashore, they become subject to Geneva Convention I.[1] Further modifications have been made to the Conventions by Additional Protocol I.

DEFINITION OF THE WOUNDED AND SICK

7.2 The wounded and sick are 'persons, whether military or civilian, who, because of trauma, disease or other physical or mental disorder or disability, are in need of medical assistance or care and who refrain from any act of hostility'.[2]

7.2.1 The definition goes beyond persons wounded on the battlefield to encompass anybody in need of medical treatment. That includes 'maternity cases, new-born babies and other persons who may be in need of immediate medical assistance or care, such as the infirm or expectant mothers' who refrain from any act of hostility.[3] Those who carry on fighting despite their wounds are not included in the wounded and sick category.

PROTECTION AND CARE OF THE WOUNDED AND SICK

7.3 The wounded and sick are to be protected and respected. They may not be attacked. They must be treated humanely. They must be provided with medical care. They may not wilfully be left without medical assistance nor exposed to contagious diseases or infection. Priority of treatment is dictated by medical reasons only.[4] Violence and biological experiments are forbidden. Women must be treated with special respect[5] and no less favourably than men.[6]

---

[1] GC II, Art 4.   [2] Additional Protocol I 1977 (AP I), Art 8(a).   [3] AP I, Art 8(a).
[4] There must be no discrimination on grounds of sex, race, nationality, religion, political belief, or any other similar test. Spies, saboteurs, partisans, and illegal combatants who are wounded or sick are entitled to the same treatment.   [5] AP I, Art 76(1).
[6] GC I, Art 12 and AP I, Art 10.

The duty of respect means that the wounded and sick are not to be made the target of attack. The duty of protection imposes positive duties to assist them. The Geneva Conventions and Additional Protocol I do not seek the unattainable by what would be a vain attempt at removing all hardships arising from armed conflict affecting the groups of persons defined above; they merely seek to ameliorate their conditions. They expressly do so 'without any adverse distinction founded on race, colour, sex, language, religion or belief, political or other opinion, national or social origin, wealth, birth or other status, or on any other similar criteria'.[7]   **7.3.1**

Paragraph 7.3 applies to all wounded and sick, whether United Kingdom, allied or enemy, military or civilian. They are entitled to respect and protection, humane treatment, and, to the fullest extent practicable and with the least possible delay, the medical care and attention required by their condition. It is forbidden, for example, to give the treatment of United Kingdom and allied wounded priority over the treatment of wounded enemy personnel. The only distinction which is permitted in dealing with the wounded or sick is that founded on real medical need.[8] There is no absolute obligation on the part of the military medical services to accept civilian wounded and sick—that is to be done only so far as it is practicable to do so. For example, the commander of a field hospital placed to deal with casualties from an impending battle would be entitled to refer non-urgent cases elsewhere, even if the hospital had the capacity to treat them at the time. Once the treatment of a civilian patient has commenced, however, discrimination against him on other than medical grounds is not permissible.   **7.3.2**

COLLECTION OF THE WOUNDED AND SICK

The parties to a conflict are under an obligation 'at all times, and particularly after an engagement . . . without delay [to] take all possible measures to search for and collect the wounded and sick, to protect them against pillage and ill-treatment, and to ensure their adequate care'.[9] The Convention envisages 'whenever circumstances permit', an armistice, suspension of fire, or local arrangements to permit the removal, exchange, and transport of the wounded left on the battlefield. Similarly, local arrangements may be concluded to enable the removal or exchange of wounded and sick from a besieged or encircled area, and for the passage of medical and religious personnel and equipment on their way to that area.   **7.4**

[7] AP I, Art 9.
[8] GC I and II, Art 12; GC III, Art 13; GC IV, Art 27; AP I, Arts 9, 10, and 11.
[9] GC I, Art 15.

PERMITTED MEDICAL TREATMENT

7.5 'The physical or mental health and integrity of persons who are in the power of an adverse Party or who are interned, detained or otherwise deprived of liberty' as a result of armed conflict 'shall not be endangered by any unjustified act or omission'. 'Any medical procedure which is not indicated by the state of health of the person concerned and which is not consistent with generally accepted medical standards which would be applied under similar medical circumstances to persons who are nationals of the Party conducting the procedure and who are in no way deprived of liberty' is prohibited.[10]

7.5.1 In dealing with medical treatment on the basis of real medical need on the part of the patient, the law repeats fundamental medical ethics. The aim is to prevent experiments or unjustified medical operations on persons who are in no position to give their free consent. This protection extends to all those in the hands of an enemy or other party and even to citizens of the detaining power who are interned for reasons related to the armed conflict. In the absence of real medical justification, all persons are protected from physical mutilations, medical or scientific experiments, or removal of tissue or organs for transplantation *even with their consent* unless these acts are justified under the general principles outlined in paragraph 7.5.[11]

7.5.2 The only exceptions to the express prohibitions mentioned above relate to the voluntary donation of blood for transfusions or skin for grafting. Such donations must be for 'therapeutic purposes,[12] under conditions consistent with generally accepted medical standards and controls designed for the benefit of both the donor and the recipient'. 'Voluntary' means that the donor must be capable of expressing his complete agreement, without any coercion or inducement.[13]

---

[10] AP I, Art 11(1).

[11] AP I, Art 11(2). It would seem therefore that one prisoner of war (PW) could not consent to the donation of a kidney for the benefit of another PW, even his brother. In such a case, it would be necessary to arrange for the accommodation in a neutral state (GC III, Art 110(2)) or the repatriation of the two PW concerned so that they would cease to be subject to this article (see GC III, Art 109).

[12] This would preclude any transfusion or graft being taken for experimental purposes.

[13] AP I, Art 11(3). See Y Sandoz, C Swinarski, and B Zimmermann (eds), *Commentary on the Additional Protocols of 8 June 1977 to the Geneva Conventions of 12 August 1949* (1987) (*ICRC Commentary*) 486.

Medical records relating to all medical procedures should, if possible, be **7.5.3**
kept.[14] These medical records must be available at all times for inspection
by the protecting power.[15]

RIGHT TO REFUSE CONSENT

Persons protected under paragraph 7.5 have the right to refuse any surgical **7.6**
operation. In cases of refusal, medical personnel must try to obtain 'a written
statement to that effect, signed or acknowledged by the patient'.[16] The right
still exists to carry out surgery necessary to save life in an emergency without obtaining the consent of the patient in accordance with medical ethics
and on the same basis as for the general population under domestic law.[17]

CARE OF THE WOUNDED AND SICK WHO HAVE
TO BE ABANDONED

A party to a conflict compelled to abandon wounded or sick to his advers- **7.7**
ary, must, so far as military considerations permit, leave with them a part of
his medical personnel and equipment to help in caring for them.[18] Their
presence does not, however, exempt the detaining power from providing
any additional assistance that may be necessary.

STATUS OF THE WOUNDED AND SICK WHO ARE CAPTURED

Wounded and sick members of the armed forces who are captured become **7.8**
prisoners of war and are therefore also covered by the provisions dealing
with prisoners of war.[19] Medical personnel who are captured do not become
prisoners of war but may be retained by the capturing power in so far as the
state of health and the numbers of prisoners of war require. Such 'retained
personnel' are entitled, as a minimum, to treatment equivalent to that of
a prisoner of war.[20]

NON-RENUNCIATION OF RIGHTS

The wounded and sick, as well as medical personnel and chaplains, may in **7.9**
no circumstances renounce in whole or in part, the rights secured to them
by the Convention or by Additional Protocol I.[21]

---

[14] Records of voluntary blood and skin donations, however, *must* be kept, see AP I, Art 11(6).
[15] AP I, Art 11(6).   [16] AP I, Art 11(5).   [17] See ICRC *Commentary*, 495–496.
[18] GC I, Art 12.
[19] GC I, Art 14. For the direct repatriation, or the accommodation in a neutral country, of
seriously wounded and sick prisoners, see para 8.146 onwards.
[20] GC I, Art 28 and GC III, Art 33. See also paras 8.8–8.10 and 8.58.
[21] See GC I–IV, Common Art 7, 7, 7, 8.

B. PROTECTION OF MEDICAL PERSONNEL, UNITS, AND TRANSPORT

DEFINITIONS

Medical units

7.10   Medical units are[22] 'establishments and other units, whether military or civilian, organized for medical purposes, namely the search for, collection, transportation, diagnosis or treatment—including first-aid treatment—of the wounded, sick and shipwrecked, or for the prevention of disease. The term includes, for example, hospitals and other similar units, blood trans-fusion centres, preventive medicine centres and institutes, medical depots and the medical and pharmaceutical stores of such units. Medical units may be fixed or mobile, permanent or temporary'.

7.10.1   It follows that the definition of medical units is sufficiently comprehensive to include those on land, sea, and in the air. It includes civilian medical units provided that they (a) belong to one of the parties to the conflict; (b) are recognized and authorized by the competent authority of one of the parties to the conflict; or (c) while belonging to a neutral or other state not a party to the conflict, or a recognized and authorized aid society of such a state or an impartial international humanitarian organization, have been made available to a party to the conflict for humanitarian purposes.[23]

Medical personnel

7.11   'Medical personnel' means 'those persons assigned, by a Party to the conflict, exclusively to the medical purposes enumerated in paragraph 7.10 or to the administration of medical units or to the operation or administra-tion of medical transports. Such assignments may be either permanent or temporary'.[24]

7.11.1   The term embraces not only doctors and nurses but also a wide range of spe-cialists, technicians, maintenance staff, drivers, cooks, and administrators. It expressly includes military and civilian personnel and those assigned to civil defence organizations as well as medical personnel of national red cross or red crescent or other duly authorized and recognized national voluntary aid societies. Personnel of medical units and transports of neutral and other

---

[22] AP I, Art 8(e). AP I re-defines a number of expressions relating not only to those who need medical care but also both to those who provide it and the means of doing so. In this, it clarifies the law and removes some anomalies.   [23] AP I, Art 12(2).

[24] AP 1, Art 8(c).

states not parties to the conflict, national aid societies of such states, and impartial international humanitarian organizations are also included within the definition if made available to a party to the conflict for humanitarian purposes.[25] While the expression includes dental personnel and chaplains in medical units and part-time medical personnel while engaged on medical duties, it excludes qualified medical and dental practitioners who are not assigned exclusively to medical purposes.[26]

Medical transport

Medical transport means[27] any means of transportation, whether military or **7.12** civilian, permanent or temporary, assigned exclusively to the conveyance by land, water, or air of the wounded, sick, shipwrecked, medical or religious personnel, medical equipment, or medical supplies protected by the Geneva Conventions and Additional Protocol I and under the control of a competent authority of a party to the conflict. In Additional Protocol I, reference to 'medical vehicles' expressly means 'any medical transports by land'. Similarly, 'medical ships and craft' means 'any medical transports by water' and 'medical aircraft' means 'any medical transports by air'.[28]

The assignment to medical purposes must be exclusive, although it may be **7.12.1** permanent or temporary. The word 'exclusive' is intended to restrict the definition of medical transport and its use so that the essential protection will not be eroded by abuses. 'Permanent' means for an indeterminate period; 'temporary' means limited periods but devoted exclusively to medical tasks during the whole of such periods.[29]

PROTECTION OF MEDICAL UNITS

Medical units are to be 'respected and protected at all times and shall not be **7.13** the object of attack'.[30] Medical units, personnel, and transport must not be used for non-medical purposes, otherwise their protection will be jeopardized. In addition, medical units must not 'be used in an attempt to shield military objectives from attack' and, where possible, should be so sited that attacks against military objectives do not imperil their safety.[31]

---

[25] AP I, Art 9(2).

[26] eg, a qualified medical practitioner serving as an adjutant in an infantry unit. But see GC III, Art 32 and para 8.10 in relation to their status as PW.   [27] AP I, Art 8(f), (g).

[28] AP I, Art 8(h)–(j).

[29] AP I, Art 8(k). However, see the somewhat more stringent provisions that apply to hospital ships in GC II, Arts 22–35, particularly Art 33 in respect of converted merchant vessels.

[30] AP I, Art 12; GC I, Arts 19–23; GC II, Arts 22–35; GC IV, Art 18.

[31] GC I, Art 19; GC IV, Art 18; AP I, Art 12(4).

The improper use of medical units to kill, injure, or capture the enemy amounts to the war crime of perfidy.[32]

7.13.1 Medical units are given this general protection to enable them to perform their humanitarian functions. Thus, the protection given to medical units ceases if 'they are used to commit, outside their humanitarian function, acts harmful to the enemy'.[33] Protection may only be withdrawn, however, after due warning has been given, setting, whenever appropriate, a reasonable time-limit and after such warning has remained unheeded.

General Protection of Medical Duties

7.14 It is forbidden to punish anyone who carries out 'medical activities compatible with medical ethics regardless of the person benefiting therefrom'.[34]

7.14.1 This covers not only 'medical personnel' as defined above but all persons engaged in medical activities, including not only civilian medical and dental practitioners and their ancillary staff but also unqualified persons who administer first aid. Similarly those 'engaged in medical activities shall not be compelled to perform acts or to carry out work contrary to the rules of medical ethics or to other medical rules'.[35] Nor may a person engaged in medical activities be compelled 'to give to anyone belonging either to an adverse Party, or to his own Party except as required by the law of the latter Party, any information concerning the wounded and sick who are, or who have been, under his care, if such information would, in his opinion, prove harmful to the patients concerned or to their families'. However, regulations for the compulsory notification of communicable diseases must be respected.[36]

Permitted Functions in Medical Units

Weapons

7.15 Medical personnel may be equipped with 'light individual weapons for their own defence or for that of the wounded and sick in their charge'.[37]

7.15.1 Light individual weapons are those that can be handled and fired by one person and primarily intended for personnel targets. It follows that medical personnel may be armed with sub-machine guns, self-loading rifles,

---

[32] See para 5.9.   [33] AP I, Art 13(1); GC I, Art 21; GC II, Art 34; GC IV, Art 19.
[34] AP I, Art 16(1). See also GC I, Art 18.   [35] AP I, Art 16(2).   [36] AP I, Art 16(3).
[37] AP I, Art 13(2); GC 1, Art 22; GC II, Art 35. GC I also provided for the continuation of protection where civilian wounded or sick are being treated in a military medical unit. This provision has now been rendered obsolete by the removal of the distinction between civilians and military wounded and sick in AP I.

and handguns. It should be stressed that the provision and use of these arms must be merely for defensive purposes as outlined above. Medical personnel (and chaplains) are non-combatants so they are not otherwise entitled to take part in hostilities.[38] Medical personnel may use their weapons only if they, or those in their care, are attacked.[39]

Armed guards

The unit itself may be 'guarded by a picket or by sentries or by an escort'.[40] **7.16** However, the guard also may only act in a purely defensive manner and may not oppose the occupation or control of the unit by the enemy.

Weapons and ammunition taken from the wounded

Small arms and ammunition taken from the wounded and sick may be **7.17** temporarily stored in medical units until they can be disposed of to the appropriate authorities.[41] Arrangements should be made to avoid an excessive accumulation of such weapons, particularly in medical units where large numbers of wounded and sick are likely to gather or pass through.[42]

Visits by members of the armed forces

Members of the armed forces or other combatants may be in the unit for **7.18** medical reasons,[43] including visits to the wounded and sick. However, medical personnel must be careful that the protected status of their unit is not put at risk by the presence of a disproportionate number of visiting combatants.[44]

Occupied Territory

In occupied territory, the occupying power has a duty to ensure that **7.19** the medical needs of the civilian population continue to be satisfied. Restrictions are therefore imposed on the power to requisition, for military purposes, civilian medical units, equipment, materiel, or the services of their personnel.[45]

---

[38] See para 4.2.
[39] An act which, if deliberate, would be unlawful in itself. For chaplains, see para 7.30.
[40] AP I, Art 13(2)(b); GC I, Art 22(2).
[41] AP I, Art 13(2)(c); GC I, Art 22(3); GC II, Art 35(3); GC IV, Art 19.
[42] See AP I, Art 13(2)(c).   [43] AP I, Art 13(2)(d); GC IV, Art 19.
[44] See AP I, Art 13(2)(d).
[45] AP I, Art 14. See also para 11.44; HR, Art 52; GC IV, Arts 55 and 57.

MEDICAL TRANSPORT[46]

Protection

7.20 The general rule is that medical transport is entitled to similar respect and protection as is given to medical units.[47] However, there remain some practical difficulties, especially in the case of medical ships and craft and medical aircraft. These categories are dealt with below.

Hospital ships

7.21 Ships that are built, converted, or equipped specially and solely with a view to assisting the wounded, sick, and shipwrecked and to treating them and transporting them are regarded as hospital ships.[48] For a more detailed description of the provisions relating to such ships, including coastal rescue craft and chartered vessels, see Chapter 13.

Medical aircraft[49]

7.22 Aircraft duly assigned to medical purposes,[50] flying in combat zones are protected as soon as they are recognized as such.[51] Medical aircraft flying over areas physically controlled by an adverse party, or over areas the control of which is not clearly established, may be ordered to land or to alight on water as appropriate to permit inspection. Medical aircraft must obey such orders. They must be given reasonable time for compliance but in default of such obedience the aircraft may be attacked.[52] In all cases, protection for medical aircraft can be fully effective only by prior agreement between the competent military authorities of the parties to the conflict.[53]

---

[46] Medical transport and its protection have developed since the Geneva Convention 1864 provided for the neutrality of ambulances, which were then horse-drawn. Even as late as 1949, it was provided that the protection of a medical unit was not lost by the co-location of personnel and materiel of the veterinary services (military veterinary personnel being combatants). Evacuation by helicopter is now common.

[47] GC I, Arts 35, 36, and 37; GC II, Arts 38, 39, and 40; GC IV, Arts 21 and 22; AP I, Arts 21–27. See para 7.13.   [48] GC II, Art 22.

[49] This topic is dealt with in detail in Ch 12 (see paras 12.28, 12.29, and 12.104 onwards) and only a brief resumé is given here. Until AP I, medical aircraft were only protected when 'flying at heights, times and on routes specifically agreed upon between the belligerents concerned' (GC I, Art 36, GC II, Art 39). Unless agreed otherwise, flights over enemy or enemy-occupied territory were prohibited. In view of the increasing use of aircraft, mainly helicopters, for the evacuation of casualties and the lack of communication between belligerents in the combat zone, this requirement of permission became increasingly unrealistic. Air defences are complex and difficulties in identifying aircraft in flight remain.   [50] See para 7.10.

[51] AP I, Art 26.   [52] AP I, Arts 27(2) and 30.   [53] AP I, Arts 26(1), 27(1) and 29.

IDENTIFICATION OF MEDICAL UNITS, PERSONNEL, AND TRANSPORT

Distinctive emblems

For the identification of medical and religious personnel, medical units, and **7.23**
transports, protective emblems are recognized by the Geneva Conventions
and Additional Protocol I.[54] They are the red cross on a white ground, the red
crescent on a white ground, and the red lion and sun on a white ground.[55]
The red crescent may be depicted with the points of the crescent facing either
way. United Kingdom armed forces use the red cross emblem.[56]

The emblems should be as large as appropriate under the circumstances.   **7.23.1**

Israel entered a reservation that she would use the red star of David (the **7.23.2**
Magen David Adom) as her distinctive emblem. This is a red, six-pointed
star on a white ground, and is used by Israel instead of the emblems
mentioned above.

The distinctive emblem may also be used by the International Committee of **7.23.3**
the Red Cross, by national red cross and red crescent societies and by their
International Federation. For national societies (unless they fall within the
definition of medical units, personnel, or transport) the emblem is merely
indicative of a link with the red cross and red crescent society movement
rather than protective, and in that case it should be relatively small in size.

Purpose of the distinctive emblems and the distinctive signals

As a protective emblem, these emblems may only be used to identify and **7.24**
protect medical and religious personnel, units, installations, vehicles, ships,
or aircraft.[57] In addition to the use of the emblems, there is provision for
medical units and transports to signal their identity by means of 'distinctive
signals': flashing blue lights, a radio signal, radar, and other electronic identification.[58] These distinctive signals are also intended to enhance protection.

---

[54] eg, GC I, Art 38; GC II, Art 41; GC IV, Arts 18 and 20; AP I, Art 18 and Annex I, as amended
on 30 November 1993, Arts 4 and 5: see Appendix E. Strictly, when the Geneva Conventions were
adopted, only those countries which 'already use[d]' the red crescent emblem were entitled to
continue its use. However, as new states have achieved independence, no objection has been
made to their adoption of the red crescent emblem. Neither the red cross nor the red crescent
emblem is intended to have any religious significance—they are symbols of neutral protection.

[55] The red lion and sun on a white ground is not in current use. Illustrations of the emblems
are in Appendix E.

[56] During the Gulf conflict 1991, both red cross and red crescent flags were flown at some
UK medical units in Saudi Arabia as a courtesy to the host state.

[57] Also medical equipment and supplies, see AP I, Art 8(l). See also GC I, Art 44; AP I,
Art 18(6).   [58] AP I, Arts 8(m) and 18; Annex I (amended), Arts 6–9. See Appendix E.

7.24.1 The wrongful use of a distinctive emblem may constitute perfidy and thus a war crime.[59] The use of the emblems, and the distinctive signals, is also strictly controlled in time of peace.[60]

Camouflage

7.25 Whilst medical units, personnel, and transport are normally marked with the protective emblem, it is not mandatory to do so. The parties to a conflict are exhorted to 'endeavour to ensure' that they are marked.[61] Thus, the use of camouflage is permitted, though it is obvious that this in practice affects the protection of camouflaged objects.

7.25.1 If a party to the conflict has knowledge that a person or facility is protected under the Geneva Conventions, the protected status of the person or facility must be respected, regardless of whether the emblem is displayed.

7.25.2 NATO standardization agreements (STANAG) provide that medical units and transports may be camouflaged as a temporary measure at the discretion of the competent combat commander to be exercised on the basis of a balance of due protection and operational need.[62]

IDENTIFICATION AND STATUS ON CAPTURE OF SERVICE,
AUXILIARY, AND CIVILIAN MEDICAL PERSONNEL

Identification of service medical personnel

7.26 Service medical personnel[63] must be clearly identifiable as such so that they receive the protection and respect due to them. To achieve this, all service medical personnel must, in addition to normal service identity discs, wear on the left arm a water-resistant armlet (brassard) bearing the appropriate distinctive emblem. The armlet should be issued and stamped by the military authority. Service medical personnel must also carry a special identity card bearing the distinctive emblem. This card is embossed with the stamp of the military authority. These service identity cards must be uniform throughout the same armed forces and, as far as possible, of a similar type in the armed forces of all parties to Geneva Conventions I and II. Parties to a conflict must inform each other at the outbreak of hostilities which model identity card they are using. Identity cards should be made out, if possible, at least in duplicate, one copy being kept by the home country. In no circumstances may service medical personnel be deprived of their armlets

---

[59] AP I, Arts 85(3)(f) and 38(1).   [60] Geneva Conventions Act 1957, s 6.
[61] eg, GC I, Arts 39–43; AP I, Art 18.   [62] NATO STANAG 2931.
[63] For medical personnel, see para 7.11.

(or the right to wear them) or of their identity cards. In the case of loss they are entitled to receive duplicates of the cards and to have the insignia replaced.[64]

The card is illustrated at Appendix A. The version currently used by the United Kingdom is F Ident 107.   **7.26.1**

Status on capture of service medical personnel

In the event of capture, medical personnel do not become prisoners of war but are 'retained personnel'.[65]   **7.27**

Auxiliary medical personnel

Auxiliary medical personnel[66] are members of the armed forces who are specifically trained for employment, when the need arises, as hospital orderlies, nurses, or auxiliary stretcher-bearers in the search for or the collection, transport, or treatment of the wounded and sick. Auxiliary medical personnel are issued with a special identity card. Auxiliary medical personnel become prisoners of war on capture. They may be required to exercise their medical functions in the interests of prisoners of war of their own state. In that case, they are exempt from any other work.[67]   **7.28**

The identity card for auxiliary medical personnel currently used by the United Kingdom is F Indent 106.   **7.28.1**

Civilian medical personnel

Civilian medical personnel are to be accorded the same protection as service medical personnel and, in occupied territory and areas where fighting is taking place or is likely to take place, they should be recognizable by the distinctive emblem and carry an identity card certifying their status.[68] This card differs from that issued to service medical personnel.[69] Civilian medical personnel who fall into the hands of the enemy should not be detained and should be allowed to continue their medical duties. If any security measures have to be taken, civilian medical personnel have all the protection of protected persons.[70]   **7.29**

---

[64] GC I, Art 40; GC II, Art 42 is almost identical. Curiously, the Conventions refer to the 'insignia' rather than the 'armlet' being replaced.

[65] GC III, Art 33. See also paras 8.8 and 8.58.   [66] GC I, Arts 25 and 41.

[67] GC III, Art 32.

[68] AP I, Arts 15, 18(3) and Annex I (amended) Arts 2 and 3: see Appendix E.

[69] See the illustration at Appendix A.   [70] See para 9.17 onwards.

Chaplains

7.30 Chaplains are entitled to similar respect, protection, and identification to that afforded to medical personnel. The rules on armlets and identity cards in paragraph 7.26 apply equally to chaplains.[71] The Conventions are silent on whether chaplains may be armed. United Kingdom policy is that chaplains should be unarmed.

C. THE DEAD

PROTECTION OF THE DEAD

7.31 The dead must be protected against pillage and maltreatment. The looting of the property of the dead and the mutilation of their bodies are war crimes.[72]

EXAMINATION OF THE DEAD

7.32 Since some injuries sustained in, or as a result of, combat produce symptoms resembling death, the parties to a conflict are required to ensure that, in so far as circumstances permit, bodies are given an individual medical examination.[73] This is a task for medical personnel and the objects of such examination are to confirm the fact of death, to establish the identity of the deceased, and to enable a report about the death to be made.[74]

7.32.1 A medical examination is mandatory for prisoners of war,[75] and internees,[76] who die. In every case where the death of, or serious injury to, a prisoner of war or internee has been caused, or is suspected to have been caused, by a sentry, another prisoner of war or internee, or by any other person, or is due to an unknown cause, the detaining power is required to take the following action:

a. hold an official inquiry immediately;
b. inform the protecting power immediately;
c. take statements from witnesses;
d. send a report including such statements to the protecting power.

---

[71] GC I, Arts 24 and 40. The same applies, with the necessary changes, to civilian religious personnel.
[72] This is a well-established rule of customary international law, see *Schmidt Trial* (1948) 13 WCR 151 and also 13 WCR 152.   [73] GC 1, Art 17.
[74] GC I, Art 17; GC II, Art 20; GC III, Art 120; GC IV, Art 129.
[75] See para 8.172 onwards.   [76] See para 9.105 onwards.

If the inquiry indicates culpability, the detaining power must take all   **7.32.2**
necessary steps to prosecute those responsible.[77]

IDENTITY DISCS

Where the deceased is in possession of two identity discs, one disc should   **7.33**
remain on the body and the other should be sent with his personal effects
to the information bureau. If the deceased was in possession of only one
identity disc, that disc should remain on the body.[78]

PERSONAL EFFECTS AND ITEMS OF MILITARY
EQUIPMENT FOUND UPON THE DEAD

There is a well-established rule of customary international law that the dead   **7.34**
must not be plundered.[79] Looting is an offence under the Service Discipline
Acts.[80] The personal effects of the dead should be collected in identifiable
packets and sent with any available identity disc[81] to the information
bureau.[82] The personal effects that are particularly envisaged here are money,
all items of intrinsic or sentimental value, and last wills or other documents
of importance to the next of kin.[83] Articles other than personal effects, such as
military equipment, found upon the dead of a hostile party to an armed
conflict become the public property of the finding party, that is the property
of the government, not of the individuals or unit capturing them.[84]

BURIAL

The remains of the dead are to be honourably interred[85] (unless burial at sea   **7.35**
is appropriate), in so far as possible in individual graves, and, if possible,
according to the rites of the religion to which the deceased belonged. Bodies
must not be cremated[86] except for imperative reasons of hygiene or for

[77] GC III, Art 121; GC IV, Art 131. Inquiries were carried out in the case of the five
Argentinian prisoners who died and one who was seriously injured in the Falklands conflict
1982. See also para 8.176.   [78] GC I, Arts 16 and 17; GC II, Arts 19 and 20.
[79] See also para 7.31. This would preclude the stripping of clothing from a body.
[80] See NDA 1957, s 5; AA 1955, s 30; AFA 1955, s 30.   [81] See para 7.33.
[82] See para 8.182.
[83] GC I, Art 16; GC II, Art 19; GC III, Art 122; GC IV, Art 139; AP I, Art 34.
[84] *Manual of Military Law* III (1958) para 381. The taking of property found on the battlefield
as personal souvenirs is also looting and thus prohibited.
[85] This would preclude burial in quick-lime, exposure as a curiosity or to instil terror,
dissection and experiment, and grave-molestation. Post-mortem dissection to ascertain the
cause of death or to discover the nature of an epidemic would be legitimate.
[86] See GC I, Art 17; GC III, Art 120; GC IV, Art 130. This is to prevent occurrences such
as those that took place during the Second World War when captured aircrew and other

motives based on the religion of the deceased. When cremation is carried out, the circumstances and the reasons for it must be stated in the death certificate. The ashes must be respectfully treated and kept by the official graves registration service until properly disposed of according to the wishes of the home country.

GRAVES

7.36 Graves[87] must be respected and properly maintained. They must be marked so that they may always be found and should, if possible, be grouped according to the nationality of the deceased. Graves registration services must be officially established at the outbreak of hostilities and, as soon as circumstances permit, the adverse parties and any other concerned authorities are required to seek agreement for:

a. the permanent protection and maintenance of grave sites;

b. access to those grave sites by relatives of the deceased and the representatives of the official graves registration services;

c. the return of remains of the deceased to the home state on that state's request or, unless that state objects, on the request of the next of kin.

7.36.1 In the absence of agreements[88] relating either to protection and maintenance of grave sites or for the return of the deceased, the authorities of the territory in which the grave sites are situated may (a) offer to facilitate the return of the remains to the home state; and (b) if such an offer is not accepted within five years from the date of the offer, and after due notice, adopt arrangements for dealing with such remains in accordance with their own domestic laws relating to cemeteries and graves.

EXHUMATION[89]

7.37 Exhumation is permitted only (a) in accordance with an agreement on the matters dealt with in paragraph 7.36; or (b) in accordance with overriding public necessity (which may include 'medical or investigative necessity'). In such circumstances, the authorities of the territory in which the grave sites are situated are required to respect the remains and to give notice to the home state of the intended exhumation together with details of the intended place of re-interment. However, these provisions do not prevent the exhumation of temporary graves for the purpose of moving the remains

prisoners of war were murdered and their bodies cremated to avoid discovery of the method of killing. See the *Stalag Luft III Case* (1947) 11 WCR 31–52.

[87] GC I, Art 17; GC II, Art 20; GC III, Art 120; GC IV, Art 130; AP I, Art 34.

[88] AP I, Art 34(3).   [89] GC I, Art 17; AP I, Art 34(4).

to permanent graves in dignified, properly maintained cemeteries, such as those of the Commonwealth War Graves Commission.

D. TRACING THE MISSING

Each party must search for persons reported missing by an adverse party and also facilitate such searches by the provision of relevant information.[90] **7.38**

Additional Protocol I encourages the parties to try to make arrangements for joint teams from both sides to search for, identify, and recover the dead from battlefield areas, such teams to be respected and protected while carrying out those duties. The task involves the collection of the wounded and sick and their protection against pillage and ill-treatment. The living must be adequately cared for, the dead protected from despoliation. If appropriate circumstances exist, the removal of the wounded and sick from a besieged or encircled area and the passage of medical or religious personnel and equipment to the area may be agreed through an armistice or other local arrangement.[91] Additionally, the local inhabitants may assist in the collection of the wounded and sick either spontaneously or voluntarily as a result of an appeal from the military authorities for their help.[92] **7.38.1**

---

[90] GC I, Art 15; GC II, Art 18; GC IV, Art 16; AP I, Art 33. AP I, Art 32 deals with the right of families to know the fate of their relatives. This was prompted by the difficulties experienced by the United States in ascertaining the fate of missing American personnel at the end of the Vietnam conflict.   [91] See paras 10.13–10.28.
[92] GC I, Art 18; GC II, Art 21; AP I, Art 17.

8

Prisoners of War

A. INTRODUCTION

Introduction

Prisoners of war may in no circumstances renounce their rights under the **8.1**
law of armed conflict.[1] They remain members of the armed forces of
the state on which they depend and cannot agree to change their status. The
conditions of their captivity should be as reasonable as the conditions of
armed conflict will allow and must, in any event, meet the specific standards laid down by Geneva Convention III 1949.

The law on the treatment of prisoners of war is an area in which some of **8.1.1**
the most significant humanitarian advances have been made. Although
captivity is always unpleasant, the status of prisoner of war has slowly
improved from a condition of inevitable death, mutilation, or slavery to a
status recognized and protected by law. Only in the seventeenth century
did prisoners of war begin to be regarded as prisoners of the state and not
the property of the individual captors. There have been many instances,
even in the nineteenth and twentieth centuries, in which prisoners of war
have been subjected not merely to cruel neglect, unnecessary suffering, and
unjustifiable indignities, but even murdered. Maltreatment of these and
other kinds is contrary to the standards that are set by international law as
now codified chiefly in the Hague Regulations 1907,[2] Geneva Convention
III ('the Convention')[3] and Additional Protocol I 1977 (the Protocol).[4] International law may be supplemented by special agreements between the
belligerents provided that prisoners of war are not adversely affected
thereby.[5] It should always be remembered that prisoners of war are
not convicted criminals in need of corrective training or punishment. They
are members of the armed forces who, until capture, were simply doing
their duty.

Action to be Taken at the Start of Hostilities

As soon as hostilities start each party involved should, where appro- **8.2**
priate,[6] take certain immediate steps for the benefit of prisoners of war.

---

[1] GC III, Art 7.   [2] Hague Regulations 1907 (HR), Arts 4–20.
[3] GC III (in entirety); see also GC I, Arts 14 and 36; GC II, Arts 16 and 39.
[4] eg, AP I, Arts 43–47.   [5] GC III, Art 6.
[6] Some or all of these measures may not be necessary in a short conflict or in one consisting
solely of air operations.

These include:

a. appointing a protecting power, a neutral state whose duty it is to safeguard the interests of a belligerent and its nationals with regard to the enemy;[7]

b. setting up an official information bureau for the prisoners of war it holds;[8]

c. establishing in a neutral country a Central Prisoners of War Information Agency to collect and transmit information about prisoners of war;[9]

d. issuing identity cards to all persons liable to become prisoners of war;[10]

e. notifying the enemy of its rules relating to release on parole;[11]

f. notifying the enemy of titles and ranks of persons liable to become prisoners of war to ensure correct treatment according to rank;[12]

g. setting up mixed medical commissions.[13]

The following, although not mandatory, are desirable:

h. notifying the enemy of the location and marking of prisoner of war camps and transports;[14]

i. notifying the enemy of arrangements made to enable prisoners of war to exercise their right of correspondence and to receive relief supplies[15] and of any changes in those arrangements;

j. notifying the enemy of its laws relating to wills;[16]

k. establishing a graves registration service.[17]

---

[7] GC III, Art 8; GC III Art 10, and AP I, Art 5 (which enable the ICRC or any other similar organization to act as substitute where no protecting power has been appointed); Ministry of Defence, *Prisoner of War Handling* (2001) (JWP 1–10) paras 113–117. See, further, paras 16.11 and 16.12. In practice, the ICRC often carries out the humanitarian functions of a protecting power under the Convention and Protocol.

[8] GC III, Art 122; JWP 1–10, paras 118–120. See para 8.182.

[9] GC III, Art 123. See para 8.184.

[10] GC III, Arts 4 and 17. For identity cards for medical personnel and journalists, who do not become prisoners of war, GC I, Art 40, GC II, Art 42 and AP I, Art 79. See para 8.19.

[11] GC III, Art 21. See paras 8.104–8.108.   [12] GC III, Art 43.

[13] GC III, Art 112. See para 8.152.

[14] GC III, Art 23. See, respectively, paras 8.39 and 8.35(c).

[15] GC III, Art 69. See paras 8.62–8.68.   [16] GC III, Arts 77 and 120. See para 8.71.

[17] GC III, Art 120. See para 8.163.

B. PRISONER OF WAR STATUS

RULES OF ENTITLEMENT TO PRISONER OF WAR STATUS

Basic rule

The basic rule is that members of the armed forces of a party to the conflict[18] **8.3** have prisoner of war status on capture.[19] They enjoy this status from the moment that they fall into the hands of the enemy, irrespective of whether they have been formally registered as prisoners of war or whether their capture has been acknowledged by their own government.[20] In addition, there are certain non-combatants who are entitled to this status. A person does not normally forfeit prisoner of war status because of violations of the law of armed conflict.[21]

A consolidated list of those entitled to prisoner of war status is as follows: **8.3.1**

a. All members (except medical and religious personnel)[22] of the organized armed forces of a party to the conflict, even if that party is represented by a government or authority not recognized by the adversary, provided that those forces:

   (1) are under a command responsible to a party to the conflict for the conduct of its subordinates; and

   (2) are subject to an internal disciplinary system which enforces compliance with the law of armed conflict.[23]

b. Members of any other militias, volunteer corps, or organized resistance movements,[24] belonging to a party to the conflict and operating in or outside their own territory, even if it is occupied; provided that they:

   (1) are commanded by a person responsible for his subordinates;

   (2) have a fixed, distinctive sign recognizable at a distance;[25]

---

[18] See ch 4, especially paras 4.2 and 4.3.   [19] AP I, Art 44(1).

[20] During the Gulf conflict 1991, the Iraqi action in declaring that captured aircrew would only be treated as prisoners of war (PW) if the coalition forces admitted that they had been captured was a clear breach of GC III, Art 4.

[21] See, however, para 8.6. See also para 8.119.   [22] See para 8.8.

[23] GC III, Art 4; AP I, Art 43. The latter provision assimilates regular and irregular combatants. If these conditions are complied with, the definition is wide enough to cover auxiliary and reserve forces, and even irregular forces and organized resistance movements. If a party to the conflict incorporates a paramilitary or police force into its armed forces, it must notify the other belligerents (see AP I, Art 43(3)).

[24] GC III, Art 4A(2). This category was important prior to the entry into force of AP I but is now largely redundant in practice in view of the wide terms of para 8.3.1(a).

[25] During the Kosovo conflict 1999, members of the Kosovo Liberation Army (KLA) were frequently depicted in the media wearing combat fatigues with the KLA patch.

(3) carry their arms openly; and

(4) conduct their operations in accordance with the law of armed conflict.

c. Those who accompany the armed forces without actually being members thereof (for example, civilian members of military aircraft crews, war correspondents, supply contractors, members of labour units or of services responsible for the welfare of the armed forces) if duly authorized by the armed forces which they accompany. That armed force must issue these personnel with an appropriate identity card.[26]

d. Members of crews, including masters, pilots, and apprentices, of the merchant marine and crews of civil aircraft of the parties to the conflict, who do not benefit by more favourable treatment under any other provisions of international law.[27]

e. Inhabitants of non-occupied territory who, on the approach of the enemy, spontaneously take up arms to resist the invading forces without having had time to form themselves into regular armed units, provided they carry their arms openly and respect the laws of armed conflict[28] (*levée en masse*).[29]

Additional categories

8.4 In addition, two categories of personnel, though not prisoners of war, are to be treated in the same way as prisoners of war. These are persons:

a. belonging, or having belonged, to the armed forces of an occupied territory, if the occupying power considers it necessary by reason of such allegiance to intern them, even though it has originally liberated them while hostilities were going on outside the territory it occupies;[30]

b. belonging to any of the categories enumerated in paragraph 8.3.1(a) who have been received by neutral or non-belligerent powers on their territory and whom those powers are required to intern under international law.[31]

---

[26] GC III, Art 4A(4) and Annex IVA. See the specimen in Appendix C.

[27] GC III, Art 4A(5).   [28] GC III, Art 4A(6).   [29] See para 4.8.

[30] GC III, Art 4B(1). This provision was designed to prohibit the practice adopted by Germany in the Second World War (WW II) of releasing and subsequently re-arresting demobilized members of the armed forces of occupied states such as The Netherlands and then claiming to be released from the obligation to treat such persons as PW.

[31] GC III, Art 4B(2). This provision also excludes some of the provisions of the Convention but does not prevent the granting of more favourable treatment.

SPECIAL CASES

Guerrillas and militias

General rule

The general rule is that all combatants are required to distinguish them- **8.5**
selves from the civilian population when engaged in an attack or military
operation preparatory to an attack.[32]

In the case of members of the regular armed forces, the generally accepted **8.5.1**
practice of states is that they do this by wearing uniform. Other forces,
including guerrillas, must wear some distinctive form of dress or sign[33]
such as a form of uniform or combat gear that indicates that they are
combatants, not civilians.

Exception[34]

In exceptional situations of conflict where 'owing to the nature of **8.6**
the hostilities, an armed combatant cannot so distinguish himself', he
shall retain combatant, and thereby prisoner of war, status, if he carries
his arms openly during each military engagement and 'during such time
as he is visible to the adversary while he is engaged in a military
deployment preceding the launching of an attack in which he is to participate'.[35]

Where combatants are unable to bring themselves within this rule and lose **8.6.1**
prisoner of war status through failure to distinguish themselves from the
civilian population, Additional Protocol I still provides that they must be
given equivalent protection[36] and that they cannot be treated as common
criminals.[37]

Since 1949, there has been an increasing trend towards guerrilla, paramilit- **8.6.2**
ary, and similar types of warfare. As a result, it was felt necessary to make
allowance for such warfare and those who engage in it, within the para-
meters of the law of armed conflict.

---

[32] AP I, Art 44(3).   [33] GC III, Art 4A(2)(b).   [34] AP I, Art 44(3).
[35] See para 4.5. The UK government, on ratification, declared its understanding that such
exceptional situations could only arise in occupied territory or in the conflicts referred to in AP
I, Art 1(4) and that the word 'deployment' is to be interpreted as meaning 'any movement
towards a place from which an attack is to be launched'. Although the point is not included in
the UK declaration, it is understood that 'visible' includes visible through binoculars and
night-sights.   [36] See para 4.6.
[37] AP I, Art 44(4).

The wounded and sick

8.7 Wounded and sick combatants who are captured are prisoners of war, but are evacuated initially through medical channels. Until fully recovered they have the additional protection of Geneva Convention I.[38]

Service medical personnel and chaplains

8.8 The only members of the armed forces who are not combatants as defined in Additional Protocol I are medical personnel and chaplains.[39] These non-combatant members of the armed forces do not become prisoners of war but may be retained by the detaining power with a view to providing medical care or religious ministration to prisoners of war. Their special rights and privileges are set out in paragraph 8.58 and they are to be given treatment not less favourable than that given to prisoners of war.

Auxiliary medical personnel

8.9 Combatants trained as orderlies, nurses, or stretcher-bearers become prisoners of war on capture but are to be employed on their medical duties should the need arise.[40]

Combatants qualified as medical personnel or chaplains

8.10 The position of combatants who are not members of either medical or chaplaincy services but who happen to be suitably qualified is as follows:

a. physicians, surgeons, dentists, nurses, and medical orderlies who are not members of or attached to the medical service of their armed forces are prisoners of war in the event of capture. However, they may be required by the detaining power to exercise their medical functions in the interests of their fellow prisoners of war. In that event, although they remain prisoners of war, they are entitled to the same rights as retained medical personnel and are exempt from any other work;[41] and

b. ministers of religion who are not members of the chaplaincy services of their own forces are also prisoners of war in the event of capture but may, irrespective of denomination, minister freely to members of their

---

[38] GC I, Arts 12 and 14. See, further, para 7.8.
[39] GC III, Art 33; AP I, Art 43(2). See paras 4.2 and 7.15.1. See also JWP 1–10, para 306.
[40] GC I, Arts 25 and 29.   [41] GC III, Art 32.

community. For this purpose they are entitled to be treated in exactly the same way as retained chaplains and are not obliged to do any other work.[42]

Members of civil defence organizations

Members of the armed forces permanently assigned and exclusively **8.11** devoted to civil defence work are treated as non-combatants but become prisoners of war if they fall into the power of an adverse party.[43]

Mercenaries

Mercenaries[44] are not entitled to be prisoners of war[45] unless their captors **8.12** so decide. Even if not treated as prisoners of war, captured mercenaries remain entitled to the basic humanitarian guarantees provided by Additional Protocol I.[46]

Spies

A person who falls into the hands of an adverse party while engaging in **8.13** espionage,[47] does not have the right to the status of prisoner of war, although it may be given at the discretion of the detaining power. Even without the status of prisoner of war, a spy may only be subjected to punishment after trial by a court applying the prescribed safeguards.[48] Captured spies remain entitled to the basic humanitarian guarantees provided by Additional Protocol I.[49]

Deserters and defectors

Deserters in the military law sense become prisoners of war if they are **8.14** captured. On the other hand, defectors from the enemy are considered not to be entitled to be treated as prisoners of war. However, prisoners of war who defect during captivity retain their status and cannot be deprived of it.[50]

---

[42] GC III, Art 36.

[43] AP I, Art 67(1), (2). See para 5.48 and, in respect of civil defence generally, para 5.42 onwards.   [44] As defined in para 4.10.1.

[45] AP I, Art 47(1).

[46] AP I, Arts 45(3) and 75. These fundamental guarantees are set out in Ch 9 Pt B.

[47] See para 4.9. Members of the armed forces who gather intelligence in uniform are not spies.   [48] HR, Art 30; AP I, Arts 46 and 75.

[49] AP I, Art 75, see Ch 9 Pt B.   [50] See MML, part III, para 126.

Civilians

8.15 Civilians authorized to accompany the armed forces become prisoners of war on capture. Other civilians, including officials, are not prisoners of war, but have the protection of Geneva Convention IV.[51] If captured, they may for security reasons be interned or placed in an assigned residence.[52]

Diplomatic staff

8.16 Accredited diplomatic staff must be given the opportunity to leave for their own countries on the outbreak of hostilities. Where necessary, they must be assisted with their transport requirements. Diplomats only lose their privileges and immunities if they fail to leave within a reasonable time. They may then be detained or deported but nevertheless retain immunity with respect to official acts. Diplomats who directly take part in hostilities against the host state can be considered to have rejected the opportunity to make a peaceful departure and lose special protection.[53]

Neutral attachés and diplomatic agents

8.17 It is unlawful to take as prisoners of war military attachés or diplomatic agents of neutral states who accompany armed forces or are found in a captured place, provided that they are in possession of identification papers and take no part in hostilities.[54] They may be ordered to leave the theatre of war or may be handed over to their own countries.[55] If such diplomats take

[51] See Ch 9.

[52] GC IV, Arts 41–43. Heads of State, whether sovereigns or presidents, are in some cases, by the constitutional law of their own states, commanders-in-chief of the armed forces and, accordingly, entitled to PW status. Where the Head of State is actively serving in the armed forces, he may be treated as having combatant status and would, therefore, be a legitimate target for military action.

[53] GC IV, Art 35; Vienna Convention on Diplomatic Relations 1969, Arts 44 and 39(2). When enemy diplomatic agents are encountered by a state's armed forces outside its own territory, eg in territory invaded or occupied, the position in law is not clear. The practice of states on this point has not been uniform but the British view is that such persons must be allowed to retire to their own state, even at some risk to the security of the state allowing their withdrawal. In WW II, the British Ambassador to Belgium was captured by the occupying German forces and held.

[54] GC IV, Art 35.

[55] During the Russo-Japanese War 1904–5, a British naval attaché and two American military attachés with the Russian forces captured by the Japanese at Mukden were sent to Japan and handed over to the Minister of their respective countries. If, however, attachés act as 'military advisers' and as such take part in the hostilities, it could be argued that they fall within the ambit of GC III, Art 4A(4) and are thus entitled to PW status. Military advisers from neutral states who do not have diplomatic status and take no part in hostilities are 'protected persons' under GC IV (see para 9.18) if the state of which they are nationals no longer has normal diplomatic representation in the state in whose hands they are: GC IV, Art 4(2). Members of the British army who formed the Kuwait Liaison Team and who were captured by

part directly in hostilities, they would not automatically lose their diplomatic status. Rather, the host state would be entitled to declare these individuals *persona non grata*.[56]

Journalists

Apart from war correspondents accredited to the armed forces, who have **8.18** prisoner of war status on capture,[57] journalists engaged in professional missions in areas of armed conflict are entitled to the protection afforded a civilian.[58] A special identity card certifying status as a journalist may be issued by the state of which the individual is a national, or in which he resides, or where his employer is located,[59] see Appendix E.

IDENTITY CARDS

Each party to the conflict is required to issue identity cards ('ID cards')[60] to **8.19** those persons under its jurisdiction who are liable to become prisoners of war. These cards must contain all the information that a prisoner of war is required to provide to his captors[61] and may include other information such as signature and/or fingerprints of the bearer. Special cards are prescribed for civilians accompanying the armed forces,[62] journalists,[63] medical personnel[64] and chaplains,[65] and civil defence personnel.[66] As far as possible, the card for persons liable to become prisoners of war should be of a standard size, i.e. 6.5 × 10 cm, and be made out in duplicate.

DETERMINATION OF STATUS

Presumption of prisoner of war status

There is[67] a presumption in favour of entitlement to prisoner of war status if: **8.20**

a. the person concerned claims, or appears to be entitled to, that status; or

b. the party to the conflict to which he belongs claims that status on his behalf by notification to either the detaining power or the protecting power.

Iraqi forces during the invasion of Kuwait in August 1990 were repatriated to the United Kingdom following the intervention of the United Nations Secretary General. At that stage, the United Kingdom was not involved in an armed conflict with Iraq.

[56] Vienna Convention on Diplomatic Relations 1969, Art 9.   [57] See para 8.3.1(c).
[58] See Ch 9.
[59] AP I, Art 79 and Annex II. These additional protections arose from the concern expressed over the fate of journalists covering the Vietnam conflict.   [60] GC III, Art 17.
[61] See para 8.33.   [62] See para 8.3.1(c).   [63] See para 8.18.
[64] See paras 7.26–7.29   [65] See para 7.30.
[66] See AP I, Arts 66(3) and 67(1)(c) and Annex I, ch V; see also paras 5.44.1 and 5.47.
[67] AP I, Art 45(1). This expanded the provisions of GC III, Art 5, which appear to have been little used except in the Vietnam conflict.

8.20.1 In view of the difficulties discussed in paragraphs 4.4 to 4.6 of distinguishing combatants from non-combatants, it may not be easy to decide whether to give prisoner of war status to a person who has taken part in hostilities and has subsequently been captured, so the law makes this presumption in favour of prisoner of war status.

8.20.2 This presumption only relates to those captured in international armed conflicts as no provision for prisoner of war status is made in the law relating to internal armed conflicts.

Cases of doubt

8.21 In cases of doubt as to entitlement, the person concerned continues to have the protection of the Convention and Protocol until his status has been determined by a competent tribunal.[68] For the armed forces of the UK, these tribunals are boards of inquiry convened in accordance with the Prisoner of War Determination of Status Regulations 1958.[69]

Claiming prisoner of war status

8.22 Where a person in the power of an adverse party is not held as a prisoner of war and is to be tried by that party for an offence arising out of the hostilities, he has the right to claim prisoner of war status and to have that question adjudicated by a judicial tribunal. Whenever procedurally possible, this adjudication should occur before the trial for the offence. Representatives of the protecting power are entitled to attend the adjudication proceedings unless, exceptionally, in the interests of state security, they are to be held *in camera* in which event the protecting power is to be advised accordingly by the detaining power.[70]

Fundamental guarantees

8.23 Those who have taken part in hostilities but who are not entitled to prisoner of war status, and do not benefit from more favourable treatment as civilians in the hands of a party to the conflict, are nevertheless entitled to certain basic humanitarian guarantees.[71]

DURATION OF PRISONER OF WAR STATUS

8.24 The protected status of a prisoner of war begins at the moment when he falls into the power of the adverse party and continues until his final release

[68] GC III, Art 5. On the internment as PW of Iraqi nationals in the UK during the Gulf conflict 1991, see G Risius, 'Prisoners of War in the United Kingdom', in P Rowe (ed), *The Gulf War in International and English Law* (1993) 289–303.   [69] See JWP 1–10, para 126.
[70] AP I, Art 45(2).
[71] AP I, Arts 45(3) and 75. This would include, for example, mercenaries. See, further, Ch 9 Pt B.

and repatriation.[72] Prisoners of war are not permitted to renounce 'in part or in entirety' their rights as prisoners of war.[73]

The reason for this is that prisoners of war, like other victims of armed conflict, are in a poor position to bargain with their captors who might otherwise be tempted, for example, to persuade prisoners of war to 'volunteer' to enlist in the forces of the capturing power. **8.24.1**

C. INITIAL ACTION ON CAPTURE OF PRISONERS OF WAR

The following action is to be taken in respect of prisoners of war when first captured:[74] **8.25**

a. They must be treated humanely.[75]

b. If wounded or sick, they must be cared for.[76]

c. They must be disarmed and searched.[77]

d. The property listed below must remain in their possession:[78]

    (1) *clothing*, military and civilian including that for their special protection such as NBC suits;

    (2) *protective military equipment*, for example, steel helmets, flak jackets and respirators;

    (3) *feeding utensils*, ration packs, and water bottles;

    (4) *badges* of rank and nationality, military insignia;

    (5) *decorations* and medals;

    (6) *identity cards* and discs, and, where not in their possession, cards must be issued by the captor (see further, sub-paragraph i);

    (7) *personal property* which the prisoners of war are able to carry with them, such as spectacles and articles of sentimental value like personal letters and family photographs, but see sub-paragraph f.[79]

---

[72] GC III, Art 5; AP I, Arts 3(b) and 44(1). This can cause difficulty where a state withdraws from the conflict or changes side, as in the case of Italy in WW II. Release and repatriation may not be possible but, in such a case, it would still not be permissible to use even volunteer prisoners in prohibited work.   [73] GC III, Art 7.

[74] See the PW handling aide memoire in JWP 1–10, 3A.   [75] GC III, Art 13.

[76] GC I, Art 12; JWP 1–10, 3B, 2.

[77] GC III, Art 18; JWP 1–10, 3B, 3. Failure to search PW properly in the Afghanistan conflict of 2001 enabled them to stage an uprising at Mazar-i-Sherif, which was only put down with heavy loss of life.   [78] GC III, Art 18.

[79] For medicines in the possession of PW, see JWP 1–10, 3B3. See also JWP 1–10, 3F, 31–33.

e. All other items of military equipment may be confiscated. That includes arms and ammunition, non-protective military equipment, military documents such as orders, maps, and diaries containing military information. They become the property of the capturing government, not the individuals or units capturing them. Items taken should be tagged.[80]

f. Personal property may only be removed for security reasons;[81] this would include articles which could be used as weapons, such as razor blades and sharp knives, or which could affect security, such as cameras. Items of value should be dealt with in accordance with the procedure set out in sub-paragraph h.

g. Sums of money may only be taken away on the order of an officer. The amount taken must be recorded in a special register and an itemized receipt, showing the name, rank, and unit of the person issuing it, given. Money that is the private property of the prisoner of war is either credited to his account[82] or returned to him at the end of captivity.[83] Where a prisoner of war (for example, a pay clerk) is found to be in possession of money belonging to his government, the money becomes booty of war and is dealt with in accordance with sub-paragraph e.

h. Articles of value may be taken for safe custody only. A record must be made and a receipt given. The articles must be returned intact at the end of captivity.[84] This is to prevent loss of the property, especially during evacuation, and to prevent its use for bribery.

i. The identity of prisoners of war must be established and recorded. A standard form for recording such information has been agreed between NATO states.[85] Prisoners of war may be required to show their identity cards, but these may not be taken away.[86] At no time should a prisoner of war be without identity documents. The detaining power must supply identity cards to those without.[87] If a prisoner of war has no identity card but has some other means of proving his identity such as a pay book or a driving licence, he must be allowed to keep it.

j. As soon as circumstances permit, prisoners of war should be informed of their rights of correspondence.[88]

k. Prisoners of war may be segregated for interrogation.[89]

---

[80] Detailed procedures are set out in NATO STANAG 2044, see JWP 1–10, 3D, 4-1-1.
[81] GC III, Art 18.　　[82] See para 8.79.
[83] GC III, Art 18. See also NATO STANAG 2044.
[84] GC III, Art 18. See also NATO STANAG 2044.
[85] NATO STANAG 2044. For PW documentation, see JWP 1–10, 3D.　　[86] GC III, Art 17.
[87] GC III, Art 18. See also NATO STANAG 2044.　　[88] See paras 8.41–8.42 and 8.62–8.68.
[89] Detailed procedures are set out in NATO STANAG 2044. See also JWP 1–10, 3B, 8.

l. Initial interrogation is permitted, but the rules in paragraph 8.34 must be followed.[90]

m. As soon as possible after capture prisoners of war must be evacuated from the combat area.[91]

n. Minimum necessary force may be used to prevent prisoners of war from escaping. Lethal force may only be used if less severe measures would be ineffective, but a warning should first be given unless the circumstances do not permit.[92]

For prisoners of war in UK hands, the process of documenting them and **8.25.1** their military equipment is known as 'tagging'—the completion of form F/PW/778 (the PW and Personal Equipment Tag).[93]

D. RESPONSIBILITY FOR PRISONERS OF WAR

BASIC RESPONSIBILITY

The responsibility for prisoners of war lies with the capturing power and **8.26** not with the individuals or military units who captured them.[94]

The capturing power is the state whose troops effected the initial capture. **8.26.1**

This rule ensures that the capturing power, the state itself, is answerable in **8.26.2** respect of complaints and it has a strict duty to ensure observance of the law. Even in the case of multinational forces, where arrangements for handling prisoners of war are administered by several allied states, the original capturing power retains an obligation in respect of prisoners of war as set out in the following paragraph.[95] This also applies where the forces are acting under the command of the United Nations.

TRANSFER

Prisoners of war may be transferred by the capturing power to another state **8.27** which is a party to Geneva Convention III, provided that the capturing power is satisfied that the other state is able and willing to apply that

---

[90] Detailed procedures are set out in NATO STANAG 2033. See also JWP 1–10, 3B, 7, 8c.

[91] GC III, Art 19. See para 8.35.

[92] GC III, Art 42. See JWP 1–10, 3B, 6 and Appendix 3B, 1.   [93] See further JWP 1–10, 3D.

[94] HR, Art 4; GC III, Art 12; AP I, Art 44(1).

[95] In the Gulf conflict 1991, the UK established a PW Monitoring Team who were responsible for checking on the treatment of all PW captured by UK units, regardless of their final place of detention.

Convention.[96] If that state fails to carry out the provisions of the Convention in any important respect, the capturing power must, upon being notified by the protecting power, either take back the prisoners of war or take steps to correct the failure. This would include, for example, supplying food to the state holding the prisoners of war to enable it to feed them.

E. TREATMENT OF PRISONERS OF WAR

HUMANE TREATMENT

8.28 Prisoners of war must be humanely treated and their persons and honour respected at all times.[97] 'Women shall be treated with all the regard due to their sex and shall in all cases benefit by treatment as favourable as that granted to men.'[98]

8.28.1 For the treatment of juvenile prisoners of war in United Kingdom captivity, see *Prisoner of War Handling* (JWP 1–10), paragraph 308.

PROHIBITED ACTS

8.29 In relation to prisoners of war the following acts and omissions by the detaining power are *prohibited*:

a. Those unlawfully causing death or serious injury to health.[99]

b. Physical mutilation or medical or scientific experiments, even with consent.[100]

c. Any medical treatment, even with the consent of the prisoner of war, including removal of tissue or organs for transplantation, unless it is:

(1) necessitated by the health of the person concerned;

(2) consistent with generally accepted medical standards; and

(3) applied in similar circumstances to those which would apply to nationals of the detaining power.

[96] GC III, Art 12. Certain states entered reservations to this article, holding that full responsibility continues to rest with the capturing power, but the UK does not recognize their validity. See, further, A Roberts and R Guelff, *Documents on the Laws of War* (3rd edn 2000) (Roberts and Guelff, *Documents*) 367. Some of these states have since withdrawn their reservations to the Geneva Conventions 1949, see n 349.   [97] GC III, Art 13; AP I, Art 11.
[98] GC III, Art 14. See also Arts 25, 29, 49, 88, 97, and 108 and JWP 1–10, para 307. The rule could be stated as 'equal but separate' treatment, see Art 16. Due regard must be had to women's physical strength, the need to protect them against rape, forced prostitution, and indecent assault, and the special demands of biological factors such as menstruation, pregnancy, and childbirth.   [99] GC III, Art 13.
[100] GC III, Art 13; AP I, Art 11.

An *exception* to this rule is that prisoners of war may consent to give blood for transfusion or skin for grafting provided that consent is given voluntarily and without any coercion or inducement, and then only for therapeutic purposes. Generally accepted medical standards must be applied together with controls designed for the benefit of both the donor and the recipient.[101]

d. Violence or intimidation, insults, and public curiosity. Apart from prohibiting the more obvious acts of brutality, this is intended to prevent, for example, parading prisoners of war through city streets to the insults of the populace, displaying them in a humiliating fashion on television, or the failure of escorts to protect prisoners of war from acts of violence.[102]

e. Reprisals. Reprisals can never lawfully be taken against prisoners of war.[103]

Free Maintenance

The detaining power must provide for the maintenance and medical care of prisoners of war free of charge.[104] **8.30**

Non-discrimination

There must be no adverse discrimination towards prisoners of war based on race, nationality, religious belief, political opinions, or similar criteria.[105] However, the detaining power is permitted to allow privileged treatment to prisoners of war by virtue of their rank, state of health, age, or professional qualifications, as well as the special rules already mentioned relating to women. **8.31**

---

[101] GC III, Art 13; AP I, Art 11. See also para 7.5 and footnotes.

[102] GC III, Art 13. In the *Maelzer Trial* (1945) 11 WCR 53, the accused, who was the German military commander in Rome, was convicted for having exposed prisoners of war in his custody to acts of violence, insults, and public curiosity. Similarly, the IMT (Tokyo) condemned the Japanese practice of parading prisoners of war through cities and exposing them to ridicule and insults. General Schmidt, a German air force commander, was convicted for ordering that escorts provided by the armed forces should not use their weapons to protect captured allied airmen from the fury of the civilian populace. This prohibition was of general application throughout the Reich in 1944, and was known as 'The Terror Fliers Order'. As a result, many airmen were lynched by the civilian population whilst their escorts were passive spectators, see reference to *Schmidt* in (1945) 12 WCR 119. In the Gulf conflict 1991, there was condemnation of the Iraqi display on television of captured coalition aircrew reading out statements. For media access to PW, see JWP 1–10, paras 132–133.

[103] GC III, Art 13. General Müller was convicted in 1947 (unreported) for placing allied PW alongside an oil refinery in Lower Silesia as a 'reprisal' and refusing them access to air raid shelters when the allies bombed the refinery. Some PW were killed in the raids.

[104] GC III, Art 15.   [105] GC III, Art 16.

UNUSUAL CONDITIONS OF COMBAT

8.32 It is *unlawful* to kill prisoners of war on grounds of self-preservation or because holding them would impede or endanger military operations.

8.32.1 If, because of unusual conditions of combat, it is not possible to evacuate prisoners of war, they are to be released and all feasible precautions[106] taken to ensure their safety.[107] There is no obligation to release prisoners of war in circumstances in which safe evacuation is temporarily impossible. In such cases, prisoners of war may be held until release or evacuation is possible. There is, however, a continuing obligation to take all feasible measures to provide for the safety of such prisoners of war so long as they remain in the custody of the detaining power. This principle admits of no exception even in the case of airborne, commando, or special forces operations, although the circumstances of the operation may necessitate rigorous supervision of and restraint upon the movement of prisoners of war.

ESTABLISHING IDENTITY

8.33 In order that his identity can be established, every prisoner of war is bound to disclose his *service number, rank, full names*, and *date of birth*.[108]

8.33.1 The reason for this is to enable his capture to be reported to the authorities in his own country and to his family.

8.33.2 If prisoners of war are unable to state their identity because of physical or mental defects, they must be handed over to the medical service and every effort must be made to establish their identity. This may be achieved, for example, by taking fingerprints or photographs or asking fellow prisoners of war about his identity. However, no coercion may be used.

INTERROGATION

8.34 The capturing power may ask further questions to obtain tactical or strategic information but the prisoner of war cannot be forced to disclose any such information.[109] Questioning should be done in a language that the prisoner of war understands. No physical or mental torture or any other

---

[106] The word 'feasible' means that which is practicable or practically possible, taking into account all circumstances ruling at the time, including humanitarian and military considerations.

[107] AP I, Art 41(3). This may mean the provision of food and water, protective equipment, and even weapons, if necessary to preserve their lives.   [108] GC III, Art 17.

[109] See JWP 1–10, 3B, 8c. For PW documentation, see JWP 1–10, 3D.

form of coercion may be used to obtain information. Nor may those who refuse to answer be threatened, insulted, or exposed to any unpleasant or disadvantageous treatment of any kind.[110]

Wounded and sick prisoners of war may be interrogated, but not if it would **8.34.1** seriously endanger their health,[111] so medical advice should be taken in case of doubt.

Blindfolding and segregation may be necessary in the interests of security, **8.34.2** the physical restraint of prisoners of war, or to prevent collaboration prior to interrogation, but these discomforts must be truly justified and be for as short a period as possible.

The NATO states have agreed humane interrogation procedures.[112] **8.34.3** Interrogation is best done by skilled, well-briefed interrogators who are able to build up a rapport with prisoners of war.

F. EVACUATION OF PRISONERS OF WAR

The following rules are to be observed during evacuations:[113] **8.35**

a. As soon as possible after capture, prisoners of war must be evacuated to camps far enough from the fighting to be out of danger. Only those who because of wounds or sickness would run greater risks by being moved than by remaining where they are may be kept temporarily in a danger zone.[114]

b. Prisoners of war must not be exposed unnecessarily to danger whilst awaiting evacuation.

c. Evacuation must be carried out humanely and in conditions which are not inferior to those used for moving the forces of the detaining power.[115] This would rule out marches that are beyond the physical capabilities of prisoners of war or movement in overcrowded or unhygienic conditions. Where possible, their transport should be marked with large letters 'PW' or 'PG' so that they are not unwittingly attacked.[116]

d. During evacuation, prisoners of war must be supplied with sufficient food, water, clothing, and medical attention.

e. A list must be made of those evacuated.

---

[110] GC III, Art 17. In *Re Killinger and others* (1945) 3 WCR 67, some of the accused were convicted of having placed PW in excessively heated cells in order to extract information.
[111] GC III, Art 13.   [112] NATO STANAG 2033.
[113] GC III, Arts 19 and 20. See also JWP 1–10, 3B, 11–13.   [114] See also JWP 1–10, 3B, 2.
[115] See JWP 1–10, 3B, 3.
[116] Failure to mark PW transports caused many casualties during WW II.

f. If during evacuation prisoners of war have to pass through transit camps, their stay must be as short as possible. Permanent transit, screening, or interrogation camps must be fitted out like regular prisoner of war camps and the treatment of prisoners of war must be the same.[117]

G. INTERNMENT IN PRISONER OF WAR CAMPS

INTERNMENT OF PRISONERS OF WAR

8.36 Prisoners of war are normally interned in prisoner of war camps controlled by the capturing power. However, they may be interned in prisoner of war camps in a neutral country,[118] or released on parole.[119] Close confinement[120] is not permitted except as a punishment, or for medical reasons.[121]

LOCATION

8.37 Camps must be on land and in places which are healthy, hygienic, and out of danger.[122]

8.37.1 Temporary internment on board ship for the purpose of evacuation from the combat zone is permissible.[123] Former prisons may only be used once the prisoners have been removed and where that is in the interests of the prisoners of war themselves.[124] Where prisoners of war are interned in unhealthy areas or where the climate is harmful they must be moved as soon as possible to a more favourable climate.[125] Camps must not be sited so as to render military objectives immune from attack.[126]

SEGREGATION[127]

8.38 In camps, prisoners of war must be grouped according to their nationality,[128] language, and customs. Members of the same armed forces should

---

[117] GC III, Art 24. This provision would not apply to camps that are merely convenient stopping points during the evacuation but would clearly apply to camps remote from the combat zone and used primarily as bases for inter-camp transfers. See also JWP 1–10, paras 314–316 and 3E.   [118] See para 8.147.
[119] See para 8.104.   [120] GC III, Art 21. See para 8.114 onwards.   [121] See para 8.54.
[122] For layout of camps, see JWP 1–10, 3E.
[123] This was done during the Falklands conflict 1982, with the concurrence of the ICRC, because there was nowhere suitable to hold PW on the Falkland Islands and the intention was to repatriate them as quickly as possible.
[124] It follows that prisons that are still operating as such may not be used, GC III, Art 22.
[125] GC III, Art 22.   [126] GC III, Art 23.
[127] GC III, Arts 16 and 22(3). See also JWP 1–10, 3F, 34.
[128] No adverse distinction in treatment would be permissible: GC III, Art 16.

not be segregated except with their consent. Provided that the standards of the Convention are met, segregation of officers from other ranks and for security reasons is permissible.

SAFETY OF PRISONER OF WAR CAMPS[129]

Camps must be outside the combat zone. Prisoners of war must be pro- **8.39** tected to the same extent as the civilian population from the dangers of war including the provision and use of shelters.[130] Belligerents must notify each other, through the protecting power, of the location of prisoner of war camps. Whenever military considerations permit, they must be marked by the letters 'PW' or 'PG', or other agreed marking, so as to be clearly visible from the air in the day-time. Only prisoner of war camps may be so marked.

SECURITY OF CAMPS AND USE OF WEAPONS

Camps may be fenced to prevent escape.[131] However, weapons may not **8.40** be used against prisoners of war, even if attempting to escape, except as a last resort and after prior warning.[132] Orders to guards and escorts should make this clear.

INITIAL ACTION ON ARRIVAL OF PRISONERS OF WAR IN CAMPS

Prisoners' rights and documentation

If any step outlined in paragraph 8.25 has not been taken, it should be dealt **8.41** with immediately on the arrival of the prisoners of war at prisoner of war camps. In particular, they should be informed of their right to send capture cards to their families and to the Central Prisoners of War Agency and of their other rights of correspondence.[133]

Capture cards

Immediately on capture, or within one week of arrival at a camp, each **8.42** prisoner of war must be allowed to write one card to his family and another

---

[129] GC III, Art 23.

[130] This extends to the provision of respirators and protective clothing where these are on general issue. During the Gulf conflict 1991, a stock of NBC suits was set aside for issue to Iraqi PW if necessary.   [131] GC III, Art 21.

[132] GC III, Art 42. See also JWP 1–10, 3B, 6 and 3B, 1. This provision was introduced because of the many cases in which British and allied PW were shot by their guards without any justification during WW II on the pretext of escape. For a particularly flagrant example, see the *Stalag Luft III Case* (1947) 11 WCR 31–52.

[133] GC III, Art 70. See paras 8.42 and 8.62 onwards.

to the Central Prisoners of War Agency informing them of his capture, address, and state of health,[134] see the illustration in Appendix C. This also applies in cases of sickness, removal to hospital, or transfer to another camp. The cards must be forwarded as rapidly as possible.

Medical examination

8.43   An initial medical examination, though not mandatory, is recommended in the interests of both the detaining power and the prisoner of war. It enables the condition of prisoners of war during captivity to be monitored against their condition on arrival and it facilitates the maintenance of hygiene and prevention of disease.[135]

INTERNAL DISCIPLINE OF CAMPS

Camp commander

8.44   Every prisoner of war camp must be under the immediate authority of a responsible commissioned officer of the regular forces of the detaining power.[136] This prohibits camps from being commanded by members of paramilitary or even non-military organizations.[137] The camp commander must keep a copy of the Convention in his possession and ensure that the camp staff and guards know its provisions. He is responsible, under the direction of his government, for the application of the Convention[138] and has disciplinary powers over prisoners of war.[139]

Posting of Convention and orders

8.45   The text of the Convention and its annexes and any special agreements made under it must be displayed in the language(s)[140] of the prisoners of war, in places where everyone can read them.[141] Any prisoner of war who

---

[134] GC III, Art 70 and Annex IVB. See also JWP 1–10, 3F, 64. In the Gulf conflict 1991, the ICRC supplied capture cards and correspondence forms in English, French, and Arabic for use by the coalition forces. The ICRC's Central Tracing Agency normally carries out the function of the Central Prisoners of War Agency.   [135] See, further, para 8.54.

[136] GC III, Art 39. Some Japanese camps in WW II were commanded by NCOs.

[137] In WW II, German camps were sometimes commanded by members of the SS or even the Gestapo.

[138] GC III, Art 39. See PW (Disc) Regs 1958, r 1 and App 1, which meets the requirements of the convention.   [139] GC III, Art 96. See Part K of this ch.

[140] That is, the official language of the PW's state of origin, ie, the language used for official records and the publication of legislation, see Pictet, *Commentary*, 244.

[141] GC III, Art 41. See also the Prisoners of War (Discipline) Regulations 1958, reg 3 and JWP 1–10, 3F, 5.

does not have access to the posted copy must be supplied with a copy if he asks for it.[142] Regulations, orders, notices, and publications of all kinds relating to the conduct of prisoners of war must be issued to them in a language which they understand, copies being posted in a place where all may read them, and also given to the prisoners' representative.[143] Direct orders to individuals must also be given in a language that they understand.

Saluting[144]

All other-rank prisoners of war must salute and show respect to all officers of the detaining power as is provided for by the regulations applying in their own forces.[145] Officer prisoners of war must salute officers of the detaining power of higher rank and the camp commander regardless of his rank. Salutes should be returned. **8.46**

Rank of prisoners of war

Prisoners of war must be allowed to wear their badges of rank and nationality as well as their decorations.[146] They must be treated with due regard to their rank and age, especially officers and prisoners of war of officer status.[147] Promotions of prisoners of war during captivity, which have been duly notified by the power on which those prisoners of war depend, must be recognized by the detaining power.[148] **8.47**

Military status of prisoners of war

Since the camp commander's disciplinary powers cannot be delegated to prisoners of war,[149] the relationship between prisoners of war is governed by the military law of the state to which they belong. **8.48**

As regards British prisoners of war, the ordinary military relations of superior and subordinate and the military duty of obedience remain unaltered.[150] However, as the powers of commanding officers depend on a command that has ceased to exist, trials of offences under the Naval Discipline Act 1957, the Army Act 1955, and the Air Force Act 1955 cannot take place **8.48.1**

[142] In the Gulf conflict 1991, posters, supplied by the ICRC, were displayed in the compounds of the British camp. These contained the salient points of the Convention. Full copies of the Convention in Arabic were available through the camp administration.
[143] For prisoners' representative, see para 8.94.   [144] GC III, Art 39.
[145] See eg QR (Army) 2.019(b).   [146] GC III, Art 40.
[147] GC III, Arts 44 and 45. See also Art 43, in relation to equivalent ranks of civilians, merchant marine officers, etc.
[148] GC III, Art 43. See also, eg, in respect of soldiers, QR (Army) 9.146.
[149] GC III, Art 96.   [150] See, eg, QR (Army) 2.019(b).

during captivity. The enforcement of discipline as between prisoners of war can only take place after repatriation.[151]

QUARTERS, FOOD, AND CLOTHING

Quarters

8.49 Accommodation for prisoners of war is required to be at least as good as that for the forces of the detaining power billeted in the same area. Women must have separate sleeping quarters from men.[152] Sleeping quarters should have the same total area, minimum cubic space, fittings, and bedding as is provided for the detaining power's forces. Allowance must be made for special national or religious practices. All accommodation has to be dry and adequately heated and lighted, with proper fire precautions being taken. In no circumstances may conditions be damaging to health.

Food

8.50 The basic daily ration must be sufficient in quantity, quality, and variety to maintain health and prevent loss of weight or nutritional deficiencies, account being taken of the usual diet of the prisoners of war.[153] There must be an adequate supply of drinking water and those who work must have such additional rations as are necessary. Collective punishments affecting food are prohibited.

8.50.1 Because dietary needs differ in different regions of the world, no fixed scales are laid down and food ration is determined by need. A diet that may be sufficient for inhabitants of one region may prove insufficient or unsuitable for those from another.[154] Prisoners of war should be allowed to help prepare their food and may be employed for that purpose in camp kitchens.

Messing

8.51 Adequate facilities must be provided for messing and the preparation of any additional food, for example from relief parcels,[155] prisoners of war

---

[151] MML, part I, ch II, para 60; MAFL, vol I, ch III, para 64. In WW II, a number of instances occurred of 'trials' being held by tribunals set up by the PW themselves, often to try charges that the individuals accused were collaborating with the detaining power. Trials of this sort have no legal effect. PW accused of such acts should be tried by their own authorities, after repatriation.   [152] GC III, Art 25.

[153] GC III, Art 26. See the provision for medical inspection in para 8.56. See also JWP 1–10, 3F, 40.

[154] In WW II, many PW from European and Commonwealth countries and the USA suffered severely in Japanese hands because they were unable to subsist on the diet provided.

[155] GC III, Art 26.

being encouraged to manage their own messes.[156] Other ranks of the same armed forces, preferably speaking the same language, must be assigned in sufficient numbers to provide service in messes for officer prisoners of war.[157] The use of tobacco must be permitted.[158]

Canteens

Canteens must be established in all camps to enable prisoners of war to buy **8.52**
food, soap, and tobacco, and ordinary articles in daily use, for example, stationery, toilet articles, and mending materials.[159] Prices should not exceed current, local market prices.[160] The prisoners' representative has the right to participate in the management of canteens.

Clothing

The detaining power must supply prisoners of war with sufficient clothing, **8.53**
underwear, and footwear for the climatic conditions.[161] Those who work must be supplied with appropriate working clothes. There must be arrangements for regular repair and replacement.

Uniforms of enemy armed forces captured by the detaining power can be **8.53.1**
used for this purpose. Uniforms of the detaining power may also be used provided that all badges are removed.[162]

Hygiene and Medical Matters[163]

Hygiene

The detaining power must take all measures necessary to prevent epi- **8.54**
demics and to ensure that camps are kept clean, sanitary, and healthy.[164] This will be facilitated by medical examination on entry to the camp, disinfection, and inoculation. Those suffering from infectious diseases must be placed in quarantine. Hygienic conveniences, which must be separate for men and women, must be provided and kept clean and available for use by prisoners of war at all times of the day and night. Baths, showers, sufficient water and soap are to be provided so that prisoners of war may wash

---

[156] GC III, Arts 44 and 45.   [157] GC III, Art 44. See JWP 1–10, 3F, 57.

[158] GC III, Art 26. This would not prevent a no-smoking policy being implemented in parts of the camp so long as reasonable facilities for smokers were provided.

[159] GC III, Art 28. See JWP 1–10, 3F, 59–62.

[160] As to the profits from canteens, see para 8.82.   [161] GC III, Art 27.

[162] However, PW cannot be made to wear the uniform of the detaining power, see J Pictet, *Commentary on the Geneva Conventions of 12 August 1949* (1952) (Pictet, *Commentary*) 201.

[163] See also JWP 1–10, 3F, 35–51.   [164] GC III, Art 29.

themselves and their laundry. Prisoners of war must be given reasonable opportunities for using all these facilities.

Medical attention

8.55 Each camp must have an adequate infirmary where prisoners of war, including those undergoing punishment, can have the medical attention, including diet, which they need. Where necessary, there must be isolation wards for those suffering from contagious or mental diseases. Prisoners of war suffering from serious diseases or needing special treatment must be admitted to any military or civilian hospital that can give that treatment, even if they are due for repatriation in the near future. This applies particularly to the rehabilitation needs of the disabled and blind. Wherever possible, treatment should be given by retained personnel of the medical services of, or of the same nationality as, the prisoners of war.[165] Prisoners of war may not be refused medical examination. The cost of medical treatment and of remedial aids such as dentures, crutches, artificial limbs, or spectacles must be met by the detaining power.[166] Prisoners of war can be ordered to undergo medical treatment including injections to the same extent as soldiers of the detaining power,[167] but see paragraph 8.29(c).

Medical inspection

8.56 Prisoners of war must be examined at least once a month to monitor their general state of health, nutrition, and cleanliness and also to detect infection or contagion, especially tuberculosis, malaria, and venereal disease.[168] In the case of prisoners of war who work, these examinations will also verify their fitness for work. Prisoners of war who regard themselves as unfit may report sick and the doctor will make appropriate recommendations to the camp authorities.[169]

8.56.1 A daily sick parade facilitates medical care. Medical practitioners may also be concerned with the question of repatriation of prisoners of war who are seriously ill.[170] In cases of serious injury to prisoners of war there must be an official enquiry.[171]

Medical certificates

8.57 A prisoner of war who has received medical attention may insist on being given a certificate as to both the complaint and the treatment given.[172]

---

[165] As to the status and duties of such personnel, see para 8.58.
[166] GC III, Art 30. See also JWP 1–10, 3F, 43.
[167] GC III, Arts 13 and 82. See also AP I, Art 11.   [168] GC III, Art 31.
[169] GC III, Art 55.
[170] Also with sick and wounded PW who may be accommodated in neutral states. See paras 8.147–8.154.   [171] See para 8.176.
[172] GC III, Art 30.

Where the treatment relates to an accident or disease attributable to work, a certificate must be provided specifying the circumstances in which the accident or disease occurred.[173] Any certificate issued is to be copied to the Central Prisoners of War Agency.[174]

Rights and privileges of captured medical personnel

Captured medical personnel, whether they are of retained or of prisoner of **8.58** war status, who are engaged in giving medical assistance to prisoners of war have the following rights and privileges.[175]

a. As a minimum, the benefits of the Convention.

b. The facility to perform their medical duties in accordance with their professional ethics, but under the direction and control of the medical service of, and within the scope of the military laws and regulations of, the detaining power, which is ultimately responsible for the health of prisoners of war.

c. The means of treating prisoners of war, preferably of their own armed forces.

d. The facility (including the provision of transport) to make periodical visits to prisoners of war in labour detachments or hospitals outside the camp.

e. Although subject to the internal discipline of the camp, no compulsion to do work other than medical work.

f. The right to propose prisoners of war for repatriation or accommodation in a neutral country and the entitlement to attend examinations conducted by mixed medical commissions.[176]

g. If possible during hostilities, retained medical personnel have the right to be relieved and repatriated. If there is no medical work for them to do, they must be repatriated. On repatriation, they have the right to take their personal property, including medical instruments, with them.

Civilian medical personnel who fall into the hands of the enemy should not **8.58.1** be detained and should be allowed to continue with their medical duties.[177] If security measures have to be taken, civilian medical personnel have all the protection of protected persons.[178]

---

[173] GC III, Arts 54 and 68. Claims for compensation are dealt with in para 8.92.
[174] GC III, Arts 30, 54, and 68.   [175] GC III, Arts 32 and 33. See also JWP 1–10, 3F, 38.
[176] See para 8.153.
[177] For rights of access of civilian medical personnel and help where civilian medical services are disrupted by combat activity, see AP I, Art 15.
[178] AP I, Arts 15 and 16. For protected persons, see Ch 9 Pt D.

8.58.2 The senior retained medical officer is responsible to the camp military authorities for everything connected with the activities of retained medical personnel in the camp and has direct access to those authorities on all questions relating to medical duties.[179] For this purpose he must be provided with all necessary facilities for correspondence.

RELIGION[180]

Freedom of worship

8.59 Prisoners of war must be allowed complete freedom of religious worship, including attendance at services, provided that they comply with the disciplinary routine of the camp.[181] Suitable accommodation for religious services must be provided.

Chaplains

8.60 Prisoners of war may be ministered to by retained chaplains, or prisoners of war who are qualified as ministers of religion, speak the same language, and practise the same religion. Chaplains must be allocated to camps and labour detachments. The rights and privileges of retained chaplains are similar to those of retained medical personnel,[182] except that chaplains have individual right of access to the camp authorities.[183] They are permitted, subject to censorship,[184] to write to international religious organizations and the religious authorities in the country of detention on matters concerning their religious duties.[185] Those who act as chaplains may not be required to do other work.[186] If no retained chaplain or prisoner of war minister of the appropriate faith is available, one of a similar denomination or, where feasible, even a qualified layman, may be appointed at the request of the prisoners of war. The person appointed must comply with all the disciplinary and security regulations of the camp.[187]

EDUCATION AND SPORT[188]

8.61 The detaining power, while taking into account individual preferences, must encourage intellectual, educational, and recreational activities, including sport and games, and provide adequate premises and equipment.

---

[179] GC III, Art 33.   [180] See JWP 1–10, 3F, 78.   [181] GC III, Art 34.
[182] See para 8.58.   [183] GC III, Art 33.   [184] See para 8.68.
[185] GC III, Art 35. This correspondence is in addition to the quota laid down in Art 71, as to which see para 8.62. See also JWP 1–10, 3F, 69.   [186] GC III, Arts 33 and 36.
[187] GC III, Art 37. This is an important point as the person appointed may be a member of the civilian population of the detaining power.   [188] See also JWP 1–10, 3F, 79.

Every camp must contain sufficient open space for prisoners of war to be in the open air and engage in physical exercise.[189]

This provision does not permit the subjection of prisoners of war to propa- **8.61.1** ganda under the guise of education, since that would offend against the rules protecting their honour, forbidding inhumane treatment, and safe-guarding their individual preferences.

CORRESPONDENCE AND RELIEF PARCELS

Outgoing correspondence[190]

Prisoners of war must be allowed to send, in addition to the capture **8.62** cards,[191] at least two letters and four postcards every month.[192] This quota does not include complaints,[193] correspondence between prisoners' repres-entatives at labour detachments and those in the main camp,[194] and official correspondence by medical officers and chaplains.[195] Further limitations can be imposed only with the agreement of the protecting power where there is a lack of linguists for censorship. In cases of emergency or where they have been without news of their families for a long time or are a long way from home, prisoners of war must be allowed to send telegrams at their own expense.[196] Parties are under a duty to reduce telegram charges as much as possible.[197] Correspondence is normally to be in the native lan-guage of the prisoner of war.[198]

The term 'correspondence' is sufficiently wide to cover more modern **8.62.1** means of communication such as fax or e-mail.

Incoming correspondence

Prisoners of war must be allowed to receive all letters and cards addressed **8.63** to them.[199] A limitation on numbers can only be imposed by the state on

---

[189] GC III, Art 38. During the Gulf conflict 1991, many of the Iraqi PW interned in the UK were students at British universities and by the time of their release arrangements were being put in hand to enable them to continue their studies while in captivity.

[190] See also JWP 1–10, 3F, 63–72.   [191] See para 8.42.

[192] GC III, Art 71 & Annex IV C. For model correspondence card and letter, see Appendix C.

[193] See para 8.93.   [194] See para 8.97.   [195] See paras 8.58.2 and 8.60.

[196] In the interests of speed and economy, the parties to a conflict may agree a system of code words for telegrams.

[197] GC III, Art 74. The Telegraph Regulations made under the International Telecom-munications Convention 1992 recommended a special rate for PW telegrams of 25 per cent of the ordinary rate. The UK is a party to the Constitution and Convention of the International Telecommunications Union 1992.

[198] GC III, Art 71. Under this article, the parties to the conflict may allow correspondence in other languages. See PW (Discipline) Regs 1958, App I, paras 35–40 for specimen rules governing correspondence in British PW camps. See also JWP 1–10, 3F, 70.

[199] GC III, Art 71.

which the prisoners of war depend, although this might be done at the request of the detaining power.

Avoidance of delay

8.64 All correspondence must be conveyed as rapidly as possible and must not be delayed or retained for disciplinary reasons. Bags containing prisoner of war mail must be labelled as such, sealed, and addressed to offices of destination.[200]

Individual and collective relief[201]

8.65 Prisoners of war must be allowed to receive individual parcels or collective relief shipments containing items such as food, clothing, medical supplies, and religious, educational, cultural, or recreational articles. This does not absolve the detaining power from its responsibilities for the provision of such articles. Books should not be included in parcels of clothing or food. Medical supplies should, as a rule, be sent in collective parcels. Shipments may not be limited except as proposed by the protecting power in the interests of the prisoners of war themselves or the donor on account of exceptional strain on transport or communications.[202] In the absence of any special agreements between the states concerned, the regulations concerning collective relief annexed to the Convention apply, but these agreements may not restrict the right of the prisoners' representative to collect and distribute collective relief consignments.[203]

Import, postal, and transport charges

8.66 No import, customs, or other dues may be charged on relief shipments for prisoners of war. Postal dues are not to be charged on correspondence, relief shipments, or authorized remittances of money sent to or by prisoners of war through the post. This includes mail to and from the national information bureaux and the Central Prisoners of War Information Agency and to prisoners of war interned in neutral countries. If the post office cannot be used, transport costs are borne by the detaining power and the other parties to the Convention, through whose territory the consignments pass. The word 'territory' has a wide meaning and includes occupied

---

[200] GC III, Art 71. The reference to offices of destination is not explained in the Final Record of the 1949 Diplomatic Conference, nor in the Pictet, *Commentary*. It must be assumed to be a reference to the post offices of destination and, possibly, other offices such as those of the protecting power.   [201] See also JWP 1–10. 3F, 73–76.

[202] GC III, Art 72.

[203] GC III, Art 73. The Regulations Concerning Collective Relief are set out in Appendix C.

territory and territorial waters. Any additional costs must be paid by the sender.[204]

Under the Universal Postal Convention 1974, to which the United Kingdom **8.66.1** is a party, correspondence, insured letters and boxes, postal parcels, and postal money orders addressed to or sent by prisoners of war, either directly or through the information bureaux and the Central Prisoners of War Information Agency are exempt from postal charges. Items should be marked 'Prisoners of War Service'. Postal charges are waived on parcels up to five kilograms, or ten kilograms if the contents cannot be split up, or if the parcel is addressed to the camp or to the prisoners' representative for distribution to prisoners of war.[205]

Special means of transport

If military operations prevent the states concerned from carrying out their **8.67** duty to forward prisoner of war mail and relief parcels, the protecting power, the ICRC, or other approved organizations may move it and also official mail relating to prisoners of war.[206] If so, the states concerned must allow its passage, granting safe conducts[207] where necessary and, if possible, providing transport. In the absence of agreement, the costs are borne proportionately by the parties whose nationals are benefited.

Censorship

The censoring of correspondence must be done as quickly as possible, in **8.68** conditions which will not expose goods to deterioration, and then once only by the despatching and receiving states.[208] Parcels[209] must be examined in the presence of the addressee or of a fellow prisoner of war appointed by him. Relief parcels must not be delayed under pretext of censorship difficulties. If in exceptional circumstances it is necessary for military or political reasons to prohibit correspondence, this must be for as short a period as possible.

LEGAL MATTERS

Military legal status

On capture, prisoners of war become subject to the laws and regulations of **8.69** the armed forces of the detaining power.[210] However, they remain subject to

---

[204] GC III, Art 74. The Convention does not cover transport on or over the high seas otherwise than by post.   [205] Universal Postal Convention 1974, Art 16(1).

[206] GC III, Art 75.   [207] See para 10.34.   [208] GC III, Art 76.

[209] Except in the case of written or printed matter, GC III, Art 76(2).

[210] GC III, Art 82. See para 8.115.

the military law of their own countries and can be dealt with on repatriation for offences committed during captivity.[211]

Civil legal status

8.70 Prisoners of war retain their legal status as citizens of their own state. This status may not be restricted by the detaining power.[212] It means that prisoners of war are free, so far as captivity permits, to take legal steps in their state of origin, for example to dispose of property, make wills, give consent to marriage, or vote. Such action will normally be taken by appointment of an attorney or proxy.

Legal documents

8.71 The detaining power must give prisoners of war all facilities for the preparation and execution of legal documents, especially powers of attorney and wills, and for their transmission through the protecting power or Central Prisoners of War Information Agency.[213] Wills are drawn up in accordance with the law of the state of origin of the prisoner of war. That state must inform the detaining power of the necessary requirements. If the prisoner of war so wishes, the will must be sent to the protecting power and a certified copy of it to the Central Prisoners of War Information Agency. Prisoners of war must be allowed to seek legal advice about the drafting, execution, and authentication of legal documents.[214]

FINANCIAL MATTERS[215]

Camp money

8.72 Until agreement is reached with the protecting power, the detaining power may decide on the maximum amount of cash or vouchers, so-called 'camp money', which prisoners of war may have in their possession.[216] The object of this rule is to prevent prisoners of war having money that might facilitate their escape. Any amount due to prisoners of war above this maximum must be credited to their accounts.[217] This excess may consist of cash taken from prisoners of war at the time of capture,[218] advances of pay,[219] working

---

[211] In the case of members of the British armed forces, see eg, NDA 1957, s 3; AA and AFA 1955, ss 25, 145(2). See also para 8.48.1. After the Korean conflict, the USA tried several members of its armed forces for offences of collaboration whilst in North Korean PW camps.

[212] GC III, Art 14.

[213] GC III, Arts 77 and 120. For the position in respect of disciplinary proceedings, see Art 105 and para 8.133.

[214] This may be done by fellow PW with suitable legal qualifications.

[215] See also JWP 1–10, 3F, 18–30.   [216] GC III, Art 58.   [217] See para 8.79.

[218] See para 8.25(g).   [219] See para 8.74.

pay,[220] or sums sent to the prisoner of war by his government or family. These sums may not be converted into any other currency without the consent of the prisoner of war. If prisoners of war are permitted to buy goods or services outside the camp, they will either pay in cash themselves or the camp authorities will pay and debit their accounts. It is for the detaining power to lay down the appropriate rules.

Cash taken from prisoners of war[221]

Cash taken from and belonging to prisoners of war on capture falls into two **8.73** categories:

a. currency other than that of the detaining power; this is treated in the same way as articles of value and is restored to the prisoner of war on repatriation unless he has earlier requested its conversion;

b. currency of the detaining power (including currency at (a) above which is converted at the request of the prisoner of war); this is credited to his account.[222]

Advances of pay[223]

In the absence of any agreement to the contrary, the Convention provides **8.74** a scale for the monthly advance of pay to be made by the detaining power to all prisoners of war. Rates are given in Swiss francs and are to be converted into the currency of the detaining power. If the amounts designated are unduly high compared with the pay of the detaining power's own forces or are such as would seriously embarrass that power, it may, until a revised agreement has been reached between the belligerents, limit the amount which prisoners of war can draw to a reasonable sum. In the case of those below the rank of sergeant or equivalent, that must be not less than the pay of the forces of the detaining power. The reasons for the limitation must be given immediately to the protecting power. Reimbursement of these advances of pay is to be made by the state to which the prisoner of war belongs to the detaining power at the close of hostilities.[224]

Supplementary pay

The state on which prisoners of war depend may forward additional sums **8.75** for those prisoners of war on condition that they are distributed equally

---

[220] See para 8.77.
[221] GC III, Arts 18 and 59. See also para 8.25.g and JWP 1–10, 3F, 18–30.
[222] See para 8.79.
[223] GC III, Art 60. These rates are now outdated, so an agreement on the matter between the belligerents should be negotiated as quickly as possible   [224] See para 8.181.

between all prisoners of war of the same category.[225] The detaining power must credit these sums to the respective accounts. Prisoners of war must be allowed to draw on these sums in the same way as advances of pay. Supplementary payments do not absolve the detaining power from any of its other pay obligations under the Convention.

Other remittances

8.76 The detaining power must accept and credit to their accounts any other remittances of money addressed to prisoners of war individually or collectively.[226]

Working pay

8.77 Prisoners of war who work must be paid a fair working rate of pay by the detaining authorities direct.[227] The rate is to be paid in the currency of the detaining power and is to be not less than the equivalent of one quarter of a Swiss franc for a full working day. The detaining power must inform prisoners of war and their governments, through the protecting power, of the rate fixed. Since they are doing work that would otherwise have to be done by the employees of the detaining power, working pay is also to be paid to prisoners of war who are permanently assigned to duties connected with the installation and running of the camp as well as those engaged in medical and chaplaincy duties, but not to prisoners of war doing occasional fatigues. The prisoners' representative,[228] his advisers, and assistants are to be paid at a rate to be agreed between the representative and the camp authorities. Payment is made out of the special fund raised from canteen profits.[229] If there is no such fund, the detaining power must pay a fair working rate. The representative's pay could, for example, be fixed on the basis of the average amount payable to other prisoners of war. The Convention is silent as to frequency of payment but it will normally follow the practice for local civilian workers.

Deductions from pay

8.78 The Convention contains no provisions relating to deductions from pay. Therefore no deductions may be made from advances of pay unless authorized as a disciplinary punishment,[230] or by sentence of a court,[231] or in accordance with the military law of the detaining power.[232] Any attempt to avoid

---

[225] GC III, Art 61.   [226] GC III, Art 63.
[227] GC III, Art 62. The rate is now out of date, so an agreement on working pay should be negotiated between the belligerents as quickly as possible. Any national minimum wage in force in the detaining state might be used as the minimum standard for working pay.
[228] See para 8.94.   [229] See para 8.82.   [230] See para 8.127.   [231] See para 8.139.
[232] GC III, Art 82. See PW (Discipline) Regs 1958, reg 40.

these restrictions by obtaining the consent of prisoners of war to a deduction is invalid.[233]

Prisoner of war accounts

The detaining power must keep an account[234] for each prisoner of war, **8.79** showing separately at least the following:

a. amounts due to the prisoner of war or received by him as advances of pay, as working pay, or derived from any other sources;

b. sums taken from him either in the currency of the detaining power or converted into that currency;

c. payments made to the prisoner of war in cash or voucher form;

d. payments made on his behalf and at his request;

e. sums transferred to his home state.[235]

Management of prisoner of war accounts[236]

Each item entered in the account of a prisoner of war must be counter- **8.80** signed or initialled by him or by the prisoners' representative acting on his behalf. Prisoners of war must at all times have reasonable opportunities for consulting and obtaining copies of their accounts. The accounts must be open for inspection by the representatives of the protecting power when they visit the camp. The belligerents may agree to notify each other at regular intervals of the amount standing to the accounts of prisoners of war. Procedures are laid down for the case of transfer of a prisoner of war to another camp[237] and on termination of captivity.[238]

Disposal of funds

Each prisoner of war must have at his disposal the credit balance of his **8.81** account and the detaining power must make such payments as he may request, but subject to any limitations imposed by the detaining power.[239] Again, subject to any essential restrictions imposed by the detaining power, prisoners of war may also have payments made abroad. In that case payments to dependants have priority. A special procedure is laid down to enable prisoners of war to have payments made in their own country, for example to their next of kin.[240] The detaining power debits his account and

---

[233] GC III, Art 7.
[234] GC III, Art 64. Detailed instructions are contained in the Manual of Army Pay Duties.
[235] ie, in accordance with GC III, Art 63. See para 8.81.   [236] GC III, Art 65.
[237] See para 8.103.   [238] See para 8.167.   [239] See paras 8.72 and 8.74.
[240] GC III, Art 63.

sends particulars through the protecting power to his home state, which is then responsible for carrying out the request.[241]

Special fund

8.82 The profits from camp canteens must be paid into a special fund to be used for the benefit of prisoners of war. Their representative is entitled to particip-ate in the management of the canteen and of the fund.[242] The wishes of the prisoners of war should be taken into account as to how the fund should be applied. If prisoners of war are transferred *en bloc* to another camp, the canteen profits should also be transferred. When a camp is closed, any bal-ance in the special fund must be handed to an international welfare organ-ization, to be used for the benefit of prisoners of war of the same nationality as those whose purchases contributed to the fund.[243] In the case of general repatriation, the balance of the fund may be retained by the detaining power subject to any agreement to the contrary between the belligerents.

WORK OF PRISONERS OF WAR[244]

Rank

8.83 Officers may not be compelled to work, but if they ask for it should be given suitable work.[245] Non-commissioned officers can be required to do only supervisory work but may be given other suitable tasks if they so request. Other ranks can be compelled to work if they are fit, having regard to their age, health, sex, and physical aptitude. This is verified by medical examination.[246]

8.83.1 The employment of prisoners of war is of economic value to the detaining power, but is also beneficial to prisoners of war because it helps to reduce some of the harmful effects of captivity and provides a means of earning money.

Authorized work

8.84 Subject to what is said in paragraph 8.83, prisoners of war may be employed as follows:

   a. Permanent medical personnel and chaplains are to be employed only on their professional duties.[247]

---

[241] See GC III, Annex V, Model Regulations, in Annex C. However the rate of exchange for such transfers is not laid down and is subject to the domestic law of the home state.

[242] GC III, Art 28. See JWP 1–10, 3F, 29–30 and 59–62.

[243] See para 8.174. One or more of the relief societies recognized by the detaining power under GC III, Art 125, will be designated by the detaining power and will be responsible for making appropriate use of the fund.   [244] See also JWP 1–10, 3G.

[245] GC III, Art 49.   [246] See para. 8.56.   [247] GC III, Art 33(c).

b. Other personnel with medical or religious qualifications may be employed in their professional capacities, in which case they cannot be made to do any other work.[248]

c. The prisoners' representative, his advisers, and assistants are not to be required to perform any other work if the accomplishment of their duties is thereby made more difficult.[249]

d. Other prisoners may be employed on work within the following categories:[250]

  (1) administration, installation, or maintenance of prisoner of war camps;

  (2) agriculture, even if the produce is used to feed members of the enemy armed forces;

  (3) industries connected with the production or the extraction of raw materials and manufacturing industries (except metallurgical, machinery, and chemical industries); public works and building operations which have no military character or purpose;

  (4) transport and handling of stores which are not military in character or purpose; in the case of mixed war and non-war stores, prisoners of war should not be compelled to deal with them if they are mainly the former;

  (5) commercial business, and arts and crafts;

  (6) domestic service (this would include, for example, service in an officers' mess); and

  (7) public utility services without military character or purpose.

In the case of female prisoners of war, see *Prisoners of War Handling* **8.84.1** (JWP 1–10), Annex 3G, 1.

Dangerous or humiliating work

Prisoners of war may not be assigned to work which would be looked upon **8.85** as humiliating for a member of the detaining power's own forces nor, unless they volunteer, may they be employed on unhealthy or dangerous work such as mine-lifting.[251]

---

[248] GC III, Arts 32 and 36.   [249] GC III, Art 81.

[250] GC III, Art 50. See also PW (Discipline) Regs 1958, reg 4, which requires that, wherever practicable, the Defence Council is to cause a list of the approved types of work to be posted in working camps for PW. See also JWP 1–10. 3G, 3–4.

[251] GC III, Art 52. Argentinian PW who were specialist engineers were used in mine-clearance operations at the end of the Falklands conflict, but all were confirmed by the ICRC to be volunteers.

Complaints

8.86 In the event of any violation of the above provisions on appropriate work, prisoners of war may use their right of complaint.[252]

Working conditions

8.87 The working conditions of prisoners of war must be suitable, with particular regard to accommodation, food, clothing, and equipment, and not below the standard enjoyed by nationals of the detaining power employed on similar work.[253] Account must be taken of climatic conditions. National laws for the safety and protection of workers must be applied to prisoners of war. They should be given equivalent training and protective equipment to that given to nationals of the detaining power. Working conditions may not be made more arduous by disciplinary measures. Suitable working clothes[254] and appropriate additional rations[255] must be supplied. Regular medical examinations must be held to verify the fitness for work of the prisoners of war.[256] They must be paid for the work that they do.[257]

Working hours and rest periods

8.88 The length of the working day for prisoners of war, including travelling time, must not be excessive and should in no case exceed that permitted for civilian workers in the same locality.[258] In deciding what is excessive, regard should be had to work done by civilians and to the recommendations of the International Labour Organization. A rest of at least one hour must be allowed in the middle of each day's work, and another of not less than 24 hours must be allowed each week, preferably on a Sunday or other rest day as is customary in the prisoners' country of origin. Each prisoner of war who has worked for one year must be given a rest period of eight consecutive days during which he receives working pay. Working periods must not be excessive if prisoners of war are employed on piecework.

Accidents at work[259]

8.89 If a prisoner of war is injured or contracts a disease at or because of his work, he must be given the necessary medical treatment. He must also be given a medical certificate, a copy of which must be sent to the Central Prisoners of War Information Agency. This statement must show the nature of the injury or disability, the circumstances in which it arose and particulars of medical or hospital treatment given for it. Any claim for compensation

---

[252] GC III, Arts 50 and 78. See para 8.93. See also JWP 1–10, 3F, 17.   [253] GC III, Art 51.
[254] See para 8.53.   [255] See para 8.50.   [256] See para 8.56.   [257] See para 8.77.
[258] GC II, Art 53. See JWP 1–10, 3G, 10.   [259] For procedure, see JWP 1–10, 3G, 12–13.

must be submitted to the state on which the prisoner of war depends through the protecting power.[260] During captivity a prisoner of war is entitled to whatever benefits are available under the legislation of the detaining power in the event of occupational accidents or diseases.[261]

Labour detachments

For reasons of convenience, working prisoners of war may be lodged near **8.90** their place of work and away from the prisoner of war camp to which they belong. Mobile labour detachments may also be formed. The organization and administration of these detachments must be similar to that of prisoner of war camps. This includes, but is not limited to, the rules on hygiene, food, medical care, correspondence, and parcels. The detachments must be commanded by a member of the regular forces, who may be a non-commissioned officer,[262] but they remain under the control and are administratively part of a camp. The commander of the camp on which they depend retains his disciplinary powers, which cannot be delegated to a non-commissioned officer, and is responsible for ensuring that the Convention is applied to prisoners of war in labour detachments. The commander must keep an up-to-date record of these detachments, which may be visited by agents of the protecting power, the ICRC, and relief societies, as well as by retained medical personnel and chaplains.[263] Detachments should have their own prisoners' representative unless it is administratively feasible for the camp representative to undertake this responsibility.[264]

Private employers

If prisoners of war work for private employers, their treatment must not be **8.91** less favourable than that specified in the Convention.[265] They continue to be under the direct authority of the camp commander, who retains ultimate responsibility for their maintenance, care, treatment, and the payment of working pay. The precise division of responsibilities will be settled by an agreement between the military authorities and the private employer. Such prisoners of war have the right to communicate with the prisoners'

[260] GC III, Arts 54 and 68.

[261] GC III, Art 51. Despite lengthy negotiations between the United Kingdom, Germany, and Italy during WW II, no agreement on this issue could be reached. The British government considered that its domestic workmen's compensation legislation was too complex and so bound up with the conditions of free civilian workers as to make it impracticable to apply it to PW. Its view was that if injured PW received free accommodation, clothing, food, medical, and hospital treatment in respect of injuries sustained at work, they were in fact receiving the equivalent in kind of the benefits received by injured British workers.

[262] In the case of PW in UK hands, he must be at least a warrant officer, see JWP 1–10, 3G, 11.

[263] GC III, Arts 56 and 33(a) respectively.   [264] See para 8.94 onwards.

[265] GC III, Art 57.

representatives of the camp. The private employer has no disciplinary powers over prisoners of war and may not use arms against them if they try to escape, except in self-defence. This means that either military guards must be used or the prisoners of war are released on parole.[266]

CLAIMS, REQUESTS, AND COMPLAINTS

Claims for compensation

8.92 Claims arising from accidents at work are dealt with in paragraph 8.89. In cases involving death, see paragraph 8.164. Personal property, money, or valuables impounded[267] and subsequently lost through the alleged fault of the detaining power or of any of its servants, or not returned on repatriation, must be dealt with as follows:[268]

    a. Items needed by a prisoner of war during captivity, such as clothing, spectacles, or medical instruments, must be replaced by the detaining power and become the property of the prisoner of war concerned.

    b. Claims in respect of any other items must be submitted to the power on which the prisoner of war depends. The detaining power must supply him with a certificate, signed by a responsible officer, giving the reasons why the property has not been returned. The detaining power is, for example, not responsible for personal belongings of prisoners of war that they are unable to carry with them. A copy of the certificate is to be sent to the power on which the prisoner of war depends through the Central Prisoners of War Information Agency.

Requests and complaints

8.93 Prisoners of war have the right to make requests in respect of their conditions of captivity to the military authorities of the detaining power.[269] They also have the right to complain about such matters to the protecting power. This may be done either directly or through the prisoners' representative. No restrictions may be placed on requests and complaints, nor may they be included in the correspondence quota mentioned in paragraph 8.62. They must be transmitted immediately. Even if a request or complaint is unfounded, the prisoner of war making it may not be punished. This does not prevent punishment for abusive or insubordinate language or conduct accompanying a request or complaint. If it is established that complaints have been made solely in order to inconvenience the authorities of the detaining power, the immunity would not apply. Periodic reports on conditions in

---

[266] See para 8.104 onwards. See also JWP 1–10, 3G, 14f.
[267] See para 8.25(f), (g), (h).   [268] GC III, Art 68.
[269] GC III, Art 78. See also PW (Discipline) Regs 1958, reg 41.

the camps and on the needs of the prisoners of war may be sent by prisoners' representatives to the protecting power.

PRISONERS' REPRESENTATIVE

Appointment

Wherever there are prisoners of war, regardless of their number, there must **8.94** be a prisoners' representative whom prisoners of war may freely consult.[270] The representative must have the same nationality, language, and customs as the prisoners of war he represents. If there are different national groups in one camp, each group must have its own representative.

The procedure is as follows: **8.94.1**

a. In *camps for officers*[271] the senior prisoner of war officer acts as prisoners' representative, assisted by advisers chosen by the prisoners of war.

b. In *camps where commissioned and non-commissioned prisoners of war*[272] *are mixed*, the senior prisoner of war officer acts as prisoners' representative, assisted by other rank prisoners of war elected by the other ranks.

c. In *labour camps* the prisoner of war officer stationed there to carry out administrative duties may be elected prisoners' representative. If he is, his assistants must be chosen by the other rank prisoners of war from among their number.

d. In *other rank camps* the prisoners of war elect representatives by secret ballot held once every six months, or in the event of a vacancy. Representatives are eligible for re-election.

For representatives of female prisoners of war the procedure is the same, **8.94.2** see JWP 1–10, 3F, 14.

Approval by detaining power

All elected representatives must be approved by the detaining power **8.95** before they have the right to commence their duties.[273] If approval is not given the protecting power must be informed of the reasons.

Duties of prisoners' representative

The general duty of the prisoners' representative is to promote the **8.96** physical, spiritual, and intellectual welfare of his fellow prisoners of war.[274]

---

[270] GC III, Arts 79 and 81.
[271] Or those of equivalent status, eg, those falling under GC III, Art 4A(4) or (5).
[272] Or those of equivalent status, eg, those falling under GC III, Art 4A(4) or (5).
[273] GC III, Art 79.   [274] GC III, Art 80.

He represents them in dealings with the military authorities of the detaining power, the protecting power, the ICRC, and relief organizations helping prisoners of war. Although he is their spokesman he cannot be held responsible, simply because of his position, for offences committed by prisoners of war.

8.96.1 Apart from this general duty, the Convention lays down specific duties. The duties of the prisoners' representative include those listed below:

a. ensuring that the Convention is complied with and taking steps to correct breaches;

b. attending interviews with visiting agents of the protecting power or the ICRC;

c. dealing with a legal advice service and legal documents;[275]

d. dealing with requests, complaints, and periodic reports;[276]

e. ensuring that prisoners of war under detention receive proper treatment;[277]

f. proposing repatriation and participating in the mixed medical commission;[278]

g. monitoring inquiries into deaths and serious injuries of prisoners of war;[279]

h. collecting and distributing collective relief consignments[280] and holding in trust parcels and remittances for prisoners of war undergoing confinement;[281]

i. assisting in the management of canteens and their special funds;[282]

j. monitoring disciplinary sanctions imposed on prisoners of war;[283]

k. receiving communications concerning judicial proceedings against prisoners of war;[284]

l. forwarding receipts for relief consignments to relief organizations;[285]

m. arranging with the camp commander for the movement of their luggage and communal property in the event of the transfer of prisoners of war to another location;[286]

n. keeping in touch with prisoners' representatives in subordinate detachments and representing prisoners of war working for private employers;[287]

[275] See para 8.71.   [276] See para 8.93.   [277] See para 8.123.   [278] See para 8.152.
[279] See para 8.164.
[280] See para 8.65. See also GC III, Annex III, Regulations Concerning Collective Relief, in Annex C.   [281] See para 8.129 (f).
[282] See paras 8.52 and 8.82.   [283] See para 8.128.   [284] See paras 8.132 and 8.140.
[285] See para 8.174.   [286] See para 8.102.   [287] See paras 8.90 and 8.91.

o. informing prisoners of war of regulations, orders, and notices issued by the detaining power;[288]

p. counter-signing entries on prisoner of war accounts;[289]

q. counter-signing notifications of payments sent by prisoners of war to their own state.[290]

Rights of prisoners' representative[291]

The rights of the prisoners' representative include those listed below: **8.97**

a. not to do other work if to do so would interfere with his representative duties;

b. to appoint fellow prisoners of war as advisers or assistants in accordance with his requirements;

c. to have the necessary facilities to enable him to carry out his duties, including the inspection of labour detachments and the receipt of relief supplies;

d. to correspond by post and telegraph with the detaining authorities, the protecting power, the ICRC, and their delegates, mixed medical commissions, and relief organizations;[292]

e. if he is a representative at a labour detachment, to conduct correspondence with the prisoners' representative at the main camp;

f. in the event of transfer, to have a proper handover to his successor;

g. to visit locations where the prisoners of war he represents are detained and to communicate freely with them;

h. to be paid.[293]

Prisoners' representative's assistants

In larger camps a prisoners' representative may need help in discharging **8.98** his duties and his right to appoint assistants is specifically recognized.[294] The approval of the detaining power is not required. Assistants act under the general direction of the prisoners' representative and have the same privileges. These assistants may include legal advisers, interpreters, clerks, and storekeepers who will be exempt from other work and entitled to be paid[295] to the same extent as the prisoners' representative.

---

[288] See para 8.45.   [289] See para 8.80.

[290] See para 8.81 and GC III, Annex V, Model Regulations, in Appendix C.

[291] GC III, Art 81.

[292] This is in addition to the correspondence quota mentioned in para 8.62.

[293] See para 8.77.

[294] GC III, Art 81. Art 62 also refers to advisers. As indicated in para 8.98, the prisoners' representative's assistants may include advisers.   [295] See para 8.77.

Dismissal of prisoners' representative

8.99 The detaining power has the right to dismiss elected prisoners' representatives, but must inform the protecting power of its reasons.[296] The prisoners of war themselves have no right to dismiss their elected representatives but can ask the detaining power to do so. In any event the appointment lapses after six months, when a new election must be held.[297]

H. TRANSFER OF PRISONERS OF WAR[298]

Conditions for Transfer

8.100 The movement[299] of prisoners of war from one camp to another must be carried out humanely and in conditions not less favourable than those for the forces of the detaining power.[300] Account must be taken of the interests of the prisoners of war, in particular so as not to increase the difficulty of their repatriation, for example, for geographical reasons. A complete list of prisoners of war to be transferred must be made before their departure and the information bureau is to be informed of the transfer.[301] Adequate precautions must be taken for the safety and health of the prisoners of war during transfer and they must be given sufficient food, drinking water, clothing, shelter, and medical attention.[302] These provisions do not prevent the detaining power from taking reasonable steps to prevent the escape of prisoners of war whilst in transit.

Circumstances Precluding Transfer

8.101 Sick or wounded prisoners of war must not be transferred if such a move would prejudice their recovery, unless their safety imperatively demands it.[303] If fighting draws near to a camp, prisoners of war in that camp should not be moved from it unless this can be done safely or unless they would be exposed to greater danger by remaining where they are than by being transferred.

Procedure for Transfer

8.102 Prisoners of war must be officially notified in advance of impending departure and of their new postal address so that they can pack their

---

[296] GC III, Art 81. An *ex officio* prisoners' representative (eg, the senior PW officer) can only be removed by transfer to another camp.   [297] GC III, Art 79.
[298] For the procedure, see JWP 1–10, 3H.   [299] See para 8.180.   [300] GC III, Art 46.
[301] See para 8.182.1(b).
[302] In the *Heering Trial* (1946) 11 WCR 79–80, the accused was convicted of ill-treatment of prisoners on a march from Marienburg to Brunswick. See also the *Baba Masao Trial* (1946) 11 WCR 56–61.   [303] GC III, Art 47.

luggage and inform their next of kin.[304] Mail addressed to their former camp must be forwarded without delay. They must be allowed to take personal property with them. The detaining power may, if the conditions of transfer so require,[305] limit the amount of personal property to what each prisoner of war can carry, not exceeding 25 kilograms each. The camp commander is responsible for arranging, in agreement with the prisoners' representative, for the movement of luggage and common property that cannot be carried by the prisoners of war.[306] The cost of transfer must be met by the detaining power.

Accounts

When prisoners of war are transferred from one camp to another their per- **8.103**
sonal accounts[307] go with them.[308] If prisoners of war are transferred from one detaining power to another,[309] any money belonging to them which is not in the currency of the former detaining power also goes with them. Certificates must be issued showing the amount standing to their credit.

I. PAROLE OF PRISONERS OF WAR

Release on Parole

An alternative to internment in a prisoner of war camp is release on **8.104**
parole.[310] This may be either permanent or temporary provided that it is permissible under the law of the power on which the prisoner of war depends.[311] On the outbreak of hostilities, each state involved must notify the enemy of its laws and regulations relating to parole.

Effect of Parole

A prisoner of war may be partially or wholly released on parole, that is, in **8.105**
return for an undertaking not to escape and rejoin his own armed forces.[312] It is preferable for the precise terms of the parole to be in writing, signed by the prisoner of war, to avoid doubt about its conditions. A duplicate should be sent to the state on which the prisoner of war depends. Prisoners of war who are paroled are bound on their personal honour to observe scrupulously the conditions of parole. The state on which they depend is bound not to require or accept any service from them that would be incompatible with those conditions.

---

[304] GC III, Art 48.   [305] eg, in the event of transport limitations.
[306] See para 8.96.1(m).   [307] See para 8.80.   [308] GC III, Art 65.
[309] See para 8.27.   [310] GC III, Art 21; see also HR, Art 10.   [311] See para 8.108.
[312] GC III, Art 21; see also HR, Art 11.

Acceptance and Grant of Parole

8.106 A prisoner of war may not be compelled to accept release on parole,[313] nor is the detaining power obliged to grant it.[314]

Breach of Parole

8.107 Recaptured prisoners of war may be tried for the offence of breach of parole, but retain prisoner of war status.[315]

United Kingdom Practice

8.108 As a matter of United Kingdom practice, personnel of its armed forces are not permitted either to seek or to be granted parole.[316] However, temporary parole may be authorized for limited periods to enable a prisoner of war to perform acts that materially contribute to the health or welfare of himself or of his fellow prisoners of war. Other ranks may generally only give their parole through a commissioned officer of the British forces or, in the absence of such an officer, through a non-commissioned officer exercising authority, such as when acting as prisoners' representative.

J. ESCAPE OF PRISONERS OF WAR

Punishment for Escape

8.109 The law of armed conflict makes allowance for the fact that many states require members of their armed forces who become prisoners of war to endeavour to escape.[317] It therefore provides that successful escapes shall not be punished in the event of subsequent recapture and that unsuccessful escapes can only be made the subject of disciplinary action.[318]

---

[313] GC III, Art 21; see also HR, Art 11.   [314] HR, Art 11.

[315] GC III, Arts 5, 21, and 85. HR, Art 12, which provided that such conduct resulted in forfeiture of the right to be treated as a PW, has been superseded.

[316] eg, during WW II, the Army Council issued an instruction that British officers should refuse parole, remaining as PW until escape, repatriation, or exchange. Unless there were specific instructions to the contrary, this also applied to those interned in neutral countries.

[317] eg, AA 1955 and AFA 1955, s 145(2)(b) permit forfeiture of pay of a soldier or airman who as a PW fails to take reasonable steps to rejoin HM service. See also NDA 1957, s 3(1)(e), which places a duty on those subject to the NDA to escape from custody as PW, but there is no equivalent provision in the NDA permitting forfeiture of pay.

[318] GC III, Art 91. See paras 8.124–8.129.

Successful Escapes

An escape is regarded as successful[319] if a prisoner of war: **8.110**

a. joins the armed forces either of the state on which he depends or those of an ally; or

b. leaves the territory under the control of the detaining power and its allies; or

c. joins a ship flying the flag of the state on which he depends, or that of an ally, in the territorial waters of the detaining power, the ship not being under the control of the detaining power.

The general principle is that the prisoner of war must have actually gone **8.110.1** beyond the reach of the detaining power.[320] A neutral state which allows an escaped prisoner to remain in its territory may place him in an assigned residence.[321]

Unsuccessful Escapes[322]

A prisoner of war who attempts to escape but is recaptured before **8.111** 'succeeding' as defined in paragraph 8.110 is liable only to disciplinary punishment,[323] even if it is not a first offence. A recaptured prisoner of war must be handed over without delay to the competent military authority, not to a civil or quasi-military organization. He remains a prisoner of war and must be treated accordingly. Although, as a general rule, prisoners of war who have served their sentences may not be treated any differently from others,[324] those who have attempted to escape may be subjected to special surveillance. This must take place in the prisoner of war camp and must not involve the loss of any of the safeguards granted by the Convention nor have any adverse effect on their health.[325]

[319] GC III, Art 91. For PW in British hands, see PW (Discipline) Regs 1958, regs 5(3) and 39.

[320] A PW who merely escapes from the territory of the detaining power to the territory of one of that power's allies, will not be deemed to have escaped successfully. However, if he reaches neutral territory or joins a vessel belonging to his own, an allied, or neutral state beyond the territorial sea of the detaining power, the escape will be deemed to be successful. The position of an escaper who leaves that territorial sea under his own auspices, eg, on a raft, is unclear, see Y Sandoz, C Swinarski, and B Zimmermann (eds), *Commentary on the Additional Protocols of 8 June 1977 to the Geneva Conventions of 12 August 1949* (1987) (*ICRC Commentary*) vol III, 447, n 2.   [321] HC V, Art 13.

[322] GC III, Art 92. For PW in British hands, see PW (Discipline) Regs 1958, regs 5(1) and 39. See also JWP 1–10, 3F, 9b   [323] ie, those punishments listed in para 8.127.

[324] See para 8.120.

[325] One of the purposes of these articles is to render clearly unlawful the practice resorted to during WW II of handing over recaptured PW to non-military agencies such as the Gestapo or the concentration camp service, see the *Wielen and others Trial (The Stalag Luft III Case)* (1947) 11 WCR 31–52.

OFFENCES COMMITTED WHILE ESCAPING[326]

8.112 Prisoners of war who commit offences solely to facilitate escape and which do not involve violence against life or limb may only be awarded disciplinary punishment[327] for those offences.[328] In respect of other offences, the fact that they were committed in the course of an attempted escape must not be regarded as an aggravating circumstance, even if the offender is one who frequently escapes. Prisoners of war who aid or abet others to escape are also liable to disciplinary punishment only.

NOTIFICATION OF ESCAPE AND RECAPTURE

8.113 If an escaped prisoner is recaptured, the state on which he depends must be notified if his escape was notified.[329]

K. PUNISHMENT OF PRISONERS OF WAR

INTRODUCTION

8.114 The rules on this subject are dealt with under three main headings:

    a. general principles applicable at all times;[330]

    b. 'disciplinary measures',[331] which means punishment by the commander of the prisoner of war camp and is equivalent to summary disposal by a commanding officer;[332]

    c. 'judicial proceedings',[333] which means trial and punishment by a court having jurisdiction to try prisoners of war and is equivalent to trial by court-martial under the Naval Discipline Act 1957, the Army Act 1955, or the Air Force Act 1955, or by a civil court for a civil offence.[334]

GENERAL PRINCIPLES

The law applicable

8.115 Prisoners of war are subject to the laws, regulations, and orders in force in the armed forces of the detaining power and can be punished for offences they

---

[326] GC III, Art 93.   [327] That is, those punishments listed in para 8.127.
[328] Examples of such offences are those against public property, theft without intention of personal gain, the drawing up or use of false papers, and the wearing of civilian clothes.
[329] GC III, Arts 94 and 122.   [330] GC III, Arts 82–88. See paras 8.115–8.123.
[331] GC III, Arts 89–98.   [332] See paras 8.124–8.129.   [333] GC III, Arts 99–108.
[334] See paras 8.130–8.145.

commit against such laws, regulations, or orders.[335] However, no proceedings may be taken or punishments given except as permitted by the Convention.[336] A prisoner of war also remains subject to the service law of his country of origin and can be dealt with on repatriation for outstanding offences.[337]

By United Kingdom law, prisoners of war held in the custody of the United Kingdom are subject to the ordinary criminal and civil law, subject to certain modifications that follow from prisoner of war status. An example of a modification of the law is the rule that a prisoner of war, unless released on parole in the United Kingdom, is debarred from obtaining a writ of *habeas corpus* to test the lawfulness of his detention.[338] **8.115.1**

Choice of disciplinary or judicial proceedings

In deciding whether to deal summarily by disciplinary measures with offences or to proceed by way of judicial proceedings, the competent authority should exercise leniency and choose disciplinary action wherever possible.[339] **8.116**

Factors to be taken into account include the lack of allegiance[340] owed by the prisoner of war to the detaining power, his duty to escape and rejoin his armed forces, and his duty not to assist the detaining power beyond his obligations under the Convention.[341] **8.116.1**

In two circumstances the offence must be dealt with on a disciplinary basis: **8.117**

a. where an act is punishable only if committed by a prisoner of war and not if committed by a member of the armed forces of the detaining power;[342]

b. where the offence is one of attempted escape,[343] or of an act intended to facilitate escape but not involving violence, or of aiding and abetting escape.[344]

Judicial proceedings, mode of trial

Where there are to be judicial proceedings, prisoners of war are normally to be tried by military courts. If the law of the detaining power permits the trial by civil court of members of its own armed forces for particular offences, the civil courts may try prisoners of war under the same conditions. **8.118**

[335] GC III, Art 82.
[336] GC III, Art 82. See also Arts 82–108. See, further, paras 8.130–8.145.
[337] See para 8.48.
[338] *R v Superintendent of Vine Street Police Station, ex p Liebmann* [1916] 1 KB 268, upheld in *R v Bottrill, ex p Kuechenmeister* [1947] 1 KB 41.   [339] GC III, Art 83.
[340] GC III, Art 87. It is not clear whether captives of the nationality of the detaining power are entitled to PW status.   [341] See eg, AA 1955, ss 25, 145.
[342] GC III, Art 82.   [343] See para 8.111.   [344] GC III, Arts 92 and 93.

However, trial may only take place if the court is independent and impartial and the accused is given due rights of defence.[345]

8.118.1 A prisoner of war in the custody of the United Kingdom may, in certain cases, be dealt with by the civil courts,[346] but, if he is to be tried for a grave breach of the Geneva Conventions or Additional Protocol I committed in the United Kingdom, he must be tried by a civil court.[347] For such offences committed overseas, he may be tried by a military court.

Offences committed before capture

8.119 Even if convicted under the laws of the detaining power for offences, including war crimes, committed before capture, prisoners of war retain prisoner of war status and the benefits of the Convention.[348]

8.119.1 This protection only extends to persons entitled to prisoner of war status and does not include mercenaries, spies, or combatants who fail to carry their arms openly during deployments and engagements.[349]

One offence, one punishment

8.120 A prisoner of war may not be punished more than once for the same act or on the same charge.[350] Those who have served their sentences must not be treated differently from other prisoners of war.[351]

---

[345] GC III, Art 84. See para 8.133.

[346] See, eg, AA 1955, ss 70(4) (n 19 in MML I), s 133. See also GCA 1957, s 1(5).

[347] GCA 1957, s 1A. The same applies to war crimes which cannot be charged as civil offences, see PW (Discipline) Regs 1958, regs 6 and 7.

[348] GC III, Art 85. For the rights of accused persons, see para 8.133. For the special rules governing the treatment of convicted persons, see para 8.143 (death sentences) and 8.144 (imprisonment). The word 'laws' is sufficiently wide to include international law binding on the detaining power (see also GC III, Art 99). See further, *US v Noriega* (1997) 99 ILR 143.

[349] See paras 4.9, 4.10, 8.6.1, 8.12, and 8.13. Several states entered a reservation to the effect that PW convicted under the law of the detaining power 'in accordance with the principles of the Nuremberg trial, of war crimes and crimes against humanity, must be treated in the same manner as persons convicted in the country in question' that is, not as PW. The precise wording of the reservations differed slightly, see Roberts and Guelff, *Documents*, 364–365. The effect of this reservation is to deprive people of PW status once convicted of these crimes and the sentence has become legally enforceable. The UK regards these reservations as being incompatible with the spirit of the Convention and does not recognize them as being valid. The UK made declarations to that effect on ratification and subsequently, see Roberts and Guelff, *Documents*, 367. For an explanation of the reservations, see Pictet, *Commentary*, vol III, 423–425. However, several states have recently withdrawn their reservations to the Geneva Conventions 1949, namely, Belarus on 7 August 2001, Bulgaria on 9 May 1994, Czech Republic on 27 September 2001, Hungary on 31 May 2000, Romania on 24 June 2002, and Slovakia on 5 June 2000.

[350] GC III, Art 86. See, eg, AA 1955, ss 133, 134 and PW (Discipline) Regs 1958, reg 36.

[351] GC III, Art 88. But see para 8.111 as to persons punished for attempting to escape.

Punishment principles

The following punishments are forbidden: **8.121**

a. collective punishments for individual acts;
b. corporal punishment;
c. imprisonment in premises without daylight;[352]
d. any form of torture or cruelty;
e. deprivation of rank or of the right to wear badges.

Subject to the above, prisoners of war may only be sentenced to punish- **8.122**
ments that may be awarded to members of the armed forces of the detaining power for similar offences.[353] For maximum punishments awardable
on summary dealing, see paragraph 8.127. The courts and authorities of the
detaining power, in reaching decisions on punishment, must at all times
remember that the accused:

a. does not owe any allegiance[354] to the detaining power and may be, for
   example, under a duty to escape;

b. is in its power through circumstances beyond his control so that, for
   example, depression brought on by captivity should not be regarded as
   self-induced.

Courts and disciplinary authorities must be free to reduce the penalty
below the minimum prescribed for members of the armed forces of the
detaining power.

Prisoners undergoing punishment

Prisoners of war undergoing punishment must not be treated more **8.123**
severely than members of the armed forces of the detaining power of
equivalent rank undergoing the same punishment.[355] For women, treatment must neither be more severe than that for males nor more severe than
that for women members of the forces of the detaining power of equivalent
rank undergoing the same punishment. The only exception to these rules
relates to special surveillance of prisoners of war who have attempted to
escape.[356]

---

[352] This may cause problems in some modern high security prisons. See *US v Noriega* (1997),
99 ILR 143.   [353] See GC III, Art 87. See also PW (Discipline) Regs 1958, regs 5–7.

[354] It is not clear whether captives of the nationality of the detaining power are entitled to
PW status.   [355] GC III, Art 88.

[356] See para 8.111. In addition, PW who have served their sentences must not be treated
differently from other PW, see para 8.120.

DISCIPLINARY MEASURES

Authority who may take disciplinary measures

8.124 Only the camp commander or the officer acting in his place or to whom he has delegated his powers may award disciplinary punishment. Moreover, this right cannot be delegated to other ranks or to prisoners of war.[357]

Rights of accused

8.125 Before any disciplinary award is announced, the accused must be given precise information regarding the offences of which he is accused and an opportunity to explain his conduct and defend himself.[358] He must be allowed to call witnesses and, if necessary, be given the services of a qualified interpreter.

Investigation of offences and confinement before hearing

8.126 Offences against discipline must be investigated immediately.[359] The accused may not be kept in confinement pending the hearing unless either a member of the armed forces of the detaining power accused of a similar offence would be so kept, or it is essential in the interests of camp order and discipline. This period of confinement must be as brief as possible and must not exceed 14 days. The provisions of paragraph 8.129 apply equally to those in confinement awaiting disciplinary action.[360]

Powers of punishment

8.127 The only disciplinary punishments that may be awarded are:

    a. a fine not exceeding 50 per cent of advances of pay and working pay for a period of 30 days;

    b. discontinuance of any additional privileges for not more than 30 days;

    c. fatigue duties[361] not exceeding two hours a day (not applicable to officers) for not more than 30 days;

    d. confinement for not more than 30 days.

8.127.1 No punishment may be inhuman, brutal, or dangerous to health.[362] Any period of pre-trial confinement must be deducted from the award. A single punishment is to be awarded for a single offence.[363] Separate punishments

---

[357] GC III, Art 96. As to PW in British hands, see PW (Discipline) Regs 1958, reg 19.
[358] GC III, Art 96.   [359] GC III, Art 96.   [360] GC III, Art 95.
[361] The normal rules on work apply to fatigues, see paras 8.84–8.91.
[362] GC III, Arts 89 and 90. As to PW in British hands, see PW (Discipline) Regs 1958, reg 10.
[363] GC III, Art 86.

may be awarded for separate offences dealt with at the same time but the aggregate of the punishments awarded must not exceed 30 days. The period between pronouncement of an award and its execution must not exceed one month. When a further disciplinary punishment is awarded, there must be an interval of at least three days between the execution of any two of the punishments if the duration of one of them is ten days or more.[364]

Announcement of award

The decision must be announced to the accused and to the prisoners' repres- **8.128** entative. A record of disciplinary punishments must be maintained by the camp commander and must be open to inspection by representatives of the protecting power.[365]

Conditions under which summary disciplinary punishment may be served

Certain specific standards are laid down.[366] **8.129**

a. *Premises.* Prisoners of war must not be transferred to prisons, detention centres, or the equivalent. Places for service of sentences must conform to the requirements of paragraphs 8.49 and 8.54. Officers and those of equivalent status must not be lodged with other ranks. Women must be quartered separately from males and be under the immediate supervision of women.

b. *Protection.* Prisoners of war sentenced to confinement remain entitled to all the benefits of the Convention, except those necessarily rendered inapplicable by the fact of confinement. In no case, however, may they be deprived of the right to make requests and complaints or to deal with representatives of the protecting power or the ICRC.

c. *Rank.* Privileges attaching to rank may not be removed.

d. *Exercise.* Prisoners of war must be allowed to take exercise and to be in the open air for at least two hours every day.

e. *Medical.* Prisoners of war must be allowed, at their request, to attend the daily medical inspection and must be given all necessary medical attention and, if need be, removed to the camp infirmary or to a hospital.

f. *Correspondence.* The right to read, write, send, and receive letters is unaffected. Parcels and remittances of money, however, may be withheld

---

[364] GC III, Art 90. For example, a sentence of seven days fatigues pronounced on 1 January must commence not later than 1 February. If it commences on 1 January, a subsequent award of seven days confinement pronounced on 4 January may commence at any time up to 4 February. An award of ten days confinement pronounced on 4 January, however, must commence not before 11 January and not later than 4 February. [365] GC III, Art 96.
[366] GC III, Arts 97 and 98.

until completion of punishment, being entrusted meanwhile to the prisoners' representative who must hand over perishable goods to the camp infirmary.

g. *Repatriation.*[367] No prisoner of war who has been awarded a disciplinary punishment and who qualifies for repatriation or for accommodation in a neutral country may be retained on the ground that he has not completed his punishment.

JUDICIAL PROCEEDINGS

The law applicable

8.130 No prisoner of war may be tried or sentenced for an act that was not an offence under either the law of the detaining power or the international law in force at the time of its commission.[368]

Prohibition of coercion

8.131 No moral or physical coercion may be exerted on a prisoner of war to induce him to admit his guilt of any offence charged.[369] This rule would exclude, for example, the use of hypnosis, drugs, and oppressive methods of questioning.

Notification of proceedings

8.132 In any case in which the detaining power decides to institute judicial proceedings against a prisoner of war, that power must notify the protecting power and the prisoners' representative as soon as possible and at least three weeks before the opening of the trial.[370] The period of three weeks runs from the date of receipt of the notification by the protecting power and the notification must contain the following information:

a. full names, rank, number, date of birth, and profession or trade (if any) of the prisoner of war;

b. the place of internment or confinement;

c. the charge or charges on which the prisoner of war is to be arraigned with the relevant legal provisions;

---

[367] GC III, Art 115.

[368] GC III, Art 99. The reference to international law shows that the article contemplates trials for war crimes as well as for other offences. See also para 8.119.   [369] GC III, Art 99.

[370] GC III, Art 104. For PW in British hands, see PW (Discipline) Regs 1958, reg 25 and GCA 1957, s 2.

d. the court which will try the case, and the date and place for the opening of the trial.

Rights of defence[371]

In good time before the trial to enable him to exercise them, the accused **8.133** must be informed of his rights to:

a. be assisted by a fellow prisoner of war;
b. be defended by a qualified advocate or counsel of his own choice;
c. call witnesses;
d. have the services of a competent interpreter.

If he fails to choose an advocate, the protecting power must do so for him **8.133.1** and be given at least one week for that purpose. The detaining power must, on request, supply the protecting power with a list of persons qualified to conduct the defence. If neither the accused nor the protecting power appoint an advocate, the detaining power must do so.

Particulars of the charge or charges, as well as any documents which have **8.133.2** by law normally to be handed to an accused person serving in the armed forces of the detaining power, must be given to the accused in a language which he understands, and also to his defending counsel, in good time before the opening of the trial.

The defending advocate must have at least two weeks before the opening of **8.133.3** the trial for preparation of the defence. Up to the expiry of time for appeal or petition, he must be given all the necessary facilities including the following rights:

a. to visit the accused and interview him privately;
b. to interview defence witnesses, including prisoners of war.

The Convention is silent as to responsibility for payment of defence **8.133.4** counsel. In the absence of any legal aid scheme, the person or authority appointing him will be liable for such costs. Agreements for reimbursement will be a matter for negotiation between the powers concerned.

Investigation

Investigation of charges must be carried out as rapidly as circumstances **8.134** permit so that the trial can take place as soon as possible.[372]

---

[371] GC III, Arts 99 and 105. For PW in British hands, see PW (Discipline) Regs 1958, reg 26 and GCA 1957, s 3.   [372] GC III, Art 103.

Pre-trial confinement[373]

8.135 A prisoner of war must not be kept in confinement while awaiting trial unless either a member of the armed forces of the detaining power would be so confined if accused of a similar offence, or confinement is essential for reasons of national security. In no case may such confinement exceed three months. The rules set out in paragraph 8.129 also apply to prisoners of war in pre-trial confinement. The period spent in confinement awaiting trial must be deducted from any sentence of imprisonment passed on a prisoner of war and taken into account in fixing the penalty.

Bars to trial and conviction

8.136 No prisoner of war may be convicted unless he has had an opportunity to present his defence with the assistance of a legally qualified advocate or counsel.[374] At the opening of the trial, evidence must be submitted as to due receipt (at least three weeks before the opening of the trial) of the notification of the trial by the protecting power, the prisoner of war himself and the prisoners' representative.[375]Otherwise the trial cannot take place and must be adjourned.[376]

Attendance of representatives of the protecting power at the trial[377]

8.137 Representatives of the protecting power have the right to attend the hearing except when it is held *in camera* for security reasons, in which event the protecting power must be notified.

Evidence

8.138 The ordinary laws of evidence applying at trials of members of the armed forces of the detaining power also apply to trials of prisoners of war.[378]

Sentence

8.139 The general rules are set out in paragraph 8.121. Sentence may be passed on a prisoner of war only by the same courts and in accordance with the same

---

[373] GC III, Art 103. For circumstances in which members of the British armed forces are kept in pre-trial close arrest, see BR 11, Arts 0202–08, QR (Army) 6.005 and MAFL, vol I, ch III, para 16. For PW in British hands, see PW (Discipline) Regs 1958, reg 11.   [374] GC III, Art 99.
[375] See para 8.132.
[376] GC III, Art 104. This article must be read in conjunction with Art 10 (including the various reservations to that article, see Roberts and Guelff, *Documents*, 362–369) and AP I, Art 5.
[377] GC III, Art 105.
[378] GC III, Art 102. By UK service law, rules of evidence before courts-martial are those observed by civil courts in England, see BR 11, Art 1202 and NCMGO 67, AA 1955 and AFA 1955, s 99(1).

procedures as for members of the armed forces of the detaining power and only if the requirements of the Convention outlined in paragraphs 8.130–8.138 have been complied with.[379] The period spent in pre-trial confinement must be deducted from any sentence of imprisonment and taken into account in fixing any other punishment.[380] For special provisions relating to the death penalty, see paragraph 8.143.

Notification of outcome of trial

The verdict and sentence passed on a prisoner of war must be reported **8.140** immediately to the protecting power.[381] The report in the form of a summary must also indicate whether the prisoner has the right of appeal. A copy must be sent to the prisoners' representative and another to the prisoner of war, in a language that he understands, if the sentence was not pronounced in his presence.

Appeals

Every prisoner of war must be given the same rights of petition and appeal **8.141** against finding and sentence as members of the armed forces of the detaining power and must be fully informed of those rights and of any time-limits.[382] He may at any time abandon his appeal by giving notice and in that event, as in the case where a prisoner of war decides to use his right of appeal, the detaining power must notify the protecting power.[383]

Notification of final conviction[384]

When the conviction of a prisoner of war becomes legally effective or **8.142** a death sentence is pronounced, the detaining power must send the protecting power written details of:

a. the precise wording of the finding and sentence;

b. a summarized report of any preliminary investigation and of the trial, emphasizing in particular the elements of the prosecution and defence cases;

c. notification, where applicable, of the establishment where the sentence will be served or carried out.

---

[379] GC III, Art 102. For sentences which can be imposed by PW courts-martial, see PW (Discipline) Regs 1958, regs 7–9.

[380] GC III, Art 103. For PW in British hands, see PW (Discipline) Regs 1958, reg 9 and GCA 1957, s 5.   [381] GC III, Art 107.

[382] GC III, Art 106. For rights of petition and appeal of PW in British hands, see PW (Discipline) Regs 1958, reg 31 and GCA 1957, s 4, CM(A)A 1968, s 56, Sch 3.

[383] GC III, Art 107.   [384] GC III, Art 107. See also PW (Discipline) Regs 1958, reg 30.

Special rules on death sentences

8.143 Death sentences may not be imposed by United Kingdom courts, nor may United Kingdom service personnel or officials assist in any way in the implementation of death sentences, for example, by other states or by local courts. For states whose laws permit death sentences, the following rules of the Convention apply.

8.143.1 Prisoners of war and the protecting power must be informed as soon as possible of the offences that are punishable by death under the laws of the detaining power. Other offences may not thereafter be made punishable by death without the agreement of the power on which the prisoners of war depend.[385]

8.143.2 A death sentence may not be pronounced on a prisoner of war unless the attention of the court has been particularly drawn to the fact that the accused:

a. is not a national of the detaining power and is not bound to it by any duty of allegiance;[386]

b. is in the power of the detaining power through circumstances outside his control.[387]

8.143.3 A death sentence may not be carried out until at least six months from the date when the protecting power receives the detailed notification referred to in paragraph 8.142.[388]

Conditions under which sentences are served

8.144 Sentences are to be served in the same establishments and under the same conditions as for members of the armed forces of the detaining power similarly sentenced, provided that they also conform to the basic requirements of health and humanity.[389] Women sentenced to confinement are to be confined in separate quarters from men and must be under the supervision of women. All prisoners of war sentenced to confinement have the rights to:

a. make requests and complaints and deal with representatives of the protecting power or the ICRC;

b. receive and send correspondence;

---

[385] GC III, Art 100. This should have been promulgated to PW under Art 41, see para 8.45.

[386] It is not clear whether captives of the nationality of the detaining power are entitled to PW status.   [387] GC III, Art 100.

[388] GC III, Art 101.

[389] GC III, Art 108. See para 8.129. For PW in British hands, see PW (Discipline) Regs 1958, regs 32–35.

c. receive at least one relief parcel each month;

d. take regular exercise in the open air;

e. have the medical care required by their state of health;

f. have such spiritual assistance as they may desire.

Effect of sentence on repatriation

The detaining power has the discretion to postpone repatriation or accom- **8.145** modation in a neutral country in respect of prisoners of war undergoing a sentence awarded by a court, or against whom court proceedings are pending, until the proceedings are completed and the sentence served. The names of the persons so retained must be notified to the power on which they depend. However, prisoners of war may not be kept back merely on account of the imposition of disciplinary punishment.[390]

L. TERMINATION OF CAPTIVITY AND REPATRIATION

EXCHANGE OF PRISONERS OF WAR DURING HOSTILITIES

This is not a matter that is dealt with in the Convention but it is allowed by **8.146** the customary law of armed conflict on such terms as may be agreed between the states concerned.[391] The practice generally observed is to exchange soldier for soldier and rank for rank, with due allowance for differences in titles of ranks or grades. The agreement between the parties, sometimes known as a cartel,[392] may lay down other conditions, for example, that the soldiers concerned do not take any further active role in the conflict. The agreement may be negotiated during a truce by opposing commanders, or by exchange of letters between belligerent states, often through the intermediary of a neutral state.

Nowadays such an exchange would rarely be carried out except by agree- **8.146.1** ment at government level between the parties concerned and it is likely that the assistance of a protecting power or the ICRC would be sought.[393]

---

[390] GC III, Arts 115 and 119. The wording of Art 115 is wide enough to include PW held as witnesses. See also para 8.129(g).   [391] See JWP 1–10, 3H, 6.

[392] See para 10.38.

[393] During WW I, no such exchanges took place although they did during the Napoleonic and Crimean Wars, as well as the American Civil War. During WW II, some measure of agreement was reached between Germany, the United Kingdom, USA, and Switzerland, whereby a number of PW of the three belligerent states interned in Switzerland were repatriated. No formal agreement was drawn up.

REPATRIATION OR ACCOMMODATION IN A NEUTRAL
STATE DURING HOSTILITIES[394]

General principles

8.147 Parties to a conflict are bound to send back to their home state prisoners of
war who are seriously wounded or sick after having cared for them
until they are fit enough to travel.[395] However, no sick or injured prisoner
of war within this category may be repatriated against his will during hostilities.[396] In the case of those less seriously wounded or sick, parties are under
an obligation to endeavour to make arrangements for their accommodation
in neutral countries.[397] They may also conclude agreements with a view to
the direct repatriation or internment in a neutral country of able-bodied
prisoners of war who have undergone a long period of captivity.[398] This
is in addition to the general obligation to endeavour to conclude agreements that will enable all prisoners of war to be interned in a neutral
country.[399] Prisoners of war injured in accidents are subject to the same
rules as other sick and wounded unless the injuries were self-inflicted.[400]
None of this precludes the direct repatriation of prisoners of war in other
circumstances.[401]

Categories of wounded and sick for direct repatriation

8.148 The following should be repatriated direct:[402]

a. the incurably wounded and sick whose mental or physical fitness seems
to have been gravely diminished;

b. the wounded and sick who, according to medical opinion, are not likely
to recover within one year from when the wound was sustained or the
illness occurred, whose condition requires treatment and whose mental
or physical fitness seems to have been gravely diminished;

c. the wounded and sick who have recovered, but whose mental or physical fitness seems to have been gravely and permanently diminished.

---

[394] See also JWP 1–10, 3H, 7–10.   [395] GC III, Art 109.
[396] GC III, Art 109 but see para 8.170.   [397] GC III, Arts 109 and 110.
[398] GC III, Art 109.   [399] GC III, Art 111.   [400] GC III, Art 114.
[401] In the Falklands conflict 1982, both parties repatriated PW at the earliest possible opportunity. Thus the Royal Marines captured on the Falklands Islands and South Georgia during
the initial invasion were repatriated almost immediately by Argentina. In the same way, the
entire crew of the Argentine submarine *Santa Fé*, captured when the British re-took South
Georgia, were quickly returned to Argentina even though hostilities had not ceased.
[402] GC III, Art 110. Exchanges of such PW took place in Korea. During the 1956 Middle East
conflict and the 1962 Sino-Indian conflict, unilateral repatriations took place. The ICRC were
successful in arranging some limited exchanges also during the Iran–Iraq conflict of 1980–88.

Whether or not a prisoner of war's mental or physical condition has been **8.148.1** gravely diminished must, ultimately, be a matter for the opinion of the mixed medical commission.[403]

Categories of wounded and sick for accommodation in neutral states

The following may be accommodated in a neutral state:[404] **8.149**

a. wounded and sick personnel whose recovery may be expected within one year of the date of the wound or the beginning of the illness, if treatment in a neutral country might increase the prospect of a more certain and speedy recovery;

b. prisoners of war whose mental or physical health, according to medical opinion, is seriously threatened by continued captivity, but whose accommodation in a neutral country might remove such a threat.

Repatriation from a neutral state

Subsequent repatriation is a matter for agreement between the states con- **8.150** cerned but those who belong to the following categories should normally be repatriated:[405]

a. those whose state of health has deteriorated so as to fulfil the requirements for direct repatriation;[406]

b. those whose mental or physical powers remain considerably impaired even after treatment.

The conditions for prisoners of war interned in neutral countries must be **8.150.1** equal to or better than those laid down in the Convention.[407]

Procedure

The parties may make special agreements as to which cases of disablement **8.151** or sickness will be directly repatriated or accommodated in a neutral country.[408] In the absence of agreement, these matters should be settled along the lines of the principles in the Model Agreement annexed to the Convention.[409] In respect of prisoners of war serving sentences, see paragraph 8.145. In cases of doubt, determination of the medical category into which a particular prisoner of war falls is a matter for the mixed medical commission.[410]

---

[403] See para 8.152.
[404] GC III, Art 110. The predecessors of this provision were much used in WW I but, since then, belligerents have normally opted to include these categories in direct repatriation.
[405] GC III, Art 110.   [406] See para 8.148.   [407] See GC III, Arts 6 and 12.
[408] GC III, Art 110.   [409] See Appendix C.   [410] See para 8.152.

Mixed medical commissions

8.152 Upon the outbreak of hostilities, mixed medical commissions[411] are to be appointed to examine sick and wounded prisoners of war and to make appropriate decisions regarding them. The commissions consist of three members (one appointed by the detaining power and two medical practitioners from a neutral country) who visit camps at intervals of not more than six months. Their decisions are by majority and must be implemented by the detaining power. The detaining power may, of course, on medical advice repatriate manifestly injured or sick prisoners of war without referring them to the commission.

Entitlement to examination by commission

8.153 The following wounded or sick prisoners of war must be examined by the mixed medical commission:[412]

a. those selected by the medical authorities of the detaining power;

b. those submitted by a retained medical officer of the same nationality, or of an allied nation, who carries out medical duties in the camp;

c. those proposed by their prisoners' representative;

d. those proposed by the power on which they depend or by a relief society recognized by that power;

e. others who present themselves for examination after those in categories (a)–(d) have been dealt with.

8.153.1 The retained medical officer and prisoners' representative concerned have the right to attend the examination.

Expenses

8.154 The costs of repatriation or of transportation to a neutral country are borne by the detaining power up to its own frontiers. Beyond that they are the responsibility of the power on which the prisoners of war depend.[413]

Employment of repatriated prisoners of war

8.155 Repatriated prisoners of war of the categories described in paragraph 8.147,[414] may not be further employed on active military service.[415] Active military service is such as would put them at risk of recapture by their former detaining power or its allies. However, administrative and staff

---

[411] GC III, Art 112. Regulations govern the appointment and work of the commissions, see Appendix C.   [412] GC III, Art 113.

[413] GC III, Art 116.   [414] GC III, Art 110.   [415] GC III, Art 117.

work outside the combat zone and medical services anywhere would be legitimate.[416]

Repatriated prisoners of war not coming within the categories set out in paragraph 8.155 may be re-employed on active military service.[417]   **8.155.1**

BELLIGERENT FORCES TAKING REFUGE IN NEUTRAL TERRITORY

A neutral state that allows members of belligerent state armed forces to take refuge within its territory has the right to lay down the conditions upon which they may enter. In the case of large bodies of troops, it would be usual for their commander and a representative of the neutral state to draw up an agreement in which exact conditions are fixed and recorded. The first condition will be that they give up their arms. A belligerent state's military equipment and supplies, whether its own or captured, which are brought on to neutral territory must be returned at the end of the armed conflict to the state whose property they are. On the other hand, captured war material found in the possession of the troops who take refuge on neutral territory is the property of their state, regardless of its origin.[418] To the extent that the neutral state interns such personnel, the humanitarian provisions set out below apply.   **8.156**

Conditions of internment

Troops interned in neutral territory are, in many respects, in the same position as prisoners of war and the rules concerning prisoners of war apply to them as a minimum standard, subject to certain exceptions.[419] They may be confined in camps, 'fortresses', or other places assigned for the purpose, as far away as possible from the theatre of war.[420] In the absence of any special agreement, the neutral state must supply them with proper food, clothing,   **8.157**

---

[416] See Pictet, *Commentary*, vol III, 539.

[417] GC III, Art 117. Despite its apparent general application, Art 117 is taken to apply only to PW repatriated under the special rules laid down in Arts 109–110 (see Pictet, *Commentary*, vol III, 538). It does not apply to able-bodied PW who are voluntarily repatriated by the unilateral decision of the detaining power during hostilities. The UK sent members of the Royal Marine garrison of the Falkland Islands, who had been captured and then repatriated by Argentina, back into combat with the Task Force that re-took the Islands in 1982.

[418] A proposal put forward by the Dutch government that captured war material brought by the captor into neutral territory should be restored after the war to its original owner, on an analogy with prisoners of war, was not accepted by the Second Hague Conference.

[419] GC III, Art 4B(2). Where diplomatic relations exist between the neutral state and the relevant belligerent state, supervision is carried out through normal diplomatic channels rather than by use of a protecting power. For further details on the rules governing the treatment of prisoners of war, see para 8.146 onwards.   [420] Hague Convention V 1907 (HC V), Art 11.

and medical attention but is entitled to recover the cost of so doing when peace is restored.[421]

Parole

8.158   The neutral state may allow interned officers (but not non-commissioned officers and soldiers) their liberty on their giving parole not to leave the neutral territory without permission.[422]

8.158.1   No conditions are laid down under which such permission is to be given and no penalties are laid down for breaking parole.[423] The granting of leave to an interned officer to return to his own country is not dealt with either and must therefore be considered as a very exceptional measure. A neutral state minded to grant such permission would be prudent in the first instance to obtain the consent of the other belligerent state.[424]

Medical personnel

8.159   Medical personnel serving with troops which take refuge in neutral territory may be retained only in so far as the health and the numbers of such troops so require. Subject to these requirements, they must be returned as soon as possible to the state to which they belong. Chaplains are in the same position, their retention being dependent upon the spiritual needs of the troops. Medical personnel and chaplains who are retained must be accorded similar treatment to those retained under Geneva Convention III.

PRISONERS OF WAR ARRIVING IN NEUTRAL TERRITORY

Prisoners of war who have escaped

8.160   Prisoners of war who have succeeded in escaping to neutral territory regain their liberty, but they are not entitled as of right to remain there. It rests with the neutral state whether to grant or refuse them admission, and, in the

---

[421] HC V, Art 12. The most remarkable instance of this is the asylum granted by Switzerland during the Franco-German war to a French army of 82,000 men and 10,000 horses in 1871. France had, after the conclusion of the war, to pay about 11 million francs for the maintenance of this army in Switzerland during the rest of the war.

[422] HC V, Art 11(3). For the UK practice on parole, see para 8.107.

[423] It is arguable that the neutral state may have the right to demand the return of personnel who have broken their parole.

[424] A proposal by Japan that internees should not be granted parole or authorized to return to their own country except with the consent and under conditions requested by the opposing belligerent was not accepted by the Hague Conference on the ground that such permission was 'too exceptional to require regulation in express terms'. However, it was also stated that 'the Japanese proposal conforms to recent precedents and contains a useful hint for a neutral state desirous of remaining entirely free from responsibility'.

latter case, whether or not it will allow them to remain on its territory. If they are permitted to remain, the neutral state may compel them to make their residence in a specified locality to prevent them from rejoining their forces.

Prisoners of war brought in by a belligerent state

Prisoners of war brought into neutral territory by troops who take refuge **8.161** there, regain their liberty but must be treated by the neutral state in the same way as prisoners of war who have escaped.[425] The parties to a conflict may also make arrangements for the transfer to a neutral country of able-bodied prisoners of war but in these cases, the prisoners of war must be interned.

NEUTRAL TERRITORY AND THE SICK AND WOUNDED

Passage of wounded and sick

A neutral state may, without failing in its duties as a neutral, permit the **8.162** passage of sick and wounded members of belligerent forces through its territory.[426] It is under no obligation to do so but if the privilege is accorded, it must be given to all belligerent states impartially.

It is not necessary to obtain the consent of the other belligerent states to the **8.162.1** granting of permission, but it would be advisable to do so if considerable numbers are involved.[427]

Conditions of passage

If a neutral state permits the passage of sick and wounded into and through **8.163** its territory, it must ensure that no combatants or military supplies accompany them. If they do, those combatants should be interned and military supplies put into safe custody until the end of the conflict. This condition does not exclude personnel and supplies needed for the care of the wounded and sick.[428]

---

[425] HC V, Art 13(2). But see Art 14(2) in respect of the wounded and sick.

[426] HC V, Art 14(1).

[427] After the battle of Sedan in the Franco-German war of 1870–71, the German General Staff wished to send railway trains conveying wounded to Germany through Belgium and Luxembourg. The French Minister of War protested. He argued, rightly, that this would free lines to bring forward fresh soldiers and ammunition. Belgium, after consulting the British government, decided that, if one of the belligerents objected, the giving of permission would be a breach of neutrality, and therefore refused it. Luxembourg took the opposite view and granted it. Under international law, Luxembourg was correct in its reasoning but, in view of the cogent arguments put forward by France, Belgium was right in its decision.

[428] HC V, Art 14(1).

Wounded and sick remaining in a neutral state

8.164 If instead of simply transporting sick and wounded through neutral territory, the belligerent state concerned hands them over to the neutral state, they must be detained by the neutral state so as to prevent their taking any further part in the military operations.[429]

Wounded and sick prisoners of war

8.165 Wounded and sick prisoners of war belonging to the enemy who are brought into neutral territory by a belligerent state may not be carried through to the latter's territory nor may they be liberated like able-bodied prisoners of war. They must be detained by the neutral state in the same way as wounded and sick of the other party who are left in its territory.[430]

Application of Geneva Convention I

8.166 The provisions of Geneva Convention I and Additional Protocol I apply by analogy to wounded and sick who are interned in neutral territory, as well as to any dead found there.[431]

Voluntary aid societies

8.167 It is not a violation of neutrality for neutral voluntary aid societies to provide the services of medical personnel and units to a belligerent state so long as it is done with the agreement of the governments of the neutral state and the belligerent state. Both of them must notify the adverse party. Such medical personnel and units have to be placed under the control of the belligerent state to which they are lent.[432] If they fall into the hands of the adverse party, they may not be detained but must be permitted to return either to their own state or, if that is not possible, to the territory of the belligerent state in whose service they were. Until their release, they must be allowed to continue their work under the direction of the capturing power, preferably caring for the wounded and sick of the party to the conflict in whose service they were. On their departure such personnel must be allowed to take their effects, including personal articles, valuables, medical instruments, arms, and, if possible, their transport. While in the hands of the adverse party, they must be given the same food, lodging, allowances, and pay as is provided for comparable personnel of the adverse party's own armed forces. Food, in particular, must be sufficient in quantity, quality, and variety to keep them in normal health.[433]

---

[429] HC V, Art 14(2).   [430] HC V, Art 14(2).   [431] GC I, Art 4; AP I, Art 19.
[432] GC I, Art 27.   [433] GC I, Art 32.

Repatriation After Close of Hostilities[434]

Release and repatriation

Prisoners of war must be released and repatriated without delay after the **8.168** cessation of active hostilities.[435] The detailed arrangements should be included in an armistice agreement. However, if they are not, each of the detaining powers must quickly prepare and implement a repatriation scheme. In either case, the measures adopted are to be brought to the notice of all prisoners of war. By agreement between the belligerents, commissions are to be instituted for the purpose of searching for scattered prisoners of war and ensuring their repatriation with the least possible delay.[436] The duty of repatriation is absolute and may not be made conditional upon the behaviour of the state on which the prisoners depend.[437]

Cessation of hostilities

'Cessation of active hostilities' is a question of fact and does not depend on **8.169** the existence of an armistice agreement. Active hostilities have ceased where there is no immediate expectation of their resumption.[438] Cessation is not affected by isolated and sporadic acts of violence.

Involuntary repatriation

A more contentious issue is whether prisoners of war *must* be repatriated **8.170** even against their will. Recent practice of states indicates that they should not. It is United Kingdom policy that prisoners of war should not be repatriated against their will.[439]

Historically, prisoners of war were not usually repatriated against **8.170.1** their will, the point often being specifically addressed in the armistice

---

[434] See also JWP 1–10, 3H, 11–14.

[435] GC III, Art 118. There were substantial delays in the repatriation of prisoners at the end of WW II. The final repatriations took place in 1958. In the Gulf conflict 1991, however, repatriations took place soon after the end of hostilities. US President Bush announced a cease-fire on 27 February, an agreement for the release of PW was negotiated on 3 March, repatriation started the following day and by June, the ICRC had registered over 82,000 Iraqi PW and had supervised the repatriation of more than 66,000 of them. Many Iraqi PW declined to be repatriated, see para 8.170.   [436] GC III, Art 119.

[437] Following the surrender of Argentinian forces at the end of the Falklands conflict 1982, the UK repatriated a large number of PW within one month despite a refusal of the Argentine government to declare an end to hostilities.

[438] Following the Indo-Pakistan conflict 1971, the Indian government initially refused to repatriate the more than 90,000 Pakistanis held as PW, on the grounds that a renewal of hostilities could not be excluded. Repatriation did not in fact begin until late 1973, almost two years after the cessation of active hostilities. Similarly, after the Iran–Iraq conflict of 1980–88, repatriation did not begin until 1990.   [439] See JWP 1–10, 3H, 14.

agreement.[440] However, an attempt to insert such a provision into Geneva Convention III failed as it was felt that the proposal might give rise to the exercise of undue influence on the part of the detaining power. Disagreement on this issue led to a delay in the signing of the Korean armistice agreement in 1953. The Korean compromise was to have individual prisoners interviewed by representatives of neutral states and then to permit representatives of their homeland to attempt to dissuade those who chose not to return.[441]

Expenses

8.171 The cost of repatriation is apportioned by agreement between the detaining power and the state on which the prisoners of war depend.[442] Normally the former meets the costs up to its frontier but, if the frontiers are not adjoining, it is responsible only as far as the port of embarkation nearest the territory of the state on which the prisoners of war depend.

DEATH OF PRISONERS OF WAR

Wills

8.172 After the death of a prisoner of war, the detaining power must send any will in its possession to the protecting power with a certified copy to the Central Prisoners of War Information Agency.[443]

Death certificates[444]

8.173 Death certificates, in the form annexed to the Convention,[445] or lists certified by a responsible officer, of all who die whilst prisoners of war, must be forwarded by the quickest means to the information bureau.[446] These

---

[440] See the Treaty of Versailles 1919, Art 220 of which provided that PW 'who do not desire to be repatriated may be excluded from repatriation'.

[441] In the Gulf conflict 1991, this problem arose again. Repatriation was arranged through the ICRC who interviewed each PW privately. It was subsequently reported that, as at February 1992, several thousand Iraqi PW were still living in tents in Saudi Arabia, having been reclassified as 'refugees'. In the event, King Fahd of Saudi Arabia offered to take in 50,000 Iraqi refugees and PW, including army deserters. According to Pictet, a PW who objects to repatriation should not be repatriated if there are reasonable grounds for believing that there is danger to his life or liberty, especially on grounds of race, religion, social class, or political views. However, each case must be examined individually. See Pictet, *Commentary*, vol III, 547. A person subject to UK military law who refuses to be repatriated may commit an offence under the Service Discipline Acts, see NDA 1957, s 3(1)(d) or (e), AA 1955 and AFA 1955, s 25(1)(d) or (e).   [442] GC III, Arts 116 and 118.

[443] GC III, Art 120. See the procedure in JWP 1–10, 3F, 88.

[444] GC III, Art 120, Annex IVD.   [445] See Appendix C.

[446] GC III, Art 120. See para 8.182.

certificates or lists must contain as a minimum the following particulars:

a. number, rank, full names, and date of birth;
b. date and place of death;
c. cause of death;
d. date and place of burial;
e. all particulars necessary for the identification of the grave.

In the case of the death of a prisoner of war in United Kingdom hands, the **8.173.1** procedure laid down in *Prisoners of War Handling* (JWP 1–10), 3F, 84 is to be followed.

Burial or cremation

No prisoner of war may be buried or cremated without a prior medical **8.174** examination to confirm that life is extinct, to enable a report on the death to be made, and, if necessary, to establish identity.[447] If a prisoner of war was seriously wounded when captured, his identity may not have been established before death. It follows that the report should, in such cases, contain, for example, a description and measurement of the body, details of teeth and fingerprints, and a photograph. The detaining power must ensure honourable burial,[448] if possible in accordance with the rites of the deceased's religion. Wherever possible, dead prisoners of war belonging to the same state are to be buried in the same place and in individual graves unless circumstances make the use of collective graves unavoidable. A prisoner of war may not be cremated unless that accords with his religion, personal wishes, or the imperative demands of hygiene. In every such case, the fact of and the reason for cremation must be noted on the death certificate.[449]

Maintenance of graves and disposal of ashes

In order to ensure that graves may always be readily traced, particulars of **8.175** burials and of graves are to be recorded by a graves registration service to be established by the detaining power.[450] List of graves and particulars of prisoners of war interred in cemeteries and elsewhere are to be transmitted to the state with which the prisoners served. The state on whose territory graves are situated (if a party to the Convention) is responsible for the maintenance of those graves. In addition, it should keep records of bodies that are moved to other graves. The graves registration service is also responsible for identification and retention of ashes until they can be disposed of in accordance with the wishes of the home country.

---

[447] GC III, Art 120.   [448] See para 7.35.   [449] See the procedure in JWP 1–10, 3F, 86.
[450] GC III, Art 120.

Inquiries into death or serious injury

8.176 In every case of death or serious injury to a prisoner of war caused, or suspected to have been caused, by a sentry, or by any other person, and in
every case of death the cause of which is unknown, the detaining power
must immediately institute an official inquiry.[451] The protecting power
must be notified immediately. Statements must be taken from all witnesses,
especially those who are prisoners of war, and a report including such statements forwarded to the protecting power. The detaining power is to ensure
that any person or persons found to be responsible for the death or injury
are duly prosecuted.[452]

PROCEDURE ON TERMINATION OF CAPTIVITY

Notification

8.177 Prisoners of war who are to be moved must be listed before departure and
both the information bureau and the prisoners of war themselves officially
notified in advance so that they can pack their baggage and inform their
next of kin.[453]

Personal property

8.178 Impounded articles of value[454] and any currency which has not been converted into that of the detaining power must be returned to the prisoners of
war concerned and any items not returned must be sent to the information
bureau.[455] Prisoners of war must be allowed to take with them their personal property and any correspondence and parcels that have arrived for
them. If there are shortages of transport, the detaining power may limit the
amount of personal property to what each prisoner of war can carry, not
exceeding 25 kilograms each. In that event, it must forward any remaining
property, including mail, on terms agreed with the state on which the prisoners of war depend.

Accounts[456]

8.179 Unless otherwise agreed, the detaining power must:

a. give each prisoner of war a statement, signed by an authorized officer,
showing the credit balance due to him in his account;

---

[451] In the case of PW in British hands, see JWP 1–10, 3F, 82, 85.

[452] GC III, Art 121. In the Falklands conflict, an Argentinean PW was shot and killed to prevent
an attempt to sabotage the captured submarine *Santa Fé*. The British notified the Argentinian
authorities through the ICRC and established a board of inquiry to establish the facts.

[453] GC III, Art 119. See also Arts 48 and 122.   [454] See para 8.25(h).

[455] GC III, Art 119.   [456] GC III, Art 66.

b. send, through the protecting power, to the state on which the prisoners of war depend, certified lists showing the credit balances of all prisoners of war whose captivity has been terminated. The home states of the prisoners of war are then responsible for paying them these credit balances.[457]

For the disposal of canteen profits, see paragraph 8.82.   **8.179.1**

Movement[458]

This must be done humanely and in conditions that are not less favourable **8.180**
than those used for moving members of the armed forces of the detaining
power.[459] Adequate precautions must be taken for the health and safety of
prisoners of war, including provision of sufficient food, drinking water,
clothing, shelter, and medical attention.

Adjustments between belligerents[460]

Advances of pay,[461] compensation payments,[462] and payments made in their **8.181**
own states under Article 63 of the Convention,[463] are considered to be made
on behalf of the state on which prisoners of war depend and so are a matter
for adjustment between the states concerned at the close of hostilities.

M. INFORMATION BUREAUX AND RELIEF SOCIETIES

INFORMATION BUREAUX

Establishment

At the beginning of hostilities, and in all cases of occupation,[464] each party **8.182**
is to establish an official information bureau for the prisoners of war which
it holds. Neutral and other states not otherwise involved in the conflict but
which receive prisoners of war must do the same.[465]

The state concerned must: **8.182.1**

a. Ensure that the prisoners of war information bureau has the necessary
accommodation, equipment, and staff to work efficiently. Prisoners of
war may be employed in the bureau provided that the conditions of the
Convention on work are complied with.[466]

---

[457] The rate of exchange is subject to the domestic law of the home state.
[458] GC III, Art 119. See also Art 46.   [459] See also para 8.35(c), (d).
[460] GC III, Art 67.   [461] See para 8.74.   [462] See para 8.92.   [463] See para 8.81.
[464] See Ch 11.   [465] GC III, Art 122.   [466] See paras 8.84–8.93.

b. Without delay, provide the bureau with the following information about
    each prisoner of war in its hands: number, rank, full names, place and date
    of birth, state on which he depends, first name of father, maiden name of
    mother, name and address of next of kin,[467] and the address to which cor-
    respondence for the prisoner of war may be sent. Details of transfers,
    releases, repatriations, escapes, admissions to hospital, and deaths must be
    provided and information about the state of health of prisoners of war who
    are seriously ill or wounded must be given regularly, if possible, weekly.

Duties

8.183 The duties of the information bureaux are:

a. to pass information received quickly to the states concerned through the
    protecting power and the central agency;
b. to reply to all enquiries received about the prisoners of war, including
    those who have died in captivity, and to seek any necessary information
    for that purpose;
c. to ensure that its letters are properly authenticated by signature or seal;
d. to collect and forward to the states concerned[468] personal valuables,
    money, and important documents left by prisoners of war who have
    either been repatriated or released, or who have escaped or died. These
    items must be sent by the bureau in sealed packets, accompanied by
    statements giving clear and full particulars of the identity of the person
    to whom the articles belonged, together with a complete list of the con-
    tents of the parcel.

Central Prisoners of War Information Agency

8.184 A Central Prisoners of War Information Agency[469] is to be established in
    a neutral country and the ICRC may make proposals in this regard. Its func-
    tion will be to collect all information, whether obtained officially or pri-
    vately, about prisoners of war and to send it without delay to their home
    states or that with whose forces they were serving. Belligerents must give
    the agency every facility for transmitting such information and it may seek
    financial aid from any country whose nationals are benefited. This does not
    prevent similar humanitarian work from being done by either the ICRC or
    recognized relief societies, such as national red cross societies.

---

[467] The detaining power may not have all this information since, under GC III, Art 17, a PW
is not bound to disclose more than his number, rank, full names, and date of birth.

[468] Ideally also informing the protecting power and the central agency.

[469] GC III, Art 123. The ICRC's Central Tracing Agency normally fulfils the function of the
Central Prisoner of War Information Agency.

Exemption from charges

Information bureaux and the Central Agency are exempt from postal **8.185** charges, and their shipments are exempt import, customs, and other dues and transport costs to the same extent as relief supplies.[470] They should also, if possible, be given either exemption from or reduced rates of telegraphic charges.

RELIEF SOCIETIES

Religious organizations and relief societies which assist prisoners of war **8.186** must be given all necessary facilities for visiting prisoners of war and for the distribution of relief supplies and material from any source, intended for religious, educational, or recreational purposes, and for organizing their leisure time in their camps.[471] These societies or organizations may be set up in the territory of the detaining power or in any other country or they may have an international character. The special position of the ICRC in this field must be recognized and respected at all times.[472] The detaining power may limit the number of societies and organizations carrying out such activities in its territory, supervise their work, and impose reasonable security restrictions as long as this does not prevent adequate relief from reaching prisoners of war. A receipt for each consignment, signed by the prisoners' representative and by the administrative authorities of the detaining power responsible for guarding the prisoners of war, must be forwarded to the relief organization concerned as soon as possible after delivery.

---

[470] GC III, Art 124. See para 8.66.   [471] GC III, Art 125.

[472] In addition to providing relief, the ICRC has a right to visit prisoners of war, its delegates enjoying the same prerogatives as the protecting power: GC III, Art 126. The ICRC also has an important role in the operation of the Central Prisoners of War Information Agency.

9

Protection of Civilians in the Hands of a Party to the Conflict

A. INTRODUCTION

The law of armed conflict addresses in considerable detail the protection **9.1** of two classes of civilians in the hands of an adverse party to the conflict: the inhabitants of occupied territory and the nationals of a belligerent state who are in the territory of the adversary. The events of the Second World War had clearly shown that these classes of individuals were inadequately protected by the existing rules. It is above all these classes who were the subject of Geneva Convention IV 1949 (in this chapter referred to as 'the Convention'), later supplemented by certain provisions of Additional Protocol I 1977, and who form the main focus of this chapter.

Rules for the protection of civilians from the effects of hostilities are con- **9.1.1** tained mainly in Additional Protocol I and are summarized in Chapter 5. The special rules on administration of occupied territory are dealt with in Chapter 11.

Certain legal provisions apply to civilians generally: not just those in the **9.1.2** hands of the adversary but also civilians under their own government, that is, to the whole of the populations of the states engaged in a conflict. Within the law of armed conflict, see, for example, the Genocide Convention 1948, Geneva Convention IV, Articles 13–26 and Additional Protocol I, Articles 68–71. In addition, civilians will be entitled to protection under applicable human rights law. However, this topic falls outside the scope of this Manual.

B. RULES APPLICABLE TO ALL CIVILIANS IN THE HANDS OF A PARTY TO THE CONFLICT

SCOPE OF PART B

These fundamental guarantees apply as a minimum standard to all persons **9.2** who are in the power of a party to the conflict who do not benefit from more favourable treatment under the Geneva Conventions 1949 or Additional Protocol I.[1]

---

[1] Additional Protocol I 1977 (AP I), Art 75. For the applicability of this article to a state's own nationals, see Y Sandoz, C Swinarski, and B Zimmermann (eds), *Commentary on the Additional Protocols of 8 June 1977 to the Geneva Conventions of 12 August 1949* (1987) (*ICRC Commentary*), para 3017 onwards.

Basic Standards of Treatment

9.3 All persons are to be treated humanely in all circumstances and 'without any adverse distinction based upon race, colour, sex, language, religion or belief, political or other opinion, national or social origin, wealth, birth or other status or on any other similar criteria'. Their persons, honour, convictions, and religious practices must be respected.[2]

Prohibited Acts

9.4 The following acts are prohibited 'at any time and in any place whatsoever':[3]

    a. violence to the life, health, or physical or mental well-being of persons, in particular:

        (1) murder;
        (2) torture[4] of all kinds, whether physical or mental;
        (3) corporal punishment; and
        (4) mutilation;

    b. outrages upon personal dignity, in particular humiliating and degrading treatment, enforced prostitution,[5] and any form of indecent assault;

    c. the taking of hostages;

    d. collective punishments;[6]

    e. threats to commit any of the foregoing acts.

Arrest, Detention, and Internment

9.5 Where a person is arrested, detained or interned 'for actions related to the armed conflict', he must be informed promptly in a language which he

---

[2] AP I, Art 75(1).   [3] AP I, Art 75(2).

[4] In the case of *Prosecutor v Delalić et al (Čelebići Case)* (1996) 38 ILM 57, the International Criminal Tribunal for the Former Yugoslavia (ICTY) held that rape was capable of amounting to torture under international humanitarian law. This was confirmed in *Prosecutor v Furundžija* (1998) 121 ILR 218.

[5] Japan has publicly acknowledged that during the Second World War (WW II), a number of Chinese and Korean women had been compelled to become 'comfort women' for Japanese troops.

[6] This confirms the earlier prohibition in the Hague Regulations 1907 (HR), Art 50, which forbade general penalties 'inflicted upon the population on account of the acts of individuals for which they cannot be regarded as jointly and severally responsible' and also the prohibition of collective punishments in GC IV, Art 33(2)(d). It covers administrative as well as judicial punishments, eg a fine imposed on the community at large for an act committed by one of its members, or destruction of houses in a village of which the offender is an inhabitant, see *ICRC Commentary*, para 3055.

understands of the reason for these measures. Unless the arrest or detention is for penal offences, he must be released 'with the minimum delay possible and in any event as soon as the circumstances justifying the arrest, detention, or internment have ceased to exist'.[7] Pending release, he retains the protection of Additional Protocol I.[8]

TRIAL AND PUNISHMENT

Generally

In the case of penal offences relating to the armed conflict, the basic principles **9.6** of natural justice must be observed. No sentence may be passed and no penalty executed 'except pursuant to a conviction pronounced by an impartial and regularly constituted court respecting the generally recognized principles of regular judicial procedure'.[9] These principles include the following:

a. 'the procedure shall provide for an accused to be informed without delay of the particulars of the offence alleged against him and shall afford the accused before and during his trial all necessary rights and means of defence';

b. 'no one shall be convicted of an offence except on the basis of individual penal responsibility';

c. 'no one shall be accused or convicted of a criminal offence on account of any act or omission which did not constitute a criminal offence under the national or international law to which he was subject at the time when it was committed; nor shall a heavier penalty be imposed than that which was applicable at the time when the criminal offence was committed; if, after the commission of the offence, provision is made by law for the imposition of a lighter penalty, the offender shall benefit thereby';

d. 'anyone charged with an offence is presumed innocent until proved guilty according to law';

e. 'anyone charged with an offence shall have the right to be tried in his presence';

f. 'no one shall be compelled to testify against himself or to confess guilt';

g. 'anyone charged with an offence shall have the right to examine, or have examined, the witnesses against him and to obtain the attendance and examination of witnesses on his behalf under the same conditions as witnesses against him';

h. 'no one shall be prosecuted or punished by the same Party for an offence in respect of which a final judgement acquitting or convicting that

---

[7] AP I, Art 75(3).   [8] AP I, Art 75(6).   [9] AP I, Art 75(4).

person has been previously pronounced under the same law and judicial procedure';

i. 'anyone prosecuted for an offence shall have the right to have the judgement pronounced publicly'; and

j. 'a convicted person shall be advised on conviction of his judicial and other remedies and of the time-limits within which they may be exercised'.[10]

War crimes trials

9.7 Those accused of war crimes or crimes against humanity must be tried in accordance with the rules of international law, whether or not the offences amount to grave breaches of the Geneva Conventions or Additional Protocol I. As a minimum, the rules detailed in paragraph 9.6 must be applied.[11]

9.7.1 Paragraph 9.7 is of particular importance to those such as mercenaries and spies who are not entitled to prisoner of war status. They are entitled as a minimum to these protections.

PROTECTION OF WOMEN

9.8 Women must be accorded 'special respect and shall be protected in particular against rape, forced prostitution and any other form of indecent assault'.[12]

9.8.1 Women arrested, detained, or interned for reasons connected with the armed conflict must be kept in separate quarters from men and under the immediate supervision of women. In cases where families are detained or interned, they should, whenever possible, be held in the same place and accommodated 'as family units'.[13]

9.8.2 Pregnant women and mothers of dependent children who are arrested, detained, or interned for reasons related to the armed conflict must have their cases considered with the utmost priority. For these women, the pronouncement of the death penalty should be avoided, as far as that is possible, and the execution of the death penalty is forbidden.[14] In any event, United Kingdom courts may not impose death sentences.

PROTECTION AND WELFARE OF CHILDREN

9.9 Children are to be respected and protected, especially against indecent assault. The care and aid needed by children must be provided.[15]

---

[10] AP I, Art 75(4).   [11] AP I, Art 75(7).   [12] AP I, Art 76(1).
[13] AP I, Art 75(5). See also para 9.44.   [14] AP I, Art 76(2), (3).   [15] AP I, Art 77(1).

Recruitment

Steps must be taken to ensure that those aged under 15 years are not **9.9.1** recruited into the armed forces and do not take a direct part in hostilities.[16] Moreover, where there is recruitment of young persons aged between 15 and 18 years, priority is to be given to the oldest.[17] If children under 15 years do take a direct part in hostilities, they do not lose the protection of this paragraph even if they are also classified as prisoners of war.[18]

Arrest and detention

If arrested, detained, or interned for reasons connected with the armed con- **9.9.2** flict, children must be kept in separate quarters from adults unless they belong to an interned family unit.[19] Death penalties for offences related to the armed conflict are not to be carried out on those aged under 18 years at the time of the offence.[20] In any event, United Kingdom courts may not impose death sentences.

Orphans

The parties to the conflict are required to make provision for the care of chil- **9.9.3** dren under 15 years who have been orphaned or separated from their families as a result of the conflict. They must ensure the maintenance of these children and facilitate the exercise of their religion, while their education must, as far as possible, be entrusted to persons of a similar cultural tradition. Arrangements may be made, with the consent of the protecting power, for such children to be accommodated in neutral countries.[21]

Identification

Furthermore, particular steps must be taken to ensure the easy identifi- **9.9.4** cation of children under 12 years of age by, for example, the wearing of identity discs.[22]

FAMILY NEWS

The parties to the conflict are required to facilitate the giving and receipt of **9.10** personal family news.[23]

Where a postal service remains in operation, such correspondence must be **9.10.1** forwarded speedily and without undue delay. If direct postal communication

---

[16] During the Iran–Iraq conflict and in some internal conflicts in Africa, children's units were raised.   [17] AP I, Art 77(2).
[18] AP I, Art 77(3).   [19] AP I, Art 77(4).   [20] AP I, Art 77(5).
[21] Geneva Convention IV 1949 (GC IV), Art 24. See para 9.14.   [22] GC IV, Art 24.
[23] GC IV, Art 25.

is impossible, the parties to the conflict must make arrangements for correspondence to be sent through an impartial intermediary, such as the Central Information Agency, or by some alternative method. Any necessary restrictions on correspondence must at least permit the monthly use of a standard form containing 25 freely chosen words.[24]

DISPERSED FAMILIES

9.11 The belligerents, and all parties to Additional Protocol I, are required to facilitate in every possible way the reunion of families dispersed as a result of armed conflict, to deal with their enquiries, and (subject to security regulations) to facilitate the work of approved organizations engaged in this task.[25]

9.11.1 The object is to reunite families, not to deal with all displaced persons. Although the national information bureaux and the Central Information Agency[26] are primarily required to deal with protected persons,[27] they may also deal with dispersed families whose members do not fall into that category.

FREE PASSAGE OF RELIEF SUPPLIES

9.12 The parties to the conflict and all parties to Additional Protocol I must allow and facilitate the free passage of all consignments of medical and hospital stores, objects necessary for religious worship, bedding, means of shelter, and 'other supplies essential to the survival of the civilian population', such as essential foodstuffs, clothing, and tonics, intended only for civilians, even those of an adversary. In the distribution of relief consignments, children under 15, expectant mothers, and maternity cases and nursing mothers are to be given priority.[28]

9.12.1 This obligation is, however, conditional on the party being satisfied that there is no serious reason for fearing that:

a. the consignments may be diverted from their destination;

b. control may not be effective; or

---

[24] GC IV, Art 25. The ICRC's Central Tracing Agency normally carries out the role of the Central Information Agency. It has designed a special form for the exchange of family news, which may be modified to suit the specific circumstances of each armed conflict. National societies, such as the British Red Cross, normally have a role in transmitting family messages.
[25] GC IV, Art 26; AP I, Art 74.   [26] See paras 9.114–9.116.   [27] See para 9.114.
[28] GC IV, Art 23; AP I, Art 70. After Iraq's invasion of Kuwait in 1990, the UN Security Council, whilst imposing economic sanctions against Iraq, provided for an exemption in relation to medical supplies and foodstuffs. In assessing the humanitarian need for food supplies, special attention was to be given to children under the age of 15, expectant mothers, and maternity cases. See UNSCR 661(1990) and 666(1990), para 4.

c. the provision of these goods would lead to a definite advantage accruing to the military efforts or economy of the enemy.

In addition, the party retains the right to prescribe the technical arrange- **9.12.2** ments for the movement of relief supplies, including search, and to insist that distribution be supervised by the protecting power. A duty is put on all parties not to divert relief consignments, nor to delay them 'except in cases of urgent necessity in the interest of the civilian population concerned'.[29] Indeed there is a further duty to protect such consignments and to 'encourage and facilitate effective international co-ordination' of relief actions.[30]

Such relief actions shall only be undertaken 'subject to the agreement of the **9.12.3** Parties concerned'.[31] There is thus, except for those specific consignments covered by the Convention,[32] no duty to agree to them though there is a duty to consider in good faith requests for relief operations.

The provisions of paragraph 9.12 do not affect the existing rules of warfare **9.12.4** regarding naval blockade,[33] submarine warfare, or mine warfare.[34]

RELIEF PERSONNEL

Relief personnel may, where necessary, accompany relief consignments, **9.13** 'subject to the approval of the Party in whose territory they will carry out their duties'.[35] They are entitled to respect and protection[36] and parties are under an obligation to assist them 'to the fullest extent practicable'. Only 'imperative military necessity' can justify any limitation on their activities or restriction of movement, which must in any event be temporary.[37] Relief personnel are under an obligation not to exceed the terms of their mandate under Additional Protocol I and to 'take account' of the security requirements of the party in whose territory they are carrying out their duties.[38]

---

[29] AP I, Art 70(3). In the conflicts in the former Yugoslavia from 1991–95, there were many cases of obstruction of the passage of, and looting of, relief supplies. Agreements for the delivery and distribution of relief supplies must be scrupulously observed. Even where there is no agreement, looting is a war crime that should be punished.   [30] AP I, Art 70(4), (5).
[31] AP I, Art 70(1).
[32] That is, medical and hospital stores and objects necessary for religious worship; also essential foodstuffs, clothing, and tonics for children under 15, expectant mothers, and maternity cases (GC IV, Art 23). In addition, commanders should allow the passage of essential foodstuffs for all civilians to be delivered since starvation, as a method of warfare, is prohibited (AP I, Art 54(1)).   [33] However, see paras 13.93–13.95.
[34] The UK made a statement to this effect on ratification of AP I. However, see paras 13.74 and 13.75 about essential supplies that a blockading party is obliged to allow through.
[35] AP I, Art 71(1).   [36] AP I, Art 71(2).   [37] AP I, Art 71(3).   [38] AP I, Art 71(4).

C. EVACUATION OF CHILDREN TO FOREIGN COUNTRIES

WHEN EVACUATION IS PERMISSIBLE

9.14 There are no restrictions on the evacuation to a foreign country by a belligerent state of children of its own nationality. Children who are not nationals of a belligerent state may not be evacuated by that state to a foreign country unless:[39]

a. evacuation is temporary;

b. either:

(1) it is compelled by reason of the health or medical treatment of the children, or

(2) except in occupied territory, the safety of the children so demands;

c. the written consent of the parents or legal guardians[40] of each child is obtained;

d. the evacuation is made under an agreement between the state arranging for the evacuation, the state(s) receiving the children, and the state(s) whose nationals are evacuated;

e. the evacuation is supervised by the protecting power; and

f. the parties to the conflict take all feasible precautions to avoid endangering the evacuation.

EDUCATION

9.15 In the event of an evacuation of non-nationals, each child's education must be provided with the greatest possible continuity.[41] This should include moral and religious education as desired by parents.

DOCUMENTATION

9.16 In the case of evacuation of non-nationals, both the evacuating state and the receiving state must establish a card index system[42] for the evacuated children with a card, including a photograph, for each child.[43] One copy of the

---

[39] AP I, Art 78(1).

[40] If parents or guardians cannot be found, written consent is to be obtained from the persons who by law or custom are primarily responsible for the care of the children, see AP I, Art 78(1).   [41] AP I, Art 78(2).

[42] This does not have to be a manual system. A computer-based card index system may be preferred.   [43] AP I, Art 78(3).

card is sent to the Central Tracing Agency of the ICRC. Each card should include as much as possible of the following personal information about the child concerned, unless such inclusion would involve the child in risk of harm:

a. surname(s);

b. first names;

c. sex;

d. date and place of birth or estimated age;

e. father's full name;

f. mother's full name and maiden name;

g. next of kin;

h. nationality;

i. native language and any other languages spoken;

j. family address;

k. any identification number;

l. state of health;

m. blood group;

n. any distinguishing features;

o. date on which and place where the child was found;

p. date on which and place from which the child left the country;

q. religion (if any);

r. address in the receiving state; and

s. in the event of death before return, date, place, and circumstances of death and place of interment.

D. PROTECTED PERSONS

DEFINITION

Protected persons are defined as those who at any time and for any reason **9.17** find themselves 'in the hands of a Party to the conflict or Occupying Power of which they are not nationals'.[44]

Many persons are protected by the law of armed conflict: for example, the **9.17.1** wounded, sick, and shipwrecked, prisoners of war, parlementaires, medical and religious personnel, civil defence personnel, personnel assigned to the protection of cultural property, relief personnel, and civilians generally. However,

---

[44] GC IV, Art 4.

whenever the term 'protected person' is used without qualification, it means the persons defined in paragraph 9.17. They are persons considered especially at risk and, therefore, in need of special protection.

9.17.2 'In the hands of' here means simply that the person concerned is in territory which is under the control of the state in question. The most common groups within the definition are:

a. enemy nationals in one's own territory;[45]

b. the whole population of occupied territory other than nationals of the occupying power;

c. persons considered as refugees or stateless persons under international law or the law of the state of refuge or of residence.[46]

9.17.3 Apart from the special rules relating to them,[47] protected persons are entitled to all the protections set out in parts B and C of this chapter.

PERSONS NOT QUALIFYING FOR PROTECTED PERSON STATUS

9.18 Persons in the following categories are not entitled to the status of protected person:

a. Nationals of a state not bound by the Convention are not protected by it. However, a state that is a party to the Convention is bound in relation to a state that accepts and applies the provisions of the Convention. However, this is almost academic since at the time of writing the only states not party to the Convention are the Republic of the Marshall Islands and Nauru.

b. Nationals of a neutral state who find themselves in the territory of a belligerent, as well as nationals of a co-belligerent state, are also not protected persons while the state on which they depend has normal diplomatic relations with the state in whose hands they are.[48] They are entitled to be treated in the same way as nationals of the host state.[49]

---

[45] In the context of the conflict in Bosnia, it was held in *Prosecutor v Delalić et al (Čelebići Case)*, ICTY Appeals Chamber, 20 February 2001, that persons of the same nationality but of a different ethnic origin, namely, Bosnian Serb civilians at the Celebići prison camp in Bosnia, were also 'protected persons'.   [46] GC IV, Art 44; AP I, Art 73.

[47] For aliens in the territory of a party to the conflict, see Pts E–L below; for persons in occupied territory, see Pts E, G–L below, and also Ch 11.

[48] GC IV, Art 4. The British military personnel who were in Kuwait as members of a training team at the time of the Iraqi invasion in 1990 and who were captured were protected persons, not prisoners of war, as the UK was not involved in an armed conflict with Iraq at the time.

[49] See, eg, the British declaration at the Hague Conference 1907, *Actes*, vol III, 43: 'We will treat them on a footing of equality with our own countrymen'.

c. Persons who are otherwise protected under the other three Geneva Conventions.

The importance of the Convention is that it covers those not protected else- **9.18.1**
where. For example, members of resistance movements who fail to qualify
as prisoners of war would be entitled to protection under this Convention.[50]
Persons listed in paragraph 9.18 who do not qualify for protected person
status, still have the rights and protections set out in Parts B and C of the
chapter.

LOSS OF PRIVILEGES

In two cases, the privileges afforded to a protected person under the **9.19**
Convention may be restricted.[51] First, where a belligerent is satisfied that
a specific protected person in its territory 'is definitely suspected of or
engaged in activities hostile to the security of the State', that person is not
entitled to such rights and privileges under the Convention as would, if
exercised in his favour, be prejudicial to the security of the state. Secondly,
in occupied territory, where a protected person is detained as a spy or
saboteur or as a person under definite suspicion of activity hostile to
the security of the occupying power, and if 'absolute military security
so requires', such person may be deemed to have forfeited the right of
communication.[52]

In both cases, however, such persons are to be treated with humanity and, **9.19.1**
if brought to trial, must have the benefit of the rights of fair and regular trial
laid down in paragraph 9.6. At the earliest possible date consistent with
the security of the belligerent state or occupying power, such persons are
to be granted the full rights and privileges of a protected person under
the Convention.

NON-RENUNCIATION OF RIGHTS

The rights granted under the Convention to protected persons cannot **9.20**
under any circumstances be renounced by them either wholly or partially.[53]

This is to avoid the possibility of a waiver of rights under duress. It also **9.20.1**
prevents, for example, the argument that since a state has ceased to exist
because of conquest, the Convention no longer applies.

---

[50] However, see para 9.19.   [51] GC IV, Art 5.
[52] Under GC IV, Arts 106–116, with, eg, the protecting power and his relatives, see para. 9.67.
He must continue to be accorded the treatment prescribed in other articles.
[53] GC IV, Art 8.

E. RULES FOR THE TREATMENT OF PROTECTED PERSONS IN BOTH A PARTY'S OWN TERRITORY AND IN OCCUPIED TERRITORY

HUMANE TREATMENT

9.21 The person, honour, family rights, religious convictions and practices, and the manners and customs of protected persons must in all circumstances be respected. They must be humanely treated and protected against all acts or threats of violence, insults, and public curiosity. Women must be specially protected against any attack on their honour, in particular against rape, enforced prostitution, and any form of indecent assault. Subject to special provisions relating to health, age, and sex, protected persons must receive equal treatment without any adverse distinction based, in particular, on race, religion, or political opinion.[54]

SECURITY MEASURES

9.22 The parties to the conflict may take such measures of control or security in regard to protected persons as may be necessary as a result of the conflict.[55] These measures range from the carrying of identity cards and registration with the authorities to restriction to a prescribed place of residence or even internment.[56] Persons who have fled their native country and are recognized as refugees should be treated humanely.[57] They should not be subjected to controls simply because they are refugees or because of their former nationality.[58]

RELIEF ORGANIZATIONS

9.23 Every opportunity must be given to protected persons to apply to the protecting powers, the ICRC, the local national red cross (or equivalent) society, or any other organization that may assist them. Within the limits of military or security considerations, these organizations must be granted by the belligerents all necessary facilities for giving assistance. Belligerents must facilitate as much as possible visits to protected persons by delegates

---

[54] GC IV, Art 27. See also AP I, Arts 75(1) and 76. For provisions covering the arrest, detention, internment, and punishment of women, see para 9.8. [55] GC IV, Art 27.

[56] See para 9.37 onwards.

[57] Under AP I, Art 73, persons who, before the beginning of hostilities, were considered refugees or stateless persons under international law or relevant national law, are regarded as protected persons.

[58] GC IV, Art 44. In WW II, many Germans came to the UK to flee persecution in their native land.

of the protecting powers, the ICRC, and of other relief agencies providing for their spiritual or material needs.[59]

PROHIBITED ACTS

The following acts against protected persons are prohibited: **9.24**

a. using their presence to give a place or area immunity from attack or military operations;[60]

b. physical or moral coercion, especially with a view to obtaining information;[61]

c. any measure which would cause physical suffering to, or lead to the extermination of, protected persons;[62]

d. collective punishments;

e. all measures of intimidation and terrorism;

f. pillage;

g. reprisals against protected persons and their property;[63] and

h. the taking of hostages.[64]

F. PROTECTED PERSONS WHO ARE ALIENS IN THE TERRITORY OF A PARTY TO THE CONFLICT

RIGHT TO LEAVE

Unless their departure is contrary to the national interests of the state, pro- **9.25** tected persons who wish to do so must be allowed to leave the territory at the outset of, or during, a conflict.[65] Proper procedures must be established

---

[59] GC IV, Art 30. See also Art 143, under which delegates of the protecting power and the ICRC have a right of visit, and para 9.118.   [60] GC IV, Art 28; see also AP I, Art 51(7).

[61] GC IV, Art 31. Coercion would include threats against the friends or relatives of protected persons, removal of ration cards, and forcing members of the local populace to act as guides for an invading force.

[62] GC IV, Art 32; AP I, Art 75(2); see also AP I, Art 11. This prohibition applies not only to murder, torture, corporal punishment, mutilation, and medical or scientific experiments not necessitated by the medical treatment of a protected person, but also to any other measures of brutality whether committed by civilians or by military personnel.   [63] GC IV, Art 33.

[64] GC IV, Art 34.

[65] GC IV, Art 35. The term 'national interest' means that a state may prevent departure if it would be prejudicial to its security, eg, because the person concerned possesses information of military value or the circumstances of his evacuation would facilitate an attack or a piece of intelligence gathering. It would not justify such restrictions on the basis that it would make an attack on the state less likely. National interests might also cover economic reasons, eg, in states of immigration where a large exodus of aliens would cause economic problems.

to deal with their applications and decisions made as quickly as possible. Those permitted to leave must be allowed to take the necessary funds for their journey together with reasonable amounts of personal articles and effects. Applications for departure may only be refused on grounds of the national interests of the state concerned. Where permission has been refused, protected persons have the right of appeal to an appropriate court or administrative board set up by the detaining power.[66] The names of those refused permission to leave must, as quickly as possible, be passed to representatives of the protecting power unless this is contrary to either the interests of security or the wishes of the individual concerned.[67]

Conditions of Departure

9.26 Authorized departures must be carried out under satisfactory conditions of safety, hygiene, sanitation, and food. All expenses from the point of exit from the country are to be borne by the country of destination or, in the case of accommodation in a neutral country, by the state whose nationals are benefited.[68] Different arrangements may be made by special agreement between the parties to the conflict.

Persons in Confinement

9.27 Protected persons who are in pre-trial custody or serving a custodial sentence must be humanely treated and on their release may apply for permission to leave in accordance with the procedure laid down.[69]

Treatment of Protected Persons who Remain

9.28 Apart from any special controls authorized by the Convention,[70] the treatment of protected persons should be the same as that applicable in peacetime.[71] They must have the following rights:

a. to receive individual or collective relief consignments;

b. to receive the same medical attention and hospital treatment as nationals of the host state;

c. to practise their religion;

d. to the same extent as nationals of the host state, to leave areas particularly exposed to the dangers of war; and

---

[66] This provides protection against any oppressive or misguided action by a single official.

[67] The exception that permits the protected person to object to the protecting power being furnished with the reasons for refusal was inserted, eg, to meet the case of political refugees who may be jeopardized if such information is given. For a similar provision in relation to internment, see para 9.34.
[68] GC IV, Art 36.

[69] GC IV, Art 37. See para 9.25.   [70] See para 9.31 onwards.   [71] GC IV, Art 38.

e. for children aged under 15 years, pregnant women, and mothers of children aged under seven years, the same rights to preferential treatment[72] as are accorded nationals of the host state.

FINANCIAL SUPPORT

So far as security considerations permit, protected persons must be permit- **9.29** ted to carry on their normal employment. If they lose their jobs because of the conflict, they must have the same opportunities as nationals of the host state to find other paid work. If the measures of control and supervision adopted by the host state for security reasons prevent such persons from finding paid employment on reasonable conditions, the host state must ensure their support and that of their dependants. Dependants are particularly in need of such support where the head of the family has been interned or deported. Protected persons may receive allowances from their home states, from the protecting power, and from relief societies.[73]

COMPULSORY EMPLOYMENT

Protected persons may be compelled to work only to the same extent as **9.30** nationals of the host state. If they are of enemy nationality, they may only be made to do work which is normally necessary to ensure the feeding, sheltering, clothing, transport, and health of the population. They may not be required to do work directly related to the conduct of military operations. Working conditions of protected persons must be the same as those of nationals of the host state, particularly as regards wages, hours, clothing and equipment, training, and compensation for occupational accidents and diseases.[74] Protected persons who are interned may not be compelled to work.[75]

FURTHER RESTRICTIONS ON PROTECTED PERSONS

Assigned residence or internment

If the other measures of control on protected persons provided in the **9.31** Convention are inadequate,[76] the most severe additional measures that may be imposed are those of assigned residence or internment.[77] Protected

---

[72] Preferential treatment may range from the issue of supplementary rations to evacuation to safety zones. See also GC IV, Arts 14, 17, 23, 24, 89, and 132.

[73] GC IV, Art 39; see also Art 98.

[74] GC IV, Art 40. In cases of alleged infringement of these provisions, protected persons must be allowed to exercise their right of complaint under Art 30, see para 9.23.

[75] See para 9.77.   [76] See para 9.22.

[77] GC IV, Arts 41 and 42. For detailed rules on the conditions of internment, see paras 9.37–9.89. For the rules on conditions of assigned residences, see para 9.32–9.36.

persons may be interned or placed in assigned residences only if security requirements make such a course absolutely necessary. The mere fact that a person has enemy nationality and is of military age does not justify internment.[78] It is a question of whether, by reason of activities, knowledge, or qualifications, the individual represents a threat to the security of the state. If a person volunteers, through the protecting power, to be interned and his situation renders this necessary, he must be interned.[79] It will, however, be for the state concerned to decide whether the request is justified.

Assigned residence

9.32   Assigned residence may take one of two forms. The protected person may be required to stay where he is and not move outside a certain area. This is usually known as being placed under surveillance. Alternatively, he may be moved and required to live in another locality where supervision is easier. Where protected persons are required to move to an assigned residence, the detaining power must apply as many of the terms of the Convention dealing with conditions of internment as are applicable to the situation.[80]

Appeal and reconsideration

9.33   A protected person may apply to a court or administrative board designated by the detaining power for review of a decision to intern him or to place him in an assigned residence.[81] Such application must be considered as soon as possible. In any event, the court or board must review all cases of internment or assigned residence at least twice yearly with a view to 'favourable amendment of the initial decision, if circumstances permit'.

Notification

9.34   Unless the protected person objects, the detaining power must, as soon as possible, notify[82] the protecting power of:

a. the names of those interned, placed in an assigned residence, or released; and

b. any decisions of the courts or administrative boards sitting in accordance with paragraph 9.33.

---

[78] Refugees are not to be treated as enemy aliens exclusively on the basis of their nationality *de jure* of an enemy state, GC IV, Art 44.

[79] A person will usually be interned if he is penniless or where his personal safety is at risk. If a person requests internment for his own convenience, for example to be with his wife who is already interned, the state concerned is not obliged to intern him.   [80] GC IV, Art 41.

[81] GC IV, Art 43.   [82] GC IV, Art 43.

Transfer

Except for their repatriation or return to their country of residence after the   **9.35**
cessation of hostilities, protected persons must not be transferred to a state
that is not a party to the Convention. Moreover, they may only be transferred to a state that is a party if the detaining state has satisfied itself that
the receiving state is willing and able to apply the Convention.[83] In the
event of transfers taking place, the receiving state becomes responsible for
the application of the Convention.[84] Should that state fail to carry out its
obligations in any important respect, it is the duty of the state which made
the transfer either to take effective measures to correct the situation or
to request the return of the persons affected. The costs of transfer are to
be apportioned by agreement between the states concerned.[85] In no circumstances may a protected person be transferred to a state where he
has reason to fear persecution on account of his political opinions or religious beliefs. However, protected persons who are accused of offences
against the ordinary criminal law remain liable to extradition in pursuance
of extradition treaties concluded before the outbreak of the conflict.[86]

Cancellation of restrictive measures

Any restrictive measures applied to protected persons must be cancelled as   **9.36**
soon as possible after the close of hostilities. Where these measures relate to
property, cancellation is to be in accordance with the law of the detaining
power.[87]

Although the term used in the Convention is 'close of hostilities', in prac-   **9.36.1**
tice, this would mean the same as the phrase 'cessation of active hostilities'
used in the Geneva Convention III.[88]

---

[83] GC IV, Art 45.

[84] Hungary ratified the Convention with the reservation that 'in the case of the transfer of
protected persons from one Power to another, the responsibility for the application of the
Convention must rest with both of those Powers'. Hungary was joined by other Eastern
European states. These reservations are not recognized as valid by the UK. See also the
corresponding provisions on PW in para 8.27. Some of these states have since withdrawn their
reservations to the Geneva Conventions 1949: Belarus on 9 May 1994; Czech Republic on
27 September 2001; Hungary on 31 May 2000; Romania on 24 June 2002; and Slovakia on
5 June 2000.   [85] GC IV, Art 135.

[86] This is subject to refugee and human rights law. Subject also to those laws, there is
nothing to prevent a state from deporting an undesirable foreigner from its territory under
the law normally applicable in peacetime.   [87] GC IV, Art 46.

[88] See para 8.169.

G. CONDITIONS OF INTERNMENT OF PROTECTED PERSONS

GENERAL

9.37 The rules for the internment of protected persons are applicable to internees both in occupied territory and in the detaining power's own territory. In many respects, these provisions are similar to those governing the detention of prisoners of war and the layout of this section therefore is similar to that of the corresponding Part G in Chapter 8.[89]

LOCATION

9.38 The detaining power must take all necessary and possible measures to ensure that protected persons are, from the outset of their internment, 'accommodated in buildings or quarters which afford every possible safeguard as regards hygiene and health, and provide efficient protection against the rigours of the climate and the effects of the war'. Permanent internment camps must not be situated in areas which are unhealthy or where the climate is injurious to internees. Where temporary internment takes place in an unhealthy area or an area where the climate is harmful to the individual internee, that person shall be removed to a more suitable place of internment as rapidly as circumstances permit.[90]

SAFETY OF INTERNEES

9.39 The detaining power is forbidden to set up places of internment in areas that are particularly exposed to the dangers of war. It must notify the enemy state, through the protecting power, of the location of such camps. The letters 'IC', or other agreed marking, clearly visible from the air in day-time, must be used to identify them whenever military considerations permit.[91] Fire precautions must be taken and internees provided with free access to adequate shelters against air raids and other hostile action. They must also benefit from any protective measures taken in favour of the population as a whole.[92]

GROUPING OF INTERNEES

9.40 Members of the same family, particularly parents and children, must be lodged together, preferably in the same accommodation and separately

---

[89] See paras 8.36–8.99.　　[90] GC IV, Art 85.

[91] GC IV, Art 83. Only internment camps may be so marked.

[92] GC IV, Art 88. Even if no protective measures have been taken for the benefit of the local population, shelters must be installed for the internees. Internees, unlike the local population, will not normally have the opportunity to disperse into open country or to take refuge in cellars.

from other internees. Temporary separation of families is only permissible for necessary reasons of employment, health, or discipline. Grouping should accord with internees' nationality, language, and customs, nationals of the same country not being separated merely on account of language differences.[93] Internees are to be accommodated and administered separately from both prisoners of war and those deprived of liberty for other reasons.[94]

MAINTENANCE

Maintenance and medical care of interned protected persons, and of their dependants who lack adequate means of support or are unable to earn a living, must be provided free of charge by the detaining power. No deductions may be made from sums due to internees for repayment of these costs.[95]   **9.41**

INITIAL ACTION ON ARRIVAL OF INTERNEES IN CAMPS

Internees' rights[96]

Internees must be informed immediately of their rights to send an internment card[97] and of their other rights to correspondence.[98]   **9.42**

Personal property

Internees must be permitted to keep articles of personal use, especially those of a personal or sentimental value. They may also keep a certain amount of money in the form of cash or coupons to enable them to make purchases.[99] Money, other valuables, and identity documents may only be taken away in accordance with established procedures, detailed receipts being given. Internees must not be left without means of identification and those lacking an identity document must be issued with one by the detaining power. Money taken from internees is to be paid into their accounts[100] and not converted into any other currency unless the law of the detaining power permits or the internee consents.   **9.43**

Searches of internees

Women internees are to be searched only by women.[101]   **9.44**

---

[93] GC IV, Art 82.   [94] GC IV, Art 84.   [95] GC IV, Art 81.
[96] GC IV, Art 105. Under this article, the detaining power is also obliged to inform the power to which they owe allegiance and the protecting power about how it is going to implement its obligations regarding external communications for internees and about any changes to those arrangements.   [97] See para 9.45.
[98] See paras 9.61–9.63.   [99] GC IV, Art 97.   [100] See para 9.73(d).
[101] GC IV, Art 97.

Internment cards

9.45 Immediately on internment, or within one week of arrival at an internment camp, each internee must be allowed to write one card to his family and another to the Central Information Agency[102] informing them of his internment, address, and state of health.[103] This also applies in the event of sickness, admission to hospital, or transfer to another camp. Internment cards[104] must be forwarded as rapidly as possible.

INTERNAL DISCIPLINE OF CAMPS

Camp commandant

9.46 Every place of internment must be put under the immediate authority of a responsible officer of the regular forces or official of the regular civilian administration of the detaining power.[105] The camp commandant must keep a copy of the Convention in his possession and ensure that the camp staff know its provisions. He is responsible, under the direction of his government, for the application of the Convention and has disciplinary powers over internees.[106]

Posting of Convention and giving of orders

9.47 The text of the Convention and of any special agreements made under it must either be displayed in the internees' language in places where all can read them, or be in the possession of the internee committee.[107] Regulations, orders, notices, and publications of all kinds must be posted in a language understood by the internees. Similarly, direct orders to individuals must be given in a language that they understand.

General discipline

9.48 The disciplinary regime in internment camps must be humane and must not include regulations that impose physical exertion dangerous to health or involve physical or moral victimization. Identification by tattooing or other kinds of body-marking is prohibited. In particular, 'prolonged standing and roll-calls,'[108] punishment drill, military drill and manoeuvres, or the reduction of food rations' are prohibited.[109]

---

[102] See para 9.116.   [103] GC IV, Art 106, Annex III: see Appendix D.

[104] See Appendix D.   [105] GC IV, Art 99.   [106] GC IV, Art 123. See also para 9.96.

[107] GC IV, Art 99. In respect of the internee committee, see paras 9.83–9.85.

[108] Presumably this means 'prolonged roll-calls' since there can be no objection to periodic roll-calls for security reasons and to enable the detaining power to fulfil its obligations to internees.   [109] GC IV, Art 100.

QUARTERS, FOOD, AND CLOTHING

Accommodation[110]

This must be dry with adequate heat and light, particularly between dusk **9.49** and lights out. Sleeping quarters should be sufficiently spacious and well-ventilated. Internees are to have suitable bedding and sufficient blankets taking into account the climate, their age, and state of health. If it is necessary 'as an exceptional and temporary measure' to intern women who are not members of a family unit in a mixed internment camp, they must have separate sleeping quarters and sanitary conveniences.[111]

Hygiene

Accommodation must be hygienic and safeguard health.[112] Sanitary **9.50** conveniences must be provided and kept clean, being available for use by internees at all times of the day and night. Sufficient water and soap must also be provided to permit personal washing and the laundering of clothes. In this respect, showers or baths are to be made available as well as the time for washing and cleaning.

Food

The basic daily ration must be sufficient in quantity, quality, and variety to **9.51** maintain health and prevent nutritional deficiencies, regard being paid to the customary diet of the internees. There must be sufficient drinking water. Working internees as well as expectant and nursing mothers and children aged under 15 years must receive appropriate additional rations.[113]

Messing

Internees must be given the means to prepare for themselves any additional **9.52** food that they may have. The use of tobacco must be permitted.[114]

Canteens

Canteens[115] must be installed in every place of internment unless other **9.53** suitable facilities are available.[116] These canteens are to enable internees to

---

[110] GC IV, Art 85.
[111] They must also be under the immediate supervision of women, see para 9.8.1.
[112] GC IV, Art 85.   [113] GC IV, Art 89.   [114] GC IV, Art 89.
[115] GC IV, Art 87. As to the disposal of profits, see para 9.76.
[116] For example, if the internees have access to, and the opportunity to purchase from, local shops.

make purchases, at prices not higher than local market prices,[117] of food-stuffs and such everyday articles as soap and tobacco as would increase their personal well-being and comfort.

Clothing

9.54 When taken into custody, internees must be given facilities to provide themselves with necessary clothing and to procure further supplies.[118] If any internee has insufficient clothing and is unable to procure it, the detaining power must provide it for him free of charge. Clothing so provided and the outward markings placed on the internees' clothing should not be ignominious, nor liable to expose internees to ridicule. Working internees must be given suitable work clothing, including protective clothing, whenever the nature of their work so requires.

MEDICAL MATTERS

Medical attention[119]

9.55 Each internment camp must have an adequate infirmary under the personal supervision of a qualified doctor where internees may receive the medical attention that they require, as well as an appropriate diet.[120] Isolation wards must be set aside for those suffering from contagious diseases or mental illness. However, maternity cases and those suffering from serious disease, in need of special treatment, surgical operation, or hospital care must be admitted to any hospital at which such treatment or care is available and receive care not inferior to that provided for the general population. Wherever possible, internees should have the attention of medical personnel of their own nationality. Internees may not be refused medical examination. Medical treatment and remedial aids such as dentures, artificial appliances, and spectacles are to be provided free of charge.

Medical supervision[121]

9.56 A medical examination must be conducted at least once a month to monitor the general state of internees' health, nutrition, and cleanliness, to detect infection, especially tuberculosis, malaria, and venereal disease, and to

---

[117] This does not enable the internee to claim to be exempt from regulations such as those governing rationing which apply to the local civilian population.   [118] GC IV, Art 90.

[119] GC IV, Art 91.

[120] That is, a diet designed to help the patient's recovery, see JS Pictet (ed), *Commentary on the Geneva Conventions of 12 August 1949* (1958) (Pictet, *Commentary*), vol IV, 399.

[121] GC IV, Art 92.

check weight. There must be an X-ray examination at least once a year. In the case of working internees, these examinations will also verify their fitness for work.

Medical certificates[122]

An internee who has received medical attention is entitled, upon request, **9.57** to be given a certificate by the medical authorities as to the nature of the complaint and the duration and nature of the treatment given. A duplicate certificate is to be sent to the Central Information Agency.[123]

RELIGION

Freedom of worship

Internees are to enjoy complete latitude in the exercise of their religious **9.58** duties, including attendance at services, provided that they comply with the disciplinary routine of the camp.[124] Suitable accommodation for religious services must be provided.[125]

Ministers of religion

Ministers of religion who are interned must be allowed to minister freely to **9.59** members of their community.[126] The detaining power is to allocate them equitably to camps in which there are internees of the same religion and who speak the same language. Where there are too few ministers, the detaining power is to provide them with the necessary facilities, including transport and authorization, for movement from one camp to another, and this must include the means to visit internees in hospital. Ministers must be able to correspond on religious matters with the religious authorities in the country of detention and, so far as possible, with international religious organizations. This correspondence is in addition to the personal quota,[127] but is subject to censorship.[128] When internees do not have access to interned ministers of their own faith, or the numbers of such ministers are too few, the local religious authorities of that faith may appoint, in agreement with the detaining power, a substitute minister of the same faith or, if feasible, a minister of similar faith or a qualified layman. The person appointed must comply with all discipline and security regulations laid down by the detaining power but must have all the facilities granted to the ministry that he has assumed.

---

[122] GC IV, Art 91.   [123] See GC IV, Art 140 and para 9.116.   [124] GC IV, Art 93.
[125] GC IV, Art 86.   [126] GC IV, Art 93.   [127] See paras 9.61–9.63.
[128] See para 9.66.

RECREATION

Education and sport

9.60 The detaining power is required to encourage voluntary intellectual, educational, and recreational activities, including sport and games, for which purposes adequate premises and facilities must be provided. Participation, however, must be optional. Sufficient open space must be available for physical exercise with special playgrounds reserved for children and young people. The education of children and young people especially should be ensured by allowing them to attend schools either within the place of internment or outside. In general, all possible facilities shall be granted to internees to continue their studies or take up new subjects.[129]

CORRESPONDENCE AND RELIEF PARCELS

Outgoing correspondence

9.61 Internees must be permitted to send letters and cards.[130] If the detaining power deems it necessary to impose limitations, the number permitted must not be less than two letters and four cards each month.[131] This is in addition to the internment card.[132] Letters and cards must be conveyed with reasonable despatch and must not be held up as a disciplinary measure. Internees, in urgent cases, or who have been a long time without news or cannot obtain news from their relatives, as well as those who are a long distance from their homes, must be allowed to send telegrams at their own expense. States are under a duty to reduce telegram charges as much as possible.[133] Correspondence is normally to be in the internee's native language unless the detaining power authorizes correspondence in another language.

Incoming correspondence[134]

9.62 Internees must be allowed to receive all letters and cards addressed to them. Restrictions may only be imposed by the power on which they depend though this can be at the request of the detaining power.

Individual and collective relief

9.63 Internees are allowed to receive individual parcels and collective relief shipments containing items such as food, clothing, medical supplies, and

---

[129] GC IV, Art 94.   [130] GC IV, Art 107.
[131] For model correspondence cards and letter, see Appendix D.   [132] See para 9.45.
[133] GC IV, Art 110. See also Art 141 and the Universal Postal Convention 1974, Art 16(2), which provides that internees have the same facilities as PW. For PW, see para 8.62.
[134] GC IV, Art 107.

religious, educational, cultural, or recreational articles. This does not absolve the detaining power from its responsibilities for provision of such articles. Books are not to be included in parcels of clothing and food. Medical supplies should, as a rule, be sent in collective parcels. Shipments may be limited only for reasons of military necessity, in which case due notice must be given to the protecting power and to the ICRC or to any other organization responsible for shipments.[135] In the absence of any special agreement between the states concerned, the regulations concerning collective relief annexed to the Convention[136] apply. Special agreements may neither restrict the right of the internee committee[137] to collect and distribute relief consignments in the interests of recipients, nor restrict the protecting power, the ICRC, or any other organization arranging shipments, in their right to supervise their distribution.[138]

Import, postal, and transport charges[139]

No import, customs, or other dues may be charged on relief shipments for **9.64** internees. Postal dues are not to be charged on correspondence, relief shipments, or authorized remittances of money sent to internees through the post. If the post office cannot be used, transport costs are borne by the detaining power in all territories under its control and by the other parties to the Convention through whose territory the consignments pass. Any additional costs must be paid by the sender.

Special means of transport

If military operations prevent the powers concerned from carrying out **9.65** their duty to forward internees' mail and relief parcels, the protecting power, the ICRC, or other approved organizations may move it themselves as well as official mail relating to internees.[140] If so, the states concerned must allow its passage, granting safe conducts[141] where necessary and, if possible, providing transport. In the absence of agreement, the costs are borne proportionately by the parties whose nationals are benefited.

Censorship

All censoring of correspondence addressed to, or despatched by, internees **9.66** must be done as quickly as possible. Examination of consignments for

---

[135] GC IV, Art 108. The purpose of requiring notice to the protecting power of reduction in consignments is to enable alternative arrangements to be made.   [136] See Appendix D.
[137] See paras 9.83–9.85.   [138] GC IV, Art 109.
[139] GC IV, Art 110. See also Art 141 and the Universal Postal Convention 1974, Art 16(2), which provides that internees have the same facilities as PW. For PW, see para 8.66.
[140] GC IV, Art 111.   [141] See para 10.34.

internees must not be carried out in a way that exposes goods to deterioration. These examinations are to be carried out in the presence of the addressee or a fellow internee delegated by him. Censorship difficulties must not be used as a pretext for delay in the delivery to internees of their consignments.[142] Any prohibition of correspondence ordered by the parties for military or political reasons must be temporary only and of as short a duration as possible.[143]

LEGAL MATTERS

Civil legal status[144]

9.67 Internees retain their civil legal capacity and may exercise their rights in so far as these are compatible with their status as internees.

9.67.1 This means that in civil matters the internee continues to be governed by the law that applied to him before internment.[145]

Legal documents[146]

9.68 Internees must have reasonable facilities, including access to legal advice, for the preparation, execution, and transmission of legal documents, especially wills, powers of attorney, and letters of authority. Transmission of these documents will normally be through the protecting power or the Central Information Agency.

Court cases[147]

9.69 Where an internee is a party to court proceedings, and so requests, the detaining power must take steps to ensure that the court is informed of the

---

[142] GC IV, Art 112. The notion of censorship is implied in other articles dealing with correspondence between internees and 'the exterior' which do not make specific mention of it, see n 169. The detaining power may for the purposes of removing matter prejudicial to its military security, examine and censor:

a. the correspondence of ministers of religion with the religious authorities of the country of detention and international religious organizations of their faith under Art 93;

b. communications or articles sent to or by internees, including their petitions and complaints under Art 101, see para 9.82;

c. their correspondence and telegrams under Art 107, see paras 9.61–9.62; and

d. their relief shipments.

[143] Unless this provision of Art 112 is treated as referring to a temporary restriction of not more than, eg, two weeks which does not interfere with the right conferred by Art 110, it is difficult to reconcile it with Art 107, see para 9.61, which forbids restricting internees to less than two letters and four cards monthly.

[144] GC IV, Art 80.

[145] However, in respect of the law relating to offences committed by internees, see para 9.91.

[146] GC IV, Art 113.

[147] GC IV, Art 115.

fact of the detention and that the internee is not prejudiced on that account in the preparation and conduct of the case or the execution of any judgment.

Property[148]

As far as it is compatible with internment and the applicable law, internees **9.70** must be enabled to manage their property. In urgent cases and appropriate circumstances, the detaining power may permit an internee to leave the place of internment for this purpose.

Visits[149]

Every internee must be allowed to receive visitors, especially near relatives, **9.71** at regular intervals and as frequently as possible. As far as possible, internees should also be allowed to visit their homes in cases of urgency, especially death or serious illness of relatives.

Financial Matters

Allowances[150]

Apart from providing for internees' maintenance, the detaining power is **9.72** required to pay them regular allowances to enable them to purchase items such as tobacco and toilet requisites. These allowances may be in cash, credits, or purchase coupons. Additionally, internees may also receive allowances from the power on which they depend, the protecting power, relief organizations, and their families, as well as any income from property due to them under the law of the detaining power. Allowances from the state to which they owe allegiance may vary in accordance with different categories of internees (such as, for example, the infirm, the sick, and pregnant women) but no other discrimination in allocation is permissible.

Internees' accounts[151]

The detaining power must keep an account for each internee, which is to be **9.73** credited with the following:

a. allowances paid;[152]
b. wages earned;[153]
c. remittances received; and
d. sums taken from internees.[154]

---

[148] GC IV, Art 114.   [149] GC IV, Art 116.   [150] GC IV, Art 98.   [151] GC IV, Art 98.
[152] In accordance with para 9.72.   [153] See para 9.80.
[154] In accordance with para 9.43.

Management of internees' accounts[155]

9.74 Internees must be given reasonable facilities for consulting, and obtaining copies of, their accounts. A statement of accounts must be furnished to the protecting power on demand and must accompany any transferred internee.

Disposal of funds[156]

9.75 Subject to legislation in force in the territory of the detaining power, facilities are to be granted to internees to enable them to remit money to their families and other dependants. They may also withdraw amounts necessary for their personal expenses, subject to any limits fixed by the detaining power.

Welfare fund[157]

9.76 Profits from canteens go into a welfare fund for each camp for the benefit of internees. The internee committee[158] has the right to check the management of the fund. On the closure of an internment camp, the balance of the fund is to be transferred to the welfare fund of another camp for internees of the same nationality. If there is no such camp, it is to be transferred to a central welfare fund for the benefit of all internees remaining in the custody of the detaining power. In the event of a general release of internees, the balance of the fund may be retained by the detaining power unless the states concerned otherwise agree.

WORK OF INTERNEES

General

9.77 Detaining powers are forbidden to employ internees as workers unless the internees so desire.[159] Any work which, if undertaken under compulsion by a protected person not in internment, would be contrary to the terms of the Convention, or which is degrading or humiliating, is forbidden.[160] States may, however, employ, even compulsorily, interned doctors, dentists, and other medical personnel[161] in their professional capacity on behalf of their fellow internees, as well as other internees for administrative, maintenance, and domestic tasks within the camp, and also on air raid protection work, provided that their health permits.

---

[155] GC IV, Art 98.   [156] GC IV, Art 98.   [157] GC IV, Art 87.
[158] See GC IV, Art 102 and paras 9.83–9.85.   [159] GC IV, Art 95.
[160] See GC IV, Arts 40 and 51 and para 9.30.
[161] See also GC IV, Art 20 and AP I, Art 18(3) as to the need for such personnel in occupied territory and areas of fighting to be recognizable by a distinctive emblem and ID card.

Notice to terminate

Unless employed compulsorily,[162] after a working period of six weeks, **9.78** internees may give up work at any time, subject to eight day's notice.[163]

Working conditions[164]

The detaining power is responsible for working conditions, medical atten- **9.79** tion, payment of wages, and for ensuring compensation for occupational accidents and diseases. The standards are to be in accordance with national law and practice and should in no case be inferior to those applying to work of the same nature in the same district.

Wages

Wages are to be determined on an equitable basis by special agreements **9.80** between internees, the detaining power, and, where appropriate, private employers. Those engaged in medical or other internment camp work are to be paid fair wages.[165]

Labour detachments[166]

Labour detachments must remain part of, and dependent on, a place of **9.81** internment. The commandant of the internment camp is responsible for due compliance with the Convention in all labour detachments subordinate to him and must keep an up-to-date list of such detachments. Copies of that list must be sent to the protecting power, the ICRC, and any other humanitarian organization involved.[167] All of these have the right to visit detachments.

CLAIMS, COMPLAINTS, AND THE INTERNEE COMMITTEE

Complaints and petitions

Internees have the right to present to the authorities in whose power they **9.82** are petitions about the conditions of their internment. Further, they may complain about their conditions of internment, without restriction, either through their own internee committee or directly, to the representatives of the protecting power. All such petitions and complaints must be forwarded

---

[162] See para 9.77.   [163] GC IV, Art 95.   [164] GC IV, Art 95.

[165] GC IV, Art 95. It is not intended that internees should be entitled to receive the wages paid to ordinary employees because the internee, unlike the ordinary local worker, is freed from all normal financial responsibilities. See also, however, Art 81 and para 9.41 in respect of deductions.   [166] GC IV, Art 96.

[167] See GC IV, Arts 30, 142, and 143.

forthwith and unaltered. Even if they are unfounded, no punishment may be imposed on the petitioners or complainants. It is open to the internee committee[168] to send periodic reports on internment conditions and the needs of the internees to the representatives of the protecting power.[169]

Internee committee[170]

9.83 In every place of internment, internees must be able to elect members of an internee committee by secret ballot every six months. Members of the committee are eligible for re-election. Membership is subject to the approval of the detaining power, but if that is withheld or a member is dismissed, the protecting power must be informed of the reasons. It is only after approval that internees so elected can take up their duties.

Duties of the internee committee

9.84 The general duty of this committee is to further the physical, spiritual, and intellectual welfare of the internees.[171] It represents internees in dealings with the detaining and protecting powers, the ICRC, and any other organization helping internees.[172] In the event of a decision by internees to organize a mutual assistance welfare system amongst themselves, implementation would be within the competence of the internee committee. The specific tasks of the internee committee include:

a. the running of canteens;[173]
b. the transmission of complaints, petitions, and reports;[174]
c. the collection, holding, and distribution of collective relief;[175] and
d. the transportation of internees' community property and baggage.[176]

9.84.1 The internee committee must be informed of all judicial proceedings instituted against internees whom they represent, and also the result of such proceedings.[177] Any decision on disciplinary punishment against an internee must be announced in the presence of the accused and of a member of the internee committee.[178]

---

[168] See paras 9.83–9.85.

[169] GC IV, Art 101. This provision does not deprive the detaining power of the general right of censorship, which is implicit in the Convention and is referred to in Art 112, see para 9.66. Thus the duty of the authorities to transmit complaints and petitions necessarily implies a right to read the documents in question and to see whether they are in fact complaints and petitions. Moreover, since there is no obligation to transmit without alteration material that is neither a complaint nor a petition, there is no infringement of the Convention if such material is deleted from communications to representatives of the protecting power or others.

[170] GC IV, Art 102.   [171] GC IV, Art 103.   [172] GC IV, Art 102.   [173] See para 9.53.
[174] See para 9.82.   [175] See para 9.63.   [176] See para 9.88.
[177] GC IV, Art 118. See para 9.104.   [178] GC IV, Art 123.

Rights of members of the internee committee

Members of the internee committee have the following rights:[179]   **9.85**

a. not to do other work if this would interfere with their duties;[180]

b. to appoint as assistants such fellow internees as may be required;

c. to have the necessary facilities to carry out their duties including, for example, inspection of labour detachments and the receipt of relief supplies;

d. to correspond by post and telegraph with the detaining authorities, the protecting power, the ICRC, and any other organization assisting internees;[181]

e. if at a labour detachment, to conduct correspondence with the internee committee at the main camp; and

f. in the event of transfer, to have a proper handover to their successors.

TRANSFER OF INTERNEES

Conditions of transfer[182]

Transfers must be carried out humanely and under conditions at least equal **9.86** to those governing the movements of the armed forces of the detaining power on a change of station. Movement will normally be by rail or other means of transport but if, in exceptional circumstances, such transfers have to be made on foot, they may not be made unless the internees are in a fit state of health. In no case may transfers subject internees to excessive fatigue. Adequate arrangements must be made for the supply of drinking water, food, shelter, clothing, and necessary medical attention. The detaining power must take all suitable precautions to ensure the safety of internees during transfer and, before their departure, must prepare a complete list of all internees transferred.

Circumstances precluding transfer[183]

Consideration must be given to the interests of internees, so as, for example, **9.87** not to increase the difficulty of repatriating or releasing them. Sick, wounded, or infirm internees and maternity cases must not be transferred if the journey itself would be seriously detrimental to them, unless their safety imperatively demands transfer. If combat draws close to a camp,

---

[179] GC IV, Art 104.

[180] Although, in general, internees cannot be compelled to work, this provision indicates that, where they do, committee work has priority.

[181] This is in addition to the correspondence quota mentioned in para 9.61.

[182] GC IV, Art 127.   [183] GC IV, Art 127.

internees should not be moved unless either this can be done safely or they would be exposed to greater danger by remaining there.

Procedure for transfer[184]

9.88 Internees must be notified officially in advance of their impending departure and of their new postal address so that they can pack their luggage and inform their next of kin. They must be allowed to take their personal property but, if circumstances so require, the detaining power may limit the amount to not less than 25 kilograms each. The camp commandant is responsible for liaison with the internee committee in respect of the movement of the internees' community property and any luggage that cannot be taken with the internees themselves. Mail must be forwarded without delay.

Accounts

9.89 When internees are transferred, a statement of their account must be transferred with them.[185]

H. ESCAPE OF INTERNEES

ESCAPES

9.90 Internees who escape are, on recapture, to be handed over as soon as possible to the competent authorities, normally the camp commandant directly responsible for the internee before the escape.[186] Those who have attempted to escape may thereafter be subject to special surveillance[187] provided, however, that it does not affect their state of health or tend otherwise to infringe the safeguards granted by the Convention.

I. PUNISHMENT OF INTERNEES

GENERAL PRINCIPLES

The law applicable

9.91 Subject to their right to protection under the Convention, the laws in force in the territory[188] where they are interned continue to apply to internees who

---

[184] GC IV, Art 128.   [185] GC IV, Art 98. See also para 9.74.
[186] GC IV, Art 122. For punishments, see para 9.100. For offences committed during an escape, see para 9.95.1.   [187] GC IV, Art 120.
[188] GC IV, Art 117. This would include occupation legislation where the internee is interned in occupied territory. Such legislation must not exceed the powers of an occupying power as set out in Art 64. GCA 1957, ss 2–5 makes special provision for the trial of protected persons in the UK.

commit offences during internment. Offences which are punishable if committed by internees but not punishable if committed by others must, if punished, entail disciplinary punishment only.[189]

Punishment

The courts and authorities of the detaining power, in reaching decisions on **9.92** punishment, must at all times remember that the accused is not a national of the detaining power. The courts must be free to reduce the penalty below the minimum prescribed by law for the offence. The length of time for which an internee is kept in pre-trial custody must be deducted from any custodial sentence passed.[190] An internee may not be punished more than once for the same act or on the same charge.[191]

Prohibited punishments

The following punishments are forbidden: **9.93**

a. collective punishments for individual acts;[192]
b. corporal punishment;[193]
c. confinement in a place without daylight;[194] and
d. any form of torture or brutality.[195]

After sentence

Internees who have served their sentences must not be treated differently **9.94** from other internees.[196] The only exception is the rule relating to special surveillance of internees who have attempted to escape.[197]

Choice of disciplinary or judicial action

As with prisoners of war,[198] the detaining power must decide in each **9.95** case whether the offence should be tried by a court as judicial proceedings or disposed of summarily by the camp commandant taking disciplinary measures. Trials must take place in the ordinary civil courts and special

---

[189] Namely, punishments imposed by a non-judicial body or authority, eg, the commandant of an internment camp. They must be limited to the punishments set out in Art 119, see para 9.100. For serious offences against the law, the internee must be tried by the ordinary courts of the territory or, in occupied territory, by the courts set up by the occupying power. It follows that internees cannot be tried by special courts set up particularly for internees and that disciplinary punishments only may be awarded for infringements of camp discipline or orders which are not breaches of the law of the land.   [190] GC IV, Art 118.
[191] GC IV, Art 117.   [192] GC IV, Art 33.   [193] GC IV, Art 32.   [194] GC IV, Art 118.
[195] GC IV, Art 32. See also Art 119.   [196] GC IV, Art 118.
[197] GC IV, Art 120. See para 9.90.   [198] See para 8.116.

courts may not be set up for that purpose. There are two circumstances in which internees must be dealt with by way of disciplinary measures:

a. where the law provides for an act to be punishable only if committed by an internee;[199] or

b. where the offence is one of attempted escape, or of aiding and abetting either an escape or an attempted escape.[200]

9.95.1 Wherever possible, offences committed in connection with an escape should be dealt with on a disciplinary basis and the escape, even if it is a repeated offence, should not be regarded as an aggravating circumstance.[201]

DISCIPLINARY MEASURES

Authority who may take disciplinary measures

9.96 Only the camp commandant or the officer or official acting in his place or to whom he has delegated his powers may take disciplinary action.[202]

Investigation

9.97 Offences against discipline, particularly cases of escape and attempted escape, must be investigated immediately.[203]

Confinement before hearing

9.98 Confinement pending any hearing must be kept to the absolute minimum and must not, in any event, exceed 14 days.[204]

Rights of the accused

9.99 Before any disciplinary punishment is awarded, the accused must be given full details of the offence and be given an opportunity to explain his conduct and to defend himself. In particular, he must be allowed to call witnesses and, if necessary, given the services of a qualified interpreter.[205]

---

[199] GC IV, Art 117. See also GCA 1957, ss 2–5 and para 9.91.   [200] GC IV, Art 120.
[201] GC IV, Art 121.   [202] GC IV, Art 123.   [203] GC IV, Art 122.
[204] GC IV, Art 122. The provisions of para 9.103 apply equally to those in confinement awaiting disciplinary action.   [205] GC IV, Art 123.

Powers of punishment

Internees may be awarded the following disciplinary punishments:[206] **9.100**

a. a fine not exceeding 50 per cent of 30 days' pay for a working internee;[207]

b. withdrawal for up to 30 days of any privileges granted over and above the minimum provided for by the Convention;

c. fatigue duties for up to 30 days, not exceeding two hours per day and connected with the maintenance of the camp;[208] and

d. confinement for not more than 30 days.

No punishment may be inhuman, brutal, or dangerous to health and in **9.100.1** awarding punishment the internee's age, sex, and state of health must be taken into account. Any period of any single punishment must not exceed 30 days for all offences dealt with at the same time, but different punishments may be ordered to run concurrently. The period between pronouncement and commencement of the sentence must not exceed one month.[209] When a further punishment is awarded, there must be an interval of at least three days between the execution of any two of the punishments if the duration of one of them is ten days or more.

Announcement of award

The decision must be announced in the presence of the accused and a **9.101** member of the internee committee.[210]

Record

A record of disciplinary punishments must be maintained by the camp **9.102** commandant and must be available for inspection by representatives of the protecting power.[211]

Conditions under which disciplinary punishments may be served

Internees serving disciplinary punishments have the following specific rights: **9.103**

a. *Premises*:[212] the right to hygienic premises. Internees must be provided with adequate bedding and washing facilities. Women must be quartered

---

[206] GC IV, Art 119. These are all maximum punishments. A detaining power may provide for lower maximum punishments if it so wishes.

[207] See GC IV, Art 95 and para 9.80. This does not include allowances.

[208] This does not refer to an increase of working hours. Since work is voluntary for most internees, any such increase imposed as a punishment would penalize volunteers.

[209] GC IV, Art 123.   [210] GC IV, Art 123.   [211] GC IV, Art 123.   [212] GC IV, Art 124.

separately from men and under the immediate supervision of women. Internees may not be transferred to prisons or detention centres.

b. *Communication*:[213] the right to correspondence and communication with representatives of the protecting power and the ICRC.

c. *Exercise*: the right to take exercise and be in the open air for at least two hours every day.

d. *Medical Treatment*: the right to attend daily medical inspections and to receive necessary medical attention, including hospital treatment.

e. *Correspondence*: the right to read, write, send, and receive letters. Parcels and remittances of money may be withheld until after completion of the punishment, being entrusted meanwhile to the internee committee who must hand over any perishable contents to the camp infirmary.[214]

JUDICIAL PROCEEDINGS

9.104 The procedure for taking judicial action against internees is the same as that applicable in occupied territory, see paragraphs 11.56 to 11.74.[215]

J. DEATHS

DEATH OF INTERNEES

Wills

9.105 On the death of an internee, any will which he has made and given to the detaining power for safe-keeping must be sent to the person designated by the deceased.[216]

Death certificates and records[217]

9.106 Death must, in all cases, be certified by a doctor and a death certificate made out showing the causes of death and the conditions under which it occurred. An official and duly registered record of the death must be drawn up in accordance with the law of the place of internment and a certified copy sent without delay to the protecting power and to the Central Information Agency.

Burial and cremation[218]

9.107 Dead internees must be honourably buried, if possible in accordance with the rites of their religion, in individual graves unless the use of collective graves is unavoidable. Cremation may only take place either for imperative reasons

---

[213] GC IV, Arts 125, 143.   [214] GC IV, Art 125.   [215] GC IV, Art 126.
[216] GC IV, Art 129.   [217] GC IV, Art 129.   [218] GC IV, Art 130.

of hygiene, or in accordance with the religion or other expressed wishes of the deceased. The reason for cremation must be specified in the death certificate.

Maintenance of graves and disposal of ashes[219]

The detaining power must ensure that graves are respected, suitably main- **9.108** tained, and marked so that they can be found at any time. Lists of internees' graves, indicating their location, must be sent through the national informa- tion bureau, to the power on which the internees depended. Ashes are to be retained by the detaining power until they can be sent to the next of kin.

Inquiries into death or serious injury

Where the cause of death or serious injury of an internee is attributable to **9.109** another person, including a sentry, or is unknown, the detaining power must immediately hold an official inquiry and notify the protecting power. The investigation must include the recording of witness statements and, where the evidence supports criminal charges, the detaining power is under a duty to bring a prosecution. A copy of the report of the investigation must be sent to the protecting power.[220]

K. TERMINATION OF INTERNMENT

RELEASE, REPATRIATION, AND ACCOMMODATION IN NEUTRAL COUNTRIES

During hostilities or occupation[221]

As soon as the reasons for internment have ceased, an internee must be **9.110** released. The parties to the conflict must, during hostilities, seek to conclude agreements for the release, repatriation, return to places of residence or accommodation in a neutral country of certain classes of internees, particu- larly children, pregnant women, mothers of infants and young children, the wounded and sick, and those who have been detained for a long time.

After close of hostilities or occupation[222]

Internment must cease as soon as possible after the close of hostilities or the **9.111** end of occupation. The parties must endeavour to[223] ensure the return of

---

[219] GC IV, Art 130.
[220] GC IV, Art 131. For example, the record of the proceedings of either a coroner's inquest or a criminal prosecution would suffice.   [221] GC IV, Art 132.
[222] GC IV, Arts 133 and 134.
[223] The language of Art 134 makes it clear that force cannot be used to compel repatriation. Compare the corresponding provision relating to PW in GC III, Art 118 and para 8.168.

internees to their last place of residence, or facilitate their repatriation. Committees may be set up to search for dispersed internees. Internees against whom judicial proceedings are pending may be detained until the conclusion of the proceedings and any custodial sentence. Disciplinary penalties do not affect release.

Expenses[224]

9.112 In the absence of a special agreement, the expenses of dealing with released internees are borne as follows:

a. the detaining power bears the cost of:
   (1) their return to their places of residence before internment;
   (2) in respect of those interned while in transit, either completion of their journey or return to their point of departure; and
   (3) repatriation of those previously permanently domiciled in its territory but now refused permission to continue to reside there.
b. the detaining power does not bear the cost of:
   (1) movement beyond its own frontiers of those who elect to return to their own states on their own responsibility or in obedience to orders from the state on which they depend; and
   (2) repatriation of those interned at their own request.

Money and property[225]

9.113 All money and property taken from internees during internment is to be returned on release or repatriation together with any credit balances in their accounts. A detailed receipt must be given in respect of any property withheld in accordance with local legislation.

L. INFORMATION BUREAUX AND RELIEF SOCIETIES

INFORMATION BUREAUX

General[226]

9.114 At the beginning of hostilities and in all cases of occupation, each party has a duty to establish an official information bureau for receiving and transmitting

---

[224] GC IV, Art 135.   [225] GC IV, Art 97.

[226] See generally GC IV, Arts 136–141. The object of these provisions is to ensure that trace will be kept of those interned during a conflict. During WW II, large numbers of people were put in concentration camps with no attempt being made to inform any agency of their internment or their subsequent fate.

information about protected persons in its power. The party concerned must, without delay, give its bureau information about:

a. any measure which it has taken affecting any protected person who is kept in custody for more than two weeks, or who is subjected to assigned residence or interned;[227]

b. all changes affecting such protected persons, including transfers, releases, repatriations, escapes, hospital admissions, births, and deaths; and

c. details of internees' graves.[228]

The information provided[229] must be such as will assist in the exact identi- **9.114.1**
fication of the protected person concerned and must include at least:

a. surname and forenames of the individual concerned as well as the father's first name and mother's maiden name;

b. place and date of birth;

c. nationality;

d. last residence;

e. distinguishing characteristics;

f. date, place, and nature of action taken with regard to the individual;

g. name and address of the person to be informed as next of kin;

h. individual's present address for correspondence; and

i. in respect of those seriously ill or wounded, regular reports on their health, if possible weekly.

Duties of the information bureaux

These are the following: **9.115**

a. To pass information quickly to the states of which the protected persons are nationals, or the states in whose territory they resided. Information is passed through the protecting power and the Central Information Agency. If passage of the information would be detrimental to the interests of the protected person or his family, for example because this may subject them to persecution, the information is to be passed only to the Central Information Bureau.[230]

b. To reply to all enquires received about protected persons.

c. To ensure that its letters are properly authenticated by signature or seal.

d. To collect all personal valuables, including documents and wills, left by protected persons, particularly those who have been repatriated or

---

[227] GC IV, Art 136.   [228] GC IV, Art 130. See para 9.108.   [229] GC IV, Art 138.
[230] GC IV, Art 137.

released, or who have escaped or died, together, where appropriate, with certified copies of records of death. These items are forwarded either direct or, if necessary, through the Central Information Agency, to those entitled to receive them (usually the next of kin) in sealed packets with a complete list of contents and specifying clearly the identity of the owner. Detailed records must be maintained of the receipt and despatch of these items.[231]

e. Although not specifically required under the law of armed conflict, the information bureau should also supervise the documentation of children evacuated to foreign countries.[232]

Central Information Agency[233]

9.116 A Central Information Agency for protected persons, particularly for internees, must be established in a neutral country. The ICRC may make proposals in this regard. The agency may be the same one that deals with prisoners of war.[234] Its task is to collect information about protected persons from official or private channels and send it without delay to the states either of origin or of residence of the individuals concerned, except where that might be to the detriment of the protected persons concerned or their relatives. The agency must have all necessary facilities and may seek financial support from any country whose nationals are benefited. The establishment of such an agency does not prevent similar work being done by either the ICRC or relief societies such as national red cross societies.

Exemption from charges[235]

9.117 Information bureaux and the Central Information Agency are exempt from postal charges, import, customs, and other dues and transport costs. If possible, they should also be exempted from telegraphic charges or given reduced rates.

Relief Societies[236]

9.118 'Subject to the measures which the Detaining Powers may consider essential to ensure their security or to meet other reasonable need', representatives of religious organizations and other relief societies for the assistance of

---

[231] GC IV, Art 139.   [232] See paras 9.14–9.15.

[233] GC IV, Art 140. The ICRC's Central Tracing Agency normally carries out the tasks of the Central Information Agency.

[234] See para 8.184. The ICRC's Central Tracing Agency also normally carries out the tasks of the Central Prisoners of War Information Agency.   [235] GC IV, Art 141.

[236] GC IV, Art 142.

protected persons must also have the necessary facilities to enable them to visit protected persons and to distribute relief supplies and material (from whatever source received) which are intended for religious, educational, or recreational purposes. Such bodies may be set up in the territory of the detaining power or elsewhere, or they may be international. The detaining power may, however, limit the number of bodies carrying out such activities in its territory and under its supervision, as long as this does not prevent adequate relief from reaching protected persons. However, the special position of the ICRC in this field[237] 'shall be recognized and respected at all times'.

[237] The ICRC has the right to visit internees, its delegates enjoying the same prerogatives as the protecting power, see GC IV, Art 143. The ICRC also operates the Central Information Agency.

10

Negotiations Between Belligerents

A. INTRODUCTION

NEED FOR COMMUNICATION BETWEEN BELLIGERENTS

An armed conflict frequently leads to the breaking of diplomatic relations **10.1** between the parties and the cessation of direct traffic and communications between the territories controlled by the opposing forces. It is desirable, therefore, that there should remain some channels for non-hostile communications between the parties to facilitate a return to peace and for humanitarian purposes.

10.1.1 There are various ways in which such communications can be carried on: by direct contact, at local or diplomatic level, or by indirect contact, for example through a protecting power, another state, the International Committee of the Red Cross, or through the United Nations. The legal principles governing such communications are the subject of the present chapter.

PRINCIPLE OF GOOD FAITH

10.2 Whenever there are non-hostile relations between parties to an armed conflict, those relations must be conducted with the utmost good faith and any agreement reached scrupulously observed. In particular, there should be no abuse of a flag of truce or emblems of identification in dealings between belligerents.[1]

B. COMMUNICATION BETWEEN FORCES

NEED FOR COMMUNICATION BETWEEN FORCES

10.3 In addition to contacts between governments, there are occasions when it is necessary for the commanders of opposing forces to enter into communications with one another to conclude arrangements of a purely military character concerning the forces under their command.[2]

10.3.1 Occasionally such contacts, for example the arrangement of a local truce or surrender, may involve political considerations but, in view of radio and similar means of communication, these matters tend nowadays to be taken up on an inter-governmental level, avoiding actual negotiations between belligerent commanders.[3] Nevertheless, more traditional communications between commanders have not been wholly superseded. Although some of the means of communications described below may appear to be archaic,

---

[1] Hague Regulations 1907 (HR) Art 23(f); Additional Protocol I 1977 (AP I), Arts 37(1)(a) and 38(1).

[2] eg, to arrange for the collection of the dead or exchange of the wounded, see Geneva Convention I 1949 (GC I), Art 15 and AP I, Art 33(4).

[3] The meeting of military commanders at Safwan at the end of the Gulf conflict 1991 followed the suspension of hostilities announced by President Bush and the adoption of UN Security Council Resolution (UNSCR) 686(1991).

they are well established and respected in the law of armed conflict and remain of practical value.

THE PARLEMENTAIRE AND FLAG OF TRUCE

Inviolability of parlementaire

Negotiations between belligerent commanders are normally conducted, **10.4** at least in the first instance, by an intermediary, known technically as a 'parlementaire', normally operating under a flag of truce, who has been authorized in writing under the signature of the sending commander. Whilst performing their duties and provided that their conduct is correct,[4] parlementaires and those who accompany them are entitled to complete inviolability.[5] This means that they may not be attacked or taken prisoners of war and must be allowed to rejoin their own forces at the end of their mission. Inviolability of the parlementaire does not mean that all hostile activities of the opposing forces have to cease. They must cease to the extent necessary to ensure the safety of those involved in the negotiations.

The flag of truce

From time immemorial, a white flag has been used as a signal of a desire to **10.5** open communications with the enemy. This is the only meaning that the white flag possesses in the law of armed conflict.[6] Wilful abuse of a white flag that results in death or serious injury is a grave breach of Additional Protocol I.[7]

The display of a white flag means only that one party is asked whether it **10.5.1** will receive a communication from the other.[8] In some cases it may also

[4] eg, they have not indulged in espionage, see HR, Art 34.

[5] HR, Art 32. Although the reference here is to 'trumpeter, bugler or drummer, the flag bearer and interpreter who may accompany him', in modern warfare, the party is more likely to consist of a driver and radio operator, together with an interpreter. The interpreter will not necessarily be a member of the armed forces and may be a civilian. The white flag will most likely be attached to the vehicle conveying the party.

[6] In Iraq, in May 1941, a British aircraft dropped a message demanding surrender of a fort. The defenders are reported to have hoisted a white flag and then fired upon and hit the aircraft. The incident was explained later on the basis that, in Iraqi signal language, the white flag is used to call for reinforcements.   [7] AP I, Art 85(3)(f). See also Arts 37(1)(a) and 38(1).

[8] On the other hand, there is nothing in HR, Arts 32–34 to indicate that a white flag is the only method whereby one belligerent may signify to the other its desire to open communications. In modern conditions of warfare, radio, loudspeakers, or a telephone 'hotline' may also be used.

mean that the party that displays it wishes to make an arrangement for a temporary suspension of hostilities for a purpose, such as the evacuation of the wounded, but in other cases it may mean that the party wishes to negotiate for surrender. Everything depends on the circumstances and conditions of the particular case. For instance, in practice, the white flag has come to indicate surrender if displayed by individual soldiers or a small party in the course of an action.

10.5.2 Those who display a white flag should cease firing until the invitation has been answered. Any abuse of a white flag is likely to be a war crime.[9] Great vigilance must, however, always be displayed in dealing with enemy forces that have displayed a white flag, because other enemy soldiers in the vicinity may be unaware of the display of the white flag and continue firing.[10] This is especially likely where the decision to display a white flag was taken not by the enemy commander on behalf of the entire force under his command but by individual soldiers.

Procedure

10.6 Parlementaires should approach their task with caution, moving slowly and deliberately in order to be recognized. Fire must not be directed intentionally on the parlementaire or those who accompany him. Great courtesy should be observed on both sides. Parlementaires should be treated with the respect due to their rank. If it is thought desirable for their protection, a guard or escort should be provided.

10.6.1 A parlementaire may not insist on being received at a particular time or place. Since the adverse party may continue hostilities, the parlementaire should cross during a lull in the fighting or travel by a route that reduces any risk to himself or those with him.

Those accompanying parlementaires

10.7 Those accompanying the parlementaire, other than his interpreter, have no right to enter enemy lines. They should remain outside and obey any orders given to them by the adverse party. They remain entitled to protection.

---

[9] Even if it does not amount to a grave breach, see para 10.5.
[10] A British officer was killed at Goose Green during the Falklands conflict 1982 when moving towards a white flag. The shots were not fired by those displaying the white flag, but by others in the vicinity.

Obligations of the opposing commander

The commander to whom a parlementaire is sent is not obliged to receive **10.8** him in every case.[11] However, it is no longer permissible[12] for a belligerent to declare beforehand, even for a stated period, that he will not receive parlementaires. However, the commander is entitled to take all steps necessary to protect the safety of his position or unit and to prevent the parlementaire from taking advantage of his visit to secure information.

The reason for these security measures is that there may be troop movements **10.8.1** in progress[13] or, owing to the state of the defences, it may be considered undesirable to allow an envoy to approach a besieged locality. Measures taken may involve prescribing the route he takes, the hour and place of his visit, or even blindfolding. An unnecessary repetition of visits need not be allowed.

Security

A commander has the right to detain a parlementaire temporarily if the lat- **10.9** ter abuses his position.[14] In addition, a commander has, by a customary rule of international law, the right to retain a parlementaire so long as circumstances require, if the latter has seen anything, knowledge of which might have adverse consequences for the receiving forces. It is not, however, an abuse of his position for the parlementaire to report back anything he may have observed.

Loss of inviolability

A parlementaire loses his right of inviolability altogether if it is proved **10.10** beyond doubt that he has taken advantage of his privileged position to provoke or commit 'an act of treason'.[15] That includes engaging in sabotage or espionage or inducing members of the enemy armed forces to desert. Any measures taken against a parlementaire or his party should be reported at once to the enemy.

It is forbidden to make improper use of a flag of truce. Thus, a feigned inten- **10.10.1** tion to negotiate or surrender with the intention of using the white flag as

---

[11] HR, Art 33.

[12] Except in cases of reprisals for abuse of the flag of truce, see para 16.16 onwards.

[13] After the battle of Montebello in 1859, the French refused to receive parlementaires from the Austrian lines as it was essential to conceal certain movements.

[14] HR, Art 33. Examples of abuse would be the surreptitious gathering of information, the making of sketch plans, or the taking of photographs of defensive positions.

[15] HR, Art 34.

cover for the collection of information might amount to the war crime of perfidy whatever the consequences. It would amount to a grave breach of Additional Protocol I if it resulted in death or serious injury.[16] A parlementaire who abuses his position in this way can be taken as a prisoner of war and tried.

Orders to withdraw

10.11 If ordered to withdraw, the parlementaire must do so at once. If he does not do so within a reasonable time, he loses his inviolability and is liable to be fired on or to be made prisoner of war. If he does retire, however, he must not be intentionally fired on or interfered with in any other way.

Vehicles and aircraft

10.12 Vehicles and aircraft used by parlementaires have the same protection and may not be seized. These provisions extend also to naval vessels, known as cartel ships.[17] The personnel of such ships have the same rights and obligations as parlementaires. Cartel ships may also be used for the exchange of prisoners of war.[18] Such vehicles and vessels may display the white flag; aircraft carrying parlementaires may be painted white.

C. ARMISTICE, CEASE-FIRE, CAPITULATION, AND SURRENDER

GENERAL PRINCIPLES

10.13 Any agreement made by belligerent commanders must be adhered to scrupulously. A breach of its conditions might involve the international responsibility of the state concerned. The terms of any agreement, whatever the nature of its substance, should be clear and precise and take account of the troops affected by it.[19] Whenever possible it should be in writing.

10.13.1 In the past, a number of different expressions have been used to describe a suspension of hostilities in circumstances falling short of a peace treaty or a permanent end to the conflict. These expressions have included 'cease-fire', 'suspension of arms', 'cessation of hostilities', 'truce', and 'armistice' and

---

[16] AP I, Arts 37(1)(a) and 85(3)(f). See para 10.5.

[17] For the rules governing cartel ships see Ch 13, eg paras 13.33(c)(1) and 13.100(c)(1).

[18] See para 8.146.

[19] The importance of this may be seen in the case of the surrender by General Percival, on 15 February 1942, of the British Indian troops in Singapore. He stated that they were being surrendered to the Japanese whose orders were to be implicitly obeyed, but made no reference to their becoming prisoners of war (PW).

have been used in some cases almost interchangeably although all are in fact forms of armistice.

ARMISTICE

An armistice is the suspension of military operations by mutual agreement **10.14** between the belligerent parties.[20]

CEASE-FIRE; SUSPENSION OF FIRE

The term 'cease-fire' has come to have a double meaning. It may be used to **10.15** describe the situation achieved by, and central to, an armistice agreement— that is, the suspension of hostilities. In recent times it has acquired a more specialized meaning to denote an agreement to suspend hostilities. It is in the latter sense that the term is used hereafter.

In practice, a cease-fire has been a temporary suspension of military opera- **10.15.1** tions, negotiated by opposing commanders for a humanitarian purpose, such as the collection of the wounded or the exchange of prisoners of war.[21] A cease-fire may also be arranged either in consequence of a political dialogue or as a prelude to it. To this extent it may be regarded as a form of armistice. The cease-fire frequently arises from the intervention of a third party or international organization not involved in the conflict.[22] Its aim is to freeze the military operations to prevent the conflict from developing, but also to enable political discussions to be started with a view to settling the differences between the parties to the conflict. In other respects, a cease-fire is similar to an armistice agreement and the contents of a cease-fire agreement will normally follow the same pattern.

EFFECT OF ARMISTICE

An armistice is not a partial or temporary peace, though it may be the **10.16** prelude to the end of armed conflict. It does not in itself put an end to the conflict but merely suspends hostilities to the extent agreed upon by the commanders concerned. An armistice can put an end to armed conflict if that is the intention of the parties. Even without such intention, an armistice agreement can be of long duration so that the state of affairs between the parties is governed at least in part by the armistice agreement for many years.[23]

---

[20] HR, Art 36. [21] See, eg, GC I, Art 15; GC II, Art 18; GC III, Art 118; and GC IV, Art 17.

[22] eg, the UN may be involved in arranging cease-fires.

[23] eg, the Korean and Middle East armistices.

General armistice

10.17 A general armistice suspends the entire military, naval, and air operations of the belligerents.[24] It is a formal interruption of the hostilities throughout the whole region and theatre of war, although for special reasons small parts of the belligerent forces may be excluded. General armistices are of a combined political and military character. They usually precede negotiations for peace but may be concluded for other purposes.

Authority for general armistice

10.18 Since a general armistice is of vital political importance, it can only be made under the authority of the belligerent governments concerned or be subject to their subsequent approval. Indeed, general armistices are frequently arranged by diplomatic representatives.[25]

Partial armistice

10.19 A partial armistice suspends operations between portions only of the belligerent forces and within fixed operational fronts or zones. A partial armistice may be concluded for military forces only or naval forces only. However, a considerable part of the forces and of the theatre of war must be included. Anything less is likely to amount to no more than a suspension of fire.

Authority for a partial armistice

10.20 Military commanders can conclude such agreements provided that they relate to purely military matters within the commander's sphere of authority. Armistices that include political aspects require appropriate government authority.

OBLIGATIONS DURING AN ARMISTICE

10.21 During an armistice, the belligerent forces affected must stop hostilities. They must not attempt to gain ground or, in the case of a siege, they must

---

[24] The armistice of Panmunjon in Korea, signed on 27 July 1953, was a general armistice.

[25] The best examples of such armistices are probably those entered into with various Axis powers in 1943 to 1945 prior to the surrender of Germany. In particular, the armistice with Italy was signed on 3 September 1943 in Sicily by General Eisenhower 'acting by authority of the Governments of the United States and Great Britain and in the interest of the United Nations'. It was accepted by General Badoglio, as head of the Italian government.

not continue to tunnel or demolish. The belligerent forces are, however, permitted to do anything that will tend to the improvement of the situation after the expiration of the armistice and assist the continuation of the conflict, unless they are expressly prohibited from doing so by the agreement.

In short, all offensive measures of whatever nature, and any action or **10.21.1** movements which the adverse party might have been able to prevent, may constitute perfidy and are forbidden. Non-offensive measures may, however, be taken so that troops may be trained, new forces recruited, arms and ammunition manufactured, reinforcements and supplies brought up, and troops re-grouped. Arrangements for monitoring an armistice, for example by UN peacekeeping or monitoring forces, are frequently made.[26]

COMING INTO EFFECT AND DURATION

An armistice has effect from the date at which it is concluded. It must, **10.22** however, be promulgated to all relevant authorities to ensure compliance by individual members of the armed forces. It is the duty of the contracting authorities to notify an armistice officially and in good time to all commanders and to the troops.[27] Hostilities are suspended immediately after notification, or at a fixed time, as may be arranged.[28] An armistice for a limited period should state when it expires. In that case hostilities may be recommenced at the time of expiry. In the case of an armistice of unlimited duration, notice must be given to the enemy of intention to recommence hostilities,[29] in accordance with the terms of the armistice.[30]

Should anyone, ignorant of the fact that an armistice has been made, com- **10.22.1** mit an act of hostility by taking ground or capturing prisoners, he will not be punishable for that act although the state to which he belongs is bound to restore the ground or prisoners taken.[31]

AREA OF ARMISTICE

The geographical area affected should be precisely specified and any demar- **10.23** cation line and neutral zone clearly delineated.

---

[26] See also para 10.25.1.   [27] HR, Art 38.
[28] The armistice with Germany of 11 November 1918, which was signed at 0500 on that day, was stated as coming into force six hours after signature, ie, at 1100.   [29] HR, Art 36.
[30] The adverse party must be notified so that the recommencement of hostilities may not be a surprise.
[31] It is unclear whether deserters who cross over during an armistice must be returned. Some writers consider that to receive and harbour deserters is an implied act of hostility, but modern practice would appear to overrule this view.

10.23.1 Most armistices now contain provisions to prevent incidents which, however inadvertent, may lead to a fresh outbreak of hostilities. The effect of the armistice on air space and shipping should be included.

Humanitarian Arrangements

10.24 Humanitarian arrangements to be specifically agreed may include the repatriation of prisoners of war and civilian internees,[32] the provision of medical care or food supplies,[33] and the registration and burial of the dead.[34] An armistice agreement cannot take away the protection afforded to individuals[35] under the law of armed conflict, though it can improve upon that protection.

Armistice Terms

10.25 There are no stipulations under the law of armed conflict about the form and contents of armistice agreements, since much will depend on the circumstances of the case.

10.25.1 It is desirable that they are made in writing, in duplicate—with each side retaining a copy—and may be in both or all the languages of the belligerents or in the language of a neutral state. For the avoidance of doubt, armistice agreements should where possible specify what activities are permitted and deal with the other matters mentioned in paragraphs 10.21 to 10.24.

Breaches of Armistice Agreement

Effect of violation

10.26 Any serious violation of an armistice by one of the parties gives the other party the right to denounce it. In cases of urgency, hostilities can even be recommenced at once,[36] even though a certain time between giving

---

[32] See, eg, GC III, Art 118 and GC IV, Arts 133 and 134. The Agreement on the Cessation of Hostilities in Vietnam in 1954, involving the French, provided for the 'liberation and repatriation' of all civilian internees held by either side. The prisoner of war issue, on the other hand, delayed the Korean armistice for over a year after agreement had been reached on all other matters.   [33] See, eg, AP I, Arts 69 and 70.

[34] See AP I, Art 34(2).

[35] For example, PW or protected persons: GC I–IV, Arts 6, 6, 6, 7 respectively.

[36] HR, Art 40. A 'serious violation' is undefined but would clearly include a seizure of ground. It is advisable to specify in the terms of any armistice agreement, those provisions that are considered by the parties to be of such importance that a violation would be considered either 'serious' or 'urgent'.

notice of cessation and resumption of hostilities may have been stipulated in the agreement. To justify a denunciation, the violation must be grave, and to authorize an immediate resumption of hostilities, the violation must be even graver. However, in the case of a permanent armistice, which has existed for long enough that neither party can still assert that it is actively a belligerent, a resumption of hostilities might need to be considered in the light of applicable rules on the use of force including Article 2(4) of the UN Charter taken with the right of self-defence against an attack, actual or threatened.[37] Where the UN Security Council has been involved other considerations may apply, depending on the nature of any measure that it has taken for the maintenance of international peace and security.

Individual violations

Violation of the terms of an armistice by individuals acting on their own **10.27** initiative does not entitle the injured party to do more than demand the punishment of the offenders and compensation for the losses sustained, if any.[38] Soldiers captured in the act of breaking an armistice must be treated as prisoners of war. Whilst held, they may be liable to prosecution for war crimes.[39] Alternatively, an individual soldier who is captured after committing a hostile act during an armistice without authority, may conveniently be handed over to his own commander for punishment.

There is no justification in these circumstances for a renewal of hostilities **10.27.1** unless the behaviour of these individuals is approved of or sanctioned by their superiors. If, however, the violations of the armistice by individuals acting on their own initiative are repeated and it becomes evident that the adverse party is unable to repress these abuses, then, after proper protest, there may be no other way to obtain redress except by denouncing the armistice.

Perfidious activity

It would be perfidy to denounce an armistice for a specious motive or pretext **10.28** and to surprise the adverse party without giving him time to put himself on his guard. On the other hand, the existence of an armistice is no reason for relaxing either vigilance or the readiness of troops for action, or for revealing positions to the enemy that he could not detect during combat.

---

[37] See UNSCR 95(1951).   [38] HR, Art 41.

[39] In 1946, an officer in the German navy was convicted of a war crime for scuttling two submarines after they had been surrendered by the German High Command to the Allies, *Scuttled U-Boats Case* (1945) 1 WCR, 55.

CAPITULATION

10.29   A capitulation is an agreement entered into between the commanders of armed forces or belligerents concerning the terms of surrender of a body of troops, of a defended town or place, or of a particular district of the theatre of war. They are, both in character and purpose, purely and exclusively military agreements, involving the abandonment of resistance by a portion of the enemy's forces which capitulates and result, as a rule, in members of the force becoming prisoners of war. Commanders may declare or accept a capitulation only in respect of areas or troops under their command.

10.29.1   A capitulation should, therefore, contain nothing but military stipulations, though conditions concerning the civilian population and their rights may be inserted. Stipulations to the effect that the surrendering troops are forbidden from carrying arms in the future or that the sovereignty of a place or territory should change hands would be normally invalid as being outside the authority of a military commander.[40] A capitulation must take into account 'the rules of military honour'.[41]

Form of capitulation

10.30   Although no rules exist as to the form or contents of a capitulation, for the avoidance of doubt, it should be in writing and contain in the most precise and unequivocal words, the conditions which are to be observed. In particular, the agreement should state:

a. the time and date on which the capitulation is to take effect;

b. the force, locality, or object to be surrendered;

c. arrangements for the movement and administration of the surrendering forces and the taking of possession by the other party;

d. arrangements for dealing with the wounded and sick and any prisoners of war and civilian internees held by the surrendering force;

---

[40]   Art 1 of the Convention of the Capitulation of Verdun, 8 November 1870, stipulated that the surrender was made on the express condition of the retrocession of the fortress and town to France at the conclusion of peace. This exceeded the powers of the contracting commanders and created no obligations for their respective governments.

[41]   HR, Art 35. It will be rare, if not unheard of today, for terms to be given similar to those granted to the garrison of Belfort under Colonel Denfert-Rochereau in the Franco-German war in 1871. In recognition of their brave defence, the garrison was allowed free withdrawal with the honours of war. This included its eagles, colours, arms, horses, carriages, full baggage, and even the archives of the fortress.

e. the surrender of arms and equipment;

f. the prohibition of the destruction by the surrendering force of their materiel;[42]

g. information on minefields and other defence installations;[43]

h. the civilian administration of the area surrendered;

i. any orders over the surrendering force to be enforced by the other party.

Unauthorized or unnecessary surrender

A commander who surrenders unnecessarily or in violation of orders from **10.31** higher authority is liable to trial and punishment under the disciplinary code of his Service.[44]

SURRENDER

A surrender may be distinguished from a capitulation in that there is usually **10.32** no agreement stipulating the terms of the surrender. It may range from an individual soldier laying down his arms to the unconditional surrender of a nation.[45] The victor assumes an implied obligation not to resume hostilities so long as all his conditions and orders are complied with.[46]

PASSPORTS AND SAFE CONDUCTS

Passports

A passport is a document issued by a commander to a person or group of **10.33** persons permitting them unmolested movement within the territory of troops under his command. A passport may be general or limited in character and for a limited or unlimited period of time. It should also specify what persons are permitted to accompany the holder and what goods may be carried by him. Passports may be granted by an individual commander on his own authority or they may be granted as the result of agreement reached with the adverse party or a neutral or protecting power.

---

[42] During the Russo-Japanese war of 1905, General Stoessel, the commander of Port Arthur, had fortifications blown up and vessels sunk during negotiations for surrender but before the capitulation was signed. This was quite legitimate in the circumstances. The US Naval War Code, Art 52, correctly stated the principles: '*after agreeing upon or signing a capitulation*, the capitulator must neither injure nor destroy the vessels, property or stores in his possession that he is to deliver up, unless the right to do so is expressly reserved to him in the agreement of capitulation'. See *Oppenheim's International Law* (7th edn by H Lauterpacht 1952), vol II, 544, n 1.

[43] See Conventional Weapons Convention, Amended Protocol II, Art 9(2).

[44] See NDA 1957, s 2(1); AA 1955, s 24; AFA 1955, s 24.

[45] As occurred at the end of WW II.   [46] See *Oppenheim's International Law*, vol II, 552–553.

Safe conducts

10.34 Safe conducts are issued by an individual commander to enable persons or groups of persons, for a limited or unlimited period, to go to some place which cannot be reached other than by passing through an area under occupation by troops under his command, particularly when such troops are in contact with the adverse party.[47] Safe conducts may be issued in respect of goods. Such safe conducts may be licences to trade for the individual to whom they are issued or a guarantee against seizure.

10.34.1 Whilst safe conducts may also be issued to the diplomatic representatives of neutral states who are accredited to the adverse party and who may require to travel through occupied territory in order to carry out their diplomatic duties, these would normally be issued or authorized by the government rather than by a commander in the field.

Differences between passports and safe conducts

10.35 The essential difference between a passport and a safe conduct is that the former enables the holder to move freely within the area occupied by troops under the command of the authority issuing it, while a safe conduct permits the holder freely to pass through such an area, without necessarily having any cause or desire to stay within that area.

10.35.1 Arrangements are sometimes made between a military commander and an individual national or group of nationals belonging to the adverse party or to a neutral state. Such arrangements may be in the form of passports or safe conducts. Nomenclature is not significant in deciding the nature of the document issued. In fact, occasionally, the term 'pass' or 'permit' has been used. The decisive factor is the purpose for which the document has been issued, and not its terminology.

EFFECT OF PASSPORT OR SAFE CONDUCT

10.36 The person or persons to whom such documents are issued remain immune and protected as long as they comply with any conditions set out in the document and refrain from any unfriendly action which may be construed as incompatible with the purpose for which the document was issued. Such documents are not transferable and may only be used by the person or persons to whom they have been issued. In the case of goods, however, they may be transferred from one person to another unless such

---

[47] eg, to enable individuals to visit or leave an area which is besieged or about to be made the object of attack, see AP I, Art 58(a), or to permit the shipment by and for prisoners of war or civilian internees under GC III, Art 75 and GC IV, Art 111 respectively.

transfer is expressly forbidden. Passports and safe conducts may be revoked for good reasons of military expediency by the person who issued them, or his superior.[48] Until revoked, however, they are binding not only upon the person who granted them but also upon his successors. The reasons for revocation need not be given but revocation must never be used as a means of detaining the holder who must be allowed to withdraw in safety. Passports and safe conducts that have been granted only for a limited time cease to be valid with the expiration of the period designated.

SAFEGUARDS

A safeguard is a party of soldiers posted or detailed for the purpose of **10.37** safeguarding enemy or neutral persons or property when the main body of troops departs. Safeguards are only regulated by the law of armed conflict when they are the result of arrangements made between the combatants. In these cases, persons left behind as safeguards are inviolable and, if they fall into the hands of the adverse party, it is usual to allow them to rejoin their own forces as soon as military exigencies permit. Indeed, safeguards posted without prior arrangements should normally be treated in the same way provided that the circumstances of the case prove that they were posted in good faith.

CARTELS

Agreements between belligerents permitting activities between them that **10.38** would normally not occur during armed conflict[49] are known as cartels.[50] Such agreements are voidable by either party on proof of breach of their terms by the other.

SPECIAL AGREEMENTS

The Geneva Conventions and Additional Protocol I recognize that, on **10.39** a number of matters, agreements between belligerents may be desirable or necessary.[51] These cover such matters as the appointment of substitute protecting powers,[52] the repatriation of wounded and sick prisoners of war,[53] and agreements as to the location and marking of hospitals[54] and demilitarized zones.[55]

---

[48] The War Office, *The Law of War on Land being Part III of the Manual of Military Law* (1958) (MML III), para 493.   [49] Such as postal correspondence or trade in certain commodities.
[50] The word 'cartel' also has a narrower, technical meaning: an arrangement for the transfer of prisoners of war.   [51] GC I–III, Art 6; GC IV, Art 7.
[52] GC I–III, Art 10; GC IV, Art 11.   [53] GC III, Art 109.
[54] GC I, Art 23, Annex I, Arts 6 and 7. See Appendix A.   [55] AP I, Art 60.

11

Occupied Territory

A. ESTABLISHMENT OF OCCUPATION

INTRODUCTION

11.1 The military occupation of territory establishes a special relationship between the occupying power and the civilian population of the area, involving, on each side, certain rights and duties. It affects the general administration of the territory, the rights and duties of the inhabitants, and both public and private property.[1] The inhabitants of occupied territory are protected persons and entitled to the protections laid down in Chapter 9. Neutral nationals in occupied territory are entitled to treatment as protected persons under Geneva Convention IV whether or not there are normal diplomatic relations between the neutral state concerned and the occupying power.[2] However, neutral nationals not normally resident in but only on a temporary visit to occupied territory can, to a certain extent, claim different treatment from that accorded to the inhabitants in that they are as a rule exempt from requisitions. If their property is required for military needs, they must be compensated or indemnified.[3]

11.1.1 Military occupation can assume many different forms.[4] The principal concern of this chapter is 'belligerent occupation'. Classically, this refers to the occupation of enemy territory, that is, when a belligerent in an armed conflict is in control of some of the adversary's territory and is directly responsible for administering that territory. (Occupation may, of course, be exercised by

---

[1] The rules on occupation are contained in the Hague Regulations 1907 (HR), Arts 42–56, Geneva Convention IV 1949 (GC IV), Articles 27–34 and 47–78 and in Additional Protocol I 1977 (API).

[2] GC IV, Art 4. They have the right to leave the territory unless their departure is contrary to the national interests of the occupying power, see GC IV, Arts 35 and 48. For reference to the position of third party nationals in Kuwait at the time of the Iraqi invasion in 1990, see United States Department of Defence, *Report to Congress on the Conduct of the Persian Gulf War*, Appendix on the role of the law of war (1992) 31 ILM 612, 617–620.

[3] Requisitioning under HR, Art 52 is described as from 'inhabitants' and it can be argued that temporary visitors do not meet this description.

[4] For further reading, see A Roberts, 'What is a Military Occupation?' (1984) BYIL 249.

more than one belligerent, for example in the event of a coalition of forces acting together, and the term 'occupying power' has to be interpreted in relation to that possibility.) The term 'belligerent occupation' can also encompass certain other military occupations including, for example, wartime occupation of neutral territory. The provisions of the law of armed conflict that relate to occupied territory apply to belligerent occupations.

The present chapter does not cover situations where the military forces of **11.1.2** one state are in the territory of another allied state in pursuance of a treaty or agreement between allies. In those cases, the matter is governed by the treaty or agreement.[5] Nor does this chapter apply to cases of international administration of territory, for example by the United Nations or other international organizations, which will usually be governed by a complex of legal instruments establishing and regulating such administrations. In cases of liberation of allied territory, or in cases where troops are sent in to a collapsed state[6] to restore law and order, it may not always be possible to conclude a civil affairs agreement with the authorities of the country concerned in advance so that there will be *de facto* military rule by the liberating power.[7] The rules of international law applying to occupied territory should, so far as possible, be applied by analogy until an agreement is concluded. Where a belligerent liberates part of its own territory before normal civil government can be restored, the extent of the military authorities' powers is a matter of the domestic law of the belligerent concerned.[8]

DEFINITION OF OCCUPATION

Territory is considered to be occupied when it is actually placed under the **11.2** authority of external military forces. Occupation extends only to territory where that authority has been established and can in fact be exercised.[9]

EFFECTIVENESS OF OCCUPATION

To determine whether a state of occupation exists, it is necessary to look at **11.3** the area concerned and determine whether two conditions are satisfied: first, that the former government has been rendered incapable of publicly exercising its authority in that area; and, secondly, that the occupying power is in a position to substitute its own authority for that of the former government.

---

[5] Such as the NATO Status of Forces Agreement of 19 June 1951.
[6] As in Somalia in 1993 or East Timor in 1999.
[7] *Public Prosecutor v X (Eastern Java)* 1948 AD Case no 176.
[8] *Battat v R* [1951] AC 519. However, see also *Tan Tuan v Lucena Food Control Board* (1949) 18 ILR 591.   [9] HR, Art 42.

11.3.1 In some cases, occupying troops have operated indirectly through an existing or newly appointed indigenous government. This type of occupation is not discussed in detail in this chapter. In such cases, despite certain differences from the classic form of military occupation, the law relating to military occupation is likely to be applicable. Legal obligations, policy considerations, and external diplomatic pressures may all point to this conclusion.

11.3.2 Patrols, commando, and similar units, which move on or withdraw after carrying out their mission, do not normally occupy territory since they are not there long enough to set up an administration. The use of airborne forces and of mechanized warfare may make it difficult to determine whether occupation exists. When hostilities continue in enemy territory, occupation only arises in areas coming under the control of the adverse party, even if that control is only temporary, provided that measures are taken to administer the areas in question. Occupation does not take effect merely because the main forces of the country have been defeated but depends on whether authority is actually being exercised over the civilian population. However, for occupation of an area it is not necessary to keep troops permanently stationed throughout that area. It is sufficient that the national forces have withdrawn, that the inhabitants have been disarmed, that measures have been taken to protect life and property and to secure order, and that troops are available, if necessary to enforce authority in the area. The existence within an occupied area of a defended zone makes no difference so long as it is surrounded and effectively cut-off.

11.3.3 In cases where two or more states jointly occupy territory (following a coalition military campaign, for example), it is desirable that there be an agreement between them setting out the relationship between the occupying powers.

PROCLAMATION OF OCCUPATION

11.4 Mere proclamation of occupation is insufficient to bring an occupation into existence. The test in paragraph 11.3 must be satisfied.

11.4.1 Although not strictly necessary in law, a proclamation should be issued to make clear to the inhabitants the existence of the occupation, the area over which it extends, and any special regulations that have been issued by the occupying power.[10]

---

[10] See paras 11.25 and 11.58.

COMMENCEMENT OF OCCUPATION

The occupation starts when the test in paragraph 11.3 is satisfied. **11.5**

CONTINUATION OF OCCUPATION

Occupation does not cease where the forces of the occupying power con- **11.6** tinue their advance, leaving only a few troops behind, so long as they have disarmed the inhabitants and made arrangements for the administration of the occupied area. However, the authority of the occupying power should be represented by the presence of a commissioner or civil officials.

TERMINATION OF OCCUPATION

Occupation ceases as soon as the occupying power is driven out or evacu- **11.7** ates the area. Occupation will also cease when effective control transfers to a different authority, such that the territory ceases to be under the authority of external military forces.

The fact that some of the inhabitants are in a state of rebellion, or that guer- **11.7.1** rillas or resistance fighters have occasional successes, does not render the occupation at an end. Even a temporarily successful rebellion in part of the area under occupation does not necessarily terminate the occupation so long as the occupying power takes steps to deal with the rebellion and re-establish its authority or the area in question is surrounded and cut off. Whether or not a rebel movement has successfully terminated an occupation is a question of fact and degree depending on, for example, the extent of the area controlled by the movement and the length of time involved, the intensity of operations, and the extent to which the movement is internationally recognized.

APPLICABILITY OF THE LAW OF ARMED CONFLICT

The law of armed conflict applies from the outset of an occupation and con- **11.8** tinues to apply until the occupation terminates. In Geneva Convention IV (in this chapter referred to as 'the Convention') there is a provision (the 'one-year rule') for some articles of the Convention to cease to apply in occupied territory one year after the general close of military operations. However, 43 articles of the Convention continue to apply for as long as the occupying power exercises the function of government in occupied territory. The one-year rule does not apply to parties to Additional Protocol I 1977 (in this chapter referred to as 'the Protocol'), which specifies that the application of the Convention and Protocol shall cease to apply 'on the termination of the occupation'.[11]

11.8.1 Since this can result in a complex legal situation, advice about the applicability of international law to occupied territory should invariably be sought from the nearest service legal office.

B. GENERAL EFFECTS OF OCCUPATION

TEMPORARY NATURE OF OCCUPATION

11.9 Occupation differs from annexation of territory by being only of a temporary nature. During occupation, the sovereignty of the occupied state does not pass to the occupying power. It is suspended. Although there is no specific principle detailing its scope, the ousted authorities may retain some power to make legislation for the occupied territory. This legislation is restricted to legislation that does not conflict with the rights and duties of the occupying power under international law. Nevertheless, the occupying power must take all measures in its power to restore, and ensure, as far as possible, public order and safety, by respecting, unless absolutely prevented, the laws in force in the occupied state.[12] The law of armed conflict does not confer power on an occupant. Rather it regulates the occupant's use of power. The occupant's powers arise from the actual control of the area.

PROHIBITION OF ANNEXATION

11.10 Since sovereignty does not pass to the occupying power, annexation of the occupied territory is forbidden. Sovereignty can only pass in accordance with the principles of international law, usually by cession under a peace treaty. Illegal annexation does not absolve a party from complying with its obligations to protected persons under the law of armed conflict.[13]

CONSTITUTIONAL POSITION

11.11 Since sovereignty does not pass to the occupying power, that power may not change the constitution and domestic laws of the occupied territory nor set aside the rights of the inhabitants except to the extent permitted under the law of armed conflict.[14] Legislative measures may be taken for the security

---

[11] The one-year rule is in GC IV, Art 6. For parties to AP I, see Art 3(b). HR, Arts 42–56 continue to apply for the duration of the occupation. See also, JS Pictet, *Commentary on the IVth Geneva Convention* (ICRC 1956) (Pictet, *Commentary on GC IV*) 58–64.   [12] HR, Art 43.
[13] GC IV, Art 47.   [14] See paras 11.25–11.29.

of the occupying forces, the maintenance of order, the proper administration of the territory, and to enable the occupying power to carry out its obligations under the Convention for the welfare of the inhabitants. The occupying power may, however, repeal or amend laws that are contrary to international law and is also entitled to make changes mandated or encouraged by the UN Security Council.[15]

C. RESISTANCE TO OCCUPATION

BEFORE EFFECTIVE OCCUPATION

Until the occupation is effective, members of the armed forces of the occu- **11.12** pied country, of organized resistance movements, and of a *levée en masse*[16] may fight to resist the invading troops. However, they must distinguish themselves from the civilian population by, at the very least, carrying their arms openly during deployments and engagements, otherwise they run the risk of being treated as unprivileged belligerents.[17]

AFTER EFFECTIVE OCCUPATION

Even after an occupation has become effective, members of the armed forces **11.13** who have not surrendered,[18] members of organized resistance movements,[19] and members of internationally recognized liberation movements[20] may continue the fight, so long as they distinguish themselves from the civilian population or carry their arms openly during deployments and engagements.[21] A *levée en masse* is not possible after effective occupation.[22]

UNPRIVILEGED BELLIGERENTS

Only combatants have the right to participate directly in hostilities.[23] If **11.14** civilians take a direct part in hostilities without satisfying the conditions

---

[15] GC IV, Art 64. These powers may be sufficiently wide to enable repeal of laws, eg, that violate human rights treaties. In relation to UN Security Council mandates, see eg UNSCR 1483 (22 May 2003) which *inter alia* encouraged international efforts to promote legal and judicial reform by the occupying powers and others in Iraq.   [16] See para 4.8.

[17] AP I, Arts 43 and 44. For mercenaries, see AP I, Art 47.

[18] Surrender of a commander binds members of the armed forces under his command, but not those under other commands, or those serving in allied or foreign forces.

[19] GC III, Art 4A(2); AP I, Arts 43 and 44.

[20] AP I, Arts 1, 43, 44, and 96. The UK made a statement on ratification of AP I that it would only consider itself bound by a declaration of adherence by a body that is genuinely an authority representing a people engaged in a liberation conflict.   [21] AP I, Art 44(3).

[22] GC III, Art 4A(6).   [23] AP I, Art 43(2).

under which they acquire lawful combatant status,[24] they are not entitled to be treated as belligerents and may be punished by the occupying power. However, civilians taking an indirect part in hostilities by, for example, providing information or materiel, assisting escapers, and hiding weapons could only be punished if they contravened any laws or regulations passed by the occupying power.[25]

11.14.1 Unprivileged belligerents are, in any event, entitled to the protection of the Convention and Protocol,[26] although the right of communication may be forfeited in the case of spies.[27]

11.14.2 Punishing protected persons individually or collectively for offences that they have not committed is unlawful, whether or not such punishment is a reprisal measure in response to the activities of unprivileged belligerents.[28] The personal property of civilians is similarly protected.[29]

D. DUTIES OF THE POPULATION OF OCCUPIED TERRITORY

LIMITS OF LEGISLATIVE POWERS OF THE OCCUPIER

11.15 The occupying power can create punishable offences in the interests of its security or that of the population in the occupied territory.[30] It cannot compel the population of occupied territory to acknowledge its sovereignty. That means that civilians cannot be required to:

a. take part in operations against their own country;[31]

b. assist the war effort of the occupying power against their own country;[32]

c. serve in the armed or auxiliary forces of the occupying power;[33]

---

[24] See Ch 4.   [25] See paras 11.25 and 11.28.   [26] GC IV, Arts 4, 5, and 68; AP I, Art 75.

[27] GC IV, Art 5; AP I, Art 45(3). Under these articles, a state can take more severe measures against an unprivileged belligerent in its own territory than it can in occupied territory.

[28] GC IV, Art 33. Also prohibited is the practice of taking 'hostage prisoners' as a deterrent, GC IV, Art 34. The phenomenon of suicide bombing has posed problems regarding the implementation of these rules. In 2002–03, following a number of suicide bomb attacks on Israeli civilians and military personnel, Israel took severe measures in the Israeli-occupied territories against the families of certain suicide bombers.   [29] GC IV, Art 53.

[30] GC IV, Art 64. See also R Baxter, 'The Duty of Obedience to the Belligerent Occupant' (1959) BYIL 235, in particular in relation to the obligations of inhabitants, further referred to in para 11.15.1.   [31] HR, Art 23.

[32] HR, Art 52.

[33] GC IV, Art 51. Nor may any pressure or propaganda be directed at them to enlist in those forces voluntarily.

d. give information to the occupying power about their own armed forces or other defence information.[34]

While the orders of the authorities of an occupying power may be **11.15.1** lawful, and while the occupant is entitled to require obedience to lawful orders, it does not necessarily follow that failure to comply with such orders is illegal under the law of armed conflict. However, the inhabitants are liable for punishment by the occupying power should they disobey legislation, proclamations, regulations, or orders properly made by that power.

Civic Duty

In case of necessity, the inhabitants may be called upon for police duty, to **11.16** assist the regular police in the maintenance of public order, for help with fire fighting, or to perform other duties that may be required of citizens for the public good.[35]

This rule enables the occupant, in case of necessity, to conscript civilians for **11.16.1** ordinary routine public duties, eg, civilian traffic control, provided these duties do not contravene paragraph 11.15. The occupant is responsible for the orderly government of the territory.[36]

Rights of Inhabitants

The inhabitants must not be deprived, by reason of changes brought about **11.17** by the occupation, of any of the benefits to which they are entitled under the Convention.[37]

E. ADMINISTRATION OF OCCUPIED TERRITORY

Allegiance

The occupying power is forbidden to compel the inhabitants of occupied **11.18** territory to swear allegiance to it.[38]

---

[34] HR, Art 44.

[35] The War Office, *The Law of War on Land being Part III of the Manual of Military Law* (1958) (MML III), para 545.   [36] See GC IV, Art 64.

[37] GC IV, Art 47. These rights are set out in paras 9.21–9.24 and, in the case of internees, in paras 9.37–9.113.   [38] HR, Art 45.

ADMINISTRATION

11.19 The occupying power assumes responsibility for administering the occupied area.[39] Whether the administration imposed by the occupying power is called a military government or civil government is not important. The legality of its acts will be determined in accordance with the law of armed conflict. The occupying power cannot circumvent its responsibilities by installing a puppet government or by issuing orders that are implemented through local government officials still operating in the territory (see paragraph 11.7). Further, an occupying power is also responsible for ensuring respect for applicable human rights standards in the occupied territory. Where the occupying power is a party to the European Convention on Human Rights, the standards of that Convention may, depending on the circumstances, be applicable in the occupied territories.[40]

OFFICIALS, CIVIL SERVANTS, POLICE, AND JUDGES

General

11.20 Officials of the occupied territory owe no duty of allegiance to the occupying power and may refuse to serve that power.[41] If they have fled, the occupying power will have to form its own administration. Local authority officials who remain may be employed for this purpose.

Duties of officials

11.21 The occupying power may not alter the status of officials, nor apply any sanctions or take measures of coercion or discrimination against them if they decide to abstain on grounds of conscience from fulfilling their functions.[42] A belligerent cannot compel officials to take part in military operations against their own country, even if they were in the belligerent's service before the commencement of the armed conflict.[43] Those who refuse to serve may, nevertheless, be compelled to do certain types of work, see paragraph 11.52.[44]

11.21.1 Officials will normally be given instructions by their own government whether or not to remain at their posts in the event of occupation. In the

---

[39] HR, Art 43.

[40] See the decision of the European Court of Human Rights in *Banković and others v Belgium and others* (2003) 41 ILM 517.

[41] GC IV, Art 54. See also, Pictet *Commentary on GC IV*, 302–308.

[42] GC IV, Art 54. See also, Pictet, *Commentary on GC IV*, 302–308. However, see para 11.22.

[43] HR, Art 23.   [44] GC IV, Art 54. See also GC IV, Art 51(2).

absence of instructions, each must use his initiative. In making their decisions, officials must consider the need to protect life and property. The police should, so far as possible, continue their functions so as to avoid a complete breakdown of law and order. However, they cannot be required to act against lawful combatants, including properly organized resistance movements. Continuity of local administration is important if chaos is to be prevented and the welfare of the population sustained.

Dismissal of officials

The occupying power may dismiss officials, including judges, and replace **11.22** them if they refuse obedience to the occupying power.[45] However, this power should not be used arbitrarily, for example, for reasons unconnected with the official's work, or because of the official's refusal to carry out an order that is contrary to international law.[46]

Retention of officials

The occupying power is responsible for paying the salaries of officials who **11.23** continue to serve if it collects the taxes of the occupied territory.[47] Officials may, as a condition of their being permitted to continue in office, be called upon to take an oath or give an assurance that they will perform their duties conscientiously. The occupying power has no right to demand an oath of allegiance.[48]

Offences by officials

Wrongful acts by officials may lead to their dismissal. Where their acts con- **11.24** stitute ordinary crimes, they must be tried and punished according to the laws of the occupied territory. Any act calculated to injure the occupying forces may be dealt with according to security laws previously introduced by the occupying power.[49] Internment may also be ordered in the interests of the security of the occupying power.[50]

THE LAW

The law in force

There is an obligation during the occupation to respect the laws in force in **11.25** the occupied territory unless absolutely prevented.[51] An occupying power

---

[45] GC IV, Art 54. See also Pictet, *Commentary on GC IV*, 302–308.
[46] See the cases of the German military courts in Greece, 1943–45 AD Case No 149; also, *R v Maung Hmin et al*, 1946 AD Case No 139; *M P (Batavia) v Mrs S (Bandoeng)*, 1947 AD Case No 118.
[47] HR, Art 48.   [48] HR, Art 45.   [49] GC IV, Art 64.   [50] GC IV, Art 78.
[51] HR, Art 43.

would be prevented from respecting the laws in force if they conflicted with its obligations under international law, especially Geneva Convention IV 1949. The occupying power is not obliged to use the full powers available under the laws in force in occupied territory. It may suspend any of those laws that affect its own security, for example, those concerning conscription, electoral enfranchisement, rights of public assembly, the bearing of arms, and the freedom of the press. The right of the inhabitants to take legal action in the local courts must not be affected.[52] The occupying power may amend the existing law of the occupied territory or promulgate new law if this is necessitated by the exigencies of armed conflict, the maintenance of order, or the welfare of the population.[53] The domestic law of the occupying power (apart from that affecting its own armed forces) does not extend to occupied territory.

11.25.1 Since the occupying power has a duty to look after the welfare of the inhabitants, regulations, for example, fixing prices and securing the equitable distribution of food and other commodities, are permissible. The occupying power should make no more changes to the law than are absolutely necessary, particularly where the occupied territory already has an adequate legal system.

Jurisdiction

11.26 The courts of occupied territory retain jurisdiction to deal with any of the inhabitants' cases that are neither of a military nature, nor affect the safety of the occupying forces. Jurisdiction in the latter two cases is a matter for the authorities of the occupying power. Members of the occupying forces and their civilian component are normally not subject to the jurisdiction of the local courts but remain under that of their own military authorities.[54]

Local courts

11.27 The local courts may be suspended only if necessitated by the judges' or magistrates' refusal to act or on account of the behaviour of the inhabitants. In those circumstances, the occupying power must establish and duly publicize its own courts. Local courts, where functioning, have an obligation to enforce the proper laws and orders of the occupying power, but before doing so are entitled to determine whether those laws and regulations are within the competence of the occupying power under international law.

---

[52] HR, Art 23(h).   [53] HR, Art 43.

[54] All states are under an obligation to try persons who have committed grave breaches of the Geneva Conventions. In theory, both the local courts and those of the occupying power would have jurisdiction to try members of the occupying forces for grave breaches. In practice, jurisdiction in those cases would usually be exercised by the occupying power.

Publication of measures

The suspension, modification, or replacement of law or courts must be **11.28** published to the population of the occupied territory in their own language.

Criminal law

The special rules of the Convention dealing with the administration of **11.29** criminal law in occupied territory are dealt with in paragraphs 11.56 to 11.74.

THE ECONOMY

Occupation costs

The economy of an occupied country can only be required to bear the **11.30** expenses of the occupation and these should not be greater than the economy of the country can reasonably be expected to bear.[55]

Taxation

If the occupying power collects taxes, duties, and tolls which were **11.31** payable in the occupied state, it is bound to apply them towards the cost of administering that territory.[56] As far as possible, it must do so in accordance with the existing tax laws but any balance may be applied towards the maintenance of the occupying forces. However, local rates may only be used for the purposes for which they were levied. If tax officials continue to work normally, taxes will be collected by them in the usual way. Otherwise, the occupying power may impose an obligation on each local authority to collect and pay a proportion of total revenue. The occupying power can levy contributions from the inhabitants, which may only be applied to the needs of the occupying forces or to the adminis- tration of the territory and only in so far as those requirements are not met by existing taxation. Funds raised must not be used for the enrichment of the occupying power or its personnel,[57] nor be used as a collective punishment.[58] Contributions from towns and productive areas may be used to support poorer areas. Contributions may only be collected on the written order of the commander-in-chief of the occupying forces. Generally, fund-raising must accord as far as possible with the system for assessing taxes in the occupied territory. A receipt must be given to each individual contributor.[59]

---

[55] Judgment of the International Military Tribunal sitting at Nuremberg, Trial of the Major War Criminals before the International Military Tribunal (IMT), vol XXII, 482.

[56] HR, Art 48.   [57] HR, Art 49.   [58] HR, Art 50.   [59] HR, Art 51.

Commerce

11.32 The occupying power may place on the occupied territory such restrictions and conditions in respect of commercial dealings as may be necessary for military purposes. For the same reasons it may remove existing restrictions, such as current customs tariffs.

Currency

11.33 The occupying power's own currency may be used in addition to that of the occupied territory. Currency regulations may be issued by the occupying power. These measures must be necessitated by the situation in the occupied territory and must not be for the purpose of enriching the occupying power or damaging the local economy. It follows that attempts to debase the currency or impose artificial exchange rates would be unlawful. The occupying power may also issue vouchers for use by members of its forces and civilian component in the occupying forces' installations, shops, and canteens.

SECURITY MEASURES

Censorship

11.34 For legitimate reasons of security only, censorship may be imposed on the press, films, radio, television, theatres, and public entertainment, or to limit or prohibit telegram, postal, or telecommunications. To the same extent, existing press laws need not be respected, the publication of newspapers may be prohibited or subjected to restrictions, and the distribution of newspapers to unoccupied parts of the country or neutral countries may be stopped.

Postal facilities

11.35 Subject to the exigencies of the armed conflict, existing postal services must be permitted to continue. The occupying power is not obliged to provide postal facilities for the inhabitants except in accordance with specific obligations under international law, such as, for example, prisoner of war and internee mail, relief consignments, communications with the protecting power, and the ICRC.

Transport

11.36 All means of transport, whether public or private, come under the authority of, and so may be regulated by, the occupying power and are subject to requisitioning.[60]

---

[60] HR, Art 53. See paras 11.82 and 11.90.

Restrictions on civilians

Although the occupying power can impose various restriction on civilians, **11.37** including restricting freedom of movement within the occupied territory, forbidding changes of residence, visits to particular districts or immigration, and may require the possession of an identity card, these are all subject to the safeguards set out in the Convention.[61] Protected persons[62] who are not nationals of the state whose territory is occupied have the right to leave, subject to similar conditions and procedures as those under which they would be entitled to leave the territory of a belligerent.[63]

Internment or assigned residence

If other measures are insufficient, and it is required by imperative reasons **11.38** of security, civilians in occupied territory may be placed in an assigned residence or may be interned.[64] Such action must accord with procedures prescribed by the occupying power and the requirements of the Convention set out in paragraphs 9.31 to 9.36.

Appeals

The prescribed procedures must include a right of appeal. Appeals are to be **11.38.1** decided with the minimum of delay, decisions being subject to periodical review, if possible every six months, by a competent body set up by the occupying power.

Financial support

Persons subjected to assigned residence orders and required to leave their **11.38.2** homes must be given an opportunity (subject to the interests of security) of finding paid employment. If they are unable to support themselves and their dependants, the occupying power must ensure that they are supported and must permit them to receive allowances from their home country, the protecting power, or relief societies.

RELIGION

Public worship must be permitted by the occupying power and religious **11.39** convictions respected,[65] ministers of religion being permitted to give spiritual assistance to members of their religious communities. The occupying power must also accept consignments of books and articles needed for religious purposes and facilitate their distribution within the territory.[66]

---

[61] eg, Arts 47–78.   [62] See para 9.17.   [63] GC IV, Art 48. See para 9.25.
[64] GC IV, Arts 42, 43, and 78.   [65] HR, Art 46.   [66] GC IV, Art 58.

If the salaries of the clergy are paid by the state and the occupying power collects the taxes, it must continue to pay them.[67]

CHILDREN AND EDUCATION

Schools

11.40 Schools and other educational establishments must be permitted to continue their ordinary activities.[68] The occupying power must, with the co-operation of the national and local education authorities, facilitate the proper working of schools and other institutions devoted to the care and education of children. In certain circumstances an occupying power may be within its rights in temporarily closing educational institutions, but only when there are very strong reasons for doing so, these reasons are made public, and there is a serious prospect that the closure will achieve important and worthwhile results.

Children

11.41 The occupying power must do all that it can to facilitate the identification of children[69] and registration of their parentage. A special section of the national information bureau must be given responsibility for identifying children whose identity is in doubt. Particulars of their parents or other near relatives must always be recorded, if available. The personal status of children may not be changed and they may not be enlisted in formations or organizations controlled by the occupying power. If local institutions are inadequate, the occupying power must make arrangements for the maintenance and education of children who are orphaned or separated from their parents and who cannot adequately be looked after by relatives or friends. Persons entrusted with the maintenance and education of children must, if possible, have the same nationality, language, and religion as the children. Any measures introduced prior to the occupation in favour of children aged under 15 years, expectant mothers, and mothers of children under seven years in respect of food, medical care, and protection against hostilities must not be obstructed by the occupying power.[70]

MEDICAL CARE AND HYGIENE

Responsibility of occupying power

11.42 The occupying power has a responsibility for the medical care of the inhabitants of occupied territory.[71] It must ensure, so far as possible, that existing hospitals, medical, public health, and hygiene services in the

---

[67] HR, Art 48.   [68] GC IV, Art 50.   [69] See para 9.9.   [70] GC IV, Art 50.
[71] GC IV, Art 56; AP I, Art 14.

territory are continued. It has a special responsibility to prevent the spread of disease. The medical and health authorities and personnel of the occupied territory must assist in this process. It follows that medical personnel of all categories must be allowed to carry out their duties. In doing so, the occupying power must take account of the moral and ethical standards of the population. If the occupying power sets up and operates new hospitals, they are entitled to protection from attack and to display the protective emblem.[72] Medical transports and personnel are similarly protected.[73] The occupying power may issue such regulations as are necessary for compliance with its obligations under this paragraph.

Requisitioning of medical units

The occupying power must not requisition civilian medical units,[74] their **11.43** equipment, and personnel as long as they are needed for the treatment of civilians. If not, they may be requisitioned provided that:

a. it is necessary to do so for the adequate and immediate treatment of military wounded and sick;

b. requisitioning only lasts as long as the need continues;

c. immediate arrangements are made to ensure that the medical needs of the civilian population, as well as those of any wounded and sick under treatment who are affected by the requisition, continue to be satisfied.[75]

FOOD AND OTHER ESSENTIAL SUPPLIES

The occupying power is bound to ensure, to the fullest extent of the available **11.44** means, that the civilian population are supplied with food, medical supplies, clothing, bedding, means of shelter, other supplies essential to their survival, and objects necessary for religious worship.[76] If the resources of the occupied territory are insufficient, these items must be supplied by the occupying power. The occupying power must not requisition[77] food, medical supplies, or other articles in occupied territory except for use by the occupation forces and their civilian component, and then only if the needs of the civilian population have first been taken into account. Receipts must be given for requisitioned property and a fair price paid.[78] The protecting power must be given the opportunity at any time to verify the state of the food and medical supplies in occupied territory, subject to any temporary restrictions imposed by imperative military requirements.

---

[72] GC IV, Art 18. See para 7.23.   [73] GC IV, Art 56.   [74] For definition, see para 7.10.
[75] GC IV, Art 57; AP I, Art 14.   [76] GC IV, Art 55; AP I, Art 69.
[77] See paras 11.83 and 11.84.   [78] See also, HR, Arts 52 and 53.

11.44.1 These provisions are intended to prevent economic exploitation of occupied territories.

RELIEF

Relief schemes[79]

11.45 If the whole or part of the population of occupied territory suffers from a shortage of supplies, the occupying power must agree to relief schemes being put into operation. Such schemes must be implemented without delay, the occupying power facilitating them by all available means.[80] Relief schemes relate particularly to the provision of food, medical supplies, and clothing and may be undertaken by neutral states[81] or impartial humanitarian organizations such as the ICRC. All parties to the Convention and Protocol must permit the free passage of relief supplies and guarantee their protection. A state permitting the passage of relief supplies to territory occupied by an adverse party is entitled to search the consignments, regulate their passage according to prescribed times and routes, and be reasonably satisfied, through the protecting power, that the consignments are to be used for the relief of the population of occupied territory and not for the benefit of the occupying power.[82]

Diversion of relief supplies

11.46 Relief supplies may only be diverted from the purposes for which they were intended, with the consent of the protecting power, in cases of urgent necessity and in the interests of the population of occupied territory.[83]

11.46.1 Diversion of relief supplies might be necessary if, for example, an epidemic ceased in one area but spread to another, or if insuperable difficulties prevented supplies from getting through to the original destination.

Distribution

11.47 The co-operation and supervision of the protecting power must be sought with regard to the distribution of relief supplies. If the protecting and occupying powers agree, this responsibility may be delegated to another neutral state, the ICRC, or other impartial humanitarian body. The occupying power must facilitate the rapid distribution of relief consignments.[84]

---

[79] AP I, Art 69.   [80] GC IV, Art 59; AP I, Art 70.

[81] Although GC IV, Art 59, refers to 'States', Pictet, *Commentary on GC IV*, 321 suggests that only neutral states are capable of providing the essential guarantees of impartiality. AP I, Art 70 is capable of more flexible interpretation.   [82] GC IV, Art 59; AP I, Art 70.

[83] GC IV, Art 60.   [84] GC IV, Art 61.

Taxes, duties, and costs

In occupied territory, relief supplies must be exempted from all charges, **11.48** taxes, or customs duties unless these are essential to the economy of that territory. All other parties to the Convention and Protocol are required to do their best to permit transit and transport of relief supplies to occupied territories free of charge.[85]

Relief personnel

The provisions of paragraph 9.12 apply equally to relief personnel in occu- **11.49** pied territory.[86]

Individual relief

Unless there are imperative security reasons to the contrary, the occupying **11.50** power must also permit protected persons in occupied territory to receive individual relief consignments.[87]

Relief societies

Subject to temporary and exceptional measures imposed for urgent reasons **11.51** of security by the occupying power, the latter has a duty to permit re- cognized national red cross and red crescent societies and other similar organizations to continue their humanitarian activities in accordance with established principles. The occupying power may not require any changes in the personnel or structure of these societies that would prejudice their activities. The same principles apply to non-military organizations that are already in existence in the occupied territory, or which may be established, for the maintenance of essential public utility services, distribution of relief, and organization of rescues.[88]

Labour

Permitted work

Protected persons aged 18 years and over who are not interned may **11.52** be required by the occupying power to do work necessary for the occupy- ing forces, the public utility services, or the feeding, sheltering, clothing, transport, or health of the population of the occupied country.[89]

---

[85] GC IV, Art 61; AP I, Art 70.   [86] AP I, Art 71.

[87] GC IV, Art 62. An example would be a civil defence organization, see also AP I, Art 63.

[88] GC IV, Art 63.   [89] GC IV, Art. 51. See para 9.77 in respect of internees.

11.52.1 To meet the needs of the occupying forces or for the administration of occupied territory, the occupying power may enlist the aid of the local population in such capacities as, for example, engineers, doctors and nurses, clerical staff, carpenters and builders, butchers, bakers, and lorry drivers. Employees of railways, haulage contractors, airlines, canal, river, tug, and shipping companies, telephone, postal, and broadcasting authorities may also be enlisted. So too may labourers involved in repairing roads, bridges, or railways, those involved in the burial of the dead or the removal of refuse.

11.52.2 Refusal to do permitted work may be punished if the occupying power first passes legislation to that effect.

Prohibited work

11.53 The following types of work are prohibited:[90]

    a. compulsory service in the armed forces of the occupying power;[91]

    b. compulsory work by persons under 18 years;

    c. compulsory work involving participation in military operations;

    d. work outside the occupied country of which the workers concerned are nationals;

    e. employment in organizations of a military or semi-military character;

    g. any other work outside the categories listed in paragraph 11.52.

11.53.1 Protected persons may not be compelled to use forcible means to ensure the security of installations where they are performing compulsory labour,[92] nor may they be compulsorily employed in, for example, the construction of military defences or airfields, the production of munitions, the movement of military supplies, or the laying or lifting of minefields.

Conditions of work

11.54 As far as possible, workers should remain in their usual places of employment and be paid a fair wage. The work must be appropriate to their physical and intellectual capacities. The legislation in force in the occupied territory concerning working conditions such as wages, hours of work, equipment, training, and compensation for occupational accidents and illnesses continues to apply.[93] Contracts and regulations may not prevent workers from seeking the assistance of the protecting power. Measures

---

[90] GC IV, Art 51. See para 9.77 in respect of internees.
[91] This is a grave breach of GC IV, see Art 147.
[92] GC IV, Art 51. Except, to some extent, for police duties, see para 11.21.
[93] GC IV, Art 51. See para 9.77 onwards in respect of internees.

aimed at creating unemployment or restricting opportunities so as to induce people to work for the occupying power are prohibited.[94]

DEPORTATION AND MOVEMENT OF CIVILIANS

11.55 The occupying power is forbidden to transfer forcibly or deport protected persons from an occupied country either to its own territory or to that of any other state. Members of the occupying power's own civilian population may not be transferred to occupied territory. Protected persons may not be detained in an area that is especially exposed to the dangers of armed conflict, unless the security of the population or imperative military reasons so demand. An area may be totally or partially evacuated by the occupying power if:

a. such evacuation is required either for the security of the population or for reasons of imperative military necessity; and

b. protected persons are not moved outside occupied territory, unless there is no alternative; and

c. the evacuees are returned to their homes as soon as hostilities in the area have ceased; and

d. to the greatest extent practicable:

   (1) proper accommodation is provided, and

   (2) movement takes place under satisfactory conditions of hygiene, health, safety, and nutrition, and

   (3) members of the same family are not separated; and

e. the protecting power is informed of transfers and evacuations as soon as they have taken place.[95]

11.55.1 Unlawful deportation or transfer is a grave breach of the Convention.[96]

ADMINISTRATION OF CRIMINAL LAW

Continuation of criminal law

11.56 During the occupation, the existing criminal law of the occupied territory remains in force. It may be amended, suspended, or repealed by the occupying power only if it constitutes a threat to security or impedes compliance with international law. To the same extent, the courts of occupied territory may continue to administer the criminal law.[97]

---

[94] GC IV, Art 52.   [95] GC IV, Art 49.   [96] GC IV, Art 147; AP I, Art 85(4)(a).
[97] GC IV, Art 64.

Power to enact new legislation

11.57 The occupying power may introduce new criminal laws as necessary to enable it to fulfil its international obligations, maintain orderly government, and ensure the security of the occupying power, its forces, administration, establishments, and lines of communication.[98]

Publication of new legislation

11.58 New criminal law enacted by the occupying power comes into force only after it has been duly published to the inhabitants in writing in their own language. It must not be retroactive.[99]

Competent courts

11.59 The occupying power may set up its own non-political, military courts to try offences created by its own legislation. These courts, sometimes known as occupation courts, are in addition to the existing criminal courts and others that have to be established by the occupying power to administer the law of the occupied territory if officials and judges have left their posts. Occupation courts must sit in the occupied territory. So, whenever possible, should courts dealing with appeals from occupation courts.[100]

11.59.1 The rule set out in paragraph 11.59 prohibits the occupying power from extending its own civil court system to occupied territory. The occupation courts may consist of either military or civilian judges, but they must be responsible to the military authorities of the occupying power. If they are authorized to do so in accordance with laws made by the occupying power, these courts may also try cases of alleged war crimes.[101] All of these courts are subject to the rules set out in paragraphs 9.6 and 11.60 to 11.74.

Applicable law

11.60 Occupation courts may only apply those provisions of law applicable at the time of the commission of the offence and which accord with general principles of law and with human rights guarantees in the occupant's law and human rights instruments by which the occupying power is bound.[102] In the absence of more specific rules, the principles in the Universal Declaration of Human Rights 1948 will apply. In particular, the penalty must be proportionate to the offence. Courts must also take into account the fact that the accused is not a national of the occupying power.[103]

---

[98] GC IV, Art 64.   [99] GC IV, Art 65.   [100] GC IV, Art 66.
[101] MML III, para 568. See para 9.7.   [102] See para 11.19.   [103] GC IV, Art 67.

Prosecution of nationals of the occupying power

Nationals of the occupying power who, before the outbreak of hostilities, **11.61**
sought refuge in the territory of the occupied state, must not be arrested,
prosecuted, convicted, or deported from the occupied territory, except for
offences committed:

a. after the outbreak of hostilities; or

b. before the outbreak of hostilities which, according to the law of the occupied state, would have justified extradition in peacetime.[104]

Notification of proceedings

The protecting power must be informed of all proceedings brought by the **11.62**
occupying power against protected persons and involving possible sentences of imprisonment for two years or more or the death penalty.[105] It is
entitled to have information at any time about the state of such proceedings
and also to obtain full particulars of any other proceedings brought by the
occupying power against protected persons. Notification of cases involving the death penalty or imprisonment for two years or more must reach the
protecting power at least three weeks before the date of the first hearing and
must include the following particulars:

a. a description of the accused;

b. the place of residence or detention;

c. details of the charge or charges and particulars of the law or laws alleged
   to have been violated;

d. details of the court that will try the accused; and

e. the date and place of the first hearing.[106]

Rights of defence

Accused persons are entitled to the following: **11.63**

a. prompt written notification, in a language that they understand, of the
   particulars of the charges against them;[107]

b. personal presence at the trial including the facility to present necessary
   evidence for the defence, calling witnesses as required;

c. assistance by a qualified advocate or counsel of their choice who must be
   able to visit them freely and have all necessary professional facilities for
   preparation of the defence; and

---

[104] GC IV, Art 70. [105] Death sentences may not be imposed by UK courts.
[106] GC IV, Art 71. [107] GC IV, Art 71.

d. an interpreter to assist both during the preliminary investigation and at the trial, together with the right to object to the interpreter at any time and to ask for his replacement.[108]

11.63.1 If the accused fails to choose an advocate, the protecting power may provide one for him. If the protecting power is not functioning and the accused faces a serious charge, the occupying power has a duty to provide an advocate or counsel, subject to the accused's consent.[109]

Avoidance of delay

11.64 The accused shall be brought to trial as rapidly as possible.[110]

Bar to trial

11.65 Before the trial can commence, evidence must be submitted at its opening that due notice was given to the protecting power.[111]

Procedure at trial

11.66 Sentence may not be pronounced until the accused has been properly tried. The minimum requirements of a proper trial are set out in paragraph 9.6.[112]

Attendance of the protecting power at trial

11.67 Representatives of the protecting power have the right to attend the hearing, unless it is held *in camera* for security reasons. In that case, the protecting power must be notified of the fact and of the place and date of trial.[113]

Punishment

11.68 The following rules on punishments must be observed:

a. protected persons who commit an offence aimed only at harming the occupying power, but not amounting to an attempt on the life or limb of members of the occupying forces or administration, a grave collective danger, or a cause of serious damage to the property of those forces, their administration or installations, are subject to the maximum punishment of internment or simple imprisonment, provided that the duration of such internment or imprisonment is proportionate to the offence;[114]

b. military courts of the occupying power may, at their discretion, convert a sentence of imprisonment to one of internment for the same period;[115]

---

[108] GC IV, Art 72; AP I, Art 75(4)(e), (g).   [109] GC IV, Art 72; AP I, Art 75(4)(a).
[110] GC IV, Art 71.   [111] In accordance with para 11.62: GC IV, Art 71.
[112] GC IV, Art 71; AP I, Art 75(4). It is a grave breach to deprive wilfully a protected person of the rights to a fair and regular trial, see GC IV, Art 147, AP I, Art 85(4)(e).
[113] GC IV, Art 74. The reference number of the pre-trial notice should be given.
[114] GC IV, Art 68.   [115] GC IV, Art 68.

c. the death penalty may only be pronounced:[116]

    (1) in respect of offences against laws introduced by the occupying power where the accused has been convicted of espionage, serious acts of sabotage against military installations of the occupying power, or intentional offences which have caused death;[117]

    (2) on a protected person if the attention of the court has been drawn to the fact that the accused is not a national of the occupying power and, therefore, owes it no duty of allegiance;[118]

    (3) on a protected person who was aged 18 years or over at the time of the offence;[119]

d. protected persons must not be arrested, prosecuted, or convicted for acts committed or for opinions expressed before the occupation or during a temporary interruption of the occupation;[120] and

e. any period spent under arrest by the protected person while awaiting trial or punishment has to be deducted from any sentence of imprisonment.[121]

The reference in sub-paragraph (a) to 'internment or simple imprisonment' **11.68.1** does not preclude non-custodial penalties, such as fines, not involving the loss of an individual's liberty. Some breaches of legislation made by the occupying power, even if not intended solely to harm that power, may also be punished by internment or imprisonment, since they adversely affect the orderly government of the territory for which the occupying power is responsible under the Convention. Examples of such offences include contravention of regulations on blackout, curfew, traffic or exchange control.[122]

Notification of outcome of trial

The protecting power must be notified of any sentence of imprisonment for **11.69** two years or more or of death and of the grounds for that sentence. The notification must refer to the pre-trial notification and, in the case of imprisonment, must identify the place where the sentence is to be served.[123]

Appeals

Although a convicted person has no specific right of appeal under the law of **11.70** armed conflict, a right of appeal may exist under the law applied by the court. Even where that law makes no provision for appeal, the convicted person has a right to petition the competent authority of the occupying power in respect

---

[116] A death penalty may not be pronounced by a UK court.
[117] GC IV, Art 68 continues with the proviso that such offences had to have been punishable by death under the law of the occupied territory in force before the occupation began.
[118] GC IV, Art 68.   [119] GC IV, Art 68. For death sentences on women, see para 9.8.2.
[120] GC IV, Art 70. This does not apply to violations of the laws and customs or war.
[121] GC IV, Art 69.   [122] MML III, para 566, n 3.   [123] GC IV, Art 74.

of finding and sentence. He must be fully informed of his rights of appeal and of any time-limits within which he must present his appeal or petition.[124]

Time limits for appeals

11.71 Any time-limit for appeals in cases of death sentences or imprisonment for two years or more does not begin to run until the notification of the judgment has been received by the protecting power.[125]

Death sentences

11.72 Death sentences may not be imposed by United Kingdom courts, nor may United Kingdom service personnel or officials assist in any way in the implementation of death sentences, for example, by other states or by local courts. For states whose laws permit death sentences, the following rules of the Convention apply.

11.72.1 Persons sentenced to death may not be deprived of the right to petition for pardon or reprieve. Death sentences may not be carried out before at least six months have expired from the date of receipt by the protecting power of notification of final confirmation of the death sentence or of any order denying pardon or reprieve. The six-month period may, however, be reduced in particular cases in circumstances of grave emergency involving an organized threat to the security of the occupying power or its forces. But even so, the protecting power must be notified of the reduced period and must be given a reasonable time and opportunity to make representations to the occupying authorities about the death sentence.[126]

Record of judgments

11.73 A record of all judgments must be maintained by the courts and made available for inspection by representatives of the protecting power.[127]

Treatment of detainees

11.74 Protected persons who are detained either because they are awaiting trial or as a result of a custodial sentence are entitled to have the following treatment:

a. their sentences must be served in the occupied country;

b. their accommodation must, if possible, be separate from that of other categories of detainee;

---

[124] GC IV, Art 73; AP I, Art 75(4)(j). Denial of the right of appeal would be a violation of the International Covenant on Civil and Political Rights 1966, Art 14, unless a specific derogation had been made under Art 4 of that Covenant.   [125] GC IV, Art 74.
[126] GC IV, Art 75.   [127] GC IV, Art 74.

c. their conditions of food and hygiene must be sufficient to keep them in good health and must not be less favourable than those in force in prisons in the occupied country;

d. they must have the medical attention required by their state of health;

e. they have the right to spiritual assistance;

f. women must be kept in separate quarters from men and under the direct supervision of women;

g. minors must be looked after appropriately;

h. detainees have the right to be visited by representatives of the protecting power and the ICRC;

i. detainees have the right to receive at least one relief parcel per month; and

j. detainees have the right at the conclusion of the occupation to be handed over with relevant records to the authorities of the liberated territory.[128]

F. ENEMY PROPERTY IN OCCUPIED TERRITORY

DESTRUCTION PROHIBITED

Any destruction of enemy property, whether it belongs to private indi- **11.75** viduals or the state, is prohibited unless the destruction is absolutely necessitated by military operations.[129] Extensive destruction and appropriation not justified by military necessity and carried out unlawfully and wantonly is a grave breach of the Convention.[130]

There is no unrestricted right to seize and take enemy property of every **11.75.1** kind. This part of this chapter deals with the question of enemy property in occupied territory.[131]

PRIVATE PROPERTY

Respect for private property

Private property must be respected. Requisitions must be proportionate **11.76** to the resources of the occupied territory and limited to the needs of the occupying power.[132] Seizure is limited to certain types of property, see paragraphs 11.77 and 11.81.

---

[128] GC IV, Arts 76 and 77.   [129] HR, Art 23(g); GC IV, Art 53.   [130] GC IV, Art 147.
[131] For the protection of civilian property on the battlefield, see paras 5.23–5.25; for the treatment of property taken from prisoners of war, see para 8.25; and for the treatment of internees' property, see para 9.43.   [132] HR, Art 52. See also HR, Art 46.

11.76.1 Private property includes not only what would be regarded in common parlance as private property but also property, regardless of ownership, which is dedicated to religion, charity, education, or to the arts or sciences.[133]

11.76.2 The requirement to respect private property is subject to conditions necessitated by armed conflict. For example, military operations inevitably cause damage to private property and occupying forces are entitled to requisition property for necessary military purposes. Nevertheless, the principle of respect is important. Nothing is more subversive of military discipline than plundering or looting. Theft and robbery remain punishable crimes in peace and war.[134] The soldier in an enemy country must observe the same respect for civilian property as he would at home.

Permanent seizure of land and buildings

11.77 Land and buildings (whether belonging to private individuals or to corporations) must not be appropriated or otherwise disposed of, nor even used, leased, or hired for private or public profit. This prohibition also protects the private property of ruling families, so long as it is private and not the property of the state.[135]

Temporary use of land and buildings

11.78 Land and buildings may be used temporarily for the needs of the occupying power, even if that use impairs its value. Military use would include, for example, use for quartering, construction of defensive positions, or for the accommodation of the wounded and sick. Buildings may be used for observation, reconnaissance, cover, and defence. If necessary, houses, fences, and woods may be cleared to open up a field of fire or the materials used for bridges, roads, or fuel imperatively needed by the occupying forces. The owner of property used in this way may claim neither rent nor compensation but, if possible, a note of the use or damage should be kept or given to the owner so that, if compensation becomes available at the close of hostilities, there will be evidence to support the claim. If, however, a private owner has been compelled to accommodate troops or the sick or wounded in his home, this constitutes requisitioning for which payment should be made.[136]

Quartering of troops

11.79 When troops are quartered in private accommodation, some rooms should be left for the inhabitants who should be evicted only if that is imperatively

---

[133] HR, Art 56.
[134] HR, Art 47; GC IV, Art 33. See also NDA 1957, ss 5, 35A; AA 1955, s 30, and AFA 1955, s 63.
[135] Previously dealt with in MML III, para 591.
[136] L Oppenheim, *International Law* (7th edn by H Lauterpacht 1952), vol II, 411.

dictated by military necessity. In that event, some effort should be made to give the inhabitants notice and facilities for taking essential baggage with them. When unoccupied buildings are used, care should be taken of the structure and the internal fixtures and fittings. An owner's absence does not excuse theft or damage. If items are taken for military purposes, a note should be left to that effect.[137]

Reprisals

Reprisals against the property of protected persons are prohibited.[138]   **11.80**

Seizure of movable property

All private movable property used for the transmission of news or to trans- **11.81** port people or goods, whether by land, sea, or air, and private arms or munitions of war, may be temporarily seized but must be restored to the owners when peace is made.[139] The peace treaty will also deal with the question of compensation for property that has been lost, destroyed, or damaged.[140] Submarine cables connecting an occupied territory with a neutral state may only be seized or destroyed if that step becomes absolutely necessary. In that event, they have to be restored, and arrangements for compensation made, when peace is made.[141]

Items falling within paragraph 11.81 include cables, telegraph and tele- **11.81.1** phone equipment, buses, trucks, cars, trailers, railway rolling-stock and other such equipment, ships in port, river and canal craft, aircraft, arms, munitions, and all kinds of property that could serve as war materiel. That includes raw materials such as crude oil. Arms and ammunition includes sporting weapons owned by civilians. Medical transports are excluded.

Method of seizure

The law of armed conflict does not specify in detail the exact form that noti- **11.82** fications of seizure should take. Administrative effort at the conclusion of hostilities will be reduced if a detailed receipt is given at the time of seizure.

Requisitioning of private property

The occupying force may requisition commodities and services needed for **11.83** its maintenance. Requisitioning must take into account the needs of the civilian population.[142]

---

[137] Previously dealt with in MML III, para 595.   [138] GC IV, Art 33.   [139] HR, Art 53.
[140] HR, Art 53. However, the obligation to pay compensation is not dependent on a peace treaty.
[141] HR, Art 54.   [142] HR, Art 52; GC IV, Art 55.

11.83.1 Commodities that may be requisitioned include food and fuel, liquor and tobacco, material for uniforms and boots. Although alcoholic liquor and tobacco may be regarded as luxuries, they are included amongst the sorts of items that may be requisitioned since they would provide an element of comfort to occupying forces. The status of other luxury items like jewellery can be distinguished on the basis that they are not 'needed' by such forces.

11.83.2 The authorities of the occupying power must always act in good faith in requisitioning, whether for the needs of the occupying forces or for the needs of the civilian population. Exploitation of the economy of the occupied territory and private enrichment are forbidden.

11.83.3 The occupying power has a duty to ensure the provision of food and medical supplies for the civilian population and maintain orderly government. If the resources of the occupied territory are insufficient, the occupying power must import the necessary supplies. If, for example, large stocks of food and medical supplies were stored in private ownership, perhaps to force up prices or distort the economy, the occupying power could not reasonably be expected to contribute or import goods from its own resources. To avoid the absurdity of the occupying forces having to release their own stores for the civilian population, only to requisition others from the civilian population for their own use, it would be lawful for the occupying power to requisition or order compulsory sales at proper prices of hoarded foodstuffs, medical supplies, and other essential items needed for the civilian population.

Method of requisitioning

11.84 Requisitioning may only take place on 'the authority of the commander in the locality occupied'. If possible, goods and services should be paid for immediately. Otherwise, a receipt must be given and subsequent payment made without undue delay.[143]

11.84.1 Requisitioned goods become the property of the occupying power. Local authorities may be asked to assist in procuring supplies, but, if this is impossible, special units, under an officer, should be detailed for the purpose. Supplies may be requisitioned in bulk or, alternatively, local inhabitants may be required to complete a return giving details of quantities in their possession of which a proportion may then be requisitioned. Householders on whom soldiers have been quartered may also be required to feed those troops. The prices to be paid for requisitioned supplies and for commodities on sale may be regulated by the local commander.

---

[143] HR, Art 52. See also AA 1955, Pt IV in MML, Pt I.

PUBLIC PROPERTY

Military land and buildings

Military land and buildings belonging to the state, such as supply depots, **11.85** arsenals, dockyards, and barracks, as well as airfields, ports, railways, canals, bridges, piers, and their associated installations, remain at the disposal of the occupying power until the end of the conflict. Structures of this type may only be destroyed or damaged if that is imperatively demanded by military operations.[144]

Civilian land and buildings

Land and buildings that belong to the state but that are essentially civilian **11.86** or non-military in character, such as public buildings, land, forests, parks, farms, and coal mines, may not be damaged or destroyed unless that is imperatively necessitated by military operations. The occupying power is the administrator, user, and, in a sense, guardian of the property. It must not waste, neglect, or abusively exploit these assets so as to decrease their value. The occupying power has no right of disposal or sale but may let or use public land and buildings, sell crops, cut and sell timber, and work mines. It must not enter into commitments extending beyond the conclusion of the occupation and the cutting or mining must not exceed what is necessary or usual.[145]

Land and buildings of local authorities

Exceptionally, the property of local authorities (including, for example, that **11.87** of provincial, county, municipal, and parochial authorities) is treated as if it were private. Similarly, property of institutions dedicated to religion, charity, education, art, and science is also treated as private property, even if it belongs to the state. The seizure, destruction, or damage of such property, historic monuments, and works of art or science is forbidden.[146]

Examples of buildings in this latter category include places of worship, alms- **11.87.1** houses, hospitals, schools, museums, and libraries. If it is cultural property, it is protected anyway.[147] Use of property mentioned in paragraph 11.87 for other, humanitarian purposes, such as the treatment of the wounded and sick in a church, is quite proper if suitable alternative accommodation cannot be found. Cultural property is not to be used for military purposes.[148]

---

[144] GC IV, Art 53.   [145] HR, Art 55.   [146] HR, Art 56.
[147] Under HR, Art 27; AP I, Art 53; see paras 5.25 and 5.26.   [148] AP I, Art 53.

Public movable property

11.88 Occupying forces may only seize three types of movable property belonging to the occupied state:

a. cash, funds, and negotiable securities which are strictly the property of that state;[149]

b. stores of arms and supplies, means of transport, and other movable property which can be used for military operations, together with appliances for the transmission of news, wherever situated;[150]

c. public revenue and taxation raised in occupied territory, although the consequence is that the occupying power becomes liable for the costs of administering the occupied territory.[151]

11.88.1 It is the actual appropriation of such property, rather than mere occupation, that transfers ownership to the occupying power.[152] Since the seizure of funds in the hands of banks but belonging to private individuals or corporations is not permitted, banks should not be ordered to part with funds and securities until their ownership has been determined.

Other public movable property

11.89 Other public movable property, not of use for military purposes, must be respected and not appropriated.[153]

11.89.1 Official documents and papers connected with the armed conflict may be seized, even if they are part of official archives, because they will be of military significance. However, other types of archival documents, as well as crown jewels, pictures, and art collections may not be seized.

Property of questionable ownership

11.90 Where there is any doubt about whether property found in the possession of the enemy is public or private, as may occur in the case of bank deposits and stores and supplies obtained from contractors, it must be considered to be public property unless and until its private character is clearly shown. However, account should be taken of difficulties of proof of ownership, for example, if records have been destroyed or are unavailable. Where a public authority holds property on behalf of a private individual, for example, private bank deposits in state-owned banks, the property must be regarded as private. Where both public and private interests in property exist together,

---

[149] HR, Art 53. See also *French State v Etablissement Monmousseau* 1948 AD 197.
[150] HR, Art 53.   [151] HR, Art 48. See para 11.31.
[152] *Public Prosecutor v N,* 1941 AD Supplementary vol 11, 296.   [153] HR, Art 53.

the occupying power may seize or confiscate the property but must compensate private individuals to the extent of the value of their interest.

GENERAL DEVASTATION

Extensive destruction not justified by military necessity, particularly of things **11.91** indispensable to the survival of the civilian population (including food, agricultural areas, drinking water installations, irrigation works, and the natural environment) with a view to denying them to the civilian population or the adverse party is prohibited and may amount to a grave breach.[154]

The cumulative effect of this is to ban the type of general destruction known **11.91.1** as a 'scorched earth policy' in occupied territory. The distinction between prohibited general devastation and permissible destruction necessitated by military operations is one of fact and degree to be determined in each case.[155]

---

[154] GC IV, Art 147. See also AP I, Arts 35(3), 54, and 55 and para 11.75.
[155] See the *High Command Trial* (1949) 12 WCR 93; XXII IMT 571; and the *Case of von Lewinski (called von Manstein)* (1949) AD 192.

12

Air Operations

A. INTRODUCTION

SCOPE OF CHAPTER

12.1 This chapter states the law of armed conflict as it applies to air operations. It should not be considered in isolation, as it is not a self-contained handbook but an integral part of the whole Manual. Nor does it consider air operations in situations short of armed conflict or those in support of multi-national peacekeeping operations. For the legal constraints applying to the latter, see Chapter 14.

12.2 It should be emphasized that action against third states' shipping or aircraft may only be taken where justified as a measure of self-defence or otherwise in accordance with the UN Charter.

B. GENERAL PROVISIONS

DEFINITIONS

12.3 For the purposes of this chapter certain terms are defined below.

Aircraft

12.4 There is no formal definition of the term 'aircraft' either in United Kingdom domestic law or in international law. Table 12.1 is adapted from that in the Air Navigation Order 2000[1] (the 'Air Navigation Order').[2]

12.4.1 The Order regards remotely piloted vehicles (RPVs) as aircraft.[3] Microlight aeroplanes are included within the category of 'aeroplane (landplane)', and, since 1 July 1983, must be registered by the Civil Aviation Authority. The Naval Discipline Act 1957, the Army Act 1955, and the Air Force Act 1955 state that an aircraft is 'any machine for flying, whether propelled by mechanical means or not, and includes any description of balloon'.[4] The

---

[1] SI 2000/1562.   [2] SI 2000/1562, Sch 2, part A.   [3] SI 2000/1562, Art 129(2)(b).
[4] NDA 1957, s 1135(1); AA 1955, s 225(1); AFA 1955, s 223(1).

TABLE 12.1 General classification of aircraft

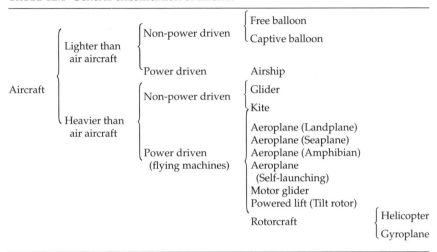

following definition of aircraft in certain annexes to the Convention on International Civil Aviation 1944 (the Chicago Convention), 'Any machine that can derive support in the atmosphere from the reactions of the air other than the reactions of the air against the earth's surface' excludes hovercraft.[5]

Auxiliary aircraft

'Auxiliary aircraft' means an aircraft, other than a military aircraft, that is **12.5** owned by or under the exclusive control of the armed forces of a state and used for the time being on government non-commercial service.[6]

Civil aircraft

'Civil aircraft' means an aircraft that is not a military, auxiliary, or other **12.6** state aircraft (such as a customs or police aircraft) and that is engaged in commercial or private service. (Definition adapted from the *San Remo Manual*).

---

[5] See Martin, Balfour, Margo, McClean, Martin (eds), *Shawcross and Beaumont Air Power* (1991) V/1.
[6] L Doswald-Beck (ed), *San Remo Manual on International Law Applicable to Armed Conflicts at Sea* (1995) (*San Remo Manual*) para 13(k). In the notes to this chapter, paras of the *San Remo Manual* will be referred to thus: SRM 13.

12.6.1 The Chicago Convention distinguishes between civil aircraft and state aircraft. The Convention applies only to civil aircraft.[7] In United Kingdom domestic law a civil aircraft is any aircraft which is not a military aircraft.[8] However, aircraft used in military, customs and police services are deemed to be state aircraft under Article 3(b) of the Chicago Convention. Thus, what is regarded under UK domestic law as a civil aircraft may be regarded under Article 3 of the Chicago Convention as a state aircraft and will be treated as such for the purposes of that Convention. State aircraft are entitled to immunity from the jurisdiction of the courts of a territorial state. One important consequence of this is that state aircraft may not be impounded in enforcement, for example, of alleged debts. If during peacetime a state aircraft, including a military aircraft, strays into the territorial airspace of another state without permission, it should be asked to leave or expelled. Force should only be used as a last resort.

12.6.2 Civil aircraft[9] may legitimately be used for support missions such as transporting troops or supplies. When so used they lose their protection and become legitimate military objectives. Whether civil aircraft on the ground are legitimate objects of attack depends upon whether they are legitimate military objectives.[10]

Civil airliner

12.7 'Civil airliner' means a civil aircraft that is clearly marked and engaged in carrying civilian passengers in scheduled or non-scheduled services along air traffic service routes.[11]

Contraband

12.8 'Contraband' means goods which are ultimately destined for territory under the control of the enemy and which may be susceptible for use in armed conflict.[12]

Medical aircraft

12.9 'Medical aircraft': see paragraph 12.104.

---

[7] Aircraft used in military, customs, and police services shall be deemed to be state aircraft, see the Chicago Convention 1944 (CC), Art 3(b). International Civil Aviation Organization (ICAO) flight procedures are established under the terms of the CC. As military aircraft are not subject to this Convention, they are not bound by ICAO regulations, other than the requirements to operate with due regard to the safety of civil aircraft.

[8] For the definition of 'military aircraft', see para 12.10.   [9] See para 12.6.

[10] AP I, Art 52; see para 12.20.   [11] SRM 13(m).   [12] SRM 148.

Military aircraft

'Military aircraft' means an aircraft operated by commissioned units of the **12.10** armed forces of a state having the military marks of that state, commanded by a member of the armed forces, and manned by a crew subject to regular armed forces discipline.[13]

The Hague Rules 1923 classified aircraft into two broad categories, public **12.10.1** and private. The following were deemed to be public aircraft:

a. 'military aircraft';
b. 'non-military aircraft exclusively employed in the public service'.

All other aircraft were deemed private aircraft.[14]

The term 'military aircraft' is not defined in any treaty but the Air **12.10.2** Navigation Order, the Chicago Convention, and the custom and practice of international law taken together give some guidelines. The Air Navigation Order states that 'military aircraft' means the naval, military, or air force aircraft of any country and:

a. 'any aircraft being constructed for the naval, military or air force of any country under a contract entered into by the Secretary of State'; and

b. 'any aircraft in respect of which there is in force a certificate issued by the Secretary of State that the aircraft is to be treated for the purpose of this Order as a military aircraft'.[15]

Generally, the status of the aircraft will be determined by its uses. **12.10.3**

Military aircraft can include, for example, transport, reconnaissance, and **12.10.4** meteorological aircraft of the armed forces of a particular state whether or not they are used in a direct combatant role. These aircraft must bear external markings indicating clearly their nationality and military character.[16] In most air forces, the same marking indicates both nationality and military character, for example, the Royal Air Force roundel. Additional markings to indicate an international grouping such as NATO are permissible but modifications of this nature adopted by any state must be promptly notified to all other states.[17] The captain and crew of military aircraft must wear clearly recognizable uniform with badges of rank at all times, as should any military passengers.[18] For this purpose, regulation flying clothing is

---

[13] SRM 13(j). The UK Air Navigation Order, see para 12.4, refers to foreign military aircraft as 'the naval, military or air force aircraft of any country'. The elements in this definition are useful in identifying such aircraft. Military aircraft in the UK would comply with these requirements. For military markings, see para 12.10.4.   [14] Hague Rules 1923, Art 2.
[15] SI 2000/1562.   [16] Hague Rules 1923, Art 3.   [17] Hague Rules 1923, Art 8.
[18] AP I, Art 44

recognized as uniform. Article 19 of the Hague Rules 1923 prohibited the use of false external marks on aircraft. Additional Protocol I now prohibits the use at any time by any party to a conflict of the flags, military emblems, insignia, or uniforms of neutral or other states not party to the conflict.[19] The use of flags, military emblems, insignia, or uniforms of an adverse party is prohibited 'while engaging in attacks or in order to shield, favour or impede military operations'.[20]

Neutral

12.11 'Neutral' has traditionally meant any state not party to the conflict.[21] However, see the discussion on neutrality in paragraphs 1.42 and 1.43.

C. REGIONS OF OPERATIONS

AIRSPACE

Lateral extent of airspace

12.12 The Chicago Convention provides 'that every State has complete and exclusive sovereignty over the airspace above its territory'.[22] For the purposes of the Convention 'the territory of a State shall be deemed to be the land areas and territorial waters adjacent thereto under the sovereignty, suzerainty, protection or mandate of such State'.[23]

12.12.1 Despite the fact that this Convention applies only to civil aircraft,[24] this definition reflects accepted customary law regarding the lateral extent of airspace.

Vertical extent of airspace

12.13 Views differ as to the precise vertical and horizontal extent of airspace. For practical purposes, it can be said that the upper limit to a state's rights in airspace is above the highest altitude at which an aircraft can fly and below the lowest possible perigee of an earth satellite in orbit. The result is that anything in orbit or beyond can safely be regarded as in outer space.

International airspace

12.14 Aircraft have freedom of overflight over exclusive economic zones (EEZs) of other states and over the high seas. The airspace in question is often

---

[19] AP I, Art 39(1).   [20] AP I, Art 39(2). See, further, para 5.10.   [21] SRM 13(d).
[22] CC, Art 1.   [23] CC, Art 2.   [24] CC, Art 3(a).

known as 'international airspace'. There is no equivalent in air law to the maritime doctrine of the contiguous zone. It is lawful for a military aircraft of one state to fly in international airspace adjacent to the national airspace of another state, for example, for the purpose of surveillance and observation of activities within that other state's national airspace or territory.

Neutral airspace

Belligerent military and auxiliary aircraft may not enter neutral airspace. **12.14A** Should they do so, the neutral State shall use the means at its disposal to require the aircraft to land within its territory and shall intern the aircraft and its crew for the duration of the armed conflict. Should the aircraft fail to follow the instructions to land, it may be attacked, subject to the special rules relating to medical aircraft in Paragraphs 12.14B to 12.14D.[24A]

Belligerent medical aircraft shall not enter neutral airspace except by prior **12.14B** agreement. When within neutral airspace pursuant to agreement, medical aircraft shall comply with the terms of the agreement. The terms of agreement may require the aircraft to land for inspection at a designated airfield within the neutral State. Should the agreement so require, the inspection and follow on action shall be conducted in accordance with Paragraphs 12.14C and 12.14D.[24B]

Should a medical aircraft, in the absence of an agreement or in deviation **12.14C** from the terms of an agreement, enter neutral airspace, either through navigational error or because of an emergency affecting the safety of the flight, it shall make every effort to give notice and to identify itself. Once the aircraft is recognised as a medical aircraft by the neutral State, it shall not be attacked but may be required to land for inspection. Once it has been inspected, and if it is determined in fact to be a medical aircraft, it shall be allowed to resume its flight.[24C]

If the inspection reveals that the aircraft is not a medical aircraft, it may be **12.14D** captured, and the occupants shall, unless agreed otherwise between the neutral State and the parties to the conflict, be detained in the neutral State where so required by the rules of international law applicable in armed conflict, in such a manner that they cannot again take part in the hostilities.[24D]

Air defence regions, air policing areas, and air defence identification zones

Air defence identification zones (ADIZs) do not constitute an extension **12.15** of national sovereignty. Their primary purpose is identification and they

[24A] SRM 18   [24B] SRM 181   [24C] SRM 182   [24D] SRM 183 are, in practical terms, a means of early warning of suspicious activity. Non-compliance with their procedures does not in itself justify the use of force against an aircraft still in international airspace or even when it later enters the airspace of the state concerned.[25]

12.15.1 During the Cold War, the UK operated an air defence region. This nationally defined area could be entered without violating British sovereignty, but any intruding aircraft was liable to interception by the RAF. Other states, including the USA and Canada, have established ADIZs extending several hundred miles seaward into international airspace above the high seas adjacent to their territorial seas. Generally, aircraft on a course to enter the airspace of these countries are required to identify themselves on entering these zones. NATO air policing areas are similar in character to ADIZs.

Warning zones[26]

12.16 From time to time, and for temporary purposes, states have declared certain areas of international airspace to be 'warning zones'.

12.16.1 These have been declared, for example, where exercises are taking place or, prior to the Nuclear Test Ban Treaty 1963, in nuclear test areas.

12.16.2 Appropriate international notices to airmen (NOTAMs) must be issued, which should keep the airspace and time restrictions involved to the minimum consistent with safety. When a state declares an area above the high seas to be hazardous, it does not purport to have authority to prohibit aircraft of other states from flying through that airspace or to have authority to punish the owners or operators of such aircraft.[27] The warnings are cautionary, not mandatory.

The control of airspace in situations short of armed conflict

12.17 There is no equivalent, for aircraft, of the naval right of innocent passage through the territorial sea of another state. Suitable preventive measures may be taken against aircraft that do intrude. These would not include an immediate attack or attempt to impound the intruder in the absence of significant aggravating circumstances. Indeed, when ships exercise this right, they are not permitted to launch, land, or take on board any aircraft.[28]

---

[25] See para 12.81.   [26] These are also referred to, eg, in CC, as prohibited zones.
[27] See also para 12.58.
[28] UN Convention on the Law of the Sea 1982 (UNCLOS), Art 19. Aircraft do enjoy rights of transit passage through international straits, by virtue of UNCLOS, Art 38, and rights of achipelaegic sea lanes passage in the air route above such lanes, by virtue of UNCLOS, Art 53(2).

Not all unauthorized incursions into sovereign airspace by foreign military aircraft will amount to aggressive acts justifying the use of force in self-defence. Much will depend on the individual circumstances, including whether any threat is posed, whether alternative possible responses exist, or whether the incident appears to be deliberate or an isolated error.

12.17.1 As a result of the shooting down of a Korean Airlines Boeing 747 by the Soviet Union on 1 September 1983, the Assembly of the International Civil Aviation Organization (ICAO) approved an amendment to the Chicago Convention recognizing the principle that 'states must refrain from resorting to the use of weapons against civil aircraft in flight and . . . in the case of interception the lives of persons on board and the safety of aircraft must not be endangered'.[29] This amendment came into force on 1 October 1998. It does not amount to an absolute prohibition on the use of force,[30] as the rights of states under the UN Charter, including the inherent right of self-defence, remains unaffected.[31]

12.17.2 The procedures for dealing with intruding aircraft, the doctrine of 'hot pursuit', and the control of airspace in peacetime generally are not governed by the law of armed conflict.

D. BASIC RULES AND TARGET DISCRIMINATION

BASIC RULES

12.18 In any armed conflict the right of the parties to the conflict to choose methods or means of warfare is not unlimited.[32]

12.19 Parties to the conflict shall at all times distinguish between civilians or other protected persons and combatants, and between civilian or exempt objects and military objectives.[33]

12.20 In so far as objects are concerned, military objectives are limited to those objects which by their nature, location, purpose, or use make an effective contribution to military action and whose total or partial destruction,

---

[29] CC, Art 3 *bis*.

[30] It is, however, an indication of the strong international sentiment that followed the shooting down of the Korean Airlines Boeing 747 in 1983.

[31] Article 3 *bis* of the Chicago Convention, as amended, confirms that the amendment shall not be interpreted as modifying in any way the rights and obligations of states set forth in the UN Charter.   [32] AP I, Art 35(1); SRM 38.

[33] AP I, Art 48, see para 2.5; SRM 39.

capture, or neutralization, in the circumstances ruling at the time, offers a definite military advantage.[34]

12.21 Attacks shall be limited strictly to military objectives.[35] Merchant vessels and civil aircraft are civilian objects unless they are military objectives in accordance with the principles and rules set forth in this chapter.[36]

12.22 In addition to any specific prohibitions binding upon the parties to a conflict, it is forbidden to employ methods or means of warfare which:

    a. are of a nature to cause superfluous injury or unnecessary suffering;[37] or

    b. are indiscriminate, in that:

        (1) they are not, or cannot be, directed against a specific military objective; or

        (2) their effects cannot be limited as required by international law as reflected in this chapter.[38]

12.23 It is prohibited to order that there shall be no survivors, to threaten an adversary therewith or to conduct hostilities on this basis.[39]

12.24 Methods and means of warfare should be employed with due regard for the natural environment, taking into account the relevant rules of international law. Damage to or destruction of the natural environment not justified by military necessity and carried out wantonly is prohibited.[40]

12.25 Aircraft are bound by the same principles and rules.[41]

12.25.1 The basic rules set out above apply to all forms of warfare, whether on land, at sea, or in the air. In addition, Articles 48 to 67 of Additional Protocol I contain detailed rules for warfare which may affect civilians or civilian objects on land.[42] Those detailed rules are set out in Chapter 5, Parts C, D, E, and F, and apply equally to attacks from the air against targets on the ground.

AIR BOMBARDMENT

12.26 In the conduct of attacks against targets on land, the following rules are of importance:

    a. Attacks are only to be directed against military objectives: see paragraph 5.4.

---

[34] SRM 40. The same definition is used for warfare affecting targets on land: AP I Art 52(2), see para 5.4. See also AP I, Arts 49(3) and 52(2).

[35] For attacks affecting targets on land, see para 5.4.   [36] SRM 41.

[37] AP I, Art 35(2); see para 6.1.

[38] SRM 42. This language derives from AP I, Art 51(4) although that article only applies to attacks affecting targets on land, see AP I, Art 49(3).

[39] AP I, Art 40, see also para 5.5; SRM 43.   [40] SRM 44. See also AP I, Arts 35 and 55.

[41] SRM 45.   [42] AP I, Art 49(3).

b. The civilian population and individual civilians must not be attacked and must be protected against the dangers arising from military operations; civilian objects are similarly protected: see paragraphs 5.3 and 5.20 onwards.

c. Indiscriminate attacks are prohibited: see paragraph 5.23.

d. Cultural objects are specially protected: see paras 5.25 and 5.26.

e. Air bombardment must not destroy or render useless objects indispensable to the survival of the civilian population: see paragraph 5.27.

f. The natural environment is specially protected: see paragraph 5.29.

g. Works and installations containing dangerous forces are protected from attack: see paragraph 5.30.

h. Attacks on non-defended localities and zones under special protection are prohibited: see paragraph 5.31.

i. Precautions must be taken in air bombardment to avoid civilian death or injury and damage to civilian objects: see paragraph 5.32.

j. Unless circumstances do not permit it, effective advance warning must be given of air bombardment that may affect the civilian population: see paragraph 5.32.8.

Enemy Vessels and Aircraft Exempt from Attack

Classes of vessels exempt from attack

See paragraph 13.33 onwards. **12.27**

Classes of aircraft exempt from attack

The following classes of enemy aircraft are exempt from attack: **12.28**

a. medical aircraft;

b. aircraft granted safe conduct by agreement between the parties to the conflict; and

c. civil airliners.[43]

Conditions of exemption for medical aircraft

Medical aircraft are exempt from attack only if they: **12.29**

a. have been recognized as such;[44]

---

[43] SRM 53.

[44] When flying over areas physically controlled by an adverse party, medical aircraft are obliged to obey orders to land, or alight on water, for inspection. If they fail to do so, they are at risk of being attacked: AP I, Arts 27(2) and 30. See, further, para 12.118.

    b. are acting in compliance with an agreement as specified in paragraph 12.112;

    c. fly in areas under the control of own or friendly forces; or

    d. fly outside the area of armed conflict.

12.29.1 In other instances, medical aircraft operate at their own risk.[45]

12.29.2 For further information about medical aircraft and their protection, see paragraph 12.104 onwards.

Conditions of exemption for aircraft granted safe conduct

12.30 Aircraft granted safe conduct are exempt from attack only if they:

    a. are innocently employed in their agreed role;

    b. do not intentionally hamper the movements of combatants; and

    c. comply with the details of the agreement, including availability for inspection.[46]

Conditions of exemption for civil airliners

12.31 Civil airliners are exempt from attack only if they:

    a. are innocently employed in their normal role; and

    b. do not intentionally hamper the movements of combatants.[47]

Loss of exemption

12.32 If aircraft exempt from attack breach any of the applicable conditions of their exemption as set forth in paragraphs 12.29 to 12.31, they may be attacked only if:

    a. diversion for landing, visit and search, and possible capture, is not feasible;

    b. no other method is available for exercising military control;

    c. the circumstances of non-compliance are sufficiently grave that the aircraft has become, or may be reasonably assumed to be, a military objective; and

    d. the collateral casualties or damage will not be disproportionate to the military advantage gained or anticipated.[48]

---

[45] SRM 54.   [46] SRM 55.   [47] SRM 56.   [48] SRM 57.

In case of doubt whether a vessel or aircraft exempt from attack is being **12.33** used to make an effective contribution to military action, it shall be presumed not to be so used.[49]

OTHER ENEMY VESSELS AND AIRCRAFT

Only military aircraft may carry out attacks

Only military aircraft may attack military objectives. If it is intended to use **12.34** civilian aircraft for combat purposes, they must be embodied into the air force and correctly marked. The classification in the Hague Rules 1923 of public and private aircraft[50] has legal implications for the rights of visit, search, and capture.

Enemy merchant vessels

See paragraph 13.40 onwards. **12.35**

Enemy civil aircraft

Enemy civil aircraft may only be attacked if they meet the definition of **12.36** a military objective in paragraph 5.4.1.[51]

The following activities may render enemy civil aircraft military objectives: **12.37**

a. engaging in acts of war on behalf of the enemy, eg, laying mines, minesweeping, laying or monitoring sensors, engaging in electronic warfare, intercepting or attacking other civil aircraft, or providing targeting information to enemy forces;

b. acting as an auxiliary aircraft to an enemy's armed forces, eg, transporting troops or military cargo, or refuelling military aircraft;

c. being incorporated into or assisting the enemy's intelligence gathering system, eg, engaging in reconnaissance, early warning, surveillance, or command, control, and communications missions;

d. flying under the protection of accompanying enemy warships or military aircraft;

e. refusing an order to identify itself, divert from its track, or proceed for visit and search to a belligerent airfield that is safe for the type of aircraft involved and reasonably accessible, or operating fire control equipment that could reasonably be construed to be part of an aircraft weapon system, or on being intercepted clearly manoeuvring to attack the intercepting belligerent military aircraft;

---

[49] SRM 58.   [50] See para 12.4.   [51] SRM 62.

    f. being armed with air-to-air or air-to-surface weapons; or

    g. otherwise making an effective contribution to military action.[52]

12.38 Any attack on these aircraft is subject to the basic rules set out in paragraphs 12.18 to 12.25.[53]

12.38.1 Civil aircraft[54] are entitled to the general protection afforded civilians and civilian objects and may only be attacked if they meet the definition of a military objective.[55] In times of armed conflict, and subject to any specific restrictions which may be imposed, civil aircraft may fly in their own national airspace, in international airspace, and, subject to authorization, over the territory and territorial waters of neutral states. During armed conflict, the provisions of the Chicago Convention do not affect the freedom of action of any of the states involved, whether as belligerents or as neutrals.[56] The same principle applies in the case of a party to the Chicago Convention that declares a state of national emergency and notifies the fact to the Council of the International Civil Aviation Organization.[57] Civil aircraft of a belligerent, if they enter enemy airspace, are likely to be deemed a military threat, with all the risks that this implies. Any decision to attack must be based on military necessity.[58] It is, therefore, of particular importance that in time of armed conflict the external markings and radio and radar procedures of civil aircraft comply strictly with international requirements. Civil aircraft, wherever encountered by military aircraft of the adverse party, are required to identify themselves and to act on instructions in order to certify their status and preclude their involvement in hostilities.

Enemy warships and military aircraft

12.39 Unless they are exempt from attack under paragraphs 13.33 or 12.29, enemy warships and military aircraft and enemy auxiliary vessels and aircraft are military objectives.[59]

12.40 They may be attacked, subject to the basic rules in paragraphs 12.18 to 12.25.[60]

12.41 For attacks on military aircraft, see paragraph 12.62 onwards.

---

    [52] SRM 63.   [53] SRM 64.   [54] See para 12.6.

    [55] See the definition in para 5.4. Various activities may render enemy civil aircraft military objectives including engaging in acts of war, transporting troops or military cargo, engaging in the enemy's intelligence gathering system, or refusing to identify itself or divert from its track, see SRM 63.   [56] CC, Art 89.

    [57] CC, Art 89.   [58] As to which, see para 2.2.   [59] SRM 65.

    [60] SRM 66.

Neutral merchant vessels

See paragraph 13.46 onwards and the comments on neutrality in paragraphs **12.42** 1.42 to 1.43.

Neutral civil aircraft

Civil aircraft bearing the marks of neutral states may only be attacked if **12.43** they meet the definition of a military objective in paragraph 5.4.1.[61]

The following activities may render neutral civil aircraft military objectives: **12.43.1**

a. if they are believed on reasonable grounds to be carrying contraband, and, after prior warning or interception, they intentionally and clearly refuse to divert from their destination, or intentionally and clearly refuse to proceed for visit and search to a belligerent airfield that is safe for the type of aircraft involved and reasonably accessible;

b. if they engage in belligerent acts on behalf of the enemy;

c. if they act as auxiliaries to the enemy's armed forces;

d. if they are incorporated into or assist the enemy's intelligence system; or

e. if they otherwise make an effective contribution to the enemy's military action, eg, by carrying military materials, and, after prior warning or interception, they intentionally and clearly refuse to divert from their destination, or intentionally and clearly refuse to proceed for visit and search to a belligerent airfield that is safe for the type of aircraft involved and reasonably accessible.[62]

Any attack on these aircraft is subject to paragraph 12.2 and the basic rules **12.44** in paragraphs 12.18 to 12.25.[63]

Civil aircraft should avoid areas of potentially hazardous military **12.45** activity.[64]

In the immediate vicinity of naval operations, all civil aircraft shall comply **12.46** with instructions from the belligerents regarding their heading and altitude.[65]

---

[61] SRM 62. But see also the comments on neutrality at paras 1.42–1.43.
[62] SRM 70. [63] SRM 71. [64] SRM 72. [65] SRM 73.

12.47 Belligerents and neutral states concerned, and authorities providing air traffic services, should establish procedures whereby commanders of warships and military aircraft are aware on a continuous basis of designated routes assigned to or flight plans filed by civil aircraft in the area of military operations, including information on communication channels, identification modes and codes, destination, passengers, and cargo.[66]

12.48 Belligerent and neutral states should ensure that a notice to airmen (NOTAM) is issued providing information on military activities in areas potentially hazardous to civil aircraft, including activation of danger areas or temporary airspace restrictions. This NOTAM should include information on:

a. frequencies upon which the aircraft should maintain a continuous listening watch;

b. continuous operation of civil weather-avoidance radar and identification modes and codes;

c. altitude, course, and speed restrictions;

d. procedures to respond to radio contact by the military forces and to establish two-way communications; and

e. possible action by the military forces if the NOTAM is not complied with and the civil aircraft is perceived by those military forces to be a threat.[67]

12.49 Civil aircraft should file the required flight plan with the cognizant air traffic service, complete with information as to registration, destination, passengers, cargo, emergency communication channels, identification modes and codes, updates en route, and carry certificates as to registration, airworthiness, passengers, and cargo. They should not deviate from a designated air traffic service route or flight plan without air traffic control clearance unless unforeseen conditions arise, eg, safety or distress, in which case appropriate notification should be made immediately.[68]

12.50 If a civil aircraft enters an area of potentially hazardous military activity, it should comply with relevant NOTAMs. Military forces should use all available means to identify and warn the civil aircraft, by using, *inter alia*, secondary surveillance radar modes and codes, communications, correlation with flight plan information, interception by military aircraft, and, when possible, contacting the appropriate air traffic control facility.[69]

---

[66] SRM 74.   [67] SRM 75.   [68] SRM 76.   [69] SRM 77.

E. METHODS AND MEANS OF WARFARE

MEANS OF WARFARE

Air-to-surface missiles

The employment of 'dumb' bombs has not been rendered unlawful by the **12.51** advent of precision guided or 'smart' bombs, but developing technology does bring with it a change in the standards affecting the choice of munitions when taking the precautions[70] referred to in paragraph 5.32.

The employment of tracer bullets by or against aircraft is not prohibited.[71] **12.51.1** In relation to air operations against any ground target, such employment is customarily regarded as lawful when its essential purpose is to ensure accuracy, and therefore discrimination, as it would be, for instance, when the aircraft is in flight.

Remotely delivered mines

This subject is dealt with in detail in paragraphs 6.13 and 6.14. **12.52**

Incendiary weapons

It is in all circumstances prohibited 'to make any military objective located **12.53** within a concentration of civilians the object of attack by air-delivered incendiary weapons'.[72]

This subject is dealt with in detail in paragraph 6.12. **12.53.1**

Laser weapons

It is prohibited[73] 'to employ laser weapons specifically designed, as their **12.54** sole combat function or as one of their combat functions, to cause permanent blindness to unenhanced vision'.[74]

Systems which use lasers for range-finding, missile guidance, and target **12.54.1** laying, not being so designed as above, are unaffected.

---

[70] AP I, Art 57(2).   [71] See para 6.10.
[72] CCW, Protocol III, Art 2(2). This provision should not be taken to imply that air delivery of incendiary or other weapons, projectiles, or munitions is less accurate or less capable of being carried out discriminately than any other means of delivery: see UK statement on ratification of CCW, Protocol III.   [73] CCW, Protocol IV, Art 1.
[74] See para 6.14.

Nuclear weapons

12.55 See paragraph 6.17.

BLOCKADE

12.56 For blockade, see paragraph 13.65 onwards.

MARITIME ZONES

12.57 For maritime zones, see paragraph 13.77 onwards.

WAR ZONES RESTRICTIONS[75]

12.58 Parties to a conflict may establish zones of immediate operations or exclusion zones[76] within which they intend to pursue or are actively pursuing hostilities. Notice of the existence of these war zones must give the extent, location, duration, and associated risks, see paragraph 13.78. The right to fire upon any aircraft disregarding a general prohibition of entry into such a zone must be based on military necessity. That requires an assessment as to whether in all the circumstances the aircraft is a military objective and whether an attack upon it can be carried out without disproportionate loss of civilian life or civilian property.

12.58.1 These zones may exist over the territories and territorial waters of any state involved in the armed conflict and, where military necessity justifies it, may include airspace over the high seas. Both civil and military aircraft, including those of neutral states, which operate in support of the enemy are liable to attack in a war zone. But due allowance should be made for the continuance of neutral traffic by allowing freedom of transit, at least between neutral countries, along alternative routes where the normal route lies through a zone which is temporarily closed.

12.58.2 The presumption, in Additional Protocol I,[77] of civilian status in cases of doubt does not, strictly speaking, apply in air-to-air combat.[78] Nevertheless,

---

[75] See JM Spaight, *Air Power and War Rights* (3rd edn 1947) (Spaight, *Air Power*) 400 onwards.
[76] During the Falklands conflict 1982, a total exclusion zone of 200 nautical miles radius was established around the Islands. It applied, *inter alia*, to any aircraft, military or civil, operating in support of the illegal occupation by the Argentine forces, and any aircraft (military or civil) found within the zone without authority from the Ministry of Defence would be regarded as operating in support of the illegal occupation and thus hostile and liable to be attacked by the British forces. The zone was imposed in exercise of the right to self-defence as recognized by Art 51 of the UN Charter.   [77] Arts 50(1) and 52(3).
[78] AP I, Art 49(4).

attacks on ostensibly civil aircraft should only be carried out as a last resort when there is reason to believe that it is itself deployed on an attack. An example might be when, during an armed conflict, an exclusion zone has been established around the United Kingdom and an apparently civilian airliner enters the zone on a course set for a major city, all required notification and other procedures to establish the zone have been meticulously completed, and all attempts to communicate with the aircraft, including buzzing, have failed or been ignored.

DECEPTION, RUSES OF WAR, AND PERFIDY

Military and auxiliary aircraft are prohibited at all times from feigning exempt, civilian, or neutral status.[79] **12.59**

Ruses of war are permitted, see paragraph 5.17. **12.60**

'It is prohibited to kill, injure or capture an adversary by resort to perfidy', see paragraph 5.9. **12.61**

AIR-TO-AIR COMBAT

Enemy military aircraft

In time of armed conflict, enemy military aircraft that are not exempt (see paragraph 12.28) may be attacked and destroyed in any airspace other than that of a neutral state.[80] Such enemy military aircraft may be captured anywhere except in the jurisdiction of a neutral state. Ownership passes to the capturing state by virtue of the capture and prize procedure. **12.62**

However, the possibility of effecting capture in air-to-air combat is not a realistic one. The extent and manner of air-to-air attacks depends, in practice, upon many factors including military, political, and geographical considerations and the level of intensity of the conflict. For example, when it is desired to maintain the conflict at low intensity, the air forces of a party to a conflict may be authorized to attack only military aircraft that are involved in direct combat operations. They may be instructed not to attack military aircraft engaged only in transporting supplies, even though these aircraft are not protected by international law and are legitimate targets. **12.62.1**

An enemy military aircraft is a legitimate target in armed conflict unless it is entitled to protection as a medical aircraft (see Part G below), or to specific protection as a result of an agreement between belligerents. Such agreements[81] would include non-hostile use of aircraft in connection with, for **12.62.2**

---

[79] SRM 109.   [80] But see para 1.43(a).   [81] See, generally, Ch 10.

example, negotiations to conclude hostilities, parlementaires, cease-fires, surrenders, exchange of prisoners of war, and exchanges of official communications. Agreements should include provisions about appropriate markings and other means of identification. The individual status of personnel carried on military aircraft is subsumed in the military character of the aircraft until such time as they leave it.

Method of attack

12.63 Military aircraft and other aircraft that are military objectives may be attacked by any method, means, or weapon not otherwise prohibited, including air-to-air missiles and explosives or incendiary projectiles.

12.63.1 Although by the St Petersburg Declaration 1868, the signatories renounced the use by their military or naval forces of any projectile below 400 grammes in weight, which is either explosive or charged with fulminating or inflammable substances, a customary practice of using such weapons in air-to-air combat has developed. During the First World War it was found that the most effective means of destroying enemy balloons was by incendiary bullets, and the Hague Rules1923, recognized this practice: 'the use of tracer, incendiary or explosive projectiles by or against aircraft is not prohibited'. This provision was declared to apply equally to states party to the St Petersburg Declaration and those that are not.[82] This provision, though never ratified, is regarded as declaratory of customary international law.

Surrender by enemy aircraft

12.64 Although it is forbidden to 'kill or wound an enemy who, having laid down his arms, or having no longer means of defence, has surrendered at discretion',[83] in air-to-air combat, surrender is usually impracticable and occurs very infrequently.

12.64.1 In the special circumstances of air-to-air combat the continuation of an attack after an indication by the opponent of a wish to surrender is not inconsistent with the rule in paragraph 12.64, as the enemy pilot who remains in his aircraft cannot be said to have 'laid down his arms' or to have 'no longer a means of defence'. However, if the surrender is offered in good faith and in circumstances that do not prevent enforcement, for example, when the engagement has not taken place over enemy territory, it must be respected and accepted. Surrenders of enemy aircraft and crews should not be discouraged because not only is a psychological advantage gained, but an enemy

---

[82] Hague Rules 1923, Art 18.   [83] HR, Art 23(c).

aircraft and defecting aircrew can provide intelligence which, if promptly and properly evaluated, may be of inestimable benefit to operations planning.

Surrender by ground troops

The basic rules of international law relating to air-to-ground combat are **12.65** set out in paragraphs 12.26 and 12.51 to 12.55. The rule on surrender is in paragraph 12.64.

Although there were examples[84] in both World Wars where aircraft accepted **12.65.1** surrenders from armed forces on the ground, there were practical difficulties in accepting such surrenders. The surrender of ground troops to an aircraft crew occurred on at least one occasion during the 1990–91 Gulf conflict. With the advent of close support and ground-attack helicopter units, the surrender of ground troops to aircraft has become a more practical proposition.

AIRCRAFT IN DISTRESS

General

If it is clear that an enemy aircraft is disabled beyond recovery and is unable **12.66** to continue and will not resume combat, or indeed is unarmed, and its immediate destruction would offer no military advantage, then the attack must be broken off to allow its crew and passengers to evacuate.

A topic very closely related to that of surrender in the air is whether an **12.66.1** attack should be continued against a disabled aircraft. The rule of the law of armed conflict forbidding the killing or wounding of an enemy who is *hors de combat*[85] is difficult to apply in the context of aerial warfare. Sometimes pilots simulate disability or loss of control.[86] It is frequently necessary in aerial combat to pursue to destruction an enemy aircraft apparently in distress because of the impossibility of verifying its condition.[87] Despite its apparent condition the aircraft may not have lost the use of all its offensive systems.

---

[84] Spaight, *Air Power*, 131–132.   [85] See para 5.6.

[86] An action which simply replicates the apparent symptoms of distress and which is intended to induce an adverse belligerent aircraft to call off an attack is a legitimate ruse of war. To go further, however, eg, by falsely using an international distress signal, or any internationally recognized sign or signal for distress or surrender in order to gain a combat advantage, would amount to perfidious conduct, see Hague Rules for the Control of Wireless Telegraphy in Time of War 1923, Art 10.

[87] See L Oppenheim, *International Law* (7th edn by H Lauterpacht 1952), vol II, 521; Spaight, *Air Power*, 127.

Parachutists

12.67 No 'person parachuting from an aircraft in distress shall be made the object of attack during his descent'. A person who has parachuted from an aircraft in distress must, upon reaching the ground in territory controlled by an adverse belligerent, be given an opportunity to surrender before being attacked unless it is apparent that he is engaged in a hostile act. Airborne troops do not fall under this protection.[88]

12.67.1 The destruction or an attempt at destruction of the aircraft, any part of its equipment, or related documents would constitute a hostile act.

AIRMEN IN ENEMY-HELD TERRITORY

'Downed' airmen

On land[89]

12.68 On land, a 'downed' airman from an aircraft in distress must be afforded a reasonable opportunity to surrender before the attack upon him is resumed. Clearly if the 'downed' airman is incapacitated he is *hors de combat* and the general rule[90] will apply. The attack may be resumed immediately if he offers violence, attempts to escape, or if, suffering no incapacity, he is in territory controlled by his own forces. The pilot who has crash-landed his aircraft and is attempting to complete its destruction or the destruction of any part of his or its equipment is committing a hostile act and may be attacked immediately.[91]

Combat rescue of 'downed' aircrew on land

12.69 The use of, for example, military assets to rescue aircrew who have been 'downed' on territory under the control of the enemy is a combat activity. It is therefore legitimate for an enemy in such circumstances to attack the rescuers or by some other means to impede or prevent the rescue activity.[92] However, that would not apply in the case of medical personnel, units or transports collecting the sick or wounded, see Chapter 7.

12.69.1 The mere fact that a rescue service saves enemy personnel as well as its own does not entitle it to immunity from attack. Once taken prisoner, such

---

[88] AP I, Art 42(3); but see para 5.7.1.   [89] AP I, Art 42(2).   [90] See para 5.6.

[91] See paras 5.7 and 12.51. During the Gulf conflict 1991, the *London Evening Standard* of 21 January 1991 reported that the Iraqi government was offering rewards for the capture alive of enemy pilots. Such a policy would not, in itself, be unlawful particularly if it dissuaded the local population from attacking them.

[92] See Spaight, *Air Power*, 166. During WW II, the British government properly asserted the right to drive off or destroy craft assigned to the rescuing service.

enemy personnel should be accorded all the rights of a prisoner of war,[93] at least until their status has been determined. Arguably, any communication by 'downed' aircrew with their national authorities constitutes a hostile act, which would at that point justify an attack upon that aircrew. Such justification may also arise from other conduct indicating that the 'downed' individual is seeking to continue the fight.

Combat rescue at sea

A 'downed' airmen at sea falls within the definition of 'shipwrecked' so that **12.70** he must not be attacked if he refrains from hostile acts.[94]

Although it can be argued that search and rescue by aircraft used exclus- **12.70.1** ively for rescuing airmen 'downed' at sea in areas either not controlled by friendly forces or not occupied by enemy forces should be regarded as a protected activity under the provisions of Geneva Convention II 1949, it has been the general practice not to afford such protection.[95]

Evasion, capture, and escape

Evasion before capture

A 'downed' airman who evades capture in enemy-held territory is, until **12.71** he surrenders, a lawful target for attack. Provided that he has not at any time fallen into the power of the enemy[96] and remains in his uniform, he may conduct himself as a combatant but will be subject to all the legal constraints which that status involves.[97] If he discards his uniform but nevertheless engages in an attack or in a military operation preparatory to an attack, he may be an unlawful combatant.[98] If he is captured when not in uniform he runs the risk of being treated as a spy.[99]

---

[93] These are set out in GC III and AP I, see Ch 8.

[94] GC II, Art 12.   [95] See further para 12.122.2.   [96] See para 12.72.

[97] See para 4.2 and, generally, Ch 5. In particular, he must not attack civilians or civilian objects.

[98] AP I, Art 44(7). A combatant member of the regular armed forces of a party to a conflict is obliged to wear uniform while engaging in an attack or in a military operation preparatory to an attack, AP I, Art 44(7). The statement (g) made by the UK on ratification may considerably restrict the circumstances in which a 'downed' airman can legitimately conduct himself as a combatant when out of uniform. See, more generally, para 4.5.

[99] AP I, Art 46(2) provides that a member of the armed forces of a party to the conflict shall not be regarded as engaging in espionage when wearing his uniform, which for these purposes includes his ordinary flying suit.

Capture

12.72 An airman who falls into the power of an adverse party becomes a prisoner of war.[100] This applies equally to authorized civilian members of military aircraft crews.[101] These persons are prisoners of war from the time that they fall into the power of the enemy and until their final release and repatriation.[102] If the captured airman does not appear to be entitled to prisoner of war status, but claims it or it is formally claimed on his behalf, he is to be presumed to be a prisoner of war, and therefore protected, until his status is determined by a competent tribunal.[103]

12.72.1 Whether a combatant has fallen into the power of the enemy is a question of fact. It is from the moment of capture that the airman becomes entitled to the protection and rights arising from his status as a prisoner of war, see Chapter 8. Airmen who become prisoners of war are entitled to the same protections as are afforded to prisoners of war who are members of the other armed services.

Conduct after capture

General

12.73 The responsibility of the detaining power for the handling of prisoners of war is dealt with in Chapter 8. The duties and constraints placed upon the captor by virtue of Geneva Convention III 1949 exist for the benefit and protection of the captive as a protected person. The duties placed upon the prisoner of war by the Convention are dealt with in Chapter 8. In addition, particular responsibilities relating to his conduct when in the power of the enemy may have been laid upon a prisoner of war as a member of the armed forces of a state by way of regulation or instruction of his own service. These may have the force of national law and breach of them may be the subject of criminal or disciplinary action against the prisoner of war once he has rejoined his own force.[104] They are, however, national in character

---

[100] AP I, Art 44. See, generally, Ch 8. The status of prisoner of war (PW) and the provisions of GC III do not apply in circumstances of non-international armed conflict unless applied by agreement between the parties.

[101] GC III, Art 4A(4). The latter should be authorized by their armed forces and should hold an appropriate identity card.

[102] GC III, Art 5.   [103] AP I, Art 45. See also para 8.21.

[104] See, eg, AFA 1955, s 25(1)(c). A person subject, in this instance, to air force law who, having been captured by the enemy, knowingly and without lawful excuse fails to take any reasonable steps which are available to him to rejoin Her Majesty's Service commits an offence.

and form no part of the international law of armed conflict. It is important for the prisoner of war to be aware of the provisions of the Convention[105] and, if and when his national instructions and the circumstances permit or demand, to remind his captors of its requirements.[106]

F. MEASURES SHORT OF ATTACK: INTERCEPTION, VISIT, SEARCH, DIVERSION, AND CAPTURE

If a ship or aircraft resists measures short of attack and force is consequently used, the rules in Part D are applicable, in particular that the vessel or aircraft to be attacked must be a military objective. **12.74**

DETERMINATION OF ENEMY CHARACTER OF VESSELS AND AIRCRAFT

The fact that a merchant vessel is flying the flag of an enemy state or that a civil aircraft bears the marks of an enemy state is conclusive evidence of its enemy character.[107] The fact that a merchant vessel is flying the flag of a neutral state or a civil aircraft bears the marks of a neutral state is *prima facie* evidence of its neutral character.[108] **12.75**

If the commander of a warship suspects that a merchant vessel flying a neutral flag in fact has enemy character, the commander is entitled to exercise the right of visit and search, including the right of diversion for search under paragraph 13.111.[109] **12.76**

If the commander of a military aircraft suspects that a civil aircraft with neutral marks in fact has enemy character, the commander is entitled to exercise the right of interception and, if circumstances require, the right to divert for the purpose of visit and search.[110] **12.77**

If, after visit and search, there is reasonable ground for suspicion that the merchant vessel flying a neutral flag or a civil aircraft with neutral marks has enemy character, the vessel or aircraft may be captured as prize, subject to adjudication.[111] **12.78**

The United Kingdom has not used prize courts for many years and is unlikely to do so in the future. Where a vessel or aircraft is captured by United Kingdom armed forces it will normally be deemed to be the property of Her Majesty's government. **12.78.1**

---

[105] GC III, Art 127, requires that study of the Convention be included in programmes of military and, if possible, civil instruction. This requirement was restated in AP I, Art 83.
[106] GC III, Art 78.   [107] SRM 112.   [108] SRM 113.   [109] SRM 114.
[110] SRM 115.   [111] SRM 116.

12.79 Enemy character can be determined by registration, ownership, charter, or other criteria.[112]

<h2 align="center">Visit and Search of Merchant Vessels</h2>

12.80 See paragraph 13.91 onwards.

<h2 align="center">Interception, Visit, and Search of Civil Aircraft[113]</h2>

Basic rules

12.81 In exercising their legal rights in an international armed conflict, belligerent military aircraft have a right to intercept civil aircraft outside neutral airspace where there are reasonable grounds for suspecting they are subject to capture. Any such action is subject to paragraph 12.2. If, after interception, reasonable grounds for suspecting that a civil aircraft is subject to capture still exist, belligerent military aircraft have the right to order the civil aircraft to proceed for visit and search to a belligerent airfield that is safe for the type of aircraft involved and reasonably accessible. If there is no belligerent airfield that is safe and reasonably accessible for visit and search, a civil aircraft may be diverted from its declared destination.[114]

12.81.1 Crews of civil aircraft are entitled to prisoner of war status if they fall into the power of an enemy unless they qualify for more favourable treatment under any other provision of international law.[115]

12.82 As an alternative to visit and search:

a. an enemy civil aircraft may be diverted from its declared destination;

b. a neutral civil aircraft may be diverted from its declared destination with its consent.[116]

Civil aircraft under the operational control of an accompanying neutral military aircraft or warship

12.83 A neutral civil aircraft is exempt from the exercise of the right of visit and search if it meets the following conditions:

a. it is bound for a neutral airfield;

b. it is under the operational control of an accompanying:

(1) neutral military aircraft or warship of the same nationality; or

---

[112] SRM 117.

[113] For the procedure when exercising rights of visit and search, see the RAF *Law of Air Operations Manual*.   [114] SRM 125.

[115] Geneva Convention III 1949 (GC III), Art 4A(5).   [116] SRM 126.

(2) neutral military aircraft or warship of a state with which the flag state of the civil aircraft has concluded an agreement providing for such control;

c. the flag state of the neutral military aircraft or warship warrants that the neutral civil aircraft is not carrying contraband or otherwise engaged in activities inconsistent with its neutral status; and

d. the commander of the neutral military aircraft or warship provides, if requested by the commander of an intercepting belligerent military aircraft, all information as to the character of the civil aircraft and its cargo as could otherwise be obtained by visit and search.[117]

Measures of interception and supervision

Belligerent states should promulgate and adhere to safe procedures for intercepting civil aircraft as issued by the competent international organization.[118] **12.84**

Civil aircraft should file the required flight plan with the cognizant air traffic service, complete with information as to registration, destination, passengers, cargo, emergency communication channels, identification modes and codes, updates en route and carry certificates as to registration, airworthiness, passengers, and cargo. They should not deviate from a designated air traffic service route or flight plan without air traffic control clearance unless unforeseen conditions arise, eg, safety or distress, in which case appropriate notification should be made immediately.[119] **12.85**

Belligerents and neutrals concerned, and authorities providing air traffic services, should establish procedures whereby commanders of warships and military aircraft are continuously aware of designated routes assigned to and flight plans filed by civil aircraft in the area of military operations, including information on communication channels, identification modes and codes, destination, passengers, and cargo.[120] **12.86**

In the immediate vicinity of naval operations, civil aircraft shall comply with instructions from the combatants regarding their heading and altitude.[121] **12.87**

In order to avoid the necessity of visit and search, belligerent states may establish reasonable measures for the inspection of the cargo of neutral civil aircraft and certification that an aircraft is not carrying contraband.[122] **12.88**

The fact that a neutral civil aircraft has submitted to such measures of supervision as the inspection of its cargo and grant of certificates of **12.89**

---

[117] SRM 127.   [118] SRM 128.   [119] SRM 129.   [120] SRM 130.
[121] SRM 131.   [122] SRM 132.

non-contraband cargo by one belligerent is not an act of unneutral service with regard to an opposing belligerent.[123]

12.90 In order to obviate the necessity for visit and search, neutral states are encouraged to enforce reasonable control measures and certification procedures to ensure that their civil aircraft are not carrying contraband.[124]

CAPTURE OF ENEMY VESSELS AND GOODS

12.91 See paragraph 13.99 onwards.

CAPTURE OF ENEMY CIVIL AIRCRAFT AND GOODS

12.92 Subject to the provisions of paragraph 12.93, enemy civil aircraft and goods on board such aircraft may be captured outside neutral airspace. Prior exercise of visit and search is not required.[125]

12.93 The following aircraft are exempt from capture:

a. medical aircraft; and

b. aircraft granted safe conduct by agreement between the parties to the conflict.[126]

12.94 Aircraft listed in paragraph 12.93 are exempt from capture only if they:

a. are innocently employed in their normal role;

b. do not commit acts harmful to the enemy;

c. immediately submit to interception and identification when required;

d. do not intentionally hamper the movement of combatants and obey orders to divert from their track when required; and

e. are not in breach of a prior agreement.[127]

12.95 Capture is exercised by intercepting the enemy civil aircraft, ordering it to proceed to a belligerent airfield that is safe for the type of aircraft involved and reasonably accessible and, on landing, taking the aircraft as a prize for adjudication. As an alternative to capture, an enemy civil aircraft may be diverted from its declared destination.[128]

12.96 If capture is exercised, the safety of passengers and crew and their personal effects must be provided for. The documents and papers relating to the prize must be safeguarded.[129]

---

[123] SRM 133.　　　[124] SRM 134.　　　[125] SRM 141.　　　[126] SRM 142.
[127] SRM 143.　　　[128] SRM 144.　　　[129] SRM 145.

Capture of Neutral Merchant Vessels and Goods

See paragraph 13.106 onwards and also the comments on neutrality at **12.97** paras 1.42 to 1.43.

Capture of Neutral Civil Aircraft and Goods

Subject to paragraph 12.2, neutral civil aircraft are subject to capture **12.98** outside neutral airspace if they are engaged in any of the activities in paragraph 12.43 or if it is determined as a result of visit and search or by any other means, that they:

a. are carrying contraband;

b. are on a flight especially undertaken with a view to the transport of individual passengers who are embodied in the armed forces of the enemy;

c. are operating directly under enemy control, orders, charter, employment, or direction;

d. present irregular or fraudulent documents, lack necessary documents, or destroy, deface, or conceal documents;

e. are violating regulations established by a belligerent within the immediate area of naval operations; or

f. are engaged in a breach of blockade.[130]

Goods on board neutral civil aircraft are subject to capture only if they are **12.99** contraband.[131]

The rules regarding contraband as prescribed in paragraph 13.106 onwards **12.100** shall also apply to goods on board neutral civil aircraft.[132]

Capture is exercised by intercepting the neutral civil aircraft, ordering it to **12.101** proceed to a belligerent airfield that is safe for the type of aircraft involved and reasonably accessible and, on landing and after visit and search, taking it as prize for adjudication. If there is no belligerent airfield that is safe and reasonably accessible, a neutral civil aircraft may be diverted from its declared destination.[133]

---

[130] SRM 153. See also the comments on neutrality at paras 1.42–1.43.   [131] SRM 154.
[132] SRM 155.   [133] SRM 156.

12.102 As an alternative to capture, a neutral civil aircraft may, with its consent, be diverted from its declared destination.[134]

12.103 If capture is exercised, the safety of passengers and crew and their personal effects must be provided for. The documents and papers relating to the prize must be safeguarded.[135]

G. MEDICAL AIRCRAFT

Definitions

12.104 The term 'medical aircraft' is defined as any means, whether service or civilian, of conveying by air the wounded, sick, shipwrecked, medical personnel, religious personnel, medical equipment, or medical supplies protected by the Geneva Conventions and Additional Protocol I. Whether assigned on a permanent or temporary basis, such an aircraft must be assigned exclusively to that purpose and must be under the control of a competent authority of a party to the conflict.[136] The term 'shipwrecked' includes personnel in the sea or other waters after forced landing by or from aircraft.[137] Helicopters used for medical purposes within the above conditions come within the definition of medical aircraft. Hovercraft do not.[138]

12.104.1 The first specific provisions for medical aircraft, some of which survive today, were made in the Geneva Convention for the Amelioration of the Condition of the Wounded and Sick in Armed Forces in the Field 1929. Although sanitary aircraft and flying ambulances, as they were then called, were used to a limited extent in the First World War, these aircraft were ordinary combat aircraft not exclusively committed to the evacuation of the wounded. In the Second World War, aircraft were used extensively for the evacuation of the wounded and sick and the transport of medical personnel and material. They did not, however, usually conform to the provisions for the marking of medical aircraft in the Geneva Convention 1929. The Convention required that such aircraft should be painted white and carry a red cross or other distinctive emblem alongside their national colours. During the Second World War, the British practice was, except to a small extent in the Mediterranean and the Middle East, to evacuate the wounded in aircraft used also for other purposes. Military transport aircraft were used on the outward journey for the conveyance of military supplies and personnel and on the return journey for the evacuation of the wounded and sick. The practice of the USA was similar. The aircraft used were not marked with the emblem of the red cross and could not

---

[134] SRM 157.   [135] SRM 158.   [136] AP I, Art 8(f), (g), (i).
[137] GC II, Art 12; AP I, Art 8(b).   [138] See para 12.4.1.

have claimed the protection of the Convention. However, the risk was considered acceptable in view of the Allies' air supremacy.

The increased potential of aircraft for collecting intelligence and the difficulties of identifying medical aircraft at a distance and ensuring that they are being properly used for exclusively medical purposes has resulted in detailed provisions for facilitating recognition and checking the validity of the claim to protected status in Additional Protocol I. **12.104.2**

IDENTIFICATION

Medical aircraft shall be respected and protected as specified in this section of the Manual.[139] To obtain this respect and protection, they must be recognized as medical aircraft and the following measures are prescribed for this purpose. **12.105**

Distinctive emblem

Medical aircraft must be clearly marked with the distinctive emblem of the red cross or red crescent[140] on their lower, upper, and lateral surfaces.[141] The marking indicating nationality must also appear on each surface together with any other markings or means of identification which may be agreed between the belligerents at the outbreak of, or during the course of, hostilities.[142] The improper use of the red cross and other protective markings on any aircraft is forbidden.[143] Temporary medical aircraft, which cannot, either for lack of time or because of their characteristics, be marked with the distinctive emblem, should use the most effective means of identification available.[144] Means of identification are intended only to facilitate identification and do not, of themselves, confer protected status. **12.106**

In identifying medical aircraft of other states, distinctive emblems other than the red cross[145] must be remembered. **12.106.1**

Light signal[146]

An optional means of visual identification of medical aircraft consists of a flashing blue light. No other aircraft is allowed to use this signal but, in the absence of a special agreement between the parties to the conflict reserving the use of flashing blue lights for the identification of medical vehicles, ships, and craft, the use of such signals for other vehicles or ships is not prohibited. **12.107**

---

[139] AP I, Art 24.   [140] See para 7.23 and Appendix E.
[141] In the case of HM aircraft the emblem used is the red cross on a white ground.
[142] GC I, Art 36; GC II, Art 39.   [143] AP I, Art 38.   [144] See SRM 175.
[145] Which are dealt with in para 7.23.   [146] AP I, Annex I, Art 6, see Appendix E.

12.107.1 The blue colour is obtained by using trichromatic co-ordinates:

$$\text{green boundary} \quad y = 0.065 + 0.805x$$
$$\text{white boundary} \quad y = 0.400 - x$$
$$\text{purple boundary} \quad x = 0.133 + 0.600y$$

12.107.2 The recommended flashing rate of the blue light is between 60 and 100 flashes per minute and the aircraft should be fitted with as many lights as are necessary to make the signal visible from as many directions as possible.

Radio signal

12.108 Provision is also made for a radio signal consisting of a radio-telephonic or a radio-telegraphic message, preceded by a distinctive priority signal. This distinctive priority signal, to be designated and approved by a World Administrative Radio Conference of the International Telecommunications Union, must be transmitted three times before the call sign of the aircraft.[147] The message must be transmitted at appropriate intervals in English, irrespective of which state is operating the medical aircraft.

12.108.1 The radio message, preceded by the distinctive priority signal, must convey the following information:

a. the call sign of the medical transport;
b. the position of the medical transport;
c. the number and type of medical transports;
d. the intended route;
e. the estimated time *en route* and of departure and arrival, as appropriate; and
f. any other information such as flight altitude, radio frequencies guarded, languages used (other than English), and secondary surveillance radar modes[148] and codes.

12.108.2 Although not specifically mentioned, it is essential that 'other information' should include details of the occupants and cargo in support of the status of medical aircraft. The omission of this information may create suspicion and lead to instructions to land for search.[149]

12.108.3 So long as they are used in accordance with established standards, practices and procedures, medical units and transports may also use the codes and

---

[147] See ITU, Radio Regulations, ch IX, Art 40.   [148] See para 12.109.
[149] AP I, Annex I, Art 8 (as amended 30 November 1993): see Appendix E.

signals laid down by the International Telecommunications Union, the International Civil Aviation Organization, and the International Maritime Organization.[150] When two-way radio communication cannot be established, the signals provided for in the International Code of Signals adopted by the International Maritime Organization or in the appropriate Annex to the Chicago Convention 1944 may be used.[151]

Electronic identification

Secondary surveillance radar (SSR) may also be used to identify and follow **12.109** the course of medical aircraft. The SSR system is specified in Annex 10 to the Chicago Convention 1944.[152] The SSR mode and code to be reserved for the exclusive use of medical aircraft are to be established by the states party to Additional Protocol I or by the parties to an armed conflict, either by agreement or by one of the parties unilaterally.[153]

It would be advisable for such agreements and declarations to conform **12.109.1** to the recommended procedures of the International Civil Aviation Organization.

PROTECTION OF MEDICAL AIRCRAFT

Friendly territory

In and over land areas physically controlled by friendly forces, or in and **12.110** over sea areas not physically controlled by an adverse party, the respect and protection of medical aircraft of a party to the conflict is not dependent on any agreement with an adverse party.[154]

Where, however, proposed flight plans of medical aircraft will bring them **12.110.1** within the range of an adverse party's surface-to-air weapons systems it is only sensible for the party operating the aircraft to notify the adverse party.[155] In any circumstances, specific agreement between the adversaries, and any other states involved, is, in practice, the most effective guarantee of the safety of medical aircraft.

Contact and similar zones[156]

In and over those parts of the contact zone which are physically controlled **12.111** by friendly forces, and in and over those areas the physical control of which

---

[150] AP I, Annex I, Arts 10, 11, and 12 (as amended): see Appendix E.
[151] AP I, Annex I, Art 12 (as amended): see Appendix E.
[152] See CC, Annex 10 (Aeronautical Telecommunications), paras 2.5, 3.8, Attachment B.
[153] AP I, Annex I, Arts 8, 9 (as amended): see Appendix E.   [154] API, Art 25.
[155] See para 12.112 onwards.   [156] AP I, Art 26.

is not clearly established, protection for medical aircraft can only be effective in so far as this has been agreed in advance by the parties. In the absence of an agreement medical aircraft operate at their own risk but they must nevertheless be respected when recognized.

12.111.1 The 'contact zone' is any area on land where the forward elements of opposing forces are in contact with each other, especially where they are exposed to direct fire from the ground.

Areas controlled by an adverse party

Prior agreement[157]

12.112 Medical aircraft continue to be protected whilst flying over land or sea areas physically controlled by an adverse party so long as there are prior agreements to that effect. Parties to the conflict are encouraged to notify such flights and to conclude such agreements, particularly in areas where control is not clearly established. Agreements should specify the altitudes, times, and routes for safe operation and should include means of identification and communications.

12.112.1 A medical aircraft which flies over an area physically controlled by an adverse party either without prior agreement or in breach of the terms of an agreement, either through navigational error or because of an emergency affecting the safety of the flight, must make every effort to identify itself and to inform the adverse party of the circumstances. As soon as a medical aircraft has been recognized by an adverse party, that party is to make all reasonable efforts to give the order to land or to alight on water for inspection, or to take other measures to safeguard its own interests. In any case, the aircraft concerned must be allowed time for compliance before it is attacked. It is likely that any such agreement would be for a specific flight or series of flights rather than a general agreement lasting for a period of time. The necessity for having an agreement and adhering rigidly to its terms cannot be overstressed. A medical aircraft, no matter how well-marked and in how many ways it indicates its status, which enters enemy airspace without agreement or in breach of the terms of an agreement is at risk of attack even if it has been recognized as claiming medical status. Before attacking, an adverse party must make all reasonable efforts to give the order to land or alight on water for inspection. This obligation arises only where there has been navigational error or an emergency affecting the safety of the flight and the circumstances have been communicated to the adverse party.

[157] AP I, Art 27.

Absence of prior agreement

Whether a belligerent orders a medical aircraft to land for inspection **12.113** or takes other measures to safeguard its interests, for example, ordering a change of route, an increase in altitude, or requesting more information about the nature of the medical aircraft's difficulties, it must allow that aircraft time for compliance before attacking. The degree of deviation from an agreement or from instructions that an enemy may claim as justification for an attack might be very slight.[158] The captain of a medical aircraft must take great care to ensure that his aircraft does not enter enemy airspace without prior agreement and that, when it does enter by agreement, that the terms of the agreement are closely adhered to. The captain of a medical aircraft who finds that his aircraft has strayed into enemy airspace must make every effort to identify his aircraft to the enemy and to indicate his submission to that adverse party's air traffic instructions. If, owing to an emergency, it is necessary to enter enemy airspace without prior agreement or contrary to the terms of an agreement, contact should, if possible, be made with the enemy in order to obtain agreement to the proposed course of action.

Medical aircraft in neutral airspace[159]

Belligerent medical aircraft shall not enter neutral airspace except by prior **12.114** agreement. When within neutral airspace pursuant to agreement, medical aircraft shall comply with the terms of the agreement. The terms of the agreement may require the aircraft to land for inspection at a designated airport within the neutral state. Should the agreement so require, the inspection and follow-on action shall be conducted in accordance with paragraphs 12.115 to 12.116.

Should a medical aircraft, in the absence of an agreement or in deviation **12.115** from the terms of an agreement, enter neutral airspace, either through navigational error or because of an emergency affecting the safety of the flight, it shall make every effort to give notice and to identify itself. Once the aircraft is recognized as a medical aircraft by the neutral state, it shall not be attacked but may be required to land for inspection. Once it has been inspected, and if it is determined in fact to be a medical aircraft, it shall be allowed to resume its flight.

If the inspection reveals that the aircraft is not a medical aircraft, it may **12.116** be captured, and the occupants shall, unless agreed otherwise between

---

[158] What this means is that a relatively slight deviation from the disclosed route might be used, rightly or wrongly, as the justification for an attack, thus emphasizing how important it is that medical aircraft keep to the intended route.   [159] AP I, Art 31.

the neutral state and the parties to the conflict, be detained in the neutral state where so required by the rules of international law applicable in armed conflict, in such a manner that they cannot again take part in the hostilities.

Summary of rules

12.117 The rules that must be observed by the captain of a medical aircraft in relation to overflight of the territory of an adverse party may be summarized as follows:

a. no overflying without agreement;

b. where there is an agreement, its terms must be adhered to strictly;

c. there must be no deviation from the terms of an agreement for any reason other than an emergency affecting the safety of the flight;

d. if there is accidental overflight, in the absence of an agreement, every effort must be made to contact the adverse party, to identify the aircraft, its status, and the circumstances of its flight, and to submit to the adverse party's air traffic instructions;

e. if an emergency affecting the safety of a flight necessitates overflying without agreement or in breach of an agreement, every attempt must be made to inform the adverse party and to seek its agreement. If time does not permit this course of action, a medical aircraft may proceed but must identify itself and its status to the adverse party and must immediately notify the adverse party of the circumstances and proposed course of action; and

f. the adverse party's instructions, including instructions to land, must be obeyed.

Interception of enemy medical aircraft

12.118 If there is no agreement concerning the operation of an apparent enemy medical aircraft and it fails to respond to instructions then, if it constitutes an immediate military threat and other methods of control are impracticable, it may be attacked. Similarly, an apparent medical aircraft may be attacked if it is beyond reasonable doubt that its claim to protection is unjustified or indeed if it initiates an attack.

12.118.1 Any attack on an enemy aircraft recognized as claiming medical status should be instituted only as a last resort. If a purported medical aircraft is not known to be engaged in any activity inconsistent with medical status and obeys the instructions of its interceptor, it must not be attacked even if there has been no prior agreement as to its activity.

Restrictions on Use of Medical Aircraft

Military advantage[160]

Parties to an armed conflict must not use medical aircraft in an attempt to **12.119** acquire a military advantage. Their presence must not be used in an attempt to render military objectives immune from attack.

For example, areas where medical aircraft are loaded or unloaded, includ- **12.119.1** ing helicopter pads, should be as far away as practicable from areas of normal military operations. Medical aircraft should not be parked adjacent to buildings or other installations which themselves are not entitled to protection.

Intelligence[161]

Medical aircraft must not be used to collect or transmit intelligence data **12.120** or carry any equipment intended for such purposes. The persons and cargo that may be carried by medical aircraft are restricted to the wounded, sick, shipwrecked, medical and religious personnel, and medical supplies. Personal effects and equipment intended solely to facilitate navigation, communication, or identification are permissible.

The *presence* of communications and encryption equipment in an aircraft **12.120.1** operating as a medical aircraft is not precluded. Nor is the *use* of such equipment wholly to facilitate navigation, identification, and communication in support of the operation of medical aircraft. Neither such presence nor such use negates the protection to which the medical aircraft is entitled.[162]

Arms[163]

Medical aircraft must not carry any armament. However, small arms and **12.121** ammunition collected from the wounded, sick, and shipwrecked on board and not yet handed over to the proper service authority, together with such light individual weapons as may be necessary to enable medical personnel on the aircraft to defend themselves and the wounded, sick, and shipwrecked in their charge, are permissible.[164]

---

[160] AP I, Art 28(1).   [161] AP I, Art 28(2).

[162] On ratification of AP I, the UK made the following statement: 'given the practical need to make use of non-dedicated aircraft for medical evacuation purposes, the UK does not interpret this paragraph as precluding the presence on board of communications equipment and encryption materials or the use thereof solely to facilitate navigation, identification or communication in support of medical transportation'. For the definition of medical transport, see para 7.12 and AP I, Art 8(f).   [163] AP I, Art 28(3).

[164] See also para 7.15.

Search and rescue

12.122 Whilst flying over contact or similar zones[165] or over areas controlled by an adverse party, medical aircraft must not, without prior agreement with the adverse party, be used to search for the wounded, sick, and shipwrecked.[166]

12.122.1 This restriction does not relate to the use of medical aircraft for such search purposes in areas controlled by friendly forces or not physically controlled by an adverse party. In these circumstances, the medical aircraft is, when recognized, entitled to protection.

12.122.2 An agreement to operate medical aircraft in a search and rescue role will be more readily achieved following a specific engagement when search and rescue is considered necessary. A speculative search and rescue operation when there are no known casualties is more likely to be construed as a reconnaissance exercise and an agreement is thus less likely to be achieved.

NOTIFICATION AND AGREEMENTS[167]

Giving notification

12.123 Notification may be given to an adverse party when medical aircraft propose to fly in and over land areas physically controlled by friendly forces, or in and over sea areas not physically controlled by an adverse party. Where it is sought to establish complete protection, agreements may be entered into when medical aircraft propose to:

a. fly in and over parts of the contact zone which are physically controlled by friendly forces and in and over those areas the physical control of which is not clearly established;[168]

b. fly over land and sea areas physically controlled by an adverse party;[169]

c. fly in search of the wounded, sick, and shipwrecked in the areas referred to in sub-paragraphs (a) and (b) above; and

d. fly over or land in the territory of a neutral or other state not participating in the armed conflict.[170]

12.123.1 Notifications and requests for prior agreements must state:

a. the proposed number of medical aircraft;
b. flight plans; and
c. means of identification.

---

[165] See para 12.111.   [166] AP I, Art 28(4).   [167] AP I, Art 29.
[168] See para 12.111.   [169] See para 12.112.   [170] See para 12.114 onwards.

It is an implicit term of every such notification or request that every flight **12.123.2** will abide by the rules of use for medical aircraft set out in paragraphs 12.119 to 12.122.

Receipt of notification

A belligerent party receiving a notification must acknowledge receipt **12.124** immediately. A belligerent receiving a request for prior agreement to the operation of medical aircraft in the areas referred to in paragraph 12.123 must immediately notify the party making the request:

a. that it is agreed to; or

b. that the request is denied; or

c. putting forward reasonable alternative proposals to the request. It may also propose a prohibition or restriction of other flights by the requesting party in the area concerned during the period of time involved. If the requesting party accepts the alternative proposals it must notify the second party of that acceptance.

The detailed provisions of an agreement may properly take into account the **12.124.1** nature and flight characteristics of the particular aircraft, for example, helicopters operating at low level in a local area or a fixed-wing aircraft in transit at higher altitude. Parties must take all necessary measures to ensure that notifications and agreements can be made rapidly. This necessitates the establishment of channels of communication and recognized procedures so that delays in the operation of medical flights are minimized.

LANDING AND INSPECTION OF MEDICAL AIRCRAFT

Landing and inspection

A medical aircraft flying over areas which are either physically controlled **12.125** by an adverse party or over which physical control has not been clearly established may be ordered to land for inspection. Medical aircraft must obey such an order.[171]

Whether a medical aircraft has landed in response to such an order or **12.125.1** whether it has landed for other reasons, an inspection must be commenced without delay and must be conducted expeditiously. The party carrying out the inspection may not order the removal of the wounded and sick from the aircraft unless their removal is essential for the inspection. It must, in any event, ensure that the condition of the wounded and sick is not

---

[171] AP I, Art 30.

adversely affected by the inspection or the removal. Although there is no provision prohibiting the removal of crews, medical attendants, or medical supplies from the aircraft during the inspection, the inspection should be carried out as expeditiously as possible and with the minimum of inconvenience and should be carried out in a reasonable and unprovocative manner, always bearing in mind the humanitarian mission of the aircraft involved.

Medical status confirmed

12.126 If the inspection discloses that an aircraft:

   a. is a medical aircraft as defined in paragraph 12.104;

   b. has not violated any of the restrictions set out in paragraphs 12.119 to 12.121; and

   c. has not flown without, or in breach of, a prior agreement where such an agreement is required (see paragraph 12.123);

the aircraft and those of its occupants who belong to the adverse party operating the aircraft or to a neutral state or other state which is not a party to the conflict must be allowed to continue the flight without further delay.

Medical status not confirmed

12.127 If, however, an inspection discloses that an aircraft:

   a. is not a medical aircraft as defined in paragraph 12.104;

   b. has violated any of the restrictions set out in paragraphs 12.119 to 12.121; or

   c. has flown without, or in breach of, a prior agreement where such an agreement is required (see paragraph 12.123);

the aircraft may be seized. A seized aircraft that has been assigned as a permanent medical aircraft may be used thereafter by the capturing power as, and only as, a medical aircraft. Each occupant of the aircraft is treated according to his status.

Other aircraft on humanitarian missions

12.128 Other aircraft, military or civilian, belligerent or neutral, that are employed in the search for, rescue, or transport of the wounded, sick, and shipwrecked, operate at their own risk, unless pursuant to prior agreement between the parties to the conflict.[172]

   [172] SRM 179.

13

Maritime Warfare

A. INTRODUCTION

SCOPE OF CHAPTER

13.1 This chapter states the law of armed conflict as it applies to maritime operations. It does not deal with attacks from the sea against targets on land; that is dealt with in Chapter 5. This chapter should not be considered in isolation; it is not self-contained but an integral part of the whole Manual. Nor does it consider maritime operations in situations short of armed conflict.[1]

13.2 International law regarding armed conflicts at sea is to be found mainly in rules of customary law derived from state practice. It has not been codified or developed in treaty form to anything like the same extent as the law of armed conflict on land, although there are various treaties, mostly dating from the early twentieth century, which may continue to be of some importance. In addition, several of the principles stated in treaties on land warfare constitute rules of customary law which are also applicable in naval warfare. *The San Remo Manual on International Law Applicable to Armed Conflicts at Sea* ('the *San Remo Manual*'),[2] produced in 1995 by a group of international lawyers and naval experts, attempts to provide 'a contemporary restatement of the law, together with some progressive development, which takes into account recent state practice, technological developments and the effect of related areas of the law'.[3] The *San Remo Manual* is a valuable reference work and much of the present chapter reflects its content.[4] When appropriate and possible the text of the *San Remo Manual* has been repeated in this chapter. However, where necessary the wording used in this chapter departs from the precise *San Remo* text either because that text does not reflect United Kingdom practice or because the *San Remo* text requires clarification or amplification.

13.3 In considering the rules set out in this chapter, it is necessary to bear in mind at all times one point of central importance, namely that the conduct of armed conflict at sea is subject to the limitations imposed by the UN Charter on all use of force. One particularly important aspect of those limitations is that even when resort to force is justified, it should not exceed what is

---

[1] Such as internal disturbances, see para 15.2.1.

[2] L Doswald-Beck (ed), *San Remo Manual on International Law Applicable to Armed Conflicts at Sea* (1995) (*San Remo Manual*). In the notes to this chapter, paragraphs of the *San Remo Manual* will be referred to thus: SRM 137. [3] SRM, ix.

[4] Where appropriate, rules based on the *San Remo Manual* text but not reflecting its precise wording will be referred to in notes as 'Adapted from SRM'.

necessary and proportionate to the achievement of the goal for which force may be used. In a conflict of limited scope, this may mean that a belligerent state is constrained, to a greater extent than the rules set out in the present chapter might suggest, in the action that it may lawfully take against the shipping or aircraft of states not involved in the conflict. In cases where those constraints apply, further guidance will be given by the Ministry of Defence.

It should also be borne in mind that there is a degree of controversy regard- **13.4** ing the extent to which some of the older rules, such as those relating to the presence of belligerent warships in neutral waters, retain their legal force. For example, while there is general agreement that belligerent warships must not conduct operations in the territorial and internal waters of neutral states,[5] the United Kingdom takes the view that the old rule which prohibited belligerent warships from remaining in neutral ports for more than 24 hours except in unusual circumstances, is no longer applicable in view of modern state practice.

B. GENERAL PROVISIONS

DEFINITIONS

For the purposes of this chapter certain terms are defined below: **13.5**

a. 'aircraft': see paragraph 12.4;

b. 'attack' means an act of violence, whether in offence or in defence;[6]

c. 'auxiliary aircraft': see paragraph 12.5;

d. 'auxiliary vessel' means a vessel, other than a warship, that is owned by or under the exclusive control of the armed forces of a state and used for the time being on government non-commercial service;[7]

e. 'civil aircraft': see paragraph 12.6;

f. 'civil airliner': see paragraph 12.7;

g. 'collateral casualties' or 'collateral damage' means the loss of life of, or injury to, civilians or other protected persons, and damage to or the destruction of the natural environment or objects that are not in themselves military objectives;[8]

---

[5] See para 13.8.
[6] Additional Protocol I 1977 (API), Art 49(1), see para 5.20; SRM 13(b).   [7] SRM 13(h).
[8] SRM 13(c).

h. 'contraband' means goods which are ultimately destined for territory under the control of the enemy and which may be susceptible for use in armed conflict;[9]

i. 'hospital ships, coastal rescue craft and other medical transports' means vessels that are protected under Geneva Convention II 1949 and Additional Protocol I 1977;[10]

j. 'medical aircraft': see paragraph 12.104;

k. 'merchant vessel' means a vessel that is not a warship, an auxiliary vessel, or other state vessel (such as a customs or police vessel) and that is engaged in commercial or private service;[11]

l. 'military aircraft': see paragraph 12.10;

m. 'neutral' means any state not party to the conflict. Commanders should follow instructions issued by the Ministry of Defence;

n. 'warship' means a ship belonging to the armed forces of a state bearing the external marks distinguishing the character and nationality of such a ship, under the command of an officer duly commissioned by the government of that state and whose name appears in the appropriate service list or its equivalent, and manned by a crew which is under regular armed forces discipline.[12]

AREAS OF NAVAL WARFARE

13.6   The following are areas of naval warfare:

a. Subject to other applicable rules of international law contained in this chapter or elsewhere, hostile actions by naval forces may be conducted in, on, or over the territorial sea, internal waters, land territories, continental shelf, exclusive economic zone, and, where relevant, archipelagic waters of belligerent states (both enemy and allied).[13] It should be noted that it is only internal waters and the territorial sea that together with the land territories constitute the territory of a belligerent. Other zones of maritime jurisdiction (eg continental shelf and exclusive economic zone) lying beyond the limits of the territorial sea do not form a part of the territory of the state.

b. Subject to other applicable rules of international law contained in this chapter or elsewhere, hostile actions by naval forces may also be

---

[9] SRM 148.
[10] SRM 13(e). Hospital ships must be marked and notified, see para 13.33.1.
[11] Adapted from SRM 13(i).   [12] SRM 13(g).
[13] The legal basis for conducting operations in the waters of an allied state would be the agreement of that state.

conducted in, on, or over the high seas and those waters falling beyond the territorial limits of all states.

c. Except where the contrary is expressly provided in this chapter, hostile actions by naval forces may not be conducted in, on, or over the territorial sea, internal waters, land territories, or, where relevant, archipelagic waters of any state which is not a belligerent.

The principle in paragraph 13.6(c) does not prohibit hostile actions by naval **13.6.1** forces in, on, or over the continental shelf or exclusive economic zone of any state that is not a belligerent. In carrying out operations in those areas, however, there is a duty to conduct operations with due regard for the rights and duties of the coastal state and other states which may have rights in those waters.[14]

C. REGIONS OF OPERATIONS

NEUTRAL WATERS

Neutral waters consist of the internal waters, territorial sea, and, where **13.7** applicable, the archipelagic waters of neutral states. Neutral airspace consists of the airspace over neutral waters and the land territory of neutral states.[15]

Within and over neutral waters, including neutral waters comprising an **13.8** international strait and waters in which the right of archipelagic sea lanes passage may be exercised, hostile actions by belligerent forces are forbidden. A neutral state must take such measures as are consistent with paragraphs 13.10 to 13.20, including the exercise of surveillance, as the means at its disposal allow, to prevent the violation of its neutrality by belligerent forces.[16]

Hostile actions within the meaning of paragraph 13.8 include, among **13.9** others:

a. attack on or capture of persons or objects located in, on, or over neutral waters or territory;

b. use as a base of operations, including attack on or capture of persons or objects located outside neutral waters, if the attack or seizure is conducted by belligerent forces located in, on, or over neutral waters;

c. laying of mines; or

d. visit, search, diversion, or capture.[17]

---

[14] See para 13.21.   [15] SRM 14.   [16] SRM 15.   [17] SRM 16.

13.9A Belligerent forces may not use neutral waters as a sanctuary.[17A]

13.9B Subject to Paragraphs 13.16 and 13.20, a neutral State may, on a non-discriminatory basis, condition, restrict or prohibit the entrance to or passage through its neutral waters by belligerent warship and auxiliary vessels.[17B]

13.9C Subject to the duty of impartiality, and to Paragraphs 13.9D and 13.10–13.20, and under such regulations as it may establish, a neutral State may, without jeopardising its neutrality, permit the following acts within its neutral waters:

a. passage through its territorial sea, and where applicable its archipelagic waters, by warships, auxiliary vessels and prizes of belligerent States; warships, auxiliary vessels and prizes may employ pilots of the neutral State during passage;

b. replenishment by a belligerent warship or auxiliary vessel of its food, water and fuel sufficient to reach a port in its own territory; and

c. repairs of belligerent warships or auxiliary vessels found necessary by the neutral State to make them seaworthy; such repairs may not restore or increase their fighting strength.[17C]

13.9D A belligerent warship or auxiliary vessel exercising rights of passage through neutral waters should do so continuously and expeditiously unless unable to do so on account of damage, the stress of weather or by *force majeure*.

13.9E Should a belligerent State be in violation of the regime of neutral waters, as set out in this manual, the neutral State is under an obligation to take the measures necessary to terminate the violation. If the neutral State fails to terminate the violation of its neutral waters by a belligerent, the opposing belligerent must so notify the neutral State and give that neutral State a reasonable time to terminate the violation by the belligerent. If the violation of the neutrality of the State by the belligerent constitutes a serious and immediate threat to the security of the opposing belligerent and the violation is not terminated, then that belligerent may, in the absence of any feasible and timely alternative, use such force as is strictly necessary to respond to the threat posed by the violation.[17D]

[17A] SRM 17.   [17B] SRM 19.   [17C] SRM 20.   [17D] SRM 22.

INTERNATIONAL STRAITS AND ARCHIPELAGIC SEA LANES

General rules

Belligerent warships and auxiliary vessels and military and auxiliary **13.10** aircraft may exercise the rights of passage through, under, or over international straits and of archipelagic sea lanes passage provided by general international law, even if one or more of the littoral states or the archipelagic state are neutral.[18]

The neutrality of a state bordering an international strait is not jeopardized **13.11** by the transit passage of belligerent warships, auxiliary vessels, or military or auxiliary aircraft, nor by the innocent passage of belligerent warships or auxiliary vessels through that strait.[19]

The neutrality of an archipelagic state is not jeopardized by the exercise of **13.12** archipelagic sea lanes passage by belligerent warships, auxiliary vessels, or military or auxiliary aircraft.[20]

Neutral warships, auxiliary vessels, and military and auxiliary aircraft may **13.13** exercise the rights of passage provided by general international law through, under, and over international straits and archipelagic waters, even though one or more of the littoral states or the archipelagic state is a belligerent.

There is no requirement for any ships, including warships, to give notice of **13.13.1** intention to exercise rights of passage. However, there may be circumstances where it would be prudent to inform a state that a ship is undertaking such passage purely as a precautionary measure and without accepting that there is any legal obligation attached to the provision of that information.

Transit passage and archipelagic sea lanes passage

The rights of transit passage and archipelagic sea lanes passage applicable **13.14** to international straits and archipelagic waters in peacetime continue to apply in times of armed conflict. The laws and regulations of states bordering straits and archipelagic states relating to transit passage and archipelagic sea lanes passage adopted in accordance with general international law remain applicable.[21]

Belligerent and neutral surface ships, submarines, and aircraft have **13.15** the rights of transit passage and archipelagic sea lanes passage through,

[18] SRM 23.   [19] SRM 24.   [20] SRM 25.   [21] SRM 27.

under, and over all straits and archipelagic waters to which these rights generally apply.[22]

13.16 Neutral states may not suspend, hamper, or otherwise impede the right of transit passage nor the right of archipelagic sea lanes passage.[23]

13.17 A belligerent vessel in transit passage through, under, or over an international strait, or in archipelagic sea lanes passage through, under, or over archipelagic waters, is required to proceed without delay, to refrain from the threat or use of force against the territorial integrity or political independence of a neutral littoral or archipelagic state, or in any other manner inconsistent with the purposes of the UN Charter, and otherwise to refrain from any hostile actions or other activities not incident to their normal modes of continuous and expeditious transit.

13.18 Belligerents passing through, under, and over neutral straits or waters in which the right of archipelagic sea lanes passage applies are permitted to take defensive measures consistent with their security, including launching and recovery of aircraft (including for the purpose of combat air patrol), screen formation steaming, and acoustic and electronic surveillance. Belligerents in transit or archipelagic sea lanes passage may not, however, conduct offensive operations against enemy forces, nor use such neutral waters as a place of sanctuary nor as a base of operations.[24]

13.19 Neutral vessels may likewise exercise the rights of transit passage and archipelagic sea lanes passage through belligerent international straits and archipelagic waters.[25]

13.20 The right of non-suspendable innocent passage ascribed to certain international straits by international law may not be suspended in time of armed conflict.[26]

Exclusive Economic Zone and Continental Shelf

13.21 If hostile actions are conducted within the exclusive economic zone or on the continental shelf of a neutral state, belligerent states shall, in addition to observing the other applicable rules of the law of armed conflict at sea, have due regard for the rights and duties of the coastal state, *inter alia*, for the exploration and exploitation of the economic resources of the exclusive economic zone and the continental shelf and the protection and preservation of the marine environment. They shall, in particular, have due regard for artificial islands, installations, structures, and safety zones established by

---

[22] SRM 28.   [23] SRM 29.   [24] Adapted from SRM 30.   [25] SRM 32.
[26] SRM 33.

neutral states in the exclusive economic zone and on the continental shelf,[27] as well as vessels engaged in fishing. Belligerents shall also take care to avoid damage to cables and pipelines laid on the seabed which do not exclusively serve other belligerents.

HIGH SEAS AND SEABED BEYOND NATIONAL JURISDICTION

Hostile actions on the high seas shall be conducted with due regard for the **13.22** rights of others in their use of the high seas.[28]

Belligerents shall take care to avoid damage to cables and pipelines laid on **13.23** the seabed which do not exclusively serve the belligerents.[29]

D. BASIC RULES AND TARGET DISCRIMINATION

BASIC RULES

In any armed conflict the right of the parties to the conflict to choose methods **13.24** or means of warfare is not unlimited.[30]

Parties to the conflict shall at all times distinguish between civilians or other **13.25** protected persons and combatants and between civilian or exempt objects and military objectives.[31]

In so far as objects are concerned, military objectives are limited to those **13.26** objects which by their nature, location, purpose, or use make an effective contribution to military action and whose total or partial destruction, capture, or neutralization, in the circumstances ruling at the time, offers a definite military advantage.[32]

Attacks shall be limited strictly to military objectives.[33] Merchant ves- **13.27** sels and civil aircraft are civilian objects unless they qualify as military objectives in accordance with the principles and rules set forth in this chapter.[34]

---

[27] Adapted from SRM 34.   [28] SRM 36.   [29] SRM 37.
[30] AP I, Art 35(1); SRM 38.   [31] AP I, Art 48, see para 2.5; SRM 39.
[32] SRM 40. The same definition is used for warfare affecting targets on land: AP I, Art 52(2), see para 5.4. See also AP I, Arts 49(3) and 52(2).
[33] For attacks affecting targets on land, see para 5.4.   [34] SRM 41.

13.28 In addition to any specific prohibitions binding upon the parties to a conflict, it is forbidden to employ methods or means of warfare which:

    a. are of a nature to cause superfluous injury or unnecessary suffering;[35] or

    b. are indiscriminate, in that:

        (1) they are not, or cannot be, directed against a specific military objective; or

        (2) their effects cannot be limited as required by international law as reflected in this chapter.[36]

13.29 It is prohibited to order that there shall be no survivors, to threaten an adversary therewith, or to conduct hostilities on this basis.[37]

13.30 Methods and means of warfare should be employed with due regard for the natural environment taking into account the relevant rules of international law. Damage to or destruction of the natural environment not justified by military necessity is prohibited.[38]

13.31 Submarines and aircraft are bound by the same principles and rules.[39]

Precautions in Attack[40]

13.32 With respect to attacks, the following precautions shall be taken:

    a. those who plan, decide upon, or execute an attack must take all feasible measures to gather information which will assist in determining whether or not objects which are not military objectives are present in an area of attack;

    b. in the light of the information available to them, those who plan, decide upon, or execute an attack shall do everything feasible to ensure that attacks are limited to military objectives;

    c. they shall furthermore take all feasible precautions in the choice of methods and means in order to avoid or minimize collateral casualties or damage; and

    d. an attack shall not be launched if it may be expected to cause collateral casualties or damage which would be excessive in relation to the concrete and direct military advantage anticipated from the attack as a whole; an attack shall be cancelled or suspended as soon as it

---

    [35] AP I, Art 35(2); see para 6.1.

    [36] SRM 42. This language derives from AP I, Art 51(4) although that article only applies to attacks affecting targets on land, see AP I, Art 49(3).

    [37] AP I, Art 40, see also para 5.5; SRM 43.   [38] SRM 44. See also AP I, Arts 35 and 55.

    [39] SRM 45.   [40] SRM 46.

becomes apparent that the collateral casualties or damage would be excessive.[41]

Paragraphs 13.43 to 13.48 provide additional precautions regarding civil **13.32.1** aircraft.

ENEMY VESSELS AND AIRCRAFT EXEMPT FROM ATTACK

Classes of vessels exempt from attack

The following classes of enemy vessels are exempt from attack:[42]   **13.33**

a. hospital ships;[43]

b. small craft used for coastal rescue operations and other medical transports;

c. vessels granted safe conduct by agreement between the belligerent parties including:

   (1) cartel vessels, eg, vessels designated for and engaged in the transport of prisoners of war;

   (2) vessels engaged in humanitarian missions, including vessels carrying supplies indispensable to the survival of the civilian population, and vessels engaged in relief actions and rescue operations;

d. vessels entitled to be identified by the emblem of the red cross or red crescent;

e. vessels engaged in transporting cultural property under special protection;[44]

f. passenger vessels when engaged only in carrying civilian passengers;

g. vessels charged with religious, non-military scientific or philanthropic missions[45] (vessels collecting scientific data of likely military applications are not protected);

[41] The language of paragraph 13.32 is similar to that of AP I, Art 57, which applies to attacks affecting targets on land, by virtue of AP I, Art 49(3), as to which, see para 5.33.

[42] This composite list of vessels represents a combination of those vessels listed in SRM 47 and 110. The SRM contains two slightly different lists in the two paragraphs but there appears to be no satisfactory reason why they should be different and every reason why the list of exempt vessels in SRM 47 should also be reflected in the list of vessels that cannot be simulated as a legitimate ruse of war.

[43] Provided they have been notified in accordance with paragraph 13.33.1. Reprisals against such ships are prohibited, GC II, Art 47.

[44] Special protection is provided by the Cultural Property Convention 1954 and accompanying regulations.

[45] Such vessels are presumed to be genuinely charged with such missions unless, when challenged, they fail to demonstrate their exempt status.

    h. small coastal fishing vessels and small boats engaged in local coastal trade, but they are subject to the regulations of a belligerent naval commander operating in the area and to inspection;

    i. vessels designed or adapted exclusively for responding to pollution incidents in the marine environment;

    j. vessels which have surrendered;

    k. life rafts and life boats;

    l. vessels protected by the UN flag.

13.33.1 Hospital ships must be distinctively marked (exterior surfaces shall be white, the red cross or red crescent emblem must be painted on each side and on the horizontal surfaces so placed as to afford the greatest possible visibility from the sea and from the air; a white flag with the red cross or red crescent must be flown as high as possible and the national flag should also be flown),[46] and parties to a conflict have an obligation to notify the other parties that particular vessels are hospital ships.[47] That notification shall include details of registered gross tonnage,[48] length from stem to stern, and numbers of masts and funnels, and must be made at least ten days before the ships are employed. The parties are, of course, free to notify further details.[49]

Conditions of exemption

13.34 Vessels listed in paragraph 13.33 are exempt from attack only if they:

    a. are innocently employed in their normal role;

    b. submit to identification and inspection when required; and

    c. do not intentionally hamper the movement of combatants and obey orders to stop or move out of the way when required.[50]

Hospital ships

13.35 The exemption from attack of a hospital ship may cease only by reason of a breach of a condition of exemption in paragraph 13.34 and, in such a case,

---

  [46] GC II, Art 43. Consideration should also be given to the use of flashing blue lights, radio signals, radar transponders, and acoustic underwater identification methods, see AP I, Annex I (as amended on 30 November 1993), Arts 6–9 in Appendix E.   [47] GC II, Art 22.

  [48] GC II, Art 26 encourages the use of ships of over 2,000 tons gross for transportation over longer distances and on the high seas.

  [49] Additional information can usefully include call signs and radio frequencies used; whether the hospital ship is equipped with means of self-defence, as well as positional and routing information.   [50] SRM 48.

only after due warning has been given naming in all appropriate cases a reasonable time-limit to discharge itself of the cause endangering its exemption, and after such warning has remained unheeded.[51]

If after due warning a hospital ship persists in breaking a condition of its exemption, it renders itself liable to capture or other necessary measures to enforce compliance.[52] **13.36**

A hospital ship may only be attacked as a last resort if: **13.37**

a. diversion or capture is not feasible;

b. no other method is available for exercising military control;

c. the circumstances of non-compliance are sufficiently grave that the hospital ship has become, or may be reasonably assumed to be, a military objective; and

d. the collateral casualties or damage will not be disproportionate to the military advantage gained or expected.[53]

All other categories of vessels exempt from attack

If any other class of vessel exempt from attack breaches any of the conditions of its exemption in paragraph 13.34, it may be attacked only if: **13.38**

a. diversion or capture is not feasible;

b. no other method is available for exercising military control;

c. the circumstances of non-compliance are sufficiently grave that the vessel has become, or may be reasonably assumed to be, a military objective; and

d. the collateral casualties or damage will not be disproportionate to the military advantage gained or expected.[54]

Classes of aircraft exempt from attack

See paragraph 12.28 onwards. **13.39**

OTHER ENEMY VESSELS AND AIRCRAFT

Enemy merchant vessels

Enemy merchant vessels which do not fall into the category of exempt vessels are liable to attack in a wider range of circumstances. Nevertheless, **13.40**

---

[51] SRM 49.   [52] SRM 50.   [53] SRM 51.   [54] SRM 52.

they may only be attacked if they fall within the definition of a military objective.[55]

13.41 The following activities may, depending on the circumstances, render enemy merchant vessels military objectives:

a. engaging in belligerent acts on behalf of the enemy, eg, laying mines, minesweeping, cutting undersea cables and pipelines, engaging in visit and search of neutral merchant vessels, or attacking other merchant vessels;

b. acting as an auxiliary to an enemy's armed forces, eg, carrying troops or replenishing warships;

c. being incorporated into or assisting the enemy's intelligence gathering system, eg, engaging in reconnaissance, early warning, surveillance, or command, control, and communications missions;

d. sailing under convoy of enemy warships or military aircraft;

e. refusing an order to stop or actively resisting visit, search, or capture;

f. being armed to an extent that they could inflict damage to a warship; this excludes light individual weapons for the defence of personnel, eg, against pirates, and purely deflective systems such as 'chaff'; or

g. otherwise making an effective contribution to military action, eg, carrying military materials.[56]

13.42 Any attack on these vessels is subject to the basic rules set out in paragraphs 13.24 to 13.31.[57]

Enemy civil aircraft

13.43 See paragraph 12.36 onwards.

Enemy warships and military aircraft

13.44 Unless they are exempt from attack under paragraphs 13.33 or 13.39, enemy warships and military aircraft and enemy auxiliary vessels and aircraft are military objectives within the meaning of paragraph 13.31.[58]

13.45 They may be attacked, subject to the basic rules in paragraphs 13.24 to 13.31.[59]

---

[55] In so far as objects are concerned, military objectives are limited to those objects which by their nature, location, purpose, or use make an effective contribution to military action and whose total or partial destruction, capture, or neutralization, in the circumstances ruling at the time, offers a definite military advantage: see para 13.26.

[56] Adapted from SRM 60.   [57] SRM 61.   [58] SRM 65.   [59] SRM 66.

For further information about attacks on military aircraft, see paragraph 12.39 **13.45.1** onwards.

Neutral Merchant Vessels and
Civil Aircraft

Neutral merchant vessels

Particular care must be taken before initiating hostile action against neutral **13.46** vessels. Any attack on these vessels is subject to paragraph 13.3 and the basic rules in paragraphs 13.24 to 13.31.[60]

Merchant vessels flying the flag of neutral states may only be attacked if **13.47** they fall within the definition of military objectives.[61] They may, depending on the circumstances, become military objectives if they:

a. are believed on reasonable grounds to be carrying contraband or breaching a blockade, and after prior warning they intentionally and clearly refuse to stop, or intentionally and clearly resist visit, search, or capture;

b. engage in belligerent acts on behalf of the enemy;

c. act as auxiliaries to the enemy's armed forces;

d. are incorporated into or assist the enemy's intelligence system;

e. sail under convoy of enemy warships or military aircraft; or

f. otherwise make an effective contribution to the enemy's military action, eg, by carrying military materials, and it is not feasible for the attacking forces first to place passengers and crew in a place of safety. Unless circumstances do not permit, they are to be given a warning, so that they can re-route, offload, or take other precautions.[62]

The mere fact that a neutral merchant vessel is armed provides no grounds **13.48** for attacking it.[63]

Neutral civil aircraft

See paragraph 12.43 onwards. **13.49**

---

[60] Adapted from SRM 68.

[61] In so far as objects are concerned, military objectives are limited to those objects which by their nature, location, purpose, or use make an effective contribution to military action and whose total or partial destruction, capture, or neutralization, in the circumstances ruling at the time, offers a definite military advantage: see para 13.26.   [62] Adapted from SRM 67.

[63] SRM 69.

E. METHODS AND MEANS OF WARFARE

Means of Warfare

Missiles and other projectiles

13.50 Missiles and projectiles, including those with over-the-horizon capabilities, shall be used in conformity with the principles of target discrimination as set out in paragraphs 13.24 to 13.31.[64]

Torpedoes

13.51 It is prohibited to use torpedoes that do not sink or otherwise become harmless when they have completed their run.[65]

Mines

13.52 Mines may only be used for legitimate military purposes including the denial of sea areas to the enemy.[66]

13.53 Without prejudice to the rules set out in paragraph 13.54, the parties to the conflict shall not lay mines unless they become harmless when they have become detached or control over them is otherwise lost.[67]

13.54 It is forbidden to use free-floating mines unless:

a. they are directed against a military objective; and
b. they become harmless within an hour after loss of control over them.[68]

13.55 The laying of armed mines or the arming of pre-laid mines must be notified unless the mines can detonate only against vessels which are military objectives.[69]

13.56 Belligerents shall record the locations where they have laid mines.[70]

13.57 Mining operations in the internal waters, territorial sea, or archipelagic waters of a belligerent state should provide, when the mining is first executed, for free exit of shipping of neutral states.[71]

13.58 Mining of neutral waters by a belligerent is prohibited.[72]

---

[64] SRM 78.
[65] Hague Convention VIII of 1907 Relative to the Laying of Automatic Submarine Contact Mines (HC VIII), Art 1(3); SRM 79.   [66] SRM 80.
[67] HC VIII, Art 1(1), (2); SRM 81.   [68] HC VIII, Art 1(2); SRM 82.
[69] Adapted from SRM 83.   [70] SRM 84.   [71] SRM 85.   [72] SRM 86.

Mining shall not have the practical effect of preventing passage between **13.59** neutral waters and international waters.[73]

The minelaying states shall pay due regard to the legitimate uses of the seas **13.60** beyond territorial limts by, *inter alia*, providing safe alternative routes for shipping of neutral states.[74]

Transit passage shall not be impeded. Passage through waters subject to the **13.61** right of archipelagic sea lanes passage shall not be impeded unless safe and convenient alternative routes are provided.[75]

After the cessation of active hostilities, parties to the conflict shall do their **13.62** utmost to remove or render harmless the mines they have laid, each party removing its own mines. With regard to mines laid in the territorial seas of the enemy, each party shall notify their position and shall proceed with the least possible delay to remove the mines in its own territorial sea or otherwise render the territorial sea safe for navigation.[76]

In addition to their obligations under paragraph 13.62, parties to the **13.63** conflict shall endeavour to reach agreement, both among themselves and, where appropriate, with other states and with international organizations, on the provision of information and technical and material assistance, including in appropriate circumstances joint operations, necessary to remove minefields or otherwise render them harmless.[77]

Neutral states do not commit an act inconsistent with the laws of neutrality **13.64** by clearing mines laid in violation of international law.[78]

Methods of Warfare

Blockade

A blockade shall be declared and notified to all belligerents and neutral **13.65** states.[79]

The declaration shall specify the commencement, duration, location, and **13.66** extent of the blockade and the period within which vessels of neutral states may leave the blockaded coastline.[80]

A blockade must be effective. The question whether a blockade is effective **13.67** is a question of fact, and is of significance because of the need to distinguish between legitimate blockading activity and other activities (including visit and search) that might be carried on illegitimately on the high seas under the guise of blockade.[81]

---

[73] SRM 87.   [74] SRM 88. See comment at para 13.58.   [75] SRM 89.
[76] HC VIII, Art 5; SRM 90.   [77] SRM 91.   [78] SRM 92.   [79] SRM 93.
[80] SRM 94.   [81] Adapted from SRM 95.

13.68 The force maintaining the blockade may be stationed at a distance determined by military requirements.[82]

13.69 A blockade may be enforced and maintained by a combination of legitimate methods and means of warfare provided this combination does not result in acts inconsistent with the rules set out in this chapter.[83]

13.70 Merchant vessels believed on reasonable grounds to be breaching a blockade may be captured. Merchant vessels which, after prior warning, clearly resist capture may be attacked if they are military objectives.[84]

13.71 A blockade must not bar access to the ports and coasts of neutral states.[85]

13.72 A blockade must be applied impartially to the vessels of all states.[86]

13.73 The cessation, temporary lifting, re-establishment, extension, or other alteration of a blockade must be declared and notified as in paragraphs 13.65 and 13.66.[87]

13.74 The declaration or establishment of a blockade is prohibited if:

   a. it is intended to starve the civilian population or deny it objects essential for its survival; or

   b. the damage to the civilian population is, or may be expected to be, excessive in relation to the concrete and direct military advantage anticipated from the blockade.[88]

13.75 If the civilian population of the blockaded territory is inadequately provided with food and other objects essential for its survival, the blockading party must provide for free passage of such foodstuffs and other essential supplies, subject to:

   a. the right to prescribe the technical arrangements, including search, under which such passage is permitted; and

   b. the condition that the distribution of such supplies shall be made under the local supervision of a protecting power or a humanitarian organization which offers guarantees of impartiality, such as the International Committee of the Red Cross.[89]

13.76 The blockading belligerent shall allow the passage of medical supplies for the civilian population or for the wounded and sick members of the armed forces, subject to the right to prescribe technical arrangements, including search, under which such passage is permitted.[90]

---

[82] SRM 96.   [83] SRM 97.   [84] See paras 13.46–13.48.   [85] SRM 99.
[86] SRM 100.   [87] SRM 101.   [88] AP I, Art 54; SRM 102.   [89] SRM 103.
[90] SRM 104.

Security zones

Security zones may be established by belligerents as a defensive measure or **13.77** to impose some limitation on the geographical extent of the area of conflict. However, a belligerent cannot be absolved of its duties under the law of armed conflict by establishing zones in such a manner that they adversely affect the legitimate uses of defined areas of the sea.[91]

Maritime exclusion zones and total exclusion zones are legitimate means of **13.77.1** exercising the right of self-defence and other rights enjoyed under international law. However, in declaring the zones, the exact extent, location, duration, and risks associated should be made clear in accordance with paragraph 13.78.

Should a belligerent, as an exceptional measure, establish such a zone: **13.78**

a. the same body of law applies both inside and outside the zone;
b. the extent, location, and duration of the zone and the measures imposed shall not exceed what is strictly required by military necessity and the principle of proportionality;
c. due regard shall be given to the rights of neutral states to legitimate uses of the seas; necessary safe passage through the zone for neutral vessels and aircraft shall be provided:
   (1) where the geographical extent of the zone significantly impedes free and safe access to the ports and coasts of a neutral state;
   (2) in other cases where normal navigation routes are affected, except where military requirements do not permit; and
d. the commencement, duration, location, and extent of the zone, as well as the restrictions imposed, shall be publicly declared and appropriately notified.[92]

Compliance with the measures taken by one belligerent in the zone shall **13.79** not be construed as an act harmful to the opposing belligerent.[93]

Nothing in paragraphs 13.65 to 13.79 should be deemed to derogate from **13.80** the customary belligerent right to control neutral vessels and aircraft in the immediate vicinity of naval operations.[94]

DECEPTION, RUSES OF WAR, AND PERFIDY

Military and auxiliary aircraft are prohibited at all times from feigning **13.81** exempt, civilian, or neutral status.[95]

[91] Adapted from SRM 105.   [92] SRM 106.   [93] SRM 107.   [94] SRM 108.
[95] SRM 109.

13.82   Ruses of war[96] are permitted. Warships and auxiliary vessels, however, are prohibited from launching an attack whilst flying a false flag, and at all times from actively simulating the status of those vessels exempt from attack listed in paragraph 13.33.[97]

13.82.1   Paragraph 13.82 is without prejudice to the obligations to notify and identify hospital ships, see paragraph 13.33.1.

13.83   'It is prohibited to kill, injure or capture an adversary by resort to perfidy.'[98] Acts inviting the confidence of an adversary to lead it to believe that it is entitled to, or is obliged to accord, protection under the rules of international law applicable in armed conflict, with intent to betray that confidence, constitute perfidy. Perfidious acts include the launching of an attack while feigning:

a. exempt, civilian, neutral, or protected United Nations status;

b. surrender or distress by, eg, sending a distress signal or by the crew taking to life rafts.

F. MEASURES SHORT OF ATTACK: INTERCEPTION, VISIT, SEARCH, DIVERSION, AND CAPTURE

13.84   If a ship or aircraft resists measures short of attack and force is consequently used, the rules in Part D are applicable, in particular that the vessel or aircraft to be attacked must be a military objective.

DETERMINATION OF ENEMY CHARACTER OF VESSELS AND AIRCRAFT

13.85   The fact that a merchant vessel is flying the flag of an enemy state or that a civil aircraft bears the marks of an enemy state is conclusive evidence of its enemy character.[99]

13.86   The fact that a merchant vessel is flying the flag of a neutral state or a civil aircraft bears the marks of a neutral state is *prima facie* evidence of its neutral character.[100]

13.87   If the commander of a warship suspects that a merchant vessel flying a neutral flag in fact has enemy character, the commander is entitled to exercise

---

[96] For a definition of ruses of war, see para 5.17. Deception at sea has been a feature of naval history. Warships were entitled to disguise themselves if they so wished by, for instance, flying other colours. Aircraft, on the other hand, have never been entitled to bear false markings. The UK position is that ruses of war—disguising ships to appear to be different (for example by using different or no lights)—are permissible subject to the rules in this paragraph.

[97] See also n 42.

[98] AP I, Art 37(1), see para 5.9. SRM 111 states that perfidy is prohibited, but this goes beyond AP I.   [99] SRM 112.

[100] SRM 113.

the right of visit and search, including the right of diversion for search under paragraph 13.94.[101]

If the commander of a military aircraft suspects that a civil aircraft with neutral marks in fact has enemy character, the commander is entitled to exercise the right of interception and, if circumstances require, the right to divert for the purpose of visit and search.[102] **13.88**

If, after visit and search, there is reasonable ground for suspicion that the merchant vessel flying a neutral flag or a civil aircraft with neutral marks has enemy character, the vessel or aircraft may be captured as prize.[103] **13.89**

Enemy character can be determined by registration, ownership, charter, or other criteria.[104] **13.90**

Visit and Search of Merchant Vessels

Basic rules

In exercising their legal rights in an international armed conflict at sea, belligerent warships and military aircraft have a right to visit and search merchant vessels outside neutral waters where there are reasonable grounds for suspecting that they are subject to capture.[105] Any such action is subject to paragraph 13.3. **13.91**

As an alternative to visit and search, a neutral merchant vessel may, with its consent, be diverted from its declared destination, thereby obviating the need for visit and search. This does not imply that the vessel's consent is required for the exercise of visit and search if that is deemed necessary.[106] **13.92**

Merchant vessels under convoy of accompanying neutral warships

A neutral merchant vessel is exempt from the exercise of the right of visit and search if it meets the following conditions: **13.93**

a. it is bound for a neutral port;

b. it is under the convoy of an accompanying neutral warship of the same nationality or a neutral warship of a state with which the flag state

---

[101] SRM 114.   [102] SRM 115.

[103] SRM 116 adds that capture as prize is 'subject to adjudication'. However, the United Kingdom has not used prize courts for many years and is unlikely to do so in the future. Where a vessel or aircraft is captured by United Kingdom armed forces it may be deemed to be the property of Her Majesty's government.

[104] SRM 117. According to the SRM, p 194, an example of other criteria might be the transfer to a neutral flag for the purpose of evading belligerent capture, and that a transfer would only be genuine if it resulted in complete divestiture of enemy ownership and control. See also para 13.47 concerning activities that may render neutral vessels military objectives.

[105] SRM 118.   [106] SRM 119. See also para 13.94.

of the merchant vessel has concluded an agreement providing for such convoy;

c. the flag state of the neutral warship warrants that the neutral merchant vessel is not carrying contraband or otherwise engaged in activities inconsistent with its neutral status; and

d. the commander of the neutral warship provides, if requested by the commander of an intercepting belligerent warship or military aircraft, all information as to the character of the merchant vessel and its cargo as could otherwise be obtained by visit and search.[107]

Diversion for the purpose of visit and search

13.94 If visit and search at sea is impossible or unsafe, a belligerent warship or military aircraft may divert a merchant vessel to an appropriate area or port in order to exercise the right of visit and search. As an alternative to visit and search, diversion may be considered more practical and appropriate.[108]

Measures of supervision

13.95 In order to avoid the necessity for visit and search, belligerent states may establish reasonable measures for the inspection of cargo of neutral merchant vessels and certification that a vessel is not carrying contraband.[109]

13.96 The fact that a neutral merchant vessel has submitted to such measures of supervision as the inspection of its cargo and grant of certificates of non-contraband cargo by one belligerent is not an act of unneutral service with regard to an opposing belligerent.[110]

13.97 In order to obviate the necessity for visit and search, neutral states are encouraged to enforce reasonable control measures and certification procedures to ensure that their merchant vessels are not carrying contraband.[111]

INTERCEPTION, VISIT, AND SEARCH OF CIVIL AIRCRAFT

13.98 See paragraph 12.81 onwards.

CAPTURE OF ENEMY VESSELS AND GOODS

13.99 Subject to the provisions of paragraph 13.100, enemy vessels, whether merchant or otherwise, and goods on board such vessels may be captured outside neutral waters. Prior exercise of visit and search is not required.[112]

---

[107] SRM 120.   [108] SRM 121. See also para 13.92.   [109] SRM 122.   [110] SRM 123.
[111] SRM 124.   [112] SRM 135.

The following vessels are exempt from capture: **13.100**

a. hospital ships[113] and small craft used for coastal rescue operations;[114]

b. other medical transports, so long as they are needed for the wounded, sick, and shipwrecked on board;

c. vessels granted safe conduct by agreement between the belligerent parties including:

    (1) cartel vessels, eg, vessels designated for and engaged in the transport of prisoners of war; and

    (2) vessels engaged in humanitarian missions, including vessels carrying supplies indispensable to the survival of the civilian population, and vessels engaged in relief actions and rescue operations;

d. vessels engaged in transporting cultural property under special protection;

e. vessels charged with religious, non-military scientific or philanthropic missions; vessels collecting scientific data of likely military applications are not protected;

f. small coastal fishing vessels and small boats engaged in local coastal trade,[115] but they are subject to the regulations of a belligerent naval commander operating in the area and to inspection; and

g. vessels designed or adapted exclusively for responding to pollution incidents in the marine environment when actually engaged in such activities.[116]

Vessels listed in paragraph 13.100 are exempt from capture only if they: **13.101**

a. are innocently employed in their normal role;

b. do not commit acts harmful to the enemy;

c. immediately submit to identification and inspection when required; and

d. do not intentionally hamper the movement of combatants and obey orders to stop or move out of the way when required.[117]

Capture of a merchant vessel is exercised by taking such vessel as prize. If **13.102** military circumstances preclude taking such a vessel as prize at sea, it may be diverted to an appropriate area or port in order to complete capture. As an alternative to capture, an enemy merchant vessel may be diverted from its declared destination.[118]

---

[113] Any hospital ship in a port that falls into the hands of the enemy shall be authorized to leave that port, GC II, Art 29.

[114] Neither category is classed as a warship when in a neutral port, GC II, Art 32.

[115] HC XI, Art 3, describes these categories as 'Vessels used exclusively for fishing along the coast or small boats employed in local trade'.   [116] SRM 136.

[117] SRM 137.   [118] SRM 138. See also n 103.

13.103 Subject to paragraph 13.104, a captured enemy merchant vessel may, as an exceptional measure, be destroyed[119] when military circumstances preclude taking or sending such a vessel as an enemy prize. The vessel must be deemed capable of making a contribution to the enemy's war effort and may be destroyed only if the following criteria are met beforehand:

   a. the safety of passengers and crew is provided for; for this purpose, the ship's boats are not regarded as a place of safety unless the safety of the passengers and crew is assured in the prevailing sea and weather conditions by the proximity of land or the presence of another vessel which is in a position to take them on board;

   b. documents and papers relating to the prize are safeguarded; and

   c. if feasible, personal effects of the passengers and crew are saved.[120]

13.104 The destruction of enemy passenger vessels carrying only civilian passengers is prohibited at sea. For the safety of the passengers, such vessels shall be diverted to an appropriate area or port in order to complete capture.[121]

Capture of Enemy Civil Aircraft and Goods

13.105 See paragraph 12.92 onwards.

Capture of Neutral Merchant Vessels and Goods

13.106 Subject to paragraph 13.3, neutral merchant vessels are liable to capture outside neutral waters if they are engaged in any of the activities referred to in paragraph 13.47 or if it is determined as a result of visit and search or by other means, that they:

   a. are carrying contraband;

   b. are on a voyage especially undertaken with a view to the transport of individual passengers who are embodied in the armed forces of the enemy;

   c. are operating directly under enemy control, orders, charter, employment, or direction;

   d. present irregular or fraudulent documents, lack necessary documents, or destroy, deface, or conceal documents;

   e. are violating regulations established by a belligerent within the immediate area of naval operations; or

   f. are breaching or attempting to breach a blockade.

---

[119] If it is a military objective, see para 13.84.   [120] SRM 139.   [121] SRM 140.

Capture of a neutral merchant vessel is exercised by taking such vessel as prize.[122]

Subject to paragraph 13.3, goods on board neutral merchant vessels are liable to capture only if they are contraband.[123]   **13.107**

In order for goods to be designated as contraband, they have to be included in the list of prohibited goods published by the belligerent, see also paragraph 13.110.   **13.108**

In order to exercise the right of capture referred to in paragraph 13.106(a) and 13.107, the belligerent must have published contraband lists. The precise nature of a belligerent's contraband list may vary according to the particular circumstances of the armed conflict. Contraband lists shall be reasonably specific.[124]   **13.109**

Goods not on the belligerent's contraband list are 'free goods', that is, not subject to capture. As a minimum, 'free goods' shall include the following: **13.110**

a. religious objects;

b. articles intended exclusively for the treatment of the wounded and sick and for the prevention of disease;

c. clothing, bedding, essential foodstuffs, and means of shelter for the civilian population in general, and women and children in particular, provided there is not serious reason to believe that such goods will be diverted to other purpose, or that a definite military advantage would accrue to the enemy by their substitution for enemy goods that would thereby become available for military purposes;[125]

d. items destined for prisoners of war, including individual parcels and collective relief shipments containing food, clothing, educational, cultural, and recreational articles;

e. goods otherwise specifically exempted from capture by international treaty or by special arrangement between belligerents; and

f. other goods not susceptible for use in armed conflict.[126]

The destruction of captured neutral passenger vessels carrying civilian passengers is prohibited at sea. For the safety of the passengers, such vessels shall be diverted to an appropriate port in order to complete capture as provided for in paragraph 13.106.[127]   **13.111**

Capture of Neutral Civil Aircraft and Goods

See paragraph 12.98 onwards.   **13.112**

---

[122] SRM 146. See also n 108.   [123] SRM 147.   [124] SRM 149.
[125] See GC IV, Art 23.   [126] SRM 150.   [127] SRM 152.

G. PROTECTED PERSONS, MEDICAL TRANSPORTS

GENERAL RULES

13.113 Except as provided for in paragraph 13.125, the provisions of Part G are not to be construed as in any way departing from the provisions of Geneva Convention II 1949 and Additional Protocol I 1977, which contain detailed rules for the treatment of the wounded, sick, and shipwrecked and for medical transports.[128]

13.114 The parties to the conflict may agree, for humanitarian purposes, to create a zone in a defined area of the sea in which only activities consistent with those humanitarian purposes are permitted.[129]

13.114.1 Such an agreement need not be in writing, nor need the zone exist indefinitely.[130] Permissible activities within the zone would include those necessary to carry out the humanitarian work for which the zone was created, and would include military helicopter flights for the transport of the wounded. Activity inconsistent with the agreed purpose of the zone, such as using the area as a sanctuary for submarines, would be an abuse of the humanitarian agreement.

PROTECTED PERSONS

13.115 Persons on board vessels and aircraft having fallen into the power of a belligerent or neutral shall be respected and protected. While at sea and thereafter until determination of their status, they shall be subject to the jurisdiction of the state exercising power over them.[131]

13.116 Members of the crews of hospital ships may not be captured during the time they are in the service of these vessels. Members of the crews of rescue craft may not be captured while engaging in rescue operations.[132]

13.117 Persons on board other vessels or aircraft exempt from capture listed in paragraphs 13.100 and 13.99 may not be captured.[133]

13.118 Religious and medical personnel assigned to the spiritual and medical care of the wounded, sick, and shipwrecked shall not be considered prisoners

---

[128] SRM 159.   [129] SRM 160.

[130] Although there is no provision of this kind in GC II, this concept was successfully used by the UK during the Falklands conflict 1982. A neutral zone was established, approximately 20 nm in diameter, on the high seas, to enable the exchange of the wounded of both sides to take place.   [131] SRM 161.

[132] SRM 162.   [133] SRM 163.

of war. They may, however, be retained as long as their services for the medical or spiritual needs of prisoners of war are needed.[134]

Nationals of an enemy state, other than those specified in paragraphs 13.116 to 13.118, are likely to be entitled to prisoner of war status and may be made prisoners of war if they fall into any of the categories listed in paragraph 8.3.1.[135] **13.119**

In the context of maritime warfare, these categories may include: **13.119.1**

a. crew members of auxiliary vessels or auxiliary aircraft;

b. crew members of enemy merchant vessels or of civil aircraft not exempt from capture, unless they benefit from more favourable treatment under other provisions of international law;

c. crew members of neutral merchant vessels or civil aircraft that have taken a direct part in the hostilities on the side of the enemy, or served as an auxiliary for the enemy.

Nationals of a neutral state: **13.120**

a. who are passengers on board enemy or neutral vessels or aircraft are to be released and may not be made prisoners of war unless they fall into any of the categories listed in paragraph 8.3.1 or have personally committed acts of hostility against the captor;

b. who are members of the crew of enemy warships or auxiliary vessels or military aircraft or auxiliary aircraft are entitled to prisoner of war status and may be made prisoners of war;

c. who are members of the crew of enemy or neutral merchant vessels or civil aircraft are to be released and may not be made prisoners of war unless the vessel or aircraft has committed an act covered by paragraphs 13.41, 13.43, 13.47, or 13.49, or the member of the crew falls into any of the categories listed in paragraph 8.3.1 or has personally committed an act of hostility against the captor.[136]

Civilian persons other than those specified in paragraphs 13.116 to 13.120 are to be treated in accordance with Geneva Convention IV 1949[137] and Additional Protocol I.[138] **13.121**

For persons who have fallen into the power of a neutral state, see part L of Chapter 8. **13.122**

---

[134] SRM 164.

[135] For handling prisoners of war (PW) captured at sea, see United Kingdom Ministry of Defence, *Prisoner of War Handling* (JWP 1–10, 2001), Annex 3c. For general rules on PW handling, see Ch 8.   [136] SRM 166.

[137] SRM 167.   [138] Especially Arts 72–79.

MEDICAL TRANSPORTS

13.123 In order to provide maximum protection for hospital ships from the moment of the outbreak of hostilities, states must beforehand make general notification of the characteristics of their hospital ships as specified in Article 22 of Geneva Convention II 1949. Such notification should include all available information on the means whereby the ship may be identified.[139]

13.123.1 Names of hospital ships shall be notified at least ten days before they are used, see paragraph 13.33.1.

13.124 Hospital ships may be equipped with purely deflective means of defence, such as chaff and flares. The presence of such equipment should be notified.[140] Crew members of hospital ships may carry light individual weapons for the maintenance of order and for their own protection.[141]

13.125 In order to fulfil most effectively their humanitarian mission, hospital ships should be permitted to use cryptographic equipment. The equipment shall not be used in any circumstances to transmit intelligence data nor in any other way to acquire any military advantage.[142]

13.126 Hospital ships, small craft used for coastal rescue operations, and other medical transports are encouraged to implement the means of identification set out in Annex I of Additional Protocol I 1977.[143]

13.127 These means of identification are intended only to facilitate identification and do not, of themselves, confer protected status.[144]

MEDICAL AIRCRAFT

13.128 Medical aircraft are to be protected and respected as specified in paragraph 12.104 onwards.

THE WOUNDED, SICK, SHIPWRECKED, AND DEAD

Protection and care

13.129 The wounded, sick, and shipwrecked are to be respected and protected. They may not be attacked[145] under any circumstances.[146] They must be treated

---

[139] SRM 169. See para 13.33.1.   [140] SRM 170.   [141] GC I, Art 35(1).

[142] SRM 171. GC II, Art 34(2), states that hospital ships may not possess or use a secret code for their wireless or other means of communication. This general wording has caused difficulties. British forces in the Falklands conflict 1982 found that having to give orders to their hospital ships 'in the clear' risked giving away their own positions or likely movements. The rule stated in paragraph 13.128 is a legitimate interpretation of Art 34(2).   [143] SRM 172.

[144] SRM 173.   [145] See para 7.3, GC II, Art 12 and AP I, Art 10.

[146] No consideration of, eg, 'operational necessity' can excuse the unlawful killing of survivors: *The Peleus Case* (1946) 1 WCR 1 .

humanely. They must be provided with medical care. They may not wilfully be left without medical assistance nor exposed to contagious diseases or infection. Priority of treatment is dictated by medical reasons only. Violence and biological experiments are forbidden. Women must be treated with respect, with due regard to their sex and no less favourably than men.[147] The parties to a conflict are also under an obligation, particularly after an engagement, to take all possible measures, consistent with their own security, 'to search for and collect the shipwrecked, wounded and sick, to protect them against pillage and ill-treatment, to ensure their adequate care, and to search for the dead and prevent their being despoiled'.[148]

For the definition of 'wounded and sick', see paragraph 7.2. The term 'shipwreck' means shipwreck from any cause and includes forced landings at sea by or from aircraft.[149] **13.129.1**

In the care of the wounded, sick, shipwrecked, and dead, the guidance in Chapter 7 should be followed until they are landed. **13.129.2**

Burial at sea

Burial at sea of the dead is to be carried out individually as far as circumstances permit and is to be preceded by a careful examination, preferably a medical examination, of the bodies to confirm death, establish identity, and to enable a report to be made. Where a double identity disc is used, one half of the disc should remain on the body.[150] **13.130**

---

[147] GC II, Art 12; AP I, Art 10.   [148] See para 7.4 and GC II, Art 18.
[149] GC II, Art 12.   [150] GC II, Art 20.

14

Application of the Law of Armed Conflict During Peace Support Operations

THE LEGAL FRAMEWORK FOR PEACE SUPPORT OPERATION FORCES

Peace support operations ('PSOs') are subject to a number of different legal **14.1** regimes, amongst others those derived from:

a. the United Nations Charter;

b. the decisions of the United Nations Security Council establishing the operation and defining the mandate of the PSO force;

c. the agreements between the United Nations and the host state or states on the territory of which the PSO is to be conducted and between the United Nations and the states which have agreed to contribute units to the PSO force;

d. the United Nations Convention on the Safety of United Nations and Associated Personnel 1994 (UN Safety Convention); and

e. the Convention on Privileges and Immunities of the United Nations 1946.

In addition, the law of the host state or states will generally be applicable, although the agreements between those states and the United Nations will usually specify the extent to which the PSO force and its members are immune from the jurisdiction of host state courts. United Kingdom forces taking part in PSOs are also subject to the relevant rules of United Kingdom law.

The present chapter, however, is concerned only with the application of the **14.2** law of armed conflict during PSOs. Guidance on the application of other rules of national and international law will be given in each operation. Reference may also be made to JWP 3–50 *Peace Support Operations*.

PEACE SUPPORT OPERATION FORCES WHICH BECOME PARTY TO AN ARMED CONFLICT

14.3 The extent to which PSO forces are subject to the law of armed conflict depends upon whether they are party to an armed conflict with the armed forces of a state or an entity which, for these purposes, is treated as a state.[1] Although the United Nations (and regional organizations) are not states and are not parties to the various treaties on the law of armed conflict, states providing contingents to PSOs remain bound by the treaties to which they are parties.[2]

14.4 Where PSO forces become party to an armed conflict with such forces, then both sides are required to observe the law of armed conflict in its entirety.[3] In those circumstances, recourse must be had to the whole of this Manual.

14.5 A PSO force can become party to an armed conflict, and thus subject to the law of armed conflict:

   a. where it was mandated from the outset to engage in hostilities with opposing armed forces as part of its mission (which will be the case, for example, with certain types of enforcement action under Chapter VII of the United Nations Charter); and

   b. where its personnel, though not originally charged with such a task, become involved in hostilities as combatants (whether as a result of their own initiative or because they are attacked by other forces) to such a degree that an armed conflict comes into being between the PSO force

---

[1] For example, during the 1950–53 Korean conflict, United Nations forces were instructed to comply with the provisions of the Geneva Conventions 1949 notwithstanding that North Korea was not, at that time, recognized as a state by the United Nations or by any of the states contributing to the United Nations forces in Korea.

[2] In this context, note the provisions of Common Art 1 of the Geneva Conventions, which requires states parties 'to respect and to ensure respect for the present Convention in all circumstances' and Art 1(1) of Additional Protocol I, which is in the same terms.

[3] The applicability of the law of armed conflict in such circumstances was recognized in the Korean conflict. It is assumed by Art 2(2) of the UN Safety Convention, which refers to 'an enforcement action under Chapter VII of the Charter of the United Nations in which any of the personnel are engaged as combatants against organized armed forces and to which the law of international armed conflict applies'. The applicability of the law of armed conflict is not, however, confined to enforcement actions; as explained in para 14.5, a United Nations peacekeeping force may become party to an armed conflict even though that was not its original mandate. It is the fact of being a party to an international armed conflict, not the nature of the original mandate or the provisions under which the force was established, which is determinative.

and the opposing forces. The latter situation may arise in any type of PSO.[4]

On the other hand, a PSO force which does not itself take an active part in **14.6** hostilities does not become subject to the law of armed conflict simply because it is operating in territory in which an armed conflict is taking place between other parties. That will be the case, for example, where a force with a mandate to observe a cease-fire finds that the cease-fire breaks down and there is a recurrence of fighting between the parties in which the PSO force takes no direct part.

It is not always easy to determine whether a PSO force has become a party **14.7** to an armed conflict or to fix the precise moment at which that event has occurred. Legal advice and guidance from higher military and political levels should be sought if it appears possible that the threshold of armed conflict has been, or is about to be, crossed.

Responsibility for ensuring compliance with the law of armed conflict by **14.8** the members of a PSO force is divided between the national authorities of each contingent and the United Nations or other international organization under whose auspices the operation is conducted. The United Nations (or other international organization) will usually issue rules of engagement which will require compliance with the law of armed conflict and its commanders will issue their orders accordingly. However, the model agreement between the United Nations and contributor states requires the contributor state to ensure that the contingent which it contributes complies with the law of armed conflict. Since only states possess a criminal jurisdiction, violations of the law of armed conflict can usually be punished only by national courts and disciplinary authorities. A member of a contingent in a PSO force who violates the law of armed conflict will, therefore, normally stand trial before the courts of his own state, although if the violation amounts to a grave breach of the Geneva Conventions or Additional Protocol I, any national court will possess jurisdiction.[5]

PEACE SUPPORT OPERATION FORCES WHICH HAVE NOT BECOME PARTY TO AN ARMED CONFLICT

A PSO force which has not become a party to an armed conflict is not sub- **14.9** ject to the law of armed conflict as such. That will be so even though there may be incidents in which acts of violence are directed against the force and

---

[4] The various categories into which legal and military writers tend to divide PSOs are not, therefore, decisive in determining whether the law of armed conflict is applicable, since any force is capable of becoming involved as a party in an armed conflict, although such a consequence is obviously more likely in some operations than in others.

[5] For further information about enforcement of the law of armed conflict, see Ch 16, especially Pt G.

members of the force take action in self-defence, so long as the threshold of armed conflict is not crossed. It follows that, below that threshold, members of a PSO force may be involved in fighting without being subject to the law of armed conflict.

14.10 Nevertheless, such fighting does not take place in a legal vacuum. Quite apart from the fact that it is governed by national law and the relevant provisions of the rules of engagement, the principles and spirit of the law of armed conflict remain relevant.

14.11 In the case of United Nations PSOs, that has been formally recognized by the Bulletin on the Observance by United Nations Forces of International Humanitarian Law issued by the United Nations Secretary-General on 6 August 1999.[6] The bulletin, with which all members of United Nations forces are required to comply, applies 'to United Nations forces when in situations of armed conflict they are actively engaged therein as combatants, to the extent and for the duration of their engagement'.[7] The bulletin sets out a non-exhaustive list of fundamental principles with which any recourse to force by members of a United Nations force must comply.[8]

14.11.1 The bulletin has been the subject of criticism by the United Nations Committee on Peacekeeping. In its report of March 2000, it stressed that the bulletin ought accurately to reflect the terms of international humanitarian law. It requested the Secretary-General to undertake further consultations to this end.

PROTECTION ACCORDED TO PSO FORCES BY THE LAW OF ARMED CONFLICT

14.12 Since members of PSO forces may frequently find themselves caught up in an armed conflict to which the PSO force is not a party, the law of armed conflict affords them certain protections.

14.13 The parties to an armed conflict are prohibited to make use of the emblem of the United Nations except as authorized by the United Nations.[9] In addition, it is prohibited to kill, injure, or capture an adversary by feigning protected status by the use of signs, emblems, or uniforms of the United Nations and to do so constitutes the war crime of perfidy.[10]

---

[6] A Roberts and R Guelff, *Documents on the Laws of War* (3rd edn 2000) (Roberts and Guelff, *Documents*) 725.   [7] Section 1(1).

[8] Section 2 makes clear that the bulletin does not set out an exhaustive list and does not replace the provisions of national laws by which military personnel remain bound throughout the operation.

[9] Additional Protocol I 1977 (AP I), Art 38(2); Rome Statute 1998, Art 8(2)(b)(vii).

[10] AP I, Arts 37(1)(d) and 85(3)(f). The provision was not intended to apply where members of United Nations armed forces intervene as combatants in an armed conflict. See Y Sandoz,

Insofar as a party to an armed conflict is not subject to a more extensive **14.14** prohibition or restriction on the use of landmines,[11] the Mines Protocol to CCW requires it to take certain steps to protect United Nations forces from mines and booby-traps.[12]

More generally, where a United Nations force or other PSO force is not **14.15** engaged as a party to an armed conflict, its personnel and equipment would not constitute a military objective[13] and attacks on them will therefore be unlawful.[14] While it falls outside the scope of the present Manual, the United Nations Convention on the Safety of United Nations and Associated Personnel 1994 outlaws a series of actions against United Nations personnel and national personnel associated with certain types of United Nations operation and requires all states party to the Convention to extradite or prosecute those accused of such crimes.

ENFORCEMENT OF THE LAW OF ARMED CONFLICT BY PSO FORCES

In some circumstances, members of a PSO force may be expressly or im- **14.16** pliedly charged with certain responsibilities for ensuring the compliance of others with the law of armed conflict. For example, they may have a responsibility to intervene so far as feasible to prevent the commission of grave breaches or other war crimes or to arrest persons indicted for such offences.[15] In addition, there is a duty on states party to Additional Protocol I to co-operate with the United Nations in response to serious violations of the law of armed conflict.[16]

C Swinarski, and B Zimmermann (eds), *Commentary on the Additional Protocols of 8 June 1977 to the Geneva Conventions of 12 August 1949* (1987) para 1509.

[11] See para 6.13.

[12] Protocol II, Art 8 and Amended Protocol II, Art 12(2), see Roberts and Guelff, *Documents*, 531, 545.   [13] See para 5.4.

[14] See the decision of the International Criminal Tribunal for the Former Yugoslavia in *Prosecutor v Karadžić and Mladić*, 108 ILR 85. See also Rome Statute, Art 8(2)(b)(iii), (e)(iii).

[15] For example, members of the Stabilization Force (SFOR) deployed in Bosnia and Herzegovina under the terms of the Dayton Agreement 1995 have arrested a number of persons indicted by the International Criminal Tribunal for the Former Yugoslavia.

[16] AP I, Art 89.

15

Internal Armed Conflict

A. INTRODUCTION

THE LAW APPLICABLE

15.1 The rules, set out in this chapter, relating to internal conflicts are more limited than those applying to international armed conflicts. The rules are to be found mainly[1] in:

a. Common Article 3 to the Geneva Conventions 1949, which applies to all internal armed conflicts;

b. Additional Protocol II 1977, which applies to armed conflicts within a state 'between its armed forces and dissident armed forces or other organized

---

[1] Other treaties also apply to internal armed conflicts such as the Cultural Property Convention 1954 (CPC), the Second Hague Protocol 1999, the Amended Mines Protocol 1996, and the Rome Statute of the International Criminal Court 1998 (Rome Statute). They will be referred to as necessary in the relevant paragraphs of this chapter.

armed groups which, under responsible command, exercise such control over part of its territory as to enable them to carry out sustained and con-certed military operations and to implement' the Protocol. The Protocol supplements the basic rules in Common Article 3.

In addition, there are certain principles of customary international law which are applicable to internal armed conflicts.[2] These are set out in Part B below.

15.1.1   In practice many conflicts since 1945 have had the characteristics of both international and non-international armed conflicts.[3] For example, in many cases, outside states have become involved in support of the rival parties in what may have originated as an internal conflict. In such cases, the more fully developed rules applicable in international armed conflict may be applied to certain phases and aspects of the conflict. Outside parties in such conflicts have in many cases accepted the applicability of those rules. The discussion that follows relates to conflicts, or aspects of them, that remain essentially non-international in character.

15.1.2   In the past, the application of the law of armed conflict in non-international armed conflict was largely dependent on 'recognition of belligerence'. The law of armed conflict, or parts of it, could be brought into effect if a govern-ment recognized the belligerent status of an insurgent faction opposing it, or if foreign states recognized the belligerent status of that faction. The doc-trine has declined to the point where recognition of belligerency is almost unknown today. The rules outlined in this chapter are applicable in internal armed conflicts irrespective of any question of recognition.

TYPES OF INTERNAL CONFLICT

15.2   The law of armed conflict makes a distinction between the following situa-tions arising within the borders of a state, the law applicable to them being different in each case:

a.   internal disturbances and tensions, such as riots and isolated and spor-adic acts of violence, to which the law of armed conflict does not apply;[4]

b.   internal armed conflicts between the armed forces of a state and one or more armed factions in that state or internal armed conflict between such armed factions;[5]

c.   internal armed conflicts between the armed forces of a state and an organ-ized armed faction which have reached the level at which Additional Protocol II comes into operation;[6]

---

[2] *Prosecutor v Tadić (Jurisdiction)* (1995) 105 ILR 419; Art 8(2) of the Rome Statute.
[3] See the judgment of the ICTY Appeals Chamber in *Prosecutor v Tadić*, on 15 July 1999, (1995) 38 ILM 1518.   [4] See para 15.2.1.
[5] See Pt B below.   [6] See Pt C below.

d. armed conflicts referred to in Additional Protocol I 1977, Article 1(4);
   these are treated as international armed conflicts.[7]

Of these situations, only the legal aspects of those listed at (b) and (c)—internal armed conflicts—are dealt with in detail in this chapter.

Internal disturbances

'Situations of internal disturbances and tensions, such as riots, isolated and **15.2.1**
sporadic acts of violence and other acts of a similar nature' do not amount
to armed conflict.[8] These situations are covered mainly by the municipal
laws of states. The main body of international law applicable to these situations is human rights law,[9] including the law relating to crimes against
humanity and genocide, but, in addition, as a matter of policy, states have
sometimes taken the view that, even if a particular situation is not an armed
conflict under international law, the relevant principles and rules of the law
of armed conflict will be applied.

Conflicts referred to in Additional Protocol I, Article 1(4)

Additional Protocol I specifically applies to 'armed conflicts in which **15.2.2**
peoples are fighting against colonial domination and alien occupation and
against racist régimes in the exercise of their right of self-determination, as
enshrined in the Charter of the United Nations and the Declaration on
Principles of International Law concerning Friendly Relations and
Co-operation among States in accordance with the Charter of the United
Nations'.[10] However, the Protocol only applies if the authority representing
the 'peoples' engaged in the armed conflict makes a special declaration
undertaking to apply the Geneva Conventions and Additional Protocol I.[11]
The effect of any such declaration would be that such conflicts are treated as
international armed conflicts.

The background to this development in Additional Protocol I was the emer- **15.2.3**
gence of a large number of post-colonial states, many of which had only
gained independence from their former colonial rulers after long struggles
and wished to see certain ongoing struggles recognized as essentially international in character. It was against this background that the International

---

[7] See paras 1.33.6 and 15.2.2.
[8] See Additional Protocol II 1977 (AP II), Art 1(2); Rome Statute, Art 8(2)(d).
[9] Such as the European Convention on Human Rights 1950 and the International Covenant
on Civil and Political Rights 1966, though derogations are permissible even from parts of
human rights law 'in time of public emergency which threatens the life of the nation', see
Art 4(1) of the International Covenant and similar wording in Art 15(1) of the European
Convention.   [10] Additional Protocol I 1977 (AP I), Art 1(4).
[11] In accordance with AP I, Art 96(3).

Covenants on Economic, Social and Cultural Rights and on Civil and Political Rights, both of which were drawn up in 1966, put emphasis on 'the right of self determination'.[12] The UN General Assembly had on several occasions from 1968 onwards urged the application of Geneva Conventions III and IV in particular conflicts of a wholly or partly anti-colonial character.[13] There was thus an increasing body of opinion that viewed such 'wars of liberation' as internationalized, if not international, armed conflict.

15.2.4   In the negotiations that resulted in Additional Protocols I and II, this trend was formally recognized and provision was made for armed conflicts of this type to be assimilated into the definition of international conflicts, to which the full scope of all four Geneva Conventions and Additional Protocol I would apply.[14]

15.2.5   However, the United Kingdom made a declaration on ratification of Additional Protocol I that it would not be bound 'in consequence of any declaration purporting to be made' in such cases 'unless the UK shall have expressly recognised that it has been made by a body which is genuinely an authority representing a people engaged in an armed conflict' of this type. A similar statement made by Germany; and the statements of Belgium, Canada, Ireland, and South Korea indicated that recognition of the authority by the appropriate regional inter-governmental organization was regarded as a relevant factor.

B. ALL INTERNAL ARMED CONFLICTS

APPLICABILITY OF COMMON ARTICLE 3

15.3   Once the level of violence has reached the intensity of an armed conflict, the provisions of Common Article 3 to the Geneva Conventions apply.[15]

15.3.1   The point at which situations of internal disturbances and tensions develop into an armed conflict is open to interpretation. Attempts to define the term 'armed conflict' have proved unsuccessful and although Common Article 3 specifically provides that its application does not affect the legal status of the parties to a conflict, states have been, and always will be, reluctant to admit that a state of armed conflict exists. Factors that may determine whether an

---

[12] See Common Art 1 to the International Covenant on Economic, Social and Cultural Rights 1966 and the International Covenant on Civil and Political Rights.

[13] eg, UNGAR 2383(XXIII), 2508(XXIV), 2547(XXIV), and 2796(XXVI) on Southern Rhodesia; UNGAR 2707(XXV) and 2795(XXVI) on territories under Portuguese administration.

[14] AP I, Art 1(4).   [15] See para 15.4.

internal armed conflict exists include whether rebels possess organized armed forces, control territory, and ensure respect for the law of armed conflict.[16] In the case of *Prosecutor v Tadić (Jurisdiction)* it was held that:

an armed conflict exists whenever there is a resort to armed force between States or protracted armed violence between governmental authorities and organized armed groups or between such groups within a State. International humanitarian law applies from the initiation of such armed conflicts and extends beyond the cessation of hostilities until a general conclusion of peace is reached; or, in the case of internal conflicts, a peaceful settlement is achieved. Until that moment, international humanitarian law continues to apply in the whole territory of the warring States or, in the case of internal conflicts, the whole territory under the control of a party, whether or not actual combat takes place there.[17]

The terms of Common Article 3 are really no more than 'rules which were **15.3.2** already recognized as essential in all civilized countries, and embodied in the national legislation of the States in question, long before the Convention was signed'. It follows that whilst states may not be willing to admit to the application of Common Article 3 as a matter of law, its provisions are frequently applied in practice.[18]

PROVISIONS OF COMMON ARTICLE 3

Under the terms of Common Article 3, the parties[19] to a non-international **15.4** armed conflict occurring in the territory of a party to the Conventions are obliged to apply 'as a minimum', the following provisions:

(1) Persons taking no active part in the hostilities, including members of armed forces[20] who have laid down their arms and those placed hors de combat by sickness, wounds, detention, or any other cause, shall in all circumstances be treated humanely, without any adverse distinction founded on race, colour, religion or faith, sex, birth or wealth, or any other similar criteria.

---

[16] JS Pictet, *Commentary on the Geneva Conventions of 12 August 1949* (Pictet, *Commentary*) (1952) vol I, 49, lists these among possible criteria but at the same time thinks it was wise to abandon the attempt to define internal armed conflict. He goes on to say: 'Speaking generally, it must be recognized that the conflicts referred to in Article 3 are armed conflicts, with armed forces on either side engaged in hostilities—conflicts, in short, which are in many respects similar to an international war, but take place within the confines of a single country. In many cases, each of the Parties is in possession of a portion of the national territory, and there is often some sort of front'. [17] (1995) 105 ILR 419, 488.

[18] See Pictet, *Commentary* (1960) vol III, 35–37; and 76 ILR 446–449.

[19] This purports to bind *all* parties, both states and insurgents, whether or not the latter have made any declaration of intent to apply the principles. Enforcement, however, would be under the terms of national domestic law, unless the International Criminal Court has jurisdiction, see para 16.33. [20] This includes both government and insurgent armed forces.

To this end, the following acts are and shall remain prohibited at any time and in any place whatsoever with respect to the above-mentioned persons:

(a) violence to life and person, in particular murder of all kinds, mutilation, cruel treatment and torture;

(b) taking of hostages;

(c) outrages upon personal dignity, in particular, humiliating and degrading treatment;

(d) the passing of sentences and the carrying out of executions without previous judgement pronounced by a regularly constituted court affording all the judicial guarantees which are recognized as indispensable by civilized peoples.

(2) The wounded and sick shall be collected and cared for.

15.4.1 These provisions do not preclude the application of the relevant national law—except to the extent that a particular rule of national law directly conflicts with any of the provisions of Common Article 3. Thus captured insurgents, whether nationals of the state or not, may be tried for offences they have committed, provided that the basic requirements of the law of armed conflict for humane treatment and judicial guarantees are observed. Captured insurgents are not legally entitled to be treated as prisoners of war.[21] Common Article 3 does, however, state that the parties should 'further endeavour to bring into force, by means of special agreements, all or part' of the main provisions of the Conventions. Thus there is nothing to prevent greater application of the Conventions, for example, the conferring of status akin to that of prisoners of war, where agreed and appropriate.[22]

15.4.2 There is an express provision in Common Article 3 that 'an impartial humanitarian body, such as the International Committee of the Red Cross, may offer its services to the Parties to the conflict'. However, the involvement of the ICRC does not of itself indicate that Common Article 3 is deemed to apply.

BASIC PRINCIPLES OF THE LAW OF ARMED CONFLICT

Introduction

15.5 There has been no consensus between states as to the extent to which rules of the law of armed conflict other than those specifically laid down in

---

[21] In the Algerian civil conflict, France tried, condemned, and executed armed militants for bearing arms against the state and other crimes, though seeming to expect the Algerian Revolutionary Front (FLN) to provide prisoner of war (PW) treatment for captured French soldiers. By 1958, however, the French had abandoned the systematic prosecution of FLN militants and began establishing PW-like camps for them.

[22] See para 15.56 with regard to supplementary agreements.

treaties[23] apply to internal armed conflicts. The jurisprudence of the International Criminal Tribunal for the former Yugoslavia suggests that some of those rules do apply and the Rome Statute of the International Criminal Court 1998 (Rome Statute) lists a series of acts which, if committed in internal armed conflicts, are considered war crimes.[24] While it is not always easy to determine the exact content of the customary international law applicable in non-international armed conflicts, guidance can be derived from the basic principles of military necessity, humanity, distinction, and proportionality explained in Chapter 2. The remaining paragraphs of Part B of this chapter, therefore, represent an attempt to set out guidelines in the form of practical rules that can be applied in internal armed conflicts to enable those engaged in an internal armed conflict to act within the law of armed conflict.

Combatants and non-combatants

A distinction is to be drawn between those who are taking a direct part in hostilities, who may be attacked, and those who are not taking a direct part in hostilities, who are protected from attack.[25] **15.6**

The law relating to internal armed conflict does not deal specifically with combatant status or membership of the armed forces. That is because in internal armed conflict, the law of the place where the conflict takes place continues to apply. In practice, dissident armed forces may be the result of members of the armed forces of the state breaking away to oppose the government, ad hoc armed opposition groups may be established, or civilians may take up arms to overthrow the government. In any of these cases, the political aim may be to take over the whole country or to set up an autonomous region within it. The nature of these armed opposition groups is such that, unless they control territory or have an operating base in a neighbouring country, they probably operate clandestinely and do not have a transparent and public structure. They may be connected to a political party or movement. **15.6.1**

Unlike combatants in an international armed conflict, members of dissident armed forces remain liable to prosecution for offences under domestic law. These can include normal acts of combat—for example, a dissident combatant who kills or injures a member of the government forces may be **15.6.2**

---

[23] Common Art 3 and Additional Protocol II are not the only legal rules applicable in internal armed conflict. Some treaties on weapons apply in both international and internal armed conflicts, see, eg, Amended Protocol II of 1996 to the Conventional Weapons Convention 1980, Art 1(2). [24] Rome Statute, Art 8(2)(e).
[25] Customary law, as confirmed by Geneva Conventions 1949 I–IV, Art 3. Other measures under national law, such as arrest and trial, may be taken.

prosecuted for murder or other offences against the person—and even membership of the dissident group. A member of the security forces who kills a dissident or a civilian will also have to justify his actions under domestic law and may be tried before the courts for any offence he may have committed.

15.6.3 A captured member of dissident fighting forces is not legally entitled to prisoner of war status. He may be dealt with according to the law of the state for any offences he may have committed. A member of the security forces who is captured by the dissidents is not entitled to prisoner of war status but any mistreatment of him is likely to amount to an offence against the law of the state. He may take such legal action to secure his release as is permitted by the law of the state.[26] His status depends a great deal on the situation at the time. If, as is likely, the rebels do not control territory, have to operate clandestinely, and do not have proper facilities for internment, they must disarm, question, and release detainees. Wherever possible, treatment equivalent to that accorded to prisoners of war should be given. Of course, the situation is different if the parties to the conflict have agreed to apply Geneva Convention III in its entirety, as they are encouraged but not required to do.

15.6.4 Nevertheless, the law of non-international armed conflict clearly requires that any person (whether a combatant or a civilian) detained by either dissident or government forces must be treated humanely.[27]

15.6.5 In carrying out attacks, there should be a distinction between those who take an active part in hostilities and those who do not. The use of the words 'are taking' emphasizes that a potential or future fighter may not be attacked as such. However, being a person who takes a direct part in hostilities does not give rise to any special legal immunity or prisoner of war status.

Child soldiers

15.7 It is prohibited to conscript or enlist 'children under the age of fifteen years into armed forces or groups' or to use them 'to participate actively in hostilities'.[28]

15.7.1 Recent internal conflicts, particularly in West Africa, have been marked by the recruitment, arming, and deployment on military missions of children, many of whom have been involved in the commission of atrocities. Such recruitment and use is a war crime under the Rome Statute. Such child soldiers are to be treated humanely on capture, see paragraph 15.30.

---

[26] Although this may be difficult or impossible in practice.
[27] See para 15.29 onwards.   [28] Rome Statute, Art 8(2)(e)(vii).

Civilian immunity

Those who do not take an active part in hostilities are to be spared from **15.8** direct attack and, so far as possible, from the incidental effects of military operations.[29] Attacks aimed at terrorizing civilians are prohibited.

Military targets

Attacks are to be directed only against objects or areas which, at the time the **15.9** attack is launched, are of tactical or strategic military importance.

There is no definition of military objectives or attacks in the treaty law dealing **15.9.1** with non-international armed conflicts. Nevertheless, the definitions used in respect of international armed conflicts should be treated as applicable.[30]

Safeguard of civilians and other persons *hors de combat*

Persons who take no active part in the hostilities are to be protected and **15.10** respected.

That includes not only civilians and the civilian population, as persons **15.10.1** taking no active part in hostilities, but also fighters who have surrendered or who are *hors de combat* (placed out of action) because of sickness, wounds, detention, or for any other reasons. It is prohibited to make any adverse distinction founded on race, colour, religion or faith, sex, birth, or wealth, or any other similar criteria.

Detainees should be provided with sufficient food and drinking water, facil- **15.10.2** ities for health and hygiene, and shelter from the weather and the dangers of armed conflict.

Quarter

It is prohibited to conduct military operations on the basis of a denial of **15.11** quarter.[31]

Treachery

It is prohibited to kill or wound by resort to treachery.[32] Ruses of war are **15.12** permitted.

---

[29] GC I–IV, Art 3; Rome Statute, Art 8(2)(e)(i).   [30] See paras 5.4 and 5.20.
[31] Hague Regulations 1907 (HR), Art 23(d); Rome Statute, Art 8(2)(e)(x).
[32] HR, Art 23(b); Rome Statute, Art 8(2)(e)(ix).

15.12.1 The definition of perfidy in paragraph 5.9.1 may also be used as guidance as to the meaning of 'treachery' in internal armed conflicts.

Recognized emblems

15.13 It is prohibited to make improper use of the flag of truce or the red cross or red crescent emblems.[33]

Prohibition of displacement of civilians

15.14 It is prohibited to order the displacement of the civilian population for reasons related to the conflict, unless the security of the civilians involved or imperative military reasons so demand.[34]

15.14.1 It may be necessary to evacuate civilians temporarily from areas of danger, from encircled areas, or for the better conduct of military operations. It is prohibited to move them for reasons based on race, colour, religion or faith, sex, birth, or wealth or any similar criteria or in order to shield military targets from attack.

15.14.2 Recent armed conflicts have been blighted by the use of 'human shields' to protect military installations from attack and by the practice known as 'ethnic cleansing' when people of a certain racial origin or religious beliefs have been murdered or expelled from their homes, which have been destroyed. These practices violate the basic law of armed conflict principles of targeting, discrimination, and humane treatment of those *hors de combat*, as well as the basic human rights law principles of non-discrimination on racial or ethnic grounds and in freedom of thought, conscience, and religion.[35] They are likely to be war crimes. Depending on the circumstances, these practices may also amount to crimes against humanity or even genocide.

Indiscriminate attacks

15.15 Attacks that are not directed against military targets are prohibited.

15.15.1 There is no specific rule on indiscriminate attacks under customary law but the principle of distinction prohibits attacks that are not aimed at a specific target.

Immunity of civilian objects

15.16 Civilian property must not be attacked.

[33] HR, Art 23(f).   [34] Rome Statute, Art 8(2)(e)(viii).
[35] GC I–IV, Art 3; International Covenant on Civil and Political Rights, Arts 6, 7, 16, and 18; European Convention on Human Rights, Arts 9 and 10.

There is no definition of civilian objects nor is the term used in the treaties **15.16.1** dealing with internal armed conflicts, but the principles of military necessity and humanity require attacks to be limited to military objectives. Thus attacks on the following are prohibited unless they are being used for military purposes: civilian dwellings, shops, schools, and other places of non-military business, places of recreation and worship, means of transportation, cultural property, hospitals, and medical establishments and units.

UN General Assembly Resolution 2675, which was unanimously adopted[36] **15.16.2** and applies to all armed conflicts, can be regarded as evidence of state practice. Paragraph 5 of the resolution states: 'dwellings and other installations that are used only by the civilian population should not be the object of military operations'. The principle of military necessity demands that civilian property may only be destroyed, or requisitioned for use, for necessary military purposes.

The old practices that tolerated during sieges the bombardment of civilian **15.16.3** buildings (other than places of worship), hospitals, cultural property, indispensable objects, and works containing dangerous forces,[37] have not survived.

Destruction and seizure of property

It is prohibited to destroy or seize the property of an adversary unless such **15.17** destruction be imperatively demanded by the necessities of the conflict.[38]

Property may not be destroyed unless it is a military objective and it is mil- **15.17.1** itarily necessary to do so.

The word 'property' covers all kinds of property, whether public or private, **15.17.2** fixed or portable. It may be permissible to destroy a house in order to clear a field of fire or because it is being used as an enemy military observation or sniper post. It would not be permissible to burn down a house simply to prevent its being inhabited by persons of a different ethnic group or religious persuasion.

Protection of cultural objects and places of worship

It is prohibited: **15.18**

a. to commit any act of hostilities against cultural property, so long as it is not being used for military purposes.

---

[36] UNGAR 2675 was passed on 9 December 1970 by 109 votes to none with 18 states absent or abstaining.   [37] The exceptions are to be found in HR, Art 27; AP II, Arts 14–16.
[38] HR, Art 23(g); Rome Statute, Art 8(2)(e)(xii).

As a corollary, the better view is that the law also prohibits:

b. the use of cultural property for purposes which are likely to expose it to destruction or damage in armed conflict, unless there is no feasible alternative to such use;

c. the stealing, misappropriating, confiscation of, or wilful damage to, cultural property.[39]

15.18.1 Cultural property includes places of worship, institutions dedicated to religion, charity, education, the arts and sciences, historic monuments, and works of art and science.[40]

15.18.2 Cultural property that is civilian property must be respected in any event. In addition, the Cultural Property Convention 1954 and the Second Hague Protocol 1999[41] apply in internal armed conflicts.[42]

15.18.3 Intentionally directing attacks against buildings dedicated to religion, education, art, science, or charitable purposes, and historic monuments, provided they are not military objectives, is a war crime.[43]

Starvation; objects indispensable to survival

15.19 Starvation of civilians as a method of warfare is prohibited.

15.19.1 The right to life is a non-derogable human right.[44] Violence to the life and person of civilians is prohibited,[45] whatever method is adopted to achieve it. It follows that the destruction of crops, foodstuffs, and water sources, to such an extent that starvation is likely to follow, is also prohibited. The same applies to sieges, blockades, embargoes, or the blocking of relief supplies with the intention of causing starvation.

Environmental protection

15.20 Regard must be had to the natural environment in the conduct of all military operations.

[39] It is unlikely that the removal of works of art to prevent them falling into the hands of the opposing party would violate this principle. [40] HR, Art 27.

[41] The United Kingdom is not yet a party to the Convention or Protocol.

[42] See para 5.26. [43] Rome Statute, Art 8(2)(e)(iv).

[44] International Covenant on Civil and Political Rights, Arts 4 and 6; European Convention on Human Rights, Art 2. Deaths resulting from lawful acts of war are excepted from the latter (Art 15(2)) as are cases arising from the use of minimum necessary force in defence of any person from unlawful violence, to effect arrest, or prevent the escape of a person lawfully detained, or lawfully to quell a riot or insurrection. [45] GC I–IV, Art 3.

Works and installations containing dangerous forces

In accordance with the general principles of targeting set out above, objects **15.21** such as dams, dykes, and nuclear power stations which contain forces, the escape of which would be likely to endanger the civilian population, may only be attacked if they (a) constitute military objectives and (b) care is taken to minimize the risk to the civilian population. The latter requirement is of special importance with such targets because of the danger that they can pose.

The protection given to these objects in international conflicts is much more **15.21.1** detailed.[46]

Precautions in attack

In planning or carrying out attacks, precautions must be taken to limit **15.22** attacks to military objectives and to minimize incidental loss or damage.

The need to take precautions can be inferred from the principle of propor- **15.22.1** tionality and the principle of distinction, which require some care to be taken in the planning and execution of an attack. Attacks must be cancelled, suspended, or re-planned if the rule in paragraph 15.21 cannot be complied with. The same applies in sieges.

Pillage

Pillaging a town or place, even when taken by assault, is forbidden.[47]   **15.23**

Pillage, also known as plunder or looting, is the same as stealing, which is **15.23.1** an offence in peace or war. It must be distinguished from the lawful requisitioning of property for military, rather than private, purposes.

Precautions against the effects of attacks

Military commanders and the civilian authorities should do everything **15.24** that they feasibly can do to protect civilians and civilian objects in their area of control from the effects of war.

Nothing is laid down in customary law or in the treaties dealing with internal **15.24.1** armed conflicts about precautions in defence. This is a matter of common humanity. The use of human shields is prohibited.[48]

---

[46] See para 5.32.   [47] HR, Art 28; Rome Statute, Art 8(2)(e)(v).   [48] See para 15.14.2.

Undefended localities

15.25 It is prohibited to attack or bombard, by whatever means, towns, villages, dwellings, or buildings that are undefended.[49]

15.25.1 If a town, village, or building is undefended and can be occupied without resistance, there is no need to attack it and it is prohibited to do so. It is also prohibited to attack buildings unless they are military objectives. Undefended towns and villages that cannot be occupied because they are behind enemy lines or are in areas controlled by enemy forces may also not be attacked as such. Attacks against specific military objectives in those towns and villages are permitted, though precautions must be taken to minimize incidental loss or damage.

15.25.2 The other rules on protective zones applicable in international armed conflicts[50] may be applied by analogy to internal armed conflicts.

Civil defence

15.26 Civil defence personnel, installations, transports, and equipment are not to be attacked.

15.26.1 The treaties dealing with internal armed conflict make no special provision for civil defence. Civil defence personnel and installations that are civilian in character share the general civilian immunity. Military personnel engaged on civil defence duties pose no threat to the opposing party.

Humanitarian assistance and peacekeeping missions

15.27 It is prohibited to attack the 'personnel, installations, material, units or vehicles involved in a humanitarian assistance or peacekeeping mission in accordance with the Charter of the United Nations, so long as they are entitled to the protection given to civilians or civilian objects under the international law of armed conflict'.[51]

15.27.1 The protection and delivery of relief supplies will usually be dealt with in agreements between the state concerned and the relief agencies in question.

15.27.2 Whenever the military situation permits, the delivery and distribution of humanitarian aid to people in need must be permitted. Starvation as a method of warfare is prohibited.[52]

---

[49] HR, Art 25.   [50] See para 5.39 onwards.   [51] Rome Statute, Art 8(2)(e)(iii).
[52] See para 15.19.

Weapons[53]

It is prohibited to use: **15.28**

a. weapons of a nature to cause unnecessary suffering or superfluous injury;[54]
b. bacteriological weapons;[55]
c. chemical weapons, including riot control agents, as a method of warfare;[56]
d. poison or poisoned weapons;[57]
e. anti-personnel land mines.[58]

The wounded, sick, and dead, medical and religious personnel

It is prohibited to attack: **15.29**

a. the wounded, sick, and shipwrecked, who are to be collected and cared for;[59]
b. medical and religious personnel;[60]
c. medical buildings, including hospitals and places where the wounded and sick are cared for, medical material, medical units, and transport.[61]

The wounded, sick, and shipwrecked must be protected against pillage and **15.29.1** ill-treatment, treated humanely, and given the medical treatment they need without discrimination for non-medical reasons. The dead must not be despoiled or ill-treated and must be decently disposed of. Medical units, personnel, and transports must be protected from attack and are entitled to display the protective emblem of the red cross or red crescent on a white background.

Treatment of persons in the hands of a party to the conflict

Humane treatment

Persons in the hands of a party to the conflict, whether the government side, **15.30** dissident armed forces, or other armed groups, are entitled to humane treatment at all times. They must not be discriminated against on grounds of race, colour, religion or faith, sex, birth, or wealth, or similar criteria. The

---

[53] For more information about the law relating to weapons, see Ch 6.   [54] AP II, Art 35(2).
[55] Biological Weapons Convention 1972.
[56] Chemical Weapons Convention 1993, Art 1.   [57] HR, Art 23(a).
[58] Ottawa Convention 1997, Art 1. See also Amended Mines Protocol, Arts 1(2), (3).
[59] GC I–IV, Art 3.   [60] Rome Statute, Art 8(2)(e)(ii).
[61] Rome Statute, Art 8(2)(e)(ii), (iv).

following acts are always prohibited with respect to these persons:

a. violence to life and person, in particular murder of all kinds, mutilation, cruel treatment, and torture;

b. taking of hostages;

c. 'rape, sexual slavery, enforced prostitution, forced pregnancy,[62] forced sterilization, and any other form of sexual violence also constituting a serious violation of' Common Article 3;[63]

d. other outrages upon personal dignity, in particular humiliating and degrading treatment;

e. 'physical mutilation or . . . medical or scientific experiments of a kind which are neither justified by medical, dental or hospital treatment of the person concerned nor carried out in his or her interest, and which causes death to or seriously endangers the health of' that person;[64]

f. the passing of sentences and the carrying out of executions without previous judgment pronounced by a regularly constituted court, affording all the judicial guarantees which are recognized as indispensable by civilized peoples.[65]

15.30.1 The treatment of civilians outside the combat zone is principally governed by the domestic law of the country concerned, any human rights treaties binding on that state, and the basic humanitarian principles set out in paragraph 15.30.

15.30.2 Members of the opposing armed forces or groups who are captured are to be treated humanely and given the treatment set out in paragraph 15.30. They are still subject to domestic law and may be tried for offences such as treason or murder that they have committed but may not be punished except after conviction in a fair trial.[66]

15.30.3 Prisoner of war status does not arise in internal armed conflicts unless the parties to the conflict agree, or decide unilaterally as a matter of policy, to accord this status to detainees. Otherwise, the treatment of detainees is governed by the domestic law of the country concerned, any human rights treaties binding on that state in time of armed conflict and the basic humanitarian principles mentioned in paragraph 15.30. It is recommended that while detained in military custody, persons who have taken a direct part in hostilities should be given the same treatment as if they were prisoners of war.

---

[62] ' "Forced pregnancy" means the unlawful confinement of a woman forcibly made pregnant, with the intention of affecting the ethnic composition of any population or carrying out other grave violations of international law': Rome Statute, Art 7(2)(f).
[63] Rome Statute, Art 8(2)(e)(vi).   [64] Rome Statute, Art 8(2)(e)(xi).
[65] GC I–IV, Art 3.   [66] See para 15.30(d).

Outrages on personal dignity include acts such as rape, indecent assault, **15.30.4**
enforced pregnancy or sterilization, enforced prostitution, and slavery.
Hostage taking and any form of summary punishment are prohibited. It
is prohibited to order that there should be no survivors or to order that
prisoners will not be taken.

Indispensable judicial guarantees include as a minimum:[67]   **15.30.5**

a. individual criminal responsibility (so that collective punishments would
   be unlawful);

b. the right of the accused not to be compelled to testify against himself;

c. the presumption of innocence until proved guilty;

d. notification to the accused of the charges against him;

e. adequate time and opportunity for the accused to prepare his defence;

f. the attendance of both prosecution and defence witnesses and, if necessary, an interpreter;

g. trial in person and public judgment.

Death penalties must not be pronounced or carried out.[68]   **15.30.6**

Enforcement of the law of armed conflict in internal armed conflicts

Assistance of the ICRC

See paragraph 15.4.2.   **15.31**

War crimes

Although the treaties governing internal armed conflicts contain no grave **15.32**
breach provisions, customary law recognizes that serious violations of those
treaties can amount to punishable war crimes.[69]

It is now recognized that there is a growing area of conduct that is criminal in **15.32.1**
both international and internal armed conflict. This is reflected in Article 8 of
the Rome Statute.

'Customary international law imposes criminal liability for serious viola- **15.32.2**
tions of Common Article 3, as supplemented by other general principles
and rules on the protection of victims of internal armed conflict, and for

---

[67] International Covenant on Civil and Political Rights, Art 14. See also the European
Convention on Human Rights, Art 6.

[68] Although death penalties are envisaged under international law (but *not* on persons under
18, nor on pregnant women or nursing mothers, because of the right to life of the embryo or
child). Under UK law, death penalties have been abolished, even for military related offences.

[69] Rome Statute, Art 8, see para 16.29.

breaching certain fundamental principles and rules regarding means and methods of combat in civil strife.'[70]

Denunciation

15.33 The provisions of Common Article 3 apply at all times and cannot be denounced. The same applies to the basic principles of the law of armed conflict.

C. ADDITIONAL RULES IN PROTOCOL II

APPLICABILITY

15.34 Additional Protocol II applies to all armed conflicts which meet the threshold outlined in paragraph 15.1.b but fall outside Additional Protocol I. When it applies, it supplements the rules in Part B.

15.34.1 Additional Protocol II extends the provisions of Common Article 3 by spelling out the rules in greater detail. It also contains more specific provisions about its scope of application. The criteria laid down in paragraph 15.1.b exclude guerrilla or partisan activities where the dissidents are unable to establish control over any particular place or area. These activities, if amounting to armed conflict, would be covered by Common Article 3 and the basic principles set out in Part B above. Protocol II does not replace Common Article 3; it develops and supplements it in those conflicts where it is applicable. However, just as Common Article 3 specifically provides that its applicability does not affect the legal status of the parties, so Protocol II expressly states that nothing within it 'shall be invoked for the purpose of affecting the sovereignty of a State or the responsibility of the government, by all legitimate means, to maintain or re-establish law and order in the State or to defend the national unity and territorial integrity of the State'.[71] Similarly, nothing in the Protocol can be invoked 'as a justification for intervening, directly or indirectly, for any reason whatever, in the armed conflict or in the internal or external affairs of the High Contracting Party in the territory of which that conflict occurs'.[72]

---

[70] *Prosecutor v Tadić (Jurisdiction)* (1995) 105 ILR 453, 523.

[71] AP II, Art 3(1): 'legitimate' must be interpreted as legitimate under international law. A state could not rely on domestic legislation at variance with the provisions of the Protocol.

[72] AP II, Art 3(2). In the absence of any other justification in international law, this would appear to preclude assistance to either party. However, it only binds states, not organizations, and it would therefore not be an infringement of this provision for the UN to intervene where permissible under the terms of its Charter or for states to intervene under the authority of the UN Security Council, by invitation of the government in question, or on humanitarian grounds. Indeed, recognition of a breakaway state and admittance as a member of the UN, as happened with Bangladesh in 1971, would otherwise clearly be a breach of the Protocol's provisions.

CONTENTS

The Protocol itself is split into four main parts: scope,[73] humane treatment,[74] **15.35**
wounded, sick, and shipwrecked,[75] and civilian population.[76] It concludes
with formal provisions on ratification and like matters. There are no provisions on enforcement, which remains a matter for domestic law, for the
International Criminal Court, or for international tribunals when they have
jurisdiction.[77]

SCOPE

The 'material field of application', namely the type of conflict to which the **15.36**
Protocol is applicable, has already been addressed.[78] In addition, there is a
'personal field of application' in that the Protocol applies 'without any
adverse distinction founded on race, colour, sex, language, religion or
belief, political or other opinion, national or social origin, wealth, birth or
other status, or on any other similar criteria' to all persons affected by an
armed conflict to which the Protocol applies.[79]

HUMANE TREATMENT

General protection

'All persons who do not take a direct part or who have ceased to take part **15.37**
in hostilities, whether or not their liberty has been restricted, are entitled to
respect for their person, honour and convictions and religious practices.
They shall in all circumstances be treated humanely, without any adverse
distinction. It is prohibited to order that there shall be no survivors.'[80]

Prohibited acts

The following acts against protected persons[81] 'are and shall remain pro- **15.38**
hibited at any time and in any place whatsoever'.[82] These are:

a. violence to the life, health, and physical or mental well-being of persons,
   in particular murder as well as cruel treatment such as torture, mutilation, or any form of corporal punishment;

b. collective punishments;

c. taking of hostages;

---

[73] AP II, Arts 1–3.   [74] AP II, Arts 4–6.   [75] AP II, Arts 7–12.
[76] AP II, Arts 13–18.
[77] The tribunal for Rwanda was specifically given jurisdiction over violations of AP II, see
ICTR Statute, Art 4.   [78] AP II, Art 1. See para 15.34.
[79] AP II, Art 2(1).   [80] AP II, Art 4(1).   [81] See para 15.37.   [82] AP II, Art 4(2).

d. acts of terrorism;[83]

e. outrages upon personal dignity, in particular humiliating and degrading treatment, rape, enforced prostitution, and any form of indecent assault;

f. slavery and the slave trade in all their forms;

g. pillage;

h. threats to commit any of the foregoing acts.

Protection of children

15.39   In general, 'children shall be provided with the care and aid they require' but the Protocol also lays down particular requirements.[84] These include an education which makes provision for their religious and moral care, steps to facilitate family reunions, and a ban on their recruitment or participation in the hostilities while under the age of 15. However, if children under that age do take part in hostilities, they continue to benefit from the general protections provided in the Protocol, including the special protection of them as children.[85] If necessary, measures should be taken, where possible with the consent of their parents or guardians, 'to remove children temporarily from the area in which hostilities are taking place to a safer area within the country and ensure that they are accompanied by persons responsible for their safety and well-being'.[86]

15.39.1   Particular attention is given to the position of children because they are likely to be at special risk in internal conflicts.

Protection of detainees and internees

15.40   Internees or detainees continue to benefit from the basic fundamental guarantees outlined in paragraphs 15.37 and 15.38 and, if wounded and sick, in paragraph 15.43. However, in addition and again as a minimum, they are entitled:[87]

a. to food and drinking water, health and hygiene safeguards, protection against the rigours of the climate and the dangers of the armed conflict to the same extent as the civilian population;

---

[83] The term 'terrorism' is undefined and is used here in a non-technical sense. See also AP II, Art 13(2).   [84] AP II, Art 4(3).

[85] Together with any other protection to which they may be entitled, for example, as PW.

[86] AP II, Art 4(3)(e). This would not permit the removal of children out of their home country.

[87] AP II, Art 5(1). Internees and detainees are *not* PW. The provisions on treatment if wounded or sick, and on relief and religion, apply to anyone whose liberty has been restricted in any way whatsoever for reasons relating to the armed conflict, see Art 5(3), even if not interned or detained, eg, those under house arrest or in an assigned residence.

b. to receive individual or collective relief;

c. to practise their religion and, if requested and appropriate, to receive spiritual assistance from chaplains or similar persons;

d. if made to work, to have the benefit of working conditions and safe-guards similar to those enjoyed by the local civilian population.

This protection applies, even after the end of the conflict 'until the end of such deprivation or restriction of liberty'.[88]   **15.40.1**

Internal armed conflicts, since they are principally governed by domestic law, will inevitably lead to an increase in detentions and other restrictions being imposed by that law for security reasons related to the conflict. The Protocol therefore protects those whose liberty has been restricted, whether detained, interned, or subjected to any control on their freedom.   **15.40.2**

Further protection of detainees and internees

Those responsible for the internment or detention are also placed under an obligation 'within the limits of their capabilities' to 'respect' some further provisions relating to persons interned or detained for reasons relating to the armed conflict.[89] These are: **15.41**

a. that except when men and women of a family are accommodated together, women shall be held in quarters separated from those of men and shall be under the immediate supervision of women;

b. that all persons whose liberty has been restricted in any way whatsoever for reasons related to the armed conflict shall be allowed to send and receive letters and cards, the number of which may be limited by the competent authority if it deems necessary;

c. that places of internment and detention shall not be located close to the combat zone; protected internees and detainees shall be evacuated when the places where they are interned or detained become particularly exposed to danger arising out of the armed conflict, if their evacuation can be carried out under adequate conditions of safety;

d. the benefit of medical examinations;

e. that the physical or mental health and integrity of protected internees and detainees shall not be endangered by any unjustified act or omission. Accordingly it is prohibited to subject them, or indeed anyone whose liberty has been restricted in any way whatsoever for reasons related to the armed conflict, to any medical procedure which is not indicated by the state of health of the person concerned and which is not

---

[88] AP II, Art 2(2).   [89] AP II, Art 5(2).

consistent with the generally accepted medical standards applied to free persons under similar medical circumstances.

In addition, if it is decided to release persons deprived of their liberty, necessary measures to ensure their safety shall be taken by those so deciding.[90]

Requirement of fair trials

15.42 The general principle is that 'no sentence shall be passed and no penalty shall be executed on a person found guilty of an offence except pursuant to a conviction pronounced by a court offering the essential guarantees of independence and impartiality'.[91] There follows a list of particular requirements:[92]

a. the procedure shall provide for an accused to be informed without delay of the particulars of the offence alleged against him and shall afford the accused before and during his trial all necessary rights and means of defence;

b. no one shall be convicted of an offence except on the basis of individual penal responsibility;[93]

c. no one shall be held guilty of any criminal offence on account of any act or omission which did not constitute a criminal offence, under the law[94] at the time when it was committed; nor shall a heavier penalty be imposed than that which was applicable at the time when the criminal offence was committed; if after the commission of the offence, provision is made by law for the imposition of a lighter penalty, the offender shall benefit thereby;

d. anyone charged with an offence is presumed innocent until proved guilty according to law;

e. anyone charged with an offence shall have the right to be tried in his presence;

f. no one shall be compelled to testify against himself or to confess guilt.

After the trial, 'a convicted person shall be advised on conviction of his judicial and other remedies and of the time limits within which they may be

---

[90] AP II, Art 5(4). For example, there may be a need to protect them from attacks by the civil population.

[91] AP II, Art 6(2). This replaced the wording to be found in Common Article 3, which referred to a 'regularly constituted court'. It has been argued that no court established by an insurgent authority could be 'regularly constituted' and so wider wording based on GC III, Art 84 was adopted.   [92] The list is not exhaustive.

[93] This reiterates, in different language, the provision in AP II, Art 4(2)(b).

[94] The French text '*le droit national ou international*' has been abbreviated in the English text, though the use of the bare word 'law' must be taken to include both national and international law. It could also be wide enough to cover 'laws' passed by an insurgent authority.

exercised'.[95] Regardless of the offence committed, the death penalty is not to be imposed by UK courts.[96] At the end of hostilities, the authorities in power, whoever they might be, 'shall endeavour to grant the broadest possible amnesty to persons who have participated in the armed conflict, or those deprived of their liberty for reasons related to the armed conflict, whether they are interned or detained'.[97]

This protection applies, even after the end of the conflict 'until the end of such deprivation or restriction of liberty'.[98] **15.42.1**

The Protocol thus lays down minimum standards in relation to the prosecution and punishment of criminal offences related to the armed conflict. The right of the established authorities to prosecute, try, and convict persons charged with such offences is left intact but the necessity for some form of minimal judicial guarantee is evident in that situations involving non-international armed conflict also often bring with them the suspension of constitutional guarantees, the promulgation of special laws, and the creation of special jurisdictions. **15.42.2**

WOUNDED, SICK, AND SHIPWRECKED

Treatment

All wounded, sick, and shipwrecked persons, 'whether or not they have taken part in the armed conflict shall be respected and protected.[99] In all circumstances, they shall be treated humanely and shall receive, to the fullest extent practicable and with the least possible delay, the medical care and attention required by their condition'. The only permitted distinction in their care and treatment is that made on medical grounds.[100] **15.43**

The basic provision in Common Article 3 that 'the wounded and sick shall be collected and cared for' has been expanded in Additional Protocol II. It attempts to 'make explicit what was implicit . . . in Article 3 . . . by formulating a number of derivative rules specifying the protection to be given to medical personnel, unit and installations, the standard of care and so **15.43.1**

---

[95] AP II, Art 6(3).

[96] AP II provides that the death penalty is not to be pronounced on persons who were under the age of 18 years at the time of the offence and shall not be carried out on pregnant women or mothers of young children: AP II, Art 6(4). The term 'young children' is left undefined although some guidance may be obtained from GC IV, Art 14, which refers to children under seven. However, UK personnel are bound by the prohibition on death penalties under UK law.

[97] AP II, Art 6(5). The wording here is vague. It is understood to relate to offences under domestic law but not to those guilty of crimes under international law. Amnesties have taken place in both Zimbabwe and South Africa at the end of an extended period of internal conflict.

[98] AP II, Art 2(2).   [99] AP II, Art 7(1).   [100] AP II, Art 7(2).

forth'.[101] No definitions are included but, as the provisions re-iterate the essential substance of Part II of Additional Protocol I, the definitions contained there[102] can be used as a guide even though they have no binding force.

Search

15.44 'Whenever circumstances permit, and particularly after an engagement, all possible measures shall be taken without delay to search for and collect the wounded, sick, and shipwrecked, to protect them against pillage and ill-treatment, to ensure their adequate care, and to search for the dead, prevent their being despoiled and decently dispose of them.'[103]

Medical and religious personnel

15.45 Medical and religious personnel must be 'respected and protected and shall be granted all available help for the performance of their duties. They shall not be compelled to carry out tasks which are not compatible with their humanitarian mission'.[104] In particular, in the performance of their duties, medical personnel may not be required to give priority to anyone other than on medical grounds.[105]

General protection of medical duties

15.46 'Under no circumstances shall any person be punished for having carried out medical activities compatible with medical ethics, regardless of the person benefiting therefrom.'[106] This general principle is expanded in three areas.

    a. Persons engaged in medical activities shall neither be compelled to perform acts or to carry out work contrary to, nor be compelled to refrain from acts required by, the rules of medical ethics or other rules designed for the benefit of the wounded and sick, or the Protocol.[107]

    b. The professional obligations of persons engaged in medical activities regarding information which they may acquire concerning the wounded and sick under their care shall, subject to national law, be respected.[108]

---

[101] See the Official Records of the Diplomatic Conference on the Reaffirmation and Development of International Humanitarian Law applicable in Armed Conflicts, Geneva, 1974–1977, vol XI, 209.   [102] See AP I, Art 8.

[103] AP II, Art 8. See paras 7.4–7.5 and 7.33 for similar though more detailed provisions in international armed conflict.

[104] AP II, Art 9(1). Such tasks could include medical experiments.

[105] AP II, Art 9(2). This is a re-iteration of the principle outlined in Art 7(2), see para 15.43.

[106] AP II, Art 10(1).   [107] AP II, Art 10(2).

[108] AP II, Art 10(3). The reservation referring to 'national law' substantially weakens the effect of this and the following provision. However, the final text was a compromise to avoid a perceived violation of the principle of non-interference with the internal affairs of states, as affirmed in Art 3.

c. Subject to national law, no person engaged in medical activities may be penalized in any way for refusing or failing to give information concerning the wounded and sick who are, or have been, under his care.[109]

The position of those engaged in medical activities in non-international **15.46.1** armed conflict has always been delicate, particularly on the sensitive issue of the release of information. The drafters of the Protocol negotiated the above compromise to guarantee the principle of the 'neutrality' of medical activities.

Medical units and transports

Medical units and transports 'shall be respected and protected at all times **15.47** and shall not be the object of attack'.[110] However, this protection may cease if 'they are used to commit hostile acts, outside their humanitarian function'.[111] Even then, the protection will only cease 'after a warning has been given setting, whenever appropriate, a reasonable time limit, and after such warning has remained unheeded'.

Distinctive emblems[112]

Subject to the directions of the competent authority,[113] the distinctive **15.48** emblem of the red cross, red crescent, or red lion and sun on a white background[114] 'shall[115] be displayed by medical and religious personnel and medical units, and on medical transports. It shall be respected in all circumstances. It shall not be used improperly'.

CIVILIAN POPULATION

General protection from hostilities

The special rules[116] for the protection of civilians from hostilities are: **15.49**

a. 'The civilian population and individual civilians shall enjoy general protection against the dangers arising from military operations'.[117]

---

[109] AP II, Art 10(4).   [110] AP II, Art 11(1).

[111] AP II, Art 11(2). This mirrors the provisions of AP I, Art 13(1) in relation to international armed conflict. Again the examples in AP I, Art 13(2) of acts which shall not be considered as 'harmful to the enemy', the phraseology used in AP I, may provide guidance in the interpretation of this provision.   [112] AP II, Art 12.

[113] In the case of insurgents, this will be the *de facto* authority.

[114] The red lion and sun emblem is not in current use, see para 7.23.

[115] Although in the English text, the word 'shall' implies a mandatory requirement, the French text, by using the future tense rather than the imperative, makes clear that this is a right rather than a requirement.   [116] That is, in addition to those set out in Pt B above.

[117] AP II, Art 13(1). See also AP I, Art 51(1).

b. 'The civilian population as such, as well as individual civilians, shall not be the object of attack. Acts or threats of violence the primary purpose of which is to spread terror among the civilian population are prohibited'.[118]

c. 'Civilians shall enjoy the protection afforded by [the Protocol] unless and for such time as they take a direct part in hostilities'.[119]

15.49.1 These general principles are expanded by a number of rules which 'shall be observed in all circumstances',[120] and are set out in the following paragraphs.

15.49.2 The need to extend the basic protection offered to the civilian population by Common Article 3 in non-international armed conflict has been recognized by the General Assembly of the United Nations.[121] However, the nature of such conflicts made very difficult the drafting of provisions that would not be seen as an unwarranted intrusion into national sovereignty. The result has been a simplified version of the provisions contained in Additional Protocol I for international armed conflicts.[122] Indeed the general principles are a miniature replica of those contained in Protocol I. However, the provisions of Additional Protocol II have to some extent been overtaken by the now higher standards of customary law, as set out in Part B above.

Prohibition of starvation

15.50 Starvation of civilians as a method of combat is prohibited. Similarly, it is prohibited 'to attack, destroy, remove or render useless, for that purpose, objects indispensable to the survival of the civilian population, such as foodstuffs, agricultural areas for the production of foodstuffs, crops, livestock, drinking water installations and supplies and irrigation works'.[123]

Protection of dams, dykes, and nuclear power stations

15.51 It is forbidden to attack dams, dykes, and nuclear electrical generating stations 'even where these objects are military objectives, if such attack may cause the release of dangerous forces and consequent severe losses among the civilian population'.[124]

---

[118] AP II, Art 13(2). See also AP I, Art 51(2) and paras 5.3 and 5.21.
[119] AP II, Art 13(3). See also AP I, Art 51(3) and para 5.3.2.   [120] AP II, Art 13(1).
[121] See UNGAR 2675(XXV) of 9 December 1970, reaffirming UNGAR 2444(XXIII) of 19 December 1968.   [122] See AP I, Arts 48–56.
[123] AP II, Art 14. See also AP I, Art 54(1), (2) and para 5.28. This provision does not affect the law on naval blockade, see para 13.91 onwards. It would, however, prevent government forces from adopting a 'scorched earth' policy as a method of pressure against civilians supporting insurgents.
[124] AP II, Art 15. See AP I, Art 56(1) and para 5.30. The exemptions in AP I, Art 56(2) and the other detailed provisions of that article, though relevant, are not repeated here.

This would not, however, prevent an attack on a nuclear, chemical, or bac- **15.51.1**
teriological research centre, even though such an attack might release dangerous forces, provided that the attack was not made illegal by some other
provision of the Protocol.

Protection of cultural property

It is prohibited 'to commit any acts of hostility directed against historic monu- **15.52**
ments, works of art or places of worship which constitute the cultural or spiritual heritage of peoples and to use them in support of the military effort'.[125]

Prohibition of displacement

It is forbidden to displace the civilian population for reasons related to the **15.53**
conflict unless their security or 'imperative military reasons so demand'. If
they do have to be displaced, 'all possible measures' must be taken to provide
satisfactory conditions of shelter, hygiene, health, safety, and nutrition.[126]
In no circumstances may civilians be compelled to leave their own territory
for reasons connected with the conflict.[127]

See, further, paragraph 15.14.2. **15.53.1**

Relief actions

Relief societies such as red cross or red crescent societies and similar organ- **15.54**
izations, located in the territory where the conflict is taking place, may offer
their services for the benefit of the victims of the conflict. Indeed, the civilian population itself may, on its own initiative, offer 'to collect and care
for the wounded, sick, and shipwrecked'.[128] If a lack of essential supplies
causes undue hardship to the civilian population, other exclusively
humanitarian and impartial action for their relief may be mounted with the
consent of the state concerned.[129]

---

[125] AP II, Art 16. See AP I, Art 53 and para 5.26. The intentional targeting of mosques and
other cultural objects in the war in former Yugoslavia is a clear breach of these provisions.

[126] AP II, Art 17. Similar provisions do not appear in AP I, though they can be found in
GC IV, Art 49. The practice in the Malayan insurgency of collecting civilians into 'protected
villages' would now require justification under the terms of this article.

[127] This forbids 'ethnic cleansing' as seen in the conflicts during the breakup of the Yugoslav
Federation. The word 'territory' is sufficiently wide to cover areas controlled by different factions.

[128] AP II, Art 18(1). This paragraph makes it clear that the primary responsibility for relief
during non-international armed conflict rests on the authorities within the state itself. This again
complies with the principle of non-intervention. Indeed, the article only allows organizations,
and the civilian population, to 'offer' relief. The final decision remains with the relevant authorities.

[129] AP II, Art 18(2). International intervention by humanitarian organizations is seen as a
last resort and again is subject to the consent of the state concerned. However, the withholding
of consent could in itself be a breach of AP II, Art 14.

15.55 High Contracting Parties may denounce the Protocol but any denunciation will not take effect for six months. If, on the expiry of that six months, that party is involved in a conflict to which the Protocol applies, the denunciation will not take effect until the end of that armed conflict.[130]

D. SUPPLEMENTARY AGREEMENTS

15.56 Because there are relatively few legal rules relating to internal armed conflicts, the parties to the conflict are encouraged to enter into special agreements to supplement those basic rules.[131] In some cases this has been done in the past,[132] most recently in the armed conflict in Bosnia in 1992–95.[133] Military personnel need to be aware of the contents of those special agreements and apply them in addition to the rules in this Manual.

---

[130] AP II, Art 25(1). Persons deprived of liberty or whose liberty has been restricted for reasons related to the conflict continue to benefit from the provisions of the Protocol until their final release.   [131] GC I–IV, Art 3.

[132] In an ad hoc agreement, the belligerent groups in the Nigerian civil conflict 1967–70 undertook to apply GC I–IV.

[133] For example, the Agreement of 22 May 1995 between the parties to the Bosnian conflict, set out in M Sassoli and A A Bouvier, *How Does Law Protect in War* (1999) 1112.

16

Enforcement of the Law of Armed Conflict

A. INTRODUCTION

MEANS OF ENFORCEMENT

16.1 Enforcement of the law of armed conflict can involve a wide variety of measures. 'Enforcement' is taken here to mean action to ensure observance of the law and also action that may be taken following alleged or actual violations. Action aimed at effective enforcement of the law can include, but is not limited to the following:

a. Disseminating knowledge of the law within the armed forces, training and equipping forces in accordance with legal requirements, and establishing an effective system for taking legal considerations into account in military planning and decision-making.

b. Media publicity about alleged violations. This can have a powerful effect and often leads to the taking of other action.

c. High-level formal inquiries into alleged violations. These inquires may be conducted by commissions established by individual states, by international commissions established by the United Nations Security Council or other bodies, or by the International Fact-Finding Commission,[1] which has been established for the purpose. The reports of such inquiries often propose specific legal action to deal with violations or to prevent their recurrence.

d. International legal adjudication of disputes between states concerning the meaning and implementation of the law, for example by the International Court of Justice.

e. Monitoring of the conduct of parties to an agreement, for example by aerial surveillance by a third party, or by an international presence on the ground, to verify, among other things, that violations of the law do not take place.[2]

f. Good offices and mediation, for example, by neutral states and intermediaries, including protecting powers and independent humanitarian bodies, with a view to ensuring that belligerents comply with the law of armed conflict.

g. Administrative controls over the careers of individuals.[3]

---

[1] The Commission, set up under Additional Protocol I 1977, Art 90, is now known as the International Humanitarian Fact-Finding Commission.

[2] For example, the Belgrade Accords of 15–16 October 1998 for the NATO Air Verification Mission over Kosovo. These accords were mentioned in UN Security Council Resolution (UNSCR) 1203/98.

[3] For example, the decision of the Argentinean government, announced on 27 January 1998, to strip Alfredo Astiz of his rank of retired captain, his uniform, and his naval pension. As an

h. Penal and disciplinary measures, such as trials before civil courts or courts-martial or appropriate disciplinary action by commanding officers. Trials may be either within a single state or organized on an international basis.[4]

i. Measures, which may include economic sanctions, arms embargoes, and various types of military action, taken under the authority of international bodies, including the UN Security Council, against offending states or armed groups.

j. Demands for compensation in respect of violations.[5]

k. Reprisals by an aggrieved state.[6]

This chapter concentrates on the formal provisions about enforcement in the relevant treaties and on the enforcement mechanisms of greatest relevance to decision-making by members of the armed forces. However, these need to be seen against the background of the wide variety of enforcement measures indicated above. **16.1.1**

Complaints of unlawful acts and omissions alleged to have been committed by individuals or by commanders are an almost inevitable feature of warfare. All sides will be striving to win the battle for public and world opinion and no state can afford to ignore this. Hostile opinion can lead to loss of political goodwill and public support and damage morale amongst the forces concerned. Failure by belligerent governments to investigate and, where appropriate, punish the alleged unlawful acts of members of their armed forces can contribute to the loss of public and world support, leading to isolation for the state involved. **16.1.2**

In earlier times, hostages were often taken, given, or exchanged to ensure observance of treaties, armistices, and other agreements. The taking of hostages, whether civilian or military, is now prohibited.[7] **16.1.3**

On a practical basis, the compliance with the law by one party can, in itself, be a strong inducement to the adverse party to comply with the law. If one party treats prisoners properly and conducts its operations within legal constraints, the adverse party will have less incentive to breach the law and **16.1.4**

---

officer, he had been involved in the so-called 'dirty war' in the 1970s and had continued to defend the horrors of that period.

   [4] eg, the establishment of the international tribunals in relation to the Former Yugoslavia and Rwanda, and the Rome Statute of the International Criminal Court 1998 ('Rome Statute') with jurisdiction over war crimes, genocide, and crimes against humanity.

   [5] See Hague Convention IV 1907 (HC IV), Art 3 and para 16.15.

   [6] See paras 16.16–16.19.

   [7] See Common Art 3 to Geneva Conventions I–IV 1949 (GC); GC IV, Art 34; Additional Protocol I 1977 (AP I), Art 75(2)(c).

indeed could be severely disadvantaged, not least through world opinion, by so doing.[8]

B. KNOWLEDGE, DISSEMINATION, LEGAL ADVISERS

Orders and Instructions

16.2 States are under a general obligation to issue orders and instructions requiring compliance with the law of armed conflict and to take steps to see that those orders and instructions are observed.[9] There is a specific provision in relation to the handling of the wounded, sick, and shipwrecked, extending to a requirement to provide for unforeseen situations 'in conformity with the general principles' of the Geneva Conventions 1949. These are that the wounded, sick, and shipwrecked should be cared for and treated without any adverse distinction.[10]

16.2.1 Whilst ignorance of the law is not generally accepted as a defence, the first step to enforcement of the law of armed conflict must be to ensure as wide a knowledge of its terms as possible both within the armed forces and outside.

Dissemination

16.3 States are also required to disseminate the texts of the Geneva Conventions 1949 and the two Additional Protocols 1977 as widely as possible in peace and war so that the general population can learn about them.[11]

16.3.1 The manner in which dissemination is done is left to the states themselves and may be by means of orders, courses of instructions, commentaries, or manuals.[12] There is a specific requirement to instruct medical personnel, chaplains, and those responsible for handling prisoners of war and the administration of protected persons. There is a general requirement to disseminate to the armed forces as a whole. Any military or civilian authorities with responsibility for applying the Conventions or Protocol must be fully acquainted with the text.[13]

---

[8] eg, the international condemnation of the actions of Iraq, in the Gulf conflict 1990–91, for taking hostages, launching indiscriminate attacks by SCUD missiles, and failing to allow ICRC access to prisoners of war (PW).   [9] HC IV, Art 1; AP I, Art 80.

[10] GC I, Art 45; GC II, Art 46.

[11] GC I, Art 47; GC II, Art 48; GC III, Art 127; GC IV, Art 144; AP I, Art 83; AP II, Art 19.

[12] In the UK, apart from courses, and manuals such as this, the texts of the Conventions are annexed to the Geneva Conventions Act 1957 (GCA 1957). The texts of AP I and II were added by the Geneva Conventions (Amendment) Act 1995 (GC(A)A 1995).   [13] AP I, Art 83(2).

Additional Protocol I also requires states to endeavour, with the assistance **16.4**
of their national red cross or red crescent societies, to train qualified persons
'to facilitate the application of the Conventions and of this Protocol, and in
particular the activities of the Protecting Powers'.[14] The parties are encouraged to send lists of such qualified persons to the International Committee
of the Red Cross (ICRC).[15]

LEGAL ADVISERS

Legal advisers are required to be available, when necessary, to advise milit- **16.5**
ary commanders at the appropriate level on the application of the law of
armed conflict and also on the appropriate instruction to be given to members of the armed forces in this subject.[16]

C. COMPLAINTS, MEDIATION, FACT-FINDING

COMPLAINTS

In view of the lack of diplomatic relations between states involved in an **16.6**
armed conflict, complaints cannot normally be made through the usual
diplomatic channels. However, other methods are available, depending
on the degree of publicity required. The traditional method of complain-
ing under the protection of a flag of truce[17] remains, although modern
communications have meant that the message is more likely now to be
transmitted by radio or television. Complaints may be made also through
neutral states, whether or not the complainant also seeks their good offices
to mediate with a view to making the adverse party observe the law of
armed conflict.[18]

MEDIATION

Good offices and mediation by neutral states for the purpose of settling **16.7**
differences are friendly acts, in contradistinction to intervention, which is

[14] AP I, Art 6(1). For the role of the protecting power, see paras 16.11–16.12.
[15] AP I, Art 6(3).
[16] AP I, Art 82. In the UK, this is mainly achieved through the service legal branches. The
'appropriate level' will depend on the circumstances but in the Army, it will normally be at
divisional level. In an air campaign, there will normally be a legal adviser on the staff of the
theatre air commander.   [17] See para 10.5.
[18] Although complaints lodged with neutral states, good offices, and mediation are
diplomatic means, they are of sufficient interest to require brief mention here.

dictatorial interference for the purpose of making the belligerents comply with the laws of armed conflict.[19] Specific provision is also made in the Geneva Conventions for conciliation by the protecting powers.[20]

Role of the UN

16.8   The UN, and in particular the Security Council, has taken a wide range of measures regarding the enforcement of the law of armed conflict. These measures have included investigation of violations, urging parties to observe the law, authorizing military action to prevent or respond to violations, the establishment of criminal tribunals.

16.8.1 During the Cold War, with frequent uses of the veto by the two super-powers, the Security Council was not active in taking such measures, the power was rarely used, and the principal role of the UN was in acting through the 'good offices' of the Secretary-General. Successive Secretaries-General intervened and mediated with varying degrees of success and whilst their primary role was conflict resolution, efforts were also made in 'humanitarian' missions such as those to secure the release of Western hostages in the Lebanon during the Lebanese civil conflict. The Security Council itself has raised the issue of violations of 'international humanitarian law' in numerous conflicts, including the Iran–Iraq conflict 1980–88, the Gulf conflict 1990–91,[21] the conflicts in former Yugoslavia 1991–99,[22] and the events in Rwanda in 1994.[23] Such violations led to the Security Council taking coercive action under Chapter VII of the UN Charter as well as using the consent provisions of Chapter VI.

International Co-operation

16.9   Ensuring respect for the law of armed conflict is a universal responsibility.[24] International co-operation is encouraged by Additional Protocol I, which provides for:

a. meetings to consider general problems concerning the application of the Geneva Conventions and Additional Protocol I;[25]

---

[19] See L Oppenheim, *International Law* (7th edn by H Lauterpacht 1952) vol II, 559.

[20] GC I, II, and III, Art 11; GC IV, Art 12. See also para 16.12.

[21] See UNSCR 666(1990), 670(1990), and 674(1990).

[22] See UNSCR 764(1992), 771(1992), 780(1992), and, in particular, 827(1993) establishing an international tribunal for the prosecution of war crimes.

[23] See UNSCR 935(1994) and in particular 955(1995) establishing a further international tribunal for the prosecution of war crimes.   [24] Common Art 1 of GC I–IV.

[25] AP I, Art 7.

b. exchange of official translations of the Protocol as well as any implementing domestic legislation[26] with similar provisions applying in relation to the Conventions;[27]

c. mutual assistance in criminal proceedings brought in respect of grave breaches of the Conventions or Protocol,[28] including assistance with evidence and extradition;

d. co-operation, jointly or individually, with the UN in situations of serious violations of the Conventions or Protocol.[29]

FACT-FINDING

Additional Protocol I also provides for the establishment of a permanent **16.10** International Fact-Finding Commission.[30] This, now known as the International Humanitarian Fact-Finding Commission, came into existence in 1991 after 20 states party to the Protocol had agreed to accept its competence. It is competent to enquire into an allegation that a grave breach or other serious violation of the Conventions or Protocol has occurred but only in regard to the conduct of a party that has accepted its competence whether permanently or ad hoc. With the consent of the parties concerned, the Commission can also enquire into other violations of the laws of armed conflict and, in all cases, can offer its good offices to assist in helping to restore respect for the Conventions and Protocol.

There are detailed rules as to the composition and administration of the **16.10.1** Commission.

It often said that the truth is the first victim of war. Propaganda and counter- **16.10.2** propaganda often result in a distortion of facts and statistics. Allegations of war crimes and atrocities are often found, on investigation, to be untrue or exaggerated. An independent fact-finding mission or inquiry can play an important part in establishing the facts, so that appropriate steps to rectify the situation can be taken by an international body.[31] The UN Security Council has been particularly active in this area and has established ad hoc commissions of experts to conduct inquiries. These UN commissions have issued reports on violations, for example, during the Iran–Iraq conflict in 1984–88, in the conflicts in the former Yugoslavia, in 1993–94, and in

---

[26] AP I, Art 84.	[27] GC I, Art 48; GC II, Art 49; GC III, Art 128; GC IV, Art 145.

[28] AP I, Art 88.	[29] AP I, Art 89.

[30] AP I, Art 90. The UK accepted the competence of the commission on 17 May 1999.

[31] Although the International Fact-Finding Commission has not yet been called into action, a similar body, called a Commission of Experts, was established by UNSCR 780(1992) adopted on 6 October 1992 to investigate violations of international humanitarian law in the territory of the former Yugoslavia.

Rwanda in 1994. In addition, the international criminal tribunals established by the UN for the former Yugoslavia and Rwanda have been heavily involved in fact-finding.

D. INDEPENDENT SUPERVISION

THE PROTECTING POWER

Appointment

16.11 The parties to a conflict are under a duty at the beginning of the conflict or any occupation to appoint a protecting power. If this is not done, or the appointment is not accepted by the adverse party, all parties must accept mediation from the ICRC and, if that fails, accept the ICRC as a substitute.[32] Once protecting powers have been appointed, the parties must permit them to fulfil their role.[33] This includes facilitating to the greatest extent possible the activities of the representatives of the protecting power, only restricting those activities exceptionally and temporarily for reasons of imperative military necessity.[34]

16.11.1 Although the concept of a protecting power had long been familiar in international law for the protection of a state's nationals abroad, it was only applied in the law of armed conflict after the First World War when the Geneva Prisoners of War Convention 1929 was drafted. Initially, the protecting power had the right to visit prisoner of war centres, contact the prisoners, and offer good offices to the belligerent parties on the application of the Convention. The role developed during the Second World War, where the world-wide nature of the conflict led at one stage to one country, Switzerland, acting simultaneously for as many as 35 states, including opposing parties, and thereby assuming a function more akin to that of an umpire.[35] Although the powers and functions of the protecting power have been expanded in the Geneva Conventions 1949 and again in Additional Protocol I, formal use of the system since 1945 has for the most part been restricted to 'textbook' conflicts such as the Falklands conflict 1982.[36] As the protecting power must be acceptable to both sides,[37] failure to agree on or appoint a protecting power has led to an increasing use of the ICRC as a substitute body, exercising the same role and function.[38]

---

[32] AP I, Art 5.   [33] GC I, II, and III, Art 10; GC IV, Art 11; AP I, Art 5.

[34] GC III, Art 126; GC IV, Art 143.

[35] See J Pictet, *Commentary on the Geneva Conventions of 12 August 1949* (Pictet, *Commentary*) vol III (1960) 95–96.

[36] Switzerland acted for the UK and Brazil for Argentina. No appointments were made in the Gulf conflict 1990–91, possibly because this conflict was of short duration.

[37] See AP I, Art 5(2).   [38] AP I, Art 5(4).

Duties of the protecting power

The specific duties of protecting powers are laid down in various articles **16.12**
of the Geneva Conventions 1949 and Additional Protocol I. These are dealt
with in detail in the relevant chapters of this Manual. However, their
general responsibilities may be summarized as follows:

a. to safeguard the interests of the parties, applying the Conventions and
   Protocol with the co-operation of the parties and under the scrutiny of
   the other protecting powers;[39]

b. to lend their good offices with a view to settling disagreements between
   the parties to the conflict;[40] and

c. to visit prisoners of war and civilian internees, including the conducting
   of interviews personally or through an interpreter. It is for the protecting
   power to select the places for these visits. These may be prohibited only
   exceptionally and temporarily for reasons of imperative military necessity. If mutually agreed and necessary, compatriots of those interned
   may be permitted to participate in these visits.[41]

INTERNATIONAL COMMITTEE OF THE RED CROSS

The ICRC has, since its establishment, had an important humanitarian role **16.13**
in armed conflict.[42] It is responsible for operating the Central Tracing
Agency; maintaining records of prisoners of war, inspecting their camps,
and providing relief; providing humanitarian assistance to the civilian
population of countries in conflict;[43] and it also works behind the scenes to
settle disputes and help states comply with the law of armed conflict.[44] The
parties to a conflict are under an obligation to give the ICRC all possible
facilities to enable it to carry out its humanitarian functions. As far as possible, similar facilities should also be granted to national red cross and red
crescent societies.[45]

The role of the ICRC has taken on an increasing importance in the light of the **16.13.1**
failure of states to appoint protecting powers. The ICRC has developed a
wider role working for 'fundamental human rights' in areas on the peri-
phery of armed conflict. Humanitarian assistance to refugees and displaced
persons, visits to detainees held under emergency laws in situations falling
short of armed conflict, and disaster relief, are amongst these activities.

---

[39] GC I, II, and III, Art 8; GC IV, Art 9.   [40] GC I, II, and III, Art 11; GC IV, Art 12.
[41] GC III, Art 126; GC IV, Art 143.
[42] GC I, II, and III, Arts 9 and 11; GC IV, Arts 10 and 12; AP I, Art. 5.
[43] GC III, Arts 123, 125, and 126; GC IV, Arts 140, 142, and 143.
[44] GC I–III, Art 11; GC IV, Art 12.   [45] AP I, Art 81.

This has led to the ICRC being linked with, and compared to, other agencies, both inter-governmental and non-governmental. However, in international armed conflict, the ICRC fulfils a unique role that requires total impartiality. This can lead to misunderstandings and ill-informed criticism.

INQUIRIES

16.14 There are provisions[46] for inquiries into alleged violations of the Conventions to be initiated at the request of a party to the conflict. However, since this procedure depends upon mutual agreement between the parties as to method, procedures, and choice of an 'umpire', it is unlikely to be of great practical significance. The provisions have never been invoked.[47]

E. COMPENSATION

16.15 It is a principle of international law that a state responsible for an internationally wrongful act is obliged to make full reparation for the injury caused by that act.[48] This principle extends to the law of armed conflict in that a state is responsible for violations of the law committed by persons forming part of its armed forces and, if the case demands, is liable to pay compensation.[49]

F. REPRISALS

NATURE OF REPRISALS

16.16 Reprisals are extreme measures to enforce compliance with the law of armed conflict by the adverse party. They can involve acts which would normally be illegal, resorted to after the adverse party has itself carried out illegal acts and refused to desist when called upon to do so. They are not retaliatory acts or simple acts of vengeance. Reprisals are, however, an extreme measure of coercion, because in most cases they inflict suffering upon innocent individuals.

---

[46] GC I, Art 52; GC II, Art 53; GC III, Art 132; GC IV, Art 149.

[47] To some extent they have been superseded by those relating to the International Fact-Finding Commission under AP I, Art 90; see para 16.10; see also para 16.11.

[48] See Art 31 of the draft articles on Responsibility of States for Internationally Wrongful Acts, adopted by the International Law Commission in 2001.

[49] HC IV, Art 3. This provision is repeated in AP I, Art 91. After the Gulf conflict 1990–91, a UN Compensation Commission was set up under UNSCR 687(1991) and 692(1991) to deal with the processing and payment of claims against Iraq 'as a result of its unlawful invasion and occupation of Kuwait'. Its establishment, however, was based on violations of the *jus in bello* as well as the *jus ad bellum*.

Nevertheless, in the circumstances of armed conflict, reprisals, or the threat of reprisals, may sometimes provide the only practical means of inducing the adverse party to desist from its unlawful conduct.

CONDITIONS FOR REPRISAL ACTION

In order to qualify as a legitimate reprisal, an act must comply with the **16.17** following conditions when employed:

a. It must be in response to serious and manifestly unlawful acts, committed by an adverse government, its military commanders, or combatants for whom the adversary is responsible.[50]

b. It must be for the purpose of compelling the adversary to observe the law of armed conflict. Reprisals serve as an ultimate legal sanction or law enforcement mechanism. Thus, if one party to an armed conflict breaches the law but then expresses regret, declares that it will not be repeated, and takes measures to punish those immediately responsible, then any action taken by another party in response to the original unlawful act cannot be justified as a reprisal.

c. Reasonable notice must be given that reprisals will be taken. What degree of notice is required will depend upon the particular circumstances of the case.

d. The victim of a violation must first exhaust other reasonable means of securing compliance before reprisals can be justified.

e. A reprisal must be directed against the personnel or property of an adversary.

f. A reprisal must be in proportion to the original violation. Whilst a reprisal need not conform in kind to the act complained of, it may not significantly exceed the adverse party's violation either in degree or effect. Effective but disproportionate acts cannot be justified as reprisals on the basis that only an excessive response will forestall further violations.

g. It must be publicized. Since reprisals are undertaken to induce an adversary's compliance with the laws of armed conflict, any action taken as a reprisal must be announced as such and publicized so that the adversary is aware of the reason for the otherwise unlawful act and of its own obligation to abide by the law.[51]

h. As reprisals entail state responsibility, they must only be authorized at the highest level of government.[52]

---

[50] See the findings of the Italian Military Tribunal in the *Ardeatine Cave Massacre Case (Trial of Kappler)* (1948) AD 471, 473.   [51] See the *Bruns Trial* (1948) 3 WCR 21–22.
[52] See also para 16.19.2.

    i. Reprisal action may not be taken or continued after the enemy has ceased to commit the conduct complained of.

UNLAWFUL REPRISALS

16.18 Reprisals are never lawful if directed against any of the following:

    a. the wounded, sick, and shipwrecked, medical personnel and chaplains, medical units, establishments and transports;[53]

    b. prisoners of war;[54]

    c. protected persons and their property.[55]

16.19 Additional Protocol I extends the categories of persons and objects against whom reprisals are prohibited to:

    a. civilians and the civilian population;[56]

    b. civilian objects;[57]

    c. historic monuments, works of art or places of worship which constitute the cultural or spiritual heritage of peoples;[58]

    d. objects indispensable to the survival of the civilian population such as foodstuffs, crops, livestock, drinking water installations and supplies, and irrigation works;[59]

    e. the natural environment;[60]

    f. works or installations containing dangerous forces, namely dams, dykes, and nuclear electrical generating stations.[61]

16.19.1 However, on ratification of Additional Protocol I, the United Kingdom made the following statement:

The obligations of Articles 51 to 55 are accepted on the basis that any adverse party against which the United Kingdom might be engaged will itself scrupulously

---

[53] GC I, Art 14; GC II, Art 16; GC III, Art 13; AP I, Art 20.   [54] GC III, Art 13.

[55] GC IV, Art 33. For a definition of 'protected person' in this context, see para 9.17.

[56] AP I, Art 51(6).   [57] AP I, Art 52(1).

[58] AP I, Art 53(c). See also a similar provision, though with a different definition of 'cultural property', in the Cultural Property Convention 1954 (CPC), Art 4(4). The UK has not yet ratified this Convention.   [59] AP I, Art 54(4).

[60] AP I, Art 55(2).

[61] AP I, Art 56. The UK made a separate statement on ratification in respect of this article, in the following terms: 'The United Kingdom cannot undertake to grant absolute protection to installations which may contribute to the opposing Party's war effort, or to the defenders of such installations, but will take all due precautions in military operations at or near the installations referred to in paragraph 1 of Article 56 in the light of the known facts, including any special marking which the installation may carry, to avoid severe collateral losses among the civilian populations; direct attacks on such installations will be launched only on authorisation at a high level of command'. See also para 5.30.

observe those obligations. If an adverse party makes serious and deliberate attacks, in violation of Article 51 or Article 52 against the civilian population or civilians or against civilian objects, or, in violation of Articles 53, 54 and 55, on objects or items protected by those Articles, the United Kingdom will regard itself as entitled to take measures otherwise prohibited by the Articles in question to the extent that it considers such measures necessary for the sole purpose of compelling the adverse party to cease committing violations under those Articles, but only after formal warning to the adverse party requiring cessation of the violations has been disregarded and then only after a decision taken at the highest level of government. Any measures thus taken by the United Kingdom will not be disproportionate to the violations giving rise thereto and will not involve any action prohibited by the Geneva Conventions of 1949 nor will such measures be continued after the violations have ceased. The United Kingdom will notify the Protecting Powers of any such formal warning given to an adverse party, and if that warning has been disregarded, of any measures taken as a result.

This means that reprisals taken in accordance with the statement are per- **16.19.2** missible by and against the United Kingdom.[62] However, commanders and commanders-in-chief are not to take reprisal action on their own initiative. Requests for authority to take reprisal action must be submitted to the Ministry of Defence and require clearance at Cabinet level.[63]

G. WAR CRIMES ·

INTRODUCTION

The principle of individual responsibility for violations of the law of armed **16.20** conflict goes back to early civilization. However, although the Lieber Code during the American Civil War specifically imposed individual responsibility,[64] the Hague Conventions 1907 were silent on the point. This did not prevent the Allied powers, at the end of the First World War, seeking the trial 'before military tribunals [of] persons accused of having committed acts in violation of the laws and customs of war' in the Treaty of Versailles.[65] Indeed Kaiser Wilhelm II of Germany was himself 'arraigned' in the same treaty.[66]

---

[62] Although the Yugoslav Tribunal has stated that attacks on civilians by way of reprisal can never be justified (*Prosecutor v Kupreskić*, ICTY Case No IT-95-16 of 14 January 2000 at part V of para 20), the court's reasoning is unconvincing and the assertion that there is a prohibition in customary law flies in the face of most of the state practice that exists. The UK does not accept the position as stated in this judgment.

[63] Statement, set out in para 16.19.1, by UK on ratification of AP I.

[64] See Art 71. Wirz, the commandant of a Confederate prisoner of war camp, was put on trial and sentenced to death for a series of atrocities committed against Unionist prisoners in his charge.

[65] Art 228, XIII (1919) AJIL 251. No such persons were handed over although Germany herself held a few trials including the *Llandovery Castle Case* (1921) AD Case No 235.

[66] Art 227.

16.21 Following the Second World War, the London Charter[67] established the Nuremberg Tribunal to try war crimes, crimes against humanity, and crimes against peace. War crimes were defined as:

> violations of the laws or customs of war. Such violations shall include, but not be limited to, murder, ill-treatment or deportation to slave labour or for any other purpose of civilian population of or in occupied territory, murder or ill-treatment of prisoners of war or persons on the seas, killing of hostages, plunder of public or private property, wanton destruction of cities, towns or villages, or devastation not justified by military necessity.[68]

16.22 Although there is some overlap with war crimes, crimes against humanity and crimes against peace are not covered in this Manual.

GRAVE BREACHES AND WAR CRIMES

16.23 The Geneva Conventions 1949 introduced a new concept, that of 'grave breaches'. These are war crimes of such seriousness as to invoke universal jurisdiction.[69] Universal jurisdiction entitles any state to exercise jurisdiction over any perpetrator, regardless of his nationality or the place where the offence was committed. In the case of grave breaches, states are obliged to introduce legislation to this effect. See also paragraph 16.30. Additional Protocol I extended the definition of grave breaches.[70] Other serious offences against 'the laws and customs of war' whether proscribed by treaty or by customary law, remain war crimes and are punishable as such, see paragraph 16.26.

GRAVE BREACHES

16.24 Grave breaches under the Geneva Conventions consist of any of the following acts against persons or property protected under the provisions of the relevant Convention:

a. wilful killing;

b. torture or inhuman treatment, including biological experiments;

c. wilfully causing great suffering or serious injury to body or health;

d. extensive destruction and appropriation of property, not justified by military necessity and carried out unlawfully and wantonly;[71]

e. compelling a prisoner of war or other protected person to serve in the forces of a hostile power;

---

[67] HMSO, Cmd 6668.   [68] Art 6(b).
[69] GC I, Art 49; GC II, Art 50; GC III, Art 129; GC IV, Art 146.   [70] AP I, Art 85.
[71] GC I, Art 50; GC II, Art 51; GC III, Art 130; GC IV, Art 147.

f. wilfully depriving a prisoner of war or other protected person of the rights of fair and regular trial;[72]

g. unlawful deportation or transfer or unlawful confinement;

h. taking hostages.[73]

Additional Protocol I extends[74] the definition of grave breaches to include **16.25** the following:

a. any wilful act or omission which seriously endangers the physical or mental health or integrity of any person who is in the power of a party other than the one on which he depends and involves:[75]

(1) subjecting that person to any medical procedure which is not indicated by the state of health of the person concerned and which is not consistent with generally accepted medical standards which would be applied under similar medical circumstances to persons who are nationals of the party conducting the procedure and who are in no way deprived of liberty;[76]

(2) carrying out on such persons, even with their consent, physical mutilations, medical or scientific experiments, or removal of tissue or organs for transplantation, except where these acts are justified in conformity with the conditions provided for in (1) above,[77] or, in the case only of donations of blood for transfusion or of skin for grafting, that they are given voluntarily and without any coercion or inducement, and then only for therapeutic purposes, under conditions consistent with generally accepted medical standards and controls designed for the benefit of both the donor and the recipient.[78]

b. any of the following acts, when committed wilfully, in violation of the relevant provisions of the Protocol, and causing death or serious injury to body or health:[79]

(1) making the civilian population or individual civilians the object of attack;[80]

(2) launching an indiscriminate attack[81] affecting the civilian population or civilian objects in the knowledge that such attack will cause excessive loss of life, injury to civilians, or damage to civilian objects;[82]

---

[72] GC III, Art 130; GC IV, Art 147.   [73] GC IV, Art 147.

[74] Whilst there is, in some cases, considerable overlap between these provisions and those in the Conventions, the protection given is generally broader in scope.

[75] AP I, Art 11(4).   [76] AP I, Art 11(1).   [77] AP I, Art 11(2).   [78] AP I, Art 11(3).

[79] AP I, Art 85(3).

[80] See AP I, Art 51(2). This does not, of course, exclude the possibility of collateral or incidental damage to civilians arising out of an attack directed against a legitimate military objective.

[81] As defined in Art 51(4).   [82] As defined in Art 57(2)(a)(iii).

(3) launching an attack against works or installations containing dangerous forces[83] in the knowledge that such attack will cause excessive loss of life, injury to civilians, or damage to civilian objects;

(4) making non-defended localities[84] and demilitarized zones[85] the object of attack;

(5) making a person the object of attack in the knowledge that he is *hors de combat*;[86]

(6) the perfidious use[87] of the distinctive emblem of the red cross, red crescent or of other protective signs recognized by the Conventions or the Protocol;[88]

c. the following, when committed wilfully and in violation of the Conventions or the Protocol:[89]

(1) the transfer by the occupying power[90] of part of its own civilian population into the territory it occupies, or the deportation or transfer of all or parts of the population of the occupied territory within or outside this territory;[91]

(2) unjustifiable delay in the repatriation of prisoners of war[92] or civilians;[93]

(3) practices of *apartheid* and other inhuman and degrading practices involving outrages upon personal dignity, based on racial discrimination;[94]

(4) making the clearly recognized historic monuments, works of art, or places of worship which constitute the cultural or spiritual heritage of peoples and to which special protection has been given by special arrangement,[95] the object of attack, causing as a result extensive destruction thereof, where there is no evidence that the adverse party is using such objects in support of the military effort[96] and when such historic monuments, works of art, and places of worship are not located in the immediate proximity of military objectives;[97]

(5) depriving a protected person of the rights of fair and regular trial.[98]

---

[83] See Art 56(1). See also UK statement at n 61. [84] As defined in Art 59.
[85] As defined in Art 60.
[86] As defined in Art 41. This has always been a war crime under customary law.
[87] In violation of Art 37. [88] See paras 5.9 and 5.10. [89] AP I, Art 85(4).
[90] See para 11.55.
[91] In violation of GC IV, Art 49. Such transfers are permitted on a temporary basis if the security of the civilian population or imperative military reasons require this.
[92] See also GC III, Art 118. [93] See also GC IV, Art 132.
[94] See also GC I and II, Art 12; GC III, Art 16; GC IV, Arts 13 and 27; AP I, Arts 9 and 75.
[95] For example, by direct agreement between the belligerents or within the framework of a competent international organization. See CPC and the role of UNESCO within that Convention.
[96] See AP I, Art 53(b). [97] As defined in Art 52(2). [98] See Art 75(3)–(6).

WAR CRIMES

Serious violations of the law of armed conflict, other than those listed as **16.26** grave breaches in the Conventions or Protocol, remain war crimes and punishable as such. A distinction must be drawn between crimes established by treaty or convention and crimes under customary international law. Treaty crimes only bind parties to the treaty in question, whereas customary international law is binding on all states. Many treaty crimes are merely codifications of customary law[99] and to that extent binding on all states, even those that are not parties.

War crimes may be committed by nationals both of belligerent and of **16.26.1** neutral states. A state may elect to deal with its own nationals under the appropriate municipal law for acts that amount to war crimes. Members of the British armed forces can be dealt with under the relevant sections of the Service Discipline Acts for offences such as murder or manslaughter.

The Hague Regulations

The Hague Regulations 1907 are now recognized as part of customary **16.27** law.[100] Those regulations provide that the following acts are 'especially forbidden':[101]

a. to employ poison or poisoned weapons;[102]

b. to kill or wound treacherously individuals belonging to the hostile nation or army;[103]

c. to kill or wound an enemy who, having laid down his arms, or having no longer means of defence,[104] has surrendered at discretion;[105]

d. to declare that no quarter will be given;[106]

e. to employ arms, projectiles, or material calculated to cause[107] unnecessary suffering;[108]

---

[99] See AP I, Art 41.

[100] See the Judgment of the Nuremberg Tribunal (IMT), part 22, 467.

[101] Many of these acts are now grave breaches under the Conventions or AP I. However, as customary law, they bind all, even those who are not parties to the Conventions or the Protocol.

[102] This would include the poisoning of wells, streams, and other sources of water supply.

[103] See also AP I, Art 37.

[104] This would include airmen, who have abandoned their aircraft in distress, whilst descending by parachute, see AP I, Art 42(1).

[105] This is also a grave breach under AP I, Art 85(3)(e).

[106] See also AP I, Art 40. This is not, however, a grave breach.

[107] AP I, Art 35(2), renders this as 'of a nature to cause'.

[108] This has been expanded by AP I, Art 35(2) to include 'weapons, projectiles and material and methods of warfare of a nature to cause superfluous injury or unnecessary suffering'.

   f. to make improper use of a flag of truce,[109] of the national flag or of the military insignia and uniform of the enemy,[110] as well as the distinctive emblems of the Geneva Convention;[111]

   g. to destroy or seize the enemy's property,[112] unless such destruction or seizure be imperatively demanded by the necessities of war;

   h. to declare abolished, suspended, or inadmissible in a court of law the rights and actions of the nationals of the hostile party;[113]

   i. to compel the nationals of the hostile party to take part in the operations of war directed against their own country, even if they were in the belligerent's service before the commencement of the war.[114]

16.28 In addition, the Hague Regulations forbid pillage[115] and the punishment of spies without proper trials.[116] They also provide that a violation of the terms of an armistice by an individual acting on his own initiative[117] entitles the injured party to demand the punishment of the offender.[118] If the party injured captures the offender, it may try him for a war crime.[119]

Customary law

16.29 Among other war crimes traditionally recognized by the customary law of armed conflict are:

   a. mutilation or other maltreatment of dead bodies;[120]

   b. looting;[121]

In view of the somewhat subjective nature of this test, state practice has been to negotiate specific treaties to ban weapons systems that might be held in breach, see, eg, the Conventional Weapons Convention 1980 (CCW). However, the principle remains important in relation to modifications of legitimate weapons systems, see para 6.1 onwards. UK forces are entitled to presume that they will not be issued with weapons which, used as instructed, contravene this provision.

   [109] See also AP I, Art 37(1)(a). This is not a grave breach.   [110] See also AP I, Art 39.

   [111] See also AP I, Art 85(3)(f) by which perfidious use of the emblems is made a grave breach.

   [112] AP I, Art 85(3)(b) makes an indiscriminate attack affecting civilian objects, knowing that such attack will cause excessive damage to such objects, a grave breach. There is no reference in either the Conventions or the Protocol to enemy property as such.

   [113] See GC IV, Arts 47, 54, and 64.

   [114] It is a grave breach to compel a PW or a protected person to serve in the forces of a hostile power, see GC III, Art 130; GC IV, Art 147. See also GC IV, Art 51.

   [115] Hague Regulations 1907 (HR), Arts 28 and 47.

   [116] HR, Art 30. See also AP I, Arts 46 and 75.

   [117] This is to distinguish the case from action taken on the orders of a party to the armistice. Any serious violation of an armistice by a party to it entitles the injured party to denounce the armistice, see HR, Art 40.   [118] HR, Art 41.

   [119] See *Scuttled U-Boats Case (Trial of Grumpelt)* (1945) 1 WCR 55.

   [120] See also AP I, Art 34(1). The taking of body parts, eg ears, as proof of a body count is clearly forbidden.   [121] Also an offence under military law, see Army Act (AA) 1955, s 30.

c. use of a privileged building for improper purposes;[122]
d. attacking a privileged or protected building;
e. attacking a properly marked hospital ship or medical aircraft;
f. firing on shipwrecked personnel;[123]
g. using bacteriological methods of warfare.[124]

The Rome Statute of the International Criminal Court contains a longer list **16.29.1** of war crimes[125] including offences committed in international and non-international armed conflict, see paragraph 16.33. Though it is not necessarily an exclusive list,[126] it is indicative of current international thinking in this area.

JURISDICTION

Mode of trial

International law permits any state to try those accused of war crimes, what- **16.30** ever their nationality and wherever the offence was committed. However, the exercise of jurisdiction will depend on whether the particular crime or the particular offender can be tried according to the domestic law of the state concerned. In the case of grave breaches, states have an obligation to enact legislation to provide effective penal sanctions for persons committing or ordering the commission of any of the acts or omissions concerned.[127] It is a fundamental principle of law that no person may be tried for a war crime unless the act in question was an offence at the time of its commission.[128]

Members of otherwise properly regulated armed forces who contravene the **16.30.1** law of armed conflict are also likely to be in breach of their own service disciplinary codes for which they may be tried by court-martial, if that is appropriate, in accordance with those codes.[129] Alternatively, they may be tried under their own domestic civil law. Prisoners of war charged with war crimes must be tried by the same courts, applying the same procedures, as would be

---

[122] Hospitals, churches, schools, and other civilian installations, as well as cultural objects, lose their protection if used, for example, as a sniper's post, though the rule of proportionality requires steps to be taken to minimize incidental damage to such objects if the sniper post is attacked.

[123] See *The Peleus Trial (the Case of Eck)* (1946) 1 WCR 1.

[124] See also the Biological Weapons Convention 1972, which the UK has ratified.

[125] Rome Statute of the International Criminal Court 1998 ('Rome Statute'), Art 8. See also para 16.33.   [126] Rome Statute, Art 10.

[127] GC I, Art 49; GC II, Art 50; GC III, Art 129; GC IV, Art 146; AP I, Art 85(1). If the party concerned does not institute proceedings against offenders, it may, subject to the provisions of its own law, hand such persons over for trial by any party to the Conventions, which has made out a *prima facie* case.   [128] This includes offences under international law.

[129] As in the case of Lt William Calley, arising from the My Lai massacre in Vietnam, and tried by a US military court-martial.

applicable to members of the armed forces of the detaining power.[130] Civilians so charged may be tried either by the ordinary courts of the state concerned or in courts set up by an occupying power.[131] Persons accused of war crimes are entitled to a proper trial and have rights of defence.[132]

16.30.2 The civil courts of the United Kingdom can try persons of any nationality who are accused of committing any grave breach of the Geneva Conventions[133] or of Additional Protocol I. Prisoners of war who have committed grave breaches whether before or after capture can be tried by court-martial.[134] Furthermore, the Royal Warrant of 14 June 1945 provides for the trial by military tribunal of any person who commits a violation of the 'laws and usages of war . . . during any war in which [Her] Majesty has been or may be engaged at any time since the 2nd September 1939'.[135] This extends not only to members of the enemy armed forces, but also to enemy civilians and others of any nationality, including British, as well as civilians and members of the armed forces of allied or neutral states. For such trials, the victims do not have to be British subjects.[136] Members of the British armed forces who commit war crimes would normally be tried under the appropriate provisions of their own service disciplinary code. A member of the British armed forces, or a person who is subject to service discipline, can be tried by court-martial for an offence under the Geneva Conventions Act 1957, except for offences committed in the United Kingdom.[137]

16.30.3 In addition, the International Criminal Court Act 2001 gives jurisdiction to the civil courts of England, Wales, and Northern Ireland to try any United Kingdom national or resident, or any person subject to service jurisdiction, for any offence listed in the Rome Statute of the International Criminal Court, wherever committed.[138] In respect of persons subject to service jurisdiction, service courts will also have jurisdiction over such offences except when they are committed within the United Kingdom.[139]

[130] GC III, Art 82; see also para 8.114.
[131] GC IV, Arts 64–75 and 146. See also paras 11.59–11.60.
[132] GC I, Art 49; GC II, Art 50; GC III, Art 129; GC IV, Art 146; AP I, Art 75(7).
[133] GCA 1957, s 1, as amended by the GC(A)A 1995.
[134] See the Prisoners of War (Discipline) Regulations 1958.
[135] In theory, there was no requirement for the War Crimes Act 1991 as trials could have taken place under the Royal Warrant. However, it was not considered appropriate to bring such cases before military tribunals nearly 50 years after the crimes had allegedly been committed.
[136] Thus in the *Zyklon B Case (In Re Tesch and others)* (1946) 1 WCR 93, tried before a British military court in Hamburg, the accused, who were German civilians, were found guilty of supplying poison gas for use in extermination chambers, the victims being Polish, Belgian, Dutch, French, and Czech nationals.
[137] GCA 1957, s 1A (inserted by International Criminal Court Act (ICCA) 2001, s 70(2)).
[138] ICCA 2001, ss 51, 58. Scotland has its own legislation, see International Criminal Court (Scotland) Act (ICC(S)A) 2001.
[139] ICCA 2001, s 74, amending the existing provisions of the Service Discipline Acts.

Extradition

Persons accused of grave breaches may be extradited to another state if that accords with the law of the place where they happen to be and also if the state demanding extradition makes out a *prima facie* case.[140] This applies to neutral states as well as belligerents. **16.31**

In the United Kingdom, extradition is governed by the Extradition Act 1989. This requires that a court must, subject to an exception in relation to certain countries where there are special provisions,[141] be satisfied that the evidence would be sufficient to warrant the accused's trial if the extradition crime had taken place within the jurisdiction of the court.[142] Extradition generally depends on the existence of an extradition treaty between the states involved, whether bilateral or multilateral. Special rules apply in relation to international tribunals.[143] **16.31.1**

International tribunals

War crimes may also be tried by international tribunals.[144] **16.32**

The Nuremberg International Military Tribunal[145] was established by agreement between the USA, UK, France, and the USSR to try the major war criminals of the Second World War. It followed the abortive attempts to bring war criminals to justice after the First World War. The International Military Tribunal supplemented the military tribunals and national tribunals established by the authorities of the Allied states.[146] A further international military tribunal was established in Tokyo.[147] **16.32.1**

---

[140] GC I, Art 49; GC II, Art 50; GC III, Art 129; GC IV, Art 146; AP I, Art 85(1). AP I, Art 88 requires parties to assist one another in connection with grave breaches including co-operation in matters of extradition.   [141] See Extradition Act 1989, s 4.

[142] Extradition Act 1989, s 9.

[143] eg, in respect of the International Tribunal for former Yugoslavia, see SI 1996/716, Art 6.

[144] The earliest example is the trial of Peter Hagenbach at Breisach on 4 May 1474 for crimes he had committed whilst installed as governor by Duke Charles of Burgundy. The trial was ordered by the Archduke of Austria in whose territory Hagenbach was captured and the bench before which he was tried consisted of judges from Austria and the allied cities as well as 16 knights representing the order of knighthood.   [145] See also para 16.21.

[146] The USA and UK, in particular, established military courts in their zones of occupied Germany and Italy. In Belgium, France, Holland, Norway, Czechoslovakia, Poland, Yugoslavia, and some other countries, national tribunals pronounced sentence upon war criminals surrendered by virtue of arrangements made by the United Nations War Crimes Commission, an important inter-Allied body set up by a diplomatic conference in October 1943.

[147] By a proclamation issued on 19 January 1946, by the Supreme Commander for the Allied Powers in the Pacific. In 1948, the Supreme Court of the USA decided that the tribunal was not a tribunal of the USA, having been set up by General MacArthur acting as an agent of the Allied powers. For that reason, the Supreme Court held that it had no power to review or set aside judgments of the Tribunal, see *Hirota and others v Douglas MacArthur* (1948) AD Case No 154, 485.

16.32.2 The principles of international law recognized in the Nuremberg Charter and judgment were unanimously affirmed by the UN General Assembly in 1946.[148] In 1948, the General Assembly requested the International Law Commission to study the desirability and feasibility of an international criminal court.[149] This work led to a draft statute for such a court,[150] but the project foundered at the time owing to the absence of an internationally accepted definition of the crime of 'aggression' and the onset of the Cold War.

16.32.3 The end of the Cold War and the serious offences in former Yugoslavia and subsequently Rwanda again raised the public profile of the war crimes issue. In response to the atrocities committed in former Yugoslavia, the Security Council, acting under Chapter VII of the UN Charter, established an International Tribunal for the Prosecution of Persons Responsible for Serious Violations of International Humanitarian Law Committed in the Territory of the Former Yugoslavia since 1991.[151] The Report of the Secretary-General on which the establishment was based stated 'In the view of the Secretary-General, the application of the principle *nullum crimen sine lege* requires that the international tribunal should apply rules of international humanitarian law which are beyond any doubt part of customary law so that the problem of adherence of some but not all states to specific conventions does not arise. This would appear to be particularly important in the context of an international tribunal prosecuting persons responsible for serious violations of international humanitarian law'.[152] Its statute gave the court jurisdiction over, among other things, grave breaches of the 1949 Geneva Conventions, genocide, and 'violations of the laws or customs of war' defined as including 'but not . . . limited to':

a. employment of poisonous weapons or other weapons calculated to cause unnecessary suffering;

b. wanton destruction of cities, towns, or villages, or devastation not justified by military necessity;

c. attack or bombardment, by whatever means, of undefended towns, villages, dwellings, or buildings;

d. seizure of, destruction of, or wilful damage done to institutions dedicated to religion, charity and education, the arts and sciences, historic monuments, and works of art and science;

e. plunder of public or private property.[153]

---

[148] UN General Assembly Resolution (UNGAR) 95(1).   [149] UNGAR 260B(III).

[150] UN General Assembly, 9th Session 1953–1954, *Official Records*, Supplement No 12 (A/2645).   [151] UNSCR 827(1993), 32 ILM 1203.

[152] Para 34 of Report of the Secretary-General pursuant to para 2 of UNSCR 808(1993), 32 ILM 1159.

[153] Statute of the International Criminal Tribunal for the former Yugoslavia (ICTY Statute), Art 3. The non-exhaustive nature of the wording has enabled the court to introduce other parts

The Yugoslav Tribunal was followed by the establishment of a similar **16.32.4** tribunal for Rwanda.[154] This Tribunal covered new ground since it was established in relation to an exclusively internal armed conflict and was given jurisdiction under its Statute over serious violations of Common Article 3 of the Geneva Conventions and of Additional Protocol II.[155] This was the first time that the international community had made express provision for individual criminal responsibility for breaches of international law in internal armed conflict. The traditional view which had prevailed until then was that internal armed conflict was a matter for domestic law enforcement and that Common Article 3 and Additional Protocol II did not create individual criminal responsibility in themselves.

International Criminal Court

At the same time as the Tribunals for former Yugoslavia and Rwanda **16.33** were established, fresh attempts were made to resurrect the idea of an International Criminal Court. The International Law Commission produced a draft statute[156] and a diplomatic conference resulted in the Rome Statute, which provides for the establishment of such a court.[157]

The statute came into force on 1 July 2002. The United Kingdom ratified the **16.33.1** statute on 4 October 2001 following adoption of the necessary legislation.[158]

The court will have jurisdiction only where states having jurisdiction them- **16.33.2** selves are 'unwilling or unable genuinely' to exercise that jurisdiction.[159] It is thus complementary to national jurisdictions and does not have primacy over them as in the case of the Yugoslav and Rwanda Tribunals.[160] Indeed, under the Statute, a state may exclude war crimes committed by its nationals or on its territory for a period of seven years after the entry into force of the Statute for that state.[161]

When operative, the court will have jurisdiction over genocide, war crimes, **16.33.3** and crimes against humanity as defined in the Statute. It will also have jurisdiction over the crime of aggression, although this cannot be exercised until a definition has been agreed and adopted by a formal review conference.[162]

---

of the law of armed conflict including AP I, to which all the states of former Yugoslavia had become parties by 1993. See *Prosecutor v Tadić (Jurisdiction)* (1997) 105 ILR 419.

[154] See UNSCR 955(1994), 33 ILM 1598.

[155] Statute of the International Criminal Tribunal for Rwanda 1994 (ICTR Statute), Art 4.

[156] See (1996) 33 ILM 253.   [157] See (1996) 37 ILM 999.

[158] The International Criminal Court Act 2001 and the International Criminal Court (Scotland) Act 2001.

[159] See Rome Statute, Art 17. The words 'unwilling or unable' are closely defined.

[160] See ICTY Statute, Art 9(2); ICTR Statute, Art 8(2).

[161] See Rome Statute, Art 124. The UK, on ratification, did not claim the 7-year opt-out for war crimes provided for in Art 124 of the Statute.   [162] See Rome Statue, Art 5.

International Criminal Court's jurisdiction over war crimes

16.34 After detailing grave breaches of the Geneva Conventions, Article 8 of the Rome Statute lists other war crimes that are within the jurisdiction of the court as follows.

International armed conflict

(b) Other serious violations of the laws and customs applicable in international armed conflict, within the established framework of international law,[163] namely, any of the following acts:

   (i) Intentionally directing attacks against the civilian population as such or against individual civilians not taking a direct part in hostilities;

  (ii) Intentionally directing attacks against civilian objects, that is, objects which are not military objectives;

 (iii) Intentionally directing attacks against personnel, installations, material, units or vehicles involved in a humanitarian assistance or peacekeeping mission in accordance with the Charter of the United Nations, as long as they are entitled to the protection given to civilians or civilian objects under the international law of armed conflict;

 (iv) Intentionally launching an attack in the knowledge that such attack will cause incidental loss of life or injury to civilians or damage to civilian objects or widespread, long-term and severe damage to the natural environment which would be clearly excessive in relation to the concrete and direct overall military advantage anticipated;

  (v) Attacking or bombarding, by whatever means, towns villages, dwellings or buildings which are undefended and which are not military objectives;

 (vi) Killing or wounding a combatant who, having laid down his arms or having no longer means of defence, has surrendered at discretion;

(vii) Making improper use of the flag of truce, of the flag or of the military insignia and uniform of the enemy or of the United Nations, as well as of the distinctive emblems of the Geneva Conventions, resulting in death or serious personal injury;

(viii) The transfer, directly or indirectly, by the Occupying Power of parts of its own civilian population into the territory it occupies, or the deportation or transfer of all or parts of the population of the occupied territory within or outside this territory;

---

[163] On ratification of the Rome Statute, the UK made the following declaration: 'The United Kingdon understands the term "the established framework of international law", used in Article 8(2)(b) and (e), to include customary international law as established by State practice and *opinio juris*. In that context the United Kingdom confirms and draws to the attention of the Court its views as expressed, *inter alia*, in its statements made on ratification of relevant instruments of international law, including the Protocol Additional to the Geneva Conventions of 12 August 1949, and relating to the Protection of Victims of International Armed Conflicts (Protocol I) of 8 June 1977'.

(ix) Intentionally directing attacks against buildings dedicated to religion, education, art, science or charitable purposes, historic monuments, hospitals and places where the sick and wounded are collected, provided they are not military objectives;

(x) Subjecting persons who are in the power of an adverse party to physical or medical or scientific experiments of any kind which are neither justified by the medical, dental or hospital treatment of the person concerned nor carried out in his or her interest, and which cause death to or seriously endanger the health of such person or persons;

(xi) Killing or wounding treacherously individuals belonging to the hostile nation or army;

(xii) Declaring that no quarter will be given;

(xiii) Destroying or seizing the enemy's property unless such destruction or seizure be imperatively demanded by the necessities of war;

(xiv) Declaring abolished, suspended or inadmissible in a court of law the rights and actions of the nationals of the hostile party;

(xv) Compelling the nationals of the hostile party to take part in the operations of war directed against their own country, even if they were in the belligerent's service before the commencement of the war;

(xvi) Pillaging a town or place, even when taken by assault;

(xvii) Employing poison or poisoned weapons;

(xviii) Employing asphyxiating, poisonous or other gases, and all analogous liquids, materials or devices;

(xix) Employing bullets which expand or flatten easily in the human body, such as bullets with a hard envelope which does not entirely cover the core or is pierced with incisions;

(xx) Employing weapons, projectiles and material and methods of warfare which are of a nature to cause superfluous injury or unnecessary suffering or which are inherently indiscriminate in violation of the international law of armed conflict, provided that such weapons, projectiles and material and methods of warfare are the subject of a comprehensive prohibition . . . ;[164]

(xxi) Committing outrages upon personal dignity, in particular humiliating and degrading treatment;

(xxii) Committing rape, sexual slavery, enforced prostitution, forced pregnancy, . . . enforced sterilization, or any other form of sexual violence also constituting a grave breach of the Geneva Conventions;

(xxiii) Utilizing the presence of a civilian or other protected person to render certain points, areas or military forces immune from military operations;

[164] But only when added to the Statute by formal amendment procedure under the relevant articles.

(xxiv) Intentionally directing attacks against buildings, material, medical units and transport, and personnel using the distinctive emblems of the Geneva Conventions in conformity with international law;

(xxv) Intentionally using starvation of civilians as a method of warfare by depriving them of objects indispensable to their survival, including wilfully impeding relief supplies as provided for under the Geneva Conventions;

(xxvi) Conscripting or enlisting children under the age of fifteen years into the national armed forces or using them to participate actively in hostilities;

All internal armed conflicts

(c) In the case of an armed conflict[165] not of an international character, serious violations of article 3 common to the four Geneva Conventions of 12 August 1949, namely, any of the following acts committed against persons taking no active part in the hostilities, including members of armed forces who have laid down their arms and those placed hors de combat by sickness, wounds, detention or any other cause:

(i) Violence to life and person, in particular murder of all kinds, mutilation, cruel treatment and torture;

(ii) Committing outrages upon personal dignity, in particular humiliating and degrading treatment;

(iii) Taking of hostages;

(iv) The passing of sentences and the carrying out of executions without previous judgement pronounced by a regularly constituted court, affording all judicial guarantees which are generally recognized as indispensable.

(d) [omitted]

Internal armed conflicts that take place in the territory of a state when there is protracted armed conflict between governmental authorities and organized armed groups or between such groups

(e) Other serious violations of the laws and customs applicable in armed conflicts not of an international character, within the established framework of international law,[166] namely, any of the following acts:

(i) Intentionally directing attacks against the civilian population as such or against individual civilians not taking direct part in hostilities;

(ii) Intentionally directing attacks against buildings, material, medical units and transport, and personnel using the distinctive emblems of the Geneva Conventions in conformity with international law;

(iii) Intentionally directing attacks against personnel, installations, materials, units or vehicles involved in a humanitarian assistance or peacekeeping mission in accordance with the Charter of the United Nations, as long as

---

[165] This does not include situations of internal disturbances and tensions, such as riots, isolated and sporadic acts of violence, or other acts of a similar nature.

[166] See n 163.

they are entitled to the protection given to civilians or civilian objects under the international law of armed conflict;

(iv) Intentionally directing attacks against buildings dedicated to religion, education, art, science or charitable purposes, historic monuments, hospitals and places where the sick and wounded are collected, provided they are not military objectives;

(v) Pillaging a town or place, even when taken by assault;

(vi) Committing rape, sexual slavery, enforced prostitution, forced pregnancy, . . . enforced sterilization, and any other form of sexual violence also constituting a serious violation of article 3 common to the four Geneva Conventions;

(vii) Conscripting or enlisting children under the age of fifteen years into armed forces or groups or using them to participate actively in hostilities;

(viii) Ordering the displacement of the civilian population for reasons related to the conflict, unless the security of the civilians involved or imperative military reasons so demand;

(ix) Killing or wounding treacherously a combatant adversary;

(x) Declaring that no quarter will be given;

(xi) Subjecting persons who are in the power of another party to the conflict to physical mutilation or to medical or scientific experiments of any kind which are neither justified by the medical, dental or hospital treatment of the person concerned nor carried out in his or her interest, and which causes death to or seriously endanger the health of such person or persons;

(xii) Destroying or seizing the property of an adversary unless such destruction or seizure be imperatively demanded by the necessities of the conflict.

CRIMINAL RESPONSIBILITY

Individual criminal responsibility

Individuals are responsible for the war crimes that they commit themselves **16.35** or which they order or assist others to commit.

Article 7 of the Statute of the International Criminal Tribunal for the former **16.35.1** Yugoslavia provides that 'a person who planned, instigated, ordered, committed or otherwise aided and abetted in the planning, preparation or execution of a crime . . . shall be individually responsible for the crime'.

The Rome Statute of the International Criminal Court also confirms that an **16.35.2** individual is responsible for a war crime if he:

a. commits the crime himself, on his own or jointly with others, or

b. orders, solicits, or induces a crime which is committed or attempted, or

c. aids, abets, or otherwise assists in the commission of the crime, including providing the means for its commission, or

d. contributes to the commission or attempted commission of the crime by a group of persons acting with a common purpose.[167]

16.35.3 The fact that a subordinate was ordered to do an act, or make an omission, which was illegal does not, of itself, absolve the subordinate from criminal responsibility.[168]

Responsibility of commanders

16.36 Military commanders are responsible for preventing violations of the law (including the law of armed conflict) and for taking the necessary disciplinary action.[169] A commander will be criminally responsible if he participates in the commission of a war crime himself in one of the ways set out in paragraph 16.35.2, particularly if he orders its commission. However, he also becomes criminally responsible if he 'knew or, owing to the circumstances at the time, should have known' that war crimes were being or were about to be committed and failed 'to take all necessary and reasonable measures within his or her power to prevent or repress their commission or to submit the matter to the competent authority for investigation and prosecution'.[170]

16.36.1 The concept of command responsibility was first enunciated in the case of General Yamashita.[171] In that case, General Yamashita was held to have failed to exercise 'effective control' of his troops who were carrying out widespread atrocities in the Philippines. The Tribunal held that the nature of the crimes themselves provided *prima facie* evidence of knowledge and laid down a test that was reflected in the text of the *Manual of Military Law* Part III of 1958. According to that test, a commander was considered responsible if 'he has actual knowledge or should have knowledge, through reports received by him or through other means'.[172]

16.36.2 The Statute of the International Criminal Tribunal for the former Yugoslavia dealt with command responsibility as follows:

the fact that any of the acts . . . was committed by a subordinate does not relieve his superior of criminal responsibility if he knew or had reason to know that the

---

[167] Art 25, para 3.   [168] See para 16.47.

[169] HC IV, Art 3; GC I, Art 49; GC II, Art 50; GC III, Art 129; GC IV, Arts 29 and 146; AP I, Art 91.

[170] Rome Statute, Art 28; see also AP I, Art 86(2).

[171] *Case of General Yamashita* (1946) AD Case No 111. The judgment of the military commission that tried General Yamashita was reviewed and upheld by the US Supreme Court.

[172] *Manual of Military Law*, Part III (1958) (MML), para 631.

subordinate was about to commit such acts or had done so and the superior failed to take the necessary and reasonable measures to prevent such acts or to punish the perpetrators thereof.[173]

The Statute of the International Criminal Court deals with command res- **16.36.3** ponsibility as follows:[174]

(a) A military commander or person effectively acting as a military commander shall be criminally responsible for crimes . . . committed by forces under his or her effective command or control, or effective authority and control as the case may be, as a result of his or her failure to exercise control properly over such forces, where:

   (i) That military commander or person either knew or, owing to the circumstances at the time, should have known that the forces were committing or about to commit such crimes; and

   (ii) That military commander or person failed to take all necessary and reasonable measures within his or her power to prevent or suppress their commission or to submit the matter to the competent authorities for investigation and prosecution.

(b) With respect to superior and subordinate relationships not described in paragraph (a), a superior shall be criminally responsible for crimes . . . committed by subordinates under his or her effective authority and control, as a result of his or her failure to exercise control properly over such subordinates, where:

   (i) The superior either knew, or consciously disregarded information which clearly indicated, that the subordinates were committing or about to commit such crimes;

   (ii) The crimes concerned activities that were within the effective responsibility and control of the superior; and

   (iii) The superior failed to take all necessary and reasonable measures within his or her power to prevent or repress their commission or to submit the matter to the competent authorities for investigation and prosecution.

Despite the various formulations of the test, there is general agreement on **16.36.4** the nature of command and the degree of knowledge required.

The test of command in this context is one of 'effective control' over a **16.36.5** subordinate.[175] There need not be proof of command in the sense of formal organizational structures 'so long as the fundamental requirement of an effective power to control the subordinate, in the sense of preventing or punishing criminal conduct is satisfied'.[176]

---

[173] ICTY Statute, Art 7(3).   [174] ICC Statute, Art 28.
[175] See *Yamashita Case*. See also *Prosecutor v Delalić and others (Čelebići Case)* (Appeals Chamber) (1999) 40 ILM 677, para 198.   [176] See *Čelebići Case*, para 254.

16.36.6 Similarly, it is now accepted that an element of knowledge has to be proved, as command responsibility is not a form of strict liability.[177] Actual knowledge is clearly sufficient, but it is also sufficient if a commander 'had reason to know'. This has been described as 'where he had in his possession information of a nature, which at the least, would put him on notice of the risk of such offences by indicating the need for additional investigation in order to ascertain whether such crimes were committed or were about to be committed by his subordinates'.[178] It follows that possession of the means of knowledge may be regarded, in appropriate circumstances, as being the same as knowledge itself.

Responsibility of civilian authorities

16.37 Civilian superiors will also be liable for the acts of their subordinates in the same way as military commanders, though the difference in the command relationship means that a court is likely to require evidence of actual knowledge or a conscious disregard of information which would have enabled him to know.[179]

Responsibility of states

16.38 Parties to a conflict are obliged to instruct military commanders to prevent breaches of the law of armed conflict and ensure that their subordinates know of their obligations under that law.[180] This provision is based on the principle that an effective disciplinary system to prevent breaches is the best way of ensuring compliance with the law of armed conflict. But failure to do so does not of itself give rise to criminal responsibility.

16.38.1 Heads of state and their ministers are not immune from prosecution and punishment for war crimes.[181] Their liability is governed by the same principles as those governing the responsibility of civilian authorities.[182]

MENTAL ELEMENT OF WAR CRIMES

16.39 A person is normally only guilty of a war crime if he commits it with intent and knowledge.[183]

---

[177] See *Čelebići Case*, para 239.

[178] See *Čelebići Case*, paras 223, 239, upholding the Trial Chamber's findings.

[179] Rome Statute, Art 28(b). See also *Čelebići Case*, para 240.   [180] AP1, Art 7.

[181] See the ICTY decision of 11 July 1996 in its review of the indictment in the case of Karadžić and Mladić, 108 ILR 85.

[182] See para 16.37. Under the Rome Statute, Art 28, the standards differ between civilian authorities (28(b)) and military commanders (28(a)) to reflect the different hierarchical structures.   [183] This is confirmed by the Rome Statute, Art 30.

However, some war crimes contain an integral mental element. An example **16.39.1**
is the grave breach of *wilful* killing. This word can be interpreted as extending beyond intent and knowledge. The International Committee of the Red
Cross explain wilfulness as follows:

wilfully: the accused must have acted consciously and with intent, i.e. with his mind
on the act and its consequences and willing them . . .; this encompasses the concepts
of 'wrongful intent' or 'recklessness', viz., the attitude of an agent who, without
being certain of a particular result, accepts the possibility of it happening; on the
other hand, ordinary negligence or lack of foresight is not covered, i.e., when a man
acts without having his mind on the act or its consequences.[184]

In the decided cases, the issue of recklessness has not been relevant, as the
offences were so obviously committed with intent, except in those cases
where command responsibility is invoked where there is a different
test.[185]

The governing provisions for international tribunals and courts have not, **16.39.2**
in the past, sought to outline general principles of law but to concentrate on
substantive matters. Thus it has been left to the tribunals and courts to
develop their own jurisprudence on a case by case basis. The Statute of the
International Criminal Court, for the first time, has sought to rectify this
and provides, in Article 30, that 'unless otherwise provided' the material
element of an offence must be committed 'with intent and knowledge'.
Both 'intent' and 'knowledge' are separately defined. This text, however,
implies that there are occasions when this test may be inappropriate and,
indeed, in the elements of crimes there are provisions which depart from
Article 30, introducing a 'should have known' test.[186]

National tribunals will normally be governed by the general principles of law **16.39.3**
contained in their own domestic legislation although these will undoubtedly
be influenced by any international jurisprudence that may exist. The United
Kingdom has adopted, for the purposes of offences under the International
Criminal Court Act 2001, the definition of 'intent' contained in the Rome
Statute[187] as well as the provisions on command/superior responsibility.[188]
On other issues, such as general defences, the ordinary criminal law will
apply.[189]

---

[184] Y Sandoz, C Swinarski, and B Zimmermann (eds), *Commentary on the Additional Protocols
of 8 June 1977 to the Geneva Conventions of 12 August 1949* (1987) (*ICRC Commentary*) 994.
[185] See para 16.36.
[186] See elements for Art 8(2)(b)(xxvi), using, conscripting, or enlisting children, Report of
the Preparatory Commission for the International Criminal Court, *Finalized Draft Text of the
Elements of Crimes*, UN Doc PCNICC/2000/1/Add 2, 2 November 2000.
[187] ICCA 2001, s 66; and ICCA(S)A 2001, s 6.   [188] ICCA 2001, s 65; ICC(S)A 2001, s 5.
[189] ICCA 2001, ss 56 and 63; ICC(S)A 2001, s 9.

DEFENCES TO WAR CRIMES CHARGES

Introduction

16.40 War crimes are not absolute offences and persons accused of such crimes are entitled to raise such defences as are recognized by the tribunal before which they appear. This may be a domestic tribunal governed by the domestic law of the state concerned[190] or an international tribunal,[191] in which case the matter will be governed by the statute or charter of the tribunal concerned. This section deals with the defences that are most likely to be raised in connection with war crimes.

Accident

16.41 The fact that death or damage was caused by accident may be a defence to a war crimes charge, because of lack of intent.

16.41.1 If the death or damage was caused by a mistake, malfunction, accident, or collateral damage, for example, a civilian being hit by a stray bullet or shell or as a result of a ricochet, that would be a defence. This would be an issue of fact for a tribunal to determine. If they consider that death, damage, or injury may have been caused by a mistake, the accused would be entitled to acquittal on that charge. Of course, the excuse of mistake may wear thin if raised in case after case, especially if the prosecution can prove that it is being put forward by a well-trained and equipped army with good target intelligence and ample opportunity and practice to direct fire accurately.

Duress

16.42 Persons acting under duress have a defence if they act necessarily and reasonably as a result and do not intend to cause greater harm than the one sought to be avoided.[192]

16.42.1 Duress means a threat of imminent death or of continuing or imminent serious bodily harm to the person threatened or another person. It can arise through direct threats or through force of circumstances over which the person under duress has no control.

---

[190] As in the case of *US v Calley*, arising out of the My Lai massacre in Vietnam, or in the cases tried by the German Reichsgericht at Leipzig after the First World War (WW I).

[191] As in the Nuremberg Tribunal or the international tribunals established for the prosecution of war crimes committed in former Yugoslavia and Rwanda.

[192] Rome Statute, Art 31(1)(d). The ICTY Appeals Chamber held, in the *Erdemović Case* (1996) 111 ILR 298, that duress was not a defence to war crimes charges involving the killing of innocent persons.

Duress by threats

Although duress is a long-standing defence under English law, it is less **16.42.2** well formulated in international law. A person accused of a war crime is entitled to plead that he was under an immediate and real fear for his life. However, the more serious the crime, or the accused's part in it, the greater and more irresistible must be the duress before it can be regarded as affording a defence. It is a general principle of law that an individual is not permitted to avoid suffering or even to save his own life at the expense of the life of another. If duress does not amount to a defence, it may be considered in mitigation of punishment.[193]

Duress by circumstances

Compulsion arising from circumstances has developed as a concept under **16.42.3** English law. This occurs where the necessity arises otherwise than by the threats or physical compulsion of a third party, for example, where A in extremity of hunger kills B in order to eat him.[194] This is quite separate from military necessity, dealt with in paragraph 16.44. The principles for such a defence are the same as for duress generally, and thus the occasions on which such a defence is likely to be relevant will be limited to those where the violation was of a technical nature and the accused acted reasonably and had used his best endeavours to avoid a violation. For example, where a country suffers a severe food shortage, the commander of a prisoner of war camp who cannot obtain relief supplies or assistance may have no alternative other than to put prisoners of war on rations that are below the minimum standards laid down in Geneva Convention III. In such circumstances, the accused, on the principles outlined above, would not be held criminally responsible. As with duress by threats, duress by circumstances may be considered in mitigation of punishment.

Ignorance of the law

Ignorance of the law is no excuse, but if the law is unclear or controversial, **16.43** an accused should be given the benefit of that lack of clarity by the award of a lesser or nominal punishment.

---

[193] This defence sometimes referred to as 'compulsion' was raised in a number of trials after the Second World War (WW II), often linked to superior orders, see the cases of *Fuerstein*, *Jepson*, and *Holzer*, all referred to at (1947) 15 WCR 172–173. In the *Holzer* case, the judge advocate advised the Canadian military court as follows: 'There is no doubt on the authorities that compulsion is a defence when the crime is not of a heinous character. But the killing of an innocent person can never be justified . . . In most if not all cases the fact of compulsion is a matter of mitigation of punishment and not a matter of defence'. See also the case of *Erdemović* before the ICTY Appeals Chamber, 111 ILR 298.

[194] See *R v Dudley and Stephens* (1884) 14 QBD 273, referred to in the case of *Fuerstein* 15 WCR 173.

16.43.1 The Statute of the International Criminal Court also makes allowance for the possibility that a mistake of law may negate the mental element of a war crime.[195]

Military necessity

16.44 Since the conventional laws of armed conflict have been drafted with the concept of military necessity in mind,[196] it is not open to a person accused of a war crime to plead this as a defence unless express allowance is made for military necessity within the provision allegedly breached.[197] Even where allowance is made, it will be open to the court to assess whether military necessity required the specific acts committed, bearing in mind the rule of proportionality[198] in which the military need for the operation has to be weighed against humanitarian interests. The greater the incidental damage, the greater the military need required to justify the action taken.[199]

Mistake of fact

16.45 Mistake of fact is a defence if it negates the mental element required for a crime.[200]

16.45.1 So, for example, if an artillery commander is ordered to fire at an enemy command post in a particular building and he does so believing that it is a command post but it later turns out that, unbeknown to him, it was a school, he would not be guilty of a war crime because he did not intend to attack a school.

16.45.2 Although a failure to take reasonable steps to verify information might give rise to criminal responsibility, the responsibility of the officer—and of the military commander who gave him the order—would be assessed in the light of the facts as he believed them to be, on the information reasonably available to him from all sources. The position is similar for indiscriminate attacks. The defence of mistake of fact cannot succeed where the accused was ordered to do something which was manifestly illegal,[201] such as killing prisoners of war.

---

[195] ICC Statute, Art 32.

[196] See the Preamble to HC IV which states 'According to the views of the high contracting Parties, these provisions, the wording of which has been inspired by the desire to diminish the evils of war, as far as military requirements permit . . . '.

[197] eg, HR, Art 23(g); GC III, Arts 23, 75, and 126; GC IV, Arts 5, 42, 53, and 147; CPC, Art 4(2); AP I, Art 54(5).   [198] See paras 2.6–2.8.

[199] See *In re List* (1948) 9 WCR 34. Any assessment must be based on the information available to the commander at the time and not on a distortion arising from hindsight.

[200] Rome Statute, Art 32.

[201] See *The Dover Castle* (1921) 2 AD 429 Case No 231; *The Llandovery Castle* (1921) 2 AD 436 Case No 235.

Physical compulsion

Criminal responsibility is not incurred by a person for such acts as he is phys-   **16.46**
ically compelled to perform against his will and despite his resistance.[202]

Superior orders

The Statute of the International Criminal Court states[203] that superior orders   **16.47**
do not relieve a person of criminal responsibility unless:

a. 'The person was under a legal obligation to obey orders of the
   Government or the superior in question';
b. 'The person did not know that the order was unlawful'; and
c. 'The order was not manifestly unlawful'.[204]

The reference to a legal obligation to obey orders is a reference to the require-   **16.47.1**
ments of national law, for example, military law, which, in many countries,
makes it an offence for soldiers not to obey orders. However, orders to commit
genocide or crimes against humanity are considered to be manifestly unlawful.

Even where superior orders do not in themselves provide a defence to war   **16.47.2**
crimes charges, they may be relevant to other defences such as lack of *mens rea*,
mistake of fact, or duress, and may be taken into account in mitigation of
punishment.[205]

---

[202] 'If there be an actual forcing of a man, as if A by force takes the arm of B and the weapon in his hand and therewith stabs C whereof he dies, this is murder in A but B is not guilty': Sir Matthew Hale, *The History of the Pleas of the Crown* (1736) vol I, 534.

[203] ICC Statute, Art 33.

[204] The background to this provision is of importance to members of the armed forces for whom obedience to orders is a fundamental rule. In the first edition of L Oppenheim, *International Law* (1906) 264, it was stated that members of the armed forces who commit breaches of the law in conformity with orders of their superiors are not war criminals and it is their superiors alone who carry responsibility. This statement also appeared at para 443 of the 1914 edition of the *Manual of Military Law*. In the *Llandovery Castle Case* (1920) 2 AD 436, however, it was held that superior orders offer no defence where the rule of international law involved is simple and universally known. Despite this, the reference to the superior orders defence in the Manual was not amended until 1944. The defence of superior orders was denied in the IMT Charter, Art 8; the Charter of the International Military Tribunal (Tokyo), Art 6; the ICTY Statute, Art 7(4); and the ICTR Statute, Art 6(4). Perhaps the reason for this blanket denial of the defence of superior orders was because, following the *Llandovery Castle Case*, the offences to be dealt with by the tribunals concerned were clearly war crimes. Nevertheless, it led to some uncertainty, some academic writers arguing that superior orders may yet be a defence where the orders are not manifestly illegal, others that superior orders only went to the question of intent. It will be noted that the Rome Statute now moves away from a total denial of the defence of superior orders.

[205] The ICTY took superior orders into account in mitigation in its sentencing judgment on 29 November 1996 in the case of *Erdemović* (1996) 37 ILM 1182. Such mitigation would

16.47.3 Orders from a superior in this context include those of a government, a superior—military or civilian—or a national law or regulation. A serviceman is under a duty *not* to obey a manifestly unlawful order.

PUNISHMENT

Customary law

16.48 Corporal punishment and cruelty in any form are prohibited. Death penalties may not be pronounced on accused persons who were under the age of 18 years at the time of the offence,[206] nor carried out on pregnant women or mothers of dependent infants.[207] There are particular safeguards and requirements in respect of death and custodial sentences for:

a. prisoners of war;[208]
b. women and children, whether or not protected persons;[209]
c. protected persons generally.[210]

16.48.1 A death sentence may not be imposed by any UK court.

Treaty law

16.49 The maximum penalty available to the International Criminal Tribunals for Yugoslavia and Rwanda and to the International Criminal Court is life imprisonment.[211]

16.49.1 The maximum sentence for those convicted of offences under the International Criminal Court Act 2001 (and the Scottish equivalent) which involve murder or offences ancillary to murder is life imprisonment. There is a maximum sentence of 30 years imprisonment in all other cases.[212] The same sentences apply to those convicted of grave breaches of the Geneva Conventions or Additional Protocol I under the Geneva Conventions Act 1957.[213]

RELEASE

16.50 Convicted offenders, whether prisoners of war or civilians, serving sentences for war crimes have no right to release at the cessation of hostilities.[214] This is a matter that should be dealt with in peace treaties. These

not apply where shocking and extensive crimes are committed consciously, ruthlessly, and without military excuse or justification, see IMT Judgment, part 22, 493 (Keitel).

[206] AP I, Art 77(5).   [207] AP I, Art 76(3).   [208] See paras 8.142–8.143.
[209] See paras 9.8–9.9.   [210] See Ch 9, Pt D.
[211] ICTY Statute, Art 24; ICTR Statute, Art 23; Rome Statute, Art 77.
[212] ICCA 2001, ss 53(5), (6) and 60(5), (6); ICC(S)A 2001, s 3(4), (5).
[213] GCA 1957, s 1A (inserted by ICCA 2001, s 70(2)). The sentencing provisions laid down for prisoners of war under the PW (Discipline) Regs 1958 are different as they have not yet been amended.   [214] See para 8.144.

should also deal with the disposal of cases involving persons accused of war crimes who were not charged or dealt with before cessation of hostilities. Any amnesty must be considered of doubtful effect as, although it would be binding as between parties to the treaty, it would not bind other states or the International Criminal Court, particularly in respect of grave breaches of the Geneva Conventions or of Additional Protocol I.[215]

H. OFFENCES IN OCCUPIED TERRITORY

As mentioned in paragraph 11.57 onwards, an occupying power may make **16.51** regulations in the interests of public order and safety of its own forces which provide for the punishment of those who contravene them.[216] For such acts to be punishable, they must have been published and brought to the notice of the inhabitants in their own language, and notices may not be retroactive.[217] Unlike war crimes, these offences must be tried locally and are not subject to extradition.

---

[215] Indeed, it would appear to contradict the provisions on enforcement contained in the Conventions and AP I, see GC I, Art 49; GC II, Art 50; GC III, Art 129; GC IV, Art 146; AP I, Art 85(1). To the contrary in internal armed conflict, see AP II, Art 6(5).

[216] GC IV, Art 64.   [217] GC IV, Art 65.

APPENDICES

Documents and Materials

It is considered unnecessary to include all the law of armed conflict treaty texts in this Manual as they are reproduced in the book, A Roberts and R Guelff, *Documents on the Laws of War* (3rd edn 2000). These Appendices therefore contain only those necessary documents and materials that are not to be found in Roberts and Guelff.

Appendix A

Geneva Convention I 1949: Annexes

ANNEX I. DRAFT AGREEMENT RELATING TO HOSPITAL ZONES AND LOCALITIES

Art 1. Hospital zones shall be strictly observed for the persons named in Article 23 of the Geneva Convention for the Amelioration of the Condition of the Wounded and Sick in the Armed Forces in the Field of 12 August 1949, and for the personnel entrusted with the organization and administration of these zones and localities, and with the care of the persons therein assembled.

Nevertheless, persons whose permanent residence is within such zones shall have the right to stay there.

Art 2. No persons residing, in whatever capacity, in a hospital zone shall perform any work, either within or without the zone, directly connected with military operations or the production of war material.

Art 3. The Power establishing a hospital zone shall take all necessary measures to prohibit access to all persons who have no right of residence or entry therein.

Art 4. Hospital zones shall fulfil the following conditions:

(a) They shall comprise only a small part of the territory governed by the Power which has established them.

(b) They shall be thinly populated in relation to the possibilities of accommodation.

(c) They shall be far removed and free from all military objectives, or large industrial or administrative establishments.

(d) They shall not be situated in areas which, according to every probability, may become important for the conduct of the war.

Art 5. Hospital zones shall be subject to the following obligations:

(a) The lines of communication and means of transport which they possess shall not be used for the transport of military personnel or material, even in transit.

(b) They shall in no case be defended by military means.

Art 6. Hospital zones shall be marked by means of red crosses (red crescents, red lions and suns) on a white background placed on the outer precincts and on the buildings. They may be similarly marked at night by means of appropriate illumination.

Art 7. The Powers shall communicate to all High Contracting Parties in peacetime or on the outbreak of hostilities, a list of the hospital zones in the territories governed by them. They shall also give notice of any new zones set up during hostilities.

As soon as the adverse Party has receive the above-mentioned notification, the zone shall be regularly constituted.

If, however, the adverse Party considers that the conditions of the present agreement have not been fulfilled, it may refuse to recognize the zone by giving immediate notice thereof to the Party responsible for the said Zone, or may make its recognition of such zone dependent upon the institution of the control provided for in Article 8.

Art 8. Any Power having recognized one of several hospital zones instituted by the adverse Party shall be entitled to demand control by one or more Special Commissioners, for the purpose of ascertaining if the zones fulfil the conditions and obligations stipulated in the present agreement.

For this purpose, the members of the Special Commissions shall at all times have free access to the various zones and may even reside there permanently. They shall be given all facilities for their duties of inspection.

Art 9. Should the Special Commissions note any facts which they consider contrary to the stipulations of the present agreement, they shall at once draw the attention of the Power governing the said zone to these facts, and shall fix a time limit of five days within which the matter should be rectified. They shall duly notify the Power who has recognized the zone.

If, when the time limit has expired, the Power governing the zone has not complied with the warning, the adverse Party may declare that it is no longer bound by the present agreement in respect of the said zone.

Art 10. Any Power setting up one or more hospital zones and localities, and the adverse Parties to whom their existence has been notified, shall nominate or have nominated by neutral Powers, the persons who shall be members of the Special Commissions mentioned in Articles 8 and 9.

Art 11. In no circumstances may hospital zones be the object of attack. They shall be protected and respected at all times by the Parties to the conflict.

Art 12. In the case of occupation of a territory, the hospital zones therein shall continue to be respected and utilized as such.

Their purpose may, however, be modified by the Occupying Power, on condition that all measures are taken to ensure the safety of the persons accommodated.

Art 13. The present agreement shall also apply to localities which the Powers may utilize for the same purposes as hospital zones.

ANNEX II. IDENTITY CARD FOR MEMBERS OF MEDICAL AND RELIGIOUS PERSONNEL ATTACHED TO THE ARMED FORCES

Front

Reverse side

Appendix B

Geneva Convention II 1949: Annex

ANNEX. IDENTITY CARD FOR MEMBERS OF MEDICAL AND RELIGIOUS PERSONNEL ATTACHED TO THE ARMED FORCES AT SEA

Front

(Space reserved for the name of the country and military authority issuing this card)

IDENTITY CARD

for members of medical and religious personnel attached to the armed forces at sea

Surname..

First names...

Date of Birth ....

Rank...

Army Number...

The bearer of this card is protected by the Geneva Convention for the Amelioration of the Condition of the Wounded, Sick and Ship-wrecked Members of Armed Forces at Sea of August 12, 1949, in his capacity as

....

Date of issue	Number of Card

Reverse side

Photo of bearer

Signature of bearer or fingerprints or both

Embossed stamp of military authority issuing card

Height	Eyes	Hair

Other distinguishing marks

Appendix C

Geneva Convention III 1949: Annexes

ANNEX I. MODEL AGREEMENT CONCERNING DIRECT REPATRIATION AND ACCOMMODATION IN NEUTRAL COUNTRIES OF WOUNDED AND SICK PRISONERS OF WAR (SEE ART 110)

I. PRINCIPLES FOR DIRECT REPATRIATION AND ACCOMMODATION IN NEUTRAL COUNTRIES

A. Direct Repatriation

The following shall be repatriated direct:

(1) All prisoners of war suffering from the following disabilities as the result of trauma: loss of a limb, paralysis, articular or other disabilities, when this disability is at least the loss of a hand or a foot, or the equivalent of the loss of a hand or a foot.

Without prejudice to a more generous interpretation, the following shall be considered as equivalent to the loss of a hand or a foot:

(a) Loss of a hand or of all the fingers, or of the thumb and forefinger of one hand; loss of a foot, or of all the toes and metatarsals of one foot.

(b) Ankylosis, loss of osseous tissue, cicatricial contracture preventing the functioning of one of the large articulations or of all the digital joints of one hand.

(c) Pseudarthrosis of the long bones.

(d) Deformities due to fracture or other injury which seriously interfere with function and weight-bearing power.

(2) All wounded prisoners of war whose condition has become chronic, to the extent that prognosis appears to exclude recovery—in spite of treatment—within one year from the date of the injury, as, for example, in case of:

(a) Projectile in the heart, even if the Mixed Medical Commission should fail, at the time of their examination, to detect any serious disorders.

(b) Metallic splinter in the brain or the lungs, even if the Mixed Medical Commission cannot, at the time of examination, detect any local or general reaction.

(c) Osteomyelitis, when recovery cannot be foreseen in the course of the year following the injury, and which seems likely to result in ankylosis of a joint, or other impairments equivalent to the loss of a hand or a foot.

(d) Perforating and suppurating injury to the large joints.

(e) Injury to the skull, with loss or shifting of bony tissue.

(f) Injury or burning of the face with loss of tissue and functional lesions.

(g) Injury to the spinal cord.

(h) Lesion of the peripheral nerves, the sequelae of which are equivalent to the loss of a hand or foot, and the cure of which requires more than a year from the date of injury, for example: injury to the brachial or lumbosacral plexus median or sciatic nerves, likewise combined injury to the radial and cubital nerves or to the lateral popliteal nerve (N. peroneous communis) and medial popliteal nerve (N. tibialis); etc. The separate injury of the radial (musculo-spiral), cubital, lateral or medial popliteal nerves shall not, however, warrant repatriation except in case of contractures or of serious neurotrophic disturbance.

(i) Injury to the urinary system, with incapacitating results.

(3) All sick prisoners of war whose condition has become chronic to the extent that prognosis seems to exclude recovery—in spite of treatment— within one year from the inception of the disease, as, for example, in case of:

(a) Progressive tuberculosis of any organ which, according to medical prognosis, cannot be cured or at least considerably improved by treatment in a neutral country.

(b) Exudate pleurisy.

(c) Serious diseases of the respiratory organs of non-tubercular etiology, presumed incurable, for example: serious pulmonary emphysema, with or without bronchitis; chronic asthma*; chronic bronchitis* lasting more than one year in captivity; bronchiectasis*; etc.

(d) Serious chronic affections of the circulatory system, for example: valvular lesions and myocarditis*, which have shown signs of circulatory failure during captivity, even though the Mixed Medical Commission cannot detect any such signs at the time of examination; affections of the pericardium and the vessels (Buerger's disease, aneurisms of the large vessels); etc.

(e) Serious chronic affections of the digestive organs, for example: gastric or duodenal ulcer; sequelae of gastric operations performed in captivity; chronic gastritis, enteritis or colitis, having lasted more than one year and seriously affecting the general condition; cirrhosis of the liver; chronic cholecystopathy*; etc.

(f) Serious chronic affections of the genito-urinary organs, for example: chronic diseases of the kidney with consequent disorders; nephrectomy because of a tubercular kidney; chronic pyelitis or chronic cystitis; hydronephrosis or pyonephrosis; chronic grave gynaecological conditions; normal pregnancy and obstetrical disorder, where it is impossible to accommodate in a neutral country; etc.

(g) Serious chronic diseases of the central and peripheral nervous system, for example: all obvious psychoses and psychoneuroses, such as serious hysteria, serious captivity psychoneurosis, etc., duly verified by a specialist*; any epilepsy duly verified by the camp physician*; cerebral arteriosclerosis; chronic neuritis lasting more than one year; etc.

(h) Serious chronic diseases of the neuro-vegetative system, with considerable diminution of mental or physical fitness, noticeable loss of weight and general asthenia.

(i) Blindness of both eyes, or of one eye when the vision of the other is less than 1 in spite of the use of corrective glasses; diminution of visual acuity in cases where it is impossible to restore it by correction to an acuity of 1/2 in at least one eye*; other grave ocular affections, for example: glaucoma, iritis, choroiditis; trachoma; etc.

(k) Auditive disorders, such as total unilateral deafness, if the other ear does not discern the ordinary spoken word at a distance of one metre*; etc.

(l) Serious affections of metabolism, for example: diabetes mellitus requiring insulin treatment; etc.

(m) Serious disorders of the endocrine glands, for example: thyrotoxicosis; hypothyrosis; Addison's disease; Simmonds' cachexia; tetany; etc.

(n) Grave and chronic disorders of the blood-forming organs.

(o) Serious cases of chronic intoxication, for example: lead poisoning, mercury poisoning, morphinism, cocainism, alcoholism; gas or radiation poisoning; etc.

(p) Chronic affections of locomotion, with obvious functional disorders, for example: arthritis deformans; primary and secondary progressive chronic polyarthritis; rheumatism with serious clinical symptoms; etc.

(q) Serious chronic skin diseases, not amenable to treatment.

(r) Any malignant growth.

(s) Serious chronic infectious diseases, persisting for one year after their inception, for example: malaria with decided organic impairment, amoebic or bacillary dysentery with grave disorders; tertiary visceral syphilis resistant to treatment; leprosy; etc.

(t) Serious avitaminosis or serious inanition.

[NOTE] * The decision of the Mixed Medical Commission shall be based to a great extent on the records kept by camp physicians and surgeons of the same nationality as the prisoners of war, or on an examination by medical specialists of the Detaining Power.

B. Accommodation in Neutral Countries

The following shall be eligible for accommodation in a neutral country:

(1) All wounded prisoners of war who are not likely to recover in captivity, but who might be cured or whose condition might be considerably improved by accommodation in a neutral country.

(2) Prisoners of war suffering from any form of tuberculosis, of whatever organ, and whose treatment in a neutral country would be likely to lead to recovery or at least to considerable improvement, with the exception of primary tuberculosis cured before captivity.

(3) Prisoners of war suffering from affections requiring treatment of the respiratory, circulatory, digestive, nervous, sensory, genito-urinary, cutaneous, locomotive organs, etc., if such treatment would clearly have better results in a neutral country than in captivity.

(4) Prisoners of war who have undergone a nephrectomy in captivity for a non-tubercular renal affection; cases of osteomyelitis, on the way to recovery or latent; diabetes mellitus not requiring insulin treatment; etc.

(5) Prisoners of war suffering from war or captivity neuroses. Cases of captivity neurosis which are not cured after three months of accommodation in a neutral country, or which after that length of time are not clearly on the way to complete cure, shall be repatriated.

(6) All prisoners of war suffering from chronic intoxication (gases, metals, alkaloids, etc.), for whom the prospects of cure in a neutral country are especially favourable.

(7) All women prisoners of war who are pregnant or mothers with infants and small children.

The following cases shall not be eligible for accommodation in a neutral country:

(1) All duly verified chronic psychoses.

(2) All organic or functional nervous affections considered to be incurable.

(3) All contagious diseases during the period in which they are transmissible, with the exception of tuberculosis.

II. GENERAL OBSERVATIONS

(1) The conditions given shall, in a general way, be interpreted and applied in as broad a spirit as possible. Neuropathic and psychopathic conditions caused by war or captivity, as well as cases of tuberculosis in all stages, shall above all benefit by such liberal interpretation. Prisoners of war who have sustained several wounds, none of which, considered by itself, justifies repatriation, shall be examined in the same spirit, with due regard for the psychic traumatism due to the number of their wounds.

(2) All unquestionable cases giving the right to direct repatriation (amputation, total blindness or deafness, open pulmonary tuberculosis, mental disorder, malignant growth, etc.) shall be examined and repatriated as soon as possible by the camp physicians or by military medical commissions appointed by the Detaining Power.

(3) Injuries and diseases which existed before the war and which have not become worse, as well as war injuries which have not prevented subsequent military service, shall not entitle to direct repatriation.

(4) The provisions of this Annex shall be interpreted and applied in a similar manner in all countries party to the conflict. The Powers and authorities concerned shall grant to Mixed Medical Commissions all the facilities necessary for the accomplishment of their task.

(5) The examples quoted under (1) above represent only typical cases. Cases which do not correspond exactly to these provisions shall be judged in the spirit of the provisions of Article 110 of the present Convention, and of the principles embodied in the present Agreement.

ANNEX II. REGULATIONS CONCERNING MIXED MEDICAL COMMISSIONS (SEE ART 112)

Art 1. The Mixed Medical Commissions provided for in Article 112 of the Convention shall be composed of three members, two of whom shall belong to a neutral country, the third being appointed by the Detaining Power. One of the neutral members shall take the chair.

Art 2. The two neutral members shall be appointed by the International Committee of the Red Cross, acting in agreement with the Protecting Power, at the request of the Detaining Power. They may be domiciled either in their country of origin, in any other neutral country, or in the territory of the Detaining Power.

Art 3. The neutral members shall be approved by the Parties to the conflict concerned, who shall notify their approval to the International Committee of the Red Cross and to the Protecting Power. Upon such notification, the neutral members shall be considered as effectively appointed.

Art 4. Deputy members shall also be appointed in sufficient number to replace the regular members in case of need. They shall be appointed at the same time as the regular members or, at least, as soon as possible.

Art 5. If for any reason the International Committee of the Red Cross cannot arrange for the appointment of the neutral members, this shall be done by the Power protecting the interests of the prisoners of war to be examined.

Art 6. So far as possible, one of the two neutral members shall be a surgeon and the other a physician.

Art 7. The neutral members shall be entirely independent of the Parties to the conflict, which shall grant them all facilities in the accomplishment of their duties.

Art 8. By agreement with the Detaining Power, the International Committee of the Red Cross, when making the appointments provided for in Articles 2 and 4 of the present Regulations, shall settle the terms of service of the nominees.

Art 9. The Mixed Medical Commissions shall begin their work as soon as possible after the neutral members have been approved, and in any case within a period of three months from the date of such approval.

Art 10. The Mixed Medical Commissions shall examine all the prisoners designated in Article 113 of the Convention. They shall propose repatriation, rejection, or reference to a later examination. Their decisions shall be made by a majority vote.

Art 11. The decisions made by the Mixed Medical Commissions in each specific case shall be communicated, during the month following their visit, to the Detaining Power, the Protecting Power and the International Committee of the Red Cross. The Mixed Medical Commissions shall also inform each prisoner of war examined of the decision made, and shall issue to those whose repatriation has been proposed, certificates similar to the model appended to the present Convention.

Art 12. The Detaining Power shall be required to carry out the decisions of the Mixed Medical Commissions within three months of the time when it receives due notification of such decisions.

Art 13. If there is no neutral physician in a country where the services of a Mixed Medical Commission seem to be required, and if it is for any reason impossible to appoint neutral doctors who are resident in another country, the Detaining Power, acting in agreement with the Protecting Power, shall set up a Medical Commission which shall undertake the same duties as a Mixed Medical Commission, subject to the provisions of Articles 1, 2, 3, 4, 5 and 8 of the present Regulations.

Art 14. Mixed Medical Commissions shall function permanently and shall visit each camp at intervals of not more than six months.

ANNEX III. REGULATIONS CONCERNING COLLECTIVE RELIEF (SEE ART 73)

Art 1. Prisoners' representatives shall be allowed to distribute collective relief shipments for which they are responsible, to all prisoners of war administered by their camp, including those who are in hospitals, or in prisons or other penal establishments.

Art 2. The distribution of collective relief shipments shall be effected in accordance with the instructions of the donors and with a plan drawn up by the prisoners' representatives. The issue of medical stores shall, however, be made for preference in agreement with the senior medical officers, and the latter may, in hospitals and infirmaries, waive the said instructions, if the needs of their patients so demand. Within the limits thus defined, the distribution shall always be carried out equitably.

Art 3. The said prisoners' representatives or their assistants shall be allowed to go to the points of arrival of relief supplies near their camps, so as to enable the prisoners' representatives or their assistants to verify the quality as well as the quantity of the goods received, and to make out detailed reports thereon for the donors.

Art 4. Prisoners' representatives shall be given the facilities necessary for verifying whether the distribution of collective relief in all subdivisions and annexes of their camps has been carried out in accordance with their instructions.

Art 5. Prisoners' representatives shall be allowed to fill up, and cause to be filled up by the prisoners' representatives of labour detachments or by the senior medical officers of infirmaries and hospitals, forms or questionnaires intended for the donors, relating to collective relief supplies (distribution, requirements, quantities, etc.). Such forms and questionnaires, duly completed, shall be forwarded to the donors without delay.

Art 6. In order to secure the regular issue of collective relief to the prisoners of war in their camp, and to meet any needs that may arise from the arrival of new contingents of prisoners, prisoners' representatives shall be allowed to build up and maintain adequate reserve stocks of collective relief. For this purpose, they shall have suitable warehouses at their disposal; each warehouse shall be provided with two locks, the prisoners' representative holding the keys of one lock and the camp commander the keys of the other.

Art 7. When collective consignments of clothing are available, each prisoner of war shall retain in his possession at least one complete set of clothes. If a prisoner has more than one set of clothes, the prisoners' representative shall be permitted to withdraw excess clothing from those with the largest number of sets, or particular articles in excess of one, if this is necessary in order to supply prisoners who are less well provided. He shall not, however, withdraw second sets of underclothing, socks or footwear, unless this is the only means of providing for prisoners of war with none.

Art 8. The High Contracting Parties, and the Detaining Powers in particular, shall authorize, as far as possible and subject to the regulations governing the supply of the population, all purchases of goods made in their territories for the distribution of collective relief to prisoners of war. They shall similarly facilitate the transfer of funds and other financial measures of a technical or administrative nature taken for the purpose of making such purchases.

Art 9. The foregoing provisions shall not constitute an obstacle to the right of prisoners of war to receive collective relief before their arrival in a camp or in the course of transfer, nor to the possibility of representatives of the Protecting Power, the International Committee of the Red Cross, or any other body giving assistance to prisoners which may be responsible for the forwarding of such supplies, ensuring the distribution thereof to the addressees by any other means that they may deem useful.

ANNEX IV

(A) Identity Card (see Art 4)

NOTICE

This identity card is issued to persons who accompany the Armed Forces of but are not part of them. The card must be carried at all times by the person to whom it is issued. If the bearer is taken prisoner, he shall at once hand the card to the Detaining Authorities, to assist in his identification.

Fingerprints (optional)

(Right forefinger)

(Left forefinger)

Any other mark of identification ....

Official seal imprint

Religion

Blood type

Hair

Eyes

Weight

Height

(Name of the country and military authority issuing this card)

Photograph of the bearer

IDENTITY CARD

FOR A PERSON WHO ACCOMPANIES
THE ARMED FORCES

Name ....

First names ....

Date and place of birth ....

Accompanies the Armed Forces as ....

Date of issue   Signature of bearer

....

Remarks—this card should be made out for preference in two or three languages, one of which is in international use. Actual size of the card: 13 by 10 centimetres. It should be folded along the dotted line.

ANNEX IV

(B) Capture Card (see Art 70)

1. Front

PRISONER OF WAR MAIL | Postage free |

CAPTURE CARD FOR PRISONER OF WAR

IMPORTANT

This card must be completed by each prisoner immediately after being taken prisoner and each time his address is changed (by reason of transfer to a hospital or to another camp).

This card is distinct from the special card which each prisoner is allowed to send to his relatives.

CENTRAL PRISONERS
OF WAR AGENCY

INTERNATIONAL COMMITTEE
OF THE RED CROSS

GENEVA
SWITZERLAND

---

2. Reverse side.

| Write legibly and in block letters | 1. Power on which the prisoner depends .... |

2. Name   3. First names (in full)   4. First name of father

....

5. Date of birth .... 6. Place of birth ....

7. Rank ....

8. Service number ....

9. Address of next of kin ....

---

*10. Taken prisoner on: (or)
      Coming from (Camp No., hospital, etc.) ....

*11. (a) Good health—(b) Not wounded—(c) Recovered—(d) Convalescent—
      (e) Sick—(f) Slightly wounded—(g) Seriously wounded.

---

12. My present address is: Prisoner No. ....

      Name of camp ....

13. Date .... 14. Signature ....

---

* Strike out what is not applicable—Do not add any remarks—See explanations overleaf.

Remarks—this form should be made out in two or three languages, particularly in the prisoner's own language and in that of the Detaining Power. Actual size: 15 by 10.5 centimetres.

ANNEX IV

(C) CORRESPONDENCE CARD AND LETTER (SEE ART 71)

1. Front   I. Card

PRISONER OF WAR MAIL
_____

POST CARD

| Postage free |

To ....

Sender: Name and first names	....
Place and date of birth	Place of Destination ....
Prisoner of War No.	Street ....
Name of camp	Country ....
Country where posted	Province or Department ....

2. Reverse side.

NAME OF CAMP .... Date ....

....

....

....

....

....

....

....

....

Write on the dotted lines only and as legibly as possible.

Remarks—this form should be made out in two or three languages, particularly in the prisoner's own language and in that of the Detaining Power. Actual size of form: 15 by 10 centimetres.

ANNEX IV

(C) Correspondence Card and Letter (see Art 71)

2. Letter

PRISONER OF WAR MAIL

Postage free

To ....

Place ....

Street ....

Country ....

Department or Province ....

Country where posted

Name of camp

Prisoner of War No.

Date and place of birth

Name and first names

Sender:

****

Remarks—this form should be made out in two or three languages, particularly in the prisoner's own language and in that of the Detaining Power. It should be folded along the dotted line, the tab being inserted in the slit (marked by a line of asterisks); it then has the appearance of an envelope. Overleaf, it is lined like the postcard above (Annex IV C1); this space can contain about 250 words which the prisoner is free to write. Actual size of the folded form: 29 by 15 centimetres.

ANNEX IV

(D) Notification of Death (see Art 120)

<table>
<tr><td>

(Title of responsible
authority)

</td><td>

NOTIFICATION OF DEATH

Power on which the
prisoner depended ....

</td></tr>
</table>

Name and first names ....

First name of father ....

Place and date of birth ....

Place and date of death ....

Rank and service number (as given on identity disc) ....

Address of next of kin ....

Where and when taken prisoner ....

Cause and circumstances of death ....

Place of burial ....

Is the grave marked and can it be found later by the relatives? ....

Are the personal effects of the deceased in the keeping of the Detaining Power or are they being forwarded together with this notification?

If forwarded, through what agency? ....

Can the person who cared for the deceased during sickness or during his last moments (doctor, nurse, minister of religion, fellow prisoner) give here or on an attached sheet a short account of the circumstances of the death and burial?

(Date, seal and signature of responsible authority.)   Signature and address of two witnesses

....

Remarks—this form should be made out in two or three languages, particularly in the prisoner's own language and in that of the Detaining Power. Actual size of the form: 21 by 30 centimetres.

ANNEX IV

(E) REPATRIATION CERTIFICATE (SEE ANNEX II, ART 11)

REPATRIATION CERTIFICATE

Date :

Camp :

Hospital :

Surname :

First names :

Date of birth :

Rank :

Army number :

P. W. number :

Injury-Disease :

Decision of the Commission :

Chairman of the
Mixed Medical Commission :

A = direct repatriation
B = accommodation in a neutral country
NC = re-examination by next Commission

ANNEX V. MODEL REGULATIONS CONCERNING PAYMENTS SENT BY PRISONERS TO THEIR OWN COUNTRY (SEE ART 63)

(1) The notification referred to in the third paragraph of Article 63 will show:

(a) number as specified in Article 17, rank, surname and first names of the prisoner of war who is the payer;

(b) the name and address of the payee in the country of origin;

(c) the amount to be so paid in the currency of the country in which he is detained.

(2) The notification will be signed by the prisoner of war, or his witnessed mark made upon it if he cannot write, and shall be countersigned by the prisoners' representative.

(3) The camp commander will add to this notification a certificate that the prisoner of war concerned has a credit balance of not less than the amount registered as payable.

(4) The notification may be made up in lists, each sheet of such lists being witnessed by the prisoners' representative and certified by the camp commander.

Appendix D

Geneva Convention IV 1949: Annexes

ANNEX I. DRAFT AGREEMENT RELATING TO HOSPITAL AND SAFETY ZONES AND LOCALITIES

Art 1. Hospital and safety zones shall be strictly reserved for the persons mentioned in Article 23 of the Geneva Convention for the Amelioration of the Condition of the Wounded and Sick in Armed Forces in the Field of 12 August 1949, and in Article 14 of the Geneva Convention relative to the Protection of Civilian Persons in Time of War of 12 August 1949, and for the personnel entrusted with the organization and administration of these zones and localities, and with the care of the persons therein assembled.

Nevertheless, persons whose permanent residence is within such zones shall have the right to stay there.

Art 2. No persons residing, in whatever capacity, in a hospital and safety zone shall perform any work, either within or without the zone, directly connected with military operations or the production of war material.

Art 3. The Power establishing a hospital and safety zone shall take all necessary measures to prohibit access to all persons who have no right of residence or entry therein.

Art 4. Hospital and safety zones shall fulfil the following conditions:

(a) they shall comprise only a small part of the territory governed by the Power which has established them

(b) they shall be thinly populated in relation to the possibilities of accommodation

(c) they shall be far removed and free from all military objectives, or large industrial or administrative establishments

(d) they shall not be situated in areas which, according to every probability, may become important for the conduct of the war.

Art 5. Hospital and safety zones shall be subject to the following obligations:

(a) the lines of communication and means of transport which they possess shall not be used for the transport of military personnel or material, even in transit

(b) they shall in no case be defended by military means.

Art 6. Hospital and safety zones shall be marked by means of oblique red bands on a white ground, placed on the buildings and outer precincts.

Zones reserved exclusively for the wounded and sick may be marked by means of the Red Cross (Red Crescent, Red Lion and Sun) emblem on a white ground.

They may be similarly marked at night by means of appropriate illumination.

Art 7. The Powers shall communicate to all the High Contracting Parties in peacetime or on the outbreak of hostilities, a list of the hospital and safety zones in the territories governed by them. They shall also give notice of any new zones set up during hostilities.

As soon as the adverse party has received the above-mentioned notification, the zone shall be regularly established.

If, however, the adverse party considers that the conditions of the present agreement have not been fulfilled, it may refuse to recognize the zone by giving immediate notice thereof to the Party responsible for the said zone, or may make its recognition of such zone dependent upon the institution of the control provided for in Article 8.

Art 8. Any Power having recognized one or several hospital and safety zones instituted by the adverse Party shall be entitled to demand control by one or more Special Commissions, for the purpose of ascertaining if the zones fulfil the conditions and obligations stipulated in the present agreement.

For this purpose, members of the Special Commissions shall at all times have free access to the various zones and may even reside there permanently. They shall be given all facilities for their duties of inspection.

Art 9. Should the Special Commissions note any facts which they consider contrary to the stipulations of the present agreement, they shall at once draw the attention of the Power governing the said zone to these facts, and shall fix a time limit of five days within which the matter should be rectified. They shall duly notify the Power which has recognized the zone.

If, when the time limit has expired, the Power governing the zone has not complied with the warning, the adverse Party may declare that it is no longer bound by the present agreement in respect of the said zone.

Art 10. Any Power setting up one or more hospital and safety zones, and the adverse Parties to whom their existence has been notified, shall nominate or have nominated by the Protecting Powers or by other neutral Powers, persons eligible to be members of the Special Commissions mentioned in Articles 8 and 9.

Art 11. In no circumstances may hospital and safety zones be the object of attack. They shall be protected and respected at all times by the Parties to the conflict.

Art 12. In the case of occupation of a territory, the hospital and safety zones therein shall continue to be respected and utilized as such.

Their purpose may, however, be modified by the Occupying Power, on condition that all measures are taken to ensure the safety of the persons accommodated.

Art 13. The present agreement shall also apply to localities which the Powers may utilize for the same purposes as hospital and safety zones.

ANNEX II. DRAFT REGULATIONS CONCERNING COLLECTIVE RELIEF

Art 1. The Internee Committees shall be allowed to distribute collective relief shipments for which they are responsible to all internees who are dependent for administration on the said Committee's place of internment, including those internees who are in hospitals, or in prison or other penitentiary establishments.

Art 2. The distribution of collective relief shipments shall be effected in accordance with the instructions of the donors and with a plan drawn up by the Internee Committees. The issue of medical stores shall, however, be made for preference in agreement with the senior medical officers, and the latter may, in hospitals and infirmaries, waive the said instructions, if the needs of their patients so demand. Within the limits thus defined, the distribution shall always be carried out equitably.

Art 3. Members of Internee Committees shall be allowed to go to the railway stations or other points of arrival of relief supplies near their places of internment so as to enable them to verify the quantity as well as the quality of the goods received and to make out detailed reports thereon for the donors.

Art 4. Internee Committees shall be given the facilities necessary for verifying whether the distribution of collective relief in all subdivisions and annexes of their places of internment has been carried out in accordance with their instructions.

Art 5. Internee Committees shall be allowed to complete, and to cause to be completed by members of the Internee Committees in labour detachments or by the senior medical officers of infirmaries and hospitals, forms or questionnaires intended for the donors, relating to collective relief supplies (distribution, requirements, quantities, etc.). Such forms and questionnaires, duly completed, shall be forwarded to the donors without delay.

Art 6. In order to secure the regular distribution of collective relief supplies to the internees in their place of internment, and to meet any needs that may arise through the arrival of fresh parties of internees, the Internee Committees shall be allowed to create and maintain sufficient reserve stocks of collective relief. For this purpose, they shall have suitable warehouses at their disposal; each warehouse shall be provided with two locks, the Internee Committee holding the keys of one lock, and the commandant of the place of internment the keys of the other.

Art 7. The High Contracting Parties, and the Detaining Powers in particular, shall, so far as is in any way possible and subject to the regulations governing the food supply of the population, authorize purchases of goods to be made in their territories for the distribution of collective relief to the internees. They shall likewise facilitate the transfer of funds and other financial measures of a technical or administrative nature taken for the purpose of making such purchases.

Art 8. The foregoing provisions shall not constitute an obstacle to the right of internees to receive collective relief before their arrival in a place of internment or in the course of their transfer, nor to the possibility of representatives of the Protecting Power, or of the International Committee of the Red Cross or any other humanitarian organization giving assistance to internees and responsible for forwarding such supplies, ensuring the distribution thereof to the recipients by any other means they may deem suitable.

ANNEX III

I. Internment Card

<table>
<tr>
<td>1. Front</td>
<td>

CIVILIAN INTERNEE MAIL | Postage free |

POST CARD

IMPORTANT

This card must be completed by each internee immediately on being interned and each time his address is altered by reason of transfer to another place of internment or to a hospital.

This card is not the same as the special card which each internee is allowed to send to his relatives.

CENTRAL INFORMATION AGENCY
FOR PROTECTED PERSONS

INTERNATIONAL COMMITTEE
OF THE RED CROSS

</td>
</tr>
<tr>
<td>2. Reverse side</td>
<td>

Write legibly and in block letters—1. Nationality

2. Surname   3. First names *(in full)*   4. First name of father

5. Date of birth   6. Place of birth

7. Occupation

8. Address before detention

9. Address of next of kin

*10. Interned on :
    (or)
    Coming from (hospital, etc.) on :

*11. State of health

12. Present address

13. Date   14. Signature

*Strike out what is not applicable — Do not add any remarks — **See explanations** on other side of card

</td>
</tr>
</table>

(Size of internment card— 10 × 15 cm)

ANNEX III

II. Letter

CIVILIAN INTERNEE SERVICE
___

Postage free

To

Street and number

Place of destination *(in block capitals)*

Province or Department

Country *(in block capitals)*

Internment address

Date and place of birth

Surname and first names

Sender :

(Size of letter — 29 × 15 cm)

ANNEX III

III. Correspondence Card

1. Front

CIVILIAN INTERNEE MAIL

Postage free

POST CARD

To

Street and number

Place of destination *(in block capitals)*

Province or Department

Country *(in block capitals)*

Sender:

Surname and first names

Place and date of birth

Internment address

2. Reverse side

Date :

....

....

....

....

....

....

Write on the dotted lines only and as legibly as possible.

(Size of correspondence card — 10 × 15 cm)

Appendix E

Additional Protocol I 1977: Annexes

ANNEX I AS AMENDED ON 30 NOVEMBER 1993: REGULATIONS CONCERNING IDENTIFICATION

ARTICLE 1 GENERAL PROVISIONS (NEW ARTICLE)

1. The regulations concerning identification in this Annex implement the relevant provisions of the Geneva Conventions and the Protocol; they are intended to facilitate the identification of personnel, material, units, transports and installations protected under the Geneva Conventions and the Protocol.

2. These rules do not in and of themselves establish the right to protection. This right is governed by the relevant articles in the Conventions and the Protocol.

3. The competent authorities may, subject to the relevant provisions of the Geneva Conventions and the Protocol, at all times regulate the use, display, illumination and detectability of the distinctive emblems and signals.

4. The High Contracting Parties and in particular the Parties to the conflict are invited at all times to agree upon additional or other signals, means or systems which enhance the possibility of identification and take full advantage of technological developments in this field.

CHAPTER I IDENTITY CARDS

ARTICLE 2 IDENTITY CARD FOR PERMANENT CIVILIAN MEDICAL AND RELIGIOUS PERSONNEL

1. The identity card for permanent civilian medical and religious personnel referred to in Article 18, paragraph 3, of the Protocol should:

(a) bear the distinctive emblem and be of such size that it can be carried in the pocket;

(b) be as durable as practicable;

(c) be worded in the national or official language and, in addition and when appropriate, in the local language of the region concerned;

(d) mention the name, the date of birth (or, if that date is not available, the age at the time of issue) and the identity number, if any, of the holder;

(e) state in what capacity the holder is entitled to the protection of the Conventions and of the Protocol;

(f) bear the photograph of the holder as well as his signature or his thumbprint, or both,

(g) bear the stamp and signature of the competent authority;

(h) state the date of issue and date of expiry of the card;

(i) indicate, whenever possible, the holder's blood group, on the reverse side of the card.

2. The identity card shall be uniform throughout the territory of each High Contracting Party and, as far as possible, of the same type for all Parties to the conflict. The Parties to the conflict may be guided by the single-language model shown in Figure 1. At the outbreak of hostilities, they shall transmit to each other a specimen of the model they are using, if such model differs from that shown in Figure 1. The identity card shall be made out, if possible, in duplicate, one copy being kept by the issuing authority, which should maintain control of the cards which it has issued.

3. In no circumstances may permanent civilian medical and religious personnel be deprived of their identity cards. In the event of the loss of a card, they shall be entitled to obtain a duplicate copy.

Article 3 Identity Card for Temporary Civilian Medical and Religious Personnel

1. The identity card for temporary civilian medical and religious personnel should, whenever possible, be similar to that provided for in Article 1 of these Regulations. The Parties to the conflict may be guided by the model shown in Figure 1.

2. When circumstances preclude the provision to temporary civilian medical and religious personnel of identity cards similar to those described in Article 2 of these

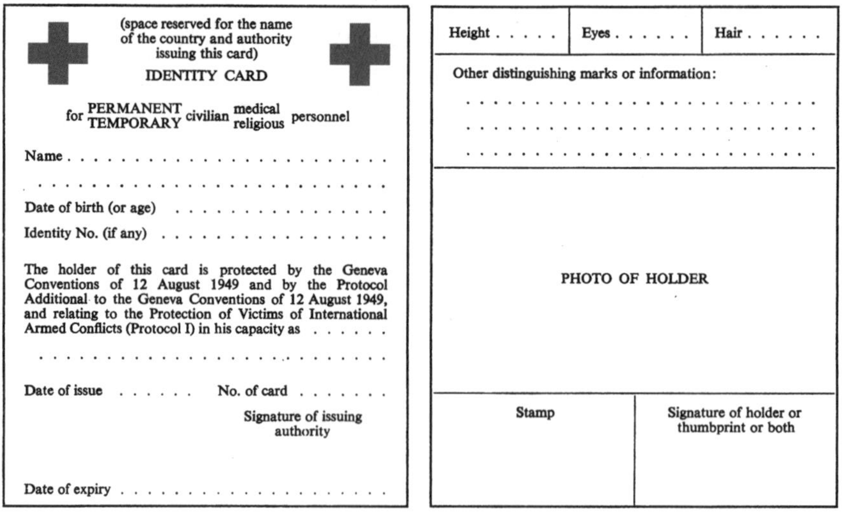

Fig 1: Model of identity card (74 mm × 105 mm)

Regulations, the said personnel may be provided with a certificate signed by the competent authority certifying that the person to whom it is issued is assigned to duty as temporary personnel and stating, if possible, the duration of such assignment and his right to wear the distinctive emblem. The certificate should mention the holder's name and date of birth (or if that is not available, his age at the time when the certificate was issued), his function and identity number, if any. It shall bear his signature or his thumbprint, or both.

CHAPTER II THE DISTINCTIVE EMBLEM

ARTICLE 4 SHAPE

The distinctive emblem (red on a white ground) shall be as large as appropriate under the circumstances. For the shapes of the cross, the crescent or the lion and sun*, the High Contracting Parties may be guided by the models shown in Figure 2.

ARTICLE 5 USE

1. The distinctive emblem shall, whenever possible, be displayed on a flat surface, on flags or in any other way appropriate to the lay of the land, so that it is visible from as many directions and from as far away as possible, and in particular from the air.

2. At night or when visibility is reduced, the distinctive emblem may be lighted or illuminated.

3. The distinctive emblem may be made of materials which make it recognizable by technical means of detecting. The red part should be painted on top of black primer paint in order to facilitate its identification, in particular by infrared instruments.

4. Medical and religious personnel carrying out their duties in the battle area shall, as far as possible, wear headgear and clothing bearing the distinctive emblem.

FIG 2: Distinctive emblems in red on a white ground

* No State has used the emblem of the lion and sun since 1980.

CHAPTER III DISTINCTIVE SIGNALS

ARTICLE 6 USE

1. All distinctive signals specified in this Chapter may be used by medical units or transports.

2. These signals, at the exclusive disposal of medical units and transports, shall not be used for any other purpose, the use of the light signal being reserved (see paragraph 3 below).

3. In the absence of a special agreement between the Parties to the conflict reserving the use of flashing blue lights for the identification of medical vehicles, ships and craft, the use of such signals for other vehicles, ships and craft is not prohibited.

4. Temporary medical aircraft which cannot, either for lack of time or because of their characteristics, be marked with the distinctive emblem, may use the distinctive signals authorized in this Chapter.

ARTICLE 7 LIGHT SIGNAL

1. The light signal, consisting of a flashing blue light as defined in the Airworthiness Technical Manual of the International Civil Aviation Organization (ICAO) Doc. 9051, is established for the use of medical aircraft to signal their identity. No other aircraft shall use this signal. Medical aircraft using the flashing blue light should exhibit such lights as may be necessary to make the light signal visible from as many directions as possible.

2. In accordance with the provisions of Chapter XIV, para. 4 of the International Maritime Organization (IMO) International Code of Signals, vessels protected by the Geneva Conventions of 1949 and the Protocol should exhibit one or more flashing blue lights visible from any direction.

3. Medical vehicles should exhibit one or more flashing blue lights visible from as far away as possible. The High Contracting Parties and, in particular, the Parties to the conflict which use lights of other colours should give notification of this.

4. The recommended blue colour is obtained when its chromaticity is within the boundaries of the International Commission on Illumination (ICI) chromaticity diagram defined by the following equations:

$$\text{green boundary } y = 0.065 + 0{,}805x;$$
$$\text{white boundary } y = 0.400 - x;$$
$$\text{purple boundary } x = 0.133 + 0{,}600y.$$

The recommended flashing rate of the blue light is between sixty and one hundred flashes per minute.

ARTICLE 8 RADIO SIGNAL

1. The radio signal shall consist of the urgency signal and the distinctive signal as described in the International Telecommunication Union (ITU) Radio Regulations (RR Articles 40 and N 40).

2. The radio message preceded by the urgency and distinctive signals mentioned in paragraph 1 shall be transmitted in English at appropriate intervals on a frequency or frequencies specified for this purpose in the Radio Regulations, and shall convey the following data relating to the medical transports concerned:

(a) call sign or other recognized means of identification;

(b) position;

(c) number and type of vehicles;

(d) intended route;

(e) estimated time en route and of departure and arrival, as appropriate;

(f) any other information, such as flight altitude, guarded radio frequencies, languages used and secondary surveillance radar modes and codes.

3. In order to facilitate the communications referred to in paragraphs 1 and 2, as well as the communications referred to in Articles 22, 23 and 25 to 31 of the Protocol, the High Contracting Parties, the Parties to a conflict, or one of the Parties to a conflict, acting in agreement or alone, may designate, in accordance with the Table of Frequency Allocations in the Radio Regulations annexed to the International Telecommunication Convention, and publish selected national frequencies to be used by them for such communications. The International Telecommunication Union shall be notified of these frequencies in accordance with procedures approved by a World Administrative Radio Conference.

ARTICLE 9 ELECTRONIC IDENTIFICATION

1. The Secondary Surveillance Radar (SSR) system, as specified in Annex 10 to the Chicago Convention on International Civil Aviation of 7 December 1944, as amended from time to time, may be used to identify and to follow the course of medical aircraft. The SSR mode and code to be reserved for the exclusive use of medical aircraft shall be established by the High Contracting Parties, the Parties to a conflict, or one of the Parties to a conflict, acting in agreement or alone, in accordance with procedures to be recommended by the International Civil Aviation Organization.

2. Protected medical transports may, for their identification and location, use standard aeronautical radar transponders and/or maritime search and rescue radar transponders.

It should be possible for protected medical transports to be identified by other vessels or aircraft equipped with secondary surveillance radar by means of a code transmitted by a radar transponder, e.g. in mode 3/A, fitted on the medical transports.

The code transmitted by the medical transport transponder should be assigned to that transport by the competent authorities and notified to all the Parties to the conflict.

3. It should be possible for medical transports to be identified by submarines by the appropriate underwater acoustic signals transmitted by the medical transports.

The underwater acoustic signal shall consist of the call sign (or any other recognized means of identification of medical transport) of the ship preceded by the single group YYY transmitted in morse on an appropriate acoustic frequency, e.g. 5 kHz.

Parties to a conflict wishing to use the underwater acoustic identification signal described above shall inform the Parties concerned of the signal as soon as possible, and shall, when notifying the use of their hospital ships, confirm the frequency to be employed.

4. Parties to a conflict may, by special agreement between them, establish for their use a similar electronic system for the identification of medical vehicles, and medical ships and craft.

CHAPTER IV COMMUNICATIONS

ARTICLE 10 RADIOCOMMUNICATIONS

1. The urgency signal and the distinctive signal provided for in Article 8 may precede appropriate radiocommunications by medical units and transports in the application of the procedures carried out under Articles 22, 23 and 25 to 31 of the Protocol.

2. The medical transports referred to in Articles 40 (Section II, No. 3209) and N 40 (Section III, No. 3214) of the ITU Radio Regulations may also transmit their communications by satellite systems, in accordance with the provisions of Articles 37, N 37 and 59 of the ITU Radio Regulations for the Mobile-Satellite Services.

ARTICLE 11 USE OF INTERNATIONAL CODES

Medical units and transports may also use the codes and signals laid down by the International Telecommunication Union, the International Civil Aviation Organization and the International Maritime Organization. These codes and signals shall be used in accordance with the standards, practices and procedures established by these Organizations.

ARTICLE 12 OTHER MEANS OF COMMUNICATION

When two-way radiocommunication is not possible, the signals provided for in the International Code of Signals adopted by the International Maritime Organization or in the appropriate Annex to the Chicago Convention on International Civil Aviation of 7 December 1944, as amended from time to time, may be used.

ARTICLE 13 FLIGHT PLANS

The agreements and notifications relating to flight plans provided for in Article 29 of the Protocol shall as far as possible be formulated in accordance with procedures laid down by the International Civil Aviation Organization.

ARTICLE 14 SIGNALS AND PROCEDURES FOR THE INTERCEPTION OF MEDICAL AIRCRAFT

If an intercepting aircraft is used to verify the identity of a medical aircraft in flight or to require it to land in accordance with Articles 30 and 31 of the Protocol, the standard visual and radio interception procedures prescribed by Annex 2 to the Chicago Convention on International Civil Aviation of 7 December 1944, as amended from time to time, should be used by the intercepting and the medical aircraft.

CHAPTER V CIVIL DEFENCE

ARTICLE 15 IDENTITY CARD

1. The identity card of the civil defence personnel provided for in Article 66, paragraph 3, of the Protocol is governed by the relevant provisions of Article 2 of these Regulations.

2. The identity card for civil defence personnel may follow the model shown in Figure 3.

Front	Reverse side

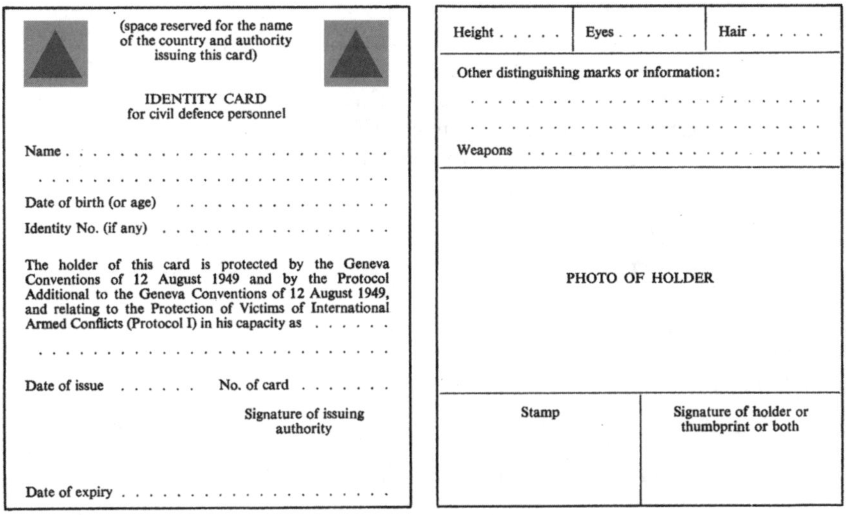

(space reserved for the name of the country and authority issuing this card)

IDENTITY CARD
for civil defence personnel

Name . . . .

. . . .

Date of birth (or age) . . . .

Identity No. (if any) . . . .

The holder of this card is protected by the Geneva Conventions of 12 August 1949 and by the Protocol Additional to the Geneva Conventions of 12 August 1949, and relating to the Protection of Victims of International Armed Conflicts (Protocol I) in his capacity as . . . . . .

. . . .

Date of issue . . . . . . No. of card . . . .

Signature of issuing authority

Date of expiry . . . .

Height . . . . . | Eyes . . . . . . | Hair . . . . . .

Other distinguishing marks or information:

. . . .
. . . .

Weapons . . . .

PHOTO OF HOLDER

Stamp | Signature of holder or thumbprint or both

FIG 3: Model identity card for civil defence personnel (format: 74 mm × 105 mm)

3. If civil defence personnel are permitted to carry light individual weapons, an entry to that effect should be made on the card mentioned.

Article 16 International Distinctive Sign

1. The international distinctive sign of civil defence provided for in Article 66, paragraph 4, of the Protocol is an equilateral blue triangle on an orange ground. A model is shown in Figure 4.

Fig 4: Blue triangle on an orange background

2. It is recommended that:

(a) if the blue triangle is on a flag or armlet or tabard, the ground to the triangle be the orange flag, armlet or tabard;

(b) one of the angles of the triangle be pointed vertically upwards;

(c) no angle of the triangle touch the edge of the orange ground.

3. The international distinctive sign shall be as large as appropriate under the circumstances. The distinctive sign shall, whenever possible, be displayed on flat surfaces or on flags visible from as many directions and from as far away as possible. Subject to the instructions of the competent authority, civil defence personnel shall, as far as possible, wear headgear and clothing bearing the international distinctive sign. At night or when visibility is reduced, the sign may be lighted or illuminated; it may also be made of materials rendering it recognizable by technical means of detection.

CHAPTER VI WORKS AND INSTALLATIONS CONTAINING DANGEROUS FORCES

Article 17 International Special Sign

1. The international special sign for works and installations containing dangerous forces, as provided for in Article 56, paragraph 7, of the Protocol, shall be a group of three bright orange circles of equal size, placed on the same axis, the distance between each circle being one radius, in accordance with Figure 5 illustrated below.

2. The sign shall be as large as appropriate under the circumstances. When displayed over an extended surface it may be repeated as often as appropriate under

FIG 5: International special sign for works and installations containing dangerous forces

the circumstances. It shall, whenever possible, be displayed on flat surfaces or on flags so as to be visible from as many directions and from as far away as possible.

3. On a flag, the distance between the outer limits of the sign and the adjacent sides of the flag shall be one radius of a circle. The flag shall be rectangular and shall have a white ground.

4. At night or when visibility is reduced, the sign may be lighted or illuminated. It may also be made of materials rendering it recognizable by technical means of detection.

ANNEX II. IDENTITY CARD FOR JOURNALISTS ON DANGEROUS PROFESSIONAL MISSIONS

NOTICE

This identity card is issued to journalists on dangerous professional missions in areas of armed conflicts. The holder is entitled to be treated as a civilian under the Geneva Conventions of 12 August 1949, and their Additional Protocol I. The card must be carried at all times by the bearer. If he is detained, he shall at once hand it to the Detaining Authorities, to assist in his identification.

ملصوطة

تصرف هذه البطاقة للصحفيين المكلفين بمهمات مهنية خطرة في مناطق المنازعات المسلحة ويحق لصاحبها أن يعامل معاملة الشخص المدني وفقاً لاتفاقيات جنيف المؤرخة ١٢ آب / أغسطس ١٩٤٩ ولحقها (بروتوكولها) الإضافي الأول. ويجب أن يحتفظ صاحب البطاقة بها دوما وإذا اعتقل فيجب أن يسلمها فوراً إلى سلطة الاعتقال لتساعد على تحديد هويته.

NOTA

La presente tarjeta de identidad se expide a los periodistas en misión profesional peligrosa en zonas de conflictos armados. Su titular tiene derecho a ser tratado como persona civil conforme a los Convenios de Ginebra del 12 de agosto de 1949 y su Protocolo adicional I. El titular debe llevar la tarjeta consigo, en todo momento. En caso de ser detenido, la entregará inmediatamente a las autoridades que lo detengan a fin de facilitar su identificación.

AVIS

La présente carte d'identité est délivrée aux journalistes en mission professionnelle périlleuse dans des zones de conflit armé. Le porteur a le droit d'être traité comme une personne civile aux termes des Conventions de Genève du 12 août 1949 et de leur Protocole additionnel I. La carte doit être portée en tout temps par son titulaire. Si celui-ci est arrêté, il la remettra immédiatement aux autorités qui le détiennent afin qu'elles puissent l'identifier.

ПРИМЕЧАНИЕ

Настоящее удостоверение выдается журналистам, находящимся в опасных профессиональных командировках в районах вооруженного конфликта. Его обладатель имеет право на обращение с ним как с гражданским лицом в соответствии с Женевскими Конвенциями от 12 августа 1949 г. и Дополнительным Протоколом I к ним. Владелец настоящего удостоверения должен постоянно иметь его при себе. В случае задержания он немедленно вручает его задерживающим властям для содействия установлению его личности.

(Name of country issuing this card)

(اسم القطر المصدر لهذه البطاقة)

(Nombre del país que expide esta tarjeta)

(Nom du pays qui a délivré cette carte)

(Название страны, выдавшей настоящее удостоверение)

IDENTITY CARD FOR JOURNALISTS ON DANGEROUS PROFESSIONAL MISSIONS

بطاقة الهوية الخاصة بالصحفيين المكلفين بمهمات مهنية خطرة

TARJETA DE IDENTIDAD DE PERIODISTA EN MISION PELIGROSA

CARTE D'IDENTITÉ DE JOURNALISTE EN MISSION PÉRILLEUSE

УДОСТОВЕРЕНИЕ ЖУРНАЛИСТА, НАХОДЯЩЕГОСЯ В ОПАСНОЙ КОМАНДИРОВКЕ

Front

Issued by (competent authority)
صدرت من (السلطة المختصة)
Expedida por (autoridad competente)
Délivrée par (autorité compétente) -------------
Выдано (компетентными властями)

Photograph of bearer / صورة صاحب البطاقة / Fotografía del titular / Photographie du porteur / Фотография предъявителя

Place / المكان / Lugar / Lieu / Место
Date / التاريخ / Fecha / Date / Дата

(Official seal imprint)
(الخاتم الرسمي)
(Sello oficial)
(Timbre de l'autorité délivrant la carte)
(Официальная печать)

(Signature of bearer)
(توقيع صاحب البطاقة)
(Firma del titular)
(Signature du porteur)
(Подпись владельца)

Name / اسم الشهرة / Apellidos / Nom / Фамилия

First names / الاسم / Nombre / Prénoms / Имя, Отчество

Place & date of birth / مكان وتاريخ الولادة / Lugar y fecha de nacimiento / Lieu & date de naissance / Дата и место рождения

Correspondent of / مراسل / Corresponsal de / Correspondant de / Корреспондент

Specific occupation / الهيئة المحددة / Categoría profesional / Catégorie professionnelle / Род занятий

Valid for / يبقى المفعول إلى / Válido por / Durée de validité / Действительно

Height / الطول / Estatura / Taille / Рост
Eyes / العينان / Ojos / Yeux / Глаза

Weight / الوزن / Peso / Poids / Вес
Hair / الشعر / Cabello / Cheveux / Волосы

Blood type / فصيلة الدم / Grupo sanguíneo / Groupe sanguin / Группа крови
Rh factor / عامل التخثط / Factor Rh / Facteur Rh / Rh-фактор

Religion (optional) / الديانة (اختياري) / Religión (optativo) / Religion (facultatif) / Религия (факультативно)

Fingerprints (optional) / البصمات (اختياري) / Huellas dactilares (optativo) / Empreintes digitales (facultatif) / Отпечатки пальцев (факультативно)

(Left forefinger) / (البابة اليسرى) / (Dedo índice izquierdo) / (Index gauche) / (Левый указательный палец)

(Right forefinger) / (البابة اليمنى) / (Dedo índice derecho) / (Index droit) / (Правый указательный палец)

Special marks of identification / العلامات المميزة لتحديد الهوية / Señas particulares / Signes particuliers / Особые приметы

Reverse side

Appendix F

Hague Cultural Property Convention 1954, Article 16

CULTURAL PROPERTY EMBLEM AND IDENTITY CARD

CHAPTER V THE DISTINCTIVE EMBLEM

EMBLEM OF THE CONVENTION

Art 16.1. The distinctive emblem of the Convention shall take the form of a shield, pointed below, per saltire blue and white (a shield consisting of a royal-blue square, one of the angles of which forms the point of the shield, and of a royal-blue triangle above the square, the space on either side being taken up by a white triangle).

2. The emblem shall be used alone, or repeated three times in a triangular formation (one shield below), under the conditions provided for in Article 17.

Appendix G

Annex to the Amended Mines Protocol

TECHNICAL ANNEX

1. Recording

(a) Recording of the location of mines other than remotely-delivered mines, mine-fields, mined areas, booby-traps and other devices shall be carried out in accordance with the following provisions:

    (i) the location of the minefields, mined areas and areas of booby-traps and other devices shall be specified accurately by relation to the coordinates of at least two reference points and the estimated dimensions of the area containing these weapons in relation to those reference points;

    (ii) maps, diagrams or other records shall be made in such a way as to indicate the location of minefields, mined areas, booby-traps and other devices in relation to reference points, and these records shall also indicate their perimeters and extent;

    (iii) for purposes of detection and clearance of mines, booby-traps and other devices, maps, diagrams or other records shall contain complete information on the type, number, emplacing method, type of fuse and life time, date and time of laying, anti-handling devices (if any) and other relevant information on all these weapons laid. Whenever feasible the minefield record shall show the exact location of every mine, except in row minefields where the row location is sufficient. The precise location and operating mechanism of each booby-trap laid shall be individually recorded.

(b) The estimated location and area of remotely-delivered mines shall be specified by coordinates of reference points (normally corner points) and shall be ascertained and when feasible marked on the ground at the earliest opportunity. The total number and types of mines laid, the date and time of laying and the self-destruction time periods shall also be recorded.

(c) Copies of records shall be held at a level of command sufficient to guarantee their safety as far as possible.

(d) The use of mines produced after the entry into force of this Protocol is prohibited unless they are marked in English or in the respective national language or languages with the following information:

    (i) name of the country of origin;
    (ii) month and year of production; and
    (iii) serial number or lot number.

The marking should be visible, legible, durable and resistant to environmental effects, as far as possible.

2. Specifications on Detectability

(a) With respect to anti-personnel mines produced after 1 January 1997, such mines shall incorporate in their construction a material or device that enables the mine to be detected by commonly-available technical mine detection equipment and provides a response signal equivalent to a signal from 8 grammes or more of iron in a single coherent mass.

(b) With respect to anti-personnel mines produced before 1 January 1997, such mines shall either incorporate in their construction, or have attached prior to their emplacement, in a manner not easily removable, a material or device that enables the mine to be detected by commonly-available technical mine detection equipment and provides a response signal equivalent to a signal from 8 grammes or more of iron in a single coherent mass.

(c) In the event that a High Contracting Party determines that it cannot immediately comply with sub-paragraph (b), it may declare at the time of its notification of consent to be bound by this Protocol that it will defer compliance with sub-paragraph (b) for a period not to exceed 9 years from the entry into force of this Protocol. In the meantime it shall, to the extent feasible, minimize the use of anti-personnel mines that do not so comply.

3. Specifications on Self-Destruction and Self-Deactivation

(a) All remotely-delivered anti-personnel mines shall be designed and constructed so that no more than 10% of activated mines will fail to self-destruct within 30 days after emplacement, and each mine shall have a back-up self-deactivation feature designed and constructed so that, in combination with the self-destruction mechanism, no more than one in one thousand activated mines will function as a mine 120 days after emplacement.

(b) All non-remotely delivered anti-personnel mines, used outside marked areas, as defined in Article 5 of this Protocol, shall comply with the requirements for self-destruction and self-deactivation stated in sub-paragraph (a).

(c) In the event that a High Contracting Party determines that it cannot immediately comply with sub-paragraphs (a) and/or (b), it may declare at the time of its notification of consent to be bound by this Protocol, that it will, with respect to mines produced prior to the entry into force of this Protocol defer compliance with sub-paragraphs (a) and/or (b) for a period not to exceed 9 years from the entry into force of this Protocol.

During this period of deferral, the High Contracting Party shall:

 (i) undertake to minimize, to the extent feasible, the use of anti-personnel mines that do not so comply, and

(ii) with respect to remotely-delivered anti-personnel mines, comply with either the requirements for self-destruction or the requirements for self-deactivation and, with respect to other anti-personnel mines comply with at least the requirements for self-deactivation.

4. INTERNATIONAL SIGNS FOR MINEFIELDS AND MINED AREAS

Signs similar to the example attached[1] and as specified below shall be utilized in the marking of minefields and mined areas to ensure their visibility and recognition by the civilian population:

(a) size and shape: a triangle or square no smaller than 28 centimetres (11 inches) by 20 centimetres (7.9 inches) for a triangle, and 15 centimetres (6 inches) per side for a square;

(b) colour: red or orange with a yellow reflecting border.

[1] See Roberts and Guelff, *Documents*, 732.

BIBLIOGRAPHY

Yamashita Trial, 1948 AD (Case No 111)

Zyklon B Case (in re Tesch and Others), 1 WCR 93

Books, reports, articles, and other sources

R Bernhardt (ed), *Encyclopaedia of Public International Law* (1992–2000)

M Bothe, K-J Partsch, and WA Solf, *New Rules for Victims of Armed Conflicts* (Nijhoff 1982) (Bothe, Partsch, and Solf, *New Rules*)

J Cameron (ed), *The Peleus Trial* (1948)

EJ Castren, *The Present Law of War and Neutrality* (1954)

Defence Committee Report, see United Kingdom

Despatch, see United Kingdom

L Doswald-Beck (ed), *San Remo Manual on International Law Applicable to Armed Conflicts at Sea* (1995) (*San Remo Manual*)

JW Garner, *International Law and the World War* (1920) (Garner, *International Law*)

Germany, Federal Ministry of Defence, *Humanitarian Law in Armed Conflicts* (1992)

Grotius, *De Jure Belli ac Pacis* (1625)

M Hale, *The History of the Pleas of the Crown* (1736)

House of Commons Defence Committee, see United Kingdom

ICRC Commentary, see Sandoz etc

M Lachs, *War Crimes* (1945)

H Lauterpacht, see Oppenheim; United Kingdom

Lieber Code, see United States

L Oppenheim, *International Law*, vol 2 (7th edn by H Lauterpacht 1952) (Oppenheim)

J Pictet (ed), *Commentary on the Geneva Conventions of 12 August 1949* (1952–60) (Pictet, *Commentary*)

A Roberts, 'What is a Military Occupation?' (1984) BYIL 249

A Roberts and R Guelff, *Documents on the Laws of War* (3rd edn 2000) (Roberts and Guelff, *Documents*)

PJ Rowe (ed), *The Gulf War 1990–91 in International and English Law* (1993) (Rowe, *Gulf War*)

San Remo Manual, see Doswald-Beck

Y Sandoz, C Swinarski, and B Zimmermann (eds), *Commentary on the Additional Protocols of 8 June 1977 to the Geneva Conventions of 12 August 1949* (1987) (*ICRC Commentary*)

M Sassoli and AA Bouvier (eds), *How Does Law Protect in War?* (1999)

D Schindler, 'Transformations in the Law of Neutrality Since 1945' in AJM Dillessen and GJ Tanja, *Humanitarian Law of Armed Conflict: Challenges Ahead* (1991)

WA Solf and JA Roach (eds), *Index of International Humanitarian Law* (1987)

JM Spaight, *War Rights on Land* (1911) (Spaight, *War Rights*)

JM Spaight, *Air Power and War Rights* (2nd edn 1933) (Spaight, *Air Power*, 1933)

JM Spaight, *Air Power and War Rights* (3rd edn 1947) (Spaight, *Air Power*, 1947)

Switzerland, *Official Records of the Diplomatic Conference on the Reaffirmation and Development of International Humanitarian Law Applicable in Armed Conflicts* (1978)

United Kingdom, Correspondence respecting the Peace Conference held at The Hague in 1899 (Cmnd 9534)

United Kingdom, Despatch by the Joint Commander of Operation Granby, Second Supplement to the *London Gazette*, 18 June 1991 (Despatch)

United Kingdom, Ministry of Defence, *Prisoner of War Handling* (JWP 1–10, 2001)

United Kingdom, *Preliminary Lessons of Operation Granby*, House of Commons Defence Committee Tenth Report (HMSO 1991)

United Kingdom, The War Office, *The Law of War on Land being Part III of the Manual of Military Law* (1958) (MML)

United Kingdom, Ministry of Defence, *United Kingdom Compendium of National Rules of Engagement* (JSP 398)

United Nations, *Report of the Secretary-General Pursuant to General Assembly Resolution 53/35: the Fall of Srebrenica*, UN doc A/54/549 (1999)

United States, Department of Defense, *Conduct of the Persian Gulf War*, Final Report to Congress (1992) (Department of Defense Report)

United States, Instructions for the Government of Armies of the United States in the Field, General Order 100, 1863 (the Lieber Code)

E de Vattel, *Le Droit des Gens* (1758)

Index

emblems, insignia and badges (*cont.*):
  aircraft (*cont.*):
    military 12.10.4
    neutral 12.10.4
  armlets 7.26
  booby-traps 6.7.5
  captains' badges 12.25.4
  cultural property 5.25.2
  Cultural Property Convention 1954
    5.25.2, 5.26.6, App F
  distinctive App E
  Geneva Conventions 1949 5.10, 16.34
  grave breaches 5.9.2 n37, 16.25, 16.27 n111
  hospitals
    Red Cross emblems and 5.10.1
    ships 5.41.1
  hostilities, conduct of 5.10–5.10.1
  identity cards on 7.26
  internal armed conflicts 15.13, 15.48
  International Criminal Court 16.34
  medical aircraft 12.104.1, 12.106–12.106.1
  medical personnel 7.23–7.24, 7.26,
    7.29, 15.48
  medical transport 7.23–7.24, 15.29.1
  medical units 7.23–7.24, 15.29.1
  negotiations between belligerents 10.2
  neutrality 5.11
  orange circles, three bright 5.30.1
  peace support operations 14.13
  perfidy 5.9.2 n37, 16.25, 16.27 n111
  prisoners of war 8.25, 8.47
    punishment of 8.121
  protective 5.10
  punishment by deprivation of 8.121
  ranks 8.47
  recognized 5.10
  Red Cross, Red Crescent, Red Lion
    and Sun and Red Star of David,
    use of 5.10
  religious personnel 15.48
  removal of 5.11.1, 5.17.2
  shipwrecked 15.48
  surrender, feigning 5.10.1
  three shield emblem, cultural property
    and 5.26.6
  truce, misuse of the flag of 5.10.1
  uniforms, removal from 5.11.1, 5.17.2
  United Nations, making use of 5.10,
    14.13
  use of App E
  war crimes
    Geneva Conventions 1949 16.34
    improper use 16.27
    Red Cross badges and 5.10 n40
  works and installations containing
    dangerous forces 5.30.1–5.30.3
  wounded and sick 15.48

**embrittlement or entanglement, weapons
  causing** 6.18.2
emergencies
  accommodation 5.43.2
  civil defence tasks 5.43.2
  distressed areas, assistance in 5.43.2
  European Convention on Human Rights
    3.5.1 n18
  medical aircraft 12.112.1–12.113, 12.115,
    12.117
  supplies 5.43.2
emplacements, incendiaries used against
  6.12.6
employment *see* **work**
encircled areas *see* **sieges and encircled
  areas**
encryption equipment 12.120.1
end of application of armed conflict law
  3.10–3.11
enemy aircraft
  air to air combat 12.62–12.62.2
  auxiliary aircraft 12.37
  capture 12.62–12.62.1,12.92–12.98
  civil aircraft 12.36–12.38, 12.75,
    12.77–12.78, 12.92–12.98
  classes of aircraft 12.28
  conditions for exemption from attack
    12.29–12.31
  determination of enemy character of
    12.75, 12.77–12.79
  exemption from attack 12.27–12.32
  identification 12.62.2
  interception 12.37, 12.78, 12.82
  loss of exemption 12.32–12.33
  maritime warfare 12.95, 13.88–13.89
  markings 12.62.2, 12.75, 12.77–12.78,
    12.95, 13.88–13.89
  military aircraft 12.62–12.62.2
  military objectives 12.36–12.38
  neutral aircraft 12.75, 12.77–12.78
  neutral states, marks of 12.75,
    12.77–12.78
  surrender by 12.64–12.64.1
  visits and searches 12.77
**enemy armed forces, conduct of military
  operations against**
  aircraft, occupants of 5.7
  assassination 5.13
  emblems, recognized 5.10–5.10.1
  food and water used by enemy armed
    forces, attacking 5.19–5.19.1
  Gulf conflict 1991 8.3 n20
  hors de combat, safeguard of persons 5.6,
    5.7.2
  intelligence gathering 5.15–5.15.1
  outlawry 5.14–5.14.1
  parachutists 5.7

exemptions from attack (*cont.*):
  passenger ships 13.33
  philanthropic missions, ships on 13.33
  pollution incidents, ships dealing
    with 13.33
  scientific missions, ships on 13.33
  ships 13.33–13.39
  surrender 13.33
  UN, ships flying flag of 13.33
exercise
  internment of protected persons 9.60,
    9.103
  prisoners of war 8.61, 8.129, 8.144
  punishment 8.129, 8.144
exhumation 7.37
expectant mothers *see* **pregnant women**
experiments *see* **medical experiments**
explosive remnants of war, clearance of
    6.21–6.21.2
explosives
  air forces 6.10.2
  air operations 12.63.1
  anti-materiel 6.10.2
  bullets 6.10–6.10.2
  Chemical Weapons Convention
    6.21–6.21.2
  clearance 6.21–6.21.2
  customary law 6.10
  explosive remnants of war, clearance of
    6.21–6.21.2
  Hague Rules of Aerial Warfare 1923
    6.10.2, 12.63.1
  improvised 6.16.1
  incendiaries 6.12.4
  precautions, explosive remnants of war
    and 6.21.2
  snipers 6.10.2
  St Petersburg Declaration 1868 6.10.2
  strafing 6.10.2
  tracer 6.10.1, 6.10.2
  weight limit 6.10.2
extradition
  evidence 16.31.1
  grave breaches 16.31
  neutral states 16.31
  protected persons 9.35
  treaties 16.31.1
  UK 16.31.1
  war crimes 16.31–16.31.1

fact-finding
  Additional Protocol I 1977 16.10
  allegations 16.10.2
  armed conflict law, enforcement of
    16.10–16.10.2
  commissions of experts, *ad hoc* 16.10.2
  reports of 16.10.2

  complaints 16.10–16.10.2
  inquiries 16.14 n47
  international co-operation 16.10–16.10.2
  International Criminal Tribunal for
    Rwanda 16.10.2
  International Criminal Tribunal for the
    former Yugoslavia 16.10.2
  International Fact-Finding Commission
    16.1, 16.14 n47
    Additional Protocol I 1977 16.10
    administration 16.10.1
    competence of 16.10
    composition 16.10.1
    establishment of 16.10
    grave breaches 16.10
  International Humanitarian Fact-Finding
    Commission 16.1
  propaganda 16.10.2
  UN Security Council 16.10.2
    commissions of experts, establishment
    of *ad hoc* 16.10.2
  war crimes, allegations of 16.10.2
factions, conflict between 15.2
factories 2.6.3, 5.4.2, 5.4.4, 5.24.2
fair trials *see also* **judicial guarantees,**
    minimum
  amnesties 15.42
  appeals, time limits and 15.42
  charges, informed of 15.42
  collective responsibility, prohibition of
    15.42
  criminal law in occupied territory,
    administration of 11.66 n112
  death penalty 15.4, 15.42
  defence, right of 15.42
  detainees 9.99, 15.42
  discipline 9.99
  grave breaches 16.25
  humane treatment 15.42–15.42.2
  independent and impartial tribunals
    8.118, 15.42
  individual responsibility 15.42
  innocence, presumption of 15.42
  internal armed conflicts 15.42–15.42.2
  internment of protected persons 15.42
  minimum judicial guarantees 15.42.2
  presence of accused 15.42
  protected persons 9.19.1
  remedies, advised of 15.42
  retrospectivity 15.42
  self-incrimination 15.42
  war crimes 16.30.1
Falklands conflict
  dead 7.32.2 n77
  hospital ships 13.125 n142
  humanitarian zone, establishment of
    13.114.1 n130

punishment of war crimes (*cont.*):
International Criminal Court 16.49.1
International Criminal Tribunal for
Rwanda 16.49
International Criminal Tribunal for the
former Yugoslavia 16.49
life imprisonment 16.49–16.49.1
maximum offences 16.49–16.49.1
treaty law 16.49–16.49.1
purpose of the law of armed conflict 1.8

quarantine 8.54
quarter 5.5
garrison 5.5 n26
grave breaches 16.27 n106
hostilities, conduct of 5.5
internal armed conflicts 15.11
International Criminal Court 16.34
outlawry 5.14.1 n51
refusal of 5.5 n26
war crimes 16.27, 16.34
quartering of troops 8.49, 11.78, 11.79,
11.84.1

racist regimes, fights against
Additional Protocol I 1977 3.4
internal armed conflicts 15.2.2
international armed conflicts, as 3.4.1
liberation movements, legitimacy of 3.4.2
violence, threshold of 3.4.2
radar
Additional Protocol I 1977 App E
identification
medical aircraft 12.109
medical units, personnel and transport
7.24
Secondary Surveillance Radar (SSR)
12.109, App E
ships 13.33.1 n46
transponders 13.33.1 n46
weather 12.48
radio
complaints 16.6
Additional Protocol I 1977 App E
frequencies 13.33.1 n49
identification
medical aircraft 12.108–12.109
medical units, personnel and transport
7.24
International Telecommunications Union
12.108
propaganda 5.15.1 n58
radiocommunications App E
ships 13.33.1 n49
signals 7.24, 12.108–12.109, 13.33.1 n46,
App E
warnings 5.32.8

World Administrative Radio Conference
12.108
radioactivity, release of 5.29.3 n154
rafts and boats, life 13.33
railways and rolling stock 11.81.1
range-finding, tracers used for 6.10.2
Ranger system 6.14.1 n57
ranks
badges 8.47
commissioned officers 8.94.1, 8.108
deprivation of rank 8.121
non-commissioned officers 8.94.1,
8.108
prisoners of war 8.2, 8.31, 8.38, 8.46–8.47,
8.108
punishment 8.121, 8.129
representatives 8.94.1
work and 8.83
privileges associated with, removal of
8.129
promotion during captivity 8.47
saluting officers 8.46
segregation 8.38, 8.47, 8.129
rape 8.28 n98, 9.4 n4, 9.8
ratification of treaties 1.14
rations, reduction in 9.48
raw materiels 11.81.1
rebellions *see also* **liberation movements**
incitement to 5.15.1
occupied territories 11.7.1
receipts 11.44, 11.84
recklessness, war crimes and 16.39.1
recognition of state of war 1.30.1
recommencement of hostilities 8.158.1,
10.22, 10.26
reconnaissance
aircraft 5.15.1, 12.10.4, 12.37
drones 4.9.3
occupied territory used for, enemy
property in 11.78
patrols 4.9.2
satellites 4.9.3, 5.15.1
ships 13.41
spies 4.9.2–4.9.3
records
anti-vehicle mines 6.14.6
booby-traps 6.7.8–6.7.9, 6.14.6
Central Information Agency 9.105
deaths 9.105
discipline 8.128, 9.102
judgements 11.73
medical 7.5.3
mines 6.7.9, 6.14.6, 13.56
prisoners of war
discipline and 8.128
punishment 8.128
punishment 8.128

remuneration *see* **pay**
rent 11.78
repatriation *see also* **termination of
    captivity and repatriation of
    prisoners of war**
  armed conflict law, applicability of
      3.10, 3.11
  armistices 10.24
  civilians 16.25
  delay, unjustifiable 16.25
  duration of armed conflict 3.10, 3.11
  grave breaches 16.25
  internees 9.110–9.113, 10.24
  involuntary 8.170–8.171
  wounded and sick 7.5.1 n11, 7.8 n19
reprieves 11.72.1
reprisals
  Additional Protocol I 1977 16.19–16.19.1
  aims of 16.17
  armed conflict law, enforcement of 16.1,
      16.16–16.19
  art, works of 16.19
  assassination 5.13 n49
  authority to take, requests for 16.19.2
  chaplains 16.18
  Chemical Weapons Convention 6.8 n24
  civilian objects 16.19–16.19.1
    immunity of 5.24 n100
  civilians 16.19–16.19.1, 16.19.2 n62
  conditions for 16.17
  cultural property 16.19
  Cultural Property Convention 1954 5.26.3
  customary law 16.19.2 n62
  dams and dykes 5.30.8, 16.19
  definition 5.18
  enforcement 16.1, 16.16–16.19
  environment 5.29, 16.19
  exhaustion of other methods of securing
      compliance 16.17
  Geneva Conventions 1949 16.19.1
  historic monuments 16.19
  hostilities, conduct of 5.18
  illegal acts 16.19–16.19.2
    following 16.16
    serious and manifestly 16.17
  incendiaries 6.12.3 n41
  medical personnel 16.18
  medical transport 16.18
  medical units 16.18
  Ministry of Defence, requests to 16.19.2
  nature of 16.16
  notice 16.17, 16.19.1
  nuclear power stations 5.30.8, 16.19
  occupied territory 11.14.2
    enemy property in 11.80
  personnel of adversaries, against 16.17
  prisoners of war 8.29, 16.18

  property of adversaries, against 16.17
  proportionality 16.17, 16.19.1
  protected persons 9.24, 16.18, 16.19.1
  publicity 16.17
  punishment 11.14.2
  shipwrecked 16.18
  state responsibility 16.17
  survival, objects indispensable to 5.27,
      16.19
  UK 16.19.1–16.19.2
    armed forces, by 5.18
  unlawful 16.19–16.19.2
  warnings 16.19.1
  works or installations containing
      dangerous forces 5.30.8, 16.19
  worship, places of 16.19
  wounded and sick 16.18
requisitioning
  civil defence 5.48 n306
  civilian objects, immunity of 15.16.2
  Cultural Property Convention 1954 5.26.3
  food 11.44
  good faith 11.83.2
  medical equipment and materiels 7.19
  medical personnel 7.19
  medical units 7.19, 11.43
  methods of 11.84–11.84.1
  occupied territory 11.1, 11.43–11.44
    enemy property in 11.76, 11.78,
        11.83–11.83.3, 11.84–11.84.1
    payment for 11.78, 11.84–11.84.1
  pillage 15.23.1
  private property 11.76, 11.83–11.83.3
  quartering of troops 11.84.1
  receipts 11.44, 11.84
rescue
  airmen in enemy territory 12.69–12.69.1,
      12.70–12.70.1
  attacks on rescuers 12.69
  capture 13.100, 13.116
  civil defence tasks 5.43.2
  coastal rescue craft
    Additional Protocol I 1977 13.126
    capture 13.100, 13.116
    definition 13.5
    exemption from attack 13.33
    exemption from capture 13.100
    identification of 13.126–13.127
  combat 12.69–12.69.1, 12.70–12.70.1
  immunity 12.69.1
  land, on 12.69–12.69.1
  life rafts and boats 13.33
  medical aircraft 12.122–12.122.2, 12.123
  protected activities 12.70.1
  sea, at 12.70–12.70.1
  search and 12.70.1
  self-defence 1.5